MARKETING

James L. Burrow

SOUTH-WESTERN
★
THOMSON LEARNING

Australia • Canada • Mexico • Singapore • Spain • United Kingdom • United States

SOUTH-WESTERN

THOMSON LEARNING

Marketing
by James L. Burrow

Vice President/Executive Publisher
Dave Shaut

Team Leader
Karen Schmohe

Executive Editor
Eve Lewis

Project Manager
Enid Nagel

Production Manager
Patricia Matthews Boies

Editor
Darrell E. Frye

Executive Marketing Manager
Carol Volz

Channel Manager
Nancy A. Long

Marketing Coordinator
Yvonne Patton-Beard

Manufacturing Coordinator
Kevin L. Kluck

Art and Design Coordinator
Tippy McIntosh

Cover and Internal Design
Bill Spencer

Editorial Assistant
Stephanie L. White

Production Assistant
Nancy Stamper

Compositor
Custom Editorial Productions Inc.

Printer
RR Donnelley, Willard

About the Author

James L. Burrow, Ph.D., is the coordinator of the graduate Training and Development Program at North Carolina State University in Raleigh, North Carolina. He has been a faculty member at the community college and university levels in marketing and human resources development as well as a consultant to business and public organizations. Dr. Burrow has also served on the board of directors of the Marketing Education Association.

COPYRIGHT © 2002 South-Western, a division of Thomson Learning, Inc. Thomson Learning™ is a trademark used herein under license.

ISBN: 0-538-43232-2

Printed in the United States of America

2 3 4 5 6 06 05 04 03 02

For permission to use material from this text, contact us by

Tel: (800) 730-2214
Fax: (800) 730-2215
Web: www.thomsonrights.com

For more information, contact South-Western, 5191 Natorp Boulevard, Mason, OH, 45040. Or you can visit our Internet site at www.swep.com.

ENGAGE STUDENT INTEREST

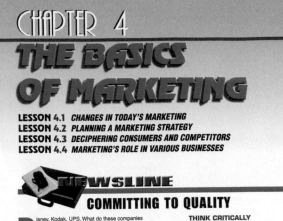

CHAPTER 4
THE BASICS OF MARKETING

LESSON 4.1 CHANGES IN TODAY'S MARKETING
LESSON 4.2 PLANNING A MARKETING STRATEGY
LESSON 4.3 DECIPHERING CONSUMERS AND COMPETITORS
LESSON 4.4 MARKETING'S ROLE IN VARIOUS BUSINESSES

NEWSLINE
COMMITTING TO QUALITY

Disney, Kodak, UPS. What do these companies have in common? They were all recognized in a consumer survey as top brand names. Respondents believed they offer "extraordinary quality." That image is just what those companies want, and they've worked hard to get it. Their marketing mixes are focused on meeting customer needs.

Some brands clearly reflect their companies' commitment to quality. Fisher-Price toys, Levi's jeans, and Chiquita bananas hold top spots in the survey. The survey shows that brands' ratings go up and down as customers see quality changing.

There are some well-known brands, however, that do not do well in the quality survey. In a number of cases, a lower ranking may be due to a target market that is focused on something other than quality, such as low prices, service, or convenience. Sometimes factors that are difficult for a company to control account for a poor showing. Many Japanese brands dropped when U.S. customers were encouraged to "Buy American."

In other instances, strong marketing has repaired poor images. Chrysler's quality rating once jumped 23 places in one year.

THINK CRITICALLY

1. Name three brands or local businesses whose focus is on something other than quality.

2. Name a car company that you think has a high-quality image.

3. Why is a quality image difficult to achieve and maintain?

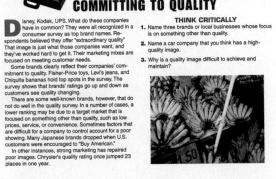

84

CORPORATE VIEW

CAREER OPPORTUNITY
CHANNEL MANAGER

POINT YOUR BROWSER
www.corpview.com

TeleView is looking for someone who possesses the following attributes.

- Excellent interpersonal and customer relations skills
- Strong problem solving and time management skills
- Technical communications proficiency
- Drive and flexibility
- Ability to work in an invigorating, team-oriented environment
- Ability to motivate others in a highly competitive environment
- Familiarity with Hispanic and Latin American cultures
- Self-starter who is motivated by opportunities and financial incentives

The main responsibilities of the job include the following.

- Achieve quarterly sales quota for the sales region
- Develop and implement the Sales and Marketing plans for the region
- Create a demand for TeleView products
- Create partnerships with sales partners to increase the flow of TeleView products to customers in Latin America and Spain
- Conduct sales and sales training seminars, marketing events, and sales/marketing briefings
- Manage channel relationships
- Work with the Brand Marketing Workgroup to extend the brand-name recognition of TeleView and Corporate View brands
- Help create exciting sales seminars and organize field marketing events

- Use press kits effectively and circulate press releases to key media in your channel region
- Insure appropriate localization of TeleView products, promotional materials, and support information

The job requires the following education, skills, and experience.

- B.S. or B.A. degree
- Minimum three years of experience in channel sales or related area
- Background and knowledge of sales and distribution systems in Latin America and in Spain
- Spanish/English fluency required
- Demonstrated strong presentation and communications skills
- Willingness to travel as much as 60 percent of the time, mostly out of the country
- Relocation to Miami, Florida

The position has a base salary and benefits. Commissions and bonuses are awarded based on successful and profitable channel management. A portable computer and remote Intranet connection will be provided.

THINK CRITICALLY

1. Prepare a cover letter written by a person who is qualified for this job and interested in applying for it.

2. Which aspects of this job are attractive to you? Which aspects do you find unattractive?

3. Search the Internet for a job similar to TeleView's channel manager. What type of compensation package is being offered for the job?

85

4.1 CHANGES IN TODAY'S MARKETING

GOALS

- **Explain** how marketing today differs from the way things were done in the past.
- **Show** why understanding customer needs is crucial, even with a superior product.

MARKETING MATTERS

Marketing as it is practiced today is much different than it was just a few decades ago. It's more complex, more interconnected with other business functions, focused on creating opportunities, and valued as an investment in the future. For all of those reasons it is even more important that businesses focus on marketing from the very beginning. It must be an integral part of business planning, because creating products and services that satisfy customer needs has to be the primary objective. Even the best products and services will fail if they do not fit the needs of their markets.

Make a list of four products or services that you've purchased recently which provided you with a high degree of satisfaction. What characteristics do these products or services have in common?

RECOGNIZING HOW
MARKETING HAS CHANGED

Marcos and Camilla are waiting for the start of their career seminar. As they look at the course outline, they see that they are beginning a study of marketing today. They begin to talk about their interest in marketing careers.

Camilla: Marketing seems to be an area where there are a lot of jobs. You hear about marketing all the time and several of my friends are planning to major in marketing.

Marcos: I'm not sure I'm interested in a marketing job. It seems like you have to be a salesperson and you know what people think of salespeople. It doesn't seem like it takes anything to be a retail salesperson. You know how many people work

long hours for no money in retail. What is your image of an automobile salesperson or of the person who calls you on the telephone at home to sell something? Even the good sales jobs in industry require you to travel all of the time. It seems like you have to be able to out-think and out-talk your customers to convince them to buy your products.

Camilla: It does seem that way, but there are other marketing jobs. Advertising is a part of marketing. Don't you think it would be exciting to create television commercials? I know some of them are weird or boring, but a lot of the advertisements are really creative and get me interested in the products they are selling.

4 THE BASICS OF MARKETING

86

NEWSLINE
Real-World Feature
Describes marketing trends or examples from real companies or industries.

CORPORATE VIEW
Career Feature
Describes marketing-related career opportunities in Corporate View.

MARKETING MATTERS
Bell-Ringer Feature
Inspires brain-storming and group discussion to motivate learning the lesson concepts.

FEATURES ENHANCE LEARNING

One-Stop Convenience

Personal computers liberated individuals and businesses from mainframes and computer operators by allowing them to process information from their desks. The Internet allowed people and businesses to buy and sell products via a web site. Now application service providers, or ASPs, give service businesses the ability to provide highly personalized services over the Internet.

Financial consultants can now subscribe to Internet-based planning services that allow them to merge clients' financial records in real time from multiple sources. Up-to-the-minute account data from banks, insurance companies, stockbrokers, mortgage lenders, and retirement plans are downloaded into a consolidated financial planning program with a few keystrokes.

With ASPs, clients and consultants no longer have to worry about working with outdated or incomplete information. Moreover, they can each view and analyze current data simultaneously from their own offices. So if someone wants to jump at a hot investment opportunity, the investor can run it by an adviser to see what overall affect it could have without either of them leaving their desks.

THINK CRITICALLY

1. How are Internet-based ASPs superior to software programs that are installed on stand-alone personal computers?

2. What kinds of concerns might arise from having highly personal and confidential data floating around cyberspace?

WORLD VIEW
Multi-Cultural Feature
Discusses marketing techniques in the rest of the world and within minority communities in the U.S. and how they differ from traditional U.S. marketing techniques.

E-MARKETING
Internet Feature
Provides specific information about how the Internet is changing traditional ways of marketing and new ways to reach customers using the Internet.

Global Advertising Techniques

One of the most important techniques for advertising in the United States is through television commercials. In 1996, advertisers spent nearly $36 billion on TV ads. That total represents about 54% of all advertising spending in 1996. As much as one-quarter of a program's broadcast time can be devoted to commercials.

However, in other countries the opportunities for television advertising can be limited. For example, in the United Kingdom two of the largest national channels have no paid commercials at all. Other channels have strict limits on the amount of broadcast time they are allowed to devote to commercials. Advertisers generally must resort to other techniques to get the word out about their products and services.

Many other countries also have little to no television commercial advertising. The broadcasters in a number of countries agree to air few or no commercials in exchange for receiving subsidies from the government.

THINK CRITICALLY

1. In a country with limited TV advertising, what techniques would you use to advertise? Would you use the same techniques in a small country and a large country?

2. Use the Internet and other resources to find out how advertising on TV is handled in another country.

SPECIAL FEATURES FOR

REACHING THE HISPANIC MARKET

The Spanish-speaking population of the United States is growing at a steady rate. There is no one formula for marketing to Hispanics, a diverse and dynamic cultural group. However, language, values, lifestyles, and social systems that are shared by the Hispanic culture can influence promotional strategies.

Hispanic respondents in focus groups tested advertisements for several products and services. The results showed that some important techniques for reaching Hispanics include testimonials, expressions of happiness, family, and the Spanish language.

Marketers who target Hispanic markets should develop promotional strategies that are responsive to the wants and needs of the consumers. While individual markets will have differences, Hispanics want recognition of their culture and values.

THINK CRITICALLY

1. What elements would you include in an advertisement targeted at the Hispanic market?

2. What types of factors would affect how you would advertise to Hispanics differently from other demographic groups?

3. Search the Internet or other resources for examples of advertisements targeting Hispanics.

GET THE MESSAGE
Communication Feature

Describes challenges, techniques, devices, and media used to convey product information to customers.

FIGURE THIS
Math Feature

Teaches mathematical concepts important for successful marketers.

E-Commerce Statistics

The top five retail web sites in January 2001 determined by the number of buyers were

Company	Number of Buyers
Amazon.com	2,300,000
Barnesandnoble.com	638,000
Ticketmaster.com	636,000
Half.com	567,000
Jcpenney.com	545,000

There were an estimated total of 10 million people who made retail purchases on the Internet that month.

THINK CRITICALLY

1. What was the combined number of buyers represented by the top five web retailers?

2. What is the percentage of all Internet customers represented by the combined total of the top five web retailers?

3. If each customer spent on average $135 on Internet purchases during the month, calculate the total amount spent by each of the retailers listed.

FUTURE MARKETERS

DIGITAL DIGEST
Technology Feature

Presents different technologies, software, hardware, and their computer-related issues useful to marketers.

Direct Mail Databases

Many businesses rely on direct mail to reach potential customers. Direct mail can include catalogs, promotional fliers, coupons, and free samples. Customers often refer to direct mailings as "junk mail." However, junk mail is big business and the technology that is required to support it is impressive.

Companies have developed a wide array of database software for storing and sorting addresses for direct mailings. In addition to a person's address, marketers determine the best time to send a piece of direct mail, and what the mailing should contain. By planning a direct mailing carefully, companies hope to maximize the sales generated, and minimize costs by weeding out customers who are unlikely to purchase.

THINK CRITICALLY

1. Describe three pieces of direct mail sent to you recently. What products were they promoting? What effect did the mailing have on your purchasing decisions?

2. Search the Internet for companies that provide direct mail database services. What services does each provide?

Bribery Common but Not Legal

Offering bribes or demanding kickbacks to facilitate international business transactions is widespread, even though it is outlawed in virtually every country. Because it is so common and so difficult to fight, it is one of the toughest barriers to international trade faced by American businesses.

Unlike in other countries, United States law makes it illegal for a U.S. company to bribe a foreign official. So Americans generally have no good choices when they encounter foreign officials who demand payment before they will award them a contract or issue necessary permits. They can either break the law to get the contract, or they can decline to pay and lose the business.

Some U.S. businesses opt to transact foreign business through foreign partners or subsidiaries. Then foreign employees handle the distasteful transactions while the parent company looks the other way and avoids violating U.S. laws.

THINK CRITICALLY

1. If a businessperson encounters a foreign citizen who expects an illicit payment to facilitate a business deal, what options does he or she have?

2. Why are attempts to combat bribery in international trade so difficult?

JUDGMENT CALL
Law and Ethics Feature

Examines laws that control the marketing industry and ethical dilemmas faced by marketing professionals.

ASSESSMENT AND REVIEW

CHECKPOINT
Short questions within lessons to assist with reading and to test your understanding.

checkpoint

When the marketing concept is followed, what is the initial focus of the planning process?

END-OF-CHAPTER ACTIVITIES

SUMMARY
Provides a comprehensive summary of key concepts.

REVIEW MARKETING CONCEPTS
Provides questions that cover all the main points.

REVIEW MARKETING TERMS
Reinforces your comprehension of key terms.

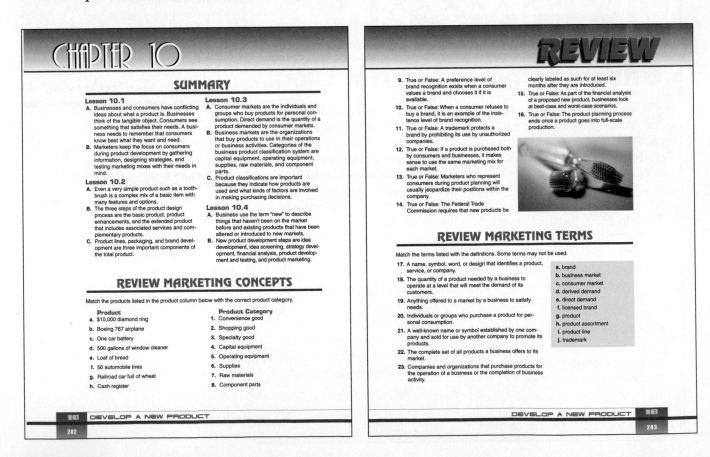

CHAPTER 10

SUMMARY

Lesson 10.1
A. Businesses and consumers have conflicting ideas about what a product is. Businesses think of the tangible object. Consumers see something that satisfies their needs. A business needs to remember that consumers know best what they want and need.
B. Marketers keep the focus on consumers during product development by gathering information, designing strategies, and testing marketing mixes with their needs in mind.

Lesson 10.2
A. Even a very simple product such as a toothbrush is a complex mix of a basic item with many features and options.
B. The three steps of the product design process are the basic product, product enhancements, and the extended product that includes associated services and complementary products.
C. Product lines, packaging, and brand development are three important components of the total product.

Lesson 10.3
A. Consumer markets are the individuals and groups who buy products for personal consumption. Direct demand is the quantity of a product demanded by consumer markets.
B. Business markets are the organizations that buy products to use in their operations or business activities. Categories of the business product classification system are capital equipment, operating equipment, supplies, raw materials, and component parts.
C. Product classifications are important because they indicate how products are used and what kinds of factors are involved in making purchasing decisions.

Lesson 10.4
A. Business use the term "new" to describe things that haven't been on the market before and existing products that have been altered or introduced to new markets.
B. New product development steps are idea development, idea screening, strategy development, financial analysis, product development and testing, and product marketing.

REVIEW MARKETING CONCEPTS

Match the products listed in the product column below with the correct product category.

Product	Product Category
a. $10,000 diamond ring	1. Convenience good
b. Boeing 767 airplane	2. Shopping good
c. One car battery	3. Specialty good
d. 500 gallons of window cleaner	4. Capital equipment
e. Loaf of bread	5. Operating equipment
f. 50 automobile tires	6. Supplies
g. Railroad car full of wheat	7. Raw materials
h. Cash register	8. Component parts

REVIEW

9. True or False: A preference level of brand recognition exists when a consumer values a brand and chooses it if it is available.
10. True or False: When a consumer refuses to buy a brand, it is an example of the insistence level of brand recognition.
11. True or False: A trademark protects a brand by prohibiting its use by unauthorized companies.
12. True or False: If a product is purchased both by consumers and businesses, it makes sense to use the same marketing mix for each market.
13. True or False: Marketers who represent consumers during product planning will usually jeopardize their positions within the company.
14. True or False: The Federal Trade Commission requires that new products be

clearly labeled as such for at least six months after they are introduced.
15. True or False: As part of the financial analysis of a proposed new product, businesses look at best-case and worst-case scenarios.
16. True or False: The product planning process ends once a product goes into full-scale production.

REVIEW MARKETING TERMS

Match the terms listed with the definitions. Some terms may not be used.

17. A name, symbol, word, or design that identifies a product, service, or company.
18. The quantity of a product needed by a business to operate at a level that will meet the demand of its customers.
19. Anything offered to a market by a business to satisfy needs.
20. Individuals or groups who purchase a product for personal consumption.
21. A well-known name or symbol established by one company and sold for use by another company to promote its products.
22. The complete set of all products a business offers to its market.
23. Companies and organizations that purchase products for the operation of a business or the completion of business activity.

a. brand
b. business market
c. consumer market
d. derived demand
e. direct demand
f. licensed brand
g. product
h. product assortment
i. product line
j. trademark

HOW TO USE THIS BOOK

IS INTEGRAL AND ONGOING

LESSON REVIEW

Provides exercises that test and apply your understanding of the concepts in the lesson.

APPLY MARKETING FUNCTIONS

Provides in-depth exercises that allow you to apply your knowledge to Marketing Research, Marketing Planning, Marketing Management, and Marketing Technology.

LESSON REVIEW

1. How does the timing of product development differ in businesses that use the marketing concept compared with those that do not?

2. Name three reasons it is difficult to meet customer needs.

3. What is market opportunity analysis?

4. What are the four elements of the marketing mix?

5. Name several ways businesses can alter the prices they charge.

6. What are the most common forms of promotion?

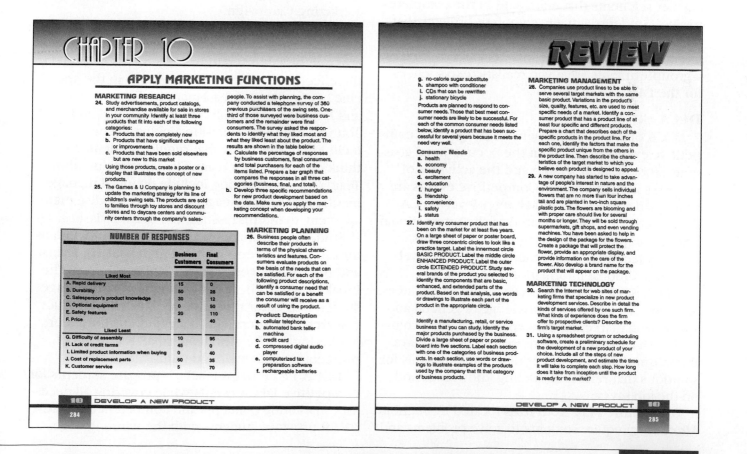

CHAPTER 10

APPLY MARKETING FUNCTIONS

MARKETING RESEARCH

24. Study advertisements, product catalogs, and merchandise available for sale in stores in your community. Identify at least three products that fit into each of the following categories:
   a. Products that are completely new
   b. Products that have significant changes or improvements
   c. Products that have been sold elsewhere but are new to this market

   Using those products, create a poster or a display that illustrates the concept of new products.

25. The Games & U Company is planning to update the marketing strategy for its line of children's swing sets. The products are sold to families through toy stores and discount stores and to daycare centers and community centers through the company's sales-people. To assist with planning, the company conducted a telephone survey of 360 previous purchasers of the swing sets. One-third of those surveyed were business customers and the remainder were final consumers. The survey asked the respondents to identify what they liked most and what they liked least about the product. The results are shown in the table below:
   a. Calculate the percentage of responses by business customers, final consumers, and total purchasers for each of the items listed. Prepare a bar graph that compares the responses in all three categories (business, final, and total).
   b. Develop three specific recommendations for new product development based on the data. Make sure you apply the marketing concept when developing your recommendations.

NUMBER OF RESPONSES

	Business Customers	Final Consumers
Liked Most		
A. Rapid delivery	15	0
B. Durability	50	28
C. Salesperson's product knowledge	30	12
D. Optional equipment	0	50
E. Safety features	20	110
F. Price	5	40
Liked Least		
G. Difficulty of assembly	10	95
H. Lack of credit terms	45	0
I. Limited product information when buying	0	40
J. Cost of replacement parts	60	35
K. Customer service	5	70

MARKETING PLANNING

26. Business people often describe their products in terms of the physical characteristics and features. Consumers evaluate products on the basis of the needs that can be satisfied. For each of the following product descriptions, identify a consumer need that can be satisfied or a benefit the consumer will receive as a result of using the product.

Product Description
   a. cellular telephone
   b. automated bank teller machine
   c. credit card
   d. compressed digital audio player
   e. computerized tax preparation software
   f. rechargeable batteries
   g. no-calorie sugar substitute
   h. shampoo with conditioner
   i. CDs that can be rewritten
   j. stationary bicycle

   Products are planned to respond to consumer needs. Those that best meet consumer needs are likely to be successful. For each of the common consumer needs listed below, identify a product that has been successful for several years because it meets the need very well.

Consumer Needs
   a. health
   b. economy
   c. beauty
   d. excitement
   e. education
   f. hunger
   g. friendship
   h. convenience
   i. safety
   j. status

27. Identify any consumer product that has been on the market for at least five years. On a large sheet of paper or poster board, draw three concentric circles to look like a practice target. Label the innermost circle BASIC PRODUCT. Label the middle circle ENHANCED PRODUCT. Label the outer circle EXTENDED PRODUCT. Study several brands of the product you selected to identify the components that are basic, enhanced, and extended parts of the product. Based on that analysis, use words or drawings to illustrate each part of the product in the appropriate circle.

   or

   Identify a manufacturing, retail, or service business that you can study. Identify the major products purchased by the business. Divide a large sheet of paper or poster board into five sections. Label each section with one of the categories of business products. In each section, use words or drawings to illustrate examples of the products used by the company that fit that category of business products.

MARKETING MANAGEMENT

28. Companies use product lines to be able to serve several target markets with the same basic product. Variations in the product's size, quality, features, etc. are used to meet specific needs of a market. Identify a consumer product that has a product line of at least four specific and different products. Prepare a chart that describes each of the specific products in the product line. For each one, identify the factors that make the specific product unique from the others in the product line. Then describe the characteristics of the target market to which you believe each product is designed to appeal.

29. A new company has started to take advantage of people's interest in nature and the environment. The company sells individual flowers that are no more than four inches tall and are planted in two-inch square plastic pots. The flowers are blooming and with proper care should live for several months or longer. They will be sold through supermarkets, gift shops, and even vending machines. You have been asked to help in the design of the package for the flowers. Create a package that will protect the flower, provide an appropriate display, and provide information on the care of the flower. Also develop a brand name for the product that will appear on the package.

MARKETING TECHNOLOGY

30. Search the Internet for web sites of marketing firms that specialize in new product development services. Describe in detail the kinds of services offered by one such firm. What kinds of experience does the firm offer to prospective clients? Describe the firm's target market.

31. Using a spreadsheet program or scheduling software, create a preliminary schedule for the development of a new product of your choice. Include all of the steps of new product development, and estimate the time it will take to complete each step. How long does it take from inception until the product is ready for the market?

REVIEW

10 DEVELOP A NEW PRODUCT

284

DEVELOP A NEW PRODUCT 10

285

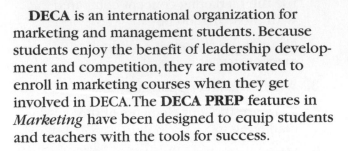

CASE STUDY

South-Western Marketing provides two features to help students experience marketing in action—Case Studies and Deca Prep activities.

DECA is an international organization for marketing and management students. Because students enjoy the benefit of leadership development and competition, they are motivated to enroll in marketing courses when they get involved in DECA. The **DECA PREP** features in *Marketing* have been designed to equip students and teachers with the tools for success.

DECA PREP

DECA PREP provides marketing students with winning strategies for competition at all levels. The role play situations, team events, and written events included are correlated to actual DECA events. Students gain valuable problem solving experience by presenting their ideas to a judge (teacher/business person). Written projects that seemed overwhelming are now assigned in smaller segments that culminate in the complete project. Students actually complete projects that are ready for competition. Team projects focus attention on extemporaneous decision making by a group. Students are given realistic experiences for the DECA team events.

DECA COMPETITION

DECA offers a comprehensive program of competitive events based upon the occupational goals of its student membership and the activities of chapters in high schools. Competitive events are replicated at the state and chapter level. **DECA PREP** activities are correlated to the International DECA Competitive, Team, and Written Events. Each project makes reference to the DECA web site for additional information.

DECA Series Events cover occupational areas. Students validate their knowledge of general and specialized marketing concepts by taking a comprehensive exam and participating in role plays that require them to use critical thinking skills for solutions that reflect marketing knowledge and on-the-job savvy.

DECA Role Play Activities located throughout *Marketing* require students to solve problems and create marketing strategies. The teacher/business person (judge) plays the role of manager, customer, or marketing specialist. Students present their solutions to the judges who evaluate the effectiveness of the presentation.

Written DECA events challenge students to conduct research, devise creative marketing strategies, and to prepare projects that are ready for DECA competition. Projects are broken into smaller segments that are culminated into the final project.

Marketing Research Events provide students with opportunities to demonstrate competencies needed by managers. Research projects included in *Marketing* include Business and Services Marketing Research, General Marketing Research, Hospitality and Recreation Marketing Research, Retail Marketing Research, and the Advertising Marketing Campaign.

Management Team Decision-Making Events provide participants opportunities to analyze one or a combination of elements essential to the effective operation of a business in the specific occupational area. Financial Services, Sports and Entertainment Marketing, and Travel and Tourism are Team Decision-Making Events included in this book that require students to think creatively as a team. Elements included in Team Decision Making include financial management, personnel management, merchandise management, marketing issues, and security issues.

Students are challenged to write business plans for the **Entrepreneurship Participating Event** and the **Entrepreneurship Written Event**. The break down of these assignments will encourage students to enter this category. Students conduct research and interview successful entrepreneurs. Marketing teachers evaluate small segments of projects as students build them.

DECA PREP helps teachers prepare students for competitive DECA events while covering all necessary marketing concepts and competencies. **DECA PREP** provides students with the winning edge.

YOUNG ENTREPRENEUR IN THE WEB DESIGN WORLD

Matt Douglas became interested in designing web sites when he was 13 years old. He liked the idea of making information available to the entire world, and the thought of designing his own web pages was exciting.

Learning how to design web sites was a fun challenge for Matt. He started with a small site about himself. Even though Matt did not have much experience with the Web, he was eager to learn something new. Through hours of trial and error, Matt taught himself the essentials of web site development.

Locating customers is the most difficult part of a web designer's job. Matt's experience taught him the most effective method of finding customers is networking. He was very fortunate because his dad was a very successful manufacturer's representative with hundreds of contacts, many of whom needed web sites. About half of the sites Matt has created have been related to manufacturing. Friends and family have been a huge asset to Matt's business, because their contacts have accounted for most of his work.

Another less-effective method Matt used was cold calling. Matt learned that people either want a web site or they don't. In most cases, he found that there was little he could say or do to change someone's mind in that regard.

Once a web developer manages to get his foot in the door, it is important to ask the right kinds of questions in order to design a site that meets the client's requirements. A web designer must determine what type of site customers are looking for. Is it a general information site for their business, or do they want to use the site to sell products?

When young Matt started designing web pages, he often faced the problem of gaining the trust of older clients. It was difficult for some of them to accept Matt as a serious businessperson because he was so young. Matt helped overcome this obstacle by being extremely polite and professional and responding to customer requests immediately.

Matt learned the hard way that the price should be established before beginning work on a site. When he began working as a web designer, Matt did not quote prices up front. Then when he wrote up his final invoices, he would under-price them to avoid any bad feelings from clients. Consequently, clients would get great sites for half what they should have paid. Now Matt establishes a price range at the outset.

Often a site will take a month or more to complete. Clients are usually busy, and Matt might be out of contact with them for weeks. When this happens, Matt sends an invoice for the work that he has completed, even though the site is not finished. This helps to remind a client that work is in progress, and it brings money into Matt's business in the meantime.

To keep up to date with the latest Internet market information, Matt pays close attention to the news. Many articles proclaim new products as the "future of the Internet." Matt analyzes these articles and researches products to find out if they could help his business grow. Also, Matt learns new techniques of web design by searching the Web and studying other business web sites.

Matt has served many clients since he launched his web design venture in the summer of 2000. Although prices vary for individual sites, Matt generally charges between $800 and $1,500 per site—a low cost considering the quality of his work.

Matt has learned to balance his business activities and the demanding workload of high school. At first it was difficult. Matt would spend either too much time on his business, or too much time on schoolwork. While one would receive all of Matt's attention, the other would suffer. Once Matt realized this, he trained himself to balance the two by designating certain times for each. By sticking to a time schedule, Matt has been successful with business and school.

THINK CRITICALLY

1. List three obstacles Matt had to overcome as an entrepreneur.

2. What factor has allowed young web designers to create work for people around the world?

3. How should billing be handled for a web design business? Why?

4. How does a young person balance school and a challenging career?

http://www.deca.org/publications/HS_Guide/guidetoc.html

TECHNICAL MARKETING REPRESENTATIVE EVENT

One of your clients is a specialty grocery store called Ideal Grocery, located in Waverly, population 25,000. Waverly's population represents two primary marketing targets: families who still own working farms, and wealthy families who commute to the nearby city for work but choose to live in spacious homes on large lots. Customers demand the grocery basics, but they also have sophisticated tastes and often request international foods and unique items. Ideal Grocery has established good relations with vendors and has been able to satisfy its customers' requests reliably. Ideal also makes a nice profit margin on all special requests.

Because it is the sole supermarket in town, Ideal Grocery can be very busy, especially on weekends. There are six cashiers using scanners that were installed 10 years ago, but all produce still needs to be weighed on a separate scale. Despite experienced cashiers, the older technology causes lines to build.

The owners of Ideal Grocery want to improve the checkout system of their store to make the lines move faster. They are interested in learning more about new cash registers and other electronic equipment for maintaining inventory, pricing, scanning, weighing, and processing checkout transactions.

Feedback from cashiers shows a need for a more user-friendly transaction display so customers can easily check price accuracy; a desire by customers to use credit cards for purchases; and a desire to continue the popular Ideal Bonus Card that provides discounts, check approval, and buying points for customer loyalty. There is also a need for at least one wider aisle to accommodate wheelchairs, strollers, and bulky items. Aisles cannot be added due to the store's size; however, increasing the width of an existing aisle would not be a problem. Due to the high profit margin on special requests, Ideal has been able to budget $100,000 for the project.

DEFINE THE PLAN Describe the product(s) and define the target customer.

PREPARE THE SALES PRESENTATION Organize appropriate information, and present/defend a sales presentation.

Case Studies

Relationship Marketing at Big Ball Sports
MADD Tackles a Big Social Issue
Young Entrepreneurs Prosper in Growing Market
What Kind of Music Do Teens Want?
You Deserve a Hotel Break Today
Gas Stations and a Whole Lot More
The Cable Television Challenge
Making Financial Services Convenient
Packaging for an International Marketplace
Coca Cola—The Expanding Brand
Selling Legal Services in Cyberspace
From Small Town Retailer to the NYSE
The Ups and Downs of the Dot.com World
Brand Recognition: The Personality of a Product
"We Love to See You Smile"
Super Bowl Advertisement Bonanza
Home Improvement Shows and Stores
Ethics and Successful International Business
Napster, Theft or Ingenuity?
Financing a Start-Up Company
The Rise of Successful Entrepreneurs
The Perfect Marriage Turns Sour
Young Entrepreneur in the Web Design World

DECA Prep

Fashion Merchandising Promotion Plan
Civic Consciousness Project
Entrepreneurship
Business and Financial Services Marketing Research Event
Hospitality and Recreation Marketing Research Event
Vehicles and Petroleum Role Play
Management Team Decision Making Event for Sports and Entertainment Marketing
Marketing Research Event for Business and Financial Services
International Marketing Event
Learn to Earn Project
Creative Marketing Research Project
Apparel and Accessories Role Play
E-commerce Marketing Research Event
Retail Marketing Research Event
Civic Consciousness Project
Travel and Tourism Team Decision Making Event
Free-Enterprise Event
Marketing Management Role Play
Business Services Role Play
Financial Services Team Decision Making Event
Entrepreneurship Written Event
Public Relations Project
Technical Marketing Representative Event

CONTENTS

CHAPTER 1

MARKETING TODAY 2

NEWSLINE

U.S. Exports Marketing Expertise 2

Corporate View: Career Opportunity
Product Marketing Manager 3

LESSONS

1.1 What Is Marketing? 4

1.2 Businesses Need Marketing 10

1.3 Understanding the Marketing Concept 16

1.4 Marketing's Role Today and Tomorrow 21

SPECIAL FEATURES

Digital Digest 22
E-Marketing 5
Figure This 14
Judgment Call 17
Marketing Matters 4, 10, 16, 21
World View 7

REVIEW AND ASSESSMENT

Checkpoint 6, 8, 9, 11, 12, 15, 18, 20, 23, 25
Lesson Review 9, 15, 20, 25
Chapter Review 26–29

MARKETING IN ACTION

CASE STUDY *Relationship Marketing at Big Ball Sports* 30

Fashion Merchandising Promotion Plan 31

CHAPTER 2

MARKETING IMPACTS SOCIETY 32

NEWSLINE

Who Is Responsible? 32

Corporate View: Career Opportunity
Sales Representative 33

LESSONS

2.1 The Impact of Marketing 34

2.2 Criticisms of Marketing 39

2.3 Increasing Social Responsibility 44

SPECIAL FEATURES

Digital Digest 38
E-Marketing 39
Figure This 49
Get the Message 36
Judgment Call 48
Marketing Matters 34, 39, 44
World View 40

REVIEW AND ASSESSMENT

Checkpoint 35, 36, 38, 42, 43, 46, 47, 49
Lesson Review 38, 43, 49
Chapter Review 50–53

MARKETING IN ACTION

CASE STUDY *MADD Tackles a Big Social Issue* 54

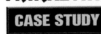

Civic Consciousness Project 55

CONTENTS

CHAPTER 3

MARKETING BEGINS WITH ECONOMICS 56

An Economic Dogfight 56

Corporate View: Career Opportunity
Marketing Director 57

LESSONS

3.1 Scarcity and Private Enterprise 58

3.2 Observing the Law of Supply and Demand 62

3.3 Types of Economic Competition 68

3.4 Enhancing Economic Utility 75

SPECIAL FEATURES

Digital Digest 59
E-Marketing 60
Figure This 73
Get the Message 77
Judgment Call 72
Marketing Matters 58, 62, 68, 75
World View 76

REVIEW AND ASSESSMENT

Checkpoint 59, 61, 64, 67, 70, 74, 76, 77
Lesson Review 61, 67, 74, 77
Chapter Review 78–81

MARKETING IN ACTION

 CASE STUDY *Young Entrepreneurs Prosper in Growing Market* 82

 Entrepreneurship 83

CHAPTER 4

THE BASICS OF MARKETING 84

Committing to Quality 84

Corporate View: Career Opportunity
Channel Manager 85

LESSONS

4.1 Changes in Today's Marketing 86

4.2 Planning a Marketing Strategy 91

4.3 Deciphering Consumers and Competitors 98

4.4 Marketing's Role in Various Businesses 103

SPECIAL FEATURES

Digital Digest 93
E-Marketing 88
Figure This 104
Get the Message 101
Judgment Call 96
Marketing Matters 86, 91, 98, 103
World View 89

REVIEW AND ASSESSMENT

Checkpoint 88, 90, 92, 94, 97, 100, 102, 104, 105
Lesson Review 90, 97, 102, 105
Chapter Review 106–109

MARKETING IN ACTION

CASE STUDY *What Kind of Music Do Teens Want?* 110

 Business and Financial Services Marketing Research Event 111

CONTENTS

USING MARKETING RESEARCH 112

Restaurants Find a Niche 112

Corporate View: Career Opportunity
Sales Administrative Assistant 113

LESSONS

5.1 Understanding the Need for Market Information 114

5.2 Finding and Managing Marketing Information 119

5.3 Using Marketing Research 128

5.4 Collecting Primary Data 134

SPECIAL FEATURES

Digital Digest 118
E-Marketing 115
Figure This 136
Get the Message 126
Judgment Call 123
Marketing Matters 114, 119, 128, 134
World View 129

REVIEW AND ASSESSMENT

Checkpoint 116, 118, 124, 127, 130, 132, 133, 135, 136, 137
Lesson Review 118, 127, 133, 137
Chapter Review 138–141

MARKETING IN ACTION

 You Deserve a Hotel Break Today 142

 Hospitality and Recreation Marketing Research Event 143

MARKETING BEGINS WITH CUSTOMERS 144

Sony Gets Close to Customers 144

Corporate View: Career Opportunity
Marketing Writer and Editor 145

LESSONS

6.1 Understanding Consumer Behavior 146

6.2 What Motivates Buyers? 150
6.3 Types of Decision Making 154

SPECIAL FEATURES

Digital Digest 157
E-Marketing 149
Figure This 155
Get the Message 153
Judgment Call 156
Marketing Matters 146, 150, 154
World View 148

REVIEW AND ASSESSMENT

Checkpoint 147, 149, 151, 153, 155, 157
Lesson Review 149, 153, 157
Chapter Review 158–161

MARKETING IN ACTION

Gas Stations and a Whole Lot More 162

Vehicles and Petroleum Role Play 163

CONTENTS

CHAPTER 7

COMPETITION IS EVERYWHERE 164

 NEWSLINE

Saturn Stalls but Still Pleases 164

Corporate View: Career Opportunity
Large Account Sales Manager 165

LESSONS
7.1 Targeting Market Segments 166
7.2 Positioning for Competitive Advantage 171
7.3 Competing for Market Segments 175
7.4 Learning About the Competition 180

SPECIAL FEATURES
Digital Digest 172
E-Marketing 177
Figure This 170
Get the Message 181
Judgment Call 173
Marketing Matters 166, 171, 175, 180
World View 168

REVIEW AND ASSESSMENT
Checkpoint 168, 170, 173, 174, 178, 179, 182, 183
Lesson Review 170, 174, 179, 183
Chapter Review 184–187

MARKETING IN ACTION
 CASE STUDY *The Cable Television Challenge* 188

 Management Team Decision Making Event for Sports and Entertainment Marketing 189

CHAPTER 8

MARKETING FOR E-COMMERCE 190

 NEWSLINE

Consumers Say No to Pets.com 190

Corporate View: Career Opportunity
Art Director 191

LESSONS
8.1 What is E-Commerce? 192
8.2 The Growing Importance of E-Commerce 197
8.3 Impact of E-Commerce on Distribution Channels 201
8.4 Role of Promotion for E-Commerce 206

SPECIAL FEATURES
Digital Digest 207
E-Marketing 198
Figure This 199
Get the Message 193
Judgment Call 204
Marketing Matters 192, 197, 201, 206
World View 202

REVIEW AND ASSESSMENT
Checkpoint 194, 196, 198, 200, 203, 205, 209, 211
Lesson Review 196, 200, 205, 211
Chapter Review 212–215

MARKETING IN ACTION
 CASE STUDY *Making Financial Services Convenient* 216

 Marketing Research Event for Business and Financial Services 217

CONTENTS

CHAPTER 9

THE MARKETING STRATEGY 218

NEWSLINE

Target Your Market 218

Corporate View: Career Opportunity
Brand Development Manager 219

LESSONS

9.1 Developing a Market Strategy 220
9.2 Assessing Marketing Mix Alternatives 224
9.3 Analyzing Product Purchase Classifications 232
9.4 Planning for Marketing 238
9.5 Developing a Marketing Plan 244

SPECIAL FEATURES

Digital Digest 246
E-Marketing 240
Figure This 222
Get the Message 221
Judgment Call 236
Marketing Matters 220, 224, 232, 238, 244
World View 227

REVIEW AND ASSESSMENT

Checkpoint 222, 223, 226, 228, 231, 235, 237, 240, 243, 247, 249, 251
Lesson Review 223, 231, 237, 243, 251
Chapter Review 252–255

MARKETING IN ACTION

CASE STUDY *Packaging for an International Marketplace* 256

International Marketing Event 257

CHAPTER 10

DEVELOP A NEW PRODUCT 258

NEWSLINE

Regulating Product Labeling 258

Corporate View: Career Opportunity
Web Site Development Manager 259

LESSONS

10.1 What is a Product? 260
10.2 Components of a New Product 265
10.3 Product Market Classifications 272
10.4 Developing Successful New Products 278

SPECIAL FEATURES

Digital Digest 280
E-Marketing 275
Figure This 276
Get the Message 262
Judgment Call 267
Marketing Matters 260, 265, 272, 278
World View 261

REVIEW AND ASSESSMENT

Checkpoint 261, 264, 266, 268, 271, 273, 276, 277, 278, 281
Lesson Review 264, 271, 277, 281
Chapter Review 282–285

MARKETING IN ACTION

CASE STUDY *Coca Cola—The Expanding Brand* 286

Learn to Earn Project 287

CONTENTS

CHAPTER 11

SERVICES NEED MARKETING 288

Promoting Lawyers 288

Corporate View: Career Opportunity
General Administrative Assistant **289**

LESSONS

11.1 What Are Services? **290**

11.2 Classifying Types and Evaluating Quality **295**

11.3 Developing a Service Marketing Mix **300**

SPECIAL FEATURES

Digital Digest **298**
E-Marketing **301**
Figure This **294**
Get the Message **302**
Judgment Call **297**
Marketing Matters **290, 295, 300**
World View **293**

REVIEW AND ASSESSMENT

Checkpoint **291, 294, 298, 299, 302, 303**
Lesson Review **294, 299, 303**
Chapter Review **304–307**

MARKETING IN ACTION

 CASE STUDY *Selling Legal Services in Cyberspace* **308**

Creative Marketing Research Project **309**

CHAPTER 12

PRODUCTS FOR RESALE 310

Coding System Unlocks Business Markets **310**

Corporate View: Career Opportunity
Customer Service Specialist **311**

LESSONS

12.1 Business-to-Business Exchange Process **312**

12.2 Making Purchasing Decisions in Business **318**

12.3 Business Purchasing Procedures **324**

12.4 Retail Purchasing **330**

SPECIAL FEATURES

Digital Digest **314**
E-Marketing **326**
Figure This **319**
Get the Message **331**
Judgment Call **333**
Marketing Matters **312, 318, 324, 330**
World View **313**

REVIEW AND ASSESSMENT

Checkpoint **313, 317, 320, 321, 323, 327, 328, 329, 332, 333**
Lesson Review **317, 323, 329, 333**
Chapter Review **334–337**

MARKETING IN ACTION

 CASE STUDY *From Small Town Retailer to the NYSE* **338**

Apparel and Accessories Role Play **339**

CONTENTS

CHAPTER 13

GET THE PRODUCT TO CUSTOMERS 340

The Shift from Image to Value **340**

Corporate View: Career Opportunity
Support Specialist **341**

LESSONS
13.1 Marketing through Distribution **342**
13.2 Assembling Channels of Distribution **347**
13.3 Wholesaling **354**
13.4 Retailing **359**
13.5 Physical Distribution Keeps Things Moving **364**

SPECIAL FEATURES
Digital Digest **345**
E-Marketing **356**
Figure This **349**
Get the Message **355**
Judgment Call **360**
Marketing Matters **342, 347, 354, 359, 364**
World View **343**

REVIEW AND ASSESSMENT
Checkpoint **344, 346, 350, 353, 357, 358, 362, 363, 366, 368, 369**
Lesson Review **346, 353, 358, 363, 369**
Chapter Review **370–373**

MARKETING IN ACTION
CASE STUDY *The Ups and Downs of the Dot.com World* **374**

 E-Commerce Marketing Research Event **375**

CHAPTER 14

DETERMINING THE BEST PRICE 376

Establishing Value at HMOs **376**

Corporate View: Career Opportunity
Credit Manager and Analyst **377**

LESSONS
14.1 The Economics of Price Decisions **378**
14.2 Developing Pricing Procedures **384**
14.3 Pricing Based on Market Conditions **390**

SPECIAL FEATURES
Digital Digest **379**
E-Marketing **389**
Figure This **385**
Get the Message **391**
Judgment Call **382**
Marketing Matters **378, 384, 390**
World View **393**

REVIEW AND ASSESSMENT
Checkpoint **379, 381, 383, 385, 387, 389, 392, 394, 395**
Lesson Review **383, 389, 395**
Chapter Review **396–399**

MARKETING IN ACTION
CASE STUDY *Brand Recognition: The Personality of a Product* **400**

 Retail Marketing Research Event **401**

CONTENTS

CHAPTER 15

PROMOTION MEANS EFFECTIVE COMMUNICATION 402

Influencing What You Eat **402**

Corporate View: Career Opportunity
Public Relations Specialist **403**

LESSONS

15.1 Promotion as a Form of Communication **404**
15.2 Types of Promotion **410**
15.3 Mixing the Promotional Plan **416**

SPECIAL FEATURES
Digital Digest **407**
E-Marketing **412**
Figure This **421**
Get the Message **408**
Judgment Call **414**
Marketing Matters **404, 410, 416**
World View **420**

REVIEW AND ASSESSMENT
Checkpoint **406, 408, 409, 413, 414, 415, 418, 421**
Lesson Review **409, 415, 421**
Chapter Review **422–425**

MARKETING IN ACTION
 CASE STUDY *"We Love to See You Smile"* **426**

Civic Consciousness Project **427**

CHAPTER 16

BE CREATIVE WITH ADVERTISING 428

Where's the Consumer? **428**

Corporate View: Career Opportunity
Senior Graphic Artist **429**

LESSONS
16.1 What is Advertising? **430**
16.2 Developing an Advertising Plan **435**
16.3 Putting the Ad Plan Into Action **442**

SPECIAL FEATURES
Digital Digest **434**
E-Marketing **441**
Figure This **445**
Get the Message **443**
Judgment Call **431**
Marketing Matters **430, 435, 442**
World View **440**

REVIEW AND ASSESSMENT
Checkpoint **432, 433, 434, 437, 441, 444, 445**
Lesson Review **434, 441, 445**
Chapter Review **446–449**

MARKETING IN ACTION
 CASE STUDY *Super Bowl Advertisement Bonanza* **450**

Travel and Tourism Team Decision Making Event **451**

CONTENTS

CHAPTER 17

SELLING SATISFIES THE CUSTOMER 452

Selling With Technology **452**

Corporate View: Career Opportunity
Corporate Counsel **453**

LESSONS
17.1 The Value of Selling **454**
17.2 Preparing for Effective Selling **461**
17.3 The Selling Process and Sales Support **468**

SPECIAL FEATURES
Digital Digest **472**
E-Marketing **457**
Figure This **458**
Get the Message **462**
Judgment Call **470**
Marketing Matters **454, 461, 468**
World View **465**

REVIEW AND ASSESSMENT
Checkpoint **455, 459, 460, 464, 466, 467, 472, 473**
Lesson Review **460, 467, 473**
Chapter Review **474–477**

MARKETING IN ACTION
 Home Improvement Shows and Stores **478**

Free-Enterprise Event **479**

CHAPTER 18

MOVING INTO A GLOBAL ECONOMY 480

Are Trade Agreements Barriers or Bridges? **480**

Corporate View: Career Opportunity
Localization Engineers **481**

LESSONS
18.1 The Expanding World Economy **482**
18.2 How Businesses Get Involved **487**
18.3 Understanding International Markets **492**

SPECIAL FEATURES
Digital Digest **494**
E-Marketing **484**
Figure This **488**
Get the Message **483**
Judgment Call **496**
Marketing Matters **482, 487, 492**
World View **490**

REVIEW AND ASSESSMENT
Checkpoint **485, 486, 488, 490, 491, 495, 497, 499**
Lesson Review **486, 491, 499**
Chapter Review **500–503**

MARKETING IN ACTION
 Ethics and Successful International Business **504**

Marketing Management Role Play **505**

CONTENTS

CHAPTER 19

MANAGING RISKS 506

NEWSLINE

Successful New Products Are No Easy Task **506**

Corporate View: Career Opportunity
Senior Financial Analyst **507**

LESSONS

19.1 Assessing Business Risks **508**
19.2 Identifying Marketing Risks **513**
19.3 Managing Marketing Risks **518**

SPECIAL FEATURES

Digital Digest **521**
E-Marketing **516**
Figure This **520**
Get the Message **509**
Judgment Call **510**
Marketing Matters **508, 513, 518**
World View **515**

REVIEW AND ASSESSMENT

Checkpoint **511, 512, 514, 517, 520, 523**
Lesson Review **512, 517, 523**
Chapter Review **524–527**

MARKETING IN ACTION

CASE STUDY *Napster: Theft or Ingenuity?* **528**

Business Services Role Play **529**

CHAPTER 20

MARKETING REQUIRES MONEY 530

NEWSLINE

Frito-Lay Focuses on Finance **530**

Corporate View: Career Opportunity
Financial Analyst **531**

LESSONS

20.1 Marketing Affects Business Finances **532**
20.2 Tools for Financial Planning **538**
20.3 Budgeting for Marketing Activities **546**

SPECIAL FEATURES

Digital Digest **539**
E-Marketing **548**
Figure This **550**
Get the Message **536**
Judgment Call **544**
Marketing Matters **532, 538, 546**
World View **547**

REVIEW AND ASSESSMENT

Checkpoint **534, 537, 541, 543, 545, 551, 553**
Lesson Review **537, 545, 553**
Chapter Review **554–557**

MARKETING IN ACTION

CASE STUDY *Financing a Start-Up Company* **558**

Financial Services Team Decision Making Event **559**

CONTENTS

CHAPTER 21

WHAT IS ENTREPRENEURSHIP? 560

NEWSLINE

Avoiding the Glass Ceiling **560**

Corporate View: Career Opportunity
Inventory Analyst/Inventory Manager **561**

LESSONS

21.1 What is Entrepreneurship? **562**
21.2 Entrepreneurs' Characteristics **566**
21.3 Business Ownership Opportunities **571**
21.4 Legal Needs for Entrepreneurs **575**
21.5 Developing a Business Plan **579**

SPECIAL FEATURES

Digital Digest **576**
E-Marketing **572**
Figure This **574**
Get the Message **563**
Judgment Call **569**
Marketing Matters **562, 566, 571, 575, 579**
World View **568**

REVIEW AND ASSESSMENT

Checkpoint **564, 565, 567, 570, 573, 574, 577, 578, 580, 581**
Lesson Review **565, 570, 574, 578, 581**
Chapter Review **582–585**

MARKETING IN ACTION

 CASE STUDY *The Rise of Successful Entrepreneurs* **586**

Entrepreneurship Written Event **587**

CHAPTER 22

TAKE CONTROL WITH MANAGEMENT 588

NEWSLINE

Quality Is Top Management Responsibility **588**

Corporate View: Career Opportunity
Accounts Payable Manager **589**

LESSONS

22.1 Managing With a Purpose **590**
22.2 Managing Effectively With a Plan **596**
22.3 Managing Marketing Activities **602**

SPECIAL FEATURES

Digital Digest **606**
E-Marketing **591**
Figure This **594**
Get the Message **605**
Judgment Call **604**
Marketing Matters **590, 596, 602**
World View **598**

REVIEW AND ASSESSMENT

Checkpoint **592, 595, 599, 601, 604, 607**
Lesson Review **595, 601, 607**
Chapter Review **608–611**

MARKETING IN ACTION

 CASE STUDY *The Perfect Marriage Turns Sour* **612**

Public Relations Project **613**

CONTENTS

CHAPTER 23

CAREERS IN MARKETING 614

What Do Employees Want? 614

Corporate View: Career Opportunity
Research and Information Specialist 615

LESSONS

23.1 Benefits of a Marketing Career **616**
23.2 Job Levels in Marketing **621**
23.3 Marketing Education and Career
Paths **627**
23.4 Beginning Career Planning **632**

SPECIAL FEATURES

Digital Digest **635**
E-Marketing **625**
Figure This **633**
Get the Message **617**
Marketing Matters **616, 621, 627, 632**
World View **629**

REVIEW AND ASSESSMENT

Checkpoint **618, 620, 623, 626, 628, 631,
634, 637**
Lesson Review **620, 626, 631, 637**
Chapter Review **638–641**

MARKETING IN ACTION

 *Young Entrepreneur in the
Web Design World* **642**

 *Technical Marketing
Representative Event* **643**

REVIEWERS

Kara Adams
Marketing and
Advertising Design
Instructor
Plano, TX

Sandra Bell-Duckworth
Marketing Education
Coordinator
Westerville, OH

Monica A. Caillouet
Marketing Instructor
Gonzales, LA

Dr. David Corbin
Curriculum Supervisor,
Business Technology
Midlothian, IL

Bruce Dickinson
Business and Marketing
Instructor
Sioux Falls, SD

Chris Dunkle
Marketing Instructor
Ona, WV

Thomas Farah
Marketing Instructor
Green Bay, WI

Lisa M. Gil-de-Lamadrid
Educational Specialist,
Marketing
Miami, FL

Dennis R. Groome
Marketing Instructor
Richmond, VA

Terrie Lockwood
Marketing Coordinator
Baton Rouge, LA

Vicki McKay
Marketing Instructor
Pasadena, TX

Pam Naylor
Marketing Education
Instructor-Coordinator
Birmingham, AL

Debbi Popo
Marketing Instructor
Columbus, OH

Dr. Diane Ross Gary
Supervisor, Business
Education
Bridgeport, CT

Nancy I. Royer
Vocational Instructor
Chesapeake, VA

Gary L. Schepf
Instructor
Irving, TX

Debra Wendt
Workforce Development
Instructor
Milwaukee, WI

Sue Wyche
Tech Prep Coordinator
Shreveport, LA

CHAPTER 1

MARKETING TODAY

LESSON 1.1 *WHAT IS MARKETING?*

LESSON 1.2 *BUSINESSES NEED MARKETING*

LESSON 1.3 *UNDERSTANDING THE MARKETING CONCEPT*

LESSON 1.4 *MARKETING'S ROLE TODAY AND TOMORROW*

NEWSLINE

U.S. EXPORTS MARKETING EXPERTISE

For the United States, highly developed marketing skills are more than just a means of conducting its own enterprises. As the former Soviet and eastern European countries have continued their difficult transformation from government-controlled to free-market economies, the United States has been demonstrating international leadership. Those nations implementing new economic systems have looked to the United States for expertise in organizing and managing the marketing systems essential to competitive business success.

It became evident long ago in the United States that the capability of producing and manufacturing good products is not enough to guarantee the success of companies. Marketing activities are also necessary. Companies need to be able to identify customers, move products efficiently to those customers, develop effective communications and promotion programs, assist in financing for customers, and help the customer use the products after the sale. These activities must be done in a way that allows the company to make a profit.

In government-controlled economies, individual businesses did not have to be as concerned about profits for each product or as concerned that consumers were necessarily satisfied with each product. Therefore, marketing functions were not well developed in those countries, making it very difficult to implement the changes needed for new economic systems to succeed.

Hundreds of United States marketing experts went to work in the developing countries to help with the changes. People have been redesigning transportation systems, looking at processes for handling and storing products, developing the technology for market research, establishing credit and financing policies and procedures, and assisting with the many other activities needed for effective marketing. The United States is viewed as a model of marketing effectiveness, and U.S. marketers are in demand to assist with the development of the effective functions and activities required. Marketing expertise has become an important U.S. export.

THINK CRITICALLY

1. In a free-market economy, who ultimately determines which products and services are produced?

2. Why are most marketing skills not needed in a government-controlled economy?

3. Since organizations in a government-controlled economy do not have to devote time or resources to marketing activities, why are they not more efficient than businesses in free market economies?

CORPORATE VIEW

CAREER OPPORTUNITY
PRODUCT MARKETING MANAGER

www.corpview.com

TeleView is looking for a Product Marketing Manager. Persons interested in this position should possess the following skills.

- Problem-solving, project organization, time management, and interpersonal skills
- Drive, flexibility, and technical communications skills
- Excellent customer relations skills
- Ability to work in an invigorating, team-oriented environment

The main responsibilities of the job include the following.

- Managing every part of product development from Research and Development and testing through manufacturing, marketing, sales, and product support
- Product planning
- Coordinating marketing with a product workgroup team
- Coordinating budgets and internal resources to bring a product to market on time and within budget
- Defining and evangelizing new product directions and opportunities
- Determining product pricing, product information, advertising, and other marketing campaigns
- Driving the launch of a new product

The job requires the following education, skills, and experience.

- BA, BS, or MBA in business, marketing, management, corporate communications, or a related field

- Four years of relevant experience, ideally including a successful track record in product management as well as Web and Intranet experience
- Proven leadership skills
- Strong technical communications skills
- Demonstrated ability to manage the many small details of a major product release

THINK CRITICALLY

1. Prepare a sample resume of a person who is qualified for this job and interested in applying for it.

2. Considering your own skills and preferences, does this sound like a job you would like to have one day? Why or why not?

3. Search want ads or the Internet for a job similar to TeleView's Product Marketing Manager. What type of compensation package is being offered for the job?

3

1.1 WHAT IS MARKETING?

GOALS

- **Understand the importance of studying marketing.**
- **Explain what marketing is and describe the marketing functions.**
- **Define marketing.**

Marketing is one of the most important functions in the modern American company. For example, in 2000 companies spent more than $233 billion on advertising, which is just one piece in the large marketing pie. There are hundreds of different business activities and careers that can be classified as marketing.

Work with a group. Generate a list of 10 different business activities or careers that you feel should be classified as marketing. Explain your reasons for selecting each. Share your list and reasons with the rest of the groups.

WHY STUDY MARKETING?

Marketing is exciting, important, and profitable. Businesses, individual consumers, and our economy benefit from effective marketing. This chapter introduces marketing in a way many people will not recognize. Even though marketing is a well-known word, it is often misused or misunderstood. Marketing has changed a great deal over the past 20 years. Some businesses still do not use marketing effectively.

Marketing is a rather large category covering a number of different activities that provides broad benefits when used effectively. There are differences between effective and ineffective marketing. Marketing and marketing activities have changed dramatically over the years. Marketing is now an important activity essential not only to the success of manufacturers and retailers, but also to government agencies, hospitals, law offices, schools, and churches. Marketing has a number of major functions with numerous examples performed by almost every business. Successful businesses develop an approach to marketing planning that responds to the needs of customers so that customers will be satisfied with the products and services they purchase.

WHERE DOES MARKETING TAKE PLACE?

Marketing is one of the most visible business activities around you. You do not often see products being manufactured, accountants maintaining the financial records of a business, or human resources managers hiring and training personnel. But you see marketing every day. Marketing includes advertisements on the radio, products being transported by truck, and marketing researchers in shopping malls.

You are involved in marketing. You make marketing decisions regularly. You assist routinely in the effective marketing of products and services. Marketing activities are involved when you select the products or services you intend to purchase. You are involved in marketing activities when you decide to use cash or a credit card and when you pay for the delivery of a bulky product to your home (rather than attempt to transport it yourself).

ALL TYPES OF BUSINESSES USE MARKETING

Businesses Directly Involved in Marketing	Businesses With Major Marketing Activities	Businesses With Limited Marketing Role
advertising agencies	retailers	law offices
marketing research firms	manufacturers	physicians
sales representatives	banks	accounting firms
trucking companies	real estate agencies	government agencies
credit card companies	insurance companies	universities
telemarketing businesses	automobile dealers	construction businesses
travel agencies	farmers and ranchers	public utilities

By studying marketing, you will learn how businesses use marketing to increase their effectiveness and the profits they make. You will also improve your personal marketing skills. Those skills are useful to you as a consumer as you make better purchasing decisions. Marketing skills are used as you make an application for college. You use marketing skills when you interview with a potential employer. Marketing skills are used also when you serve as a leader of an organization. And they are the skills needed for many exciting and well-paying careers in the business world.

Every business today is involved in marketing. Over four million firms in the United States have marketing as their primary business activity (see Figure 1-1). Examples of those businesses are advertising agencies, real estate offices, marketing research businesses, finance companies, travel agencies, and retail stores. Most large businesses have marketing

E-MARKETING

Basic Internet Business Models

As web sites have developed and grown as marketing tools, several basic models have emerged for companies doing business on the Internet:

Selling goods or services online. Amazon.com is a classic example of this model. It sells everything online. Established businesses have also formed Internet ventures to complement their non-Internet sales activities.

Providing access to an audience. America Online, for example, provides advertisers access to more than 20 million people.

Selling subscriptions to a web site. A number of premium web sites require subscription payments. Some offer basic information without charges but require payment for advanced services, such as online investment research.

Selling admissions. Some Internet events are like pay-per-view television events. As streaming media technology improves, this business model is likely to become more prevalent.

THINK CRITICALLY

1. Which of these basic Internet business models does Yahoo! represent?

2. If a magazine publisher starts an Internet edition that is accessible only to people who pay for its print edition, what type of Internet business model does it represent?

departments employing many types of marketing specialists. Even small companies are finding they need to employ people who understand marketing and are able to complete a number of marketing activities.

There are many types of marketing jobs ranging from selling to inventory management. Careers in advertising, sales promotion, customer service, credit, insurance, transportation, and research require preparation in marketing. Marketers work for manufacturers, law offices, hospitals, museums, professional sports teams, and symphonies. There are marketing jobs available as you begin your career. These jobs include retail clerk, bank teller, stock person, telemarketing interviewer, and delivery person. You could advance to many marketing management jobs, some requiring a great deal of education and experience. Typically, marketing positions can be among the highest paid jobs in most companies. Because of the change and growth that has occurred in marketing, many people view it as the most diverse and exciting career area of the 21st century.

checkpoint

Name three types of businesses whose activities are almost entirely marketing.

WHAT IS MARKETING?

When many people hear the word marketing they only think of advertising and selling. However, many marketing activities need to be completed before a product or service is ever ready to be advertised and sold.

MARKETING FUNCTIONS

Marketing activities can be grouped into seven functions. These functions, Product/Service Management, Distribution, Selling, Marketing-Information Management, Financing, Pricing, and Promotion, are summarized in Figure 1-2. Don't be concerned if you don't completely understand the meaning as you read the descriptions. You will learn more about the functions and how each function is used as a part of effective marketing in later chapters.

Product/Service Management Assisting in the design and development of products and services that will meet the needs of prospective customers.

Distribution Determining the best methods and procedures to be used so prospective customers are able to locate, obtain,

FIGURE 1-2
Marketing activities can be categorized within seven functions.

Population Trends Pose Challenges

World population now exceeds 6 billion, having more than tripled since 1930. Because markets consist of people willing and able to exchange things of value, the exponential growth of population, particularly in less developed countries, puts a heavy burden on marketing. The distribution of food, for instance, is a complicated marketing problem.

The United Nations forecasts world population will reach 8.9 billion in 2050, with most of the growth occurring in less developed regions. At the same time, marketers must contend with declining population in certain regions of the world, such as western Europe. As a result, people in different areas will have vastly different economic needs and desires.

Whatever their circumstances, all areas benefit from vigorous international trade. Such trade cannot be effectively maintained unless marketers address themselves to the varying needs of people all around the world. Satisfying those disparate needs and coordinating those efforts poses a serious marketing challenge.

THINK CRITICALLY

1. How can marketers in developed countries ease the burdens posed by population growth in less developed countries?

2. Use the Internet to find information about world population trends. Prepare a graph or chart displaying the information you found.

---

and use the products and services of an organization.

Selling Direct, personal communications with prospective customers in order to assess needs and satisfy those needs with appropriate products and services.

Marketing-Information Management Obtaining, managing, and using market information to improve decision making and the performance of marketing activities.

Financing Budgeting for marketing activities, obtaining the necessary financing, and providing financial assistance to customers to assist them with purchasing the organization's products and services.

Pricing Establishing and communicating the value of products and services to prospective customers.

Promotion Communicating information to prospective customers through advertising and other promotional methods to encourage them to purchase the organization's products and services.

Each of these functions occurs every time a product or service is developed and sold. The performance of the activities described in the functions is the responsibility of marketers. So you can see that marketing is a very complex part of business and is very important to the success of businesses and to the satisfaction of customers.

COMPANIES USE THE MARKETING FUNCTIONS

You can identify the marketing functions being performed by companies as they develop new products, improve marketing procedures, and respond to customer needs. You can find examples of these functions in hundreds of different forms.

Sony used *product/service management* to develop the Video Walkman, which combines a 3-inch television with an 8-mm videocassette recorder.

Hertz uses a unique *distribution* strategy as a part its car rental service. Hertz will park a car at the exit of an airport terminal with the engine running, heated in the winter or cooled in the summer, and with all paperwork completed for selected customers to speed their departure from the airport.

Many professional firms are recognizing the importance of personal *selling* to the success of their practices. Selected executives in law offices, accounting firms, and banks are completing professional sales training in order to effectively develop new clients for the businesses.

The electronic scanners used at checkouts of supermarkets provide information on purchases so managers can instantly determine what is being purchased in order to keep the best assortment of products available for customers. This is an example of the use of *marketing-information management*.

Major automobile manufacturers, such as General Motors, demonstrate the *financing* function when they maintain their own financing organizations (like GMAC) to make loans to consumers available at the automobile dealerships.

A bakery manager notices that customers aren't purchasing pastries, cookies, and other snacks because they are too expensive. As part of the *pricing* function, she lowers the prices and places a sign in the front window advertising them.

Businesses selling expensive products such as oceanfront condominiums prepare high-quality videotapes, which provide information and *promote* products using audio and video messages. The videotapes are sent to carefully selected customers to interest them in purchasing a condominium through a unique type of promotion.

Of the seven marketing functions, which occur when a product is developed and sold?

DEFINING
MARKETING

Because of the many functions and activities that are part of marketing, it is not easy to develop a definition of marketing that effectively describes it. Marketing has changed in recent years and continues to change. A simple definition was presented in a 1960 book of marketing terms published by the American Marketing Association. Marketing was described as "the performance of business activities that direct the flow of goods and services from producer to consumer or user." As marketing developed

and was applied in a broad set of businesses and organizations, definitions became more complex. Marketing now includes customer research and product development activities. It applies to non-profit businesses and to organizations not considered businesses (churches, sororities and fraternities, schools, and libraries). Not only is marketing used for products and services, but for individuals (political candidates, artists, sports stars), and even to promote ideas (stop smoking, recycling, stay in school).

Satisfying
Exchange

The most recent definition of marketing, accepted by the American Marketing Association in 1985, is very long and complex, but it communicates how marketing has changed over the years. It defines marketing as the process of planning and executing the conception, pricing, promotion, and distribution of ideas, goods, and services to create exchanges that satisfy individual and organizational objectives.

Because marketing can be applied in very different ways in various businesses and organizations, and because marketing needs to be easily understood, the following simplified definition describes the value marketing offers to those who use it well.

Marketing is the creation and maintenance of satisfying exchange relationships.

You need to carefully consider all parts of this definition in order to understand marketing. *Creation* suggests that marketing is involved from the very beginning as products and services are being developed. *Maintenance* means that marketing must continue to be used as long as a business or organization is operating. *Satisfaction* of both the business and the customer is an important goal of marketing. When products or services are exchanged, the needs of everyone involved must be met as well as possible. Finally, *exchange relationships* applies the definition to any exchange

where people are giving and receiving something of value as shown in Figure 1-3. Marketing is needed by, but not limited to, businesses that are selling products and services.

checkpoint

What kinds of relationships are central to the modern concept of marketing?

LESSON REVIEW

1. Name three types of marketing activities that people see almost every day.

2. Identify three marketing functions and describe real-life examples of those functions that you have experienced, heard about, or read about.

3. What percentage of businesses are involved in marketing activities?

4. What has happened to the commonly accepted definition of marketing over the past 40 years?

5. What is the key attribute of the exchange relationships that marketers seek to create and maintain?

1.2 BUSINESSES NEED MARKETING

GOALS

- ● **Explain why businesses need marketing.**
- ● **Understand how marketing has developed in the business world.**
- ● **Describe the functions of business.**

MARKETING MATTERS

Marketing has developed from a set of primitive business activities into a sophisticated and vital business function. A number of simple business activities were taken for granted in the past but today are considered to be key marketing functions. For example, 100 years ago, providing credit to regular customers was common, easy to manage, and considered "good for business." Today, providing financing options, including credit, is a key marketing function, and can require entire divisions within large corporations.

Work with a group. Imagine that you are a running a business 100 years ago. Think of an activity that might have been common then. Discuss how that activity compares to its modern equivalent. Share your discussion results with the other groups.

THE NEED FOR MARKETING

Ever since the first products were exchanged, there has been a need for marketing. In the past, marketing was viewed as a simple set of activities that would help a business sell its products to more customers. The very first businesses developed marketing to improve exchanges.

Business managers know that marketing must be carefully planned. It must be coordinated with other business activities. The approach to managing marketing activities changes as businesses and other organizations implement the marketing concept.

Marketing is an important part of business. Some people believe that if a business offers a good product, marketing is not necessary. However, if the customer does not know about the product, does not know where to purchase it, is unable to get to the place where it is sold, cannot afford the price of the product, or does not believe the product is a good value, the product will not be purchased. Marketing is

required to provide a variety of activities or services so the customer will be able to purchase the product.

Marketing cannot be successful if the product is not what the customer wants or is a poor quality product. While a customer may be encouraged to buy a product through advertising, selling, or a low price, the product must be seen as satisfying a need of the customer. If the customer decides to buy the product, and it does not work the way the customer was led to believe, if it is of poor quality, or if it has a defect, the customer will likely return the product for a refund. Even if the customer does not return a product that was not satisfying, it is unlikely the customer will buy the same product again.

Businesses and other organizations use effective marketing to provide satisfying exchanges of products and services with customers. The ways marketing is used have changed over the years, but the need for marketing has not.

Why does a business need marketing if it has a good product or service?

MARKETING AND THE DEVELOPMENT OF BUSINESS

There have been times in history when people were self-sufficient. Being **self-sufficient** means you do not rely on others for the things needed in order to survive. People were able to find or produce the food and materials needed for themselves and their families. That type of lifestyle required very hard work and was very risky. Self-sufficient people had to have good hunting, fishing, or farming skills to obtain needed food as well as the capability of developing shelter, clothing, and other necessities. Often it was not possible to obtain everything needed to survive because of poor weather, competition with other people, sickness, or lack of skill.

BARTERING

Some people who found they were not successful at being self-sufficient tried to find other ways to survive. They saw that often, when they did not have certain things they needed, other people had those things. If each person had something that the other person valued, they were able to exchange, so each would be better off than before. Exchanging products or services with others by agreeing on their values is known as **bartering**. A system of bartering was developed so people could exchange with

others to obtain the things they needed. For example, in an early bartering system, someone who was a good hunter but was not able to grow grain might exchange products with another person who had extra grain but needed meat. People who had developed skills in weaving cloth might barter with people who raised animals. Exchanging products through bartering was one of the first examples of marketing. Bartering still takes place today on a limited scale, and is even taxed by the IRS.

SPECIALIZATION OF LABOR

People discovered that they had particular interests or skills in certain kinds of work, while they were not as good at or were uninterested in other types of work. If they concentrated on the work they did well, they were able to accomplish much more than if they tried to do a variety of things. Concentrating on one or a few related activities so that they can be done well is known as **specialization of labor**. Specialization of labor made it possible for people to produce larger quantities of a single product than if they were attempting to produce many different products. Therefore, more of that product would be available to exchange with other people.

MONEY SYSTEMS

As specialization of labor became more common and a greater variety and quantity of products were available, it was not always possible to barter. Not all people needed the products of others, and it was not always possible to reach agreement on what products were worth so that they could be exchanged directly. To assist with the exchange process, a money system was developed. A **money system** established the use of currency as a recognized medium of exchange. With money, people could obtain products even if they did not always have products on hand to exchange. Those with products to sell could do so for money, which could then be used for future purchases. The development of a money system is another example of marketing.

CENTRAL MARKETS

With many people producing more types of products and with people having money to purchase the items they needed, the demand for products increased. It was a difficult process to locate and accumulate all of the products people wanted and needed. A great deal of time was spent traveling to sell and purchase products. To solve that problem, central markets were developed. A **central market** is a location where people bring products to be conveniently exchanged. Central markets were often located at places where many people traveled, such as where rivers or roads met.

Towns and cities developed at those locations and became centers of trade. People brought the products they wanted to sell to the markets. Those people needing to obtain products would also travel to the market to make purchases. Developing locations where products could be bought and sold was another step in the development of marketing. (See Figure 1-4.)

OTHER MARKETING ACTIVITIES

As central markets expanded, other types of business services were created to make exchanges easier. It was not always possible for sellers and buyers to travel to the markets at the same time. Therefore, businesses were formed to purchase products from producers and hold them for sale to purchasers. Other businesses were started to loan money to buyers or sellers, to help with transportation of products, or to locate products that were not available in the market but that customers wanted. Each of those activities resulted in the development of another marketing activity and made the exchange process more effective for those who produced products and for those who purchased and consumed the products.

How did the development of central markets aid the growth of business?

FIGURE 1-4
Central locations where many people travel provide convenient places for marketing activities to be completed.

Marketing Through Central Markets

THE FUNCTIONS OF BUSINESS

The previous examples have illustrated how marketing developed to improve the exchange of products between producers and consumers. It is clear that marketing is an important part of business and that businesses cannot be effective without marketing. But marketing cannot be successful alone. A number of other activities are important to businesses. These activities are summarized in Figure 1-5.

PRODUCTION

The primary reason for a business to exist is to provide products or services to consumers and to earn a profit. The **production function** creates or obtains products or services for sale. Think of the variety of products and services available from businesses and you can see that production can take various forms.

Raw Materials   Production includes obtaining raw materials for sale to customers. Mining, logging, drilling for oil, and similar activities are examples of this type of production.

Processing   Other businesses take raw materials and change their form through processing so they can be used in the production of other products or in the operation of businesses or equipment. Examples include oil refining and the production of steel, paper, plastics, food products, and so forth.

A third example of production is agriculture, where food and other materials are grown for consumption or for processing into a variety of products.

Manufacturing businesses are also involved in production. Those businesses use raw materials and other resources to produce products for sale to consumers or to other businesses. Most of the products consumed by you, your friends, your family, and businesses have been produced by manufacturers.

FIGURE 1-5
Marketing must be planned cooperatively with many other activities in a business.

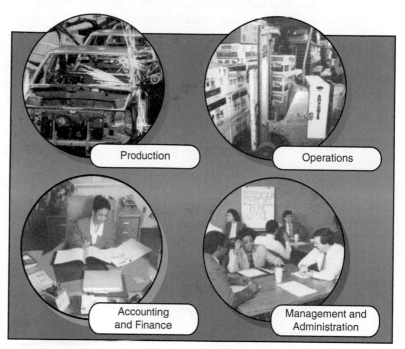

Production

Operations

Accounting and Finance

Management and Administration

Services   The development of services is also an example of the production function. While a physical product is not provided to the customer, offering a service such as preparing tax returns, cutting hair, providing lawn maintenance services, or performing a concert meets customer needs in the same way as making consumable products.

Finally, some businesses do not produce or manufacture products but accumulate products for resale to customers. Offering products produced or manufactured by others for sale to customers is known as **merchandising**. Retailers and wholesalers are examples of merchandising businesses. While merchandising is not production, it makes products available for sale in those businesses in the same way that production and manufacturing do for other businesses.

OPERATIONS

The ongoing activities designed to support the primary function of a business and to keep a business operating efficiently are known as **operations**. Many things must occur for a business to successfully produce and market products and services. Buildings and equipment must be operated, maintained, and repaired. Products must be obtained, transported, stored, and protected. Paperwork must be completed. Customer questions must be answered and customer services provided. The way operations are completed often means the difference between profit or loss for a business.

ACCOUNTING AND FINANCE

Businesses are very complex with a variety of activities occurring at the same time. A large amount of money is handled by most businesses in many forms including cash, checks, and credit. The **accounting and finance function** plans and manages financial resources and maintains records and information related to businesses' finances.

Finance begins by determining the amount of capital needed for the business and where that capital will be obtained. Budgets must be developed, watched carefully, and updated. Most businesses must regularly borrow money for major purchases as well as for some day-to-day operations. Determining sources for borrowing, interest rates, and loan payback schedules are important responsibilities of accounting and finance personnel. Without careful record keeping and an understanding of the financial situation, managers will be unable to plan the activities of the business. The accounting and finance function provides that type of information and assistance in the business.

MANAGEMENT AND ADMINISTRATION

Even the smallest businesses require that considerable time be spent in planning and organizing activities. Someone must determine what the business will do, how it can best meet the needs of customers, and how to respond to competitors' actions. Problem-solving, managing the work of employees, and evaluating the activities of the business are ongoing responsibilities of managers. The **management and administration function** involves developing, implementing, and evaluating the plans and activities of a business.

FIGURE THIS
1234567890

Marketing research, both internal and external, is an important marketing function. For professional organizations, whose members are its primary customers, analyzing membership data can provide valuable insights and help them serve their members better.

An association of business executives wanted to determine the type of positions its members had held prior to being promoted into their current positions. A clerk reviewed each member's resume and came up with the following data:

Production: 225 members
Accounting: 104 members
Finance: 160 members
Operations: 85 members
Marketing: 358 members

Becoming an Executive

Administration: 58 members
Management: 44 members
Undetermined: 32 members

THINK CRITICALLY

1. Based on the data above, how many members are there in the organization?

2. What percentage of the association membership worked in each of the business areas listed above?

3. Construct or draw a pie chart that illustrates the results of the research by depicting both the actual numbers in each category and the percentage of the overall membership that each category represents.

Managers are responsible for everything that occurs in the business including the work of the employees. They must develop objectives and plans, make sure the appropriate resources are available, be responsible for buildings and equipment, and assign responsibilities to others. Managers are held responsible for the performance of the company, including whether or not it is profitable.

MARKETING

Marketing is also an important function of business. All businesses need to complete a variety of activities in order to make their products and services available to consumers and to ensure that effective exchanges occur. Those activities are known as marketing.

COORDINATION OF BUSINESS FUNCTIONS

Each of the functions of business is dependent on the other functions if the business is to be effective. Products can be produced, but if the company is not operated or managed effectively, if adequate records are not maintained, or if marketing is not successful, the products will not be sold at a profit. In the same way, operations, management, and administration are used to coordinate the work of the business. Finance and accounting provide information to the other parts of the business to ensure that a profit is possible.

Some organizations have not been successful in coordinating the business functions. The various functions operated independently and often competed with each other. Products were produced that could not be sold. Marketing activities were planned with little attention to their costs. Managers concentrated on specific activities of the business without considering if their decisions would have negative effects on other functions. The result was that the quality of products and customer service declined while prices increased. Customers became unhappy when they found that products were declining in quality, they could not get the level of service they expected, or prices were increasing rapidly. Competitors who were better organized were able to take advantage of those situations.

Most businesses recognize that they must carefully coordinate the functions and activities if they are going to satisfy their customers and make a profit. Managers and employees are trained to work together. A great deal of planning is done to determine how activities should be organized.

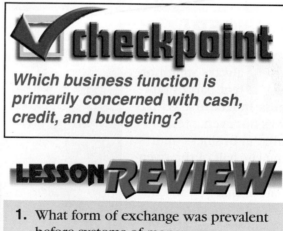

checkpoint

Which business function is primarily concerned with cash, credit, and budgeting?

LESSON REVIEW

1. What form of exchange was prevalent before systems of money were developed?

2. How does the specialization of labor make people more productive, and how does that contribute to the development of marketing activities?

3. What can people do with money that they cannot do easily by trading goods or services directly for other goods or services?

1.3 UNDERSTANDING THE MARKETING CONCEPT

GOALS

- Define the marketing concept.
- Determine how businesses implement the marketing concept.

THE MARKETING CONCEPT

Marketing was not always an important part of business. Indeed, marketing was not even a term used in business until the last half of the twentieth century. In the early part of that century, businesses were concerned about producing products that customers needed and were able to afford. Major efforts that could be considered marketing were directed at getting the products to customers. There were not many choices of transportation methods, and roads and highways were not

well developed. The primary way to sell more products was to be able to deliver them to a larger number of customers.

As consumers increased their standard of living and had more money to spend, the demand for newer and better products increased. Demand was usually greater than the available supply of products. Business people concentrated on production and seldom had to worry a great deal about marketing. Customers were often eager to buy new products and would seek out the manufacturer when they heard of a product they wanted.

Over time production processes improved, there was more competition among producers and manufacturers, and consumers had more choices of products and services available. Therefore, businesses had to compete with each other to get customers to buy their products. Businesses began to increase their attention to basic marketing activities, such as advertising and selling, to convince customers that their products were superior to those of competitors.

SATISFYING CUSTOMER NEEDS

As it became more and more difficult and expensive for businesses to sell their products, some business people began to realize an important fact. Businesses could no longer be successful by just producing more products or by increasing the amount of advertising and selling efforts for the products. They had to produce products that customers wanted. The most successful businesses were the ones that considered customers' needs and worked to satisfy those needs as they produced and marketed their products and services. That philosophy of business is now known as the marketing concept.

FIGURE 1-6
Effective marketing emphasizes customers, products, and profits.

ELEMENTS OF THE MARKETING CONCEPT

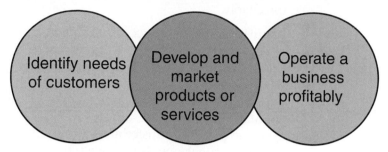

Identify needs of customers — Develop and market products or services — Operate a business profitably

The **marketing concept** is using the needs of customers as the primary focus during the planning, production, distribution, and promotion of a product or service.

Using the marketing concept is not as easy as it might sound. Three activities must be accomplished by businesses if they want to use it successfully. Those three activities are illustrated in Figure 1-6.

● First, the business must be able to identify what will satisfy customers' needs.

JUDGMENT CALL

Misuse Sullies Marketing's Image

Many people do not have a positive image of marketing, because marketing practices too often take advantage of prospective customers without satisfying their needs. That tends to occur when someone is concerned only with making a sale, not a long-term relationship.

Common examples of ways marketing is misused include:

● Stating that a price has been reduced when it really hasn't.

● Advertising a product at a low price, but only stocking a very small quantity so that it is quickly sold out.

● Sending a consumer a letter that says the person has won an expensive prize, then charging a large amount for shipping and handling costs.

● Distributing misleading depictions or descriptions of products.

● Attempting to sell people something after they participate in a phony marketing research survey.

THINK CRITICALLY
What can people do to discourage misuse of marketing when they encounter it?

- Second, the business must be able to develop and market products or services that customers consider to be better than other choices.
- Third, the business must be able to operate profitably.

Many businesses are successfully identifying and responding to needs of customers. Fast food restaurants provide breakfast menus and late night hours in order to have their products available when customers want them. Many banks provide services so customers can pay bills, transfer money, and check account balances by using a telephone or a personal computer. Hospitals offer wellness programs, weight loss clinics, and fitness centers to attract clients and broaden their image. Colleges offer courses to area high school students to allow college credits to be earned prior to graduation and to interest students in enrolling full time at the college.

THE CONSEQUENCES OF NOT SATISFYING CUSTOMER NEEDS

Businesses that do not use the marketing concept are more concerned about producing products than understanding customer needs. Once products are developed, they rely on marketing activities to try to sell those products. You may be aware of the difficulty some automobile manufacturers have selling their cars. In some cases the difficulty results because they are not producing the type, style, or quality of cars customers want. The companies then have to use extensive advertising, price reductions, rebates, and pressure selling to convince customers to buy a product that is not really what the customers prefer.

Retail stores sometimes buy products that they believe will sell, but then see that customers are not willing to buy them. The stores then have to cut prices, increase advertising, use special displays, and other strategies to convince customers to buy the products. The extra expenses of marketing products that customers may not have a strong interest in buying can lead to reductions in profit or even losses for the business. Additionally, after purchasing the product, the customer may decide it is not what was wanted and return the product to the business or become very unhappy with both the product and the company that sold it. The customer may be reluctant to buy from that company in the future and may express dissatisfaction to prospective customers, resulting in reduced sales for the company.

Under the marketing concept, what is a business's primary focus during planning, production, distribution, and promotion of a product?

IMPLEMENTING THE MARKETING CONCEPT

Companies that believe in the marketing concept operate differently than those who do not. Businesses using the marketing concept follow a two-step process.

IDENTIFY THE MARKET

The first step is to identify the market they want to serve (see Figure 1-7). A **market** refers to the description of the prospective customers a business wants to serve and the location of those customers. An example of a market for a bicycle manufacturer may be people who ride bicycles for health and fitness in the mountains. A potential market for a sports arena may be teenagers within 80 miles of the arena who attend concerts more than two times a year.

DEVELOP A MARKETING MIX

The second step is to develop a marketing mix that will meet the needs of the market and that the business can provide profitably. A **marketing mix** is the blending of four marketing elements (product, distribution, price, and promotion) by the business. The bicycle manufacturer may decide to offer a mountain bike with three choices of frames and tires. They can sell through a selected group of bicycle shops in resort towns in Colorado, Wyoming, Utah, and New Mexico. The price can range from $280–$550. It can be promoted by advertising in two fitness magazines, a cable sports channel, and by

FIGURE 1-7
The definition of a market includes people and their location.

Identifying a Market

salespeople in the bicycle shops. The sports arena manager could choose a marketing mix for concerts that includes groups that have albums in the top 40 of the pop/rock charts, scheduled on Saturday or Sunday evenings, priced at $60 for reserved seating and $32 for open seating, and promoted on the three area FM radio stations with the highest audience ratings for listeners age 15–25.

Each of the elements of the marketing mix shown in Figure 1-8 provides many

FIGURE 1-8
Businesses use the four elements of the marketing mix to satisfy customer needs.

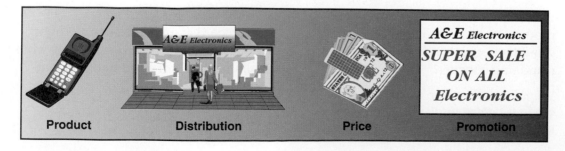

| Product | Distribution | Price | Promotion |

alternatives from which the business can select to satisfy the market better. The development and implementation of the marketing mix will be discussed in detail in other chapters. Basic definitions of each mix element are as follows.

Product is anything offered to a market by the business to satisfy needs, including physical products, services, and ideas.

Distribution includes the locations and methods used to make the product available to customers.

Price is the actual amount that customers pay and the methods of increasing the value of the product to the customers.

Promotion includes the methods and information communicated to customers to encourage purchases and increase their satisfaction.

While each of the definitions is written to describe marketing of products by a business, the mix elements are also part of services and ideas. Non-business organizations and even individuals can effectively develop marketing mixes. The strategies of effective marketing that you will be learning have very broad applications.

What four marketing elements make up what is known as the marketing mix?

LESSON REVIEW

1. What are some of the immediate consequences of producing products that customers do *not* want?

2. Beyond identifying customers' needs and developing products that they want to buy, what else must businesses do to successfully use the marketing concept?

3. If a business is the sole producer of a product that its customers need, why should it bother with implementing the marketing concept?

4. What is the first step a business takes when it begins implementing the marketing concept?

5. In identifying the market it wants to serve, what two things does a business decide?

6. If a fast food chain was expanding into a new area, decisions about where to locate each of its individual restaurants would fall under which element of the marketing mix?

7. If a record store mailed out discount coupons to nearby residents, they would fall under which element of the marketing mix?

MARKETING'S ROLE TODAY AND TOMORROW

MARKETING MATTERS

Marketing is an important tool for businesses. In addition, a number of other organizations that are not businesses also find benefits in performing marketing activities. For example, colleges routinely send recruiters all over the United States and to foreign countries to attempt to persuade students to attend their school.

Work with a group. Create a list of 5 organizations. Identify a marketing function that each can perform to their benefit. Share your results with the other groups.

GOALS

● Describe the changing role of marketing.

● Summarize how marketing is changing and why marketing is important.

THE CHANGING ROLE OF MARKETING

While marketing is necessary in all exchanges, businesses have not always believed marketing was important. They expected customers to take most of the responsibility for completing marketing activities. Only recently have many business people realized the value of effective marketing. There are several changes in the role that marketing has played in U.S. businesses during the past century. The historical development of marketing is summarized in Figure 1-9.

PRODUCTION EMPHASIS

In the early years of the last century (1900–1920), production processes were very simple and few product choices were available. People had limited money to spend on products and much of their purchasing was for basic necessities.

FIGURE 1-9
The philosophy of marketing changed throughout the past century.

Production Era	1900s-1920s	Emphasis on producing and distributing new products
Sales Era	1930s-1940s	Emphasis on using advertising and sales-people to convince customers to buy a company's products
Marketing Department Era	1950s-1960s	Emphasis on developing many new marketing activities to sell products
Marketing Concept Era	1970s-Today	Emphasis on satisfying customers' needs with a carefully developed marketing mix

Transportation systems were not well developed so it was difficult to get products from where they were manufactured to the many people throughout the United States.

In that environment, businesses believed that if they could produce products, they would be able to sell them. So they concentrated on developing new products and improving the process of production. The only real marketing effort was devoted to distribution, moving products from the producer to the customer.

SALES EMPHASIS

During the 1930s and into the 1940s, businesses became more effective at producing products. Efficient methods of producing large numbers of products at a low cost, such as assembly lines, were used. Transportation systems improved including the use of trains, boats, and trucks, making it easier to get products to more customers. At the same time, the standard of living of many Americans was improving, giving them money to spend on more products.

These changes resulted in increased competition among businesses. They could no longer rely on customers buying their products just because they were able to get the products to the customers.

Companies began to rely on salespeople to represent their products. The salespeople would attempt to convince customers that their company's products were better than the products of competitors.

MARKETING DEPARTMENT EMPHASIS

The sales emphasis continued on until well into the 1950s for many businesses and well beyond that time for others. Then after World War II, the U.S. economy expanded rapidly and wage levels increased for consumers as their hours of work declined. Consumers

Using Databases to Support Decision Making

There is an important distinction between data and information. Data are simply recorded facts, whereas information is a body of facts that have been organized in a format suitable for use in decision making.

A database is a collection of data that is arranged in a logical manner and organized in a form that can be stored and processed by a computer. A common example is a collection of customer names, addresses, prior purchases, and current orders that a company assembles internally. Internal records and reports contain a wealth of data related to costs, shipments, inventories, dollar amounts, financing, and dates. Data is used to generate reports, or information, that marketers can then use to make better decisions and improve performance.

Many commercial organizations also assemble and market computerized databases of external data, such as sales of various products, brands, and packages. Marketers can analyze that data to determine which packages sell best, what price is most effective, and how their brands are doing in relation to their competitors' brands.

Information gleaned from databases can be displayed numerically or graphically. Advances in spreadsheet and statistical software have revolutionized the analysis of marketing data.

THINK CRITICALLY

1. For a business manager, what is the important distinction between data and information?

2. What are some key differences between internal and external databases, and how do those differences affect their usefulness to businesses?

had more money to spend and more time to enjoy the use of many products. Companies increasingly found that consumers were not easily convinced to purchase products when they had many choices available to them. Therefore, businesses had to find different ways to be sure that consumers purchased their products. Companies began to develop marketing departments that were responsible for developing those new methods.

One of the first efforts of the new marketing department was to expand the use of advertising. Advertising had an important role of informing consumers about a company's products, the reasons to buy the products, and where they could be located. New methods of getting products to customers were developed including catalog sales through the mail and even the use of airplanes to move some products very rapidly. Products were distributed extensively through many retail stores. Customers were offered credit to make purchases more affordable. As companies worked to find additional methods to encourage customers to buy, the marketing department became an important part of the business.

MARKETING CONCEPT EMPHASIS

The marketing department emphasis showed that marketing could be a very important tool for businesses. A number of activities were now available that had not been used in the past.

However, just because more activities were used, companies were not always more successful. It was discovered that marketing was becoming quite expensive. Also, since the goal of the marketing department was to sell the products of the company, marketers began to misuse marketing activities. These unethical activities sometimes resulted in sales, but also led to customer complaints. Examples included high-pressure sales, misleading advertising, and customer services that were not provided as promised. These earlier actions help explain why some people have a negative attitude toward sales people and advertisements.

Marketers also discovered that no matter how hard they tried, there were products that customers did not want to buy. If customers did not believe the product would satisfy their needs, marketing was not effective. Yet marketers were not involved in developing the company's products.

In the 1970s, some companies began to realize they could be more successful if they listened to consumers and considered customer needs as they developed products and services. The marketing concept uses the needs of customers as the primary focus during the planning, production, distribution, and promotion of a product or service.

When the marketing concept was adopted, marketing became more than the work of one department. It was now a major part of the business. Marketing personnel worked closely with people in other parts of the company. Activities were completed with customer satisfaction in mind. By coordinating the efforts of the departments in the company and by focusing on satisfying customers' needs, companies were able to develop and market products that customers wanted and that could be sold at a profit. Those companies were using the marketing concept. Since its first use in the 1970s, the marketing concept has been proven as an effective method and is now used by the majority of businesses and by other organizations.

Name the four major phases in the development of marketing's role in business since 1900.

THE CHANGING DEFINITION
OF MARKETING

Marketing is very different today than it was even just fifteen or twenty years ago. If you look back over the history of business, you can see that marketing has played a role in even the simplest early businesses. But business people have not recognized the full value of marketing as a business tool until recently. Figure 1-10 shows how the definition of marketing has changed because of the progression of marketing activities.

The role of marketing in business has changed along with the definition. Previously, marketing was seen as a tool to help the business sell its products and services. It was not needed if sales were high. Today, business people see that marketing contributes in several important ways to the business. It provides information about customers and their needs through market research, which helps businesses plan more effectively. Marketing provides many ways to serve customers better including distribution, pricing, credit, and customer services. Marketing can increase customer satisfaction by solving customer problems. Finally, marketing can help the business be more profitable by coordinating activities and controlling costs.

FIGURE 1-10
As the activities of marketing have changed, marketing has become more important to businesses.

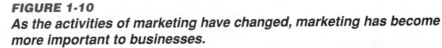

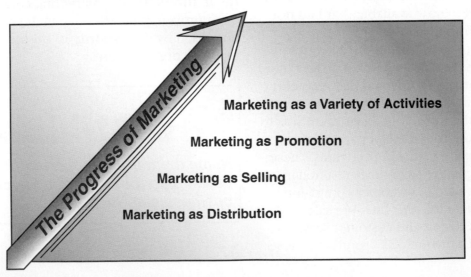

The Progress of Marketing

Marketing as a Variety of Activities

Marketing as Promotion

Marketing as Selling

Marketing as Distribution

MARKETING IN OTHER ORGANIZATIONS

Because of the successful use of marketing in businesses, other organizations now look to marketing for help. Libraries, churches, government agencies, community organizations, and the military are using marketing activities. Some use marketing very well while others do not understand marketing. They may view marketing as advertising or selling only and not as a way of satisfying their customer or client needs.

You can evaluate organizations to determine if they understand the value of marketing. If they rely on promotion with brochures, advertisements, and public service announcements, they probably view marketing as a way to convince consumers of the value of their organization. Without research to help them understand their clients, they are not able to respond to the clients' needs.

If they use marketing to determine what products and services to offer, where to make them available, how to help consumers determine the value of their services, and to communicate effectively with those consumers, they have adopted the marketing concept. The marketing concept works just as well for organizations as it does for businesses.

MARKETING IS IMPORTANT

Marketing managers are responsible for a large number and variety of activities. They must work with many people inside and outside of a company. Marketing managers are ultimately responsible for a large part of the company's budget. People involved in marketing need information about customers, competitors, and market conditions. This information helps marketers make decisions that will result in sales and profits for the business. Marketers have varied amounts of experience and education. They work in businesses to complete all of the functions and activities described in this chapter. Marketing is an exciting and challenging career area. If you are interested in marketing you must be willing to develop the needed knowledge and skills. Marketing offers many opportunities for you now and in your future.

Ultimately, marketing is important to every business for what reason?

1. What function of marketing received the most attention in the early phase that was characterized by simple production methods and limited product choice?

2. As production costs declined, people's standards of living increased, and distribution systems improved—all resulting in increased competition—to whom did businesses turn to move their products?

3. What were some of the innovative means marketing departments employed in the post-World War Two era to convince consumers to buy their products?

4. What was the key insight underlying the development of the marketing concept in the 1970s?

5. How has the role of marketing changed and expanded since it was seen primarily as a tool to help businesses sell products and services?

6. If using the marketing concept successfully entails operating profitably, how can a non-profit organization implement the marketing concept?

7. Name several reasons why marketing is important to a business or non-profit organization.

SUMMARY

Lesson 1.1

A. Studying marketing is important because of its value in the business world. Everyone benefits from marketing skills.

B. Marketing activities can be grouped into seven marketing functions that occur each time a product is developed and sold.

C. Marketing is creating and maintaining satisfying exchange relationships.

Lesson 1.2

A. Businesses need marketing to reach and serve customers effectively so they maximize sales and profits.

B. Marketing has become more complex as specialization of labor, the use of money, and the development of central markets expanded opportunities for exchanges.

C. Other business functions that must be coordinated with marketing include production, accounting, and management.

Lesson 1.3

A. The marketing concept is the philosophy that satisfying customer needs must be a business's primary focus in all that it does.

B. The marketing concept is implemented by identifying a target market and developing a marketing mix to meet that market's needs.

Lesson 1.4

A. The emphasis of marketing has evolved from production and distribution to sales to marketing departments to the marketing concept.

B. Marketing is important because marketing pervades business and marketers' decisions are key determinants of business success.

REVIEW MARKETING CONCEPTS

1. Which marketing function involves designing and developing products and services?
   a. product/service management
   b. marketing information management
   c. pricing
   d. selling

2. Which marketing function establishes the value of products and services?
   a. selling
   b. pricing
   c. product/service management
   d. marketing information management

3. Which marketing function develops procedures so customers are able to locate, obtain, and use products and services?
   a. selling
   b. promotion
   c. distribution
   d. financing

4. Which business function involves activities that make products and services available to consumers and ensure that effective exchanges occur?
   a. management and administration
   b. production
   c. marketing
   d. operations

5. Which business function involves developing, implementing, and evaluating the plans and activities of a business?
   a. management and administration
   b. accounting and finance
   c. marketing
   d. operations

6. Which business function creates or obtains products or services for sale?
   a. management and administration
   b. production
   c. marketing
   d. operations

7. Which business function represents the ongoing activities designed to support the primary function of a business and to keep it operating efficiently?
a. management and administration
b. production
c. marketing
d. operations

8. Which marketing function involves direct, personal communications with prospective customers in order to assess and satisfy needs with appropriate products and services?
a. selling
b. promotion
c. purchasing
d. marketing information management

REVIEW MARKETING TERMS

Match the terms listed with the definitions. Some terms may not be used.

9. The creation and maintenance of satisfying exchange relationships.

10. Using the needs of customers as the primary focus during planning, production, distribution, and promotion of a product or service.

11. The prospective customers a business wants to serve and the location of those customers.

12. Blending of the four marketing elements (product, distribution, price, and promotion) by the business.

13. Anything offered to a market by the business to satisfy needs, including physical products, services, and ideas.

14. The locations and methods used to make the product available to customers.

15. The actual amount customers pay and the methods of increasing the value of the product to the customers.

16. The methods and information communicated to customers to encourage purchases and increase their satisfaction.

17. Characteristic of not relying on others for the things needed in order to survive.

18. Exchanging products or services with others by agreeing on their values without using money.

19. Concentrating on one or a few related activities so that they can be completed very well.

20. Tool that established the use of currency as a recognized medium of exchange.

a. accounting and finance function
b. bartering
c. central market
d. distribution
e. management and administration function
f. market
g. marketing
h. marketing concept
i. marketing mix
j. merchandising
k. money system
l. operations
m. price
n. product
o. production function
p. promotion
q. self-sufficient
r. specialization of labor

APPLY MARKETING FUNCTIONS

MARKETING RESEARCH

21. Find and clip (or photocopy) an article from a current magazine or newspaper that describes how a company performed a marketing function as it developed a new product or service, improved a marketing procedure, and/or responded to customer needs. Prepare a brief oral report describing the function and how it does or does not illustrate the marketing concept.

22. Each of the functions of business described in the chapter provide career opportunities. There are careers available for people who have completed high school and have no experience in the area. Other careers require a college degree and and/or a great deal of experience.

Locate a newspaper, magazine, or web site that lists job opportunities or contains advertisements for employment. For each of the business functions in the following list, find at least two examples of jobs that have responsibility for that function. One example should be open to people with a high school diploma and little or no experience. The other example should require a college degree and several years of experience. Copy information about the job, including job title, description of duties, qualifications required, and level of pay (if listed).

Business Functions
Production
Operations
Accounting and finance
Management and administration
Marketing

MARKETING PLANNING

23. Write at least five examples from your own experience for each of the following:
  a. Five marketing activities you have seen in the last week.
  b. Five businesses in your community that have marketing as an important activity.
  c. Five careers in marketing.

  d. Five examples of businesses performing marketing functions.
  e. Five descriptions of markets.

24. Read each of the following statements. Then classify each statement according to which business emphases it illustrates.

Business Emphases
Production emphasis
Sales emphasis
Marketing department emphasis
Marketing concept emphasis

  a. "Our products are not selling. The salespeople must not be doing a good job."
  b. "If we could increase our advertising, more people would know about our products."
  c. "The important thing is to be able to find a way to deliver the products to people in other states."
  d. "We have the best bicycle on the market. I wonder why people are not buying more of them."
  e. "Our marketing research shows that our prices are a bit high. Let's see if we can find some ways to reduce prices while still meeting important customer needs."
  f. "Our competitors are always coming out with new products before we do. Let's give our engineers more money for product development and see what they can come up with."
  g. "We need to think of other things that could help sell our products. What about offering our own credit card to customers?"
  h. "We need to improve our level of customer satisfaction. Let's create a team of managers from production, finance, operations, and marketing to plan a new customer service program."

MARKETING MANAGEMENT

25. Managers are regularly making decisions about the price of products. They are attempting to provide a good value for customers, make a profit for the business, and insure that products are sold rather than remaining unsold in the business. Often the original price charged for a product is not the price at which it is sold.

Collect information on price reductions for at least ten products. You can gather the information from products you, your family, or friends have purchased, by checking prices in stores in your community, or from studying advertisements. Identify the original price and the reduced price for each product. Then complete the following activities.

a. Calculate the amount and percentage of decrease in price for each product. For example, if a compact disc player originally sold for $150 and is on sale for $125, the price reduction is $25 ($150 − $125). The percentage of decrease is the price reduction divided by the original price. For the compact disc player, the percentage of decrease in price is 16.7% ($25 ÷ $150).

b. Assuming the business makes 4% net profit on each sale (this may not be true for many of the products identified), determine how much reduction in profit the store will have for each product. For the CD player, at the original price the profit would have been $6 ($150 × 4%), at the reduced price the profit is $5 ($125 × 4%) The reduction in profit is $1.

c. Assuming that the business has a loss on any product that has a price reduction of more than 35% (again this may not be true of some products), identify the products on which losses will occur and the amount of that loss. In the CD example, if the business loses money on any price reduction of more than 35%, the loss will begin when the price is reduced to $97.50 ($150 × 65%).

d. Using the marketing concept, determine reasons why the manager of the business may have decided to reduce the price for the product you identified. Suggest other things the manager might have been able to do to avoid reducing the product's price.

26. Businesses may have problems when the business functions are not coordinated. An important way to increase customer satisfaction and make a profit is to organize the functions so they cooperate rather than compete. For each of the following sets of functions, identify two specific problems that might result if the functions compete, and two ways that customer satisfaction or company profits could improve if the functions are coordinated.

Business Functions
Production and marketing
Finance and marketing
Operations and production
Management and finance

MARKETING TECHNOLOGY

27. Identify 10 people who vary in age, gender, occupation, and other personal characteristics. Ask each person the following three questions. Record their answers:
   a. What do you believe the word "marketing" means?
   b. When you hear the word "marketing," are your feelings more positive, more negative, or neutral?
   c. Do you believe most people involved in marketing are attempting to meet your needs as a customer? Yes or No?

When you have completed the interview, write a summary of your findings to question a in your word-processing program. In your spreadsheet program, enter the names of those you interviewed in one column. In the next column, enter each interviewee's answer to question b, and in the next column, enter their answers to question c. Create two graphs in your spreadsheet that illustrate the answers to questions b and c.

28. The two statements below express opinions often held by people who do not understand marketing. For each of the statements, develop a paragraph of at least five sentences in your word-processing program that demonstrates why the opinion is not correct.

"My business offers high-quality products, so it does not need marketing."

"Customers have been complaining my products are not as good as they would like. I need to use marketing to be sure those poor products are sold."

MARKETING IN ACTION

RELATIONSHIP MARKETING AT BIG BALL SPORTS

Big Ball Sports evolved from a simple screen-printing shop to a multimillion-dollar mass-production operation that employed 20 computer design artists and 19 sales representatives in 1994. One of the features that made apparel unique at Big Ball Sports was wraparound screen-printing. Artwork started on the front of the t-shirt and wrapped around to the back of the shirt. Big Ball Sports also coined the phrases "Football is Life," Baseball is Life," "Soccer is Life," etc. These simple phrases

became guarded trademarks for Big Ball Sports. The company kept a watchful eye on the market to make sure there was no infringement of its trademark. Many companies and universities were tempted to copy the slogan that brought so much success to Big Ball Sports.

The company became a major player in providing national retail chains, such as JCPenney, Dillard's, and Foley's, with sports apparel. JCPenney became such a large client that Big Ball Sports built a separate warehouse for merchandise sold to the chain. Even brands such as Nike and Adidas were intrigued by the success of Big Ball Sports.

THE IMPORTANCE OF RELATIONSHIPS

Successful marketing depends upon building successful relationships between the producer, retailers, promoters, and customers. Relationship marketing played an important role in the success of Big Ball Sports. The company hired Key Collins as a players' relations specialist, who was responsible for meeting with and gaining the trust of professional athletes. In addition to supplying retailers, Big Ball Sports also provided shirts, caps, and other apparel for professional athletes' charity events such as golf tournaments. In turn, these athletes gave Big Ball Sports sales reps tickets to professional sporting events. In addition, they wore Big Ball Sports apparel while meeting fans before the game. The end result was greater sales of merchandise for Big Ball Sports and favorable publicity for the professional athletes.

As Big Ball's players' relations specialist, Collins successfully developed long-lasting relationships with professional athletes that proved to be very profitable for the company. One of Collins' strategies was to place gifts of Big Ball Sports apparel in an athlete's locker on game day. He also attended numerous professional games and visited with the athletes in the locker room after the game.

Collins frequently spoke to high school students about Big Ball's unique marketing strategies. It was not unusual for a professional athlete such as baseball player Luis Gonzales to accompany Collins. Big Ball Sports handed out free t-shirts to students, and the professional athlete signed autographs. The free t-shirts and associations with professional athletes increased the high school (target market) demand for Big Ball Sports merchandise. This marketing strategy increased the company's sales and public awareness, and professional athletes gained positive public exposure as well.

Building successful relationships is a key role of marketing. Collins and Big Ball Sports were very effective in that respect. Yet even the best

marketing strategies cannot overcome poor management of wealth and the inability to satisfy retailer demands. Department stores demanded that companies such as Big Ball Sports ticket their own merchandise and provide hangers for displaying it. Equipment that was electronically compatible with the department stores' equipment was very expensive. Mounting debt and poor management of cash flow resulted in the eventual sale of Big Ball Sports to Signal Manufacturing Co. Collins lost his job, but he didn't lose all the benefits that go with building relationships. During his

unemployment, he received a desk from Luis Gonzales.

THINK CRITICALLY

1. What is the meaning of "relationship marketing?"

2. What is the purpose of a trademark? What was the trademark that Big Ball Sports wanted to protect?

3. Why would professional athletes act as representatives of Big Ball Sports merchandise without earning any wealth?

---

http://www.deca.org/publications/HS_Guide/guidetoc.html

FASHION MERCHANDISING PROMOTION PLAN

DECA PREP

Big Ball Sports opens a retail store in an upscale shopping mall. You are a management trainee for Big Ball Sports and have been asked to develop a sales promotion plan using apparel and accessory items only. Prepare a four-week sales promotion plan for Big Ball Sports.

STORE DESCRIPTION   Give a thorough description of your store. Be sure to describe your merchandise (product), location (place), price, and target market.

CAMPAIGN OBJECTIVES   Objectives are purposes to be accomplished. Write the objectives for your promotional campaign. You must give good reasons for your promotional plan if you expect it to be accepted.

PROMOTIONAL PLAN   Develop a four-week promotional plan for September. It is important to describe a schedule of events for advertising, displays (interior and exterior), publicity, and other in-store activities. Make sure to describe your activities thoroughly. Be sure to include a projected budget for all costs.

RESPONSIBILITY TASK SHEET   A promotional plan is only as good as the people performing the tasks. A responsibility task sheet assigns positions and activities to key people in the business (Big

Ball Sports). This part of the promotion plan requires you to assign activities to key players with Big Ball Sports. Be sure to explain your assignment of tasks.

SUMMARY   You have the opportunity to close your proposal. You must summarize the benefits of your fashion merchandise sales promotion plan. You have the opportunity to convince management that your sales promotion plan will be effective.

CHAPTER 2

MARKETING IMPACTS SOCIETY

LESSON 2.1 *THE IMPACT OF MARKETING*

LESSON 2.2 *CRITICISMS OF MARKETING*

LESSON 2.3 *INCREASING SOCIAL RESPONSIBILITY*

NEWSLINE

WHO IS RESPONSIBLE?

Remember the new product that made a "splash" on the market? It was a super squirt gun with a water capacity of 2 liters or more and a range of 50–100 feet. When the inventor showed the product to several toy manufacturers, they didn't believe it would be successful. It was just another water gun and so big and heavy that most children would not want to carry it around. However, those manufacturers were very wrong!

From the time it was first introduced, it was a big hit. Stores could not keep enough in stock. It was not a product just for children. Teenagers and adults bought the super squirt guns. They were used at the beach, in the streets, and at parties. Some even showed up at schools.

However, just when the success of the new product seemed assured, many stores decided to stop selling it. What led to problems for this popular product relates to an area of business that is often unrecognized—the business' responsibility to society.

While the super squirt gun was fun to use, the force of the water from the gun was great enough that it could be harmful if it was directed at people who were close to the gun or were unaware that they were about to be hit. Stories were heard about bruises from the force of the water and car accidents caused when drivers were hit by water through an open window. Some businesses feared that they could be liable for injuries caused by the squirt guns. Several stores decided not to sell them. A few cities passed laws outlawing the sale and use of the squirt guns. Parents were reluctant to buy the toys for their children.

Although the super squirt guns continue to be manufactured and sold, sales are lower than before. Their popularity may increase again. The toys could be a very successful product in the future. The businesses that either manufacture or sell the water guns must determine how the sales will affect the business. Will the businesses be seen as irresponsible? Will they be involved in lawsuits? Will they lose money if they have a large number of guns for sale and the product is declared illegal? There are many reasons why businesses may decide not to sell a product. A large demand for the product and the possibility of high profits may not overcome social responsibility.

THINK CRITICALLY

1. If a business declines to sell a product because of possible lawsuits, is it being socially responsible, looking out for its own interests, or both? Explain.

2. Search the Internet for information on manufacturers and retailers of super squirt guns and their liability for injuries and accidents. Summarize your findings.

CAREER OPPORTUNITY
SALES REPRESENTATIVE

POINT YOUR BROWSER
www.corpview.com

TeleView is looking for an employee who possesses the following attributes.

- Excellent interpersonal and customer relations skills
- Drive, flexibility, and technical communications skills
- Ability to organize detailed proposals
- Desire to advance in a dynamic organization that is the leader in a rapidly evolving and fast-growing industry
- Ability to work in an invigorating, team-oriented environment
- Self-starter who is motivated by opportunities and incentives

The main responsibilities of the job include the following.

- Assume responsibility for sales within a specific territory
- Demonstrate products at local and national trade shows
- Foster sales through local sales channels
- Educate retail stores and outlets about the TeleView product line
- Monitor the Intranet daily for new products and price changes
- Communicate and process orders online
- Advise management regarding product pricing acceptance, market conditions, competitors' products, and consumer reaction to marketing campaigns
- Drive the launch of new products

The job requires the following education, skills, and experience.

- An Associate or BS degree or equivalent experience. Two years working in TeleView Customer

Support is considered an equivalent level of experience

- Sales experience in telecommunications or a computer-related field. Experience in telesales is a plus.
- Computer and Internet experience a plus
- Verbal and written communications skills
- Strong technical communications skills

THINK CRITICALLY

1. Prepare a cover letter written by a person who is qualified for this job and interested in applying for it.

2. The pay for this job is primarily sales commission. What are the advantages and disadvantages of that type of compensation?

3. Search want ads or the Internet for a job similar to TeleView's sales representative. What type of compensation package is being offered for the job?

2.1 THE IMPACT OF MARKETING

GOALS

- Explain how marketing affects businesses.
- Describe marketing's impact on individuals.
- Discuss ways marketing benefits society.

There are a number of factors that go into making a purchasing decision. "Is the price right?" "Is the product what I need?" "Will the product perform as expected?" "Is there a guarantee or warranty in case it is defective?" People ask themselves these and many other questions when making most purchasing decisions.

Work with a group. Have each person in the group name a product he or she has purchased recently. Then list all the important questions that went into making the purchasing decision. Do the questions differ from product to product? Are there certain questions that were the same or similar for all or most of the products? What did the manufacturers and retailers do to help you answer these questions? Summarize your results and share them with the other groups.

MARKETING AFFECTS BUSINESSES

Marketing is responsible for helping businesses find markets for their products and services and sell them profitably. But many people question the value of marketing. Some see it as adding to the cost of products. Others believe it causes people to buy things they otherwise would not want or need. Still others suggest that if businesses produce quality products and services, then there is no need for marketing.

It is important to determine if marketing plays a positive or a negative role. What does marketing contribute to businesses, to individuals, and to society? If there are problems with marketing, what can be done to eliminate those problems?

CRITICAL BUSINESS FUNCTION

Marketing is an important business function. Even though businesses have not always understood marketing and used it effectively, they could not have existed without marketing. Marketing is responsible for the activities leading to the exchange of a business' products and services for the customer's money. Transportation, financing, promotion, and the other marketing functions are needed for the exchange to occur.

Businesses that use the marketing concept benefit even more from marketing. In those businesses, marketing is responsible for identifying and understanding customers.

Through the use of market research and marketing information systems, the business is able to determine customer needs, attitudes, likes, and dislikes. Then the business can carefully develop products and services that meet the needs of the customers and earn a profit.

CUSTOMER SATISFACTION

Manufacturers developing a new brand of toothpaste will make better decisions if they are aware of what consumers like and dislike about the current brand used. The manager of a clothing store will want to know what consumers are expecting in terms of styles and prices before purchasing new items for sale.

Marketing helps a business satisfy customer wants and needs. This means that customers are more likely to be loyal and continue to purchase from the business. Marketing also helps the business make better decisions about what to sell and how to sell it. Therefore, the business is more likely to operate efficiently. So, effective marketing is important to businesses.

Why do businesses that use the marketing concept benefit more from marketing?

MARKETING
HELPS PEOPLE

Because marketing improves exchanges between businesses and consumers, individuals benefit from marketing. While many people do not easily recognize those benefits, those who understand marketing can provide examples of its value.

Consider going to a supermarket to purchase supplies for a party. If the store is conveniently located, you will not have to worry about how you will get to and from the store. You want the store to stock your favorite brands of decorations, drinks, and snacks. There should be an adequate supply of the items you need. When you get into the store, the products should be easy to locate. The prices should be clearly marked and affordable. A store employee should be able to answer your questions and help you check out and bag your purchases. The store should allow you to pay for your purchases with cash, check, credit, or debit card.

Each of the activities described for the purchase of your party supplies at the supermarket is an example of marketing. Those activities make it easier for you to shop and help to ensure that you get the items you need for your party, quickly and at a reasonable price. The business benefits because you purchase the products, and you benefit because the business is able to satisfy your needs.

BETTER PRODUCTS AT LOWER COST

Marketing provides other contributions to individuals that may not be as obvious. Because marketing is continually determining what consumers like and dislike and what needs are not satisfied, improvements are made to products and services and new products are developed. As a result of marketing activities, more products are available to meet the needs of more customers. This results in higher sales volume. The increase in sales allows businesses to produce products more efficiently and costs can actually decline. See Figure 2-1 on page 36.

The first personal computers were very basic and not very powerful, but cost several thousand dollars. Today's personal computers are hundreds of times more powerful, have many features to make them easy to use, and can be purchased for less than $1,000. This is possible because of improved technology and marketing.

Naming Rights Relieve Taxpayers

Buying naming rights for publicly owned sports stadiums and arenas is obviously good for taxpayers' wallets, and it is apparently good for business too. At the astronomical prices such rights have been selling lately, they had better be very good for businesses shelling out, in one case, more than $100 million over 15 years.

Businesses that slap their names on stadiums figure to get billions of impressions per year from fans, passers-by, and television viewers. Typically the corporate name goes on signs seen from adjacent roadways, on stadium entrances, and inside near the scoreboards. In addition, naming rights deals usually include other amenities such as luxury boxes, complimentary tickets, and game sponsorships.

In a recent survey, 9 of 10 people knew the corporate sponsors of their local sports arenas. And 6 of 10 respondents said that naming a sports venue after a corporate sponsor was good for the community. The practice has become so common that the public now expects it, and taxpayers increasingly demand it as a way to recoup costs.

THINK CRITICALLY

1. In what ways does buying naming rights differ from buying TV spots for a popular sporting event such as the Super Bowl or the World Series?

2. What are some of the possible drawbacks of putting a business's name on a public sports arena?

FIGURE 2-1
When the marketing concept is used, customer satisfaction increases, while costs of production and selling prices decrease.

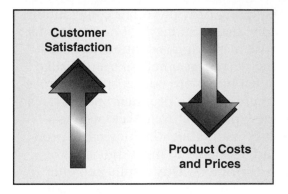

Customer Satisfaction

Product Costs and Prices

EXPANDED OPPORTUNITIES

Another contribution of marketing to individuals is a vast area of employment. Between one-fourth and one-third of all jobs in the United States are marketing jobs or have marketing as a major job responsibility. Salespeople, customer service representatives, warehouse managers, inventory specialists, marketing research personnel, and many others have interesting, financially rewarding careers because of marketing.

Finally, marketing skills are valuable to people who are not directly employed in marketing. By understanding the marketing process and using the marketing concept, you will be able to accomplish a number of your goals. Marketing skills can help you get elected to an office in a club, prepare for a job or for college, plan a fund-raising activity for an organization, or start your own business.

Through marketing, people can choose from a wide variety of products and services, find businesses that respond to their needs, have access to good jobs, and develop skills that help meet many personal goals.

What percentage of jobs in the United States involve the performance of marketing activities?

MARKETING
BENEFITS SOCIETY

Does society benefit because of marketing? There are many positive effects of marketing for society as shown in Figure 2-2.

FIGURE 2-2
All of the benefits of marketing are not obvious. However, those benefits are important to consumers, businesses, and society.

BENEFITS OF MARKETING

Businesses meet consumer needs
Consumers make better decisions
Natural resources are used more effectively
Standard of living is improved
International trade increases

NEW AND BETTER PRODUCTS

Marketing helps to identify and develop new and better products and services for consumers. Many of those products and services are beneficial to society in general. More efficient automobiles use less gasoline and cause less pollution. Biodegradable products reduce the growing need for landfill space. Products like airbags and motorcycle helmets reduce the number and severity of injuries from accidents.

Marketing encourages businesses to provide products and services that consumers want. It also helps consumers make more effective decisions about what to purchase. As a result, the natural resources and raw materials of a country should be used more efficiently rather than being wasted on products consumers will not buy.

BETTER STANDARDS OF LIVING

Marketing improves the standard of living in a country. The standard of living is based on the products and services available to consumers, the amount of resources consumers have to obtain the products and services, and the quality of life for consumers. Countries that have well-developed marketing systems are able to make more and better products available to consumers. Those countries also have more jobs for their citizens and higher wage scales as a result of marketing.

PROMOTES INTERNATIONAL TRADE

Marketing has been particularly effective in improving international trade. International trade contributes many benefits to the participating countries and to the consumers in those countries. Think of the number of products you buy that were produced in another country. Just as the United States is a large consumer of foreign products, many businesses in this country sell products internationally. Without marketing, such benefits would not be possible.

Marketing activities are essential for international trade. Marketers help to determine where products can be sold and how to sell them in countries that may have very different business procedures, money systems, and buying practices. Methods of shipping and product handling must be identified or

developed. Decisions about customer service must be made. Promotional methods appropriate for the people in each country or region have to be developed to ensure that customers understand the products and their benefits.

Feedback for Sale

Marketers seeking quick feedback from users of their products and services can turn to a number of new Internet services that serve as forums for consumer complaints and comments. Planetfeedback.com, FeedbackDirect.com, eComplaints.com, and Epinions.com all give consumers a chance to vent their frustrations when they're unhappy or give businesses a pat on the back when they do something right.

The feedback services, in turn, are building databases that can complement companies' own marketing research. They plan to make money by selling businesses the customer data they collect. The data can give businesses insight into their own products, services, and marketing efforts as well as those of their competitors.

Even though most companies already have their own customer feedback mechanisms in place, the new Internet services figure that their feedback is quicker and more cost-effective because they are actively seeking out consumers who want to get something off their chests and because they are collecting data on millions of products from consumers around the globe.

THINK CRITICALLY

1. What kinds of useful information could a company obtain from data compiled by an Internet feedback service?

2. Why might dissatisfied customers vent their frustrations through an Internet feedback service rather than writing or calling a company directly themselves?

How does marketing help the environment?

1. Name at least two things that tend to occur when the marketing concept is used effectively.

2. Today's computers are much more powerful and versatile than those of even a few years ago. Which of the following terms best describes today's computer prices compared to a few years ago: much more, more, about the same, or less?

3. Name three marketing jobs.

4. What are some of the ways in which marketing improves a society's standard of living?

5. What are some of the ways that marketing improves international trade?

CRITICISMS OF MARKETING

MARKETING MATTERS

The activities associated with marketing can sometimes cause customers and other people to get upset. Marketing has been accused of creating a false need for unnecessary products. Some feel that marketing is a waste of money and only serves to increase the price customers pay. Others claim that high-quality products don't need any marketing because the products will sell themselves.

Work with a group. Discuss each of these complaints, and reasons why they are valid. Then try to come up with reasons why they are wrong. Share your results with the other groups.

GOALS

- Discuss three common criticisms of marketing.
- Explain how marketing can be used to solve social problems.

COMMON COMPLAINTS

It would be easy to say that marketing has only positive results. That is not always the case. If not used appropriately, marketing can have negative effects. The misuse of marketing has led to some criticisms and has created a negative image for some marketing activities.

Business people must take criticisms of marketing seriously. Those criticisms often represent the attitudes of many consumers. If consumers have a negative opinion about an important part of a business, it can affect whether they will be customers or not.

Marketers and other business people need to study marketing practices to be sure they result in effective exchanges and customer satisfaction.

E-MARKETING

Surfing For Secondary Data

Many marketing researchers see the Internet as the world's largest public library. Millions of organizations post a wealth of reliable data there. For example, the Library of Congress site has the full text of all versions of congressional legislation and the full text of the *Congressional Record.* The Securities and Exchange Commission requires publicly owned corporations to file financial reports electronically so they can then be posted on the Internet. The Census Bureau runs a site with demographic data for business researchers.

Search engines allow users to quickly comb the Internet for information on virtually any topic. Most portals such as Yahoo!, Hotbot, Excite, AltaVista, and Snap contain comprehensive search engines. All a researcher has to do is type a search term in plain English or click on key words and phrases.

Anyone can access most web sites for free and without prior approval. There are also many commercial sites on the Internet that offer specialized information that might be highly valuable for some businesses. Many of those sites require users to register and pay subscription fees or document fees.

THINK CRITICALLY

1. What kinds of information can researchers gather from the Internet?
2. Name advantages of finding data from the Internet instead of the library.

MARKETING CAUSES UNNEEDED PURCHASES

Through marketing, consumers have many choices of products available for them to purchase. Those products are readily available in many stores, are displayed in ways that make them easy to purchase, and are attractively packaged to attract attention. Advertising is used extensively to encourage people to consider specific brands of products. Credit and special financing arrangements are available for most expensive products to make them seem more affordable. Marketing activities and the power of promotion can increase the sales of products and services.

Businesses using the marketing concept should carefully consider the potential impact of marketing activities on consumers. While it might seem appropriate to use any tool that will result in more sales of a product, the long-term results of the sale should be considered as well. If a customer buys a product because of marketing rather than because the product is really needed, there is a good chance the customer will be dissatisfied. How many times have you or your friends purchased something and then quickly decided you really didn't want or need the item? What was your response?

Many consumers simply return the item, and expect a refund. The business

WORLDVIEW

Cultural Pride Creates Barriers

Although cultural differences can create marketing barriers for all sorts of products, news and entertainment media face hurdles that can be even more difficult to surmount. Many countries want to develop and promote their own news and entertainment industries and are concerned about homegrown industries being overwhelmed by imports, especially those from the United States.

International products are discouraged through tariffs that can make pricing exorbitant. France is particularly protective of its film and television industries. The European Union tries to reserve at least half of its television programming for shows that are made in Europe.

The United States has no formal barriers to entertainment imports, but demand for foreign productions is limited. Foreign films with English subtitles are rarely successful here. One foreign-made show that has leaped across cultural

barriers into the hearts of Americans is Teletubbies. Produced in the United Kingdom, it chronicles the antics of four pear-shaped creatures with TV monitors in their bellies who live in a meadow and babble in baby talk.

The immense popularity of Teletubbies all over the world shows that, whatever cultural barriers do exist, there is also a fundamental commonality among cultures that transcends many international differences. It is the job of marketers to break through the former and exploit the latter.

THINK CRITICALLY

1. Why do you think foreign-language movies with English subtitles are not often successful in the United States?

2. How have the development of the Internet and the growth of cable TV helped to break down cultural barriers?

not only has lost the sale, but now has a product that is worth much less than before and perhaps cannot be resold. Even if the consumers do not return the products, they are likely to be quite dissatisfied. That is particularly true if the product cost a great deal of money. Do you believe the consumers will buy that product again? The business is left with returned merchandise, a dissatisfied customer, and possibly a bad reputation among the customer's friends.

To respond to this criticism, business people must be very sensitive to the needs and experiences of customers. Products and services should be carefully matched to customers' needs. Products that do not sell should be evaluated to determine why customers do not want them. In that way, the business can make better purchasing decisions in the future in order to offer products and services that customers want.

Marketing should start with good products. If a product is not meeting customer needs, business people should avoid using marketing strategies such as promotion and price reductions to try to sell the product. This will often lead to dissatisfaction with the product and the business.

Finally, the business must value long-term relationships with customers. One sale is not enough. The business will be successful when customers return again and again because they are satisfied with the business and believe the business is concerned about their needs.

MARKETING WASTES MONEY

As seen in Figure 2-3, the average cost of all marketing activities is about 50 percent of the price of products. For some products it is much higher and for others it is a very small percentage. Since many people think of marketing as only advertising and selling, they are upset when they believe those activities double the price of their purchases.

In reality, selling and promotion are a small part of the cost of marketing—typically about 2–10 percent of the product's price. And effective selling and promotion do increase the value to the customer. If a salesperson helps you select the best product for your needs rather than selling you something you do not want, you have spent your money more effectively. Advertising can provide product information so you can make the best choice, or inform you where a product can be purchased and when it is on sale. Advertising can even result in savings because of the information provided.

Economists who study the impact of marketing activities on product prices have demonstrated that marketing actually results in lower prices in the long run. Because products can be sold to more customers, there is greater competition among businesses. When consumers have choices of products, they will usually buy those that are reasonably priced. That encourages businesses to keep prices as low as possible in order to be competitive. According to the economists, increased sales volume and competition result in lower prices for consumers.

FIGURE 2-3
On average, total marketing expenses are about one-half of a product's price, while sales and advertising costs average about 2–10 percent of the price.

The Typical Costs of Marketing

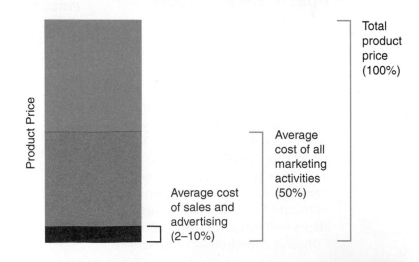

SOME PRODUCTS DON'T NEED MARKETING

There are many examples of businesses that rely on marketing to sell poor quality products. Think of the used automobile with many defects that is sold only because the salesperson convinced the unsuspecting customer that the car was really in good condition. There are numerous tales of unsuspecting people buying land for a home based on information in a brochure or videotape, only to discover that the land is in a swamp or on the side of a steep mountain. Marketing is certainly misused in those situations to misrepresent poor products.

On the other hand, consider whether or not a high-quality product needs marketing. Without marketing, it would be the responsibility of the consumer to find out that the product exists and to gather information about it. The consumer would have to locate the product, pay cash for it, and transport it from where it was manufactured to where it was to be used. The customer would assume all of the risk in handling and moving the product. If it were damaged, the customer would be responsible.

These examples and many others show that marketing is important even for quality products and services. Marketing activities must be performed in every exchange. If the business is not responsible for marketing, consumers will have to complete the activities themselves in order to purchase the product or service.

Why is a business that is committed to long-term customer relationships less likely to use high-pressure sales tactics?

MARKETING SOLVES PROBLEMS

Marketing, if misused, can have negative results, however, marketing can help to solve important problems and contribute to social improvement. There are many examples of very positive results when marketing is used effectively.

MARKETING INCREASES PUBLIC AWARENESS

There are many serious problems facing our society. Concerns about health care, crime levels, poverty, diseases, racism, education, unemployment, drug use, the environment, and teenage pregnancy all require the attention of many people if solutions are to be found. Marketing contributes to the solutions in several ways. Through communication, people are more aware of the problems and how they affect individuals and the country. Consider the number of times you have received information on using seat belts, recycling, the dangers of drugs and alcohol, and reasons to stay in school. Marketers have been responsible for developing the advertisements and public service announcements you have seen. Some of these are shown in Figure 2-4.

FIGURE 2-4
Publicity and advertising are important tools in developing public awareness of issues, problems, and solutions.

Marketing Increases Public Awareness

Marketing has encouraged people to eat low cholesterol products, quit smoking, contribute money to colleges, apply for scholarships, and support research into cures for diseases like AIDS and cancer. Marketing has encouraged people to vote and to avoid drinking and driving. You can think of many important social issues that are now receiving much attention because of effective marketing.

MARKETING HELPS MATCH SUPPLY WITH DEMAND

Products and services are not always available where they are most needed by consumers. For example, if there is a drought in one part of the country, farmers and ranchers in that area may not have enough hay and grain to feed their livestock. At the same time, there might be an excess supply in other areas. An effective distribution system can move the hay and grain quickly from one part of the country to another, matching supply and demand. See Figure 2-5.

Oil products and gasoline can be distributed throughout the country using an extensive network of pipelines. If a greater supply of natural gas or heating oil is needed in the north during an especially cold winter, it can be routed away from areas that have less demand. Marketing helps to prevent or reduce the impact of problems that could otherwise result in serious problems for society.

FIGURE 2-5
Marketing activities are important in making the economic system work.

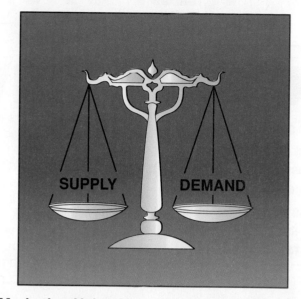

Marketing Helps Match Supply and Demand

If a heat wave in the West is causing electrical outages, how can marketing help alleviate the problem?

LESSON REVIEW

1. On average, marketing costs represent what percentage of the price that a consumer pays for a product?

2. On average, the cost of sales and promotions represent what percentage of the price that a consumer pays for a product?

3. If sellers do not perform certain marketing functions, why doesn't that reduce the final cost of a product to the consumer?

4. Name several public awareness campaigns that are intended to benefit society.

5. If cranberry growers were suffering from an oversupply of cranberries that slashed prices and threatened to put them out of business, how could marketing help them?

2.3 INCREASING SOCIAL RESPONSIBILITY

- Define consumerism.
- Explain ways by which businesses improve their own practices.
- Discuss how ethical issues affect marketers' professional responsibilities.

Most consumers have at one time purchased a product that did not live up to expectations. A shirt doesn't fit right. A vacuum cleaner doesn't remove dirt well. A potted plant wilts and dies in just a week. A new hairstyle doesn't look very good.

Work with a group. Describe an occasion when a product or service you purchased didn't live up to your expectations. How did you handle the situation? Were you satisfied with the outcome? Would you have handled another group member's situation differently than he or she did? Share a summary of your discussion with the other groups.

CONSUMER PROTECTION

Marketers cannot think only about selling products and making a profit. They must be aware of other effects of their activities. Marketing is a powerful tool that can have both positive and negative results. Marketers must be willing to pay attention to society's needs to determine how businesses can contribute to solutions.

The trend today is a greater expectation for business to be socially responsible and to aid in solving the problems facing society. Concern about the consequences of actions on others is **social responsibility**. Business people recognize that they must make decisions that consider factors beyond what their customers want and what is most profitable for the business. Most business people recognize their businesses cannot be successful in the long run if society is facing major problems.

Increasing the social responsibility of businesses is occurring in three major ways. The growth of consumerism, government

regulation, and improving business practices are each playing a role. See Figure 2-6.

FIGURE 2-6
Consumer groups, government, and business organizations all must play a role in improving society.

Social Responsibility Must Be Shared

THE GROWTH OF CONSUMERISM

Consumerism is the organized actions of groups of consumers seeking to increase their influence on business practices. Consumers as individuals can have only a small influence on the activities of a business. However, when organized as a group of consumers, they have a much greater impact by speaking out, meeting with business people to recommend changes, and using the money they spend on purchases to influence decisions.

While consumers have always attempted to influence business practices, consumerism became an important influence on business practices in the 1960s when President John F. Kennedy presented the Consumer Bill of Rights. The Consumer Bill of Rights identified four basic rights that all consumers should expect: the right to adequate and accurate information, the right to safe products, the right to product choices, and the right to communicate their ideas and opinions to business and government.

As a result of the attention focused on those rights, consumers have become very active in ensuring that their rights are protected. Some ways used to protect consumer rights are consumer education, consumer information, lobbying, and product boycotts. Consumer groups develop materials and educational programs to be used in schools and in other places to help people become better consumers. You may have used some of those materials to learn how to use banking services, purchase insurance, and apply for loans.

There are a number of consumer organizations that test products to determine whether they are safe and if they provide consumers with a good value for the price. The organizations often publish the results in books, magazines, and on the Internet or have a telephone service so people can call for product information before making a purchase. Consumer lobbyists work with national and state legislators to develop laws to protect consumer rights. Some important consumer laws are described in Figure 2-7.

FIGURE 2-7
Federal legislation is one method of increasing the social responsibility of businesses.

Legislation	Purpose
Mail Fraud Act, 1872	To protect customers from businesses using the mail to defraud
Sherman Antitrust Act, 1890	To increase competition among businesses by regulating monopolies
Food and Drug Act, 1906	To control the content and labeling of food and drug products by forming the Food and Drug Administration (FDA)
Federal Trade Commission Act, 1914	To form the Federal Trade Commission (FTC) to protect consumer rights
Robinson-Patman Act, 1936	To protect small businesses from unfair pricing practices between manufacturers and large businesses
Fair Packaging and Labeling Act, 1966	To require packages to be accurately labeled and fairly represent the contents
National Traffic and Motor Vehicle Safety Act, 1966	To set requirements for automobiles and automotive products
Consumer Credit Protection Act, 1968	To require disclosure of credit requirements and rates to loan applicants
Consumer Product Safety Act, 1972	To set safety standards and to form the Consumer Product Safety Commission (CPSC)
Fair Debt Collection Act, 1980	To prevent harassment of people who owe money by debt collectors

Finally, consumers have found they can influence business practices by the way they spend their money, their consumer vote. If a group of consumers is dissatisfied with the actions or products of a business they can organize a consumer **boycott**. A boycott is an organized effort to influence a company by refusing to purchase its products. Consumer groups also reinforce positive business practices by encouraging their members to purchase products from businesses that respond to consumer needs.

GOVERNMENT REGULATION

The United States government plays an active role in business practices. Many of the laws and regulations of government are designed to improve the social impact of business practices. Others are specifically developed to protect consumers.

What federal law is intended to protect consumers by requiring that packages be accurately labeled and contents fairly disclosed?

IMPROVING
PRACTICES

Most businesses recognize their responsibility to consumers and to society. If consumers are dissatisfied with the business' practices, they will soon stop buying the company's products. Social problems often lead to increased government regulation of business or increases in taxes to pay for programs designed to solve the problems. Businesses do not want increased regulation or taxes.

Individual businesses and business organizations are working to improve business practices in several ways. Those ways include codes of ethics, self-regulation, and social action.

CODES OF ETHICS

A **code of ethics** is a statement of responsibilities for honest and proper conduct. Business people recognize that the inappropriate or illegal behavior of one firm can have a very negative effect on the whole industry. They attempt to influence that behavior by agreeing on standards of conduct. By agreeing to a code of ethics, the business people encourage responsible behavior. In some groups, the codes of ethics are enforced by penalties, established by the industry, that are applied to businesses that violate the standards. A portion of the American Marketing Association's Code of Ethics is summarized in Figure 2-8.

SELF-REGULATION

Individual businesses and groups of businesses in the same industry have developed procedures to respond to consumer problems and to encourage customers to work directly with the businesses to solve problems. Taking personal responsibility for actions is known as **self-regulation**. The Better Business Bureau is a consumer protection organization sponsored by businesses. The purpose of the Better Business Bureau is to gather information from consumers about problems, provide information about improper business practices so consumers can make better decisions, and attempt to solve problems between businesses and their customers.

Many businesses have consumer service departments that work to solve consumer problems and to provide consumers with information about the company and its products. The General Electric Answer Center offers a 24-hour-a-day, toll-free telephone service so customers can get information, register complaints, and make

FIGURE 2-8
Organizations and industries often develop a code of ethics to promote honest and proper standards of conduct.

RESPONSIBILITIES OF THE MARKETER

IN PRODUCT DEVELOPMENT AND MANAGEMENT
- disclosing all substantial risks associated with a product or service
- identifying substitutions that change the product or impact buying decisions
- identifying extra cost-added features

IN PROMOTIONS
- avoiding false and misleading advertising
- rejecting high-pressure or misleading sales tactics and promotions

IN DISTRIBUTION
- not exploiting customers by manipulating the availability of a product
- not using coercion
- not exerting undue influence over the reseller's choice to handle a product

IN PRICING
- not engaging in price fixing
- not practicing predatory pricing
- disclosing the full price associated with any purchase

IN MARKETING RESEARCH
- prohibiting selling or fundraising disguised as conducting research
- avoiding misrepresentation and omission of pertinent research data
- treating clients and suppliers fairly

suggestions. Chrysler developed a Car Buyer's Bill of Rights and added the position of Vice President for Consumer Affairs to ensure those rights are protected.

Some industries, such as homebuilders, developed procedures that consumers can use to resolve problems with a specific builder. Problems that cannot be resolved between the customer and the business are referred to an independent panel who can help determine a fair solution.

SOCIAL ACTION

Business people are concerned about the world in which they live. Many are active in helping to solve some of society's serious problems. They use resources from their businesses to help. Members Only, a clothing manufacturer, spent more than $100 million on advertising messages directed at reducing drug abuse and increasing voter registration. More recently it directed its efforts toward alleviating the homeless problem.

Nike committed about $50 million to a literacy program. McDonalds sponsors Ronald McDonald Houses for families with children who are hospitalized with serious illnesses. Each day you can see many examples of businesses that are concerned about their communities. They invest time and money to help the community and its people.

What is a code of ethics adopted by an industry or professional group?

ETHICS IN MARKETING?

Business ethics have received a great deal of attention recently. **Ethics** is decisions and behavior based on honest and fair standards. Most business people behave ethically. However, the actions of a few people can cause customers to wonder if ethical behavior is really valued in business.

RESPONSIBILITY TO CUSTOMERS

Marketers deal directly with customers. They ask customers to spend money for products intended to satisfy needs and wants. Because of this relationship, marketers have a special responsibility to behave ethically. People place a high value on ethical business behavior. Business people are expected to be honest and fair in dealings with customers, employees, and other businesses. The American Marketing Association Code of Ethics describes specific responsibilities for marketers in the areas of product planning, promotion, pricing, distribution, and marketing research.

Each marketer is responsible for ethical behavior. Decisions and actions should be evaluated to determine if they are honest and fair. Sometimes there will appear to be conflicts in what is best for the business, for employees, for customers and competitors, and for society in general. Some people suggest the decision should be based on what is best for the most people. Others believe an action is right or wrong based on the effects on the people directly involved.

JUDGMENT CALL

Advertisers Support Education

Ethical decisions are not always clear-cut. What some people view as a useful innovation, others regard as inappropriate. Marketers must then decide whether to continue to offer the product or withdraw it. Channel One News faced that decision.

Channel One is a daily 12-minute program for students. In 2000, students in more than 12,000 schools viewed Channel One.

Channel One was developed in response to data showing that students had little understanding of current events. The show's creators believed satellite television offered a solution. In studying the market, however, they discovered that most schools did not have money for satellite receivers or the programming.

Its solution was including four 30-second commercials in the program, sold to businesses that wanted to reach the school-age market. The money bought satellite equipment, financed production, and generated profits.

The solution seemed to benefit everyone concerned, but many people objected. Lawsuits were filed in several states and some companies, fearing advertising on it would create a negative image, dropped their support.

Channel One is an example of an ethical decision that business people face. The correct decision is not always clear, because people have different priorities and perspectives.

THINK CRITICALLY

1. Why might people oppose advertiser-supported TV in schools?

2. For what reasons might advertisers hesitate to give school officials a veto over the advertising they want to show?

FIGURE THIS

Calculating How Much is Too Much

When a business sets prices artificially low to drive out competitors, it is engaging in predatory pricing. Claims of predatory pricing are common, especially when companies move into new markets or try to increase market share.

On the other hand, many economists think it is virtually non-existent. Some argue that predatory pricing is irrational, no monopoly has ever been created by it, and such claims are usually made by competitors who don't want to lower their prices. Legal restrictions on price-cutting simply hurt consumers, the very people they are supposed to help, they say.

Active competition naturally promotes price cutting, sometimes even below costs. For example, a business might cut prices to entice people to try a new product. Or a product might be perishable or becoming obsolete, so a business might sell it cheap today rather than be stuck with worthless inventory tomorrow. Or, like Henry Ford with his Model T, a seller might want to stimulate demand in order to increase volume and lower unit production costs.

THINK CRITICALLY

1. TRC, Inc. makes $1 gross profit on item WG5876 that sells for $10. Research shows it could sell three times as many if the price were $8. How much must it lower its per-unit cost to earn the same per-unit gross profit?

2. How much would TRC need to lower its per-unit costs in order to maintain its $1 profit per item if it lowered prices to $7?

HARM AND ACCOUNTABILITY

In some cases, it may appear there is no real harm in unethical behavior. If dishonesty results in a customer buying your product rather than your competitor's, or if you can conceal a mistake you made, you may believe that it does not matter. That is not the case. Marketers must remember that their emphasis must be on what is best for everyone involved in an exchange. Their actions usually affect many others, both inside and outside the business.

In other cases, unethical behavior has negative consequences for individuals and businesses. Improper marketing can harm customers. Society is hurt by businesses that have no concern for the products and services they sell or how or to whom they are marketed. Finally, many unethical business practices are also illegal. People have been fined and even imprisoned as a result of unethical actions.

Some businesses are developing education programs and operating procedures to help employees understand how to make ethical decisions. Those businesses want to improve the ethical image of all businesses and ensure customers believe they will be treated fairly by every employee.

✓ checkpoint

Why do marketers have a special responsibility for ethical behavior?

LESSON REVIEW

1. Which national elected leader proposed the Consumer Bill of Rights?

2. Name the four rights enumerated in the Consumer Bill of Rights.

3. The Better Business Bureau is an example of what kind of regulation?

4. If a public corporation is supposed to maximize its shareholders' return on investment, how can it justify giving millions of dollars to social causes?

5. Name four marketing functions covered by the American Marketing Association's code of ethics.

SUMMARY

Lesson 2.1

A. Marketing affects businesses by giving them the means of defining and understanding customers' needs so they can develop products that satisfy those needs.

B. Marketing helps individuals because it results in better products, job opportunities, and skills that can be useful in many areas.

C. Marketing benefits society by providing for more efficient use of resources, higher standards of living, and robust trade.

Lesson 2.2

A. Three common criticisms of marketing are that it makes people buy things they don't really want, that it doesn't add value, and that it is not needed for a good product.

B. Marketing can be used to solve social problems by raising public awareness and by helping to balance supply and demand.

Lesson 2.3

A. Consumer action and government regulation are used increasingly to ensure that businesses respect consumer rights.

B. Businesses adopt codes of ethics and use self-regulation to resolve customer problems and avoid greater government regulation.

C. Marketers have special ethical responsibilities since they are supposed to be cultivating satisfied customers.

REVIEW MARKETING CONCEPTS

1. True or False: With the use of marketing, businesses are able to produce products and services that consumers need.

2. Which of the following are involved in completing marketing functions?
   a. manufacturers
   b. consumers
   c. trucking companies
   d. all of the above

3. True or False: When marketing is effective, prices usually increase more than enough to cover the costs of marketing, so sellers make larger profits per unit sold.

4. True or False: An important social problem created by marketing is that it tends to result in the misuse and waste of raw materials and natural resources.

5. Effective marketing is used to encourage people to buy what kinds of things?
   a. things they otherwise would not buy
   b. things they need or want

   c. things that businesses cannot otherwise sell
   d. luxury items they cannot afford

6. On average, the cost of all marketing activities is about __?__ of the price of a product.

7. True or False: Marketing is necessary to sell the product at a profit only when a business has an inferior product or service.

8. Marketing can be an effective tool in helping society to solve some serious problems when it is used by which of the following?
   a. government
   b. business
   c. non-profit groups
   d. all of the above

9. Transporting water to an area where there is a severe drought is an example of what?
   a. self-regulation
   b. consumerism
   c. matching supply and demand
   d. public awareness

10. True or False. Business people cannot be expected to contribute to solving social problems if they are going to make a profit.

11. True or False: Individual consumers acting alone can usually be quite effective in influencing the activities of businesses.

12. The Consumer Bill of Rights was part of what?
    a. the original U.S. Constitution
    b. the first 10 amendments to the Constitution
    c. FDR's New Deal program of the 1930s
    d. President Kennedy's proposals in the 1960s

13. When a group of consumers agrees to stop buying a business's product in order to influence the actions of that business, it is called a(n) __?__ .

14. When a business cuts prices below costs in order to drive its competitors out of business, it is said to be engaging in __?__ pricing.

15. True or False: Federal laws to improve business practices and protect consumers have only been in existence since 1960.

REVIEW MARKETING TERMS

Match the terms listed with the definitions. Some terms may not be used.

16. The organized actions of groups of consumers seeking to increase their influence on business practices.

17. Taking personal responsibility for actions.

18. An organized effort to influence a company by refusing to purchase its products.

19. Concern about the consequences of actions on others.

20. Referring to decisions and behavior based on honest and fair standards.

21. A statement of responsibilities for honest and proper conduct.

a. boycott
b. code of ethics
c. consumerism
d. ethics
e. self-regulation
f. social responsibility

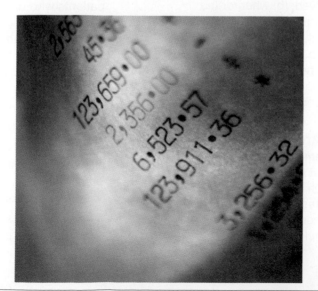

CHAPTER 2

APPLY MARKETING FUNCTIONS

MARKETING RESEARCH

22. The four consumer products in the table below have undergone significant price decreases from the time they were first sold until now. Those price decreases occurred because of improved technology and effective marketing and resulted in higher sales. The prices listed for each product are typical of the prices charged when the products were first introduced and more recent prices.

  a. For each product, find the price reduction and the percentage decrease from the introductory price to the recent price.

  b. Assume that you planned to buy all four of the items. Calculate the total cost of the purchases if all were purchased at the introductory price. Now calculate the total cost if all were purchased at the recent price. Calculate the percentage savings to you if you were able to make all purchases at the recent price.

  c. List four other products with large price decreases from the time they were first introduced until now.

Product	Introductory Price	Recent Price
Hand-held Scientific Calculator	$138	$18
Quartz Watch	320	60
Personal Computer	2,800	895
Microwave Oven	860	220

23. Review the business section in five issues of a newspaper or five issues of a business magazine (*Business Week, Fortune,* or *Money,* for example). Identify all articles that relate to the social responsibility of businesses. For each article determine (a) the primary issue involved; (b) whether the problem is being addressed by consumer groups, government, businesses, or a combination; and (c) the type of action being proposed to solve the problem. After you have collected the information, summarize your findings in a one-page written report.

MARKETING PLANNING

24. The following statements describe marketing activities that may result in a problem for society. For each statement, describe a problem that may result from the practice and one way that consumers, government, and businesses could respond.

  a. Fast-food restaurants use a large amount of packaging.

  b. Credit card companies use advertising to encourage people to use credit for more of their purchases.

  c. A hospital cannot afford to admit patients who do not have health insurance.

  d. A market research organization asks a large number of personal questions during interviews.

25. a. For each of the following criticisms of marketing, describe with specific examples why each is not always accurate.

  Marketing causes people to purchase things they otherwise would not buy.

  Marketing adds to the cost of products without providing anything of value.

  Quality products and services do not need marketing.

b. For each of the following positive results of marketing, provide specific examples demonstrating that those contributions do exist.

Marketing increases public awareness of problems and solutions.

Marketing helps match supply and demand to solve serious problems.

MARKETING MANAGEMENT

26. Work in small groups to prepare a code of ethics for students and teachers. Pattern your code of ethics after the example in the chapter or another code of ethics you can locate. When you are finished, share your group's code of ethics with the other groups. Identify the areas of agreement and disagreement in the various codes of ethics. Discuss how the students in the class could enforce the code of ethics through self-regulation.

27. Both the Newsline on super squirt guns and the Judgment Call discussing Channel One News in schools present situations in which business people must decide how their decisions can be socially responsible. Choose one and answer the following questions:
   a. What is the social responsibility issue presented?
   b. Who is affected by the decisions of the business? How is each group affected?
   c. What is a possible action that can be taken by a concerned consumer group, government, or group of businesses? By the business involved?
   d. What do you believe is the most socially responsible action? Why?

MARKETING TECHNOLOGY

28. Obtain a copy of a recent annual report issued by a public company that has been in business for at least 10 years. Copies can be obtained from the companies themselves, a library, or on the Internet. Find the section that summarizes the company's financial performance for the past 10 years.
   a. Use a spreadsheet. For each of the most recent five years listed, enter the company's revenues or total sales, its net profits or net income, and its earnings or net income per share in three separate columns of the spreadsheet.
   b. Have the spreadsheet calculate the percentage changes in each column for the most recent four years.

29. Using an Internet search engine and browser, find the FedStats home page, which is a gateway to statistics from more than 100 federal agencies. Select your state from the MapStats drop-down menu, and then locate the most recent population statistics for your state and county. What percentage of your state's total population resides in your county?

MARKETING IN ACTION

CASE STUDY

MADD TACKLES A BIG SOCIAL ISSUE

Alcohol advertising encourages students in grades 5 through 12 to drink, according to 56 percent of students surveyed. One-half of the 20 million junior and senior high school students in America drink monthly.

Underage drinking is the biggest substance abuse problem in America, killing 6.5 times more young people than all other drugs combined. Unfortunately, many young people do not realize they can die from an overdose of alcohol. U.S. life expectancy over the past 75 years has improved for every age group except people from 15 to 24 years old. Their death rate is higher today than it was 20 years ago, and drunk and drugged driving are the leading causes of death. Drunk driving is the nation's most frequently committed violent crime. Almost 15,000 people were killed and over 600,000 were injured in alcohol-related traffic crashes in 1999.

Mothers Against Drunk Driving (MADD) was

founded in 1980 by a group of California women after a 13-year-old girl was killed by a hit-and-run driver. The driver was allowed to plead guilty to vehicular manslaughter even though he had been out on bail for only two days on charges

stemming from another hit-and-run accident. He also had three previous drunk-driving arrests with two convictions.

MADD is a tax-exempt, nonprofit organization with more than 600 national chapters. Members include mothers, fathers, grandparents, and young people. The major focus of MADD is to look for effective solutions to the problems of drunk driving and underage drinking, while supporting individuals and families who have experienced the pain of senseless crimes involving alcohol.

MADD contends that individuals injured and killed in drunk-driving collisions are not "accident" victims. The impaired driver makes two choices—first to drink, and then to drive. Deaths and injuries caused by impaired drivers can be prevented, it says.

NATION'S LARGEST ORGANIZATION FOR CRIME VICTIMS

MADD is the nation's largest crime victims' assistance organization. It offers a wide range of free support services and information for victims of impaired driving. Dialing 1-800-GET-MADD connects victims to trained staff and volunteers who provide emotional support and can guide them through the criminal justice system.

MADD has helped pass more than 2,300 anti-drunk-driving and underage-drinking laws. The passage of the national 21 minimum drinking-age law in 1984 was due in part to MADD's efforts. In 1995, the group helped to pass a zero-tolerance provision making it illegal for individuals under 21 to drive after consuming alcohol.

MADD advocates passage of a federal constitutional amendment for victims' rights and stricter penalties for repeat drunk-driving offenders. National programs and public awareness campaigns conducted by MADD include *Designate A Driver* campaign, *National Sobriety Checkpoint Week,* and the *Tie One On For*

Safety holiday red ribbon campaign. MADD has focused particularly on youth with a series of educational and activism initiatives that involve young people in efforts to prevent underage drinking and impaired driving.

MADD has an informative web site that tells about its history and goals. The site also provides eye-opening statistics concerning alcohol consumption and related deaths. There are links for parents, males, and females that highlight the drawbacks of alcohol consumption.

BUSINESSES SHOULDER RESPONSIBILITY

Why should businesses care about MADD? Because beverages, both alcoholic and nonalcoholic, are the largest revenue producers for restaurants and bars. Many entertainment venues earn large sums of money from selling alcohol. Businesses that sell alcohol have responsibilities to refuse sales to minors and to make sure that customers who have drunk too much do not drive. Restaurants and bars have been held liable for accidents caused by patrons who have had too much to drink.

Bennigan's, a national restaurant franchise, is aware of its responsibility to inform customers about the consumption of alcohol. Bennigan's tries to evaporate some of the myths about alcohol consumption by displaying charts near the pay telephones that show the relationship between an individual's weight, alcohol consumed, and blood-alcohol content. The charts are an attempt to make customers aware of their blood-alcohol content, because it can lead to arrest and jail time if they choose to drive. It also is a good public-awareness campaign for health reasons.

Many cities and restaurants offer free taxi rides for patrons who have been drinking on New Year's Eve. This special service is not only good public relations, but it also makes the roadways safer and decreases the possibility of death from alcohol-related accidents.

THINK CRITICALLY

1. What are the main purposes of MADD?

2. How could high school students work effectively with MADD to increase alcohol awareness?

3. Why do you think the government has paid attention to MADD and passed legislation lobbied by MADD?

---

http://www.deca.org/publications/HS_Guide/guidetoc.html

CIVIC CONSCIOUSNESS PROJECT

Using what you have learned about MADD, you can develop a Civic Consciousness project. Your project will focus on underage drinking and the negative results of drinking and driving.

SUMMARY MEMORANDUM Write a one-page description of the project.

INTRODUCTION Write about the historic background of MADD.

CONTRIBUTIONS TO A NEEDED COMMUNITY SERVICE OR CHARITY Describe the purpose of the project. Give rationale for selecting the community service project. Describe the benefits of the project.

ORGANIZATION AND IMPLEMENTATION Prepare an organizational chart that shows member involvement and job descriptions. Describe the project and show necessary documentation. What is the impact goal for the beneficiary (community, young people, citizens)?

EVALUATION AND RECOMMENDATIONS Evaluate the project. What was the impact of the community service project? Give recommendations to improve the project in the future.

CHAPTER 3

MARKETING BEGINS WITH ECONOMICS

LESSON 3.1 *SCARCITY AND PRIVATE ENTERPRISE*

LESSON 3.2 *OBSERVING THE LAW OF SUPPLY AND DEMAND*

LESSON 3.3 *TYPES OF ECONOMIC COMPETITION*

LESSON 3.4 *ENHANCING ECONOMIC UTILITY*

NEWSLINE

AN ECONOMIC DOGFIGHT

Fly the friendly skies? Not hardly. Airlines are fighting for passengers with price cuts and discounts. Because of this competition, several major U.S. airlines have gone out of business, sold off assets, or allowed themselves to be taken over by competitors.

In the 1970s, airlines were very profitable businesses. Today the few large airlines that remain have tried to concentrate their services in "hub" cities—central locations where they can route a lot of interconnecting flights to generate a large amount of passenger traffic. That gives them a chance to dominate the competition in that region.

What transformed this industry in which fat profits once were virtually guaranteed? Much of it is the role government has played and the nature of competition faced by airlines. The federal government has traditionally provided a great deal of regulation. In addition to maintaining safety standards, in the past the

government also regulated competition. Passenger loads and profits were protected.

Then in the 1980s, the government deregulated the industry. Subsidies were no longer provided, and airlines were free to compete for routes. Inefficient airlines found they could no longer compete as better-managed companies encroached on their markets.

Airlines have tried to show customers how their services are different from one another, but many customers do not see any important differences. So airlines use price competition and costly promotions.

THINK CRITICALLY

1. Do you think increased competition in the airline industry is good or bad for air safety?

2. How many airports serve the area in which you live? How many airlines control most of the scheduled flights in those airports?

CORPORATE VIEW

CAREER OPPORTUNITY
MARKETING DIRECTOR

TeleView is looking for someone who possesses the following attributes.

- Dynamic leader who can motivate others
- Excellent interpersonal and customer relations skills
- Strong problem solving, project organization, and time management skills
- Drive, flexibility, and technical communications skills
- Ability to organize detailed proposals
- Ability to work in an invigorating, team-oriented environment
- Self-starter who is motivated by opportunities and financial incentives

The main responsibilities of the job include the following.

- Directing the overall product marketing operation for a line of TeleView products
- Assisting and directing product marketing managers as they bring products from R&D to market
- Managing the complete product life cycle of an entire line of products
- Developing marketing strategy for entire product line
- Defining new business opportunities for your line of products
- Writing and maintaining annual business plan for your team
- Hiring product marketing managers
- Training and mentoring your team
- Coordinating the relationship with marketing, sales, and support
- Responsible for P&L (Profit and Loss) and overall performance of your product line

The job requires the following education, skills, and experience.

- BA or BS degree minimum, MBA highly desired
- Eight years of product marketing and management experience with consistent growth in responsibilities
- Positive track record managing revenue growth
- Srong management experience working in teams

THINK CRITICALLY

1. Prepare a cover letter written by a person who is qualified for this job and interested in applying for it.

2. What skills do you possess that might qualify you tor this position?

3. Search want ads or the Internet for a job similar to TeleView's marketing director. What type of compensation package is being offered for the job?

3.1 SCARCITY AND PRIVATE ENTERPRISE

- Identify the basic economic problem.
- Describe how America's private enterprise economy works.

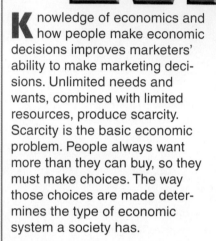

K nowledge of economics and how people make economic decisions improves marketers' ability to make marketing decisions. Unlimited needs and wants, combined with limited resources, produce scarcity. Scarcity is the basic economic problem. People always want more than they can buy, so they must make choices. The way those choices are made determines the type of economic system a society has.

The United States has a private enterprise economy, which has many of the characteristics of a free economy. America's economy is driven by consumers' independent decisions about what they want to buy and by producers' decisions about what they will produce. The government's role in making economic choices is very limited.

Make a list of the 10 things you bought most recently. List the main factors involved in your purchasing decisions.

THE IMPORTANCE OF ECONOMIC UNDERSTANDING

M any people believe that effective marketing relies almost solely on creativity. In their view, people who can create a memorable image for a product or attract the customer's attention will increase sales. People who understand marketing, however, know that the marketing process is more scientific. Effective marketing relies on the principles and concepts of economics. Knowledge of economics and how economic decisions are made improves marketing decision-making and results in increased customer satisfaction and higher profits for the company.

An understanding of the types of competition that businesses face also contributes to better marketing decisions. Marketers need to manage based on the type of competition they face. They also must learn how to interpret economic information to improve marketing decisions. Marketers and

other business people should recognize that the increased competition faced by most businesses places a whole new importance on understanding and using economic information.

THE BASIC ECONOMIC PROBLEM

People's wants and needs are unlimited. They seldom feel like their wants and needs are completely satisfied. Conversely, resources are limited. There are never enough available to meet everyone's wants and needs. For example, producing a car requires a variety of resources, including glass, rubber, steel, and plastic. Yet there is a limited supply of each of those resources, and they are also needed for things other than producing cars. So there may not be enough to make all the automobiles that people might want.

Unlimited wants and needs, combined with limited resources, result in **scarcity**. Scarcity is the basic economic problem. Because of scarcity, choices must be made. How will limited resources be used to satisfy people's unlimited wants and needs? Because wants and needs will always be greater than the available resources, choices and tradeoffs must be made. The available resources will have to be allocated to satisfy some wants and needs and not others.

Scarcity creates difficult problems for a society. Some needs and wants are satisfied while others are not. Resources are used to produce certain products and services. Other products and services are not produced. What is produced and for whom it is produced must be determined. The way those decisions are made indicates the type of economic system a society has.

WHO MAKES THE DECISIONS?

An economy is designed to facilitate the use of resources. The resources satisfy the individual and group needs of people in the economy. Economies are organized in many ways. The type of economic system determines who owns the resources. It determines how decisions are made regarding the use of resources. Which needs are satisfied and how resources are distributed depends on the type of economic system. Even the cost of that resource depends on the economic system.

In a system known as a **controlled economy**, the government attempts to own and control important resources and to make the decisions about what will be produced and consumed. In another type of economy known as a **regulated economy**, the resources and decisions are shared between the government and

Database Marketing Made Easy

Many businesses create databases that contain huge amounts of data about their existing customers and potential customers. Their marketers use the data to generate computerized mailing lists and individualized promotions as well as research for product development efforts.

Database programs store, sort, and analyze large volumes of data. They are very useful for businesses with large customer bases or even those with relatively small customer bases but a large number of customer transactions.

To build a database, you first identify each relevant bit of information you want to keep track of, and then input that information into a database field. A business might want a separate field for the customer name, phone number, each item ordered, price, the transaction date, and so forth. A collection of fields pertaining to a particular

customer or order is known as a record. All of the records combined make up the database.

The practice of using databases to make marketing decisions is known as database marketing. Databases may also be purchased from outside vendors that specialize in compiling mailing lists or sales leads, for example. Relational database software allows marketers to relate records in one database—a business's internal customer records, for instance—to records in other databases.

THINK CRITICALLY

1. What is a database field?

2. What is a collection of related fields, such as the fields that pertain to a specific customer or sales transaction?

3. Give an example of how a marketer might use a database's sorting capabilities to obtain useful information.

other groups or individuals. In a **free economy**, resources are owned by individuals rather than the government, and decisions are made independently with no attempt at regulation or control by the government.

What is the basic economic problem?

AMERICA'S PRIVATE ENTERPRISE ECONOMY

The United States has many of the characteristics of a private enterprise economy. **Private enterprise** is based on independent decisions by businesses and consumers with only a limited government role regulating those relationships.

Businesses decide what products and services to produce. Consumers decide what to purchase. Government generally regulates what is produced and what is consumed only when someone is thought to have an unfair advantage or disadvantage or when the government wants to encourage or discourage some economic activity.

CHARACTERISTICS

There are several important characteristics that describe a private enterprise economy.

- Resources of production are owned and controlled by individual producers.
- Producers use the profit motive in deciding what to produce. The **profit motive** is the use of resources toward

the greatest profit for the producer.
- Individual consumers make decisions about what will be purchased to satisfy needs.
- Consumers use value in deciding what to consume. **Value** is a decision to use resources toward the greatest satisfaction of wants and needs.
- The government stays out of exchange activities between producers and consumers unless it is clear that individuals or society are harmed by the decisions.

Because businesses have a great deal of independence in a private enterprise economy, their decisions can determine whether they succeed or fail.

Consumers   Individuals who purchase products and services to satisfy needs are consumers. They have limited resources, or money, to satisfy their needs. Consumers select products that they believe are able to provide the greatest satisfaction for the price. **Demand** is a relationship between

Online Auctions Transforming Purchasing

In a recent reader poll by *Purchasing Magazine,* only about one in four industrial buyers said they would use online auctions to make purchasing decisions. Based on the success many businesses are having with online auctions, those buyers could soon change their minds. The potential cost savings and price reductions make auctions a promising tool.

The thought of online auctions might make current suppliers jittery, but once they know that a business is accepting bids, the way an auction is conducted doesn't necessarily matter. For purchasers, auctions allow them to consider bids from a larger number of potential suppliers, rather than just two or three. Also, bidding often is used to start the

process, narrow the field and establish a basis for negotiations. There's no requirement that a business award any contract to the lowest bidder.

One purchasing executive noted that existing suppliers have won his business more than 75% of the time by bidding lower prices than he has been paying. Savings like that, plus administrative cost savings, could make online auctions the wave of the future.

THINK CRITICALLY

1. Why do online auctions make existing suppliers nervous?

2. How do online auctions cut administrative costs?

the quantity of a product consumers are willing and able to purchase and the price.

Consumers gather information about available products and services in order to select those that appear to satisfy their needs. As an example, a basic consumer need is for clothing. Some consumers will sew their own clothes. Some will buy basic and inexpensive clothing. Others will spend a great deal of money on a large and expensive wardrobe.

Producers Businesses that use the resources they control to develop products and services are producers. They hope to sell products and services to consumers for profit. **Supply** is a relationship between the quantity of a product that producers are willing and able to provide and the price.

Producers gather information on the types of products and services consumers want in order to provide those that are most likely to be purchased. An example of a producer's decision is the development of a restaurant. Consumers eat a number of their meals outside the home. There are opportunities to start businesses that respond to that need. Individual restaurant owners can determine the type of business they want to operate based on what they believe customers want.

Government Under ideal circumstances, government allows consumers and producers to make decisions without any interference. However, there are times when some consumers or producers are at a disadvantage and will not receive fair treatment, or society will be harmed by the decisions made by producers and consumers. In those situations the government enacts laws and regulations to help those who are treated unfairly.

ECONOMIC FORCES

An example of decision-making in a private enterprise economy illustrates how the system operates. One community has a variety of entertainment options, but has no social club for teenagers. Many teenagers indicate a need for some type of club and suggest they would visit it and spend

money there if one was developed. Even though it appears that the need for the new type of business exists, there is no requirement that anyone open a teen social club. It will be developed only when someone recognizes the need, determines that a club could be opened and operated profitably, wants to operate that type of business, and has the resources to do so.

Members of city government might recognize the need for a teen club. They may see teenage crime rates increasing, or have concerns expressed to them by teenagers and parents, or just want to meet important needs of city residents. Based on that concern, the government may encourage the development of a teen club through tax incentives or other economic assistance. Or they may have the city develop and operate a teen center as a city service.

Typically in a private enterprise economy, government would not get involved with the economic problem described. It would rely on the profit motive to encourage the development of a new business and on consumers expressing needs to businesses for products and services.

In a private enterprise economy, when does government get involved in exchange relationships?

1. Why is an understanding of economics more important to marketing now than it was in the past?

2. What is the cause of scarcity?

3. What are the key economic characteristics that distinguish one type of economic system from another?

4. Name three characteristics of a private enterprise economy.

3.2 OBSERVING THE LAW OF SUPPLY AND DEMAND

Explain microeconomics and the concept of consumer demand.

Identify factors that affect supply and its relationship to demand.

Microeconomics analyzes the interaction of consumer demand with producer supply to predict how changes in one affect the other. Much depends on consumers' needs and wants and on the availability of alternatives. When the independent decisions of consumers and producers are combined, they can be illustrated as curved lines on a two-dimensional graph that intersect at the market price.

Make a list of the last article of clothing you purchased, the last restaurant food you bought, and your last transportation-related expense, with the prices you paid for each. If each had cost 20% more, would you still have bought them? What if they were 50% more? Twice as much as you paid? What determines the point at which you decide not to buy something or to find an alternative?

MICROECONOMICS AND CONSUMER DEMAND

Economics attempts to understand and explain how consumers and producers make decisions concerning the allocation of their resources. That understanding helps consumers and producers to use their resources as effectively as they can. It also helps government decision-makers determine if and when they should become involved in the economy as they work to maintain an even balance between producers and consumers and to maintain a strong economy that improves the standard of living for citizens.

Economics operates on two levels, as illustrated in Figure 3-1. The first level,

known as **macroeconomics**, studies the economic behavior and relationships of the entire society. Macroeconomics looks at the big picture. It helps to determine if

FIGURE 3-1
Macroeconomics studies the whole economy while microeconomics studies the relationships between individual businesses and their consumers.

Comparing Macroeconomics and Microeconomics

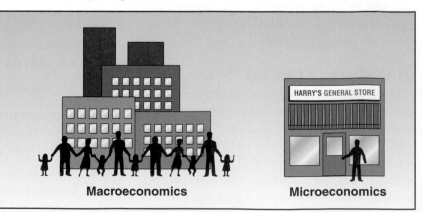

may seem very important to you. You may be willing to pay much more to buy a CD at the concert rather than waiting to make the purchase later.

Another factor that affects consumers' decisions is the available supply of products and services to satisfy their needs. If the country's resources are being used as effectively and efficiently as possible. The decisions of all consumers and producers and the effects of those decisions on the economy are studied.

The second level, **microeconomics**, is the study of relationships between individual consumers and producers. Microeconomics looks at small parts of the total economy. Microeconomics studies how individuals make decisions about what to produce and what to consume.

While a broad understanding of economics is important to marketers, they are most concerned about microeconomics. You can see that information about how consumers make decisions on what they will purchase and how much they are willing to pay can be very important in selecting target markets and developing effective marketing mixes. It is also important to understand how a business' competitors make decisions about what they will produce and the prices they are likely to charge. Microeconomics looks at supply, demand, and the level of individual product prices. The relationship between supply and consumer demand is an important tool for marketers.

FACTORS AFFECTING DEMAND

A number of factors influence consumers' decisions regarding what to purchase and how much to pay. If a need or want is particularly important or strong, a consumer might be willing to spend more money to satisfy it. For example, if you are at a concert and really like the songs you just heard, obtaining a CD

there is a very large supply of a product, consumers will usually place a lower value on it. Imagine walking through a farmers' market where a large number of producers are selling fresh fruits and vegetables. As a consumer, you see there are many choices of sellers and a large quantity of each product available. Therefore, you will probably be careful not to overpay for the fruits or vegetables you want. On the other hand, if a large number of customers are at the market and only a few farmers are there to sell their products, the customers may pay much higher prices to be sure they get the items they need.

A third factor is the availability of alternative products that consumers believe will satisfy their needs. If consumers believe there is only one product or brand that meets their needs, they are willing to pay a higher price. If several options seem to be equally satisfying, consumers are more careful about how much they pay. An example of this factor is your choice of entertainment for an evening. If there are very few things from which you and your friends can choose, you are willing to pay quite a bit for a specific activity. If you identify several options (a movie, bowling, a sporting event, renting a video) and each seems enjoyable, you may consider the cost more carefully. You might select one that is inexpensive but which you and your friends will still enjoy.

ANALYZING DEMAND CURVES

Economists try to determine how much consumers are willing and able to pay for various quantities of products or services. The relationship between price and the quantity demanded is often illustrated in a graph known as a **demand curve**. Figure 3-2 shows a sample demand curve for movies in a city. As the price of movies increases, fewer people buy tickets. As the price decreases, more tickets are sold. This relationship is known as the **law of demand**: When the price of a product is increased, less will be demanded. When the price is decreased, more will be demanded.

Just as in marketing, economists use the concept of markets. All of the consumers who will purchase a particular product or service comprise an **economic market**. Economists believe that the consumers in an economic market view the relationship of products and prices in the same way.

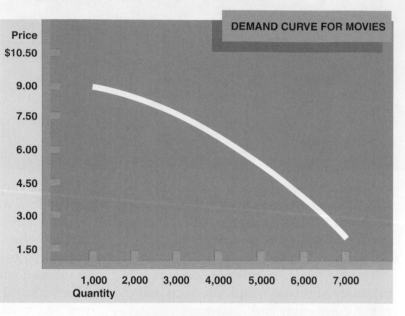

FIGURE 3-2
As the price of movies increases, the number of consumers willing and able to pay that price decreases.

DEMAND CURVE FOR MOVIES

checkpoint

How does microeconomics differ from macroeconomics?

SUPPLYING
THE PRODUCT

There are several factors that influence what and how many products or services a business will produce. Factors include the possibility of profit, the amount of competition, and the capability of developing and marketing the products or services.

One of the most important reasons for businesses to operate in a private enterprise economy is to make a profit. Businesses will try to offer products and services that have a good chance of making a large profit, rather than products and services likely to yield either a small profit or the possibility of a loss. Business managers carefully consider both the costs of producing and

marketing products and the prices they will be able to charge for those products. That analysis helps in determining the most profitable choices to produce.

HANDLING THE COMPETITION

When looking for opportunities, businesses consider the amount and type of competition. When competition is intense (with many businesses offering the same types of products or services), there are fewer opportunities for success than when there is little competition. When possible, suppliers may choose to offer products and services that have few competitors. Another

option when there is a lot of competition is to change the product to make it different from those offered by other businesses. For example, an owner of an apartment complex in a community where there are many vacant apartments may provide a sports club or athletic facility. The owner may extend short-term leases or may offer furnished apartments if those types of services are not available in other apartment complexes.

Finally, businesses use the resources available to develop products and services. **Economic resources** are classified as natural resources, capital, equipment, and labor. The specific types of resources a business has available will determine the types of products and services it can develop and sell. Some resources are very flexible so the business can change and offer new products quickly. For example, if the owners of a retail furniture store found that major appliances such as refrigerators and stoves were not profitable, they could quickly change the products sold in that part of the store to some that are more profitable. Other businesses have more difficulty changing products. Companies that own oil wells or coal mines, for instance, have few options because the natural resources they own are

their products. They have to sell the oil and coal even if those products are not very profitable.

ANALYZING SUPPLY CURVE

Some economists predict how the quantity of products and services changes at various prices. The graph of the relationship between price and quantity supplied is known as a **supply curve**. An example supply curve for watches is shown in Figure 3-3. The graph shows that as the price increases, producers will manufacture more watches. As the price goes down, fewer will be manufactured. This relationship is known as the **law of supply**: When the price of a product is increased, more will be produced. When the price is decreased, less will be produced.

FIGURE 3-3
As the price for watches decreases, so does the quantity of watches that manufacturers will be willing to supply.

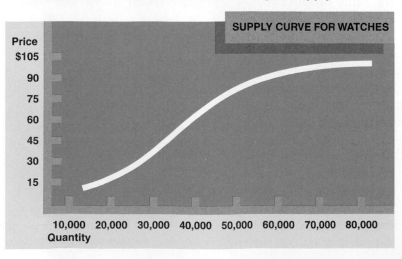

Figure 3-4 shows a demand curve and a supply curve for a particular type of notebook computer. The demand curve shows that fewer computers will be purchased as the price increases. As expected, computer manufacturers are willing to supply a larger number of computers if prices are high, fewer if prices are low.

To determine the number of computers that will actually be produced and sold, the two curves must be combined. The combined curves are shown in

Whenever possible, producers use their resources to provide products and services that receive the highest prices. Just as with demand, economists believe that all producers in a market respond in similar ways when determining what to produce. Like consumers, producers see a relationship between products and prices.

INTERSECTING SUPPLY AND DEMAND

We learned that suppliers and consumers make independent decisions. When the decisions of many consumers of the same product are combined, they form a demand curve illustrating the quantity of a product or service that will be demanded at various prices. And when the decisions of all the suppliers of the same product or service are combined, they form a supply curve. That curve illustrates the quantity of the product that will be supplied at various prices.

FIGURE 3-4
Consumers and suppliers respond very differently to price changes. The demand curve illustrates consumers' responses and the supply curve illustrates suppliers' responses.

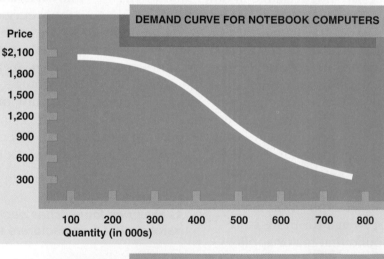

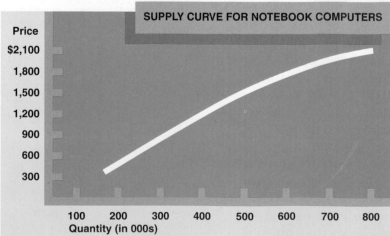

Figure 3-5. Notice that the two lines cross or intersect at a price of $1,300 and a quantity of 450,000 computers. The point where supply and demand for a product are equal is known as the **market price**. At that price, 450,000 computers will be manufactured and sold.

Each product in a specific market has its own supply and demand curves. And each market has price and quantity relationships that are unique and result in different curves on the graphs.

FIGURE 3-5

The point at which the demand curve and the supply curve for notebook computers intersect is the market price.

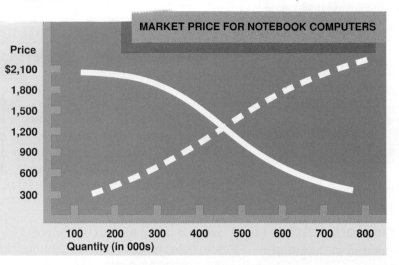

MARKET PRICE FOR NOTEBOOK COMPUTERS

Price: $2,100, 1,800, 1,500, 1,200, 900, 600, 300

Quantity (in 000s): 100, 200, 300, 400, 500, 600, 700, 800

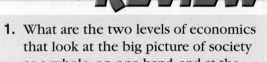

checkpoint

What are the main factors that businesses consider when deciding what and how much to produce?

LESSON REVIEW

1. What are the two levels of economics that look at the big picture of society as a whole, on one hand, and at the decision-making of individual consumers and producers, on the other?

2. What happens to the demand curve for a product when there is an influx of new consumers into the market? Give an example.

3. Name and give examples of three factors that affect consumer demand for a product or service.

4. Name and give examples of three factors that affect the supply of a product.

5. In analyzing the profit potential of a product, what two things do producers carefully consider?

6. On a graph of the supply and demand curves for a product, what point on the graph indicates the market price?

3.3 TYPES OF ECONOMIC COMPETITION

● **Define pure competition and monopoly.**

● **Explain the characteristics of oligopolies and monopolistic competition.**

Businesses' responses to consumer demands are strongly influenced by the competitive structure of the industries they are in and the markets they serve. The type of competition, or in some extreme cases the lack of competition, determines how much control businesses have over pricing and what strategies they should follow to maximize long-term profits.

Each type of competition produces a characteristic demand curve. Identifying and defining the demand curve is important in developing marketing strategies.

Make a list of six businesses, large and small, that operate in your city or town. Now rate the businesses on a point scale of 1-to-10 based on how much market control you think they have over the prices they charge, with a rating of 10 representing maximum control.

ALL-OUT COMPETITION OR NO COMPETITION AT ALL

The type of competition found in the market affects consumer and supplier decisions alike. If consumers see a variety of products that seem to be very similar, they will be less willing to pay higher prices. If suppliers are in a market with many other businesses offering similar products, they will not be able to easily increase their prices. Business people must be able to determine the type of competition they are facing, and the amount of control they have over the prices they can charge, in order to make effective production and marketing decisions.

Two characteristics are important in determining the type of economic competition in a specific market:

1. The number of firms competing in the market
2. The amount of similarity between the products of competing businesses

Economists use those characteristics to define four forms of economic competition—pure competition, monopoly, oligopoly, and monopolistic competition.

PURE COMPETITION

There are a few markets where there are a large number of suppliers and their products are very similar. In these markets, consumers have a great deal of control over choices and prices. Because the suppliers are unable to offer products that consumers view as unique, they must accept the prices that consumers are willing to pay or the consumers will buy from another business. This market condition is known as pure competition. In **pure competition** there are a large number of suppliers offering very similar products.

The traditional examples of industries in pure competition are producers of agricultural products such as corn, rice, wheat, and livestock. Each producer's products are just like every other producer's. There are many producers, so customers have no difficulty finding a business that will sell the products. Because customers have so many choices of suppliers and the products of all suppliers are similar, prices will be very competitive. No single supplier will be able to raise the price. Other examples of markets in which businesses face something close to pure competition are those for many of the low-priced consumer products you purchase—milk, gasoline, ballpoint pens, light bulbs, blank diskettes and CDs, and the like.

An example of the demand curve for a business in a purely competitive market is shown in Figure 3-6. In theory, it is a straight line at one price. That suggests that the supplier will receive the

FIGURE 3-6

In pure competition, the seller must accept the market price no matter how much of the product is sold.

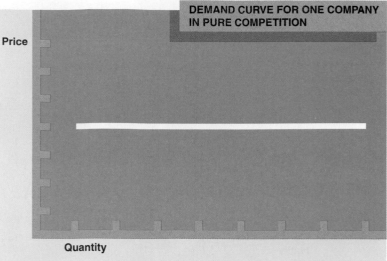

DEMAND CURVE FOR ONE COMPANY IN PURE COMPETITION

Price

Quantity

same price no matter how much of the product the supplier is willing to sell. Therefore, businesses have no control over price if they want to sell their products.

MONOPOLY

The opposite of pure competition is a monopoly. A **monopoly** is a type of market in which there is one supplier offering a unique product. In this market, the supplier has almost total control and the consumers will have to accept what the supplier offers at the price charged. That occurs because of the lack of competition.

Because of the obvious advantage a business has in monopoly markets, the government attempts to control them so there are few examples of monopolies that actually dictate prices. Utility companies that supply communities with electricity, gas, or water are typically organized as monopolies. There is only one supplier of each product since it would be very inefficient to have several companies extending gas and water lines or electrical service to every home. Once a home is supplied with the utilities, it would be easy for the company to raise the price. The consumer would have no choice but to

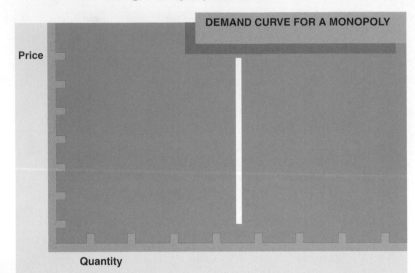

DEMAND CURVE FOR A MONOPOLY

Price

Quantity

interstate highway and there is only one gasoline station at a particular exit, that business can operate much like a monopoly for those customers who need gasoline or other automotive products. A supermarket or other retail business in an area where there is no other similar business can also operate as a monopoly for those customers who are unable to travel to a competing business. In theory, the demand curve facing a business that has a monopoly would look like the one in Figure 3-7. There is a fixed demand for the product, since there are no other businesses offering a similar product. Therefore, if unregulated, the business can charge any price it chooses. The consumer either pays the price set by the business or goes without.

pay the higher price or go without the gas, water, or electricity. So government agencies regulate the prices that can be charged by the utility companies. Other examples of markets that can operate much like a monopoly are cable television, some local telephone services, and businesses that are the only ones of their type in a particular geographic area where consumers have no choices. If you are driving down an

☑ **checkpoint**

Distinguish pure competition from monopoly based on the two characteristics that economists use to define types of competition.

BETWEEN THE EXTREMES

Between the extremes of pure competition and monopoly are two other types of economic competition. In an **oligopoly** a few businesses offer very similar products or services. As you consider the difference between an oligopoly and the other two types of markets, you might be able to see the problems and advantages facing businesses in this type of market. If the businesses work together, they will be like a monopoly and have a great deal of control in the market. On the other hand, if they are very competitive, the similarity of their products or services will give consumers choices, much like in pure competition. In that case, the consumers will have more control and prices will be lower.

OLIGOPOLIES

The airline industry is an example of an oligopoly. There are only a very few large airlines competing for national travel in the United States. It is difficult to see real important differences between two or three airlines that serve the same cities. Therefore, if one airline wants to increase the number of passengers on its flights, it will often do it by reducing prices. To counter that effort and to keep passengers from flying with the competitor, other airlines will usually have to reduce their prices as well.

One airline will not usually be successful in increasing prices alone. If the airline industry wants higher prices to cover operating expenses and contribute to profit, the competing companies will have to cooperate in raising their prices as well. Again, government agencies often attempt to regulate that type of activity, making it illegal for businesses to work together to control prices. Notice, however, that if one airline announces a price increase or decrease, the competing airlines are usually very quick to match the change.

Other examples of industries with characteristics of an oligopoly are automobile manufacturers, oil refineries, computer manufacturers, Internet service providers, and companies offering long-distance or wireless telephone services. On the local level, some businesses operate as oligopolies because there are only a few businesses offering almost identical products and services to the consumers in that market. Some examples in medium- to large-size communities are taxi services, movie theaters, banks, and hospitals.

The demand curve facing businesses in an oligopoly is difficult to describe. For an individual business, the demand curve will look like the demand in pure competition since one business cannot influence the price it can charge to any great extent. Figure 3-8 shows an example of a demand curve for one company in an oligopoly.

The demand curve for all of the businesses combined in an oligopoly will look much like that of a monopoly. Cooperatively, the businesses have a great deal of control

FIGURE 3-8
One business in an oligopoly will have little influence over the price it can charge.

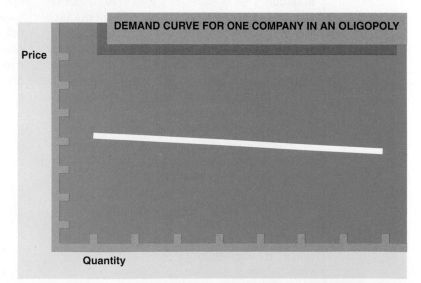

DEMAND CURVE FOR ONE COMPANY IN AN OLIGOPOLY

Price

Quantity

over price. Consumers who want the product or service will have to purchase from one of the few companies in the market or go without. An example of a demand curve for the entire industry in an oligopoly is shown in Figure 3-9.

MONOPOLISTIC COMPETITION

By far the most common type of economic competition facing most businesses is monopolistic competition. In **monopolistic competition** there are many firms competing with products that are somewhat different. The fewer the number of competitors and the greater the differences among the competitors' products or

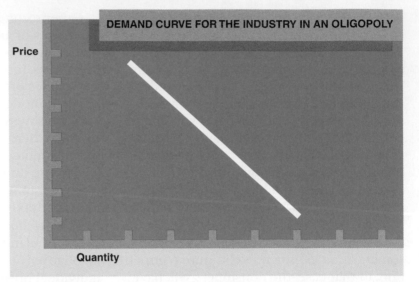

FIGURE 3-9
Because there are few firms in an oligopoly, the total industry has much more control over prices.

DEMAND CURVE FOR THE INDUSTRY IN AN OLIGOPOLY

Price

Quantity

services, the greater the control each firm will have in the market. With more competitors and only minor differences, businesses will have very limited control.

JUDGMENT CALL

When Is Cooperative Pricing Ethical?

In some industries, controlling prices is very difficult. That is especially true in an oligopoly, where a few large businesses offer products that are very similar and it is hard to attract customers with factors other than price. If a customer wants to purchase a car and several dealers sell the same models, the customer will shop to find the lowest price. Dealers know they must be competitive.

When business people see that they are competing in an oligopoly, they might be tempted to agree with other businesses to keep prices high. To protect consumers, the federal government makes it illegal for businesses to "fix" prices. Recently, several milk producers were charged with fixing prices for the milk they sold to schools. In another case, companies who sold concrete for government buildings were accused of agreeing in advance on the prices they would bid.

It is difficult for the government to regulate pricing when a few large firms compete. For example, it is not unusual for an airline to announce a price change to take place in several weeks. Then competing airlines can determine if they are going to match the price change. Likewise, automobile manufacturers typically announce new model prices months in advance. That gives competing manufacturers time to adjust their prices. While these pricing practices are not illegal, they have much the same effect as illegal price fixing.

THINK CRITICALLY

1. Do you think the legal pricing practices described for the airline and auto industries are ethical?

2. How is pricing affected when competing companies merge?

FIGURE THIS
1234567890

Measuring the Demand Curve

Economists have a way of quantifying demand curves so that businesses can use them to develop better marketing strategies. This method of quantifying is referred to as "elasticity of demand." In economics, elasticity means responsiveness to change. Elasticity of demand measures how much consumer demand for a product changes when the price is raised or lowered.

If demand is highly elastic, the demand curve is more horizontal, and a small change in price will have a big effect on consumer demand. If it is inelastic, the curve is more vertical, and demand remains relatively constant.

Elasticity is quantified by calculating the ratio of the percentage change in the quantity demanded over the percentage change in price. To illustrate, let's say a movie theater's research indicates that if it raises its price from $4 to $5, the average number of tickets it sells will decrease from 150 per night to 100. To calculate the elasticity of demand, first calculate the percentage change in tickets: 50/150 = 1/3 = 33%. Then calculate the percentage change in price: $1/$4 = 1/4 = 25%. Now calculate the ratio of the change in demand (33%) over the change in price (25%): 33/25 = 1.3.

When the ratio is greater than 1, the demand is said to be elastic, and raising prices decreases overall revenue. When it is less than 1, demand is inelastic, and raising prices increases revenue.

THINK CRITICALLY

1. Research for a bicycle shop indicates that if it lowers the price it charges for a tune-up from $30 to $20, it will sell twice as many tune-ups. Calculate its elasticity of demand.

2. Is its demand elastic or inelastic?

3. If the shop's costs per tune-up remain the same regardless of how many tune-ups it does, what should it do to maximize profits?

There are many examples of businesses in monopolistic competition. Most retail businesses in which you shop face this type of competition. Most of the products or services you buy fit the definition.

As a consumer you typically have several choices of businesses or products. Among those choices, you can identify differences. Some differences are very noticeable and important. Other differences are only minor. When you have choices as a consumer, you usually select the one providing the most satisfaction at the best value. Examples of businesses and products in monopolistic competition include restaurants, movie theaters, shopping malls, athletic shoes, soap, stereo equipment, and cosmetics.

The demand curve for businesses in monopolistic competition falls somewhere between that of pure competition and monopoly. An example of this type of demand curve is in Figure 3-10.

FIGURE 3-10
When there are few differences among products, businesses will have little price control.

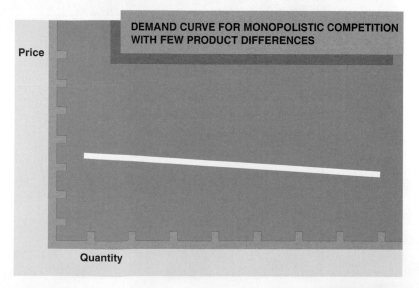

DEMAND CURVE FOR MONOPOLISTIC COMPETITION WITH FEW PRODUCT DIFFERENCES

Price

Quantity

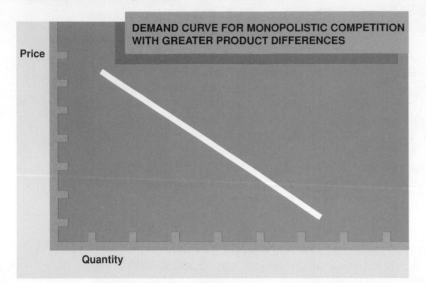

DEMAND CURVE FOR MONOPOLISTIC COMPETITION
WITH GREATER PRODUCT DIFFERENCES

Price

Quantity

economic competition they face and to act accordingly in order to maximize profits. A business in pure competition will not be able to exercise much control in the market, while one in a monopoly will have almost total control. Businesses in an oligopoly must pay careful attention to the actions of competitors. For the largest number of businesses, those in monopolistic competition, the differences between competing products will be very important. Wherever possible, marketers will want to do things that result in products that are different and better than those of competitors. In that way they will have more control in the marketplace.

The greater the differences among products and services, the more control the business has, so the demand curve is more vertical. If there are few differences, the business has less control, so the demand curve is more horizontal. An example is shown in Figure 3-11.

UNDERSTANDING THE COMPETITION

It is important for business people and especially marketers to know the type of

checkpoint

Contrast oligopolies and monopolistic competition.

LESSON REVIEW

1. In which direction, horizontally or vertically, does an individual airline's demand curve tend to run? Under what circumstances does it tend to be otherwise?

2. Which company would have a more vertical demand curve, a business that makes high-priced cosmetics sold only in boutiques and department stores or one that makes a bargain line that's sold in discount stores and supermarkets?

3. How can a business in pure competition increase profits?

4. How can a business in monopolistic competition increase profits?

5. From a marketing standpoint, why is it so important for a business to understand the type of competition it faces?

ENHANCING ECONOMIC UTILITY

MARKETING MATTERS

Although consumers rarely analyze precisely how they decide to buy products or services, they unconsciously make buying decisions based on the satisfaction they expect to derive from them. Businesses therefore strive to increase consumers' satisfaction by making improvements to products and services.

Economists have developed a concept called utility and identified various types of utility to explain why consumers get more or less satisfaction from different products. For businesses, utility is important to help them develop better products.

Identify two products in your classroom and propose changes that would increase the satisfaction they provide.

GOALS

- Define various types of economic utility.
- Explain how marketers use utility to increase customer satisfaction.

UTILITY MEANS SATISFACTION

Most people would like to purchase many more things than they are able to afford. Because of limited resources and unlimited needs, they have to choose among available products and services. People select those that provide the greatest amount of satisfaction for the money they are able or willing to spend. You may have to choose between attending a concert and purchasing a CD, for example. Saving for college may be more important than buying a car.

To analyze how people make choices among competing products, economists use a concept called economic utility. **Economic utility** is the amount of satisfaction a consumer receives from the consumption of a particular product or service. Products that provide great satisfaction have a higher economic utility, while those providing less satisfaction have a lower utility.

Businesses can use economic utility to increase the likelihood that consumers will buy their products or services. If a consumer believes that a particular product will provide higher utility than other choices, that product is the one that will likely be purchased. The four primary ways businesses can increase the economic utility of a product or service are changes in form, time, place, and possession.

Form Utility The physical product provided or the service offered is the primary way that consumer needs are satisfied. *Form utility* results from changes in the tangible parts of a product or service.

Some products and services are in a more usable form than others. They may be constructed of better or more durable materials. The product may also come with features that more consumers want.

Time Utility Even though a product is in the form a customer wants, it may not be available when the customer wants it. *Time utility* results from making the product or service available when the customer wants it.

Sorry We're Closed

Americans expect convenience, particularly when it comes to shopping. Stores and restaurants open early and close late. Many remain open 24 hours a day. With few exceptions, retailers operate seven days a week. Some people are so busy that Sunday is the only day they get a chance to do their shopping. In most industries, competition forces retailers to stay open for long hours, because if they don't, someone else will steal their customers.

In Germany, the situation is quite different. German retailers, by tradition and by law, generally are open only limited hours each day and not at all on Sundays. Most shops close between 6:00 and 6:30 in the evening. If people want groceries later than that or on

Sunday, they are out of luck. Even though the laws were recently changed to loosen restrictions on opening hours, German retailers have been slow to change because the public apparently likes things the way they are.

Only time will tell if past practices are eventually eroded by competitive pressures, possibly from foreign retailers who have fewer qualms about bucking German tradition.

THINK CRITICALLY

1. Owners of small shops tend to support restricted shopping hours in Germany. Why would they favor such restrictions?

2. German laws restricting shop hours affect what forms of economic utility?

A bank stays open in the evening and on Saturday mornings. An auto dealership opens its service department on weekends. Each of these examples illustrates improvements in time utility for a product or service.

Place Utility Just as some consumers are concerned about when a product is available, others may want to purchase or consume the product at a particular place. Making products and services available where the consumer wants them is *place utility.*

Convenience stores are successful because they are located in neighborhoods close to where consumers live. Businesses that provide mailing, photocopying, and facsimile services are becoming very popular, but they must be located conveniently to small businesses and individual consumers who need them. A convenient location for products and services is an important utility for people with busy lives.

Possession Utility Possession utility is the most difficult to understand, but it is a

very important type of economic utility. A product may be in the form a consumer wants and be available at the right time in the right place, yet the consumer still may not be able to purchase the product because of a lack of resources. *Possession utility* results from the affordability of the product or service. It is usually not possible for a business to decrease the price just so a product can be sold. It does not want to sell products at a loss. Yet there are other ways besides cutting the price to make a product more affordable.

Some people today would have a difficult time shopping without a credit card. Using credit allows people to purchase things for which they do not have enough cash at the time. They can then pay for the product when the credit bill is received or pay gradually with monthly payments.

Few people want to spend money to purchase a movie just so they can watch it more than once. Video stores are very successful because they rent movies rather than sell them. With low-cost rentals, people can watch more movies. Likewise, automobile dealerships lease new automobiles. Leases make it possible for customers to drive new cars without having to make a huge down payment. You will probably rent rather than buy a cap and gown for your graduation.

Finding ways to finance, rent, or lease products has become an important business activity today. It is a valuable way to offer possession utility to customers.

What are the four primary types of economic utility?

UTILITY AS A MARKETING TOOL

Radio Thriving In Digital Age

In this digital age, radio is still one of the fastest growing marketing media. Doomsayers have been predicting radio's demise ever since television arrived, but radio is thriving. One reason is the lifting of government restrictions that changed the nature of competition in the industry.

In the past, owners were limited to two stations in a given metropolitan area. The argument was that the number of stations is limited, so it is necessary to ensure that no single company dominates it. As a result, each major U.S. market tended to have many radio operators, few of whom made much profit. Advertising was cheap, but service was poor. Mounting a radio marketing campaign took a lot of effort by the advertiser, because the individual stations weren't much help. They concentrated on programming, not on how to help their advertisers get their message out.

After ownership restrictions were lifted, the industry changed dramatically. Suddenly, a few radio groups controlled most of the popular stations. In some cities, one group controlled virtually the entire market. Radio stations no longer battled one another so much as they competed with other media for advertisers' dollars. By consolidating sales operations, the radio groups could cut costs, deliver better service, and make more profit. Advertising sales have never been better.

THINK CRITICALLY

1. Describe the state of the radio industry in terms of the type of competition that existed before ownership restrictions were lifted and since.

2. Who are the consumers whose needs radio stations attempt to satisfy if they are using the marketing concept?

Business people who use the marketing concept try to identify customer needs and develop marketing mixes to satisfy those needs. Economic utility supports the marketing concept. It identifies ways to improve customer satisfaction through changes in form, time, place, and possession. Marketers need to determine what changes customers would like to have in products and services in order to develop an effective marketing mix. There are many possible ways to improve products. The actual product or service can be changed. In addition, a business can provide it at a more convenient time or place. Or the business can find ways to make the product more affordable for prospective customers.

How does the marketing concept relate to the concept of economic utility?

1. To illustrate the concept of economic utility, cite an example of a new or improved product or service that you have purchased recently. What improvement did it have compared to existing products or services, and what type of utility does that represent?

2. If a beverage company decides to package its product in smaller plastic bottles, what type of utility improvement would that represent?

3. Give an example of an improvement in time utility as it might be applied to a tangible product.

4. Marketers try to identify changes that customers desire in products and services in order to develop what?

SUMMARY

Lesson 3.1

A. Marketers need to manage based on the type of competition they face. They also must learn how to interpret economic information. The basic economic problem is that people have unlimited needs and wants but only limited resources. The result is scarcity.

B. In a private enterprise economy such as America's, decisions are made by independent consumers and businesses, with only limited intervention by government.

Lesson 3.2

A. Microeconomics is concerned with the relationship between individual consumers and producers and the effect of changes in price on consumer demand.

B. The likelihood of business profits and the nature of competition largely determine the supply of products and services.

Lesson 3.3

A. In pure competition, a large number of producers supply a very similar product. In a monopoly, a single producer supplies a unique product.

B. In an oligopoly, a few producers supply a similar product. In monopolistic competition, many producers compete by supplying somewhat different products.

Lesson 3.4

A. Businesses can improve customer satisfaction with their products through changes in form utility, time utility, place utility, and possession utility.

B. Economic utility supports the marketing concept by identifying ways to improve customer satisfaction, which results in more effective marketing mixes.

REVIEW MARKETING CONCEPTS

1. True or False: A private enterprise economy is heavily regulated by government.

2. True or False: Consumers have limited resources and unlimited needs and wants.

3. Changes in a product's physical features affect its __?__ utility.

4. True or False: A larger supply of a product will usually cause consumers to place a lower value on it.

5. When the price of a product is raised, a larger quantity will be purchased. That statement is known as which of the following?
   a. the law of supply
   b. the law of demand
   c. the law of the land
   d. the law of economic utility

6. True or False: Economic resources are classified as natural resources, capital, equipment, and consumers.

7. In pure competition, there are a large number of suppliers offering which of the following?
   a. very similar products
   b. somewhat different products
   c. unique products
   d. an unlimited supply of products

8. True or False: Economic utility is the amount of profit businesses make from selling a product.

9. True or False: The quantity of a product that producers are willing and able to provide at a specific price is known as demand.

10. Locating an automated teller machine in an airport is an example of improving the __?__ utility for banking services.

REVIEW MARKETING TERMS

Match the terms listed with the definitions. Some terms may not be used.

11. A system where the government attempts to own and control important resources and to make the decisions about what will be produced and consumed.

12. The relationship that dictates that when the price of something is increased, less of it will be demanded, and when the price is decreased, more will be demanded.

13. The type of market in which there is only one supplier offering a unique product.

14. The result of unlimited wants and needs combined with limited resources.

15. The type of market in which there are a few businesses offering very similar products.

16. A system where the resources and decisions are shared between the government and other groups or individuals.

17. The economic system based on independent decisions by businesses and consumers with only limited government intervention.

18. The study of economic behavior and relationships for the entire society.

19. A graph of the relationship between price and quantity demanded.

20. The use of resources toward the greatest profit for the producer.

21. All of the consumers who will purchase a particular product or service.

22. The point where supply and demand for a product are equal.

23. A graph of the relationship between price and quantity supplied.

24. The type of market in which there are a large number of suppliers offering very similar products.

25. The amount of satisfaction a consumer receives from the consumption of a product or service.

26. The study of economic relationships between individual consumers and producers.

27. The type of market in which there are many competing businesses offering products that are somewhat different.

a. controlled economy
b. demand
c. demand curve
d. economic market
e. economic resources
f. economic utility
g. free economy
h. law of demand
i. law of supply
j. macroeconomics
k. market price
l. microeconomics
m. monopolistic competition
n. monopoly
o. oligopoly
p. private enterprise
q. profit motive
r. pure competition
s. regulated economy
t. scarcity
u. supply
v. supply curve
w. value

APPLY MARKETING FUNCTIONS

MARKETING RESEARCH

28. Businesses can be classified into the four types of competition—pure competition, monopoly, oligopoly, and monopolistic competition—based on two factors: the number of competitors in the market, and the amount of similarity between the products of competing businesses.

Use the advertising section of your local telephone directory, a business directory, or copies of newspapers or business magazines to identify two businesses that fit into each of those four categories. Explain each decision based on the two factors listed.

29. Select a popular food item that is sold through your school's lunch menu or in a vending machine in your school. Determine the current price for the item. Then construct a chart showing the following price increases and decreases for the product: +10%, +25%, +50%, +100%, -10%, -25%, -50%, -90%.

Survey five people from your school. Ask each person how many of the items they typically purchase in one week at the current price. Then ask each person how many of the items they would purchase at each of the price increases and decreases. Based on the results, construct a demand curve to illustrate the effect of price changes on demand for the product.

MARKETING PLANNING

30. When a marketer analyzes a demand curve, it is important to determine what effect changes in price and quantity demanded would have on the amount of money the business will receive from selling the product. The amount received is known as the total revenue and is determined by multiplying the price by the quantity demanded.

For example, if the price of a product is $8.50 and the quantity demanded at that price is 1,550 items, the total revenue would be $13,175 ($8.50 x 1,550). The following information was taken from the demand curves for two different products. Calculate the total revenue for each price listed. Then construct a demand curve for each product.

PRODUCT 1		PRODUCT 2	
Price	Quantity Demanded	Price	Quantity Demanded
$1.00	350,000	$250	1,125
$2.50	280,000	$325	950
$3.25	225,000	$400	600
$4.00	175,000	$500	425
$4.75	75,000	$850	250
$5.50	25,000	$1,000	200

31. You have been an economist for the United Nations for the past 15 years. Now, in the year 2028, a large industrial colony is being developed on the moon. It will be started by 2,000 people initially, and there are plans to expand it until nearly a million people are living in the colony by 2050. The United Nations is studying the best form of economic system to develop on the colony.

Prepare a two-page report in which you compare the three types of economies—controlled, regulated, and free enterprise. Discuss the advantages and disadvantages of each for consumers, businesses, and the government. Make a recommendation on the most appropriate system for the colony. Consider factors like resources available, supply and demand, the amount of competition, and so forth.

MARKETING MANAGEMENT

32. The four types of economic utility can be used to improve customer satisfaction for products and services. Marketing managers must be creative in determining ways that products and services can be improved. For each of the following three items, determine changes that could be made in form, time, place, and possession utility. Then recommend the one change for each product that you believe would be the most effective in improving customer satisfaction. Provide a reason for your recommendation.

   a. Vending machine selling fresh popcorn

   b. Large-screen television

   c. College recruiting high school seniors

33. Tasha Formby is a recent graduate of Central University with a degree in Business Administration and extensive course work in computer information systems and marketing. She completed one summer internship with a computer manufacturer during which she worked in sales. She worked full time during another summer and part time during two school years at a local company that provides commercial printing services to small businesses. She was in charge of design work using computer software.

   After interviewing with several companies, Tasha decides to open her own printing business. She decides to locate in the same city in which she attended college. There are three large printing companies in the city, including the one she worked for during her college years. Those businesses compete for the printing services of the large and small companies in the area. There are eight other small printing businesses, each of which serve individual consumers rather than businesses.

   Tasha decides to compete with the larger companies for business printing rather than with the small printers. She believes there is more opportunity for larger printing jobs, and she would like her business to grow as rapidly as possible. She also believes her computer background could help her better serve the businesses' needs.

   After operating the business for six months, Tasha is becoming concerned. The prospective customers she contacts are more concerned about the prices of printing rather than the personalized service she provides. The larger printers are usually able to price lower than her business. It also seems like the larger printing businesses have much more control over the prices they charge, raising prices for some customers and lowering them for others.

   a. What type of competitive environment do you believe Tasha's business is facing? What information leads you to that answer?

   b. Do you believe she would face the same type of competition if she had chosen to sell to individual consumers? Why or why not?

   c. What do you believe Tasha can do to improve the chances of success for her new printing business? What economic concepts support your answer?

MARKETING TECHNOLOGY

34. Using a spreadsheet program, input the data contained in the table for Exercise 31 with the prices and corresponding quantities demanded for each product in separate columns. Have the spreadsheet calculate the resulting elasticity of demand for each increase in price and corresponding decrease in quantity. Use the following formula to calculate elasticity: Elasticity equals the percentage change in quantity divided by the percentage change in price.

35. Using an Internet browser or search engine, search business news sites such as PR Newswire (www.prnewswire.com) or other news sites for corporate announcements of improvements in their products or services. Find one example each of an improvement in form utility, time utility, place utility, and possession utility. For each example, summarize the change that is being announced and explain why it is an example of that type of utility.

MARKETING IN ACTION

CASE STUDY

YOUNG ENTREPRENEURS PROSPER IN GROWING MARKET

Matt Brown began mowing lawns and building good customer relationships at age 10. Matt's business grew quickly while he attended Lincoln Northeast H.S. from 1988 to 1990, thanks to favorable publicity from satisfied customers. Jason Rystrom also attended Lincoln Northeast and obtained a job at a major nursery in Lincoln because he planned to attend college majoring in horticulture. With Matt's list of satisfied customers and Jason's experience at a nursery/landscaping business, forming a partnership in 1990 was a natural.

A high level of motivation and strong work ethic contributed to the success of their business. When lawn jobs slacked off during the winter months, Matt and Jason diversified by offering snow removal services to residences and businesses. Diversification allowed the young entrepreneurs to earn money during the landscaping and lawn-mowing off-season.

Matt had started the business with one lawn mower and one trimmer. The business grew to 80 customers each week. A normal workweek during the summer was 60 hours. A third person was added to the work crew. Reasons for business success included a willingness to work long hours, experience in the landscaping/lawn service business, and reliability. Matt and Jason were able to open credit accounts at major suppliers of landscape materials. They were given purchase discounts at major suppliers because they were reliable, paying customers.

Matt's big wedding day was November 11, 1996. An unusually large snowstorm hit the night before, creating business opportunities for snow removal. Matt, Jason, and another groomsman excused themselves early from the prenuptial dinner to remove snow. They worked all night until 5 a.m. the morning of the wedding, and still made it to the church on time for the big event at 8 o'clock.

Matt and Jason graduated from the University of Nebraska in 1996 and sold their partnership. Matt earned a degree in accounting and serves as an accountant for a major bank, while Jason manages a major garden center. Both of these young entrepreneurs paid for college with their earnings from the partnership. Even today the two successful businessmen still dream of someday opening a large landscaping/lawn service in a growing city.

THINK CRITICALLY
1. What were the major personal reasons for the success of this partnership?
2. Did the growth of the city contribute to their success? Explain your answer.
3. What factors cause major population shifts to different parts of the country?
4. What opportunities are available to entrepreneurs in growing areas of the United States?

http://www.deca.org/publications/HS_Guide/guidetoc.html

ENTREPRENEURSHIP

You have learned how two young entrepreneurs successfully started and operated a lawn service/snow removal business. Unlike Matt and Jason, entrepreneurs often need financial help to get their business up and running. To obtain outside financing, you normally need to prepare a business plan (proposal) to present to prospective financiers. You will do that in this project.

INTRODUCTION   Write an introduction describing the business you plan to open.

SELF-ANALYSIS AND PROPOSED BUSINESS ORGANIZATION   Write a self-analysis that matches your strengths to the business you wish to start. Emphasize strong entrepreneurial characteristics you possess. Write about the type of business organization you will open. Will your business operate as a sole proprietorship, partnership, or corporation? Explain your rationale.

ANALYSIS OF TRADING AREA, CUSTOMER, AND LOCATION   This section of the business plan takes a close look at your trading area (demographics), target market (customer), and specific location. Remember, you are trying to get a loan for this business.

PROPOSED PRODUCT OR SERVICE Describe the product or service you will be selling. How is this product or service different from what competitors offer?

PRICING POLICIES   Specifically state your pricing strategy. Make sure to give the rationale for your decision.

PERSONAL PROMOTION, NON-PERSONAL PROMOTION, PLACE   This assignment involves three parts of the business plan. Personal promotion is directed at specific people for results. It may involve demonstration, personal selling, or selected telemarketing. Non-personal promotion is not targeted at a specific person or group. It may include television and radio commercials and newspaper advertisements. Place reminds the reader of where you will sell your product or service. Place also takes into consideration the type of distribution you will use.

PROJECTED INCOME/CASH FLOW   Visit with a business owner and/or banker to get advice in setting realistic amounts for the projected income/cash flow.

PROJECTED THREE-YEAR PLAN   Once again, visit with a banker or someone from SCORE to help develop a three-year plan. This plan is very important to lending institutions.

CAPITAL   This assignment involves three parts of the business plan. Personal capital is the money you will invest in the business. External capital comes from other sources such as financial institutions and investors. The repayment plan must show monthly payments for the term of each loan.

CHAPTER 4

THE BASICS OF MARKETING

LESSON 4.1 *CHANGES IN TODAY'S MARKETING*
LESSON 4.2 *PLANNING A MARKETING STRATEGY*
LESSON 4.3 *DECIPHERING CONSUMERS AND COMPETITORS*
LESSON 4.4 *MARKETING'S ROLE IN VARIOUS BUSINESSES*

NEWSLINE

COMMITTING TO QUALITY

Disney, Kodak, UPS. What do these companies have in common? They were all recognized in a consumer survey as top brand names. Respondents believed they offer "extraordinary quality" That image is just what those companies want, and they've worked hard to get it. Their marketing mixes are focused on meeting customer needs.

Some brands clearly reflect their companies' commitment to quality. Fisher-Price toys, Levi's jeans, and Chiquita bananas hold top spots in the survey. The survey shows that brands' ratings go up and down as customers see quality changing.

There are some well-known brands, however, that do not do well in the quality survey. In a number of cases, a lower ranking may be due to a target market that is focused on something other than quality, such as low prices, service, or convenience. Sometimes factors that are difficult for a company to control account for a poor showing. Many Japanese brands dropped when U.S. customers were encouraged to "Buy American."

In other instances, strong marketing has repaired poor images. Chrysler's quality rating once jumped 23 places in one year.

THINK CRITICALLY

1. Name three brands or local businesses whose focus is on something other than quality.

2. Name a car company that you think has a high-quality image.

3. Why is a quality image difficult to achieve and maintain?

CAREER OPPORTUNITY
CHANNEL MANAGER

POINT YOUR BROWSER

www.corpview.com

TeleView is looking for someone who possesses the following attributes.

- Excellent interpersonal and customer relations skills
- Strong problem solving and time management skills
- Technical communications proficiency
- Drive and flexibility
- Ability to work in an invigorating, team-oriented environment
- Ability to motivate others in a highly competitive environment
- Familiarity with Hispanic and Latin American cultures
- Self-starter who is motivated by opportunities and financial incentives

The main responsibilities of the job include the following.

- Achieve quarterly sales quota for the sales region
- Develop and implement the Sales and Marketing plans for the region
- Create a demand for TeleView products
- Create partnerships with sales partners to increase the flow of TeleView products to customers in Latin America and Spain
- Conduct sales and sales training seminars, marketing events, and sales/marketing briefings
- Manage channel relationships
- Work with the Brand Marketing Workgroup to extend the brand-name recognition of TeleView and Corporate View brands
- Help create exciting sales seminars and organize field marketing events

- Use press kits effectively and circulate press releases to key media in your channel region
- Insure appropriate localization of TeleView products, promotional materials, and support information

The job requires the following education, skills, and experience.

- B.S. or B.A. degree
- Minimum three years of experience in channel sales or related area
- Background and knowledge of sales and distribution systems in Latin America and in Spain
- Spanish/English fluency required
- Demonstrated strong presentation and communications skills
- Willingness to travel as much as 60 percent of the time, mostly out of the country
- Relocation to Miami, Florida

The position has a base salary and benefits. Commissions and bonuses are awarded based on successful and profitable channel management. A portable computer and remote Intranet connection will be provided.

THINK CRITICALLY

1. Prepare a cover letter written by a person who is qualified for this job and interested in applying for it.

2. Which aspects of this job are attractive to you? Which aspects do you find unattractive?

3. Search the Internet for a job similar to TeleView's channel manager. What type of compensation package is being offered for the job?

GOALS

- **Explain how marketing today differs from the way things were done in the past.**
- **Show why understanding customer needs is crucial, even with a superior product.**

MARKETING MATTERS

Marketing as it is practiced today is much different than it was just a few decades ago. It's more complex, more interconnected with other business functions, focused on creating opportunities, and valued as an investment in the future. For all of those reasons it is even more important that businesses focus on marketing from the very beginning. It must be an integral part of business planning, because creating products and services that satisfy customer needs has to be the primary objective. Even the best products and services will fail if they do not fit the needs of their markets.

Make a list of four products or services that you've purchased recently which provided you with a high degree of satisfaction. What characteristics do these products or services have in common?

RECOGNIZING HOW
MARKETING HAS CHANGED

Marcos and Camilla are waiting for the start of their career seminar. As they look at the course outline, they see that they are beginning a study of marketing today. They begin to talk about their interest in marketing careers.

Camilla: Marketing seems to be an area where there are a lot of jobs. You hear about marketing all the time and several of my friends are planning to major in marketing.

Marcos: I'm not sure I'm interested in a marketing job. It seems like you have to be a salesperson and you know what people think of salespeople. It doesn't seem like it takes anything to be a retail salesperson. You know how many people work long hours for no money in retail. What is your image of an automobile salesperson or of the person who calls you on the telephone at home to sell something? Even the good sales jobs in industry require you to travel all of the time. It seems like you have to be able to out-think and out-talk your customers to convince them to buy your products.

Camilla: It does seem that way, but there are other marketing jobs. Advertising is a part of marketing. Don't you think it would be exciting to create television commercials? I know some of them are weird or boring, but a lot of the advertisements are really creative and get me interested in the products they are selling.

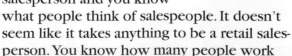

Marcos: I guess you're right. But still, it seems that marketing is used to get people to buy things they don't really need. I know companies need to sell their products to stay in business, but I'm not sure I want to be the one who has to convince someone to spend their money with my business, whether it is with advertising or selling.

Camilla: Well, I'm going to be open-minded. I want to work in business and everything I read now says that marketing is one of the fastest-growing and highest-paying career areas in business. I'll be interested to see what types of jobs are available and what it takes to be successful.

UNDERSTANDING THE DIFFERENCES

Just like Marcos and Camilla, you may have started your study of marketing with limited understanding of this important function of business. Much of our understanding comes from experience, and people have not always had positive experiences with marketing. Now that you have begun the study of marketing, you know that marketing is quite different than many consumers and business people realize. There are many marketing activities and many ways that marketing can improve exchanges between businesses and consumers.

Marketing today is quite different from marketing only a few years ago. Understanding those differences will help you use marketing more effectively. Some of the important changes are shown in Figure 4-1.

From Few to Many Marketing has expanded in scope from a few activities to a variety of activities. The earliest use of marketing was to move products from the producer to the consumer. Over time, it expanded to include a variety of promotional tools. Today, the seven marketing functions include many types of marketing activities ranging from research to offering customer credit. Effective marketers understand all of the marketing tools and know when and how to use them.

From Independent to Integrated

Marketing has evolved from a largely independent activity to a range of integrated business functions. In the past, marketing was not well understood by many business people, so they didn't know how to use and support marketing. Marketers often worked by themselves and had little contact with others in the business. Planning for marketing was done after other business planning was complete. Now, marketing is considered an essential part of the business, and marketers are involved in all important business decisions. Marketing strategies are developed as a part of the business plans.

From Problems to Opportunities

Marketing used to be handled as a problem-solving tool, but now it is regarded as an opportunity-creation tool. Marketers have often been called upon when a company

FIGURE 4-1
Marketing today is more complex and proactive.

How Has Marketing Changed?

From a few activities ....To a variety of activities

From independent ....To integrated

From problem-solver ....To opportunity-provider

| Income Statement | | Balance Sheet |

From an expense ....To an investment

E-MARKETING

Consumer Products Giant Taps Internet For New Product Launch

The Procter & Gamble Co., the world's leading marketer of consumer packaged goods, knows how to use all types of advertising and how to manipulate channels of distribution to gets its products prominently displayed on store shelves around the globe. So why did it quietly roll out an innovative new product on an Internet web site months before it was made available to retailers?

P&G sold more than 250,000 Crest Whitestrips teeth whitening treatments through dental offices and the Internet before the product completed even limited retail test marketing. The company wanted to create some buzz by word-of-mouth before the product hit store shelves.

The Internet was a good fit for Whitestrips for a number of reasons. The price—$44 for two weeks' worth of applications—was high enough to overcome consumers' reluctance to pay shipping charges for inexpensive items, yet it was low enough that people would be willing to risk that amount on a completely new product.

The web site was also used to gather information for future marketing efforts. In addition to getting buyers' names and addresses, P&G offered to forgo shipping and handling charges if a buyer gave it the names of three other people who might want to try the treatments.

THINK CRITICALLY

1. Why are consumers reluctant to pay shipping and handling charges for inexpensive items?

2. What do you think P&G hoped to gain by releasing Whitestrips months before it began retail distribution?

Marketing can be very expensive. When businesses have faced financial problems, some have looked to marketing as a place to reduce costs and save money. Most business people today recognize that companies will not be able to make a profit if products remain unsold. Effective marketing is an investment because it is responsible for matching a company's offerings with market needs. Spending money to improve marketing usually results in increased profits for the company.

Understanding and using marketing is an important business skill. Marketing is a valuable business asset in today's competitive world. People who understand the basics of marketing are in high demand in the business world. Those basics include understanding the marketing concept, planning a marketing strategy, responding to competition, and integrating marketing into the business.

faced a problem. If inventory was too high or competitors were attracting customers away from a business, marketers were asked to increase sales and promotion efforts or to find weaknesses in the competitor's programs. Today's marketers are continuously looking for new markets and for ways to improve a company's offerings in current markets. Businesses cannot afford to wait until problems occur. Marketing is responsible for identifying opportunities and helping a company to plan for those opportunities.

From Expense to Investment
What used to be thought of as an expense is now prized as a critical investment.

What are the four ways that today's marketing differs from marketing practices in the past?

COMING TO GRIPS WITH
THE MARKETING CONCEPT

The marketing concept has changed the way businesses operate. More than a new way to complete marketing activities, it requires a new approach to business planning. The marketing concept primarily focuses on customers' needs during the planning, production, distribution, and promotion of a product or service. That may seem simple, but some examples show how difficult it actually is.

RELIABLE AUTO SERVICE

Maria Santoz has always enjoyed repairing cars. As a teenager, she bought older cars, fixed them, and resold them at a profit. She studied auto mechanics in high school and became a certified mechanic at a local college. She worked for several years at a franchised auto repair center but was dissatisfied with completing repairs as quickly as possible using inexpensive repair parts rather than those specified by the manufacturer. Maria preferred to spend time with each car making sure that all problems were identified and repaired with the best available parts.

Maria decided to open her own auto repair business. She rented a small building on the edge of a large shopping center two miles from her home. She opened Reliable Auto Service and was pleased with the early response. She didn't spend a great deal on advertising, but the store's signs seemed to attract customers. Many appreciated the convenience of being able to leave their car while they were shopping. They also said they had more confidence in a business where the owner worked on their car. Now that she owned the business, Maria knew she would give each car special attention and the best possible service.

It didn't take long, however, for Maria's customers to start complaining. Many were upset when they had to leave cars overnight while Maria completed repairs. They were also concerned that repair costs were higher than they were used to paying. Maria told them that the price reflected the highest quality parts and that she guaranteed all repairs. Customers told her that

Czech Auto Maker Retools Image

Many formerly state-owned companies in Eastern Europe faced big problems as private enterprises. They had survived for years without ever having to satisfy customers or make profits. For the Czech auto maker Skoda, the situation was worse. Cars exported to Western Europe earned hard currency. But the shoddy cars became the butt of jokes: "What do you call a convertible Skoda? A dumpster."

When Germany's Volkswagen bought Skoda in 1991, it had to reshape both the company and its image. Many of the things that needed attention were marketing functions. One critical change was improving the quality of goods bought from outside suppliers. Volkswagen could impose changes directly at Skoda, but had less influence over the hundreds of smaller firms it relied on for components and supplies.

When Skoda first implemented VW's system for grading suppliers, only 1% of them earned the top mark. Within a few years, more than two thirds of them did. After that, Skoda more than doubled the number of cars sold annually in less than 10 years, even as the Czech economy struggled. More than half were exported to the West, where Skodas are no longer a joke. In fact, they rank near the very top among all brands in buyer satisfaction and retention.

THINK CRITICALLY

1. How do you think Volkswagen and Skoda persuaded vendors to improve the quality of the goods they supplied to Skoda?

2. Use the Internet to find out how buyers in Europe perceive Skoda cars.

other businesses also offered guarantees at much lower prices. Maria's business began declining. She was disappointed that customers did not seem to recognize the quality of her work.

DEE'S DESIGNS

Dee Sloan combined her talents in art and sewing to work with the community theater. She designed and made the costumes for the theater's productions. Several of the actors and actresses were so impressed with her unique designs that they asked her to create some items for their personal wardrobes.

Dee enjoyed the work and word-of-mouth from her customers soon resulted in more orders than she could fill. Because of her success, she hired several people to help her so she could expand into a full-time business. She believed she could sell her products through small businesses that would use the unique designs to compete with larger stores. She contacted several small retail chains hoping to find one who would agree to buy and distribute her fashions.

After three contacts, Dee was discouraged. Retailers said the clothing was unique and well constructed. The first retailer, however, felt the fashions did not fit thc image of her stores. The second was willing to buy one or two of the designs if Dee could produce a large volume of each in various sizes. Dee preferred to produce a variety of designs and styles. The last contact was willing to display Dee's fashions, but required a full display for each store in the chain and was unwilling to pay until 60 percent of the original order was sold. Dee could not afford that investment.

Dee could not hide her disappointment. It was hard to understand why her current customers could be so excited about her work, yet she could not interest people who were in the fashion business.

FOCUS ON CUSTOMER NEEDS

These experiences illustrate the difficulty of implementing the marketing concept. Each business had a quality product or service. Initial reactions from customcrs were positive. Yet they were unable to develop a successful business strategy. There are several reasons they were unsuccessful.

1. They were concerned only about the product or service.
2. They believed that they knew what customers would buy.
3. They did not study the market.
4. They failed to use a variety of marketing tools available to them.

Business people like Maria and Dee fail every day because they don't understand and use the marketing concept. It is not just new businesses that do not use marketing effectively. Car manufacturers, retailers, and restaurants fail, often after many years of successful operations. A business unwilling to study the needs of its customers when planning and marketing products and services is taking a big risk. Competitors who understand and use the marketing concept will turn that understanding into an advantage.

What did Maria and Dee each do wrong?

1. What is the marketing concept?

2. If a new business regards marketing as an investment rather than as an expense, what is a common mistake that it is more likely to avoid?

3. What is wrong with treating marketing mainly as a problem-solving tool?

4. When a business uses the marketing concept, what is the first step in its planning process?

PLANNING A MARKETING STRATEGY

MARKETING MATTERS

When businesses use the marketing concept, the planning process is in many ways turned on its head. Instead of starting with a product or service and then looking for customers who are willing and able to buy it, a business starts by researching potential customers and their needs. Only then does it move on to the product, but even then the product is not developed in isolation. It is planned as part of a comprehensive marketing mix, all the elements of which are focused on satisfying the customer needs that its research has identified and which it has concluded can be successfully targeted.

On paper, detail the marketing mix of a business that you have either worked for or with which you frequently do business. How do you think the mix could be improved?

GOALS

● **Understand how the marketing concept transforms business planning.**

● **Explain the importance of market segments and market opportunity analysis.**

● **Discuss how businesses develop the right marketing mix.**

PUTTING MARKETING
UP FRONT

Every business decides how it will attempt to achieve its goals. Most businesses use carefully prepared plans to guide their operations. Planning that identifies how a company expects to achieve its goals is known as a **strategy**. The strategy used by a business provides the clearest indication of whether that business understands the marketing concept.

Without the marketing concept, a business will develop a product or service and then decide how to market the product. There will be little

consideration of who the customers are or what their needs are until the product is ready to be sold. Marketing planning will occur only after the product has been designed and will typically be done by marketing specialists working apart from others in the company. The business expects that most people are potential customers of the product and that with adequate marketing those customers can be convinced to buy the product.

With the marketing concept, a very different strategy will be

FIGURE 4-2

When a firm uses the marketing concept to plan, the marketing mix is based on customer needs.

HOW DOES THE MARKETING CONCEPT AFFECT PLANNING?

Without the Marketing Concept	With the Marketing Concept
1. Develop a product.	1. Conduct research to identify potential customers and their needs.
2. Decide on marketing activities.	2. Develop a marketing mix (product, distribution, price, promotion) that meets specific customer needs.
3. Identify potential customers.	

used. The company believes it will be most successful if it can respond to needs of customers. It also recognizes that those needs may be different among various consumer groups, and that needs can change over time. As shown in Figure 4-2, the company will begin its planning by identifying potential customers and studying the needs of those customers.

Marketers will be involved in that study and in using the results to plan the products and services to be developed. The company will attempt to develop products and services that respond to customers' needs rather than what the company thinks should be offered. Marketing and product planning will occur at the same time, involving many people in all parts of the company. Marketing will be directed at meeting the identified needs of the customers rather than developing ways to convince people to buy something they may not need.

When the marketing concept is followed, what is the initial focus of the planning process?

UNDERSTANDING THE CUSTOMER

Consumers have many choices of products and services they can purchase to meet their needs. Today, most consumers are well informed, experienced in gathering information, and compare products and services before they make decisions. Even if a hurried decision is made, if the buyer is dissatisfied with the purchase or finds a better choice later, the buyer will likely return the original product for a refund.

Bringing a new product to the marketplace is very expensive for businesses. It takes time and money to develop, produce, distribute, and promote products. Once in the market, a new product competes with many other products offered by companies who also have invested a great deal and do not want to fail. The competition among products and companies is usually very intense. Companies that are not prepared for that competition have a difficult time staying in the market.

IDENTIFYING CUSTOMER NEEDS

Successful companies are usually those that meet customer needs. Think of the products you buy or the businesses you return to time after time. They are usually not your only choices, but have met your needs in specific ways better than the other choices. The reasons may be higher quality, convenience, better prices, or a unique image. Satisfying exchanges occur when you spend your money for products and services that meet your needs, and the business is able to make a profit on the sale of its products.

Meeting customer needs is not easy. First, many customers are not sure of their needs or may have conflicting needs. Second, while consumers have many needs, they typically have limited amounts of money available to satisfy those needs. They may not have enough money to buy a specific product even though they believe it is the one that best meets their needs. Finally, the needs of individuals and groups of consumers can be quite different, and their perceptions of what products or services will meet their needs are also quite different. Compare your feelings about specific products or services with your friends or family members, and you will find that there are often major differences.

Businesses tend to deal with customer needs in one of two ways as shown in Figure 4-3. Some businesses do not see the specific needs of consumers as important. They believe either that consumers don't understand their own needs or that businesses can influence consumer needs with well-designed products and effective prices and promotion. In other words, if they can effectively

Scanners Make Data Collection Quick, Easy, and Accurate

Most people are familiar with the devices that cashiers use to scan purchases in grocery store checkout lanes. The scanners read bar codes imprinted on the packages, automatically tallying purchases so the cashier doesn't have to key each price by hand into a cash register.

If ringing up prices was all scanners did, they might not be worth the hassle, much less the expense. What goes on behind the scenes, however, is even more important to the businesses that use them. Scanners are primary sources of data for stores' computerized inventory management, purchasing, accounting, and marketing research operations. Scanner-based information systems are cheap, quick, and accurate.

Every time someone buys a box of cereal or a can of soup, inventory records are automatically adjusted so that more can be purchased before it runs out. In most cases, the purchase orders are issued automatically too. And all that data is available for marketing researchers to analyze the effectiveness of sales promotions or advertisements. If a customer uses a credit card or, even better, a card issued by the store itself, the store can tell precisely who is buying what and how often.

THINK CRITICALLY

1. How might a retailer use scanner data to gauge the effectiveness of a sales promotion?

2. How does good inventory management affect customer satisfaction?

FIGURE 4-3
Consumers with different needs require specialized products and services.

Two Views of Consumers

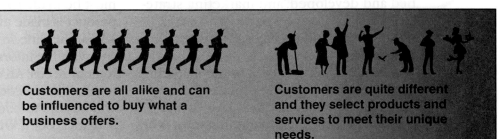

Customers are all alike and can be influenced to buy what a business offers.

Customers are quite different and they select products and services to meet their unique needs.

Gray Marketing

Controlling the channels through which a company's products are distributed and sold can be an important part of building a brand. That's particularly true for companies that sell their products internationally, because the optimum marketing mix often is different in different cultures or legal environments. In particular, controlling distribution channels allows a company to price its products based on local market conditions and maximize its profits.

Difficulties can arise if an unauthorized business imports products into a country and creates a parallel distribution channel that competes with the authorized channel. The practice is called *gray marketing*.

Manufacturers commonly complain about parallel imports and try to stop gray marketers with legal action. They claim that gray marketers damage their products' reputations, confuse consumers,

and interfere with exclusive marketing contracts that they've made with authorized distributors. Gray marketers counter that manufacturers simply want to control prices and gouge consumers for as much as they can. They say their efforts provide consumers with the same products at lower prices.

Trade liberalization in the European Union, where border inspections have been eliminated, and in North America has greatly increased gray marketing activities.

THINK CRITICALLY

1. How might gray marketing affect companies' ability to police the sale of counterfeit merchandise that violates legitimate trademark rights?

2. How does the prohibition of gray marketing enhance a company's ability to maximize its profits?

---

were not found in the businesses where you expected to find them. Products may have been damaged during shipment, poorly packaged, or assembled incorrectly.

While a few products and services are exchanged directly between the producer and the customer, most businesses must involve others in the distribution process. Manufacturers must rely on wholesalers and retailers to get products to the consumer. In the same way, a retailer must locate sources of the products its customers want and insure that those products can be obtained. Many businesses are usually involved in the production and marketing of a product.

An interesting activity is to try to trace the channel of distribution for products you purchase. Sometimes it is almost impossible to identify the companies involved in some part of the distribution process or even the company that manufactured the product. Even though many of the businesses are not obvious to the consumer, business people recognize the importance of each member of the channel and the importance of the activities they perform to the success of the marketing process. Activities such as order

processing, product handling, transportation, and inventory control must be completed well in order for companies to get the product to the customer.

Pricing Products and Services

Price is probably the most difficult marketing decision to understand and plan. Theoretically, price is determined from the interaction of supply and demand. That relationship is important in setting the best price, but it is almost impossible to set the price of a specific product in a specific business using supply and demand. Businesses must develop specific procedures to set prices that are competitive and allow the business to make a profit.

First the business needs to know its objectives in pricing its products and services. If the goal is to increase the sales volume of a particular product, a different price will be used than if the company is attempting to make the most profit possible on each sale. Many businesses set their prices so they will be the same or slightly lower than their major competitors. That may be necessary in some situations but can also create problems.

Calculating the price to be charged involves several elements. Production, marketing, and operating costs make up a great percentage of the price of most products, so the net profit available is very small. If all of the components of a price are not considered, or if prices are not calculated carefully, businesses may find that there is no profit available after expenses have been tallied. Another part of the pricing decision is how price is presented to customers. Normally, retailers use a price tag or sticker, and customers pay the price that is marked. Price may be communicated by manufacturers through catalogs or price sheets or by the salesperson representing the product.

It is common for businesses to offer discounts from their list prices to some or all of their customers. Markdowns, allowances, trade-ins, and coupons are other ways that prices can be changed. Finally, credit is commonly used to enable customers to purchase a product without paying the full price at the time they make the purchase.

In pricing products and services, marketers must try to balance the costs of the product with the customer's feelings about the value of the product. The goal is a fair price and a reasonable profit.

Planning Promotion Promotion must be planned to communicate the value and benefits of a product or service to consumers to aid them in decision-making. While advertising and other promotional methods are powerful tools if used to support effective marketing programs, they can easily be misused and can have no impact or a negative effect on consumers.

Think of promotions you believe are particularly effective or ineffective. Now try to determine the impact of a specific promotion on your purchase behavior. It is very difficult to determine the influence of just one promotion on a decision, even if you believe it is effective. If you keep track of the promotions you are exposed to in only one day, you will find that there are more messages around you than you can ever notice or to which you can actually respond.

When planning promotion, business people select from a variety of methods.

The most common are advertising, personal selling, sales promotion, visual display, and publicity. Other methods are also available that are used less frequently. The selection will be based primarily on the communication objectives the company wants to accomplish and the audience it wants to reach. Each method varies in terms of the cost per person, number of people reached, types of messages carried, and other factors. Careful planning needs to be done to reach the specific audience with an understandable message in a way that helps the consumer make appropriate decisions.

Promotion is a unique type of marketing tool. It doesn't create economic utility by itself. It is used to communicate the value and benefits of other product and marketing decisions to the consumer. Promotion cannot do a great deal to help a company that has a poor product, excessively high prices, or ineffective distribution.

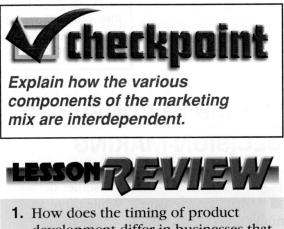

✓ **checkpoint**

Explain how the various components of the marketing mix are interdependent.

LESSON REVIEW

1. How does the timing of product development differ in businesses that use the marketing concept compared with those that do not?

2. Name three reasons it is difficult to meet customer needs.

3. What is market opportunity analysis?

4. What are the four elements of the marketing mix?

5. Name several ways businesses can alter the prices they charge.

6. What are the most common forms of promotion?

promotional activities, and demonstrating value to customers depend on the creativity of the people involved. Marketing is increasingly becoming a scientific process in which information is gathered to improve decisions and alternative methods are studied to determine which are most effective.

Conducting research is an important marketing activity. Marketers need to be skilled in organizing research and using research results. The most important type of research for most businesses is the study of potential and current customers. Companies need to be able to clearly identify their customers, characteristics that make groups of customers different from others, their important needs, and how they make purchase decisions. Additionally, research about competitors will identify the type of competition and the strengths and weaknesses of competing companies. Finally, businesses study alternative marketing strategies to determine which are most effective and most profitable.

Marketers are using more and more information to make decisions. Most companies are developing marketing information systems that collect and store a variety of information. That information is readily available, often through the use of computers, when decisions need to be made.

checkpoint

Why is it important for businesses to understand the consumer decision-making process?

RESPONDING TO COMPETITION

The private enterprise economy offers many opportunities for businesses. A person who wants to start a business and has the necessary resources can probably do so. Our economy is also good for consumers. Because of the opportunities for people to operate businesses, consumers typically have many available products and services from which to choose.

Even though private enterprise offers many opportunities, it also presents challenges to business people. When there are many businesses in a market, competition is usually very intense. Consumers can select from among a number of products and services. They expect real value from businesses or they will purchase from a competitor. Value may mean higher quality, more service, or lower prices. Businesses that are unable to meet customer expectations better than their competitors may not be able to survive.

Marketers need to be able to identify which type of competition a company faces and develop an appropriate marketing strategy.

Using the marketing concept provides direction for developing effective strategies.

INTENSE COMPETITION

The most difficult type of competition businesses face is a market in which businesses compete with others offering very similar products. One example is pure competition, where there are many businesses offering the same product. Another example is an oligopoly where only a few companies compete in the same market, but offer products in which consumers see few, if any, differences. Business people can study the customers in the market to determine if there are some groups that are not currently satisfied with the choices available.

In the past, businesses facing intense competition responded by emphasizing price or promotion. When they found customers saw no important difference among competing products, they believed they had to reduce prices to make a sale. Companies that emphasized promotion tried to convince customers that their

GET THE MESSAGE

Washroom Ads For Captive Audience

Restroom advertising had to overcome a lot of resistance just to sell itself, but it is now one of the fastest-growing advertising media. Sure, it is not the ideal environment with which most advertisers want to associate their products. Nor is it very efficient or inexpensive in terms of reaching a large number of potential buyers. Still, if an advertiser wants to target a particular demographic group—such as 18-to-35-year-old males—and be fairly well assured of their almost undivided attention for 30 seconds or more, there are few better ways of doing it than placing posters above urinals, on the inside of toilet enclosure doors, and above hand dryers. Media companies acknowledge that restroom ads are not cheap but stress that they can zero in on a niche market very accurately. The most obvious advantage is being able to differentiate ads for men and women. Moreover, by carefully choosing venues where the ads are placed, advertisers can target with pinpoint accuracy.

THINK CRITICALLY

1. Where might a retirement community place restroom ads if it wanted to reach older men and women?

2. Surveys show that young men spend most of their discretionary income in restaurants and clubs. What kinds of companies might want to advertise in the restrooms of such establishments?

3. Besides differentiating males and females, what other characteristics might advertisers zero-in on with restroom ads?

products were better than those of competitors. In some cases they created relatively minor differences and promoted those differences as being important to consumers. In other cases, they attempted to create unique brand names and images, so customers would remember the brands and select them from the available choices.

With careful study of consumer needs and their experience with available products, businesses may be able to identify ways to change or improve products, features, or the services offered with the products. New product uses might be identified. The goal of any product change is to make the product different from that of competitors and more satisfying to the target market.

There may also be opportunities in other parts of the marketing mix. Distribution can focus on making the product available at better locations and times, with more careful handling, or greater customer service. Pricing can offer alternative methods of payments, greater ease of obtaining credit, extended time for payment, or leasing rather than ownership. Promotion can provide more personalized or detailed information, use non-traditional methods or media, or communicate with the customer after the sale to aid in the use of the product.

LIMITED COMPETITION

Some businesses have the advantage of offering a product or service with little or no direct competition. In economic terms, this situation is known as a monopoly. Businesses facing limited competition often operate in very different ways than those in intense competition. They do not have to worry as much about price or even promotion since consumers are restricted in their choice of products. Therefore, a business will usually concentrate on maintaining its advantage in the market. It will attempt to keep competing businesses from entering, protect its location, and concentrate on keeping its product or service as unique as possible.

Customers using the products and services of a monopoly business often become dissatisfied with their lack of choice. They believe that without competition they pay higher prices, have poorer service, and must deal with a company more concerned about protecting its market and making a profit than about meeting the needs of consumers.

Consider the only hospital in a community where the next closest hospital is 60 miles away. That hospital would be in a market very much like a monopoly with no direct competition. It would be difficult for consumers to drive the 60 miles every time they

needed health care. The hospital administrators would not have to be particularly concerned about the people who need hospital services and could offer the services that provided the highest level of profit. Customers may not be happy, but they would have little choice of an alternative.

While it may not be as profitable in the short run, the hospital administrators could adopt the marketing concept to make operating decisions. As a result, consumers are more likely to use the local hospital and to encourage others to use it, and will be less likely to look for other places and other methods to meet their health care needs.

The same analysis could apply to the only convenience store, supermarket, or other retail business in a neighborhood, the only distributor of fuel and agricultural supplies in an area, or a government agency or school system. Each has the characteristics of a monopoly and can decide whether to adopt the marketing concept or not.

MONOPOLISTIC COMPETITION

Most businesses face competition somewhere between monopoly and intense competition. They have many competitors, but customers see some differences among the choices. The customers will attempt to determine which of the available products and services best meet their needs. It is important for the companies to have clearly identified differences that result in customers selecting their brands from among all of the available choices.

Companies in monopolistic competition find the marketing concept to be of most value. Since customers already recognize their unique choices, they attempt to select the brands that are most satisfying. Companies that use the marketing concept focus on specific groups of customers and attempt

to identify their needs. Then they will use the full range of decisions within the marketing mix to develop products and services for those customers. Changes and improvements can be made in the product, distribution, prices, and promotion that not only make the brand different from its competitors but more attractive to potential customers.

Here are some examples of the use of the marketing concept. A manufacturer of portable CD players makes its product smaller, more durable, and offers it in a variety of colors and styles. A daycare center keeps children overnight to meet the needs of parents who have evening jobs. A supermarket accepts debit cards from customers who do not want to carry cash. Information about concerts is provided through a database that can be accessed by home computer, and orders for tickets can be placed using the computer. In each case, a change is made in the marketing mix that is designed to improve the mix, make it different from the competition, and respond to an important need of the target market.

Why does monopolistic competition allow businesses to benefit most from the marketing concept?

1. Explain the five stages of the consumer decision-making process.

2. Name three things that businesses use marketing research for.

3. What is the goal of product changes?

4. What kind of competition do most businesses face?

5. From a consumer perspective, which type of competition offers the most choice? The least choice?

MARKETING'S ROLE IN VARIOUS BUSINESSES

MARKETING MATTERS

Marketing activities are performed every time an exchange of products and services occurs, whether between businesses, a business and a consumer, or even between consumers. The same basic marketing functions and activities are used in all exchanges. Each exchange involves a supplier, a consumer, and a complete marketing mix. However, there are differences in the ways that various types of businesses use those marketing tools. Moreover, the same tools are used by non-business organizations and informal groups, which recognize that marketing principles apply even when profit is not the ultimate motive.

Make a list of six products or services used in your classroom, then investigate how each was marketed by various businesses until it reached your school.

GOALS

● Explain the various marketing roles of different types of businesses.

● Examine how marketing is useful for organizations other than businesses.

DIFFERENTIATING BUSINESS ROLES

While the entire marketing mix and all marketing functions are important, each type of business will need to place special emphasis on some marketing decisions.

Producers and Manufacturers

The role of producers and manufacturers is to develop the products and services needed by other businesses and by consumers. Because of that role, the product element of the marketing mix receives the most attention. Distribution is also important as the companies develop channels that will get the products to important markets. Unless direct channels of distribution are used, other businesses have major responsibility for determining the prices consumers pay and for consumer promotion. Manufacturers and producers must respond to the needs of the people who will be the final consumers of their products. They must also be able to satisfy the needs of the businesses involved in the marketing channels for the products.

Channel Members A channel of distribution is developed in order to move products from the producer to the consumer. Channel members are used to provide many of the marketing functions during the distribution process. For those channel members, less emphasis will be placed on the product element of the marketing mix. Decisions are made about what products and services to offer and then attention is given to the other mix elements. Wholesalers emphasize distribution planning. Many wholesalers help their customers with financing and provide marketing information. Retailers are responsible for most final pricing decisions and use a variety of promotion activities to encourage consumers to purchase their

Making Sense of Markups and Margins

When people talk about saving money by cutting out the middleman, what they really want to eliminate is the markups that are applied at various stages of a distribution channel. A markup covers a business's operating expenses, taxes, and whatever profit it builds into its price before it passes a product on to another member of the channel or the end user.

Markups are often confused with gross profit margins, probably because both are commonly expressed as percentages and refer to some of the same things. However, markups and gross profit margins are measured in quite different ways and are not interchangeable terms.

A markup is the difference between the price a business pays for a product and the price it plans to sell the product for. It's expressed as a percentage of the price paid by the business.

For example, if a retailer pays $1 each for boxes of soap powder and sells them to its customers for $1.50 each, its markup is 50 cents divided by $1, or 50%.

A gross profit margin is the difference between the price a product sells for and the amount a business pays for it. It is expressed as a percentage of the selling price. For example, if a retailer pays $1 for a box of soap and sells it to customers for $1.50, its gross profit margin is 50 cents divided by $1.50, or 33%.

THINK CRITICALLY

1. If a bicycle shop buys 10 bikes for $66, $99, $124, $142, $180, $198, $210, and $300, respectively, and marks up each one by 50%, what are the resulting selling prices?

2. What would the selling prices be if the bike shop owner wanted a 50% gross profit margin?

delivered by people, making it more difficult to control the quality of the service each time it is offered. Because of the characteristics of services, the product mix element is very important. The business must develop procedures to insure that the customer receives the expected quality of service every time. Distribution planning is also important because the service must be available where and when the customer wants it. If there is not a large enough quantity available, sales will be lost. If the business is prepared to offer more services than the customers want, then expenses will be unnecessarily high.

Service businesses, like a home cleaning service, usually have more control over pricing than businesses that sell products. It is more difficult or confusing for customers to determine the appropriate price for a service, or to compare the prices of several companies, since different businesses may offer the service in a different way. Services are quite difficult to promote since the customer may not be able to see or examine them. Services that customers are not familiar with may require a great deal of promotion.

products. Channel members must be able to work cooperatively with other businesses involved in the channel while responding to the needs of the consumers in their target markets.

Service Businesses Service businesses face unique marketing challenges. Most service businesses work directly with their consumers rather than through a channel of distribution, so they are responsible for the entire marketing mix. Also, services are usually developed and

Why is quality control more difficult for a service business than for a business that makes or distributes a product?

MARKETING BY NON-BUSINESS GROUPS

The successful use of marketing has moved from the business world to other organizations. Previously many people viewed marketing in limited or negative ways. Because of those views, they were reluctant to use marketing. But today, many consumers are more aware of marketing. They see many businesses use marketing effectively. These businesses have the interests of their customers in mind. They recognize that marketing is an important tool to help organizations achieve their goals.

It is not unusual to see marketing being used by museums, libraries, symphonies, athletic teams, churches, and clubs. Just as businesses have not always understood marketing and have misused it, many organizations have made mistakes as they have tried to develop marketing plans. They often emphasized promotion and treated people as if they all have the same needs and interests. The organizations that believe marketing is simple, or which fail to study and understand marketing, may be disappointed with the results. Many organizations seek help from people who understand marketing and know how to use the marketing concept to identify target markets and develop marketing mixes. Those organizations have seen very positive results and now view marketing as an important part of their efforts.

✓checkpoint

Why should not-for-profit organizations worry about marketing?

LESSON REVIEW

1. Which element of the marketing mix generally receives the most attention from manufacturers?

2. All businesses must respond to the needs of the final consumers of their products, but most manufacturers and producers must also satisfy the needs of whom else?

3. What type of business is responsible for most final pricing decisions?

4. Which type of business is generally responsible for the entire marketing mix?

5. Why do service businesses generally have more control over pricing than businesses that make or sell products?

6. What key goal do businesses have in common with other organizations such as libraries, clubs, and civic groups?

SUMMARY

Lesson 4.1

A. Compared to past marketing practices, marketing today is involved in a larger variety of activities, is more fully integrated with other business functions, is more concerned with creating and identifying business opportunities, and is regarded as an investment.

B. Having a superior product or service is not sufficient to assure success in business. It must respond to customer needs and desires, or they will take their business elsewhere.

Lesson 4.2

A. Business planning under the marketing concept begins with research to identify potential customers and their needs. Only then is a product developed, and then as part of an overall marketing mix aimed at satisfying those customers.

B. Because consumers have unique needs, businesses must identify market segments, groups of customers with similar characteristics and needs within a larger market.

C. Businesses need to develop the right combination of elements in a marketing mix that targets the market segments they are focusing on.

Lesson 4.3

A. In making purchase decisions, consumers follow a specific sequence of steps, ranging from recognizing a need to assessing their satisfaction following purchases. Businesses that understand that process can provide consumers with the right information at the right time.

B. Businesses use marketing to identify the types of competition they face and respond accordingly to develop effective strategies.

Lesson 4.4

A. Different types of businesses have different marketing roles. For manufacturers and producers, the product element of the marketing mix is most important. For businesses in the channel of distribution, the other elements—distribution, price, and promotion—are more important depending on their role in the channel. Service businesses are generally responsible for the entire marketing mix since they tend to work directly with their final consumers.

B. Having observed how well they work for business, non-business organizations increasingly are employing marketing tools to better satisfy the needs of their customers, clients, and members.

REVIEW MARKETING CONCEPTS

1. True or False: Marketing consists of a few basic activities such as promotion and distribution.

2. True or False: In the past, marketing was used basically as a problem-solving tool, such as a way to reduce inventory.

3. True or False: Spending money to improve marketing usually results in increased profits for the company.

4. True or False: Following the marketing concept requires a total commitment to satisfying customers' needs.

5. True or False: Marketing is primarily effective for new or small businesses that can respond quickly to changes in the market or economy.

6. True or False: A marketing strategy is defined as how a company expects to achieve its goals.

7. True or False: Understanding and meeting consumer needs is relatively easy to do because most people have the same needs.

8. True or False: Groups of similar consumers within a larger market are known as market segments.

9. True or False: The marketing mix elements all act independently of each other.

10. True or False: Distribution can be described as the physical handling and transportation of a product.

11. True or False: Because of so many other variables, it is impossible to set a product or service price based strictly on the concepts of supply and demand.

12. True or False: The promotion element of the marketing mix is the communication link between the seller and the buyer.

13. True or False: Because effective marketing requires large amounts of information, most companies are now developing marketing information systems that collect and store information.

14. True or False: The most difficult type of competition faced by businesses is a market in which businesses compete with others that offer very similar products.

15. True or False: In a limited-competition situation, it is not important for marketers to pay attention to the effectiveness of their mix elements.

16. The first step in the consumer decision-making process is recognizing that a __?__ exists.

17. In monopoly situations, businesses face which type of competition?
   a. intense
   b. limited or none
   c. monopolistic
   d. all of the above

18. Service businesses face unique marketing challenges because services are delivered by people, making it difficult to assure consistent __?__ each time.

19. When businesses regard marketing as a provider of opportunities, they look for which of the following:
   a. new markets
   b. ways to improve existing products
   c. changing customer needs
   d. all of the above

REVIEW MARKETING TERMS

Match the terms listed with the definitions. Some terms may not be used.

20. Planning that identifies how a company expects to achieve its goals.

21. A group of similar consumers within a larger market.

22. Studying and prioritizing market segments to locate the best potential based on demand and competition.

a. market opportunity analysis
b. market segment
c. strategy

APPLY MARKETING FOUNDATIONS

MARKETING RESEARCH

23. Marketing involves understanding customers and their wants and needs. To demonstrate two views on customers, draw two large circles on a piece of paper. Within each circle, create a collage of pictures. One should contain customers that are all alike and would respond to a mass-marketing approach. The other circle should contain pictures of customers who are different and would respond to target marketing.

24. Brand names often have a significant impact on the consumer's perception of quality. In this exercise, you are to survey 10 people to find their perception of the quality of the following brands: Nike, Kenmore, Microsoft, Sony, and Del Monte. Use a rating scale where 1 is the worst quality and 10 is the highest quality. Record their answers in a chart like the following and find an average quality rating for each product.

MARKETING PLANNING

25. Develop a marketing mix for a house painting service. Make sure that you consult the text to include all of the variables of each mix element.

26. The study of customers and their wants and needs is primary to running a successful business. As the needs and wants of customers change, marketers are able to identify new markets or customer groups for old products or services. Now it's your turn to identify new markets. Pick-up trucks, vans, and fast food are products that have been on the market for a long time. Recently, marketers have located new markets for them. For each of those products, determine the following:

  a. Traditional markets
  b. New markets
  c. Changes in the marketing mix for new markets

Respondent	Nike	Microsoft	IBM	Sony	Del Monte
1	9	1	1	6	9
2	1	10	8	5	6
3	10	5	1	9	7
4	7	3	9	1	2
5	3	9	7	7	10
6	1	5	6	7	1
7	1	7	7	6	5
8	10	4	8	10	10
9	3	2	3	1	1
10	10	9	5	3	4
Total	55	55	55	55	55
Average Quality Rating	5.5	5.5	5.5	5.5	5.5

REVIEW

MARKETING MANAGEMENT

27. Based on the stories about Reliable Auto Service and Dee's Designs in the text, how could Maria and Dee alter their marketing mixes to make their businesses successful? Be specific and complete in answering.

28. A service that is gaining in popularity is shuttle service for children whose parents work. These shuttle services provide rides to and from after-school activities such as dancing, gymnastics, music lessons, and sports practices. The service is gaining in popularity as more families are unable to transport their children because the activities occur while both parents are still at work.

Regarding this service, what factors would you consider in:
a. Developing a satisfying product?
b. Planning your distribution?
c. Setting your price?
d. Creating your promotional plan?

MARKETING TECHNOLOGY

29. Use an Internet search engine, an online library research service, or a web site such as www.findarticles.com that searches magazines and professional journals to find a recent article on the gray marketing of parallel imports. Then use a word processor to compose a 150-to-200-word summary of the article's main points.

30. Design a spreadsheet that will calculate prices for the bicycle shop in Figure This. Input the amounts the shop paid for the 10 bikes in Question 1, and then have the spreadsheet program calculate selling prices using a 25% markup and a 25% gross profit margin. Print the results.

WHAT KIND OF MUSIC DO TEENS WANT?

How did you decide on the type of music you enjoy listening to the most? Did you count on a friend's advice, or did you listen to your favorite radio station disk jockey to determine what music is right for you?

A group of entrepreneurial music buffs in Oakland, California, carefully analyzed recordings based on fundamental elements to create a database for recommending songs to consumers. Savage Beast Technologies was one of a growing number of start-up businesses that used the Internet to try to shape the public's musical taste. It referred to its effort as the "Music Genome Project."

Companies such as Savage Beast Technologies combine cutting-edge computer technology and the opinions of experts and customers to accomplish their goals. They license their services to record retailers and other music-industry players instead of undertaking the difficult task of starting new consumer-based businesses on the Web.

Music-recommendation services believe that their work could become important in the music industry. They hope to change entirely the way that people discover music.

An underlying belief of music-recommendation companies is that today's hit-making system has flaws. Disk jockeys used to introduce new music regularly. Now centralized programming companies control playlists, and music labels focus their promotional and development dollars on artists who are proven moneymakers. Savage Beast believes that this procedure turns off listeners.

The Internet can help by giving new music groups an inexpensive means to duplicate and distribute recordings anywhere. Getting noticed among the millions of computerized tracks is not easy, though. A service like Napster mostly helps consumers who already know what they want.

SAMPLE MUSIC AND MUSIC STYLES BEFORE YOU BUY

Several service companies now allow consumers to get a taste of music before they select the CDs that appeal to them. MuBu graphically displays scores of music and plays a sample as a cursor is passed over the title. When consumers pick out a selection they like, the service suggests CDs that reflect their tastes. MoodLogic is another service that lets users search by characteristics such as "romantic R & B songs from the 1970s." GigaBeat offers a search service that displays songs or artists in a spiral pattern that indicates how they are related.

Companies such as Listen.com employ a staff of editors who review music and suggest similar artists to customers who use search tools. Other companies measure behavior of many users in order to make suggestions. The process is referred to as collaborative filtering. CantaMetrix uses digital technology that automatically picks out traits such as tempo, energy, and density of sound to categorize music. MoodLogic gets input from thousands of consumers who receive gift certificates for logging on to an affiliated site called Jaboom and classifying songs according to a large list of attributes. MuBu and

Savage Beast employ 30 music fans who spend most of their day listening on headphones and giving numerical rankings to 180 attributes, or "genes."

Using the Internet as a music recommendation tool has shown mixed results. A drawback to sounds-like approaches is that consumers must start with an existing song in mind. Recommending music is difficult since musical tastes vary for different social groups.

THINK CRITICALLY

1. What factors have contributed to the increase in music-recommendation businesses?

2. What are some of the drawbacks of using the Internet to promote and recommend music?

3. Savage Beast compared their services to those provided by Napster. What was the purpose of Napster? Why was the federal government concerned about Napster activity?

---

http://www.deca.org/publications/HS_Guide/guidetoc.html

BUSINESS AND FINANCIAL SERVICES MARKETING RESEARCH EVENT

DECA PREP

In this activity, you are a marketing representative for Savage Beast. The major purpose of your job is to encourage music retailers to use your music-recommendation service. Stiff competition in the retail music business makes it necessary to conduct research. Prospective clients want to carry the type of music their target market demands the most.

The title of your project is "Matching Merchandise to the Musical Needs of Customers." The emphasis of this project is on marketing research activities necessary to sell retail music stores on the idea of incorporating the music-recommendation service provided by Savage Beast.

DESCRIPTION OF THE PROPOSAL Prepare a description of the proposed study. Describe the business or organization as well as the community, including geographic, demographic, and psychographic factors.

DESCRIPTION OF RESEARCH METHODS Describe the research methods used. This might include sample questionnaires, letters sent and received, general background data, etc. What steps did you take to design the study and the instrument? How did you conduct the study?

PREPARE SUMMARY OF FINDINGS AND CONCLUSIONS OF THE STUDY Prepare a geographic, demographic, and psychographic

description of customers. Explain the buying behavior of customers. Summarize customer familiarity with Savage Beast. What conclusions based on the findings of the study can you make?

PREPARE A PROPOSED BUSINESS OUTLINE The outline should include goals/objectives and rationale, proposed activities and timelines, the proposed budget, and a plan to evaluate the effectiveness of marketing the services offered by Savage Beast.

CHAPTER 5

USING MARKETING RESEARCH

LESSON 5.1 *UNDERSTANDING THE NEED FOR MARKET INFORMATION*

LESSON 5.2 *FINDING AND MANAGING MARKETING INFORMATION*

LESSON 5.3 *USING MARKETING RESEARCH*

LESSON 5.4 *COLLECTING PRIMARY DATA*

NEWSLINE

RESTAURANTS FIND A NICHE

It's hot, it's fast, and it's competitive! Many Americans eat half of their meals outside the home. A large percentage are purchased from fast food or casual dining restaurants. For years, the chain restaurants all looked the same with very similar menus and service. Casual dining is changing, though, as evidenced by the success of specialty and ethnic chains.

Following its success with Red Lobster, General Mills conducted research into ethnic menus. It found that many people were looking for convenient, comfortable, sit-down restaurants where families could afford to go. They needed to offer good food, efficient service, and an ethnic atmosphere that complemented the menu. After five years and nearly $30 million of research, General Mills completed planning for the Olive Garden restaurant chain that featured an Italian theme.

What does it take to be successful in fast food? The major chains such as McDonald's, Burger King, and Wendy's have been competing with expanded menus, healthier sandwiches, salads, and more customer service. Meanwhile, a new group of chains have grown rapidly by returning to the original fast food concept of hamburgers, cheap prices, and quick service.

Chains like Rally's, Sonic, Checkers, and Daddy-O's have responded to those needs. They meet the needs of customers who want food, fast service, and low cost.

The success of these two categories of restaurants demonstrates the importance of understanding customers and responding to their needs with a tailored marketing mix. All restaurants do not have to be the same.

THINK CRITICALLY

1. Why do you think the big fast food chains such as McDonald's and Burger King have largely abandoned their original concepts on which they built so much success?

2. Name another restaurant industry category that is distinct from the ones discussed in this article.

CORPORATE VIEW

CAREER OPPORTUNITY
SALES ADMINISTRATIVE ASSISTANT

POINT YOUR BROWSER

www.corpview.com

TeleView is looking for someone who possesses the following attributes.

- Excellent interpersonal and customer relations skills
- Confidentiality and discretion in communications
- Time management skills
- Ability to prioritize events and activities and to multitask in busy office
- Ability to organize others
- Drive and flexibility
- Ability to work in an invigorating, team-oriented environment
- Willingness to relocate to Boulder, Colorado

The main responsibilities of the job include the following.

- Provide administrative support to the Director of North American Sales and Support
- Coordinate onsite and offsite sales meetings
- Prepare agendas, communicate with participants, and confirm reservations
- Prepare facilities, including conference rooms and audio-visual equipment
- Arrange for catering
- Process expense reports
- Screen incoming calls
- Manage e-mail communications
- Follow up with Corporate Communications to ensure the proper posting of sales goals, promotional pricing, and quarterly sales revenue reports from each of the seven North American regions
- Open, sort, and prioritize faxes, mail, and e-mail
- Arrange domestic and international travel
- Reconcile credit card statements
- Handle cash as needed

The job requires the following education, skills, and experience.

- Corporate communications, business, or marketing and sales training
- Must be literate in Windows and Microsoft Office Suite and willing to learn new software
- Able to use the corporate Intranet effectively
- Experience with personal information management software, such as Outlook
- Excellent word processing skills (Word or WordPerfect) a must
- Experience and ability to work with PowerPoint
- Spreadsheet (Excel) and database skills a big plus

THINK CRITICALLY

1. Prepare a cover letter written by a person who is qualified for this job and wants to apply for it.

2. What advantages and disadvantages do you think come from having a job like this?

3. Search want ads or the Internet for a job similar to this position. What type of compensation package is being offered for the job?

UNDERSTANDING THE NEED FOR MARKET INFORMATION

GOALS

- **Explain the importance of information in targeting market segments.**
- **Describe the categories of information marketers need.**

MARKETING MATTERS

People who understand the marketing concept understand why market information is important. When businesses use the production philosophy, they make all of the decisions based on their own experiences and their ideas about what is needed. By contrast, the marketing concept is based on satisfying customer needs, so it is important to know and understand customers. Information is needed to distinguish relevant market segments, particularly in today's global market, and also to understand the competition and changes taking place in the marketplace. While specific information requirements differ for each business, there are three general categories of information that all businesses need in some form.

Make a list of 10 items—hamburgers, magazines, clothes, and so on—that you buy periodically to satisfy some need or want. Then note how your preferences have changed over the years, and how those preferences have affected what you buy.

MARKETING TO SEGMENTS

Most businesses today do not use the production emphasis, nor do they try to satisfy the needs and wants of all possible consumers. Instead, they recognize that various groups of consumers have very different needs and wants, and that they can view product and service choices quite differently. As illustrated in Figure 5-1, those businesses gather specific information from consumers to determine the distinctions

FIGURE 5-1
Businesses that use the marketing concept base decisions on an understanding of customers and their needs.

"Here's what I think our customers will buy."

"What can we provide that will meet your needs as our customers?"

Businesses that use the Production Emphasis

Businesses that use the Marketing Concept

among market segments, and to decide how they can best meet the unique needs and wants of particular segments based on current market conditions.

Interactivity Propels Kiosks

At one time, retailers thought video kiosks were going to revolutionize the way people shop. But aside from bank ATMs, kiosks were slow to catch on. The development of the World Wide Web and high-speed data transfers, however, may have supplied the missing ingredients needed for kiosks to take off.

Interactive kiosks can be networked and monitored from a central location through a retailer's web site. Instead of delivering the same information or promotions to every user, they can identify individuals and customize each presentation based on their buying habits or personal preferences.

Moreover, the enhanced capabilities of interactive kiosks arrived at the same time that the cost of hardware and software was coming down dramatically. For a fraction of the monthly cost of a minimum-wage employee, a kiosk can supply customers with information, distribute coupons and other individualized promotions, or process orders and sales transactions.

For retailers and shoppers, kiosks can deliver the combined advantages of in-store and online shopping. Because they are so versatile and inexpensive, they're particularly effective for small retail chains that can react quickly to changing market signals.

THINK CRITICALLY

1. How many times in the past month have you used a kiosk? What did you use them for?

2. Name some new applications of kiosks that you have seen recently.

3. Name some new applications for kiosks that you think would be good marketing tools for retailers or other businesses.

The Global Market As businesses develop an international focus, the differences among customer groups and number of distinct market segments can become even greater. Even if businesses believe that they understand the consumers in their own country quite well, they will not have as much confidence about untested consumer groups in other countries. Gathering information about the country and its people can help determine how to become effective global business people.

Competition Competition is becoming much more intense for most businesses. It is more difficult to make decisions that will ensure customers will prefer one company's products to those of other companies. Gathering information about competitors' products and marketing activities in order to determine their strengths and weaknesses will help businesses to be more competitive.

Changing Markets Customer needs are changing, and so are the choices customers make to satisfy those needs. Many consumers are able to satisfy their basic needs much more easily than was possible in the past. Therefore they have moved beyond basic needs and devote more resources to satisfying discretionary desires, their wants. They have many choices, and much more information about those choices, so their decisions are more informed. In order to develop a marketing mix that will satisfy consumer wants, businesses must have a clear understanding of expanding consumer choices.

As consumers' wants and needs have expanded, products and services have changed as well. In the past, products may have been quite basic with few additional features or options available for consumers. Because of those limited differences, businesses often competed for sales by emphasizing such things as their location, reputation, or price. Businesses can now compete by emphasizing differences resulting from product development and technology. However, such changes can be expensive and may not always meet customer needs. The correct decisions can be very profitable, but the wrong choices can result in losses for the company. Decision makers want information so that the best and most profitable product and service improvements can be made.

When a business uses the marketing concept, what is the first thing it needs in developing a marketing plan?

CATEGORIES
OF INFORMATION

J'Borg Apparel is deciding on next year's designs for its lines of shirts and shorts. The members of the design team meet and share their ideas about possible changes. Several of the designers suggest that J'Borg should keep its basic designs from this year and simply develop new colors and some additional accessories. Another group believes that customers are moving away from their baggy cuts and will want shorter and more tailored styles. They argue that entirely new designs for its lines of apparel should be developed.

J'Borg's primary competitor is Dominique Designs. The designers at Dominique are also meeting to consider changes in product lines for the new season. However, before the meeting, they request information from the company's marketing manager. The marketing department provides records on each of the company's products. Those records identify the quantity sold by size and color for each week of the year. They also show the region of the country and the retail store in which sales were made. Original prices of products sold, markdowns, the number of items returned or unsold are also recorded.

In addition, the marketing manager distributes copies of a report that was purchased from a national apparel manufacturing association. It presents information on total consumer apparel purchases in the United States for each of the past five years for 10 major categories of apparel. Sales are broken out for four geographic regions of the country and are categorized by age and gender of consumers and by type of retail store where the products are sold. The report also identifies the top six brands of apparel and shows the percentage of total sales contributed by each brand over the five-year period. The final section of the report discusses the anticipated changes in the economy and in customer expenditures for apparel for the next year.

The final information supplied by the marketing department is the results of a marketing research study completed during the past month. Four groups of consumers from across the country were invited to a meeting to discuss their attitudes about apparel and their ideas about purchases they expected to make. The groups discussed 10 questions about designs, brands, and value. The results of the discussions are summarized in the research report. All of the designers for Dominique have carefully studied the market information and they discuss it thoroughly before deciding on next year's designs.

FIGURE 5-2
Marketers need information to make informed decisions.

TYPES OF INFORMATION NEEDED FOR EFFECTIVE MARKETING DECISIONS

Consumers	Marketing Mix	Business Environment
age	basic products	type of competition
gender	product features	competitors' strengths
income	services	competitors' strategies
education	product packaging	economic conditions
family size	guarantees	government regulations
home ownership	repairs	new technology
address	product price	consumer protection
occupation	credit choices	ethical issues
how money is spent	discounts	tax policies
attitudes	location of sale	proposed laws
primary needs	type of store used	international markets
product purchases	display procedures	
purchase frequency	use of salespeople	
brand preferences	promotion methods	
information needs	promotional message	
media preferences	promotional media	
shopping behavior		

How will each of the companies decide whether to make design changes and the types of designs to use for the next year? Which of the companies do you believe will make decisions that are most likely to be successful? What is the biggest difference in the way Dominique makes decisions compared to J'Borg?

WHAT TYPES OF INFORMATION ARE NEEDED?

Put yourself in the position of the marketing manager for a national chain of yogurt stores. It is your responsibility to collect information to help store managers decide what they can do to increase sales and profits. What information do you believe is needed?

A yogurt business is different from a ranch, a hospital, or an airplane manufacturer. Each type of business needs specific information, but there are general categories of information that all businesses should consider. Those categories are customer information, marketing mix information, and information about the business

environment. Figure 5-2 provides examples of the three categories of information.

As the marketing manager of the yogurt stores, you will need information from each of the categories. You will want to help store managers determine who their customers are, where they live, how much they spend on desserts, how they make decisions on what and when to purchase, and how they feel about your store's brand of yogurt. You also will want to know what new flavors to add, if other food products should be sold, whether specific locations or certain store layouts are more effective, the prices to charge, and the most effective promotional messages and methods. A study of internal operations such as costs of operations, training requirements for employees, and management methods may help determine the best ways to operate the stores. Your store managers will want to know if the economy will improve in the next year, if there will be new competitors or if current competitors are making important changes, if taxes or government regulations will increase, and even specific

Digital Photos Speed Products to Market

As the cost of digital photography declines and makes it affordable for more and more people, some businesses are cashing in on its advantages over film photography. PetSmart Inc., which sells pet products through stores, a web site, and a mail-order catalog, has used digital photography to slash the time it takes to bring new products to market. What used to take two or three months is now done in one month.

Digital photographs are transmitted over the Internet between the company's buyers and suppliers. Buyers show suppliers what colors they want or send sketches of new product ideas. Suppliers transmit images of products in development and get instantaneous approval to go ahead or instructions to make changes. The company not only stays on top of its market, it also saves lots of money by eliminating the need for much overseas travel.

The National Football League has also used digital photography to get products on the market quickly, taking maximum advantage of fans' Super Bowl enthusiasm before it cools off in the days after the game. Using digital photographs, it cuts at least a day off its production schedule for Super Bowl commemorative books. Those small but critical time savings can translate into a huge difference in profits.

THINK CRITICALLY

1. What are the advantages of bringing products to market more quickly?

2. What do you think might be some drawbacks to using digital photography?

information such as whether the city is planning to make street improvements in front of a store.

There are many reasons to collect information. However, all the reasons can be summarized in two statements. Effective marketing information improves the decisions of businesses, and effective marketing information reduces the risk of decision-making. If a business can make better decisions that increase the likelihood of making a profit, the time and money spent gathering information will be a good investment.

checkpoint

What are the three general categories of marketing information?

LESSON REVIEW

1. Why is information about foreign markets and foreign customers often more important than information about markets and customers in this country?

2. How does the increased affluence of society affect businesses' need for market information?

3. Name three types of customer information that are important for many business decisions.

4. Name three types of information about the business environment that are important for many business decisions.

5. What two crucial things are accomplished by having effective marketing information?

FINDING AND MANAGING MARKETING INFORMATION

MARKETING MATTERS

One of the functions of marketing is marketing information management. In Chapter 1, marketing information management was defined as obtaining, managing, and using market information to improve decision-making and the performance of marketing activities. In order to use information effectively,

businesses have to first know where to find it. Once they have it, they need to develop marketing information systems to get the most out of it.

Think of a part-time business that you would like to start, and list five sources of marketing information that would be useful in starting and operating the business.

GOALS

● Describe common sources of internal and external market information.

● Explain the five critical elements of an effective marketing information system.

SOURCES OF INFORMATION

Where do you go to find the titles of the most recent movies available on DVD? What is a good source of information to help you learn about careers or college choices? If you want to find out how much to pay for a particular model of automobile, where do you turn for help? Each of these decisions requires information. For most there may be more than one information source. You would select from the sources that are familiar and accessible. Factors that influence your selection of an information source may include its availability, how quickly it can be accessed, how complete or accurate you believe it to be, and your past experience with the source.

As business people identify data sources of marketing information, they go through a similar process. The process is summarized in the following steps:

● Identify the types of information needed.

● Determine the available sources of each type of information.

● Evaluate each source to determine if it meets the organization's needs in terms of accuracy, time, detail, and cost.

● Select the sources that best meet the identified needs.

● Enter the information into a marketing information system.

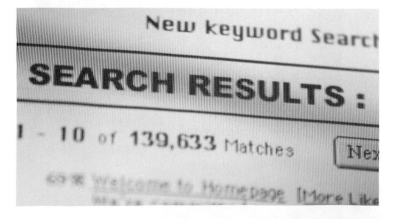

Marketing information can come from one of three sources: internal sources, external sources, and marketing research. Marketing research will be discussed in the next lesson.

INTERNAL INFORMATION SOURCES

Internal information is information developed from activities that occur within the organization. A great deal of information flows through a business. Much of it is valuable for marketing decision-making. Often, however, the information is not recorded or is not available to the right people or at the time when it would be useful for decisions. For example, salespeople learn a great deal from current and prospective customers. They get information about needs, perceptions of price, satisfaction with services, or requested changes in products. That information may never be communicated back to the company. Even if it is, it may not be part of the information reviewed when marketing plans are being developed.

Most businesses keep detailed records on production schedules and inventory levels. The people planning special promotions if they are expected to increase demand for particular products should review that information. Examples of important types of internal information are shown in Figure 5-3.

Customer Records and Sales Information

Customer information is important for effective planning.

Therefore customer records are an important information source. Many companies keep a complete record of all transactions they have with a customer. They record what is purchased, dates, and quantities purchased. If the customer purchases accessory or related products, then or at a later time, the information is also recorded and matched with the original purchase. Detailed information on payments and credit is also maintained. If the customer requires service, a service record is prepared.

To target products and marketing activities at specific customers, information more detailed than sales records is very useful. Businesses need to have demographic information such as age, family size, income, and address. They need an understanding of consumer needs, interests, and attitudes. Businesses need information regarding how the consumer makes buying decisions, such as where they gather information, what choices are considered, where they decide to purchase, and so on.

Customer information can be gathered through market research, but some businesses have discovered other ways to get it.

FIGURE 5-3
A great deal of information that is helpful when making decisions is available internally.

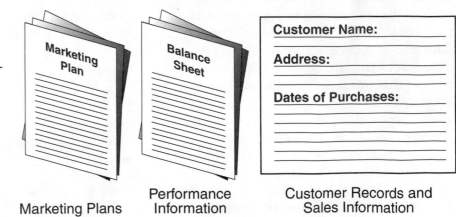

Production and Operation Reports

Marketing Plan

Balance Sheet

Customer Name:

Address:

Dates of Purchases:

Marketing Plans

Performance Information

Customer Records and Sales Information

Internal Information Sources

Detailed profiles might be completed on a customer by the salesperson as a part of the selling process. Many realtors ask prospective buyers a great deal of information in order to locate the best possible home. Salespeople who work in clothing and apparel stores develop complete information on their regular customers' needs and preferences.

A relatively new information tool used by businesses is a customer club. Prospective and current customers are provided with special incentives to join the club. In order to join, the consumer completes a detailed profile form. Based on that profile, each consumer is sent regular mailings providing new product information, special purchase opportunities and discounts, and promotional information for products and services the company believes the customer will want to buy. Some companies have used the consumer club to develop a consumer database of millions of people.

Production and Operations Reports

Production and operations activities are important to marketing. Products and services must be available when customers want them. Quality standards need to be met. Expenses need to be controlled in order to price the products and services competitively. Information about production and operations activities is collected, but it might not be shared regularly with the people planning marketing activities.

When a business is a part of a channel system working with a manufacturer, it is even more difficult to get needed information about production and operations. Often manufacturers do not believe channel members need that information or are unwilling to share it, believing it is confidential.

When companies that make up a channel of distribution work closely together and share operating information, they can meet customer needs much better and operate more efficiently. In that way all members of the channel benefit. Those companies have developed information systems that can share information about sales, costs, inventory levels, and production and delivery schedules.

Performance Information

The success of a business is judged by its performance. Some people believe the only important performance measure is the amount of profit a business makes, and managers certainly must pay attention to the bottom line. However, there are other performance measures that need to be watched along the way as well. The types of performance measures important to most businesses are sales, costs, quality, and customer satisfaction.

Performance is typically measured in one of three ways. For companies that have operated for a number of years, there are records of past performance. The current sales or costs can be compared to those of a previous month or year to determine if performance is improving.

A second method is to compare performance with that of similar businesses. Information on other businesses is available from external information sources.

The most important performance measure is the comparison of actual performance with expected performance. When managers plan marketing activities, they develop goals, performance standards, and budgets. Planning tools should be used regularly to check current performance.

EXTERNAL INFORMATION SOURCES

Marketing regularly involves other people and businesses. It is important to understand and effectively work with those outside the organization. **External information** provides an understanding of factors outside of the organization. In addition to the information gathered through marketing research, there are several valuable sources of external information that businesses can use. Those sources are reviewed in Figure 5-4.

Government Reports People often think of regulation and taxation as the major roles of government in business. However, another important activity of federal, state, and local governments is to supply information that can be used by businesses and consumers. There are a number of agencies that regularly collect information that can help businesses improve their marketing decisions.

Probably the best-known data collection agency is the U.S. Bureau of the Census. Every 10 years, the Census Bureau conducts a complete census of the country's population. The report of that census is very detailed and specific. It provides an excellent source to learn about the number of people and important characteristics of individuals and households in specific areas of the country. The Census of Population data is available in digital form for easier analysis. Also, some companies analyze census data and sell reports to businesses.

The population of the United States is not the only census completed by the federal government. Others include the Census of Manufacturers, Retail Trade, Wholesale Trade, Transportation, and County Business Patterns. Many of the studies are completed in full either every five years or every 10 years. Moreover, the Census Bureau issues yearly updates of some data that are not as comprehensive.

FIGURE 5-4
Government reports, commercial data services, business publications, and trade associations are all external sources of information.

External Information Sources

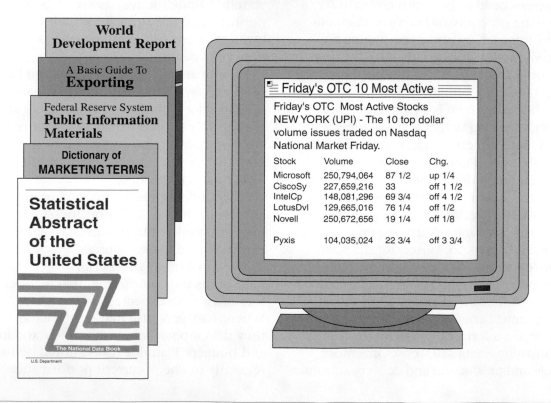

There are literally thousands of other databases, reports, and information sources available from government offices. One of the most difficult parts of using government information is determining just what is available. Information is developed on agriculture, education, housing, health, and international trade as well as many other areas of interest to businesses. Much federal government data can now be accessed through links at its comprehensive information web site at www.FedStats.gov.

Trade and Professional Associations Trade and professional associations are organized to serve people and businesses with common interests. Members of the association may be a part of the same industry such as travel, retailing, exporting, or corn producers. Other associations provide services for people in particular job categories, such as the American Management Association and the National Association of Market Developers.

Most associations provide information specific to the needs of their members. That information may be disseminated through journals, newsletters, or more-detailed research reports. Some associations have research services, libraries, or data services that can be used by members.

Business Publications Magazines and journals provide useful information for business people. Those publications include general business newspapers and magazines such as *The Wall Street Journal, Forbes,* and *Business Week,* as well as more-specialized publications such as

Black Enterprise, Advertising Age, or *American Demographics.* Business publications are useful sources of current information on the economy, legislation, new technology, or business ideas. Often the publications devote specific issues or sections to analysis of business performance. For example, *Sales & Marketing Management* publishes an annual *Survey of Buying Power* that analyzes consumer purchasing in all major U.S. markets.

★★★★★★★★★★★ JUDGMENT CALL

Dumpster Diving Legal, But Is It Really Ethical?

When it comes to business intelligence, what's legal, what's ethical, and what's expedient may not always be the same. What's more, it's often hard to determine what's what.

In July 2000, business software giant Oracle freely admitted to hiring investigators who had engaged in "Dumpster diving" to dig up dirt on consumer software giant Microsoft while the latter was battling a government antitrust lawsuit. Dumpster diving means going through people's trash searching for information that, presumably, would otherwise be secret.

Legally, trash is fair game at least in terms of criminal law, since once you throw something out, it's no longer yours. Some of the "victims" of the Oracle-induced intelligence activities, however, threatened to sue for invasion of privacy. Invasion of privacy is a civil offense that can't land anyone in jail but can result in the imposition of monetary damages and penalties.

Oracle, for its part, maintained that it had done nothing wrong. Quite the contrary, it said, it had fulfilled its civic duty in exposing what it characterized as Microsoft's attempts to manipulate public opinion by financially supporting advocacy groups that backed it in the antitrust case. Microsoft said it had never tried to hide its support of the groups.

THINK CRITICALLY

1. Ethically, is it acceptable to go through someone's trash to get information that the public ought to know about?

2. Should the government be able to go through people's trash to investigate criminal activity?

3. Should businesses go through competitors' trash to get information on new products, production processes, or marketing strategies?

4. Is it right to do anything as long as it's not illegal?

Dun & Bradstreet and Equifax provide credit information on consumers and businesses. A.C. Nielsen Co. conducts research on a number of topics and sells the information to business customers. One of the best known of their services is the Nielsen ratings for television viewing.

Commercial Data and Information Services There are a number of businesses that collect, analyze, and sell data.

What is the key difference between internal and external market information?

MARKETING
INFORMATION SYSTEMS

Certainly businesses need a great deal of information to operate successfully. With all of the information needed, business people could spend most of their time gathering and studying information. A **marketing information system** (MkIS, pronounced M-K-I-S) is an organized method of collecting, storing, analyzing, and retrieving information to improve the effectiveness and efficiency of marketing decisions.

Each business develops its own marketing information system. In some new, small businesses, an MkIS may be as simple as a filing cabinet in which the owner collects, organizes, and stores customer information, business records, and other information important to the business. In large businesses, there may be a critical operations unit with a dedicated computer system and a staff of people who collect and analyze information and prepare reports. Marketing managers carefully design MkISs to provide important information to make decisions. The information has to be complete, accurate, easy to use, timely, affordable, and cost-effective.

All effective marketing information systems contain five elements. Those elements are input, storage, analysis, output, and decision-making. They are illustrated in Figure 5-5.

FIGURE 5-5
An example of a computer-based MkIS.

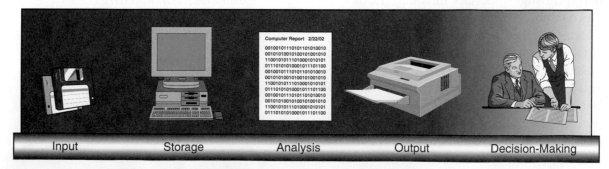

Elements of a Marketing Information System (MkIS)

DESIGNING A MARKETING INFORMATION SYSTEM

In planning an MkIS, several questions need to be answered. The questions and their results are shown in Figure 5-6.

INPUT

How do you make decisions? If you want to be as objective as possible and make good decisions, you must gather information. **Input** is the information that goes into the system that is needed for decision-making.

A great deal of information results from the regular operations of a business. It is known as routine information. Routine information about customers, competitors, and business operations is used for marketing decisions. Marketers need to know what customers purchase, in what quantities, and at what prices. They must know where customers buy their products and what factors influence them.

Marketing is influenced by the activities of competitors. Information is needed on which businesses are competing in specific markets, the marketing mixes they use, their strengths and weaknesses, their market share, and their profitability. Marketers can use information about business operations to determine what activities are effective or ineffective.

Occasionally, additional information that is not routinely collected by the business is needed for a decision. In that situation, a marketing research procedure is used to collect the information. Marketing research data provides important input for a marketing information system.

STORAGE

Have you ever rushed to a class only to discover that your assignment was not in your notebook? Many of us are very good at collecting information. We may not be as good at storing it where we can locate it when needed. **Storage** is the resources used to maintain information, including equipment and procedures, so that it can be used when needed.

A storage system in an MkIS has several characteristics. Most importantly, it must protect the information. If information is lost or damaged, it is not useful when a decision must be made. Some business information is very confidential. The storage system should be designed so that only authorized people can access the information. Finally, the storage system should be organized so information is easy to locate when it's needed.

FIGURE 5-6

A marketing information system (MkIS) is designed to help marketers obtain, store, organize, and use information to improve decisions.

DESIGNING AN MKIS

Question	MkIS Element
What information is needed to develop and implement the marketing strategy?	Input
How should the information be maintained so it is in a usable form and is easy to access when needed?	Storage
What methods should be used to organize and study the information in order to make effective marketing decisions?	Analysis
How and when should the information be made available for most effective use?	Output
What ways should the information be used to improve marketing?	Decision-Making

Tissue Packs Get In Your Face

Even in today's high-tech marketplace, sometimes the best way to get a message across is as low-tech as a . . . well, a facial tissue, Handing out pocketsize packs of tissues on the street is a common marketing tool in Japan. Promotional inserts can include coupons or informational materials. A sushi restaurant in London saw its business jump 30% when it began handing out tissue packs containing coupons for free sushi.

Tissue packs are effective because they are simple, cheap, and easy to get into the hands of a targeted audience. Since they are functional, they tend to stick around awhile, unlike unwanted promotional flyers that tend to get thrown in the trash or simply dropped on the streets. With tissues, the message gets delivered on multiple occasions each time someone tucks a pack into their pocket or purse. They also create a positive association for a product or service, one that is useful, sanitary, and environmentally friendly.

THINK CRITICALLY

1. Name some other forms of promotional handouts that you have seen.

2. Name two advantages and two disadvantages of using promotional handouts.

examine the budgets for other products or for past years. The effectiveness of one retailer in a channel of distribution may not be apparent until that company's sales are compared with those of similar companies. The costs of marketing activities for national and international activities need to be combined to determine the total marketing costs.

The type of analysis needed is usually determined when planning the marketing information system. Procedures are developed to obtain needed information from storage, to organize it for analysis, and to complete the needed analysis. Specific computer programs are available that assist with those procedures. For example, database and spreadsheet programs have procedures for analysis of the information. If statistical analysis is needed, the formulas are developed within the program or a specific statistical package is used to analyze the data quickly and accurately.

Companies that complete a large amount of data analysis usually employ people skilled in organizing and analyzing data. Most finance and accounting departments, as well as marketing research and operations units, have specialists in data analysis.

Most of the information storage in businesses today is done using computer technology. After data is entered into the computer, it is maintained on a hard or floppy disk, a CD-ROM, or on another type of storage media. Careful planning is done to make sure that back-up copies of all data are maintained and that information is secure. More traditional methods of information storage continue to be used, such as keeping documents in filing cabinets or using microphotography to make copies of information that can be stored and retrieved on microfilm or microfiche.

ANALYSIS

Information in an MkIS is maintained in order to improve decision-making. Usually the information by itself has little meaning. **Analysis** is the process of summarizing, combining, or comparing information so that decisions can be made. In order to plan a promotional budget, a manager may

OUTPUT

For managers and other decision-makers, the most important part of an MkIS is the output. Many people never see information being collected, stored, or analyzed. They are given only summaries or reports to use in decision-making. **Output** is the result of analysis given to decision-makers.

Output is usually written information or graphics. It is provided in print form or accessed by computer. Output must be useful to the people receiving the information. If it is not well organized or uses language or data that is difficult to understand, it may be misused or not used at all.

FIGURE 5-7

An effective marketing information system automates routine decisions, freeing managers to focus on the ones that aren't as easy.

Routine and Unique Decisions

| Routine Decisions | Unique Decisions |

DECISION-MAKING

The purpose of a marketing information system is to improve decision-making. Decisions should be better and made more quickly if an MkIS is well designed. The decision-making process includes who is involved in the decision, when decisions need to be made, any policies or procedures that should be considered, and the information needed by the decision-makers.

Some decisions are routine and the result of the analysis will determine the decision that should be made. For example, information in the MkIS of an office supply store shows that inventory levels of computer paper have dropped to a level where it needs to be reordered. The analysis program in the computer determines that 200 cases of paper are needed. It searches the vendor list to determine which approved vendor has the lowest current price. The vendor is selected, the reorder quantity identified, and a purchase order is sent to the vendor. No management attention to this routine decision was required as shown in Figure 5-7.

Other decisions are unique. A major credit card company considers whether to offer a money-back guarantee on all products consumers purchase using the card. The guarantee is viewed as an important service that will encourage people to use the credit card and could attract many more customers. The results will affect the company, the businesses that accept the credit card, and competing credit card companies. The decision to add the guarantee means important changes in the entire marketing mix. Once the company announces the new service, it will be difficult to end the service even if it proves to be too expensive to maintain. That decision requires a great deal of time and information, and many of the company's managers will be involved in making it.

What are the five elements of an effective marketing information system, or MkIS?

1. What is the most widely used source of demographic data on the U.S. market?

2. What are three types of performance measures commonly used by businesses?

3. What is the Internet address of the federal government's comprehensive statistics web site?

4. What does an effective marketing information system do with routine decisions?

5. Why is output the most important element of an MkIS for most managers and business executives?

6. Name three factors that influence the selection of information sources.

5.3 USING MARKETING RESEARCH

A good marketing information system should provide the information needed for regular and routine decisions. However, there are many decisions that relate to one-time problems or new situations that will require information that hasn't been anticipated or previously collected. To gather additional information needed in those circumstances, the company uses marketing research. The company will use proven problem-solving techniques.

Suppose your school needs to raise money for a new addition, and the board hires you to help decide how to continue classes during construction. What steps would you recommend?

SEEING THE PROBLEM CLEARLY

Suppose a business is considering entering a new market in which it has no previous experience, or maybe a company's engineers have suggested a product modification that is totally new. In situations like that, the company's MkIS may not have all of the information needed for the marketers to make a good decision. **Marketing research** is a procedure designed to identify solutions to a specific marketing problem through the use of scientific problem-solving.

You have probably studied and used scientific problem-solving in many other classes. If you have, you already know the steps in scientific problem-solving. Those steps are shown in Figure 5-8. The scientific method is used to ensure that a careful and objective procedure is followed in order to develop the best possible solution.

DEFINE THE PROBLEM

Marketing research is used when a business needs to solve a specific problem.

The first step is to be certain that the problem is clearly and carefully defined. That is not always an easy step. Sometimes the problem is very clear—identify the characteristics of a market or select a new advertising medium. In other cases, you may not know the real problem. If sales are declining, the problem might be that

FIGURE 5-8
A good marketing researcher plans a study by following the steps in scientific decision-making.

IMPLEMENTING A MARKETING RESEARCH STUDY

1. Define the Problem
2. Analyze the Situation
3. Develop a Data-Collection Procedure
4. Gather and Study Information
5. Propose a Solution

customers are dissatisfied with some part of the marketing mix or a competitor may have introduced a new product choice. Consumers may believe the economy is not strong and are less willing to spend money. You may have to gather some specific information before the problem is clear.

It is important to state the problem clearly and have several people review it to make sure it is understandable. The problem should be specific enough that researchers know what to study, whom to involve in the study, and the types of solutions or results that might be appropriate for the problem.

ANALYZE THE SITUATION

An important part of scientific decision-making is to understand the problem well enough to determine how to solve it. Analyzing the situation allows the researcher to identify what is already known about the problem, the information currently available, and the possible solutions that have already been attempted.

Reviewing available information and talking to people who might have ideas or additional information complete this step. Reviewing similar problems or other studies that have previously

been completed can help the researcher decide how to study the current problem.

It is possible that a careful situation analysis may result in the identification of a solution. If the decision-maker is confident in the proposed solution and has limited time or money to study the problem further, the marketing research process will come to an end. A good marketing information system will frequently provide the necessary information so that further study is not needed.

DEVELOP A DATA-COLLECTION PROCEDURE

After thoroughly reviewing the situation and the available information, the researcher decides what additional information is needed and how it should be collected. In this step, the actual marketing research study is planned. The researcher

Pepsi Fattens European Sales with Un-Diet Cola

The United States and Europe share many cultural characteristics, but marketers can get into trouble if they don't pay careful attention to differences, especially in language.

American soft drink brands such as Coke and Pepsi are popular all over the world. In most cases, the marketing for the products is the same or only slightly different than that used in the United States. Diet versions, however, have not had nearly as much success in Europe as they have in America. Marketing research indicated that Europeans were concerned about their weight, just as Americans are. Putting the word "diet" on a label, though, seemingly doomed a product.

The problem is that in many European countries, foods labeled "diet" are made for sick people. Pepsi got around the problem by developing a new sugarless soft drink called Pepsi Max. It has only one calorie, yet it's not labeled as a diet drink. It was developed specifically for the international market, and it was such a success that the company began selling it in the United States also.

THINK CRITICALLY
1. Besides language, what are some other cultural differences that marketers need to be familiar with when they try to sell products or services in multiple countries?

The results of the research are often summarized and analyzed in a variety of ways. That allows marketers to consider several possible solutions. Studying and analyzing marketing research is an important marketing skill. Marketing research departments and companies employ research analysts to complete those tasks.

PROPOSING A SOLUTION

The purpose of marketing research is to identify strategies for the company to follow in implementing and improving marketing activities. Scientific decision-making often begins with the development of a hypothesis (or possible solution) to the problem. After the research results have been organized, they need to be studied to determine if the findings support the proposed solution or suggest an alternative solution.

In most cases, market researchers do not make decisions about solutions. They prepare a report of the research results. The report is presented to managers. The marketing managers carefully study the report. They use the results to help them with decision-making. It is important that results are accurate and clearly communicated in a research report.

Marketing research reports can be presented in writing or orally. In both cases, the report should describe the study and its results in detail. Effective communication is an important skill for all marketers, especially market researchers.

Preparing Reports When a report is being prepared, two items are very important. First, the person preparing the report must know who will be receiving and studying the report. Just as a marketing mix should respond to the needs of customers, the research report must be prepared to meet the needs of its consumers. Second, the report must clearly describe the purpose of the study and the research procedures followed to collect the information in the report. Without an understanding of the

problem being studied and the methods used, those receiving the report may misunderstand or misinterpret the results.

A research report, whether written or oral, is usually organized just like the study. An outline that could be used to develop a report is shown in Figure 5-10. A research report begins with a statement of the problem or the purpose of the research and includes a brief discussion of why the study

FIGURE 5-10
A research report is clearly organized and written to communicate results to managers.

Sections of a Research Report

Statement of the Problem
_____
_____
_____

Review of Secondary Data
_____
_____
_____

Research Procedures
_____
_____
_____

Results of the Research
_____
_____
_____

Summary and Recommendations
_____
_____
_____

was needed. Then it summarizes the secondary information that was collected.

The third part is a description of the procedures used in the study. This includes the population studied and the way a sample was obtained. It will also describe the method used to collect information including surveys, observations, or experiments.

Presentation of Results The most important part of the report is the presentation of the results of the research. In a written report, the results are presented in the form of tables and graphs with brief written explanations. In an oral presentation, the results are presented using visuals. Visuals are charts, transparencies shown on an overhead projector, slides, or computer graphics displayed on a computer screen or projected onto a wall screen. The presenter provides explanations.

Finally, the research report concludes with a summary that emphasizes the most important information from the study. It may also contain recommendations for solutions if they have been requested. Sometimes the research will not completely demonstrate that a solution will be successful. Marketers will need to decide if they have enough information or if they need to continue to study the problem.

WHEN TO USE MARKETING RESEARCH

Some business people seldom use marketing research. They believe it is too expensive or requires too much time. They want to make decisions quickly and believe they have the necessary knowledge and experience to make good decisions. Companies that have a production philosophy do not believe in marketing research.

Other business people have found that marketing research is very valuable. Business people who understand the marketing concept believe that the cost and time needed for research are worthwhile if it means that the correct marketing decisions will be made and customers will be satisfied.

The decision whether to use research or not is based on how risky a decision is and how much it will cost to gather information. If there is little risk, there is no need to do research. If a business is considering investing several hundred thousand dollars in a new product or a new distribution system, marketing research can reduce the risk.

What two things are important in preparing a report?

LESSON REVIEW

1. When participants in a study are selected using random sampling, what are the chances of any particular person being selected compared to the chances of the others in the target population?

2. Which is generally easier to analyze, numerical data or non-numerical data?

3. What distinguishes secondary data from primary data?

4. What two factors determine whether or not marketing research should be used to solve a problem?

5. What type of procedure does marketing research use to arrive at a solution to a problem?

where the eyes look first, how long the customer focuses on certain products, how they search the entire display, and what they look at when making a product choice. This information can be very helpful in organizing displays and placing specific brands in the displays. The same type of equipment is used to study how consumers read magazine and newspaper advertisements.

Some observations are made without the consumer even being aware that they are being observed. Researchers are interested in learning how participants behave in normal situations. In other cases, researchers may ask people to participate in a planned situation. In these cases, the researcher wants to learn how people respond to specific, controlled activities. For example, a business might want to know how customers would react if a different type of sales presentation is used. Another example would be to study consumer responses to a new piece of equipment such as an automatic teller machine in a bank.

Why are the results of observation generally considered more accurate than survey results?

PERFORMING EXPERIMENTS

The most precise and objective information is obtained through experimentation. **Experiments** are tightly controlled situations in which all important factors are the same except the one being studied. Scientific research is done by planning and implementing experiments and then recording and analyzing the data.

Experiments are not used as often in marketing research as surveys or observations. That may be because it is difficult to manage a large number of marketing activities at the same time. It also takes a great deal of time to organize an experiment and operate it long enough to determine if significant differences occur. It is likely, however, that many

When marketers analyze research data, they'll often use an average. It might be the average age of people who buy a certain product, the average household income of a group, or the average rating given to a proposed product.

In everyday situations, average is usually defined as the arithmetic mean of a group of figures. It's derived by adding all the figures and dividing the total by the number of figures in the group. If we have the ages of 20 people, we'd add them together and divide that total by 20 to get their mean age.

There are times, though, when another type of average, the median, is more useful. The median of a group is the one in the middle when they're ranked in order by size. For example, the median of 5, 5, 7, 8, and 10 is 7. If the number of figures is even, the median is the mean of the two middle figures.

Analyzing What the Mean Means

When research data is analyzed, it's a good idea to calculate both the mean and the median to make sure they are reasonably close. If not, it might indicate that one or more unusually high (or low) figures have distorted the mean, or that someone made a mistake inputting data.

THINK CRITICALLY

1. A grocery store manager asked some customers how many movies they typically rented each month. The responses were 8, 2, 5, 12, 8, 7, 2, 3, 0, 15, 0, 8, 5, and 1. What was the mean of those responses?

2. What was the median?

3. What would she come up with for the mean and median if, in keying the figures into her calculator, the manager accidentally typed 78 instead of 7?

researchers do not recognize the real benefits of carefully planned experiments in marketing.

Implementing the marketing concept provides many opportunities for research to determine the best market segments to serve and the appropriate mix elements to provide. A company may want to determine if a customer's geographic location makes a difference in purchasing behavior. An experiment in which two groups of customers from different areas are provided the same marketing mix may help to answer the question. A business owner may be uncertain about the effect of a price increase on sales volume. An experiment can be developed in which everything except the price is held the same for two groups of customers. One group is given a 10 percent-off coupon while the other is not given a discount. The experiment can demonstrate the amount of sales change that results from the price difference.

There are other examples of possible marketing experiments. You can test two different locations for a product in a store or determine whether a radio or television commercial is more effective in maintaining customers' memory of a product. You could also analyze the effect on customer satisfaction of follow-up calls from salespeople after the purchase of an automobile.

Experiments may be quite difficult to implement successfully. However, these types of experiments can provide very important information to marketers if they are done well.

Test Markets Because of the need for control over important conditions, experiments are difficult to manage. Some companies have developed test markets. **Test markets** are specific cities or geographic areas in which marketing experiments are conducted. To prepare for a test market, companies gather information about consumers, competitors, and past marketing activities. The companies try new product ideas or make marketing changes in the test markets. They collect data on the product performance for a period of several months and compare it with previously gathered information. In this way they can attempt to predict the performance in their total market based on the results in the test market.

Simulations Sometimes experiments are not possible in actual markets. **Simulations** are experiments where researchers create the situation to be studied. For example, a business may want to see how children respond when playing with a new toy. Rather than observing children playing in their homes or schools, the business may organize a play center. Then they bring groups of children into the center and observe them under more carefully controlled circumstances. An automobile maker studying the layout of the driver's seat area does not have to build an entire new car. It can build a small area that duplicates the front seat of a car. Changing the positions of the seat and controls allows the company to determine which is most satisfying.

Many simulations are now done on computers. Computer graphics allow research participants to visualize a change and react to it. Architects can use computer software to develop a complete external view of a proposed building from all sides. The software allows the viewer to enter all doors and immediately see the interior of a room. The software could be used to test consumers' attitudes about changes in the architectural plans of the building before final design decisions are made.

What is the main benefit of using experiments compared with the other methods of collecting primary data?

1. Why is it important to keep surveys as short and sharply focused as possible?

2. What are test markets used for?

3. What are two advantages of using mechanical methods of observation?

4. What is the difference between the mean and the median of a group of numerical responses to a survey question?

CHAPTER 5

SUMMARY

Lesson 5.1

A. Market information is critical so businesses can respond to groups of customers with similar needs.

B. There are three general categories of information that marketers need: consumer information, market mix information, and information about business conditions.

Lesson 5.2

A. Common sources of market information include internal sources such as customer records and performance data as well as external sources such as government records, commercial data services, business publications, and trade associations.

B. An effective marketing information system, or MkIS, is used to organize information needed for good decision-making. An MkIS includes five elements: input, storage, analysis, output, and decision-making.

Lesson 5.3

A. The first steps toward solving marketing problems are defining the problem, analyzing the situation to get a thorough understanding of it, and developing a procedure to collect data that can be used to arrive at a solution.

B. To gather and study data relevant to a problem, it is first necessary to select participants that are representative of the population a business is trying to reach. Once the participants have been selected, data is gathered according to the established procedures. Tools and techniques for analyzing data depend largely on whether it is numerical data or non-numerical data.

C. Reports should be prepared to meet the needs of the recipients who must use them to make decisions. A report should clearly state the purpose of the study and the procedures used. It should include proposed solutions if they were requested and if the information is complete enough to do so.

Lesson 5.4

A. Marketers use surveys to gather consumer data by asking people a planned set of questions, either orally or in writing. People can be surveyed in person, through the mail, by telephone, or by other means. Survey questions can be open- or closed-ended.

B. Observation collects information by recording actions rather than having participants recall or predict their actions. This usually results in greater accuracy and objectivity.

C. Experiments are the most precise and objective way to obtain information. They are tightly controlled situations in which all the important factors are the same except the one being studied. Test markets and simulations are two common types of experiments.

REVIEW MARKETING CONCEPTS

1. True or False: Focus groups are often used to develop more specific questions to be used in a wider survey.

2. True or False: Marketing research helps businesses that are involved in international competition.

3. True or False: Businesses that have effective marketing information systems do not need to use marketing research.

4. True or False: Surveys should only ask questions that are needed to accomplish the objectives of the research.

5. True or False: Whether or not to use marketing research depends solely on its cost.

6. True or False: Close-ended questions are often used while researchers are attempting to identify the problem or are completing a situation analysis.

7. True or False: Marketing research follows the steps of scientific problem-solving.

8. True or False: The most precise and objective information about a potential market segment is obtained through focus groups.

9. True or False: A great deal can be learned about purchase behavior by observing consumers.

10. True or False: Secondary data is usually less expensive to obtain than primary data.

REVIEW MARKETING TERMS

Match the terms listed with the definitions. Some terms may not be used.

11. Offer two or more choices from which respondents can select answers.

12. A procedure in which everyone in the population has an equal chance of being selected in a sample.

13. Information collected for the first time to solve the problem being studied.

14. The results of analysis that are given to decision-makers.

15. Allow respondents to develop their own answers without information about possible choices.

16. A small number of people brought together to discuss identified elements of an issue or problem.

17. A planned set of questions to which individuals or groups of people respond.

18. All of the people in the group that a company is interested in studying.

19. Information already collected for another purpose that can be used to solve the current problem.

20. An organized method of collecting, storing, analyzing, and retrieving information to improve the effectiveness and efficiency of marketing decisions.

21. Tightly controlled situations in which all important factors are the same, except the one that's being studied.

22. Specific cities or geographic areas in which marketing experiments are conducted.

23. Information collected for the first time to solve the problem being studied.

24. A procedure to identify solutions to a specific marketing problem through the use of scientific problem-solving.

25. Collecting information by recording actions without interacting or communicating with the participant.

26. The information that goes into a marketing information system that is needed for decision-making.

27. The resources used to maintain information, including equipment and procedures, so that it can be used when needed.

28. Information developed from activities that occur within the organization.

a. analysis
b. closed-ended questions
c. experiments
d. external information
e. focus group
f. input
g. internal information
h. marketing information system
i. marketing research
j. observation
k. open-ended questions
l. output
m. population
n. primary data
o. random sampling
p. secondary data
q. simulations
r. storage
s. survey
t. test market

APPLY MARKETING FUNCTIONS

MARKETING RESEARCH

29. An important part of the marketing research process is to summarize and analyze the data after the surveys, observations, or experiments have been completed. The following chart shows the data collected from a study of store and brand choices for four age groups of consumers. A total of 1,000 people were surveyed and each respondent indicated his/her preferred store and preferred brand.

Age	Store Preference			Brand Preference		
	Bardoes	Kelvins	1–2–3	Motif	Astra	France
16–20	38	82	130	80	106	76
21–25	56	20	174	156	90	18
26–30	110	64	76	104	98	60
31–35	44	120	86	54	30	128

Calculate the following information from the data and develop tables, charts, or graphs to illustrate the results.

a. Determine the total number of participants who prefer each store and each brand. (To determine the total, add the numbers in each column of the table.)

b. Using the totals from a, calculate the percentage of the total number of participants who prefer each store and each brand. (To calculate the percentage, divide the total of each column by the total number of participants, 1,000.)

c. For each of the age categories calculate the percentage of respondents who prefer each store and each brand. (Divide the number of respondents in each preference category by the total number of participants in that age category.)

d. Illustrate the rank order of stores and the rank order of brands for each age category. (Rank order shows the store and brand that is most preferred, next most preferred, and so on.) Then illustrate the rank order of stores and brands when the responses of all age categories are combined.

e. Using the information you have summarized for a through d, develop two specific conclusions about store and brand preferences for the sample surveyed.

30. Important categories of information for marketing researchers include business data, consumer information, economic information, government data, and information about specific industries.

Use the library or the Internet to identify two specific information sources for each of the five categories of information listed above. For each of the information sources, prepare a note card that describes the name of the publication, the publisher, copyright date or frequency of publication, and the type of information that is included in the publication.

If you can obtain a copy of the publication, select a small sample of the information it contains and summarize it on your note card.

MARKETING PLANNING

31. Identify which of the five steps in scientific decision making is described by each of the following marketing research activities.

a. After receiving the surveys from the respondents, the analyst tabulates the results and prepares charts illustrating the survey results.

b. The manager reviews sales records for the past five years to see if there have been changes in the geographic location of customers during that time.

c. After considering several methods to collect information, researchers decide to organize two test markets using different distribution methods to determine which is most effective.

d. The managers listened to the report of the research results and decided to implement the top three recommendations of the research team.

e. In a discussion with salespeople, the marketing manager agrees that there has been an increase in the number of customer complaints about the cost of repair parts for the product.

32. We know a marketing information system (MkIS) is an organized method of collecting, storing, analyzing, and retrieving information to improve the effectiveness and efficiency of marketing decisions. We also know that an MkIS has five components: input, storage, analysis, output, and decision-making. The idea of an MkIS has many different applications but each should have the five components listed. You want to get a high grade on your next marketing test so you decide to develop an effective system to organize and review the information you are learning. Plan a realistic MkIS you could use. Using pictures or brief descriptions, identify your a) inputs, b) storage, c) analysis, d) output, and e) decision-making that will result in a high grade on your test.

MARKETING MANAGEMENT

33. For the situations listed, describe how you would follow each of the steps in scientific decision-making to solve the problem.

a. You are planning your schedule for your senior year in high school. You want to be sure you complete all of the requirements for graduation, meet the admissions requirements for one of your state's universities, and take several electives that will help you prepare for your current career choice.

b. You are driving down the street on your way home from school and your car's engine stalls. You are able to pull off on the side of the road and park safely.

c. You are the shift manager of the shoe department in a department store. You have one full-time and three part-time employees who work in the department; two of the employees work with you each day but it is not always the same two. During the past three weeks, the amount of receipts in the cash register at the end of the shift has not matched the total sales on five days. The amount of shortage has been as little as $6 and as high as $55.

d. As the transportation manager for a computer software business you want to find the best way to ship packages of software to customers. The method needs to be rapid, reliable, and not too expensive. You know that you have several choices of air, parcel services, truck, and the U.S. postal system.

34. The band boosters at your school are planning a fund-raising activity. They want to sell two-pocket folders that can hold full-size papers. The folders would be sold to students and faculty. The folders would be printed and assembled by a local printing company. They want your help in determining a design for the folder, the price to charge, and the best ways to promote the folder in the school to achieve a high sales volume. Prepare a proposal of three to five pages describing a marketing research study that will help the boosters answer their questions. Include the following sections in your proposal: identify the problem, design the research method, select the participants, analyze the data, and report the research results. The proposal should identify ways that include all three types of data collection —survey, observation, and experiment.

MARKETING TECHNOLOGY

35. Use the Internet to find an annual financial report of a publicly owned corporation that does business in your area. Many companies have their annual reports on their web sites. Others can be obtained from the U.S. Securities and Exchange Commission web site. In the report, find a discussion of the company's products or services and the competitive environment that it faces. Write a one-page report describing the company's products or services, the competitive environment, and its strategy.

36. Using a spreadsheet program, input the company's revenues for the last five years and have the spreadsheet calculate the percentage increase for each of the last four years and the average increase over that period. Using that average increase, project revenues ahead for the next five years. Have the spreadsheet program make a chart of the 10 years of revenue figures. Print a copy of the chart.

CHAPTER 6

MARKETING BEGINS WITH CUSTOMERS

LESSON 6.1 *UNDERSTANDING CONSUMER BEHAVIOR*

LESSON 6.2 *WHAT MOTIVATES BUYERS?*

LESSON 6.3 *TYPES OF DECISION-MAKING*

NEWSLINE

SONY GETS CLOSE TO CONSUMERS

To get an insight into consumers' behavior, Sony developed a "playground" for customers. This electronics playground in Chicago provides Sony with an opportunity to observe and listen to their customers.

The gallery is located on Michigan Avenue, Chicago's main shopping street for upscale purchasers. The two-story showroom is designed to expose customers to Sony's technology in an inviting environment. Customers are not afraid to ask questions or touch the equipment.

Sony's products are displayed in lifestyle settings, such as a bedroom or a home office. Employees encourage consumers to interact with the products. If consumers can't bear to part with something they have found and liked, they can buy it on the spot.

The showroom employees do not push Sony products. Their main responsibility is to keep an eye on which products elicit oohs and aahs and which get only fleeting glances. Sony expects to use this information to develop better marketing strategies.

The showroom staff has discovered some interesting things. One of the biggest surprises has been watching consumers discover products that have been on the market for quite a while. From this Sony can determine in which markets it is successful in advertising, and in which ones it is not.

THINK CRITICALLY

1. How does Sony's playground differ from a traditional electronics store?

2. What might customers do to experience Sony's products firsthand if they are not free to visit this playground in Chicago?

3. Visit the web site of Sony or another electronics manufacturer to find out what products and services the company offers to customers online.

CAREER OPPORTUNITY
MARKETING WRITER & EDITOR

POINT YOUR BROWSER

www.corpview.com

TeleView is looking for an employee who possesses the following skills.

- Problem solving, project organization, time management, and interpersonal skills
- Drive, flexibility, and technical communications skills
- Excellent customer relation skills
- Ability to work in an invigorating, team-oriented environment

The main responsibilities of the job include the following.

- Serving as liaison between Corporate Communications and Marketing
- Completing writing assignments in creative and exciting ways
- Preparing, as part of a team, presentations, customer Marketing information, press releases, white papers, brochures, and other product Marketing tools
- Editing documents from other workgroup team members
- Reporting progress to team leaders and departmental Editorial Manager and Product Marketing Managers
- Developing style guide information and workflow processes based on project planning goals and objectives
- Work directly with Product Marketing Managers, freelance writers, designers, artists, in-house production personnel and others to meet deadlines
- Prioritizing and managing multiple schedules
- Applying the basics of how to reach an audience with purpose
- Reflecting the corporate image and personality in your writing

- Writing in a manner that controls the length of documents
- Establishing brands as leaders in the industry

The job requires the following education, skills, and experience.

- Two to three years of professional writing experience
- BS, MS, or MA degree in corporate communications, business and technical writing, marketing, advertising, English, journalism, or related field
- Portfolio containing writing and project samples
- Editing experience

THINK CRITICALLY

1. Prepare a sample resume of a person who is qualified for this job and interested in applying for it.

2. Considering your skills and preferences, does this sound like a job you would like to have one day? Why or why not?

3. Search want ads or the Internet for a job similar to Corporate View's Marketing Writer and Editor. What type of compensation package is available for this job?

the needs at each level. Everyone must satisfy the physiological needs. They are not options. You must eat, sleep, and breathe to exist. After these needs are generally satisfied, you can start to satisfy security needs. While it's important to be secure, it is only important to be secure after you have satisfied your physiological needs. To go one level higher, social needs are certainly important, but only after you meet physiological and security needs.

Gaining respect and recognition from others satisfies esteem needs. Running for student council might be an attempt to satisfy esteem needs. The need for self-actualization usually involves intellectual growth, creativity, and accomplishment. Attending college or taking music lessons might satisfy needs for self-actualization.

Global Advertising Techniques

One of the most important techniques for advertising in the United States is through television commercials. In 1996, advertisers spent nearly $36 billion on TV ads. That total represents about 54% of all advertising spending in 1996. As much as one-quarter of a program's broadcast time can be devoted to commercials.

However, in other countries the opportunities for television advertising can be limited. For example, in the United Kingdom two of the largest national channels have no paid commercials at all. Other channels have strict limits on the amount of broadcast time they are allowed to devote to commercials. Advertisers generally must resort to other techniques to get the word out about their products and services.

Many other countries also have little to no television commercial advertising. The broadcasters in a number of countries agree to air few or no commercials in exchange for receiving subsidies from the government.

THINK CRITICALLY

1. In a country with limited TV advertising, what techniques would you use to advertise? Would you use the same techniques in a small country and a large country?

2. Use the Internet and other resources to find out how advertising on TV is handled in another country.

DIFFERENT PEOPLE, DIFFERENT LEVELS

Marketers must recognize that people are at different levels on the hierarchy of needs. Some people are focusing on security needs while others are satisfying esteem needs. Regardless of what needs individuals are attempting to satisfy, marketers must identify them if they want to satisfy them.

Housing provides a good example of how consumers' needs differ depending on where they are on Maslow's hierarchy of needs. The physiological need for housing is served by a home that provides protection from the weather. A house that is in a fairly safe neighborhood and has a security system would satisfy the need for security. For a family with young children, a house that is in a neighborhood with lots of young families might satisfy social needs. A house might satisfy esteem needs if it is well maintained and the yard is landscaped. Self-actualization needs might be satisfied by a home that is designed and built by the owner.

Global E-Commerce Opportunities

"In how many countries does your company do business?" The question is heard often among global marketers. Today, the answer is likely to be "in every country with Internet access."

Technology allows firms to buy, sell, and exchange information around the world. The Internet, automated production methods, and video conferencing are changing the way people do business. These technologies are creating global e-commerce opportunities. The scope of e-commerce includes many activities.

- Companies sell goods and services to anyone with Internet access.
- Businesses buy online from suppliers in other countries.
- Firms meet customers' geographic and cultural needs.
- People process information and distribute data worldwide.
- Marketers research global customers and markets online.

THINK CRITICALLY

1. What are some other examples of technologies that are changing the way products are marketed and sold to customers?

2. What types of marketing activities are faster and easier because of technology?

3. Find an Internet site that is used in the marketing of a product or service. How does the site provide information about the product or service to customers?

What factors determine consumer wants and needs?

LESSON REVIEW

1. What are the five levels of human needs in Maslow's hierarchy of needs?

2. When a business buys consumable products that it uses as part of its internal operations, and does not pass those products on when it sells its own products to its customers, is it a final consumer or a business consumer?

3. What is the study of consumers and how they make decisions?

4. What is the key distinction between the need for esteem and the need for self-actualization?

5. What kinds of things typically satisfy a person's physiological needs?

GOALS

- **Distinguish between different buying motives.**
- **Describe the five steps of the consumer decision-making process.**

MARKETING MATTERS

The reasons people buy things can be categorized as emotional, rational, or patronage motives. Final consumers often buy for emotional reasons such as affection or fear, while business consumers tend to be more rational and buy based on quality, price and other factors. Whatever the motivation, the consumer decision-making process generally goes through five steps, ranging from problem recognition to postpurchase evaluation.

Marketers can influence consumers' purchase decisions at each step of the process.

Describe the process you went through the last time you made a major purchase. What motivated you to make the purchase? Where did you find information on the different products or services from which you had to choose? How many different alternatives did you consider buying? How happy were you with your decision?

BUYING MOTIVES

As you decide you want or need products or services, you are motivated by what marketers call buying motives. **Buying motives** are the reasons that you buy. There are three categories of buying motives that drive consumers to purchase products or services or respond to ideas: emotional motives, rational motives, and patronage motives.

EMOTIONAL MOTIVES

Emotional motives are reasons to purchase based on feelings, beliefs, or attitudes. Forces of love, affection, guilt, fear, or passion often compel consumers to buy. Marketers realize that emotional motives are very strong. For example, Hallmark card advertisements encourage you to buy greeting cards because of love and affection. Folger's presents drinking coffee as a

relaxing social experience. AT&T used "reach out and touch someone" to give emotions to an inanimate object, a telephone.

Fear is also a motivator that is used to encourage you to buy products. You buy security systems because you are motivated by the fear of being robbed. You buy cars with optional air bags because you are motivated by fear of injury. Marketers understand your emotional motivations and use them to present their products to you.

RATIONAL MOTIVES

Sometimes emotional motivation is not appropriate or effective. **Rational motives** are reasons to buy based on facts or logic.

Rational motives include factors such as saving money, durability, and saving time. Often the products or services you purchase with rational motives are expensive. You can be swayed to purchase computer equipment because it is more powerful, faster, has more memory, includes a wireless modem, and has the best graphics. These are all attributes that affect the function of the computer. Automobile purchases are rational decisions when you consider features such as price, gas mileage, warranties, or extended mileage protection packages. But rational motives can turn into emotional motives when you really want that red Corvette.

Business people try to avoid basing purchases on emotional motives. It does not make good business sense. They base their purchasing decisions on rational motives. The best price, fastest delivery, best credit terms, and reliable products are rational motives that appeal to business consumers.

PATRONAGE MOTIVES

The third type of consumer motivation is the patronage motive. **Patronage motives** are based on loyalty. They encourage consumers to purchase at a particular business or to buy a particular brand. Consumers develop patronage motives for various reasons. They might like the low prices, high quality, friendly staff, great customer service or convenient location. Patronage purchasing is not limited to large, expensive purchases. It can involve a grocery store, gas station, hair stylist, department store, or brand of vegetables. The important point to remember is people who are motivated by patronage are very loyal to the product, service, or brand. Businesses encourage and cultivate patronage motives so they will have less competition.

Describe the different consumer buying motives.

BUYING
BEHAVIOR

The decision processes and actions of consumers as they buy and use services and products are known as **buying behavior**. Marketers know it is advantageous to understand the process customers go through when selecting goods or services so they can assist the customers in making the best possible decisions.

THE CONSUMER DECISION-MAKING PROCESS

A consumer goes through five steps when making a purchase decision, as shown in Figure 6-2. The consumer decision-making process is the process by which consumers collect information and make choices among alternatives. Decision-making, as it applies to a specific purchase, moves through problem recognition, information search, alternative evaluation, purchase, and postpurchase evaluation.

Problem Recognition First the consumer must recognize a need, desire, or problem. For example, in order to play the

piano, you recognize the need to find a good piano instructor. Once you recognize the need, you are on the decision-making path to buy a product or service.

Information Search Next the consumer gathers information about alternative solutions. After you recognize the need to hire a piano instructor, you talk to your parents, teachers, or friends about piano teachers. You might look through the phone book or search the classified section of the newspaper. You might check the bulletin boards at the library. You might ask at a music store or call the music department of the local college.

Evaluation of Alternatives After gathering information the consumer evaluates the various alternatives to determine which is best. Sometimes this involves summarizing the information, comparing the pros and cons of each choice, making trade-offs between price and various options, and ranking the alternatives. Evaluating piano instructors might involve determining whom you can afford, what hours the instructor is available, how you will get to the lesson, and the reputation of each instructor. Based on these evaluations, you will make a decision.

FIGURE 6-2
The consumer decision-making process describes how consumers make purchasing decisions.

The Decision-Making Process

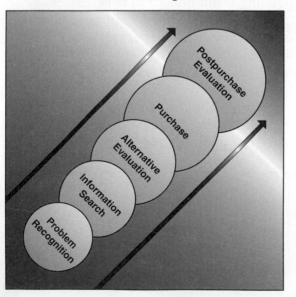

Purchase If a suitable choice is available, the consumer selects the product or service from the alternatives and makes the purchase. At this stage you have decided to take lessons at the local music store for half an hour every week. You call the instructor and register for a convenient time.

Postpurchase Evaluation At this point the consumer judges the satisfaction or dissatisfaction with the product or service purchased. You have now had several lessons, can play some simple songs, have worked with the instructor, and can tell how lessons are fitting into your schedule. If you are satisfied with your lessons, you will probably continue and may recommend your instructor to your family and friends. If you are dissatisfied, you will probably find a new instructor or quit taking lessons.

Recently, marketers have been paying more attention to postpurchase satisfaction. Toll-free telephone numbers for customer service departments let consumers easily call and ask questions or express concerns. Businesses strive to be responsive to consumer concerns by providing this service. The goal is to resolve customers' concerns and increase their satisfaction.

REACHING THE HISPANIC MARKET

The Spanish-speaking population of the United States is growing at a steady rate. There is no one formula for marketing to Hispanics, a diverse and dynamic cultural group. However, language, values, lifestyles, and social systems that are shared by the Hispanic culture can influence promotional strategies.

Hispanic respondents in focus groups tested advertisements for several products and services. The results showed that some important techniques for reaching Hispanics include testimonials, expressions of happiness, family, and the Spanish language.

Marketers who target Hispanic markets should develop promotional strategies that are responsive to the wants and needs of the consumers. While individual markets will have differences, Hispanics want recognition of their culture and values.

THINK CRITICALLY

1. What elements would you include in an advertisement targeted at the Hispanic market?

2. What types of factors would affect how you would advertise to Hispanics differently from other demographic groups?

3. Search the Internet or other resources for examples of advertisements targeting Hispanics.

What are the five stages of consumer decision-making?

1. Why do businesses try to avoid making purchases based on emotional motives?

2. Why are emotional motives such powerful motivators of so many individuals' purchasing decisions?

3. Why do businesses cultivate patronage motives in their customers and in potential customers?

4. Why is problem recognition so crucial to consumers' decision-making processes?

5. Why do you think marketers have begun to pay more attention to the postpurchase evaluation stage of the decision-making process?

Marketers need to be aware of many factors that can influence consumers' buying decisions, including personality types, social classes, cultural environments, and reference groups. How and which of those influences affect decisions depends in large part on what type of decision-making process is employed. Consumers go through three types of decision-making: routine, limited, and extensive. Marketers usually have more opportunities to sway consumers when they employ the latter two types.

List three things that you buy often and repeatedly buy the same brand. Why do you buy that particular brand? For each, list three things that would make you switch to a competitive brand.

GOALS

- Describe the influences on the consumer decision-making process.
- Explain how consumers and businesses use routine, limited, and extensive decision-making.

INFLUENCES ON THE CONSUMER DECISION-MAKING PROCESS

Knowing what influences a customer's buying decision is helpful to marketers. In order to remain profitable, businesses must provide customers with products and services that meet their wants and needs. By understanding what motivates and influences customer purchases, businesses are able to provide the products and services at the right place and the right time.

Many internal and external factors influence purchase decisions. These factors include personality, social class, cultural environment, and reference group.

Personality The first influence is personality. Personality is a well-defined, enduring pattern of behavior. Personalities influence buying decisions because everyone has individual preferences based

Breakeven Point

The breakeven point is the number of unit sales a company must make to cover the expenses of a venture. Below the breakeven point, expenses exceed revenues and a company will lose money. At the breakeven point, sales will exactly cover all expenses. Once the breakeven point is exceeded, a company will begin to make a profit.

To calculate the breakeven point, you must first find three different variables. You need to know the total fixed cost of a venture, the selling price per unit, and the variable cost per unit of a good or service. The breakeven point is the total fixed cost divided by the difference between the selling price and the variable cost per unit.

$$\text{Breakeven point} = \frac{\text{Total fixed costs}}{\text{Per unit price} - \text{per unit cost}}$$

For example, a clothing store at the mall wants to print and distribute fliers advertising their new line of sweaters. The fixed cost of the fliers is $2,400. The selling price of each sweater is $50.00 and the cost of each sweater is $10.00. The breakeven point for the flier is 60 sweaters.

$$\frac{\$2,400}{\$50.00 - \$10.00} = \frac{\$2,400}{\$40.00} = 60$$

If the store sells fewer than 60 sweaters, the store will lose money on the flier. If it sells exactly 60 sweaters, the cost of the flier will be covered exactly. If they sell more than 60, the store will make a profit.

THINK CRITICALLY

1. At the same clothing store, a display unit for jeans costs $1,800. If the jeans sell for $45.00 and cost $9.00, what is the breakeven point for the display?

2. What would be the breakeven point if the store installs a second $1,800 display unit for a different brand of jeans that sell for $54.00 and cost $18.00 each?

on their patterns of behavior. Using the example of a car purchase, personality influences the type of vehicle you prefer. You might be the flashy convertible type, the laid-back pickup truck type, or the conservative four-door sedan type. Do you prefer a particular style, color, or perhaps a certain wheel cover? All these decisions are influenced by your personality.

Social Class A second influence is social class. **Social class** refers to the lifestyle, values, and beliefs that are common to a group of people. Often social classes are identified by income level or neighborhood. Your social class affects whether you have the money or available credit to purchase a car at all and whether your choice will be acceptable to those around you. Social class exerts a strong influence on your desire for particular types and brands of goods and services.

Cultural Environment The third influence is cultural environment. **Culture** is a set of beliefs or attitudes that are passed on from generation to generation. In many parts of the United States, high school students often have a car at their disposal. This would be very different in China, where high school students rarely have access to a car.

Reference Groups **Reference groups** are groups or organizations from which you take your values and attitudes. You may currently belong to this group or you aspire to belong to it. In either case, the values of a reference group can exert a strong influence on buying behavior. Reference groups might include church groups, fraternities, work groups, civic organizations, families, or peer groups. In the case of a car purchase, you might be strongly influenced by the people in your peer group when selecting the style, model, or color.

Which of the four influences discussed in this section is an individual trait?

TYPES OF DECISION-MAKING

Consumers spend varying amounts of time and consider different factors when making decisions. It takes different decision-making skills to buy a tube of toothpaste than to buy a computer. The three types of decision-making consumers go through are routine, limited, and extensive decision-making.

Routine Decision-Making Routine decision-making is used for purchases that are made frequently and do not require much thought. For routine purchases, the consumer is familiar with the products available, often chooses the same brand repeatedly, or can make an easy substitution if the usual choice is not available. Final consumers use routine decision-making to purchase chewing gum, personal care products, and regular food purchases.

Businesses use routine decision-making when making regular purchases such as operating supplies. The business will often use one supplier and reorder from that company whenever necessary.

Limited Decision-Making Limited decision-making takes more time than routine decision-making. Often limited decision-making is associated with a product that is more expensive or is purchased less frequently. When you go to the mall to buy a pair of jeans, you might try on several styles, compare prices, and consider the fabrics of the selections before you make a decision. This is an example of limited decision-making. You need to evaluate alternatives before making a purchase.

Limited decision-making is not strictly for more-expensive items, however. If you are a Coke drinker and the store you stop at is out of Coke, what do you do? Some people easily choose another brand while others have to stop and evaluate the alternatives. Something as simple as buying a soft drink can involve limited decision-making.

Businesses use limited decision-making for many purchases, such as office equipment, furniture, fixtures, component parts, and others. For routine purchases such as supplies, limited decision-making might be used if a new supplier offers substantially lower prices or better delivery terms. Limited decision-making may be required while the purchasing agent compares the new information.

JUDGMENT CALL

The Scales Are Tipping

The United States is a nation of dieters. Diet foods, diet books, diet centers, diet therapy, diet clubs, and just plain diets are popular. Spurred by health and vanity, Americans go to great lengths to control the food and drink they consume.

However, a scientific study recently found that genes and body type, not dieting, are the keys to trimness. A National Institutes of Health panel revealed that most of the people they studied who lost weight by dieting regained the weight after five years. Many put it back on within one year.

Some marketers face legal consequences for making claims regarding the ability of their products to help consumers shed pounds. Three separate liquid diet program marketers reached agreements with the Federal Trade Commission (FTC) to settle charges that they made deceptive and unsubstantiated claims.

This anti-diet movement could have an enormous effect on the diet industry. You can be sure that marketers to the diet-conscious will be watching these developments carefully.

THINK CRITICALLY

1. What could a company do to effectively market a diet product without violating ethical guidelines?

2. Use the Internet to find companies charged with deceptive advertising. What could have been done to avoid the charges?

Extensive Decision-Making

The third type of decision-making is extensive decision-making. Extensive decision-making happens when the consumer methodically goes through all five steps of the decision-making process. Normally, extensive decision-making is for expensive purchases, like a car. Consumers do not make the decision lightly and spend time and effort evaluating alternatives and arriving at a decision.

Extensive decision-making is used in business when a purchase has not been made before or when it involves a large amount of money. Perhaps a business needs a new mainframe computer or new delivery trucks. The purchasing agent will conduct an extensive search for the best terms before a purchase decision is reached.

MARKETERS' RESPONSE

Why is this information important to marketers? Marketers want the opportunity to explain the benefits of their products and services and how they can satisfy consumer needs. When consumers stop and consider alternatives, marketers have the opportunity to explain their products through communication channels.

On the other hand, if you consistently buy the same product because you are brand-loyal, marketers want to encourage you to continue to purchase their product. They will work to insure that the product is available at the price you expect. They may even provide coupons, rebates, or other incentives to encourage continued use of the product.

Rank the decision-making types according to the time and research typically devoted to each.

Direct Mail Databases

Many businesses rely on direct mail to reach potential customers. Direct mail can include catalogs, promotional fliers, coupons, and free samples. Customers often refer to direct mailings as "junk mail." However, junk mail is big business and the technology that is required to support it is impressive.

Companies have developed a wide array of database software for storing and sorting addresses for direct mailings. In addition to a person's address, numerous pieces of data are attached. The data describes the types of products each is likely to purchase, where he or she might shop, and when a customer is likely to buy. Careful sorting of the database helps marketers determine the best time to send a piece of direct mail, and what the mailing should contain. By planning a direct mailing carefully, companies hope to maximize the sales generated, and minimize costs by weeding out customers who are unlikely to purchase.

THINK CRITICALLY

1. Describe three pieces of direct mail sent to you recently. What products were they promoting? What effect did the mailing have on your purchasing decisions?

2. Search the Internet for companies that provide direct mail database services. What services does each provide?

LESSON REVIEW

1. How might a marketer target a particular cultural group that has been identified as a large consumer of a certain product?

2. America is often referred to as a classless society. Does that mean that social class does not influence customer decision-making in the United States?

3. Under what circumstances might something that normally involves only routine decision-making suddenly require limited or even extensive decision-making?

4. Which do marketers prefer, people who use routine decision-making or more extensive decision-making?

5. How does the cost of a product correlate with the amount of time and effort spent on reaching a decision?

SUMMARY

Lesson 6.1
A. Marketers must understand consumer behavior to insure the success of a business.

B. According to Maslow's hierarchy of needs, people progress through a series of needs from physiological to security, social, esteem, and finally self-actualization.

Lesson 6.2
A. Buying motives can be emotional, rational or patronage.

B. Emotional motives are based on feelings, beliefs, or attitudes.

Rational motives are based on facts and logic. Patronage motives are based on loyalty to a particular brand or business.

Lesson 6.3
A. The decision-making process is influenced by factors such as personality, social class, culture, and reference groups.

B. Consumers make routine decisions quickly and with little thought. Extensive decision-making will be done very carefully, using much more time and information.

REVIEW MARKETING CONCEPTS

1. Marketing begins with
   a. selling a good product.
   b. understanding customers.
   c. pricing the product correctly.
   d. developing a consumer survey.

2. Dinner in a fancy restaurant and mobile telephones are usually classified as
   a. wants.
   b. needs.
   c. motives.
   d. buying decisions.

3. Maslow classified esteem needs as
   a. physical and economic safety.
   b. to realize one's potential.
   c. friends, love, and belonging.
   d. respect and recognition.

4. Motivators such as fear and guilt are classified as
   a. emotional motives.
   b. limited motives.
   c. extensive motives.
   d. affection motives.

5. Business people and purchasing agents are usually motivated by
   a. rational motives.
   b. emotional motives.
   c. buying motives.
   d. objective motives.

6. In the decision-making process, when the consumer gathers information about various products or services it is called
   a. problem recognition.
   b. information search.
   c. alternative evaluation.
   d. purchase evaluation.

7. The lifestyle, values, and beliefs that are common to a group of people is called
   a. reference group.
   b. culture.
   c. personality.
   d. social class.

8. A set of beliefs or attitudes that are passed on from generation to generation is called
   a. reference groups.
   b. social class.
   c. personality.
   d. culture.

9. When consumers choose products that they are familiar with and they often buy repeatedly, what type of decision-making do they use?
   a. The decision-making process is not necessary for these products.
   b. Limited decision-making
   c. Routine decision-making
   d. Repeated decision-making

10. When a business investigates new vendors or locates a supplier for a new component part, it uses what type of decision-making?
    a. The decision-making process is not necessary for these products.
    b. Limited decision-making
    c. Extensive decision-making
    d. Repeated decision-making

REVIEW MARKETING TERMS

Match the terms listed with the definitions. Some terms may not be used.

11. The study of consumers and how they make decisions.

12. One who buys a product or service for personal use.

13. One who buys goods and services to produce other goods and services or to resell.

14. An unfulfilled desire.

15. Anything you require to live.

16. The reasons that people buy.

17. The forces of love, affection, guilt, fear, or passion that compel consumers to buy.

18. The functional benefits to be derived from a product or service.

19. The process by which consumers collect information and make choices among alternatives.

20. Well-defined enduring patterns of behavior.

a. business consumer
b. buying behavior
c. buying motives
d. consumer behavior
e. culture
f. decision-making process
g. emotional motives
h. final consumer
i. need
j. patronage motives
k. personalities
l. rational motives
m. reference group
n. social class
o. want

APPLY MARKETING FUNCTIONS

MARKETING RESEARCH

21. In order to learn more about customers many organizations use customer feedback cards like that shown below. The organizations use that information to improve their products and services and increase customer satisfaction. An example of a customer feedback card used by a restaurant is provided.

In an effort to help your school provide better service, develop a customer feedback card to give to students at your school. The customer feedback card should be designed to find out from students what they like and dislike about your school. You may wish to ask questions about the curriculum, classes, teachers, atmosphere, spirit, extracurricular activities, grades, homework, the building, and any other items relevant to your school. Survey at least 15 students.

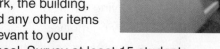

After you have completed the survey, tabulate your responses. Then find the mean, median, and mode for each question. Display the survey results in a chart or graph. Compare your results with those of your classmates and make recommendations for improvements.

22. Marketers strive to capture your attention with advertisements that use a variety of buying motives. Identify four advertisements from each of the following media: magazines, television, and radio. Two should describe emotional motives and two should describe rational motives. Clip and paste the magazine advertisements on a large piece of paper or poster board. Prepare a written description of the television ads and radio ads. Classify the type of buying motive used in each advertisement.

MARKETING PLANNING

23. Some products are sold to both business consumers and final consumers. Name at least one business consumer use and one final consumer use for each of the following items: pencils, balloons, skillet, radio, sofa, fishing lure, raisins, tractor, suitcase, and file folder. Here is an example:

Item	Business Use	Final Consumer Use
banana	restaurant	family lunches

GOOD FOOD RESTAURANT

Tell us how you like us. What did you think of our

	Poor				Excellent
Food?	1	2	3	4	5
Atmosphere?	1	2	3	4	5
Service?	1	2	3	4	5
Cleanliness?	1	2	3	4	5
Prices?	1	2	3	4	5

Thank you for sharing your views with us!

24. Telephone companies are introducing video telephones into the consumer market. Sales have been slow, because video phones are not a pressing want or need for most consumers.

Assume you are the marketing specialist for a telephone manufacturer. It is your job to develop an advertising strategy to promote video phones. Using the five steps of the decision-making process, write the advertising copy for an ad promoting video phones. After you have finished writing the ad, identify the prominent buying motive you used in the ad. Make sure you focus on an appropriate target market before you begin your work.

MARKETING MANAGEMENT

25. One of the activities of a marketing manager is to encourage the sales people to constantly keep the marketing concept in mind by paying attention to customer needs and wants. Write a letter to your sales people that reminds them of the marketing concept and motivates them to put it into action. Use the following words or phrases in your letter: customers, buying behavior, consumer decision-making process, needs, consumer behavior, wants, and final consumer. Your letter should be logical, upbeat and convincing.

20. In the past, some people thought it was unethical for marketers to exploit buying motives and the consumer decision-making process. What are your thoughts? Is identifying buying motives and using them in a promotional campaign an ethical or unethical use of marketing techniques?

Write an essay either in support of or against the use of buying motives and the decision-making process. Make sure that you use specific reasons to defend your position.

MARKETING TECHNOLOGY

27. Using Internet news services, find a corporate announcement of a new product or service. Analyze the announcement to identify which buying motives it is appealing to. Cite specific language in the announcement and explain why it appeals to the buying motive you have identified. Is the announcement aimed at businesses or final consumers? How can you tell?

28. Research the price, capacities, and important features of an expensive product that you would like to purchase, such as a car, a CD player, or a computer printer. Use a database program to keep track of information you find for each of eight different products or models. Print a copy of the research with the factual data in columns and the various models in separate rows.

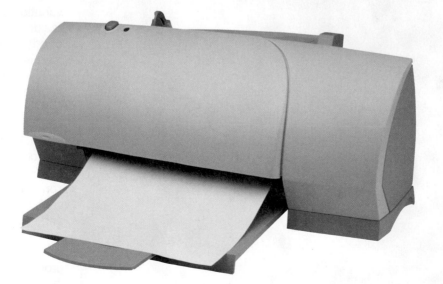

MARKETING IN ACTION

CASE STUDY

GAS STATIONS AND A WHOLE LOT MORE

The first gas stations—also known as *service* stations—offered full service to their customers. Full service included an attendant filling the vehicle with fuel, washing the windshield and windows, checking air pressure in all four tires, and making sure that oil and other fluids under the hood were at proper levels. The customer did not even have to get out of the vehicle to receive the royal treatment. Service attendants would take the money or credit card from the customer and bring back the change or receipt.

An increasingly fast-paced society demanded quicker service and more competitive prices. So, gas stations installed self-service pumps for customers who preferred to pump their own gas, at a lower price since less labor was required. Service stations became low-touch operations. The customer could simply swipe a credit card at

the pump, fill the vehicle with gas, and receive a receipt without any contact with a service attendant. Paying at the pump allows service stations to be open 24 hours a day without hiring too many employees.

Some stations continued offering full-service pumps for individuals who wanted personalized attention. And, stations began to add different kinds of services to compete for the customer's dollar.

Automated car washes were added to service stations. Customers could receive a free or inexpensive car wash when they filled their tank with gas. Service stations competed by improving the quality of car washes they offered. Customers on the go could fill their tanks and have a clean car in a matter of minutes.

As an additional convenience, ATMs (automated teller machines) were introduced at

service stations. Customers could get cash from their accounts while filling up the car with gas. ATMs at service stations provided convenience for travelers on vacation or for local residents when banks or other financial institutions were closed.

Service stations soon became one-stop fuel and food convenience stores. Not only did they sell good munchies for the road, they also sold basic convenience items such as milk, bread, and soup. Prices for the convenience items were higher than at grocery stores, since the service stations

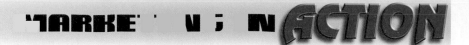
only carried small quantities. Residents of small communities could rely on service stations being open when grocery stores were closed.

The next phase for stations was the addition of fast food outlets. Service stations added scaled-down versions of Burger King, McDonald's, A & W, and Taco Bell. Some service stations even have small food courts consisting of fast food vendors such as Burger King, Kentucky Fried Chicken, and Taco Bell that are all owned by the same parent corporation. The hungry traveler can now make a quick stop for fuel and food.

All of the extra services offered by gas stations require appropriate maintenance to keep the customer happy. For example, gas pumps must be in proper working order, and customers should always receive receipts when they pay outside with a credit card at the pump. Convenience stores must be well-stocked, and restaurants must be well-run. Rising gas prices also raise customer expectations.

THINK CRITICALLY

1. Draw a timeline showing the history of service stations.

2. What do you project to be the next innovation for service stations? Why?

3. What special challenges are faced by a service station that sells fast food?

http://www.deca.org/publications/HS_Guide/guidetoc.html

VEHICLES AND PETROLEUM ROLE PLAY

DECA PREP

You are the assistant manager for a popular service station in your community. The recently added pumps that allow customers to pay with credit cards at the pump are very popular. Unfortunately, many of the pumps need repair because they do not read the credit cards correctly and/or they do not give the customer a receipt.

You have listened to many angry customers complain about having to come inside to pay for their gas. Some customers have even indicated that they will take their business to a competitor.

Your task is two-fold—you must convince the owner of the station to repair the gas pumps immediately, and you must come up with a special promotion to bring back loyal customers to your service station. You will present your proposal to the owner of the service station.

DESCRIPTION OF THE PROPOSAL
Write down the main points that you want to emphasize to the owner of the service station.

DESCRIPTION OF PROMOTION PLAN
Outline your plan for a promotion to keep loyal customers coming to your service station. Remember, they are upset with the "pay at the pump" service.

ROLE PLAY Translate what you have learned into effective, efficient, and spontaneous action, demonstrated in a role play.

CHAPTER 7

COMPETITION IS EVERYWHERE

LESSON 7.1 *TARGETING MARKET SEGMENTS*

LESSON 7.2 *POSITIONING FOR COMPETITIVE ADVANTAGE*

LESSON 7.3 *COMPETING FOR MARKET SEGMENTS*

LESSON 7.4 *LEARNING ABOUT THE COMPETITION*

NEWSLINE

SATURN STALLS BUT STILL PLEASES

General Motors' import-fighting Saturn division was so hot in the early 1990s that the Spring Hill, Tenn., factory couldn't keep up with the demand. Boasting a high-quality product and a revolutionary no-haggle sales force, Saturn dealers were selling automobiles at twice the rate of the nearest competitor, far exceeding GM's expectations.

As foreign competitors flooded the U.S. market, Saturn met them head-on. Almost overnight, Saturn became the highest quality American-made brand, with as few defects as the best imports.

GM clearly had a winner on its hands, but it forced some tough decisions at headquarters. To keep up the momentum, GM needed to pump more money into product development, money that would cut into other divisions' budgets. They objected, and Saturn had to make do. As a result, imports kept coming with innovative new products, while Saturn stalled in mid-decade.

By 2000, Saturn finally had new products in the pipeline thanks to a $1.5 billion infusion from GM. It remained to be seen if it could recapture its earlier sales momentum, however, as inventory buildup forced production cutbacks and layoffs. One thing that hadn't changed, though, was Saturn buyers' satisfaction with Saturn dealers. The division placed first among all makes in the J.D. Power sales satisfaction survey for the fifth time in six years.

Automobile Sales Satisfaction Rating

Car	Score	Car	Score
Saturn	143	Land Rover	138
Cadillac	141	Mercedes-Benz	138
Lexus	141	Volvo	138
Infiniti	139	Jaguar	137
Buick	138	Oldsmobile	137

Industry Average 124

THINK CRITICALLY

1. Why do you think other GM divisions balked at pumping more money into Saturn's product development?

2. If a business has some product lines that are surging and others that are in a slump, which lines should get preferential treatment when limited marketing funds are allocated?

CORPORATE VIEW

CAREER OPPORTUNITY
LARGE ACCOUNT SALES MANAGER

POINT YOUR BROWSER
www.corpview.com

This position has a base salary and benefits. Commissions and bonuses are awarded based on successful and profitable large account management.

TeleView is looking for someone who possesses the following attributes.

- Dynamic leader who can motivate others
- Excellent interpersonal and customer relations skills
- Strong problem solving, project organization, and time management skills
- Drive and flexibility
- Technical communications skills
- Ability to organize and multitask
- Ability to work in an invigorating, team-oriented environment

The main responsibilities of the job include the following.

- Work with large corporate accounts to sell volume product bundles
- Help organize and participate in international, national, and regional trade shows
- Create demand for TeleView products
- Work with the Brand Marketing Workgroup to extend the brand-name recognition of TeleView and Corporate View brands
- Create seminars, use press kits, organize field marketing events
- Share press releases with corporate decision makers
- Prepare corporate and executive briefings
- Partner with other regional and local events and otherwise build demand for TeleView products with large volume accounts
- Be able to demonstrate the TeleView product line

The job requires the following education, skills, and experience.

- Associate degree minimum, B.S. or equivalent preferred
- Two years sales experience, or one year TeleView Customer Support, required
- Prior sales experience with electronics and telecommunications products preferred
- Must be able to research the Internet and use e-mail
- Must know PowerPoint and video conferencing software
- Strong presentation skills required

THINK CRITICALLY

1. Prepare a resume written by a person who is qualified for this job and interested in applying for it.

2. Which parts of this job appeal to you? Which do not?

3. Search want ads or the Internet for a job similar to TeleView's large account sales manager. What type of compensation package is being offered for the job?

- **Describe how markets can be segmented by geographic location, demographic characteristics, psychographics, product usage, and benefits derived.**

- **Explain how to evaluate market potential and calculate market share.**

Businesses focus their marketing efforts to target those potential customers who are most likely to buy their products. To do so, they identify market segments or groups of consumers that share certain characteristics. Factors commonly used to segment markets include geography, demographic characteristics, psychographics, frequency of product usage, and the benefits derived from using a product. Once distinct market segments have been identified, businesses analyze them to determine which present the best opportunities. Then they choose which segments to target based on potential market share.

Make a list of six characteristics that you possess that you think would be important if you were shopping for a new car. How would each of those characteristics affect your purchasing decision?

IDENTIFYING MARKET SEGMENTS

When businesses compete, they gather their resources and put them together toward achieving a specific goal. They devise marketing strategies to compete for sales dollars, customers, market share, or whatever goal they have set. Market segments play a significant role in determining competition strategies.

A **market segment** is a group of individuals or organizations within a larger market that share one or more important characteristics. The characteristics of the market segment result in similar product or service needs. Everyone belongs to many segments. You may belong to a segment of the population who own a CD player and enjoy rock music. You might also belong to a segment that drinks a certain brand of cola or prefers to drive a certain type of car. In school, you belong to various segments depending on how you dress, how you spend your leisure time, or even the importance you place on school and grades.

Businesses use market segmentation to focus their marketing efforts. Consumers can be divided into specific, well-defined segments based on geographic location, demographic characteristics, psychographics, product usage, and benefits derived.

GEOGRAPHIC SEGMENTATION

Geographic segmentation refers to dividing consumers into markets based on where they live. These markets might be as large as a country or as small as a ZIP code designation. Remember that companies vary in size and scope and therefore the group of customers they want to reach also varies in size.

Geographic segmentation is based on the concept that for certain products, people who live in the same geographic area might have the same wants and needs. Consumers who live in Minnesota are more likely to have an interest in cold weather sports than people who live in Oklahoma. A member of a state House of Representatives might want to send a newsletter to the constituents in his or her district. This market could easily be segmented by ZIP codes.

DEMOGRAPHIC CHARACTERISTICS

Demographics refer to the descriptive characteristics of a market such as age, gender, race, income, and educational level. Figure 7-1 shows different demographic segments in the United States. Often marketers want to serve a market segment that has similar demographic characteristics. Shavers for women, skin care products for teenagers, and hair restoration products for balding men are marketed to specific demographic groups. You belong to many demographic marketing segments. Marketers have segmented you according to your age, gender, ethnic group, hair color, and possibly even your height. They have designed products that meet your needs in each of these categories.

PSYCHOGRAPHICS

Psychographics refers to people's interests and values. You are segmented psychographically by the way you spend your time and make your lifestyle choices. Psychographic segmentation is responsible for bowling alleys, sports stores, swimming pools, big screen televisions, and religious bookstores. Do you visit arcades, miniature golf, or teen centers? These products are available because business people have found segments with wants and needs that are satisfied by these products and services.

FIGURE 7-1
In the U.S. population, the demographic characteristics of education and income are closely linked.

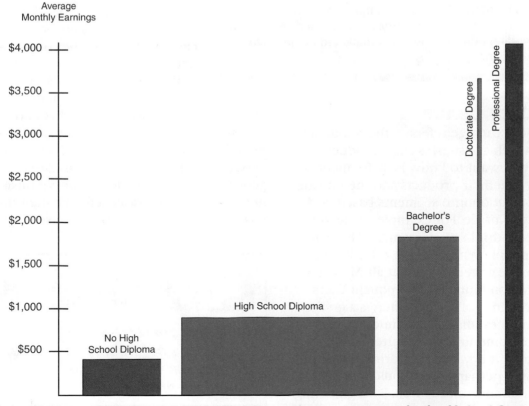

Demographic Segmentation by Education and Income in the United States

One Brand or Many?

The global economy has created quite a dilemma for global marketers. Essentially they have two choices, either support a multitude of local brands, many of which are already well established but targeted to narrow geographic market segments, or create international brands whose appeal reaches across national borders and cultural differences. Either approach is full of potential pitfalls.

Supporting lots of different local brands can be a marketing management nightmare, because each brand requires a distinct marketing mix. On a global scale, that means keeping tabs on countless permutations, or, maybe worse from a senior manager's perspective, coordinating hundreds of local marketing managers.

Creating and supporting truly global brands, however, is no simple task. In many cases, people have become quite attached to local brands. When Germany's Daimler-Benz and Chrysler merged in the late 1990s to create a family of global car brands, it initially stumbled over deep cultural differences between the two organizations. Daimler Chrysler's German chairman said a key problem was differing approaches to marketing. Americans were more apt to move quickly on a seemingly good concept and the cautious Germans preferred more research before acting.

THINK CRITICALLY

Pick a well-known international brand. Use the Internet to research how it is marketed in another country. How does it differ from the way it is marketed in the United States?

PRODUCT USAGE

Product usage refers to the frequency with which consumers use a product. Marketers want to know how frequently people use their products and then divide the population into segments based on frequency of usage. For example, some people drink soft drinks at every meal. There are other people who drink soft drinks once a day, once a week, or not at all. Marketers want to communicate to frequent users that drinking soft drinks often is a great idea and they should continue. Marketers want to communicate to infrequent users how great it is when they drink the soft drink and perhaps they would like to have the experience more often. By segmenting the market based on usage, business people approach each group differently.

BENEFITS DERIVED

As you learned earlier, each product or service on the market has a value or utility to the consumer. The **benefits derived segmentation** technique divides the population into groups depending on the value they receive from the product or service. An example is shampoo. A visit to your local drug store should convince you that there are many market segments for a product as simple as shampoo. There are segments for consumers with oily hair, dry hair, normal hair, or possibly somewhere in between. There are shampoos for people with dandruff or dry scalps. There are an equal variety of creme rinses on the market and even shampoos with creme rinse added for people who want one-step hair care. Add the number of products on the market to the variety within each product category and you can see the infinite number of segments that are created by benefits derived.

Just as marketers segment the consumer markets, they also segment business markets. Business markets are segmented by geographic location, the size of the business, the key criteria used in making purchasing decisions, or purchasing strategies.

Name five characteristics that businesses commonly use to define distinct market segments for consumer products.

ANALYZING
MARKET SEGMENTS

Once market segments have been identified, they must be analyzed. Not all segments present a marketing opportunity. Businesses select market segments that become the focus of their marketing efforts as shown in Figure 7-2. Market segments should be evaluated on the following criteria:

1. Number of potential consumers
2. Interest in the product or service and other mix elements
3. Money available to make the purchase
4. Ability to communicate with consumers through the promotional mix

Since businesses operate to make a profit, it is important to estimate the value of each market segment. This is called the market potential. The **market potential** is the total revenue that can be obtained from the market segment. Since it is unlikely that one company will attract all customers in a given market, businesses also calculate their market share. **Market share** is the portion of the total market potential that each company expects to get in relation to its competitors. Market share is usually expressed in dollars or percentages.

A typical marketing objective is to increase or maintain current market share. For example, the total market potential for 35mm film in Boise, Idaho is $3,000,000 per year. Kodak estimates that it can convince 75 percent of the total market to buy its brand. To calculate Kodak's estimated market share in Boise, multiply $3,000,000 by 0.75 for a figure of $2,250,000.

Kodak can also determine the market potential by units instead of dollars. Since the market potential is $3,000,000 and film

FIGURE 7-2

A company that sells expensive ski equipment through specialty ski shops at ski resorts would be interested in targeting consumers who they can communicate with, who have the income to support the purchase, and who will be shopping at ski resort shops.

Market Segment Analysis

People Who Like to Ski

People Who Vacation at Ski Resorts

People Who Read Ski Magazines

People With Annual Income Over $50,000

FIGURE THIS
1234567890

Rule of 72 Makes Quick Work of Projections

Calculating market share is not always as simple as it looks, even when companies have information about the current size and spending habits of a market segment they want to target. That's because market segments are always shifting, and businesses want to target those that are growing or that can be made to grow if the right stimulants are applied.

What's really important is not how big the segment is today, but how big it will be in five or 10 years. In other words, how fast can it grow?

The Rule of 72 is a simple tool that can be used to quickly estimate how fast a market share can be doubled, assuming a constant rate of annual growth. Here's the formula, where Rate is the annual rate of growth and Years is the number of years needed to double a beginning value: Years = 72 ÷ Rate.

Put the other way around, it can also tell you how fast a market needs to grow if a business wants it to double in a given number of years. In that case the formula is: Rate = 72 ÷ Years.

The Rule of 72 works well for rates of growth up to about 20% per year. For rates ranging from 20% to 36%, substitute 78 for the 72 in the above formulas.

THINK CRITICALLY

1. If Samco Inc. wants to double its Midwest sales in five years to justify a new warehouse, how fast must sales grow each year?

2. If it wants to double them in three years, what rate of growth is required?

3. If Samco's marketing manager estimates that segment sales will grow 12% annually indefinitely, how long will it take to double sales? How long will it take to quadruple sales?

has an average price of $5 per roll, the market potential in units is $3,000,000 ÷ $5 = 600,000 rolls of film. Kodak's estimated market share is 75 percent of 600,000 rolls, for a figure of 450,000 rolls of film (600,000 × 0.75 = 450,000). Kodak has the potential of selling 450,000 rolls of film in this market segment in Boise, Idaho.

checkpoint

Why is it necessary for a business to target consumers that it can communicate with effectively?

LESSON REVIEW

1. Why would a marketer want to focus on a narrow market segment rather than aim for a much broader market that encompasses many more potential buyers?

2. Name four common ways to segment people geographically.

3. How do psychographics differ from demographic characteristics?

4. What are some ways that marketers might determine how much money people in a market segment have available to make purchases of their products or services?

5. If a company currently sells $1 million of goods in a market and estimates that a new innovation will double the potential market to $10 million and triple the percentage of the market it now has, what would be its estimated future market share in dollars?

POSITIONING FOR COMPETITIVE ADVANTAGE

Businesses know that people usually consider a number of products or services as alternatives when they try to satisfy specific needs. Marketers develop methods based on marketing mix elements to influence how a product or service is perceived. Three common strategies emphasize consumer perceptions, competition, and changes in the business environment.

Make a list of a popular model of car, a brand of jeans, a restaurant, a retail chain, and a line of consumer electronics, and write a one-line description of each comparing it to its competitors.

- **Explain the various bases for positioning a product to distinguish it from the competition.**
- **Describe the three common positioning strategies.**

BASES FOR POSITIONING

Positioning is done to highlight differences between competitors in the mind of the consumer that may influence purchases. **Market position** refers to the unique image of a product or service in a consumer's mind relative to similar competitive offerings. What methods can effectively create market positions? Firms use a variety of methods for positioning: attribute, price and quality, use or application, product user, product classification, and competitor as shown in Figure 7-3.

FIGURE 7-3

Competitors develop marketing mixes that emphasize the market positions of their products. These laundry products are clearly positioned to appeal to different target markets.

MARKET POSITION		
	Laundry Product A	**Laundry Product B**
Attribute	Cleans quickly and easily	Leaves fresh scent
Price and Quality	Low price, good value	Higher price for highest quality
Use or Application	Use as pre-wash on tough stains	Use for hand-washing sweaters and delicates
Product User	Homemaker's reliable friend	New generation's discovery
Product Classification	Used by Olympic athletes	Used by professional laundries
Competitor	Gets out dirt Product B can't	Gentler on clothing than Product A

Attribute One way of positioning a product is to highlight a product feature or attribute. For example, certain toothpastes have ingredients that whiten teeth. The manufacturer says "Our toothpaste does everything every other toothpaste does, and in addition it helps make your teeth white." The positioning is accomplished with product characteristics and related promotion.

Price and Quality This position strategy may stress high price as a sign of quality, or emphasize low price as an indication of value. Mercedes Benz doesn't apologize for the high price of its automobiles. Instead, it suggests that because they are high-priced they are high quality. Wal-Mart suggests that its products are as good as or better than anybody else's plus they are available for lower prices. Again, the positioning is accomplished by creating the desired level of quality in the product and establishing an appropriate price.

Use or Application Stressing unique uses or applications can be an effective means of positioning a product. Arm & Hammer stresses uses for its baking soda in addition to being an ingredient in baking recipes. Many consumers now believe that Arm & Hammer baking soda is an effective product with uses ranging from deodorizing your refrigerator to brushing your teeth.

Product User This positioning strategy encourages use of a product or service by associating a personality or type of user with the product. Pepsi Cola for a time suggested that Pepsi products were consumed by a "Pepsi Generation," and this generation was portrayed as young and active.

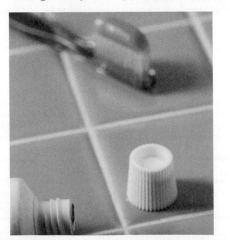

Marketers Reap New Data

The compilation of huge databases of household purchasing data is having a big impact on the way manufacturers of consumer goods allocate their marketing budgets. While it has long been easy to gauge the short-term effectiveness of marketing campaigns by analyzing data from checkout scanners, the ability to access household data now gives marketers a keen insight into long-term effects.

Household purchasing information is collected every time someone uses a frequent shopper or loyalty card. Supermarkets and discount stores make extensive use of them to encourage repeat shopping with discounts, rebates, and other promotions tied to use of the cards. With transactions identifiable by household, marketers can now piece together strings of household purchases over time.

For example, when people buy a product in response to some promotional stimulus— ad campaigns, direct mail, coupons, etc.— marketers can determine how many of them were first-time buyers; how many people continue to buy the product after trying it; how much time elapses before people buy again; and what other products the households buy or stop buying.

Marketers have long known that promotions have both short- and long-term effects on consumer buying, but until recently they could only guess at the long-term impact. Now they're getting some hard numbers.

THINK CRITICALLY

1. If a business finds that an ad campaign boosts sales by 5% over the following three months, but that 90% of new buyers continue to buy it over the next 12 months, how might that affect its marketing strategy?

2. If $2-off coupons increase monthly sales by 50%, but only one out of 10 coupon users buys the product again in the next 12 months, how might that affect a business's marketing strategy?

Product Classification   When positioning according to product class, the objective is to associate the product with a particular category of products. Railroads, for example, attempt to imitate the look, service, and scheduling associated with airlines. Pork, marketed as the "other white meat," is positioned with turkey and chicken to create an image of a healthier, leaner product.

Competitor   Sometimes marketers make an effort to demonstrate how they are positioned against competitors that hold a strong market position. Seven-Up's "Uncola Campaign" is a good example of an effort to position its product against cola soft drinks.

Anytime you see an advertisement comparing one product against one or more competitors' products or services, you can assume that a competitor positioning strategy is being used.

What are the six common bases for positioning discussed in this section? Give an example of a well-known product or service that exemplifies one of these bases.

SELECTING A
POSITIONING STRATEGY

All businesses need to develop a positioning strategy. A positioning strategy will outline how a company is going to present its product or service to the consumer and how it will compete in the marketplace. Positioning strategies usually revolve around three major areas:

1. Consumer perceptions
2. Competitors in the marketplace
3. Changes in the business environment

★★★★★★★★★★★
JUDGMENT CALL

Package Size Serves Multiple Purposes

Package size is an important part of the marketing mix for consumer goods, and it can also be crucial to a positioning strategy. Large economy-size packages may appeal to one group of people, while convenience sizes can reach a completely different segment.

Package size is strongly influenced by market standards. Twelve-ounce soft drink cans, for example, are standard because that's what consumers are used to, that's what fits into vending machines, and that's what can manufacturers are tooled to produce.

Sometimes, however, package size is also a function of the price consumers are willing to pay. If businesses think that consumers will resist a higher price they can adjust the size instead and achieve the desired price indirectly. It's particularly effective for goods that people buy in packages that are used up over a period of time. If a company reduces the size of a jar of pickles from 16 oz. to 14 oz., consumers are not likely to eat fewer pickles. Rather, they'll keep eating the same amount and buy jars a bit more frequently.

Consumer advocates often object when companies reduce sizes and keep the same price, because consumers may not notice and the price increase is hidden. Companies contend they're just trying to achieve a marketing mix that consumers want.

THINK CRITICALLY
1. If gas stations started selling gasoline in fluctuating fractions of gallons in order to cushion big swings in wholesale prices, what effect would it likely have on consumers?

CONSUMER PERCEPTIONS

Consumer perceptions are the images consumers have of competing goods and services in the marketplace. The objective is for marketers to position their products so that they appeal to the desires and perceptions of a target market. A group of consumers that has a distinct idea of the image desired for a product or service might represent a target market. A firm will do well when consumers perceive the attributes of its products as being close to the consumers' ideal image. Over the years, Hershey has done an excellent job of responding to consumer perceptions. Hershey produces a product perceived by many consumers as an ideal chocolate bar.

COMPETITION

Businesses are concerned about the perception consumers have of an organization in relation to its competitors. The ideal situation is when consumers perceive a business's products to be superior to its competitor's products or services.

A great deal of marketing effort is used in competitive positioning. The pricing, promotion, product development, and distribution strategies are all planned with an eye toward the competition. Certain products, such as soft drinks, must be carefully positioned in relation to competition because image is so important to consumers as they choose a brand. Coca-Cola and Pepsi Cola have staged a very fierce and competitive promotional battle in recent years to gain a stronger competitive position. This competition has been referred to as the "Cola Wars."

BUSINESS ENVIRONMENT

Organizations must be aware of changes in the business environment that might affect the position of its products or services. These include new products coming onto the market, changing consumer needs, new technology, negative publicity, and resource availability. Manufacturers of golf clubs have been significantly affected by the introduction of graphite as a material used in shaft construction. Ice cream companies

are well aware of the effects of fat in diets. Colleges have discovered that they must respond to the needs of non-traditional students. In each case, these business environment changes can affect the way in which goods and services are positioned.

What aspects of the market do the three major positioning strategies address?

1. Which basis or bases for positioning are illustrated by an online investment brokerage that promotes inexpensive stock trades?

2. Which basis or bases for positioning are illustrated by a sport utility vehicle with a luxury-car interior?

3. When the dairy industry runs ads showing famous athletes with milk mustaches, what positioning strategy is it employing?

4. Why might a company want to position its product as lower quality?

5. What kinds of cars do consumers generally regard as ideal?

6. How do companies in rapidly evolving fields such as information technology position themselves as superior when the industry benchmarks are constantly moving?

COMPETING FOR MARKET SEGMENTS

MARKETING MATTERS

Market segments are important because they contain the potential customers for marketers' products. Competition is the rivalry between two or more businesses to secure a dominant position in a market segment. Businesses compete for consumers' scarce dollars, and in doing so they face two types of competition when positioning their products—direct versus indirect competition, and price versus non-price competition.

They succeed by developing products that meet a market segment's wants and needs, and thereby benefit themselves as well as consumers.

List two products that you buy regularly that have been improved in the past year. What competing products are on the market? Now list two products that have not been improved in the past year, and note any competing products again. Which of these products faces the most competition?

GOALS

● Explain direct vs. indirect competition and price vs. non-price competition.

● Describe the benefits of competition to consumers.

TYPES OF COMPETITION
FOR POSITIONING

Just as there are different types of market segments and positioning strategies, there are different types of competition businesses face when positioning their products. Successful competitive strategies rely on the ability of the business to define a market position and reach a market segment. There are two major types of competition, direct versus indirect competition and price versus non-price competition.

FIGURE 7-4
Shoe stores compete directly with each other in large malls. At the same time, shoe stores compete indirectly with music stores for consumer dollars.

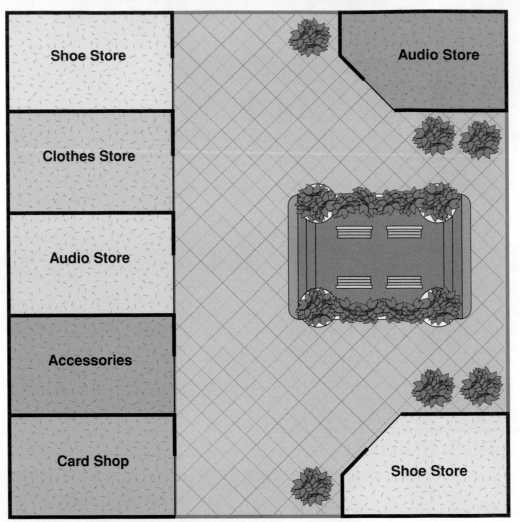

DIRECT AND INDIRECT COMPETITION

Direct competition is competition in a market segment with businesses that offer the same type of product or service. This is a common form of competition. For example, Holiday Inn and Ramada Inn compete directly with each other. Another example is laundry detergent advertisements where the two leading brands are compared by name. This is direct competition. Figure 7-4 shows different businesses in direct and indirect competition with each other.

Businesses that decide to compete directly must first decide who their competitors are. For example, McDonald's has obvious competitors such as Hardee's, Burger King, and Wendy's. It also competes against other fast food restaurants such as KFC, Taco Bell, and locally owned fast food restaurants. These are all direct competitors even though they may offer different menu items.

McDonald's competes head-on with those businesses. It tells consumers why Big Macs taste better, are economical, and easily available. McDonald's lets consumers know why they should buy McDonald's products rather than someone else's.

Indirect competition occurs when a business competes with a product that is outside its product classification group. For example, if McDonald's promotes its products as easy and convenient to obtain, then it might be in competition with meals offered at the deli counters of many grocery stores. McDonald's might also find itself competing with microwaveable meals. Remember that you have limited dollars to spend on a meal, and you only want to eat one lunch a day. How does McDonald's compete with all these similar businesses in the marketplace?

The marketing managers at McDonald's have some important decisions to make. One of the first decisions they must make is what features of their products they wish to highlight or what benefits they wish to emphasize. Remember that each market segment places value on different things, and each business must appeal to the characteristics of that segment.

E-Commerce Cools Off, Grows Up

When the price of Internet stocks dropped precipitously in the spring of 2000, many people saw it as a signal that the e-commerce boom of the late 1990s was over. Money that had been rushing into the market to back the most speculative of e-commerce ventures just as suddenly pulled out. Investors seemingly had rediscovered their affinity for profits . . . at least somewhere on the financial horizon.

Three of the most successful Internet-based dot.coms, however, performed quite well in 2000 despite experiencing sharp sell-offs in the stock market. Amazon, Yahoo!, and eBay all posted impressive revenue increases and improved fundamentals even with the loss of substantial dot.com ad revenues.

What the markets may have been implying was that, while e-commerce certainly is here to stay, as Internet businesses outgrow their dot.com roots they will increasingly be valued in ways similar to non-Internet companies. Whatever their market worth, Amazon, Yahoo!, and eBay have established themselves as viable e-business models that will persist long after the dot.com boom has settled into something akin to maturity.

THINK CRITICALLY

1. What types of direct and indirect competition do Amazon, Yahoo!, and eBay face from Internet and non-Internet competitors?

2. What advantages does the Internet give them compared to competitors that are based on more traditional business models, such as brick-and-mortar retailers, print and broadcast media outlets, and traditional auction houses and trading markets?

GOALS

- Discuss the types of information businesses need to know about their competitors.
- Describe the kinds of activities businesses engage in to gain marketing intelligence.

In order to compete effectively, businesses find out all they can about the competition. Athletic teams have used scouts for many years. They attend the competitor's games to analyze their strategies, tactics, strengths, and weaknesses. The information is used to prepare their own teams to be more effective competitors.

The same is true in business. In order to compete effectively, businesses make an effort to learn as much as they can about their competitors. To do so they engage in what is known as marketing intelligence.

Let's say you are given an assignment to observe a business in your area and write a report on its pricing strategy, distribution system, product/service planning, promotional strategy, and market position. What are the best sources of such information?

TYPES OF INFORMATION

All marketers develop each element of the marketing mix to best meet the wants and needs of their consumers. It is helpful for businesses to know how competitors are developing each element of the marketing mix and what strategies and tactics they are going to implement.

Price When businesses are in direct competition, they need to know competitors' pricing strategies. Are competitors planning a sale or are they going to raise the price and add features, options, or additional services? For example, if Chrysler reduces the price of all of its cars and trucks so there is a significant difference between their prices and the competitors', will that cause the consumer to consistently choose Chrysler brands over other brands? For some people, the answer would be yes, because for that segment, price is the most significant factor. For others, the answer would be no because there is a value in a variety of automobile features that causes them to buy the competitors' products regardless of price.

Distribution The second area to gain information about is competitors' distribution systems. Do they have wide distribution or selective distribution? Are they planning to change their distribution strategies? Part of satisfying the wants and needs of the consumer is to have the product in the right place when the customer wants to purchase it. If the competition is planning on distribution changes, their products might be more convenient to purchase than yours. It is important to know what distribution strategies your competition is planning.

Product/Service Planning The third type of information is the product/service planning process. Is your competition planning a new product introduction and do you have a product to compete effectively with it? When Pepsi introduced a clear cola, Coke did not put a comparable product on the market to compete with it. Possibly they decided it was not a significant competitor because the market segment was not large enough, or they believed the product would not succeed. It is important to know what changes and additions your competition is making in their product line.

Promotion A fourth area that is important to gather competitive information about is promotional strategies. Are they planning a large campaign or new tactics, using a new medium, or changing the times they advertise? When Sears puts coupons for carpet cleaning in newspapers, it affects the competition's business. If the competition is aware that Sears is planning this tactic, they can counter with coupons of their own or other offers that will keep them equally competitive.

GET THE MESSAGE

Outdoor Ads Attracting More Attention

With the proliferation of electronic media in the past decade, it seems paradoxical that outdoor advertising was one of the fastest-growing media for advertising and promotions. Revenues paid for the use of billboards, transit signs, banners, and other outdoor displays rose by nearly 10% per year in the 1990s.

Outdoor advertising companies boast simultaneously that they are the last "broadcast" media and also that they are the most effective at targeting narrow market segments. With all the noise created by so many electronic media, perhaps outdoor's biggest strength has been that people cannot turn it off whenever they choose. People can't help but see a billboard every time they pass it or get stuck in front of it on their way home in a rush hour traffic jam.

Outdoor advertising used to be dominated by cigarettes and alcohol, which accounted for more than half of outdoor revenues in 1979. By the 1990s, that share had dwindled to less than 15% and other industries had taken over. A study of the U.K. market in 2000 revealed that outdoor was used by 93% of the top 200 advertisers compared with just 35% a decade earlier. Creativity, low cost, and the ability to target were viewed as the medium's key strengths.

THINK CRITICALLY

1. How is outdoor advertising able to target narrow market segments effectively?

2. In what sense is outdoor advertising the last "broadcast" media?

Competitor's Market Position

There are additional factors that affect each business' competitive edge. For example, is the competition planning to enter markets in other countries? Has the competition located a new and unserved market segment? Can your company reach that market segment?

Is the competition in a good financial position? Do they have the funds available to spend on effective promotional strategies? Do they have the money available to develop new products and improve old ones? Do they have the financial flexibility to respond to pricing changes? Have your competitors located new suppliers that will make a significant difference in how their product is produced, how quickly it can be delivered, or how much it costs?

All of these factors significantly affect the competitive position among businesses. They can make the difference between success of a product or service in the marketplace or failure.

What are the five types of information that businesses need to know about their competitors?

SOURCES OF INFORMATION

Competing companies are not going to willingly exchange essential competitive information. Competing businesses must therefore find ways of obtaining information, as in Figure 7-5. Sometimes it is fairly easy and sometimes it is difficult. The process of gaining competitive market information is called **marketing intelligence**.

FIGURE 7–5
A business gains information about its competitor's strategy in order to compete more effectively and better serve its target market.

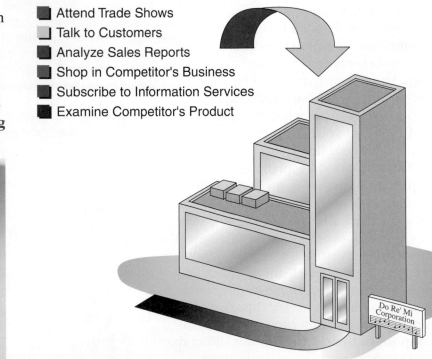

Marketing Intelligence

- Attend Trade Shows
- Talk to Customers
- Analyze Sales Reports
- Shop in Competitor's Business
- Subscribe to Information Services
- Examine Competitor's Product

Businesses engage in the following activities to gain information about their competition:

1. Ask salespeople to be alert to information about competitors' products, prices, and anticipated changes.
2. Buy competitors' products. In this way they can examine the products carefully and learn from studying them.
3. Shop in competitors' businesses or hire consultants to shop for them. It is well known that competitors are in and out of one another's businesses frequently, seeking information about pricing, promotion, and other strategies.
4. Subscribe to information services. There are business services that provide information about the activities of companies in an industry. Trade associations are a good example of this. The National Restaurant Management Association and the National Retail Merchants Association are just two examples of trade associations that offer information services to their members.
5. Study customers. As part of market research efforts, a great deal can be learned about the competition.
6. Attend trade shows. Trade shows are usually held in conjunction with conventions where vendors show their products. For example, a grocer's convention might have a trade show that includes the latest in freezer units. If you were one of the vendors attending the trade show you would be able to determine what your competitors were displaying.

COLLECTING AND ANALYZING INFORMATION

Businesses do not collect competitive information randomly. Large businesses have staffs of people whose responsibility it is to work with marketing intelligence. Their objectives are to identify the strengths and weaknesses of key competitors, to assess their current marketing strategies, and to predict their future actions.

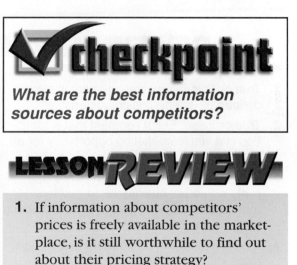

✓ checkpoint

What are the best information sources about competitors?

LESSON REVIEW

1. If information about competitors' prices is freely available in the marketplace, is it still worthwhile to find out about their pricing strategy?
2. Why is it important to know about competitors' product/service planning processes?
3. What is potentially significant about a competitor locating a new supplier?
4. Why do industry trade associations distribute information that can be used competitively against their own members?

CHAPTER 7

SUMMARY

Lesson 7.1

A. Markets can be segmented by geographic location, demographic characteristics, psychographics, product usage, and benefits derived.

B. Market segments are analyzed by evaluating market potential and calculating estimated market shares.

Lesson 7.2

A. The bases for positioning products to distinguish them from the competition are attributes, price and quality, uses or applications, users, classifications, and competitors.

B. The three common positioning strategies revolve around consumer perceptions, competitors in the marketplace, and changes in the business environment.

Lesson 7.3

A. There are two main types of competition businesses face when positioning their products: direct versus indirect competition, and price versus non-price competition.

B. Consumer benefits of competition include lower prices, product improvements, innovative new products, and a wide variety of products from which to choose.

Lesson 7.4

A. Businesses need to know several types of information about their competitors, including pricing strategies, distribution, product/service planning processes, promotional strategies, and market position.

B. Sources of information about business competitors include their own products, sales people, customers, third-party information services, and industry trade shows.

REVIEW MARKETING CONCEPTS

1. True or False: A market segment is always defined by its physical characteristics.

2. True or False: Every segment that is identified is a viable marketing opportunity for a business.

3. True or False: In order to compete effectively with other businesses, marketers must create a unique image of their product or service in the consumer's mind.

4. True or False: Market positioning is always most effective when it is based on price.

5. True or False: Marketers do not need to know how consumers are using their products, as long as they are using them.

6. True or False: An example of indirect competition would be a bowling alley and a video arcade.

7. True or False: The type of competition that stresses convenient location or ample parking is called attribute competition.

8. True or False: There are relatively few consumer benefits from competition compared to the benefits to businesses in terms of larger sales volumes.

9. True or False: In order to compete effectively, it is important to learn as much as possible about your competitor's marketing strategies.

10. True or False: Marketing intelligence is the process of gaining information about the competition.

11. True or False: A trade publication is an example of an information service that a business could use to gain competitor information.

12. True or False: Most marketing intelligence techniques are illegal or unethical.

13. True or False: Most businesses schedule information gathering on their competitors in the spring and the fall.

REVIEW MARKETING TERMS

Match the terms listed with the definitions. Some terms may not be used.

14. A group of individuals or organizations that share one or more important characteristics.

15. The total revenue that can be obtained from the target market.

16. The unique image of a product or service in a consumer's mind relative to the competition.

17. The portion of total market potential that each company expects to get in relation to its competitors.

18. The process of gaining competitive market information.

19. How people spend their time or what gives value to their lives.

20. Occurs when businesses emphasize marketing mix elements such as quality, brand, location, or service.

21. The term used to divide consumers into groups based on where they live.

22. The value a customer receives from a product or service.

23. Takes place in a market segment with businesses that offer the same type of product or service.

24. Occurs when a business competes with a product that is outside its product classification.

25. Rivalry among businesses based on price and value.

26. The term that refers to the characteristics of a market, such as age, hair color, height, and sex.

27. The frequency with which a product is consumed.

a. benefits derived segmentation
b. demographics
c. direct competition
d. geographic segmentation
e. indirect competition
f. market position
g. market potential
h. market segment
i. market share
j. marketing intelligence
k. non-price competition
l. price competition
m. product usage
n. psychographics

APPLY MARKETING FUNCTIONS

MARKETING RESEARCH

28. A medium-size city in southern Alabama has three major grocery stores that have 94 percent of the total market. The remaining 6 percent are small, locally owned stores. It is estimated that the total market potential for this town is $37.5 million. There are approximately 25,000 potential customers in this town.

a. What is the total market potential in dollars for the three major grocery stores?
b. What is the total market potential in dollars for the small, locally owned stores?
c. What is the market share in dollars for each major grocery store if they all have an equal share of the market?
d. One of the major grocery stores has recently remodeled and expanded, and

MARKETING IN ACTION

THE CABLE TELEVISION CHALLENGE

Once upon a time there were three major television networks—ABC, CBS, and NBC. Then came cable and over 200 channels. The competition has heated up, and the original three networks now have an expanded field of competitors.

Networks vie for the greatest share of the television viewing audience. Competition between television and cable networks has been great for consumers, giving them more options.

Cable television operators realized the profit-making opportunity of offering television audiences more options than the three major networks. Cable operators offered viewers numerous channels devoted to news, sports, weather, movies, and regular programming. Based on the number of channels chosen by a customer, cable charges might range from $28 per month for basic coverage to $75 for over 200 channels.

Cable networks demand fees from cable service providers such as Time Warner that carry their signals. Moreover, when people subscribe to a cable service, the programming on the major television networks is also transmitted over cable to the subscribers' TV sets.

Today there is a greater chance of seeing your favorite college playing football or basketball on Saturday, thanks to the numerous cable channels. Several decades ago, three televised football games on the three major networks was a full schedule for Saturday viewing. Today, cable subscribers can see up to 12 football games on a given Saturday. That number of possible games grows even larger with the "pay-per-view" option. Some of the major networks have established business relationships with cable channels for televising sports. For example, ABC and ESPN have an agreement for televising college football.

Sometimes competitors have secondary relationships that cause the actions of one company to have a profound effect on the competition. Disney, for example, owns ABC. Time Warner is a major cable operator and is also the parent company of CNN.

Disney had a major dispute with Time Warner when the latter did not want to include the Disney Channel as part of Time Warner's basic cable subscription. Time Warner wanted to charge its cable subscribers an additional fee for the Disney Channel. That was unacceptable to Disney, which threatened to pull ABC from the cable package if the Disney Channel would not be included as basic cable.

The dispute between these entertainment giants came to a head when Time Warner pulled ABC from 3.5 million customers across the nation. Publicity wars followed Time Warner's actions. Time Warner advertised that "Disney has taken ABC from you," while ABC countered that "Time Warner pulled ABC" and encouraged customers to call Time Warner to bring back the station.

The battle turned political when Disney communicated grave concern to the government regarding Time Warner's merger with America Online. The impasse had come after four months of fruitless discussions between the two companies and several deadline extensions to strike a deal on transmission rights. The multibillion-dollar conglomerates moved their issues to a public forum, cranking out press releases and pointing the finger of blame at each other.

ABC encouraged customers to purchase satellite dishes and dump Time Warner Cable service in order to have access to cable channels and ABC. ABC even offered to pay customers for the installation of satellite dishes that could take the place of cable service. Satellite dish sales rose at an unprecedented rate.

Time Warner lost the public relations battle when it took ABC stations away from 3.5 million subscribers in seven major cities. Time Warner's blackout was an attempt to put a serious crimp in ABC's audience, but the plan backfired. Time Warner claimed it was misunderstood, while ABC and Disney put together the network's best Monday 8–9 p.m. performance in 15 years. Eventually, Time Warner had to give in to the demands of a large customer base.

THINK CRITICALLY

1. What are the advantages of cable television?

2. What kind of promotion for satellite dishes would be effective during the Time Warner and Disney argument? Why?

3. What action by Time Warner proved to be the most fatal? Why?

http://www.deca.org/publications/HS_Guide/guidetoc.html

DECA PREP

MANAGEMENT TEAM DECISION-MAKING EVENT FOR SPORTS AND ENTERTAINMENT MARKETING

You are the commissioner for a major college football conference. You must arrange an agreement with a major cable network to televise more of your football conference games on Saturdays. The greatest benefit of having more games on television is revenue.

DESCRIPTION OF THE PROPOSAL Make a list of advantages and disadvantages associated with offering additional games on cable channels. There will be situations when a conference game on a cable network will be competing with a conference game on a major network. You must make the best decision to televise the maximum number of games possible.

Major networks pay more per game than cable networks.

DEFINE THE MARKETING AND MANAGEMENT FUNCTIONS Marketing and management functions and tasks can be applied in amateur or professional sports or sporting events, entertainment or entertainment events, selling or renting of supplies and equipment (other than vehicles) used for recreational or sporting purposes, products and services related to hobbies or cultural events, or businesses primarily engaged in satisfying the desire to make productive or enjoyable use of leisure time. Define the functions and tasks you plan to apply.

CHAPTER 8
MARKETING FOR E-COMMERCE

LESSON 8.1 *WHAT IS E-COMMERCE?*

LESSON 8.2 *THE GROWING IMPORTANCE OF E-COMMERCE*

LESSON 8.3 *IMPACT OF E-COMMERCE ON DISTRIBUTION CHANNELS*

LESSON 8.4 *ROLE OF PROMOTION FOR E-COMMERCE*

NEWSLINE

CONSUMERS SAY NO TO PETS.COM

It seemed like the ideal e-commerce business. With millions of pet owners spending money on pet supplies, toys, and food, an online business where those consumers could conveniently make purchases could not fail.

Pets.com had the financial backing of Amazon and Disney. It invested heavily in advertising featuring the famous "singing dog" hand puppet. Pets.com got worldwide attention and name recognition by spending over $1 million for advertising during the Super Bowl to introduce the puppet. The advertisement was so popular that the company was able to sell hundreds of thousands of the hand puppets.

Yet in late 2000, Pets.com announced it was closing its web site, laying off its employees, and ending business. Why did a company that appeared to have everything needed for success come to such an unfortunate end? The company's owners blamed the Internet economy, pointing to a large number of e-commerce businesses that also failed at about the same time. In a news release the CEO said, "It is well known that this is a very, very difficult environment for business-to-consumer Internet companies."

The company's failure pointed out that customer needs and choices affect the success of a product. It is true that pet owners spend millions of dollars each year buying a variety of products. It is also true that there are thousands of businesses selling those products, including local supermarkets, discount stores, and corner convenience stores. In most cases, pet owners don't need to and don't want to go online to order pet food or pet supplies and then wait a week or longer for delivery. Pet owners want to be assured of the quality of the products and are more likely to trust the businesses they shop regularly rather than a new Internet company. Even though most people knew the company's name and loved the advertising, they weren't willing to make online purchases for their pets.

THINK CRITICALLY

1. Why is the purchase of pet products less convenient using the Internet than shopping at a local business?

2. Why were consumers unwilling to buy from Pets.com even though the advertising was well recognized and well liked?

3. Search the Internet to find news reports of other Internet companies that have failed and try to determine the reasons for their failure.

CAREER OPPORTUNITY
ART DIRECTOR

POINT YOUR BROWSER
www.corpview.com

TeleView is looking for an employee who possesses the following skills.

- Proven ability to manage the development of high-quality art, design content, and short public advertising and in-house training films
- Drive, flexibility, and project organization and management skills a must
- Ability to manage a team
- Ability to work in an invigorating, team-oriented environment

The main responsibilities of the job include the following.

- Managing a workgroup team and freelance artists, film producers, and independent designers
- Working with Legal Services on related contracts
- Maintaining skills and expertise with software and graphics computer products in order to instruct and train workgroup members and new employees
- Reporting to the editorial staff on the progress of projects and products
- Designing and producing graphics, illustrations, and videos for trade shows and for online web site distribution
- Improving the communications and productivity between design and production workgroups

The job requires the following education, skills, and experience.

- BA or MA in graphic design or an equivalent seven or more years of experience
- Experience with HTML development software tools
- Highly developed project management and organizational skills

- Must submit a portfolio containing examples of design projects and short training films

THINK CRITICALLY

1. Prepare a sample resume of a person who is qualified for this job and interested in applying for it.

2. Considering your skills and preferences, does this sound like a job you would like to have one day? Why or why not?

3. Search want ads or the Internet for a job similar to Corporate View's Art Director. What type of compensation package is available for this job?

8.1 WHAT IS E-COMMERCE?

- Describe the differences between dot.com businesses and bricks and mortar businesses.
- Discuss the importance of a marketing orientation to successful e-commerce.

The beginning of e-commerce in the 1990s threatened to change the way businesses operate. After only a few years, though, many of the new companies operating solely on the Internet went out of business or were struggling to make a profit. They learned quickly that just providing easy access to their business through the Internet was not enough to ensure success. Consumers want assurance that they will get a quality product, they can make a payment with security, the product will be delivered quickly, and they can count on customer service if needed.

Make a list of the advantages and disadvantages of using the Internet to buy products and services.

THE NEW WORLD OF E-COMMERCE

It is hard to believe that the use of the Internet as a place to buy and sell products had its beginnings as recently as the mid-1990s. It seems commonplace today to use a computer to gather product information, locate businesses, compare prices, and even make purchases. But e-commerce is a new way of doing business, and companies are still learning how to use the Internet effectively.

E-commerce is the exchange of goods, services, information, or other business through electronic means. It includes the online purchase and sale of products, providing and exchanging business information, and offering customer service and support. In a very short time, e-commerce has become a multi-billion-dollar part of our economy.

The introduction of the personal computer in the late 1970s made it possible for individuals to have an important tool available at home and at work. Today, millions of people worldwide use a computer as a part of their daily activities. Much of that activity relies on the Internet. Through low-cost or free connections to the Internet, millions of people around the world can instantly access information and communicate with each other.

By 2000, nearly 50 million people in the U.S. had Internet access. However, that is a small number compared to the 500 million Internet users worldwide. Almost all businesses of significant size use computers and the Internet in their daily operations. With the growing popularity and use of the Internet, business cannot ignore its importance. Both new businesses and those that have operated for many years have begun to use e-commerce.

BUSINESS ON THE NET

Not all businesses can complete all of their activities using the Internet, but the Internet can be used for many activities. An automobile manufacturer uses video conferencing to bring designers from several countries together to work on new models of cars and trucks. A software company in California has 10 computer sites around the world where customers can access, instantly download, and pay for new computer software products. A company headquartered in the United States transmits data overnight to Ireland, where accounting specialists maintain many of the company's financial records. A Canadian telecommunications equipment producer trains technicians worldwide by connecting the desktop computers of trainees and trainers using a sophisticated audio-video system. An Iowa company processes orders, bills customers, and maintains accounts receivable for other medical supply businesses. A chemical company in

Ohio has sensors installed in the chemical tanks of customers. When the level drops to a certain point, the sensors trigger a computer program that automatically orders a new supply of the specific chemical.

FROM BRICKS TO DOT.COMS

Businesses can use the Internet for only a few activities or they can operate their entire business using the Net. A company that does almost all of its business activities through the Internet is referred to as a **dot.com business**. The name "dot.com" comes from the end of a commercial business's web address: *.com*. While a growing number of dot.com companies have received a great deal of publicity (Amazon.com, Priceline.com,

Targeting Is Essential

E-commerce businesses may believe they will not have success in selling products to African-American customers due to a widely held belief that racial and ethnic minorities have a low rate of computer and Internet use. In 2000, 29 percent of African-American households had a computer with Internet access compared to almost 50 percent of white households.

A more specific analysis shows that 83 percent of African-American households with incomes above $90,000 have Internet access and that 60 percent of blacks with a college degree use the Internet regularly at home or work. African-Americans are now purchasing new computers at the same rate as whites in the United States.

The evidence shows that e-commerce opportunities are growing rapidly in the African-American community.

THINK CRITICALLY

1. Why should a business be careful of making marketing decisions based on the types of beliefs about African-American consumers described above?

2. How can a business attempt to reach African-American households with high incomes or college degrees?

3. Search the Internet for examples of web sites or businesses that are directly trying to attract African-Americans with their products and services.

Ameritrade.com), most businesses use the Internet for only a portion of their activities. Businesses that complete most of their business activities by means other than the Internet are referred to as **bricks and mortar businesses**. The name "bricks and mortar" suggests that the company relies on real estate assets such as retail stores or factories to conduct its business.

STAGES OF DEVELOPMENT

Businesses generally progress through three stages as they develop their e-commerce presence on the Internet. They begin by offering information only. Then they progress to interactive capabilities and finally to full integration of business transactions on the Web.

Information Stage Most existing businesses first begin using the Internet for e-commerce by developing a simple web site. The web site provides basic information to help prospective customers as they gather information about products and companies. As the business gains more experience with the Internet, it will add additional information, including complete product descriptions, information on payment methods, customer services, and even product manuals.

The limitation of the information stage is that customers cannot use the web site to interact with the business. They must still visit the business in person or use the telephone or mail to obtain information that is not on the web site or to make a purchase.

Interaction Stage The second stage of e-commerce development is interaction.

In addition to providing information, the company uses its web site to interact with consumers. The simplest form of interaction is the use of e-mail. People viewing the company's web site can click on a link to bring up an e-mail form that they can use to request information, ask questions, or contact specific people in the company. In addition to e-mail, companies can add a database where customers can search for specific information about available products, features, and services. They can check product availability, calculate product costs and shipping charges, and determine how long it will take to have an order delivered. An order form may be included on the site along with a product catalog. Customers can complete, print, and then fax or mail the form to the company but cannot place an order directly from the web site using the Internet.

Integration Stage Companies that want to take full advantage of the Internet in their business move to full integration. With all of the Internet tools available, an entire business transaction can be completed on an integrated site. Customers can get necessary product, pricing, and shipping information. They can place an order and pay for the order, track their shipment until it is delivered, and obtain customer assistance following the sale—all using the Internet. Companies with integrated use of the Internet do not have to be dot.com companies. Many customers will still prefer to complete some or all of their business in traditional ways. But full integration gives customers the option to use the Internet for part or all of their business transactions with the company.

What is the primary difference between a bricks and mortar business and a dot.com business?

THE INTERNET AND MARKETING

Many of the first Internet businesses did not understand the importance of marketing. They believed that if they had an attractive web site and advertised their products extensively to prospective customers they would be successful. But they soon learned an important lesson. If customers are uncertain of the quality of a company's products, do not receive merchandise they order in a timely fashion, or are concerned about the security of using a credit card on the Internet, they will not make purchases online. A company that does not meet customer needs will not be successful, whether it is a bricks and mortar company or a dot.com. Thousands of businesses thought they could be successful in e-commerce, but a majority was not successful because they did not apply the marketing concept. Businesses that have been effective in e-commerce know that they must identify target markets and develop a marketing mix that meets the target market needs.

ADVANTAGES OF E-COMMERCE

Businesses that use the Internet have several advantages over those that do not. They have immediate access to prospective customers all over the world. They can introduce new products or update product information instantaneously. They can communicate directly with large groups of consumers or individual customers. New technologies allow the business to send video and audio messages.

The Internet allows businesses to gather very detailed and specific information about prospective and current customers that can be used to tailor a satisfying marketing mix. The Internet has become an important marketing research tool.

With the Internet, a customer concern or question can be sent to the company at any time, and a response can be developed and delivered immediately. Customers can reorder additional quantities of a product, repairs, or new products at any time of day or night, 365 days a year. They can get technical assistance or review operations manuals that have been placed online.

The Internet has resulted in the development of new products that can be delivered to customers from computer to computer. E-tickets are replacing paper tickets for travel on airlines. Tax preparation software that previously was purchased in office supply or other retail stores can now be downloaded from the Internet site of the software developer. If you want to purchase postage or tickets for a concert, you can have them sent to your computer and printed on your printer right in your own home rather than visiting the post office or box office.

The Internet has expanded competition. Small businesses can more easily compete with larger businesses because of the lower costs needed to start and operate the business and the ability to access customers easily with less promotion. Companies can enter international markets by making sure the Internet site is translated to the language of the country in which it wants to sell its products.

E-COMMERCE DISADVANTAGES

Not everything about the development of the Internet as a business tool has been positive. It provides an easy way for people to start a new business without really understanding everything that is necessary for success. Customers who placed orders with the new businesses frequently found that products were not exactly as described on the web site, were not delivered on time, or were damaged when received. Errors were made in processing the order. Customer service was difficult or impossible to obtain.

Businesses using e-commerce have found that it is much more difficult to predict demand for products when information is available worldwide on the Web. Customers expect to be able to obtain answers to questions and support any time of the day, seven days a week, putting pressure on the business to expand those services. Distribution channels, warranty and repair services, methods for accepting returns, and secure web sites for accepting credit card payments need to be developed to serve the new customers who order from the Internet.

One of the greatest disadvantages of e-commerce is the changing nature of competition and the purchasing behavior of customers. A bricks and mortar company generally competes with similar businesses in the same area. Internet businesses face competition from all other businesses offering similar products on the Web. Many consumers use the Web to gather information and compare prices, then they go to a local business to make the purchase. In this way, Internet businesses aid local businesses by providing product information and comparison prices without getting the benefit of actually selling a product.

THE MARKETING CONCEPT APPLIED TO E-COMMERCE

E-commerce has demonstrated the importance of the marketing concept to successful businesses. Many dot.com

companies have failed because they could not meet customer needs profitably. They believed that merely creating an attractive web site and providing information about their company, products, and services would result in sales and profits.

When information about a company's products and services can be viewed by people in many locations, it is especially important for the business to understand who its target market is, what their needs and wants are, and how those needs and wants can be satisfied with a marketing mix. The business must be able to offer the products and services that customers want. It also must be able to distribute them effectively, make purchases affordable and easy for the customers to order and make payments, and provide information in the form of descriptions and pictures to answer important customer questions. All parts of the marketing mix, not just promotion, are important for successful e-commerce.

How does competition change for businesses involved in e-commerce?

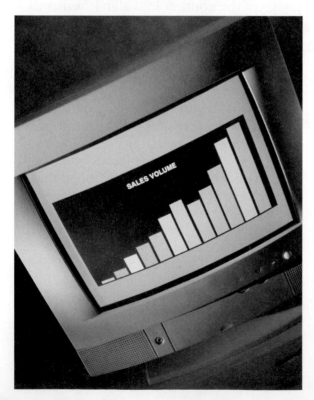

LESSON REVIEW

1. Why did e-commerce begin to grow rapidly in the late 1990s?

2. Give examples of several business activities that can be completed using the Internet.

3. How did dot.com and bricks and mortar businesses get their names?

4. Name and briefly describe the three stages of e-commerce development.

5. Why are some consumers reluctant to purchase products using the Internet?

6. List two advantages and two disadvantages of e-commerce.

THE GROWING IMPORTANCE OF E-COMMERCE

onsumers are most familiar with the businesses from which they make regular purchases or that advertise regularly. But not all businesses sell to final consumers. Many businesses serve other businesses, so consumers are less familiar with them.

Business-to-business marketing is an important part of the economy. If businesses cannot purchase the materials and supplies they need or find other businesses that will distribute, insure, and sell their products, they may not be able to operate effectively or profitably.

Use a business or telephone directory or the Internet to identify three businesses that sell directly to final consumers, three that sell to other businesses, and three that sell to both final consumers and other businesses.

GOALS

- Identify evidence of the growth of the Internet.
- Describe various business uses of the Internet for e-commerce.

GROWTH OF THE INTERNET

o one recognized the potential of the Internet when it was developed as a military and research tool in the 1950s. It developed slowly until businesses and consumers accepted and used personal computers, and technology allowed for the rapid exchange of information using specially designed software and modems.

The Internet has grown rapidly in the last decade. Over 10,000,000 web sites were available at the end of the 1990s, with millions more being added each

FIGURE 8-1
The United States easily topped all other countries in Internet usage in 2000.

COUNTRIES WITH THE HIGHEST PERCENTAGE OF INTERNET USERS IN 2000	
Country	**% of Users**
United States	42.9%
Japan	6.9
United Kingdom	5.4
Canada	5.1
Germany	4.7
Australia	2.7
Brazil	2.6
China	2.4
France	2.2
South Korea	2.2

year. An estimated 500,000,000 people around the world had access to the Internet at the beginning of this century. Almost 50 million homes in the U.S. were connected, up from just 13 million in 1995. The U.S. leads the world in Internet use, with approximately 40 percent of all users. However, people from all over the world are using the Internet, as shown in Figure 8-1.

Business use of the Internet is increasing rapidly as well. While there are many other business uses of the Internet, an important measure of Internet usage by business is the sale of products and services. According to the U.S. Department of Commerce, in 1998, U.S. Internet business-to-consumer (B2C) sales totaled $8 billion. That seems like a very large figure until it is compared to the business-to-business Internet sales in the same year. Business-to-business (B2B) sales totaled $45 billion. Still, there is a great amount of room for growth in the Internet sale of products and services. Internet sales to consumers represent less than one percent of all consumer purchases, and just over one percent of all business sales are completed using the Internet.

Internet sales worldwide are expected to reach $2 trillion by 2005, with nearly 200 million regular Internet customers. Some experts say even that estimate is low.

Are business-to-business sales on the Internet more or less than business-to-consumer sales?

BUSINESS USES
OF THE INTERNET

One of the reasons some companies are reluctant to use the Internet is that they do not believe it is useful for the type of business activities they perform. They often assume that they need to sell products using the Internet. Yet many other business activities can be completed that benefit both the business and its customers, including business communications, information gathering, and business operations.

BUSINESS COMMUNICATIONS

The Internet is a very efficient and effective communications tool for both individuals and businesses. From the beginning of the Internet, the primary way people have

Going Wireless

Consumers are attracted to new technology. Smaller, faster, and more powerful seem to be the keys to success in computer technology. Today, rather than waiting to get to the office or home to access the Internet, people are using handheld wireless devices. Personal Digital Assistants (PDAs), cell phones with wireless modems, and two-way pagers are very popular.

Companies that have spent millions of dollars on well-designed, easy-to-use web sites are now challenged to provide access for the variety of portable wireless products. A web page that looks good on a 15-inch computer screen cannot be viewed on the small screens of PDAs or cellular telephones.

THINK CRITICALLY

1. Since only a small percentage of consumers currently use the new wireless products to access the Internet, should companies try to make their web sites available to those consumers if it will involve a high cost?

2. What do you believe are the important problems companies must overcome if their customers use handheld wireless devices for communication rather than computers?

3. Use the Internet to find examples of handheld wireless products. Identify the types of Internet services that are available for use with the products.

E-Commerce Statistics

The top five retail web sites in January 2001 determined by the number of buyers were

Company	Number of Buyers
Amazon.com	2,300,000
Barnesandnoble.com	638,000
Ticketmaster.com	636,000
Half.com	567,000
Jcpenney.com	545,000

There were an estimated total of 10 million people who made retail purchases on the Internet that month.

THINK CRITICALLY

1. What was the combined number of buyers represented by the top five web retailers?

2. What is the percentage of all Internet customers represented by the combined total of the top five web retailers?

3. If each customer spent on average $135 on Internet purchases during the month, calculate the total amount spent by each of the retailers listed.

communicated is through e-mail. But many tools are currently available and new ones are regularly being developed to aid in person-to-person and business-to-business communications. Examples include chat rooms, bulletin boards, personal messengers, videophones, and online white boards that allow several people to share application software and collaborate using text and graphics tools while sitting at their computers. Businesses use the Internet to quickly and inexpensively distribute newsletters, reports, and other information to their employees.

Improved communications with current and prospective customers can occur using the Internet. Consumers use the Web to locate specific products and businesses. Companies can provide much more detailed information than is possible with traditional methods such as advertisements or business directories. Businesses post the hours they are open, identify specific contacts for information, and even offer a map showing driving directions to the business. Today, if a business has not posted information about its business, location, and products and services on the Internet, it will likely miss some customers.

The Internet has become a common way for businesses to communicate with other businesses to place orders, provide product information, or share data. Business people send e-mail messages, exchange documents, offer training, and update records with other businesses online.

INFORMATION GATHERING

Businesses also use the Internet to obtain information they need to make decisions. A great deal of information on the Internet is free and is provided by government agencies, colleges and universities, libraries, and even private businesses. Other information that businesses need can be purchased from companies specializing in research, from professional and trade associations, and from businesses that specialize in gathering and publishing information.

The Internet has improved the ability to gather information on current and prospective customers. Customers who have purchased products can complete and submit product registration and warranty cards using their computers. The registration process allows the company to collect important information about the customer, including address, telephone number, and even an e-mail address. That information is valuable in future communications and promotional activities.

Information can be obtained on where customers purchase their products, reasons for purchasing the product, and whether the customer owns or plans to purchase related products. The information can improve the company's ability to provide improved marketing mixes for their customers in the future.

Many web sites include a place where prospective customers can request information, be placed on an e-mail or mailing list,

or obtain answers to specific questions. That capability allows the company to develop a list of prospective customers and determine their specific interests. The information can be used for future communications and promotions.

Information about competitors is easier to obtain using the Internet. Businesses put a great deal of information about their products and operations on the Web. It is relatively easy to learn about competitors' products, prices, credit terms, distribution policies, and the types of customer services offered. Some web sites provide information on product tests, offer comparisons and reviews of products, and even have places for consumers to discuss their experiences with a company and it's products.

IMPROVING OPERATIONS

The performance of business and marketing activities has been improved as a result of business use of the Internet. Salespeople can log on to the company's web site and determine the availability of products to assure a customer that the order can be filled immediately. The order can be entered into the computer from anywhere in the world to speed its processing and shipping.

A production manager can access the records of a transportation company to see when an expected shipment of raw materials will be delivered. Managers in branch offices can download financial statements from the main computer to analyze their group's performance and discuss the information with other managers online. Engineers in three locations can collaborate on a new product design by examining a three-dimensional drawing online and making changes that each of them can see instantly.

Small businesses can benefit competitively from the use of the Internet. A small business usually does not have the resources to reach customers that are located in other states or countries when they have to use traditional sales and promotion methods. The Internet makes it possible for the business to compete nationally and internationally without the cost of salespeople. Several small companies are able to pool their orders through an e-wholesaler in order to get the same prices as a larger company.

What are several ways businesses use the Internet to improve operations?

1. What was the approximate number of people with Internet access worldwide in 2000?

2. What percent of total consumer purchases is represented by Internet sales?

3. Which country had the most Internet users in 2000?

4. Why are some companies reluctant to use the Internet?

5. Describe several ways businesses use the Internet for internal communications.

IMPACT OF E-COMMERCE ON DISTRIBUTION CHANNELS 8.3

GOALS

- **Describe new distribution methods using the Internet.**
- **Identify distribution problems experienced by e-businesses.**

W hen customers place an order for a product using the Internet, they want to be assured that the order is correct, that payment has been received, that the products have been shipped, and that they will be received in a reasonable time.

Work with a group. Using the Internet, identify a company that accepts product orders online. Identify the ways the company provides information to the customer about the status of their order. Compare your findings with those of other groups and discuss those that seem to be particularly effective.

DISTRIBUTION FOR

E-COMMERCE

E ffective distribution is an important part of satisfying customer needs. Customers want to locate products and services easily and conveniently. When they purchase a product, they want to make sure it is delivered quickly and undamaged. If they experience any problems with the product, customers expect prompt, reliable service.

The Internet has had an important impact on how companies distribute products. Well-planned distribution has resulted in profitable Internet sales for some companies, while inattention to distribution has contributed to business failures. The major distribution changes in e-commerce have been in access to products and services, order processing, and the methods used to distribute products from the business to its customers.

FINDING AND BUYING PRODUCTS

Before the development of the Internet, customers were limited to making most of

their purchases from businesses that were located close to the customer, those that had salespeople who would visit the customer, or companies that sold their products through catalogs, telephone sales, or advertising.

With Internet access, customers can now locate and purchase products from any company that has a web site. Consumers have many more choices of companies and products as a result of the Internet. The increase in the ease of use and effectiveness of search engines such as google.com and dogpile.com make it easy for Internet users to locate a number of suppliers for products and compare the offerings of several companies.

Companies that have integrated product purchasing into their web sites make it possible for customers to order products online. Online shopping carts have been designed to make it easy to complete an order, make immediate payment using a

Shifting Markets

While U.S. consumers currently represent over 40 percent of all Internet users worldwide, that percentage is dropping. In a report by Jupiter Research, Asian and Latin American usage rates are growing faster than in the United States.

Projections are that by 2005, U.S. Internet users will make up less than 25 percent of the worldwide market. The Asia-Pacific region will grow to 1/3 of the market, and Latin American users will move from a current 5 percent to nearly 10 percent of all users.

This may present a problem for U.S. businesses. Nearly two-thirds of American companies currently do not serve international markets over the Internet, and few of them have plans to do so in the next few years. This means that companies from other countries will have an opportunity to capture the business of the growing worldwide Internet market.

THINK CRITICALLY

1. If computer usage is increasing in the United States, why is the country's percentage of worldwide Internet users declining?

2. What recommendations would you make to U.S. businesses based on the information presented?

Usually the process just described for filling orders required many pieces of paper to be prepared and sent to every department and person involved. The Internet has streamlined order processing and reduced the amount of paper that must be handled to complete a sales transaction.

An order can be placed online by the customer, a company salesperson, or by another business who sells the company's products. When the order is received electronically, the necessary information can be directed via computer to the departments and people involved. The customer or salesperson can check on the status of the order at any time as it is processed, filled, and shipped.

The use of the Internet for order processing reduces the number of errors since the accuracy of the order can be more easily checked. There is also a large savings in order processing and distribution costs for many companies when the Internet is used. Example savings are shown in Figure 8-2.

credit card, and submit the order securely to the company. Even without online purchasing, a web site can provide an order form that can be printed and faxed or mailed to the company with payment.

ORDER PROCESSING

A sales transaction can be a complicated process. When a customer decides to purchase a product, the order must be completed and submitted to the company. It then must be directed to several locations in the business. The departments responsible for filling, packing, and shipping the order must receive the order information. Information must also be sent to the accounting department for billing and processing of payments. It may be necessary for the production department to be notified of the order so that the products are available to fill the order or to replace the inventory sold.

FIGURE 8-2
Average cost savings when customers use the Internet.

Product	Savings
Computer software	99%
Banking services	89%
Airline tickets	87%
Stocks	78%
Books	56%
Toys and gifts	48%

PRODUCT DISTRIBUTION

At first it may be difficult to see how the Internet can improve the actual physical handling and distribution of products. Many products will continue to be shipped in the same ways they have in the past. Automobiles will travel from the manufacturer to dealers by ships, trains, and trucks. Oil and gas will move thousands of miles from refineries to customers via pipelines. Express packages, fresh flowers, and gourmet foods can be transported on airplanes to insure rapid shipment. It is not possible for those types of products to be distributed using the Internet.

Many other services and some products can actually move from producer to consumer online. In some cases, the use of the Internet makes it easier and much less expensive to distribute products. Computer software companies do not have to produce diskettes or CDs with cases and packaging. Instead, customers can download the software from the company's web site. The federal and state governments do not have to print and mail tax forms and instruction booklets for those taxpayers willing to go online and access the forms and instructions from government web sites. They can print the forms or, in some cases, complete them on the computer and submit the completed forms electronically.

Some companies have had to change the form of their products to be able to distribute them using the Internet. Newspapers and magazines have created online editions of their publications. Airlines and travel agencies have developed e-tickets where paper tickets are no longer needed to travel on an airplane. Publishers have created electronic books (e-books) that can be downloaded and read on specially designed computer viewers.

Rather than printing photos on paper, film processors now offer customers the choice of having their photographs transferred to a web site where they can be viewed, stored, and e-mailed to family and friends. Or they might choose to have the digital images burned onto a CD to be viewed using a computer. Even postage can be purchased online and printed on envelopes using your computer rather than going to the post office to buy stamps.

It is likely that future technologies will make it possible for even more products and services to be distributed using computers and the Internet. As customers get more familiar and comfortable with the Internet, more and more products will be purchased online.

What are the three major areas of change in distribution resulting from e-commerce?

DISTRIBUTION PROBLEMS AND SOLUTIONS

Today, one of the concerns that keeps many people from buying products online is uncertainty about product distribution. It will be important for companies to continually improve the way they use the Internet in their distribution process. The key distribution problems facing many e-commerce businesses are the security of transactions, expanded distribution requirements, and customer service demands.

TRANSACTION SECURITY

Almost all people with Internet access use the Internet to gather information about possible purchases. They use search engines to compare products, identify where products can be purchased, and find the lowest prices. Over half of all online consumers make at least one purchase using their computer every three months.

An important statistic that should concern all e-businesses is that nearly

The Trouble with Cookies

Cookies are messages that a web server sends to your web browser when you access a site. The messages are files that transmit information from your computer back to the site. These files identify you to the web site server. Cookies may be customized to log which pages you visit and what links you connect to. Ideally, cookies benefit consumers by saving frequently entered information, allowing improved web design for easier use, and customizing products.

Some sites bar visitors who do not pemit cookies on their browsers. Because cookies are often invisible to users, and the transmitted information varies, some users regard them as an invasion of privacy and disable them in their browsers.

Privacy concerns have led some users to distrust and avoid sites that use cookies. Browsers allow users to reject cookies that get sent to any server but the original one, to be warned before accepting a cookie, or to reject all cookies.

Businesses have a legitimate desire for information about customers, but to whom does such information belong? A web site could lose traffic and potential customers, especially those who are technically oriented and wary of abuse of private information. Privacy issues will increasingly be public-relations issues for businesses, and in some cases, legal ones if data are not carefully used.

THINK CRITICALLY

1. Should a company be required to get the consent of the consumer if it sends and receives cookies from the person's computer?

2. If you operated an e-commerce business, would you favor the use of cookies with your customers?

will be stolen and misused while the information is being transmitted or while it is stored on their computer or the business' computer. The second concern is that the business will misuse the information after the order has been processed. Consumers are aware that many businesses sell customer information such as e-mail addresses to other companies, and they are afraid that their personal information will be misused or they will be contacted by many other companies as a result of the purchase.

E-commerce companies have gone to great lengths to provide security for customer information. They have purchased security technology that makes it almost impossible for information transmitted by computer to fall into the wrong hands. They offer customers the option of transmitting personal information by fax or telephone if they choose.

Companies have developed services that allow customers to prearrange transfers of payments from their bank account to the company's account so a credit card number does not have to be entered online. Credit card companies such as Visa, MasterCard, and Discover offer insurance so they will be responsible for any losses customers suffer if others misuse credit card information as a result of Internet purchases.

two-thirds of all purchases started by customers are ended before the customer submits the order. For some reason or reasons, even though customers had planned to make the purchases and began to complete the online orders, they chose not to place the orders.

One of the greatest concerns expressed by customers is the security of the information they must provide to the company when placing an order. That information includes the customer's name, address, telephone number, and their credit card number. Depending on the product being purchased, other personal information may be required in order to complete the order.

Consumers have two security concerns. The most important is that their personal information, including credit card numbers,

EXPANDED DISTRIBUTION AND CUSTOMER SERVICE

When the Internet revolution hit in the late 1990s, many people were quick to jump on the bandwagon and open their own e-businesses. It seemed all that was needed was a web page to advertise a product and a business could be successful. Even many experienced bricks and mortar businesses tried to take advantage of e-commerce by developing a web site to sell their products and services online.

Many of the e-businesses soon ran into trouble, however. If customers found their web site and placed an order, the product still needed to be packed and shipped. Customers expected the orders to be delivered quickly and undamaged. When an order was received, a customer often required answers to questions or help in assembling or using the product. If the product was damaged or not exactly what the customers wanted, they wanted to be able to return it easily for an exchange or refund.

The new e-businesses often were not prepared for the many distribution activities that had to be completed. Even experienced businesses found that they had to distribute their products in different ways to many more locations than before. As bricks and mortar businesses, they were used to customers coming to them with problems or to return and exchange merchandise. They could easily distribute products to customers who were located close to them. Their usual distribution methods no longer worked for Internet customers, however. Customers became very dissatisfied when they could not get the service they expected, so they would stop using the e-business.

Successful e-businesses have found ways to improve distribution. Companies such as UPS and FedEx have expanded their services and offer overnight shipping to meet the needs of e-commerce. They can instantly track any shipment, and customers can even go online to identify where a shipment is and when it will be delivered. Those companies make it easy for customers to return a product they do not want by providing preprinted labels, return instructions packaged with the product, and free pickup service. E-businesses offer complete return policies and procedures on their web sites.

Some e-businesses have now made arrangements for customers to be able to return unwanted merchandise to local businesses rather than having to return them by mail. That is easier for a company that is also a bricks and mortar business, but it is more difficult for a company that is completely dot.com.

Customer service centers have been developed to respond to Internet customer questions and to offer assistance while the customer is shopping and after they receive the merchandise. Well-trained customer service personnel staff telephone centers and online help centers 24 hours a day, seven days a week. Most web sites have links to FAQs (frequently asked questions) so customers can get an immediate answer to common problems without having to contact the company. Instruction manuals, product warranties and registrations, and places to order repair or replacement parts are all online.

What are the key distribution problems facing businesses using e-commerce?

LESSON REVIEW

1. What are the three major distribution changes in e-commerce?

2. Why do consumers have many more choices of products as a result of the Internet?

3. Identify the average amount of savings on distribution costs for several products resulting from the use of the Internet.

4. What are some examples of products that can be distributed totally online?

5. What percentage of customers end an online purchasing process before it is completed?

6. Identify one security concern customers have when making purchases online.

7. How do companies like FedEx and UPS help e-businesses with distribution problems?

GOALS

- Describe how companies use promotion on the Internet.
- Identify ways to increase the effectiveness of online promotion.

COMMUNICATING WITH INTERNET USERS

Most people today are not using the Internet to purchase products. In fact, only 2 percent of Internet users say they go online with the specific intention of making a purchase. Over 80 percent say their primary reason for going online is communication. If they are interested in purchasing products, consumers are more likely to use the Internet to gather information and to compare alternatives. Then many will go to a local business to make the purchase.

The purpose of promotion as a part of a company's marketing mix is to communicate information in order to encourage customers to purchase the business' products and services. Since consumers are using the Internet for communications,

promotion is an effective use of the Internet by businesses.

Both bricks and mortar and dot.com businesses can benefit from using the Internet for promotion. Online advertising by bricks and mortar businesses allows prospective customers to easily gather information and make purchase decisions before visiting the store. Dot.com businesses can use advertising to encourage customers to make online purchases rather than going to a traditional business.

ADVERTISING EXPENDITURES

Many companies use Internet advertising to promote their products and services. In 1998, businesses spent less than $2 billion for online advertising. Within four years,

The Cost of E-commerce

It is estimated that companies will spend between $5 million and $23 million each to move into e-commerce over the next five years. Those costs involve a number of types of expenditures. The companies will need to purchase computer hardware and software to manage the Web sites and offer purchase security, order processing, and customer service. They will need to develop new procedures and the necessary facilities and equipment to quickly process orders and ship them to customers. Personnel with the technology skill to perform the many new e-business activities must be hired or trained. The companies will have to create relationships with companies that will assist them with developing and operating the e-business activities. About one-third of the costs will be directed at modifying existing business activities so they can be easily integrated with the new e-commerce part of the company.

THINK CRITICALLY

1. How can companies justify spending millions of dollars to move into e-commerce?

2. Why is it necessary that current business activities such as operating traditional stores to service customers need to be integrated with the new e-commerce activities? Why shouldn't they be operated separately?

---

that figure had more than quadrupled. Among the top Internet advertisers are Microsoft, Amazon, Yahoo, eBay, Barnes and Noble, and E*Trade.

Some advertising costs are hidden, since many companies use bartering to place their ads on another web site. In return, they run advertisements for the cooperating businesses on their web site. No money is exchanged between the companies to pay for the advertising.

TYPES OF INTERNET PROMOTION

There are many ways that traditional businesses can promote their companies and their products. Those methods include all forms of advertising, from television and radio to magazines and newspapers. In addition, companies promote using salespeople, displays, promotional products (pens, travel mugs, refrigerator magnets), coupons, contests, and other methods.

Those same methods can be used by companies involved in e-commerce. The Internet also offers other ways to reach prospective customers and promote products. Four primary methods include online advertisements, web site sponsorship, priority placement in web browsers and comparison shopping services, and providing consumer information web sites.

Online Advertising Just as in newspapers and magazines, companies compete on the Web for the attention of Internet users. They will try to place their advertisements on pages that prospective customers are most likely to visit. They also use creative advertising designs. Varied sizes, colors, and placements of advertisements encourage Internet users to stop and read the company's information. Online advertising can include moving text and graphics and links to sites that contain more detailed information.

The Internet Advertising Bureau has established standards for the size and appearance of Internet advertisements. Internet advertising is measured in pixels. A pixel is the size of a small dot that is a part of the image on a video display screen

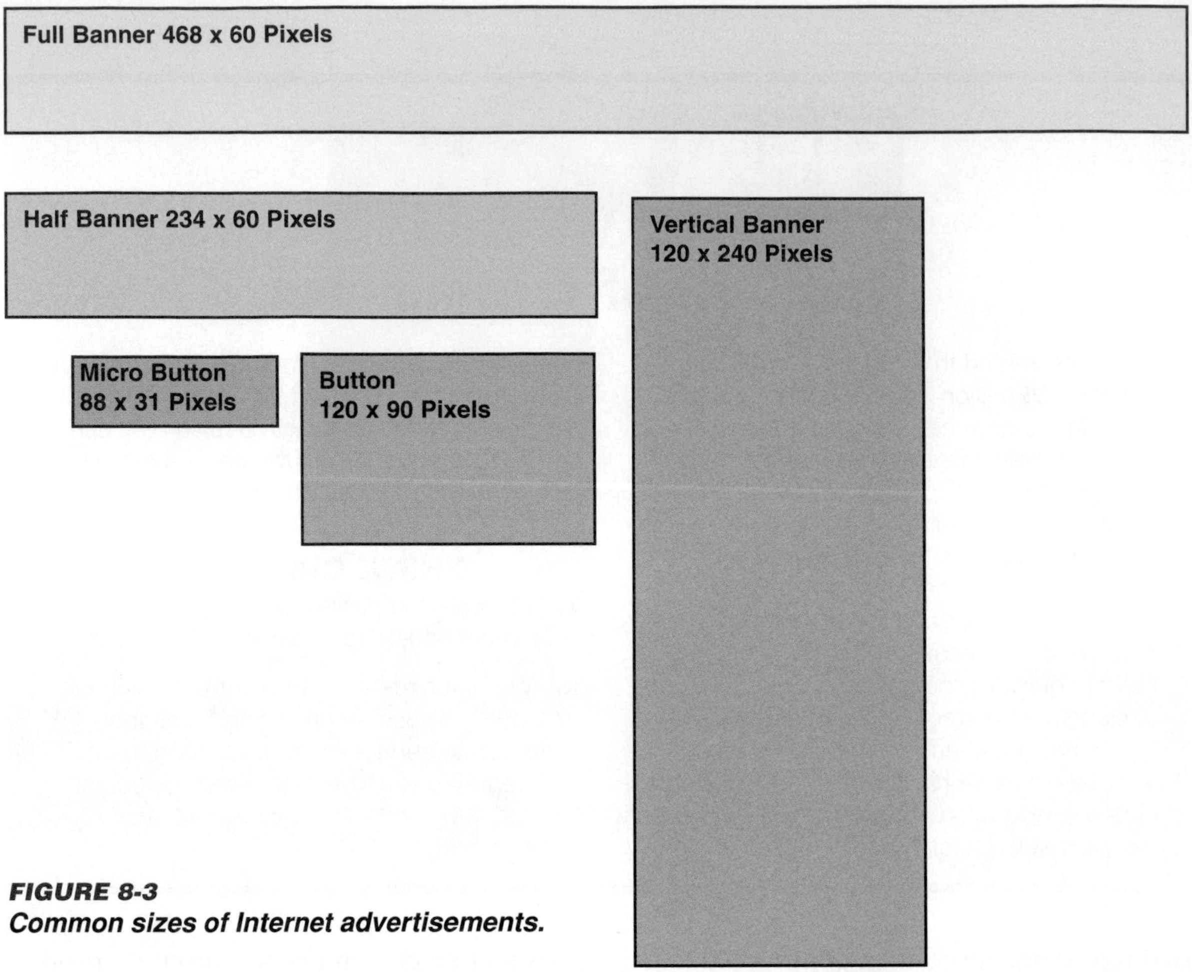

Full Banner 468 x 60 Pixels	

Half Banner 234 x 60 Pixels

Vertical Banner 120 x 240 Pixels

Micro Button 88 x 31 Pixels

Button 120 x 90 Pixels

FIGURE 8-3
Common sizes of Internet advertisements.

of a computer. Some of the common sizes of Internet ads are illustrated in Figure 8-3.

Web Sponsorship   An effective way to build recognition of a company's name and products with customers who are likely to purchase those products is to sponsor a related informational web site. The sponsor's name is included on the web site so visitors see the name each time they access the site.

A bank could benefit by sponsoring a web site that helps consumers understand how to lease or finance the purchase of an automobile. A web site dedicated to health and fitness could be sponsored by a health food store or a fitness center.

Priority Placement   When you use a web browser to find information, you might believe that the list is presented to you in random order. However, some browsers allow companies to pay to have their web site appear at the top of the list when the results of a search are shown. That placement increases the likelihood that the

Internet user will visit the company's web site to obtain additional information.

A number of web sites have been developed to help consumers identify sources for products they want to purchase and compare product features and prices (mySimon, ZDNet). While some of those web sites are independent, others will feature the products of companies who have paid to have their companies and products included on the lists. Those companies' products will appear at the top of the list, but the customer will still be able to compare features and prices of all companies.

Consumer Information   The Internet is a vast source of information on almost any topic. Consumers use the Web to gather information and learn about areas of interest. Companies and organizations develop free web sites on topics of interest to their prospective customers. The belief is that as customers become better informed and learn more about a topic, they are more likely to purchase related products and services. Examples of consumer information web sites maintained by companies are Fodors.com, which provides travel and vacation information, and Petersons.com, which offers information on choosing a college or university.

Other Types of Promotion

Businesses have developed many other ways to communicate with Internet users to promote their products and services. Companies develop e-mail lists using the addresses of people who have previously purchased products or sent inquiries to the company, and by purchasing e-mail lists from other companies. The business can then send special offers, new product information, or other communications to those consumers using e-mail.

You may have seen online coupons that are similar to the coupons you receive in the mail or that are printed in newspapers and magazines. The coupons provide a special incentive for customers to purchase a product. They are used either by printing and mailing the coupon with an order or by entering a special code on the order form when purchasing online.

Internet promotions are used to encourage consumers to request free samples, send for CDs that provide detailed product information, or visit a local store where the company's products are sold. New audio-visual technology allows businesses to provide three-dimensional views of their products online so customers can examine a product in much the same way as if they were actually handling it.

What are four primary methods a company can use to promote its products online?

PROMOTION FOR
E-COMMERCE

Most consumers are satisfied with their shopping experiences when they use the Internet to make purchases. In fact, experienced Internet shoppers are more satisfied with the online shopping experience than with the other ways they make purchases. See Figure 8-4.

FIGURE 8-4
Customer satisfaction with types of shopping.

Type	% satisfied
Shopping in stores	60%
Shopping with catalogs	56%
Shopping online	73%

The reasons customers state for their high level of satisfaction include convenience, saving time, and getting everything from one source. They also value the competitive prices they can find on the Internet.

PLANNING THE SHOPPING EXPERIENCE

Marketing using the Internet is quite different than marketing to customers who actually visit a store. When a business can talk directly to customers, identify their needs, select and demonstrate products, and immediately answer questions and concerns, the opportunity to complete the sale is much greater.

When a consumer shops using the Internet, the business typically does not have direct contact with the person. The design of the web site and effective communication principles are needed to attract consumers to the business and to help them make a purchase. To be successful, promotion must be more than well-designed advertisements on the Web. The company will need to answer the following questions to plan the shopping experience for the prospective buyer so it results in a sale and a satisfied customer.

1. How does the customer typically use the Internet to gather information? What search engines are used and what sites are visited?
2. What type of information will the customers need in order to decide if they want to purchase the company's products? Is the information easy to locate and understand?
3. Are the web pages well organized and is it easy to move forward and backward? Are the methods to locate specific product information, determine prices, purchase products, and make payments clear and easy to use?
4. Are web pages attractively designed without so much information that they are confusing? Do pictures and graphics effectively show products and how they are used?
5. Is it easy to get common questions answered? Is there a way for customers to contact the company with questions or for assistance in selecting and purchasing products?
6. Is there an easy-to-use, secure method for customers to purchase products online? Is there an alternative method for customers who don't want to buy online?
7. Are product delivery methods and costs clearly explained?
8. Are customers given information on how they can return products that don't meet their needs?

When companies carefully plan the shopping experience for Internet customers, provide needed information, and make shopping easy and enjoyable, customers will be very willing to buy online.

EFFECTIVE PROMOTION METHODS

Customers are clear about the features that are helpful in shopping online. Those features are listed in Figure 8-5.

You can see that almost all of the features customers identified involve communication between the business and the customer. So the careful planning of promotion is important to effective e-commerce. And promotion is more than just advertising to make customers aware of the business and attract them to the company's web site.

Important methods of promotion for e-commerce include the following:

● An easy-to-remember, meaningful Internet address
● Well designed online advertisements
● Advertisements in other media such as newspapers and television
● Registration with search engines to identify the company for people gathering information related to its products
● Gathering information on who visits the company's web site, when they visit, how much time they spend, which pages and links are most popular, and what information influences them to make a purchase
● Customer service personnel to help customers and answer questions
● Developing online chatrooms, discussions, and clubs to exchange information with customers
● Offering special e-mail promotions and announcements to customers to encourage regular visits to the web site

FIGURE 8-5
Features likely to increase online purchasing.

FIGURE 8-5
Features likely to increase online purchasing.

- Close-up images of products
- Information on product availability
- Product comparison guides
- An easy-to-use search function
- 1-800 Customer Service number
- Consumer reviews and product evaluations
- An easy-to-use "shopping cart" and check out feature

✓checkpoint

Are customers generally more satisfied with online shopping than with shopping in stores?

LESSON REVIEW

1. What percentage of Internet users go online with the specific intention of making a purchase?

2. How much did advertising expenditures increase in the four years since 1998?

3. What are some traditional types of promotion that can be used by e-commerce businesses?

4. How can Internet companies use consumer information web sites to promote their products and services?

5. Are consumers usually satisfied with their Internet shopping experiences?

6. List several questions a company must answer to plan shopping experiences for Web customers.

7. Identify three promotional methods e-commerce businesses can use to attract customers to their web sites.

SUMMARY

Lesson 8.1

A. Companies involved in e-commerce have advantages over those that are not. They can reach customers more rapidly and reach a larger number of customers using the Internet.

B. Many bricks and mortar companies complete some of their business online, while dot.com companies complete all or nearly all of their business using the Internet.

Lesson 8.2

A. The Internet has become an important worldwide communications and business tool. The number of Internet users continues to grow rapidly, as does both business-to-business and business-to-consumer marketing using the Internet.

B. Businesses use the Internet for many other reasons than just to buy and sell products. The Internet is used for business and consumer communications, to gather information, and to improve business operations.

Lesson 8.3

A. The Internet has helped many companies improve the distribution of products. The major distribution changes in e-commerce have been in how customers locate products and services, order processing, and the methods used to distribute products from the business to its customers.

B. Important distribution problems facing e-commerce businesses are how to insure the security of customer purchases, getting products to customers who may be located long distances from the company, and meeting customer expectations for service.

Lesson 8.4

A. Online advertising is only one way that e-commerce businesses promote their products and services. Other methods include web site sponsorship, priority placement in web browsers and comparison shopping services, and providing consumer information web sites.

B. Businesses typically do not have direct contact with customers who shop using the Internet. The design of the web site and effective communication principles are needed to attract consumers to the business and help them make a purchase.

REVIEW MARKETING CONCEPTS

1. The use of the Internet as a place to buy and sell products had its beginnings:
   a. just after World War II
   b. in the early 1970s
   c. about 1985
   d. in the mid-1990s

2. E-commerce includes all of the following except:
   a. in-store sales
   b. online product purchases
   c. exchanging business information
   d. offering customer service

3. In 2000, the number of people in the United States with Internet access was:
   a. under 1,000,000
   b. nearly 10,000,000
   c. about 50,000,000
   d. over 200,000,000

4. The difference between a dot.com and a bricks and mortar company is:
   a. the types of products sold
   b. the amount of business done online
   c. the age of the company
   d. whether computers are used or not

5. Which of the following is *not* one of the stages of e-commerce development?
   a. incorporation
   b. integration
   c. information
   d. interaction

6. Why were many of the first dot.com companies unsuccessful?
   a. They had poor web site designs.
   b. They didn't promote their products.
   c. They didn't understand the marketing concept.
   d. They set prices too low.

7. Which of the following is an advantage of e-commerce?
   a. Small companies can more easily compete with larger companies.
   b. All business expenses are lower.
   c. Businesses don't need to perform every marketing activity.
   d. There is almost no competition.

8. True or False: The United States has the largest percentage of Internet users of all countries in the world.

9. True or False: The total amount of business-to-consumer Internet sales is much larger than the amount of business-to-business sales.

10. True or False: Most businesses do not use the Internet to gather information because they have to pay for almost all of the information.

11. True or False: Some products can actually be distributed directly to consumers' homes using the Internet.

12. True or False: One of the best ways to locate companies or products on the Internet is to use a search engine.

13. True or False: While being able to process an order using the Internet is an important customer service, it actually adds to the company's costs.

14. True or False: One of the primary reasons customers do not shop online is their concern for the security of the information they must provide.

15. True or False: Most Internet shoppers go online for the purpose of gathering information rather than to make an online purchase.

16. True or False: An advantage of using the Internet for advertising is that it does not cost the business anything to place an advertisement on another business's web site.

17. True or False: Today, most consumers are satisfied with their shopping experience when they use the Internet to make a purchase.

REVIEW MARKETING TERMS

Match the terms listed with the definitions. Some terms may not be used.

18. The exchange of goods, services, information, or other business through electronic means.

19. A company that does almost all of its business activities through the Internet.

20. Businesses that complete most of their activities by means other than the Internet.

a. bricks and mortar
b. dot.com business
c. e-commerce

MAKING FINANCIAL SERVICES CONVENIENT

Financial services such as loans and investments offered by banks and other financial institutions used to be a Monday-through-Friday, 9-to-5 business. Many consumers dreaded going to the banker to request a loan, because there was always the chance of denial. Conducting financial transactions was a formal process that not many individuals enjoyed.

Deregulation of the banking industry in the 1980s required financial institutions to become more competitive. Banks were no longer the only option for financial services. Insurance companies, brokerage firms, and credit unions began to offer the same financial services previously provided by banks.

Standard business hours for financial institutions were no longer just 9 to 5. Banks and other financial institutions realized the importance of convenience for customers. Automated teller machines (ATMs) appeared in supermarkets, service stations, and many other busy locations. Consumers could now conduct many of their business transactions without communicating directly with a person in the financial institution. Soon banking by telephone and computer became common means for conducting financial transactions. Customers could replace check-writing with electronic automatic withdrawal from checking or savings accounts, and automatic payroll deposit became the option chosen by most people. Individuals receiving paychecks or Social Security checks felt comfortable having their money deposited directly to their accounts. Consumers found this type of deposit much more efficient than physically receiving a paycheck and then traveling to a financial institution to deposit it. It also reduced the chance of checks being stolen in the mail.

The Internet and telephone have allowed individuals to pay bills without writing checks. Completing the transactions by telephone or computer in real time closes the gap between receiving a payment and actually having funds available for use.

In the past, banks were the financial institutions that most consumers depended upon for financial services. It was extremely important for customers to establish a positive relationship with banks in order to receive future loans or services. Today, insurance companies, credit unions, and stock brokerage firms want to provide consumers with insurance, investments, banking services, and a whole lot more. A large brokerage firm such as Merrill Lynch offers numerous investment services, home loans, home equity loans, tax-sheltered annuities, IRAs, checking accounts, credit cards, and savings accounts. Many financial institutions have 24-hour customer service lines to compete for business. If you have a financial concern at 2 a.m., you can dial a toll-free number to get the information you need. Applying for home, automobile, or home equity loans can be handled over the telephone. Consumers no longer have to make a special trip to the financial institution and meet with a banker to find out the fate of their loan application.

Customer service is always important to gain market share in the financial world. Companies such as Merrill Lynch and State Farm Insurance spend an increasing amount of their human resource budgets to train their customer service representatives on how to communicate effectively with customers on the telephone. Most individuals are somewhat nervous when applying for credit, because they are required to share a lot of their personal financial information. Well-trained customer service representatives make the customer feel at ease while gathering all of the necessary financial data. Banking online or by telephone will not guarantee that you receive a loan, but the process has become much easier.

Merrill Lynch believes that its employees' abilities to manage themselves enhance its ability to serve its clients. The number one responsibility of Merrill Lynch is to manage client and company assets. Once Merrill Lynch earns clients'

trust, the customers reward the company with their confidence. This enables Merrill Lynch to provide customers with strategic advice and to establish long-term relationships.

THINK CRITICALLY

1. Why has competition increased for financial services?

2. Financial services are now offered on the Internet and telephone. What special concerns have these conveniences raised for consumers?

3. What promotional theme does a financial institution in a very competitive market need to relay to consumers?

http://www.deca.org/publications/HS_Guide/guidetoc.html

MARKETING RESEARCH EVENT FOR BUSINESS AND FINANCIAL SERVICES

You have learned how financial institutions today conduct much of their business over the telephone or the Internet. Do all customers really feel comfortable taking care of financial transactions with the latest technology? How do senior citizens feel about using the Internet or talking to a financial adviser on the telephone?

You have been hired by a financial institution to develop a survey. The purpose of this survey is to find out the customer comfort level using the Internet and telephone to complete financial/banking transactions. You also want to find out what the financial institution can do to make customers more likely to use the new services.

DESCRIPTION OF THE PROPOSAL Prepare a one-page description of the proposed survey. Include a description of the business or organization, as well as a description of the community (geographic, demographic, and psychographic factors).

DESCRIPTION OF RESEARCH METHODS Describe the research methods used. This might include sample questionnaires, letters sent and received, general background data, etc. What steps did you take to design the survey and the instrument? How did you conduct the survey?

PREPARE SUMMARY OF FINDINGS AND CONCLUSIONS OF THE STUDY Prepare a geographic, demographic, and psychographic description of customers. Explain the buying behavior of customers. Summarize customer familiarity with the financial institution. What conclusions based on the findings of the survey can you make?

PREPARE A PROPOSED BUSINESS OUTLINE The outline should include goals/objectives and rationale, proposed activities and timelines, the proposed budget, and a plan to evaluate the effectiveness of marketing the services offered by the financial institution.

CHAPTER 9

THE MARKETING STRATEGY

LESSON 9.1 *DEVELOPING A MARKET STRATEGY*

LESSON 9.2 *ASSESSING MARKETING MIX ALTERNATIVES*

LESSON 9.3 *ANALYZING PRODUCT PURCHASE CLASSIFICATIONS*

LESSON 9.4 *PLANNING FOR MARKETING*

LESSON 9.5 *DEVELOPING A MARKETING PLAN*

NEWSLINE

TARGET YOUR MARKET

Croemers department store opened in 1917. Over the years the store concentrated on serving an upper middle-class market segment. It offered clothing, jewelry, appliances, furniture, linens, home accessories, and a full range of customer services. Croemers developed a loyal group of customers and achieved high sales and profits. But the business almost went bankrupt learning about the importance of a marketing plan.

In 1989, two large discount stores entered the market, offering many of the same types of products as Croemers. Croemers saw an immediate impact on sales and profits as customers were attracted by lower prices at the discount stores.

The company turned to a marketing consultant who helped it complete a marketing study. Croemers learned that its primary customers viewed it as their source of attribute-based shopping goods and specialty goods. These customers were willing to pay higher prices for important purchases because of the quality and service Croemers provided.

Croemers drew up a marketing plan focused on its original target market. It developed a smaller but more profitable line of quality products that were not carried in the discount stores and reemphasized service. A new promotional program was instituted. The strategy was described in detail in a written marketing plan, and then communicated clearly to all managers and employees. Croemers was soon able to reduce costs, increase profit margins, and reestablish strong ties with its target market. Its new success was the result of careful planning and responding to customers' needs.

THINK CRITICALLY

1. Why is it that Croemers was able to succeed for years without a marketing plan but then suddenly found itself losing its customer base?

2. How is it possible for Croemers to increase profits while the discount stores are taking a big portion of the sales it used to make?

CAREER OPPORTUNITY
BRAND DEVELOPMENT MANAGER

POINT YOUR BROWSER

www.corpview.com

TeleView is looking for someone who possesses the following attributes.

- Well-developed interpersonal skills and an ability to work in an invigorating, team-oriented environment
- Excellent customer relations skills necessary to maintain customer loyalty
- Strong analytical, problem solving, and time management skills needed to manage multiple tasks simultaneously
- Technical communications proficiency
- Drive and flexibility
- Proven out-of-the-box, creative thinking abilities

The main responsibilities of this job include the following.

- Develop, implement, and maintain the TeleView brand plan
- Investigate anything and everything that impacts the TeleView brand
- Survey and review media, prepare advertising, and evaluate any other issues that impact the brand
- Develop ways to differentiate TeleView products and brands from the competition
- Invent and implement strategies for the brand to be used by Marketing, Sales and Customer Support
- Assist with marketing plans as related to marketing the TeleView and Corporate View image
- Team with the Brand Marketing Workgroup to insure consistency in the branding message
- Work with Legal Services to manage contracts and to implement new brand names

- Collaborate with Finance and Accounting on the workgroup's budget
- Report to senior management and to various marketing groups around the world
- Use the Intranet to communicate with management and other marketing groups

The job requires the following education, skills, and experience.

- B.S. or B.A. degree with an emphasis in marketing, corporate communications, rhetoric, or related fields required; advanced degree preferred
- Eight or more years in strategic marketing, creating marketing plans, and executing critical projects
- Experience in telecommunications and technology a plus
- Experience in creating business partnerships
- Strong understanding of business and how all the mission-critical functions must work together to achieve marketing goals and plans
- Negotiation skills and strong technical communications skills preferred

The position has a base salary and benefits. Bonuses are awarded based on successful and profitable brand development.

THINK CRITICALLY

1. Prepare a cover letter written by a person who is minimally qualified for this job and interested in applying for it.

2. What kinds of entry-level or lower-level jobs might prepare someone for a position such as this?

GOALS

● **Describe how market segments are defined.**

● **Understand the four criteria that an effective target market must meet.**

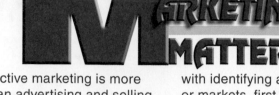

MARKETING MATTERS

Effective marketing is more than advertising and selling. At the same time, effective marketing is more than just the seven marketing functions. Effective marketing develops satisfying exchange relationships between businesses and their customers. In order to accomplish that, businesses need to develop a marketing strategy. The process begins with identifying a target market or markets, first by differentiating various segments, then by choosing a target that offers the best marketing opportunity.

Make a list of five wants or needs that you have that are different from those of most of your family members, friends, and classmates, and for each want or need name a product or service that satisfies it.

DIFFERENTIATING MARKET SEGMENTS

A marketing strategy is the way marketing activities are planned and coordinated to achieve an organization's goals. An organization that believes in the marketing concept develops marketing strategies to satisfy customer needs. In most instances, those organizations follow a two-step process, as shown in Figure 9-1.

A market includes all of the consumers a business would like to serve. It is almost impossible for a business to serve all customers well. What if a business came into your classroom to sell items for students who will be graduating next spring? It's likely that not everyone in the room is a senior, so some would automatically not be

FIGURE 9-1
Businesses that follow the marketing concept use a two-step process to develop a marketing strategy.

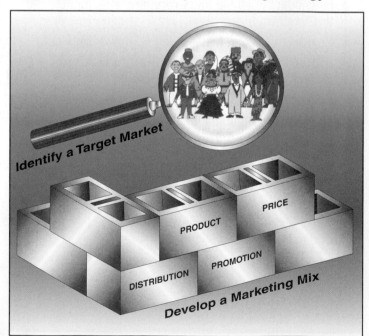

Developing a Marketing Strategy

customers. Each person has different plans for graduation. Some students have no plans yet and will not have any for several months. Others probably made plans as early as last summer and may have already purchased many of the things they will need. In some families, graduation ceremonies are an important tradition with specific procedures to be followed. In other families, it is up to each graduate to determine the plans.

Significant Differences   Your class is a very small market. It is likely that the business visiting your class will be interested in all prospective graduates from your school and from other schools in your city and state. They might want to serve graduating seniors from high schools or from colleges and universities. Some companies offer products for graduates from adult education programs, junior high schools, and even "graduates" from preschools. It is highly unlikely that those graduates all want the same things. The differences among all of the people who buy graduation products will affect purchasing decisions and the information they need.

Common Characteristics   Markets are made up of many segments. **Segments** are components of a market in which people have one or more similar characteristics. The most important characteristics of a market are the needs and wants of consumers. While needs and wants are quite different from person to person, segments of a market can be identified that have one or more strong needs or wants in common.

GET THE MESSAGE

Wireless Ads Track Moving Targets

Wireless communications has given a whole new meaning to the old adage that the three most important things in marketing are "location, location, and location." Retailers can now send location-sensitive ads to handheld wireless devices and target their messages to only those people who are nearby. The technology combines the benefits of outdoor advertising with electronic updates at almost any time.

By reaching people who are within minutes of a store or restaurant that's trying to lure customers, location-sensitive wireless advertising can be much more effective than promotions that are less targeted, such as Internet banner ads. One campaign that was used in several major metropolitan areas, placing ads at the bottom of local restaurant listings, had click-through rates of better than 10%.

More than 50 million people in North America are projected to be using wireless phones, personal digital assistants, and pagers by 2005. Wireless ads at first were simple, text-based promotions. As advances in technology increase the amount of information that can be transmitted, richer ads are more feasible.

THINK CRITICALLY

1. Wireless ad services were sensitive to users' privacy concerns and initially limited ads to people who consented to receive them. What makes wireless devices so different from PCs and other media to justify such limits?

2. What kinds of businesses benefit most from location-sensitive ads?

All Income Is Not Equal

Income is a useful tool for segmenting markets, but marketers need to be careful. Segments with very similar income levels may have quite different abilities to buy certain things. To get a true picture, marketers need to examine other factors.

Discretionary spending is the amount of total income left after paying taxes and basic living expenses. For restaurants or luxury car dealers, discretionary spending is a useful measure of income.

Young people generally have fewer obligations, so most of their income is uncommitted. People in their 30s usually have mortgages, kids, and retirement saving to worry about. Discretionary cash tends to peak when people are in their 50s, when income is high and obligations have subsided.

Discretionary spending is also influenced by economic circumstances. When energy costs spiked in 2000-2001, people cut spending on things such as restaurants, entertainment, and clothing.

Marketers generally use three age segments—18–25, 25–49, and over 50. Research indicates that the people in the youngest group have average annual income of $24,000, pay $5,000 in income taxes, spend $8,000 for housing, and save –$2,000 (which means they are accumulating debt). The middle group has average income of $43,000, pays $8,000 in taxes, $16,000 for housing, and saves $8,000. The older group takes in $41,000, pays $7,000 in taxes and $10,000 for housing, and saves $4,000.

THINK CRITICALLY

1. Based on the figures above, how much do people in each group have available for discretionary purchases?

2. How does their discretionary spending ability correlate with their income level?

A second way of identifying market segments is through demographic characteristics such as age, income, location, and educational level. Markets can also be described by psychographic or lifestyle characteristics including activities, attitudes, customs, and traditions. The attitudes of potential consumers are important in segmenting markets (see Figure 9-2). How do consumers feel about the type of products and specific brands of the products?

Another way to segment is by identifying the way consumers make their purchase decisions. These factors could include their previous experience with products, what sources of information they use, whether decisions are more rational or emotional, and how much time they take in gathering and evaluating information before a decision is made. Marketing information systems and marketing research are used to gather information in order to divide markets into segments.

FIGURE 9-2
To identify unique segments of a market, businesses must gather a variety of consumer information.

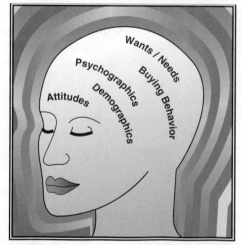

Characteristics Used to Segment a Market

How do people's different wants and needs form the basis for identifying market segments?

SELECTING
TARGET MARKETS

In order to develop an effective marketing strategy, a business should concentrate its attention on a specific market. That is known as selecting a target market. A **target market** is a clearly identified segment of the market to which the company wants to appeal. In order to be an effective target market, it must meet four criteria:

1. The people in the target market must have common important needs and respond in a similar way to marketing activities designed to satisfy those needs.
2. The people outside of the target market should have enough differences from those in the market that they will not find the marketing activities satisfying.
3. There should be adequate information about the people in the target market so they can be identified and located.
4. There should be enough information about the consumers' needs and how they make purchasing decisions that an effective marketing mix can be developed.

In the example given earlier of the firm that offers graduation products, all of the students who will be graduating should be studied. Segments can then be identified based on the type of school, its location, and when the graduation will occur. Other segments could be based on factors such as the age, gender, or even income of the graduate.

After identifying several segments, the company would study needs, attitudes, and family customs to see if they are similar or different among various segments. Also, information will be collected to see when and how each segment makes decisions about the purchase of products related to graduation. From all of the information collected, the business will identify which segment offers the best marketing opportunity. That will become the target market.

It is possible for the company to select more than one segment for a target market. To be successful, the segments must have enough common needs that they respond

in the same way to marketing efforts. For example, males and females from the same school may be a part of one target market. Or all graduating seniors from high schools in the Midwest may be similar enough to be considered one target market. Larger companies often work with several target markets at the same time. Each of the target markets requires different marketing activities because of its differences from other target markets.

What four criteria must be satisfied if a target market is to be effective?

1. What is a marketing strategy?
2. Why do businesses need a marketing strategy if they have a good product or service?
3. Does a business need to differentiate market segments if it wants to serve the entire market in a given geographic area?
4. What are psychographic characteristics?
5. What is a target market?
6. How can a business target more than one target market simultaneously?

9.2 ASSESSING MARKETING MIX ALTERNATIVES

GOALS

- Describe aspects of a basic product that can be altered to improve its market appeal.
- Discuss the considerations that marketers take into account when planning distribution, pricing, and promotions.
- Define four stages of a product life cycle.

MARKETING MATTERS

The most important work of marketers is to design and implement the marketing mix. The marketing mix is the combination of the four marketing elements—product, distribution, price, and promotion—and includes all the marketing activities the business will use to satisfy the target market. Marketers understand that there are many ways to change a product to make it more appealing to certain consumers. Those differences occur through changes in the marketing mix. An effective marketer studies each of the mix elements to understand what can be changed and which changes will be most effective in a specific target market.

Make a list of three products or services that you have bought recently and which you feel are superior to alternative products you also considered buying. What elements of those products make them superior to the others?

FINE-TUNING
THE PRODUCT

Have you had the experience of shopping for an item and finding that you have very few choices? While there may be two or three brands available, each of the brands is almost identical to the others. This is a common problem when businesses attempt to sell products to a large market. They attempt to meet the needs of the average consumer. If you are not average, you may find that there is little available that is particularly appealing to you.

For a business, it is very difficult to compete when its products are almost

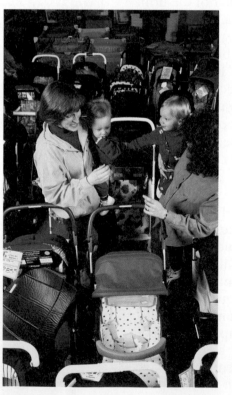

identical to those of its competitors. Such businesses are in a competitive market that is close to pure competition. When customers see few differences, they are less likely to be satisfied and will look for the lowest price. Businesses want to make their products different from the competition and more satisfying to customers. If that is accomplished, the market will be more like a monopoly.

The product or service as a marketing mix element includes anything offered to the customer by the business that will be used to satisfy needs.

This element can be very complex. There are many choices businesses can make when developing the product element of the marketing mix. Figure 9-3 illustrates the major components of a product or service that can be used to create a product that is quite different from competitors' products and that responds to the specific needs of the target market.

Not all of the components listed will be used with every product or service. In some cases, all the target market wants is the basic product. At other times services and a guarantee are important. Both research and creativity are needed to develop an effective product. Marketers need to be familiar with all of the possible changes that can be made in a product and select the most satisfying combination to serve a target market.

Basic Product The most important part of this mix element is the basic product offered. It is the first factor considered by the consumer in deciding whether or not to purchase. If a product is not viewed as need satisfying, the consumer will not consider it as a reasonable alternative. A service can also be the basic part of a marketing mix. Movie theaters, child care, home cleaning, and tax preparation businesses all offer a basic service.

Product Features After the basic product or service is identified, businesses can add features to make it different from and better than competitors' products and services. Most basic products are sold with a number of additional features. Consider the product offerings of automobile dealers. Every automobile today has hundreds of features. Some, such as seat belts, outside rearview mirrors, safety bumpers, and emission control equipment, are required by

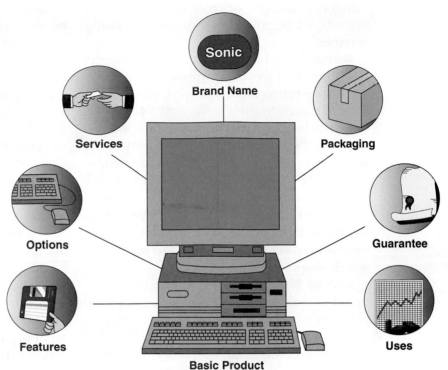

The Product Element of a Marketing Mix

law. Others are included to satisfy the common needs of automobile purchasers—carpeting, reclining seats, locking gasoline filler covers, and stereo radios.

These are examples of features on other products. A shirt offers tailoring, easy-care fabric, double-sewn buttons, and multiple color choices. A telephone has push-button dialing, 10-number memory, redial, and a volume control. Shampoo contains special moisturizers, a conditioner, and a pleasant scent. Consumers expect many of these features, and they will not buy products that do not offer the features.

Options Features are added to improve the basic product. Some businesses make decisions about the features they offer to customers. Customers are not given choices. They must accept the features the company offers. Other companies give customers choices of the features to be included on the product they purchase. Those choices are known as options. When you order telephone service you are given choices such as call waiting, call forwarding, and three-way calling. Some customers choose one or more of those options, while others choose just the basic services.

Associated Services If your family has purchased a major appliance such as a washer or refrigerator, you were probably offered a maintenance contract by the salesperson. The maintenance contract is an associated service that will pay for repair work if the appliance fails to operate properly. There are many cases where services provided with a product make the product easier to use for consumers. If you purchase a computer system, you might want someone to set it up and test it to make sure it works properly.

Brand Name/Image At first the brand name may not seem to be an important part of a product or service. You can probably identify products that you buy where the brand name is one of the most important factors in your decision. In fact, you may refuse to buy a pair of jeans, athletic shoes, or a backpack unless it is a specific brand. The brand of certain products is an important factor in making a purchase decision for many people.

Your parents may not always understand why you want to buy specific brands of certain products, but they are probably just as loyal to particular brands of automobiles, foods, athletic equipment, or magazines. Business people demonstrate brand loyalty for equipment, supplies, airlines, and hotels.

One of the important reasons for brand loyalty is the image of the brand. The **image** is a unique, memorable quality of a brand. Some brands have an image of quality, others of low price, and still others as innovative. The image must match the important needs of the consumer to be effective.

Guarantee/Warranty When customers purchase products or services, they want to receive a good value. If they are concerned the product is poorly constructed, will not work properly, or may wear out quickly, they may be unwilling to purchase

it. Companies offer guarantees or warranties with products to provide customers as insurance that the product will be repaired or replaced if there are problems.

Packaging An often-overlooked part of the marketing mix is the package. Packaging provides protection and security for the product until the consumer can use it, and it has other purposes as well. The package can provide information that helps the customer make a better purchasing decision. It can be useful in promoting the product by attracting attention, demonstrating uses of the product, and so forth. Packaging can even make the product more useful for the consumer. Producers of orange juice found that sales increased when a plastic spout with a cover that could be screwed on and off was added to their cardboard carton.

Uses The final part of the product element of the marketing mix is the use of the product. It is possible that products and services can be more satisfying to customers or can appeal to new markets if other uses are found. A classic example of expanding markets through new product uses is baking soda. Very few consumers bake their own bread today in the United States, so a manufacturer of baking soda saw sales of the product declining. In a study of consumer behavior, it was discovered that consumers use the product for many purposes other than baking. Some use it to freshen refrigerators, garbage disposals, and litter boxes for pets. Others use it to brush their teeth. Through promoting those and other uses and actually creating some new products, the company has increased their sales dramatically.

Name the seven aspects of a basic product that can be changed to improve its appeal.

DISTRIBUTION, PRICE, AND PROMOTION

The complete product or service offered by a company is certainly an important element of the marketing mix. However, unless the product is known to consumers in the target market, is available when they want it, and sells for a satisfactory price, the company will not be successful.

Distribution   Distribution is the marketing mix element that facilitates the physical exchange of products and services between businesses and their customers. Just as with product/service planning, there are many possible decisions about the locations and methods used to make products available to customers. Some important questions that should be answered in planning distribution include the following:

- Where will the customer be best able to obtain the product?
- Where will the customer use the product?
- Are there special requirements to transport, store, or display the product?
- When should distribution occur?
- Who should be responsible for each type of distribution activity?

In addition to these general distribution decisions, many products require specific attention to physical distribution factors including the type of transportation, inventory control, product handling, protective packaging, order processing, and customer service.

Price   The economic foundations of marketing identify the importance of price as a marketing mix element. People have unlimited needs and limited resources to satisfy them. They will carefully evaluate products and services to determine if the price that must be paid is appropriate.

It might appear that there is very little a marketer can do with this element of the marketing mix. A price must be set that is high enough to make a profit but not so high that customers will not want to buy. There is more to pricing, however, than setting the highest price consumers will pay.

WORLDVIEW

Mad Cows Distort Markets

Agricultural commodities tend to trade in a unified world market so that prices are pretty much the same everywhere unless the market is segmented by trade barriers. A notable exception occurred in the 1990s after an outbreak of "mad cow disease" in the UK, followed by fears that it had spread to other countries.

As a result of the ensuing health scare, beef prices were severely distorted and a highly segmented market developed. In countries where the livestock was suspected of being contaminated, such as Germany and France, export markets shrank at the same time that domestic demand shifted to imported beef. Beef prices became very volatile. In safe countries, beef producers found export demand heating up, which tended to boost prices.

To address the health concerns, the European Union began slaughtering 400,000 German cows, which also had the convenient effect of removing a lot of excess supply from the market. That tended to stabilize beef prices as well as provide a justification for the EU's protectionist agricultural policies. So politics continues to segment what would otherwise be a single world market.

THINK CRITICALLY

1. If you were a beef producer in a country where contamination was suspected, how would you benefit from a government plan to slaughter suspect livestock?

2. How do agricultural products differ from other commodities in ways that might be used to justify protectionist trade barriers?

Promotion Consumers need information about product and service choices and assistance in making the best purchasing decisions. Businesses use the promotion element of the marketing mix to provide that information and assistance. Promotion includes the methods and information communicated to customers to encourage purchases and increase their satisfaction.

Maybe more than any of the other mix elements, it is easy to see a variety of choices businesses have to change and improve the promotion mix. Some of the following decisions need to be made when planning promotion:

● Will the audience for the promotion be a general market or specific segments? Who is the decision-maker? Where are the customers in the decision-making process?
● Is the specific goal of promotion to increase knowledge, to change attitudes, or to influence behavior?
● What specific information does the audience need?
● Will promotion be most effective through advertising, personal selling, sales promotion, publicity, or some other form of communication?
● What is the total amount of money needed for effective promotion? When should the money be spent, on what activities, and for which media?
● What information does the business need from consumers? When and how can feedback be obtained to make it most useful?

Price as a marketing mix element is defined as the amount a buyer pays as well as the methods of increasing the value of the product to the customers. There are several decisions about how to develop and present the price that can affect the customer's perception of value. They include the following issues:

● Does the business want to increase sales, increase profits, or enhance the image of the product?
● Should price be based on cost, what customers are willing to pay, or what competitors are charging?
● Will there be one price for all customers? Will customers be allowed to negotiate price? Will discounts or sales be used?
● Will the price be clearly communicated through a price sticker or catalog?
● Are there things that clearly satisfy the customer and make the product better and more valuable than alternatives?

Besides the total product or service being offered, what other elements must marketers consider in developing a marketing mix?

USING LIFE CYCLE ANALYSIS

There are certainly a large number of choices available to change a marketing mix and to make it different from and better than competitors' mixes. It may seem that with all of those choices it will be difficult to determine the best combination of product, distribution, price, and promotion to use. Think of the graduation products company. If you were helping the company selling graduation products plan its marketing mix, how would you determine what mix it should use?

There are three factors to be considered each time a business plans its marketing mix. Those factors are

- the type of competition
- the purchase behavior of consumers
- the strengths and weaknesses of the business

Life cycle analysis and product/service purchase classifications can assist marketers in understanding those factors and developing effective marketing mixes.

STAGES OF A PRODUCT LIFE CYCLE

Products go through four stages in their life cycle, as shown in Figure 9-4. The stages of the life cycle are determined by changes in the type of competition the products face. By studying the competition, a business can determine the type of marketing mix needed in each stage of the life cycle.

Introduction   In the first stage of the product life cycle, a new product is introduced into the market. It is quite different from existing products so customers are not aware of it or don't realize how it can satisfy their needs. Because it is new, there are no other products that are direct competitors. It will be competing with older, established products.

As with many new things, few people will want to be the first to try the product. The business needs to identify those that are very dissatisfied with current products and those who are most likely to want to experiment with something new. These people are the target market for the new product.

The product itself will be very basic since it has just been developed. There will not likely be many features or options. In fact, if the new product is too complicated, customers may not be willing to try it. To assure the customers of the quality of the new product, the company may offer a guarantee or warranty. A well-known brand name may also encourage people to buy the new product if the experience with that brand name has been successful in the past.

The product will not have to be widely distributed in the market since only a small number of customers will buy it initially. It would be too risky and too expensive for the company to try to get widespread distribution. The company will select those

FIGURE 9-4
Analysis of the stages of a product life cycle help businesses develop effective marketing mixes.

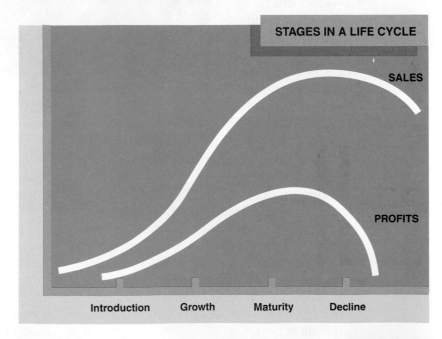

STAGES IN A LIFE CYCLE

SALES

PROFITS

Introduction   Growth   Maturity   Decline

locations where the target market would be most likely to buy this type of product.

The price usually needs to be rather high at first since the company has many expenses in developing the product and expects fewer sales immediately. People who are the first to buy a new product or have needs that are unsatisfied will often pay a higher price. They also have no other similar products to use in comparing the price.

Promotion needs to be directed at the target market to inform them that a new product is available and show how it will satisfy their needs. The audience also needs to know where they can purchase the product. Often promotion in the introductory stage of the life cycle will emphasize that the product is new and exciting to encourage people who want to be the first to own something.

Growth If a new product is successfully introduced, it attracts more customers and sales begin to grow rapidly. Competitors see that the new product offers opportunities for sales and profits, so they enter the market with their own brands of the product as soon as they can. With this growing market and increasing competition, the marketing mix must change.

Competitors need to offer something different from the first brand in order to attract customers. They will try to add features and options that make their product better than the first models. They may also provide services that support the product. Brand name will be very important as each business tries to show consumers that its offering is best.

Because more consumers are now buying the product, it must be distributed more widely in the market. To be as efficient as possible, manufacturers may use many wholesalers and retailers to sell the product. Since customers have choices of brands, each business tries to be sure its brand is available where and when the customer wants it. They concentrate on improving their order processing and handling, transportation, and customer service activities.

Customers see a range of prices during the growth stage. They have many choices of brands, features, options, and services. Brands with a quality image charge higher prices. Those just entering the market or presenting an economy image have lower prices. Businesses emphasize the value customers receive from their brand.

Promotion in the growth stage becomes more competitive. It is focused on attracting more customers into the market. It also demonstrates the advantages of specific brands. More money is spent on promotion. Unique messages are directed at specific segments of the market. The messages aim to inform prospective customers, persuade those who are making decisions, and remind those who have already purchased about the effectiveness of their decision.

Maturity During the maturity stage of the life cycle, sales peak and profits begin to decline. All of the customers who want the product and all of the companies who are offering this product are in the market. Therefore, the level of competition is very intense as companies compete for existing customers.

The products of competing companies are very similar in maturity. The features and options that were successful have been adopted by all of the companies, while those that were not successful have been eliminated. Customers are aware of brand names and images. Companies emphasize those that are successful and try to change those that are not. When possible, customer services are used to offer more value to customers.

Since customers view the products in this stage of the life cycle as very similar, they pay much more attention to price. Prices will be very competitive and businesses will regularly offer discounts or sale prices to encourage customers to purchase their brands.

Companies will increase the availability of products to make sure customers can easily obtain them. The products will be sold through many businesses, and companies will compete for the best locations.

Promotion is very important in the maturity stage. Companies want to continually remind customers of their brand name and persuade them that their company's brand is better than other choices. Because of the large number of customers in the market, mass media and advertising will be emphasized. A great deal of money is spent on promotion in the maturity stage.

Decline   A market declines when consumers decide that a product is no longer satisfying or when they discover new and better products. Sales begin to drop rapidly and there is little or no profit available to companies with products still in the market. Businesses usually try to get out of the market as quickly as possible unless they have a group of loyal customers.

For products in the decline stage of the life cycle, there is little opportunity for product improvement. Because sales and profits are declining, companies are not willing to invest in product changes. Some companies may try to identify additional uses of the product to broaden the market and retain customers.

Distribution will be cut back to only the profitable locations. Companies may save money in distribution by keeping inventory levels low and cutting back on customer service.

Price is a difficult mix element to manage in this stage of the life cycle. Since profits are declining, businesses want to keep prices high. Only the most loyal customers will pay that high price, however. In most cases, prices have to be reduced to continue to sell the product, and even that may not be enough to keep customers in the market.

Since promotion is expensive, companies reduce the amount of promotion. They are more selective in their media choices and promote much less frequently. Since there are fewer customers interested in this product, companies can use more direct methods of communication to keep their loyal customers as long as possible.

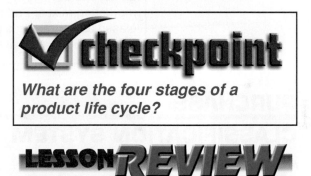

✓checkpoint

What are the four stages of a product life cycle?

LESSON REVIEW

1. What purposes does a product's package serve?

2. What is the difference between a product feature and an option?

3. What functions does the marketing mix element of distribution involve?

4. What is conveyed by product promotions?

5. How do marketers determine which life cycle stage a product or service is in?

6. Why is promotion important in the maturity stage of a product life cycle?

9.3 ANALYZING PRODUCT PURCHASE CLASSIFICATIONS

GOALS

- **Describe the four product/service purchase classifications.**
- **Explain how product/service purchase classifications affect marketing planning.**

By observing and analyzing the way consumers shop, marketers have identified four basic groups into which products and services fall based on consumers' perception of their need for them. These product/service purchase classifications—convenience goods, shopping goods, specialty goods, and unsought goods—can be used as keys to developing effective marketing mixes. Each purchase classification requires a different mix in order to effectively respond to consumers' needs and wants.

Name four things that you bought in the past month and describe the process you went through in making each purchase. What factors did you consider in making the purchase decision? Did you shop around for alternatives? How long did you shop before buying? Do you always buy the same brand, or do you merely buy whatever brand is readily available when the need arises?

PURCHASE CLASSIFICATION SYSTEM

The product/service purchase classification system is a description of the way consumers shop for products based on their needs and perception of products. See Figure 9-5 on the next page for examples of each category of the classification system.

You do not purchase all products in the same way. For some purchases you are very careful, spending a great deal of time and comparing several brands before deciding on the one to buy. For others, you know what you want and will buy it as quickly and conveniently as possible. Finally, there are some products you would not consider buying. Through careful study of the ways consumers purchase products,

marketers have developed the purchase classification system to help plan marketing strategies. The system is based on two important factors:

1. The importance of the purchase to the consumer.
2. The willingness of the consumer to shop and compare products before making the purchase.

CONVENIENCE GOODS

There are many purchases that consumers want to make in the most convenient way possible. The reason for that decision determines whether the product or service is a staple, impulse, or emergency good.

FIGURE 9-5
Marketers develop better marketing mixes by understanding how consumers shop for a product.

Classifying Products for the Consumer Market

Staple Goods Staple convenience goods include the many products you buy that are regular, routine purchases. You need to buy them frequently, you are aware of the needs they satisfy, and you probably have a preference of brands. These are products you routinely pick up when you go to a store. Staple goods include bread, milk, toothpaste, snack foods, and many other regularly purchased products.

Since you know you will need them, you make regular purchases. You will typically purchase them at a convenient location or when you make a routine shopping trip. It is not likely you will shop around from store to store in order to buy a staple good. If the store you are in does not have your favorite brand you may be willing to buy another brand, or you may wait to buy it until the next time you go shopping.

Impulse Goods How many times have you walked into a store to buy one or two items and left the store with several more purchases than you planned? These items that people purchase on the spur of the moment without advance planning are impulse goods. Some examples are candy, magazines, low-cost jewelry, unique items of clothing, and inexpensive new products. Impulse goods are often the items you see displayed near checkout counters.

Consumers do not actively shop for impulse goods. They purchase them when they see the product displayed or advertised and identify an important need that they believe can be satisfied. Because of the strong need along with a belief there is no real value to be gained in shopping and comparing other products or brands, the consumer makes the purchase immediately.

Emergency Goods You may have a favorite brand of gasoline or soft drink. When given a choice, you will probably select those brands and may even go out of your way to find them. But when the fuel gauge on your car is on empty, you will probably pull into the most convenient gasoline station and buy that brand of gas. If you are very thirsty, you may be willing to buy another brand of soft drink or even a different beverage if your favorite is not available. Products or services that are purchased as a result of an urgent need are emergency goods. Common examples of emergency goods are automobile towing services, umbrellas, ambulance services, and plumbing repair services.

As with impulse goods, consumers do not actively shop for emergency goods. They decide to purchase only because the situation creates an urgent, important need. Because of the emergency, the consumer is unable or unwilling to shop and compare products before purchasing.

SHOPPING GOODS

Most of the major purchases made by consumers are shopping goods. These products and services are typically more expensive than convenience goods. Consumers believe that the need is important, the amount of money to be spent on the purchase is significant, and that real differences exist among the choices of products and brands. Therefore they are willing to spend time shopping and comparing alternatives before making a final purchase decision. Examples of shopping goods for many people are clothing, cars, houses and apartments, stereo equipment, major appliances, colleges, dentists, and vacation locations.

Attribute-based Goods   For most shopping goods, consumers see a number of ways that choices are different. Each brand may have a different set of features or services. Prices may vary or some brands may be purchased on sale or using credit. When a variety of differences exist and the consumer considers a number of factors to determine the best value, the product is an attribute-based shopping good.

Price-based Goods   Some people evaluate major purchases and decide that several products or brands are basically alike. They will each provide the same level of satisfaction. Yet the consumer believes the price is likely to be quite different among the choices. Because the need is important and the cost is high, it is worth the time needed to shop for the best possible price. Products that consumers believe are similar but have significant price differences are price-based shopping goods.

SPECIALTY GOODS

There are some products and services consumers purchase that are so satisfying that the consumer will not consider buying anything else as a substitute. Products that have this strong brand loyalty are known as specialty goods. People often think of very well known and expensive products as specialty goods. Automobiles such as Rolls Royce, Porsche, or Lamborghini fit the description. Lear jets and Rolex watches are specialty goods.

Inexpensive and regularly purchased products are also treated as specialty goods by some customers. Do you have a favorite brand of blue jeans? Do you shop for tapes and CDs at the same store every time? Do you and your friends usually go to the same restaurant or other business after school activities? If you do and would not typically consider another choice, they would be specialty products and businesses. Even such things as chewing gum and toothpaste can be specialty goods if the customer will not buy a different brand.

The two factors that determine if a product is a specialty good are its importance in satisfying an individual's need and the willingness of the customer to delay a purchase until the specific product or brand is located. In the case of specialty goods, consumers believe the brand is the only thing that will provide satisfaction. That belief is usually based on very positive past experiences with the chosen brand and less positive experiences with other brands. Because of the strong belief in the brand, customers will not compare brands when shopping. They will not make a purchase until they can find their choice. If that means waiting or traveling to another store, the customer is willing to do so. You can see that such customer loyalty is very valuable to businesses.

UNSOUGHT GOODS

While consumers go to great lengths to find specialty goods, there are other products that consumers do not want to buy. They are known as unsought goods. If you were choosing things to purchase in the next year, would the choices include life insurance or legal services to prepare a will? Those are typically not considered important needs for young people so they would currently be unsought goods in that market. Nevertheless, when you get older with a career and a family, either of the items may become much more important and could become shopping goods or even specialty goods.

When a product or a specific brand of a product is first introduced into the market, consumers are not aware it exists. As soon as they become aware of the product, they decide if it is something that might meet a need. If a product or service does not fill a customer need, it remains unsought and unsold. Even if the business makes it easy to buy, through telephone or catalog sales or a salesperson visiting the person at home, consumers will not make the purchase.

checkpoint

What are the four product/service purchase classifications?

APPLYING PURCHASE CLASSIFICATIONS
TO MARKETING PLANNING

Just as life cycle stages provide important information about competition, purchase classifications help in the understanding of consumer behavior. That understanding is important in planning the best marketing mix. Each purchase classification requires a different mix in order to effectively respond to consumer needs.

CONVENIENCE GOODS

Consumers want to purchase convenience goods as easily as possible. They do not see important differences among products and brands that make it worth their time to shop and compare. Therefore businesses need to emphasize product location (convenience) in the marketing mix. The product mix element will focus on brand, packaging, and image.

Price is important for staple goods. Prices cannot be set higher than similar products in the same location or the consumer will switch brands. For impulse goods price is less important, and for emergency goods price is only a minor consideration. Promotion is used to remind people of brand and image for staple goods, the need to be satisfied for impulse goods, and location and availability for emergency goods.

SHOPPING GOODS

Because consumers are willing to shop and compare, the marketing mix for shopping goods is different from convenience goods. Products and services no longer have to be available in the most convenient locations. Promotion emphasizes the qualities of the product or service that consumers believe are most important. Promotion often helps consumers compare products or brands.

For attribute-based shopping goods, the product mix element is very important. Consumers are interested in the best combination of features, options, services, and uses. For price-based shopping goods, price is the most important. While customers want a quality product, they believe that several products are very similar. Therefore, they do not evaluate differences in product features. They search for the best possible price. Businesses must demonstrate that they have the lowest price or the best possible financial terms. They also need to emphasize price in promotional activities.

SPECIALTY GOODS

Specialty goods are in some ways the easiest to market and in other ways they are somewhat difficult. The emphasis in the marketing mix will depend on why consumers believe the product or service is a specialty good. Typically, that status results from a unique or quality product. In that case, the business wants to emphasize the product in marketing planning to insure that the quality or uniqueness is maintained. Promotion reminds consumers of the reasons they prefer the product.

It is possible that consumers prefer a product or service because of its location. Some people select a bank, a physician, or even a college because of its location. They would not consider another choice because it would be inconvenient. Therefore, marketing activities for that product would emphasize location more than product features. There are some instances where price is the reason for specialty status. Consumers may buy only one brand because they believe it has the best price. Once again, marketing would maintain that price so consumers remain satisfied. Marketing would emphasize the price as a part of promotion.

Market Intelligence

Kelvin Gardner is a sales representative for Agri-Gro, an agriculture chemical producer. He sells to farm supply businesses in a four-state area: Illinois, Iowa, Missouri, and Kansas. For four years, Kelvin has been number one or two in company sales. However, this year has been different. The economy is slowing, customers are delaying purchases, and Kelvin has fallen to 10th place in sales.

One company in Kelvin's territory, Farmmore, has never purchased chemicals from Agri-Gro. It has businesses in three of the four states where Kelvin works and purchases 8 percent of all chemicals sold in those states. Kelvin thinks that if he can gain Farmmore's business, he'll be back on top.

Kelvin is meeting with Farmmore's vice-president when the VP is called to meet briefly with the CEO. While he waits, Kelvin notices a copy of Farmmore's marketing plan on the desk. Kelvin knows that the document could provide keen insights into Farmmore's plans for the year. If Kelvin knew more about its plans, he could show how Agri-Gro's products would help Farmmore be more effective. But Kelvin also realizes that the marketing plan is a confidential document.

THINK CRITICALLY

1. Should Kelvin pick up the copy of the plan from the vice-president's desk and look through it, or should he respect its confidentiality?

2. What would be the likely result if he picked it up and the VP returned and caught him looking through the plan?

3. What tactic might Kelvin try to gain some insights into the company's plans without violating its confidentiality?

Occasionally, products become specialty products because of effective promotion. Promotion that is able to create excitement, a unique image, or a belief that one product is far superior to others may result in the product being treated as a specialty good for at least a short time. This is often the case with items that are considered fads.

UNSOUGHT GOODS

The marketing mix developed for unsought goods is particularly important. If the products are not well marketed, there will be no demand and the product will fail. If a product is new, the mix will emphasize promotion and distribution. Consumers must be aware of the product, how it satisfies needs, and where they can purchase it. If a business is successful with those two mix elements, the product will quickly become a convenience, shopping, or specialty good.

If customers are aware of the product or service and it remains unsought, the mix must be very carefully developed. The product is most important. The business must evaluate the product to determine why consumers do not want it. The product must be redesigned to make it more appealing to consumers and to relate to their important needs. Promotion can then be used to show consumers how the product will meet their needs.

Businesses must market unsought goods very carefully. Consumers may become quite upset if they believe a business is trying to sell them something they do not need. If consumers develop a negative attitude toward a product or a business, it will be difficult to sell them products in the future. Businesses that successfully sell unsought goods use a target market strategy. They identify the specific segments of the market that have needs related to the product or service. They then develop very personalized marketing mixes to work with those target markets at times and locations where there is a good chance to be successful. Some businesses are so effective with their marketing that a

regularly unsought good becomes a specialty good for customers. For example, people who had never purchased life insurance may be impressed by the personal attention and knowledge of one insurance agent. They not only buy one insurance policy but also buy additional products from the same agent without considering other companies.

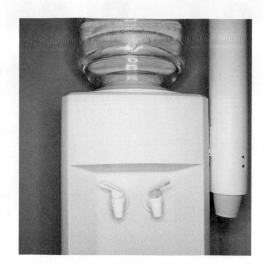

The location element of the marketing mix generally is most important for which product/service purchase classification?

1. Name the two main factors on which the product/service purchase classification system is based.

2. What are the three types of convenience goods?

3. How do shopping goods differ from convenience goods?

4. What is the main distinguishing characteristic of specialty goods?

5. Why is the development of an effective marketing mix particularly important for unsought goods?

6. Which purchase classification is generally most sensitive to changes in the price marketing mix element?

9.4 PLANNING FOR MARKETING

● Understand the benefits of marketing planning.
● Describe the steps of developing a marketing plan.

Developing a marketing plan is one of the most important steps businesses take to market their products and services. The marketing plan serves as a guide for coordinating marketing activities. Today, almost all successful businesses have a written marketing plan. Developing an effective marketing plan requires the commitment of time and attention by senior marketing managers and the gathering of information about the company, the competition, changes in the business environment, and about customers.

Write a brief but detailed description of the planning process you went through in preparing for your last exam in a class other than this one. In retrospect, how could you have applied better organization and planning to improve the results?

THE BENEFITS
OF PLANNING

When a group of friends decides to take a one-week travel vacation, they can simply start out driving and choose what to see as they go along. They might use their time effectively and have a good vacation or they might not. A better method may be for the group to agree on their destination, travel time, and activities. Then they can gather information about the planned destinations and activities. Using that information, they can develop a schedule to make the best use of their money and time.

A business person might try to get by without any planning before deciding what products to sell, how to promote them, what prices to charge, or how to respond to competition. In this case, each decision will be made when it seems important or when a problem occurs. The result might be that some decisions are made too late, without enough information, or without considering

the impact on other parts of the business. To improve decision-making, the business person gathers information about customers and competition, decides on the profit and sales goals the business can achieve, and then carefully develops a specific plan to guide the purchase, distribution, pricing, and promotion of products and services (see Figure 9-6).

In the examples above, a situation in which little planning was done was compared with one in which a great deal of planning was done to prepare for an important activity. With careful planning, the group planning a trip and the business person managing the sale of products have a much better idea of what they want to accomplish, the best ways to reach their objectives, and the likelihood that they will be able to accomplish what they planned.

WHAT IS A MARKETING PLAN?

Marketing in most businesses involves a large number of very complex activities. To be successful, the activities need to be coordinated with each other and with the activities occurring in other parts of the business. Many people are involved in carrying out the marketing activities. To make the best use of the time and work of those people, their activities should be coordinated as well.

It often takes a very long time from when a product is developed or purchased until it is sold. A great many decisions must be made and often a large amount of money and other resources must be committed by the business during the time between production and the sale of the product. Careful planning and coordination of decisions and resources will be needed in order for the business to make a profit once the products have been sold.

To aid in decision-making and the coordination of the many people, activities, and resources involved in successful marketing, businesses usually develop a marketing plan. A **marketing plan** is a clear written description of the marketing strategies of a business and the way the business will operate to accomplish each strategy.

FIGURE 9-6

Without planning, marketing efforts will not be coordinated. With planning, they are focused on satisfying customers.

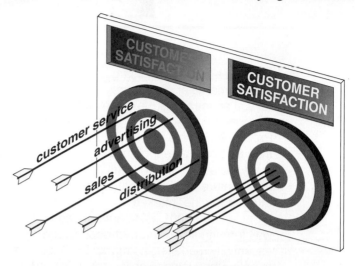

The Advantage of Planning

FROM STRATEGY TO PLAN

In a marketing strategy, the business identifies the target market to be served and develops a marketing mix. The marketing plan is based on a marketing strategy.

Marketing strategies must be developed very carefully. They need to be based on a complete study of a market and the possible ways the business can serve the market. If marketers are not careful in developing the strategy, they will be no better off than the companies with a production orientation. They will likely make decisions based on their own opinions rather than the target market's needs.

P&G On (the) Line

If you are the world's largest and most successful marketer of consumer products, how do you squeeze the maximum value from all that marketing expertise? If you are the Procter & Gamble Co., which spends more than $1 billion a year on marketing many of the world's best-known brands, you start a new venture to market that expertise over the Internet to other marketers.

In January 2001, P&G announced that it was forming a new Internet-based venture, essentially marketing its marketing expertise to help other companies launch new products. It said the venture would advise clients on all aspects of marketing, from product development to advertising and sales.

P&G partnered with Worldwide Magnifi Inc., an Internet software vendor, to build private networks that can facilitate global marketing projects. Ideally, the networks permit all marketers involved in a project to communicate simultaneously and seamlessly from different locations around the globe.

In launching the venture, P&G cited three trends in global marketing—the globalization of brands, the geographical dispersion of marketing teams, and the increasing importance of speed as a determinant of marketing success.

THINK CRITICALLY

1. Besides its investment capital, what has P&G risked by putting its marketing expertise on public display and selling it even to potential competitors?

2. How can an Internet-based network for marketers address the three trends that P&G cited in forming this venture?

A marketing plan is an organized, objective method of identifying a marketing strategy and determining how the business should operate to make sure the strategy is successful (see Figure 9-7). The process of developing a marketing plan encourages the marketer to gather and analyze information, consider alternatives, determine what competitors are likely to do, and study possible responses of customers.

Based on that study, careful procedures can be planned for the best ways to achieve the marketing strategy. It is possible to determine in advance whether the strategy can be implemented as planned. If not, the strategy can be modified before mistakes are made. You can see that the marketing strategy describes what the business wants to do and the marketing plan provides the details on how the strategy will be implemented and evaluated.

FIGURE 9-7
A marketing plan expands on a company's marketing strategy by gathering and studying information to determine actions needed to implement the strategy.

From Strategy to a Plan

What are the primary benefits of developing a written marketing plan?

PREPARING FOR MARKETING PLANNING

Just as when you plan to study for an important test or plan a vacation, marketing planning needs to be done carefully. It is a scientific process. A marketing plan is developed to solve a specific problem or accomplish an objective. Information is collected to help identify possible solutions. Alternative strategies are considered and often tested before deciding on the best one. Plans are developed so the marketing strategy selected will be implemented effectively. Finally, methods for evaluating the marketing plan are developed to insure that the marketing strategy is accomplishing the objectives or solving the problem.

FIGURE 9-8
Businesses need to be sure they have the necessary resources for effective marketing planning.

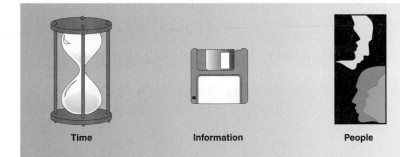

| Time | Information | People |

Resources for Effective Planning

marketing strategies, and what competitors are likely to do. They will know in advance what needs to be done to accomplish their objectives rather than waiting for problems to occur.

PLANNING TO PLAN

Marketing plans are developed for a specific time period, often one year. Plans may be quite short for a small business, but can be very long and complex for a large business with a number of products and services in many markets. The marketing plan is usually developed by the top marketing executive in the business with input and assistance from many other people. In very large companies, there may be several people working throughout the year to gather and analyze the information needed to develop the marketing plan (see Figure 9-8). Even in small companies, it takes many hours of work and the accumulation of much information to prepare an effective marketing plan.

Marketing planning is not easy. It requires time, information, and people who understand marketing planning procedures. Because of these requirements, some business people believe they do not need or cannot afford to develop marketing plans. They feel their past experience has prepared them to make marketing decisions. That attitude gives an advantage to the business people who carefully prepare marketing plans. They will know when changes are occurring in the market, how customers are likely to respond to new

PLANS ARE BUILT WITH INFORMATION

The work needed to develop a marketing plan begins long before the plan is actually written. A great deal of information is necessary to develop a good marketing plan. The people responsible for marketing planning must make sure needed information is collected and evaluated in order to begin the necessary planning.

Marketing plans developed without needed information or with limited information are likely to result in poor decisions and ineffective marketing. If the information is not available when needed and is not organized to make it easy to analyze, marketing planning will be delayed. Companies that develop marketing plans must carefully identify the information they need for those plans. Then they determine where and how the information can be obtained. They begin the data collection process long before the marketing plan is actually developed.

Each business uses somewhat different information for its marketing plan. The following types of information are usually needed for effective marketing planning.

Performance of the Company   In order to plan for the future, marketers must know what has happened in the past and what is expected to happen in the future. Information on sales and profits, effective and ineffective marketing activities, and the company's strengths and weaknesses needs to be collected and reviewed. Marketers need to know what new products are being developed, if others are being eliminated, and if resources are likely to change in the future.

Performance of Competing Companies   Customers usually have several brands of products or services from which to choose. In order to develop marketing strategies that will be successful, marketers must evaluate the products and efforts of those competing businesses and attempt to predict what competitors are likely to do in the future.

Changes Outside the Company   Many things occur that affect the potential success of a product but are outside of the immediate control of the business or its competitors. The economy can decline or improve. Laws can be passed by state and local governments that affect business activities. Additional taxes or licenses can increase costs. Newly developed technology can result in improved products or innovative production and marketing procedures. Businesses that regularly collect information to determine if changes are likely to occur are in a better position to respond to changes than businesses that do not pay attention to change.

Information About Current and Prospective Customers   Customer information is important to marketers. Understanding customers makes it possible for businesses to satisfy their needs.

Through satisfying needs, businesses hope to make a profit. Businesses must continually study information about their customers. They must learn more about who their customers are and what their needs are. A business needs to know how customers perceive the business and its competitors. Are there changes or improvements in products and services the customers would like to see? It is also important for businesses to identify other prospective customer groups. The business can gain more customers by satisfying the needs of new groups.

GATHERING NEEDED INFORMATION

Companies that successfully prepare and use marketing plans have developed procedures to gather and analyze information. Many have sophisticated marketing information systems that make it possible to quickly and objectively review large amounts of information.

Much of the information used in developing marketing plans is already available in the company. Records of production, operations, and sales are usually maintained. Detailed information on specific customers and their purchasing history is often available. In addition, many businesses regularly gather information about competitors, business trends, and the economy to use in planning.

If information is needed for marketing planning and is not currently available, procedures should be developed to obtain it. Again, some of the needed information may already be collected and available from a government agency, a trade association, or a company that specializes in market research. If those sources cannot provide the information, the business needs to complete the necessary research to obtain the information.

What four types of information are usually needed for effective marketing planning?

LESSON REVIEW

1. What is a marketing plan?

2. How is a marketing plan related to a marketing strategy?

3. Plans of all types are usually made for a certain time period. What time period do business marketing plans often cover?

4. Where do businesses obtain the information they need to develop and implement effective marketing plans?

5. Which business personnel are typically involved in developing a marketing plan?

6. What is the likely result if the information needed to implement a marketing plan is poor, limited, or unavailable?

GOALS

● Identify the five types of market analysis used in developing a marketing plan.

● Describe the elements of an effective marketing strategy.

● Explain the need for activity schedules and evaluation procedures.

MARKETING MATTERS

Marketing plans take many forms and can contain different types of information. They are developed to assist a specific business, so they are written in a way that is most useful for the people in that business.

Work with a group. If you were asked to develop a marketing plan, what steps would you need to take to complete the plan? What type of information would you need? What kinds of questions should you ask or answer before you could begin? Share your results with the other groups.

ANALYZING
THE MARKET

The first part of the marketing planning process provides an opportunity for the planners to review information to determine the most effective marketing strategy. Figure 9-9 shows a sample marketing plan outline. Sample questions are provided along the way for each major section of the outline.

Purpose and Mission The mission or purpose of the company identifies the nature of the business or the reasons the business exists. It is most often developed to describe broad categories of products or services the business provides (transportation, health care, legal services) or the types of customers the company wants to serve (business travelers, resorts in the sunbelt, single parents with children under 18). By identifying the mission or purpose, marketing planners concentrate their efforts in areas where the company is known and works best. An example of a mission statement for an auto dealership is "to offer automobiles at fair prices, to provide fast and effective service, and to treat all customers with courtesy and respect." A bank has a mission of "offering convenient and innovative financial services for the Southeast."

SAMPLE QUESTIONS

A. Purpose and Mission of the Business
   a. What is the reason this business exists?
   b. Who is the business most interested in serving?
   c. What are the important things the business is trying to accomplish?

Current Markets and Strategies

After identifying the mission, the planners briefly review the current marketing efforts of the company. The review includes an identification of the markets in which the company is operating and the marketing strategies currently being used to remind the planners of activities underway in the business. Determining the activities that are working well and those that are not helps in deciding to continue with the same strategies or to plan changes. A company might discover that its advertising costs are increasing at a rate much faster than its sales. In that case it needs to determine if the costs can be controlled or if the increased advertising might pay off later in faster sales growth.

FIGURE 9-9

A simple format for developing a marketing plan includes the three stages of development.

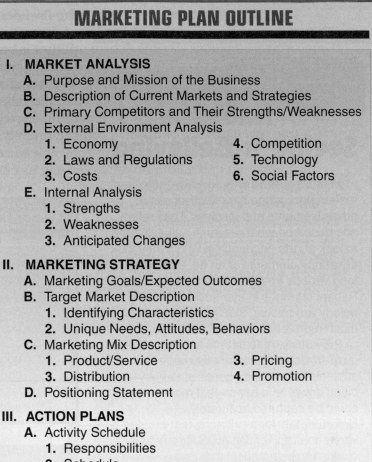

MARKETING PLAN OUTLINE

I. MARKET ANALYSIS
- **A.** Purpose and Mission of the Business
- **B.** Description of Current Markets and Strategies
- **C.** Primary Competitors and Their Strengths/Weaknesses
- **D.** External Environment Analysis
  - **1.** Economy
  - **2.** Laws and Regulations
  - **3.** Costs
  - **4.** Competition
  - **5.** Technology
  - **6.** Social Factors
- **E.** Internal Analysis
  - **1.** Strengths
  - **2.** Weaknesses
  - **3.** Anticipated Changes

II. MARKETING STRATEGY
- **A.** Marketing Goals/Expected Outcomes
- **B.** Target Market Description
  - **1.** Identifying Characteristics
  - **2.** Unique Needs, Attitudes, Behaviors
- **C.** Marketing Mix Description
  - **1.** Product/Service
  - **3.** Distribution
  - **3.** Pricing
  - **4.** Promotion
- **D.** Positioning Statement

III. ACTION PLANS
- **A.** Activity Schedule
  - **1.** Responsibilities
  - **2.** Schedule
  - **3.** Budget
- **B.** Evaluation Procedures
  - **1.** Evidence of Success
  - **2.** Method of Collecting Evidence

SAMPLE QUESTIONS

- **B.** Description of Current Markets and Strategies
  - **a.** Specifically, who are the business' current customers?
  - **b.** What are the needs and wants of the current customers?
  - **c.** How would the customers describe the important characteristics of the product, distribution, price, and promotion?

DECIDING ON STRATEGY

The most important part of the marketing plan, in terms of the company's success, is the development of a marketing strategy. The marketing strategy is the description of the way marketing will be used to accomplish the company's objectives. It includes a description of the target market and the marketing mix.

Determining Goals and Outcomes   The marketing strategy needs to include a specific statement of the goals the company plans to achieve or the expected outcomes of the marketing efforts. That way the company is able to determine whether the marketing strategy is effective. Marketing goals include such things as increasing sales or profits for certain products, increasing the market share for a product in a particular geographic area or target market, increasing the effectiveness of particular parts of the marketing mix such as distribution or customer service, or other specific results.

Defining a Target Market   The marketing strategy will clearly identify the target market to be served. The target market will be defined completely so it can be located, so people in the business understand the market's characteristics and its needs and wants, and so it is clear that the marketing mix is appropriate for the market.

While each target market is unique, it is possible for an organization to serve several target markets at the same time. When more than one market is identified, marketing planners must remember that each requires a specific marketing mix.

SAMPLE QUESTIONS

A. Marketing Goals/Expected Outcomes
   a. What are the important results the company is expecting to achieve during the time of this plan?
   b. What will be used to determine if marketing activities are successful?

SAMPLE QUESTIONS

B. Target Market Description
   a. Will the target market be the same or different from the past marketing plan?
   b. What are the obvious identifying characteristics of the target market?
   c. Is the identified market a unique segment that requires a specific marketing mix?
   d. Is this market currently purchasing the company's product or a competing product?
   e. What are the important needs and attitudes of the identified market that relate to the product to be provided?
   f. How does this target market go about making a purchase decision for the product?

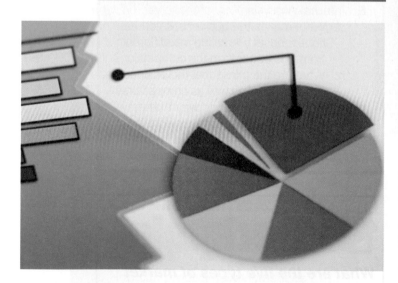

Specifying the Marketing Mix A complete description of each mix element is included in the marketing plan. Product, price, distribution, and promotion are described specifically and completely so everyone involved in implementing the mix understands what the company plans to do.

SAMPLE QUESTIONS

C. Marketing Mix Description
  a. What are the alternatives that could be developed for each of the mix elements?
  b. Of the possible choices, what are the specific and important elements of product, distribution, price, and promotion that the target market would prefer?
  c. Of the possible choices, what are the specific and important elements of product, distribution, price, and promotion that the business will be able to provide?
  d. Which of the alternative marketing mixes best meets target market needs and can be implemented effectively by the business?
  e. Who within and outside the company will need to be involved in implementing the marketing mix?

Developing a Positioning Statement One of the most interesting parts of the marketing strategy is the positioning statement. A positioning statement is a specific description of the unique qualities of the marketing mix that make it different from the competition and satisfying to the target market. For example, a discount store suggests that it provides all of the products needed in the home for a family on a budget. A manufacturer of sporting goods positions itself to serve professional sports teams with products designed to meet the specific needs of each athlete. A home improvement service specializes in working with realtors and homeowners who are planning to sell their homes. Their positioning statement may be to increase the value of the home as a result of careful cleaning and repairs.

SAMPLE QUESTIONS

D. Positioning Statement
  a. What is unique about the target market the business plans to serve?
  b. What about the company or its marketing mix are the unique and identifying qualities that are important to the target market?
  c. How can the unique qualities of the market and mix be clearly communicated in a brief statement?

What are the four elements needed for an effective marketing strategy?

PLANNING
FOR ACTION

The marketing strategy will not be successful just because it is described in a marketing plan. Many people are responsible for implementing the strategy. Their activities must be planned and procedures set up to evaluate the activities. The final section of the marketing plan identifies the actions needed to accomplish and evaluate the marketing strategy.

Activity Schedule Completing each part of the marketing strategy will require a series of activities. The needed activities must be determined along with a description of how and when the activities will be completed. Responsibility for completing each of the activities needs to be assigned.

Many people both inside and outside the company are involved in marketing. Their activities must be coordinated in order to be successful. For example, if a manufacturer is introducing a new notebook-size personal computer, the production schedule must be coordinated with distribution to retailers, the development of printed product information for the manufacturers' and retailers' salespeople, and the advertising schedule. If the computer is advertised to consumers before the retailer has a supply of the products or before salespeople are prepared to provide the necessary product information, both the consumer and retailer will be unhappy with the manufacturer.

SAMPLE QUESTIONS

A. Activity Schedule
   a. What information is needed to complete marketing planning?
   b. What activities must be completed in developing each of the mix elements?
   c. What activities are needed to implement each of the mix elements?
   d. Who will be responsible for each of the activities identified?
   e. When will each activity be initiated?
   f. When will each activity be completed?
   g. How will activities be coordinated with each other?
   h. What money and other resources will be needed for each of the activities?
   i. How and where will the necessary money be obtained?
   j. Who is responsible for preparing and managing the budget?

Evaluation Procedures To be able to determine if the action plan is effective, evaluation procedures should be developed. The evaluation procedures measure whether the marketing activities were completed on time and in the right way. They will also determine if the marketing objectives were accomplished.

Information on target markets can be collected to determine if they are responding to the marketing mix and if their needs are satisfied. Each of the mix elements can be studied to identify whether it was developed as planned. Specific activities should be evaluated to determine if the quality is acceptable and if it was accomplished within the budget available.

Information collected in the evaluation is used to make improvements in marketing activities while the plan is being implemented. As soon as problems are identified, actions should be taken to correct those problems. Evaluation information is also useful in developing the next marketing plan.

SAMPLE QUESTIONS

B. Evaluation Procedures
   a. What specific evidence will show that each of the marketing activities is successful?
   b. What evidence will demonstrate that goals and objectives have been accomplished?
   c. How and when will the evidence be collected?
   d. Who is responsible for collecting and analyzing the information?
   e. Who will need to know the results of the evaluation?

checkpoint

Why is an action plan needed once the other parts of a marketing plan are developed?

LESSON REVIEW

1. What is a mission statement?

2. Why is it important to identify primary competitors and analyze their strengths and weaknesses?

3. Name three things that might be important elements of the external environment in developing a marketing plan.

4. Why is it necessary to include a statement of goals and intended outcomes in a marketing strategy?

5. What is the function of action plan evaluation procedures?

SUMMARY

Lesson 9.1

A. When developing a marketing strategy, start by identifying common characteristics of consumers' wants and needs.

B. Next choose a target market based on which segment or segments present the best marketing opportunities based on four criteria.

Lesson 9.2

A. To develop an effective marketing mix, basic products and services can be altered to improve their appeal to various segments by adding or changing features, options, associated services, the brand name/image, guarantees/warranties, packaging, and uses.

B. Marketers need to address many issues when planning distribution, pricing, and promotion.

C. Products have four life cycle stages—introduction, growth, maturity, and decline. Each requires different marketing mixes tailored to the competitive environment characteristic of each stage.

Lesson 9.3

A. Another effective tool for marketing mixes is the product/service purchase classification system, which classifies products and services as convenience, shopping, specialty, and unsought goods.

B. Each product/service purchase classification calls for a different marketing mix based on how important consumers regard such goods and how willing they are to shop and compare alternative goods.

Lesson 9.4

A. The benefits of a marketing plan are that activities can be focused on satisfying consumers, and people who are involved in carrying out the marketing activities can make optimum use of their time.

B. Marketing plans require the careful assembling and management of information about the company, the competition strengths and weaknesses, the business environment, and customers.

Lesson 9.5

A. Marketing plans are developed in three stages. The first stage is gathering and analyzing the company's mission, markets and strategies, primary competitors, and the external environment.

B. The second stage is to form strategies based on target markets, marketing mixes, and goals and intended outcomes.

C. The final stage involves preparing a list of activities needed to implement the plan and evaluation procedures to confirm that planned activities are completed as scheduled and to assess the results.

REVIEW MARKETING CONCEPTS

The following are competitive situations faced by businesses and examples of customer purchase behavior. For each, identify the stage of the product life cycle or the product/service goods classification category being described.

1. There is little profit in the market and only the most loyal customers continue to buy.

2. The customer carefully compares product features and price at several stores before making a decision.

3. A telemarketer calls to describe a new product to a consumer. The consumer is not interested and hangs up the telephone.

4. Many companies offer a service that consumers view as quite similar. Because of the intense competition, the businesses emphasize promotion and often give customers price discounts.

5. As profits begin to increase in the market, several new companies decide to offer products for sale.

6. Driving home from work, Arthur remembers that he forgot to plan something to cook for the evening meal. Since his family will be home when he arrives, he quickly turns into the deli and purchases the evening's special to take home.

7. Franziene's tires on her automobile were almost worn out and she didn't have a lot of money to replace them. For two weeks she watched the advertisements for tires in the paper. When she saw one business offering a 20 percent discount for the purchase of four tires, she purchased them.

8. Jai needs to replace his lost calculator. He goes to several stores but cannot find the TD model 28 which he prefers. He finally locates one at the college bookstore and purchases it.

9. The Corway Company was test marketing a new transparent coating material for automobile windows that melts ice and snow at temperatures down to 10 degrees Fahrenheit. They learn that another company is developing a similar product, so they end their test market and begin selling the product in 20 northern states in order to beat the other business into the market.

10. Hector was walking through the mall when he saw an artist drawing charcoal portraits. Remembering his mother's birthday in five days, Hector had his portrait drawn to give to his mother.

Identify which of the four marketing mix elements is described in each of the following items.

11. The retail business that sells a product

12. Using telemarketing to contact prospective consumers

13. The message in an advertisement about the company's image

14. The material used in manufacturing the item

15. A new shape for the package

16. Accepting a credit card in payment for the service

17. Offering to exchange a product that was damaged by the consumer for a new product

18. Using air freight rather than trucks to get the product to the customer faster

19. A fall fashion show to inform important customers of the new apparel designs

20. A business that offers to meet or beat the price of any competitor if the customer brings in an advertisement showing that price

REVIEW MARKETING TERMS

Match the terms listed with the definitions. Some terms may not be used.

21. A description of the way consumers shop for products based on their needs and perception of products.

22. A clearly identified segment of the market to which a company wants to appeal.

23. Components of a market in which people have one or more similar characteristics.

24. The way marketing activities are planned and coordinated to achieve an organization's goals.

25. A clear written description of the marketing strategies of a business and the way the business will operate to accomplish each strategy.

26. The unique, memorable qualities of a brand.

a. image
b. marketing plans
c. marketing strategy
d. product/service purchase classification system
e. segments
f. target markets

CHAPTER 9

APPLY MARKETING FUNCTIONS

MARKETING RESEARCH

27. If a business uses a target market strategy, it needs to clearly identify the market it wants to serve in order to attract those people to the business. That is often done through advertising. Review the advertisements for several businesses. Identify three businesses that appear to be appealing to specific target markets. You will want to study several advertisements for the same business to get detailed information about their target market. Using the information from the advertisements, prepare descriptions of the target market of each business. Include information for each of the following categories if possible: demographics, needs/wants, attitudes, and purchase behavior.

28. A national association of homebuilders has collected data on the sales of various styles of manufactured windows for the past 30 years. One window style presents an interesting example of a product life cycle. It was introduced in 1971 and remained on the market until 1993. The following table summarizes its market performance during that time.

Develop a table that illustrates the following information for each of the years listed:
a. average dollar sales per manufacturer
b. average sales price of each window
c. average cost of each window
d. total profit or loss for the industry

MARKETING PLANNING

29. Select one of the following products or services to use for your work on this activity: a professional music group, athletic/running shoes, or a magazine. Identify four people to interview. Determine the information you need to obtain from each person in order to develop a target market description and to classify their purchase behavior in the product/service purchase classification system. Conduct the interviews and complete the following activities:
a. Develop target market descriptions of each person.
b. Determine whether the four people would be part of one target market or more than one.
c. Identify the appropriate product/service purchase classification category for each person interviewed and provide a brief statement describing why you selected that classification.

Year	Number of Manufacturers	Total Units Sold	Total Sales in Dollars	Total Product Cost
1971	1	800	$36,000	$38,400
1972	3	2,800	123,200	126,000
1974	5	4,500	193,500	189,000
1976	6	5,700	245,100	228,000
1978	9	10,800	464,400	410,400
1980	15	22,500	945,000	787,500
1982	15	23,000	954,500	828,000
1984	13	23,000	943,000	851,000
1986	12	22,500	877,500	855,000
1988	8	18,000	684,000	693,000
1990	4	10,500	393,750	404,250
1992	2	4,800	177,600	182,400

30. Identify a product that you own or would like to own that you consider to be a specialty good. Analyze the marketing mix of that product carefully. Using a large sheet of paper or a poster, create an illustration of the marketing mix used to sell the product. Label all parts of each mix element on the illustration.

MARKETING MANAGEMENT

31. People have different needs and different ways of shopping for products and services. Therefore it is likely that the same product or service can fit in several of the product/service purchase classification categories. For the following service and product, describe the consumer purchase behavior that would be used for each of the categories in the classification system.

     Movie
     Groceries

32. The mature stage of the product life cycle is very difficult, especially for smaller businesses. There are many competitors appealing to a arge market. They have very similar products, are increasing their distribution and promotion, and many are starting to decrease their prices to encourage consumers to switch from one business to another. Since most businesses (and especially large businesses) are appealing to the mass market, smaller businesses may have the opportunity to be successful by using the marketing concept when planning a marketing strategy.

     You are a marketing consultant for a small hotel. The business is finding it increasingly difficult to compete with the national chains that have large advertising budgets, can offer a variety of services, and are willing to cut their prices to attract business people and weekend travelers. Prepare a four-page report for the hotel owner that briefly describes the meaning of the marketing concept and why it can help the hotel develop a marketing strategy. Describe an example marketing strategy that could be implemented to help the hotel compete with the large chains. Provide a rationale to support the strategy.

MARKETING TECHNOLOGY

33. Input the window data table from Exercise 28 into a spreadsheet program. Construct a graph of the life cycle for the window illustrating total industry dollar sales and the industry's profit or loss for each year.

34. Use the Internet to search for announcements and articles about a large public corporation's plans for a new business venture. Describe the product or service the venture intends to market and its marketing strategy, including target markets and the marketing mix. What types of information did the company gather about the external environment and prospective customers in planning for the venture?

MARKETING IN ACTION

PACKAGING FOR AN INTERNATIONAL MARKETPLACE

Brand is a name, design, or symbol associated with a product. The personality of a product is associated with its brand, and packaging plays an important role in brand recognition. International business presents new challenges for packaging products. Some product packaging may need to be altered for use in foreign markets.

The package adjustment may be as simple as a name. Japanese consumers purchase *Coke Light* instead of *Diet Coke* because they do not want to be reminded that they are drinking a diet soft drink.

Color, shape, and design of the package influence consumer purchases. Millions of dollars are spent in designing the best package. Diet Coke considered numerous color combinations, lettering styles, and designs before choosing the silver can. Changing the look of a package to update it also requires a great deal of money and careful consideration. Consumers want to be assured that a new package has not changed the quality of the product inside the package.

Environmental concerns and government regulations around the world influence the package. Polystyrene foam such as Styrofoam is not popular, and biodegradable packages are considered more environmentally sound. Many companies have responded to environmental concerns by creating recyclable or reusable packages.

International businesses must consider the languages of consumers who purchase a product. Many products that require instructions for assembly or use now provide those instructions in two or more languages to meet the needs of a diverse customer base.

International marketing also involves repackaging new or used products for different reasons. Certain styles of used Levi jeans and NIKE shoes from the United States are repackaged to satisfy high demand by teenagers in Japan. Residents of developing countries may not be able to afford the price of new cars, but they may want used cars from the United States. Repackaging a used product to sell overseas presents a financial opportunity.

Every country has different product and packaging regulations. Tobacco products are required to have a warning label in the United States, while in other countries where smoking is more popular there may not be an equally high level of concern. The U.S. Food and Drug Administration must approve drugs and cosmetics for sale. Approval may require that information be provided on the package label. Some U.S. residents choose to buy more reasonably priced drugs from Mexico even though the packaging of the product is less stringent than in the United States. Product packaging has changed and improved to meet the challenges of international trade.

THINK CRITICALLY

1. List three features or characteristics that must be considered when packaging an item for international trade.

2. How have packages been changed to meet environmental concerns?

3. Give an example of a recent purchase that included label information or instructions in more than one language. What languages were included? What does this tell you about the product?

http://www.deca.org/publications/HS_Guide/guidetoc.html

INTERNATIONAL MARKETING EVENT

DECA PREP

You want to introduce a product or service to a foreign country. You have conducted a thorough investigation of the trade area and the culture. Demographics for the country indicate a good market for your idea. Now you must convince a banker to grant you the loan for your business idea.

DESCRIPTION OF PROPOSAL Prepare a one-page description of the proposal. Describe the type of business proposed and the major product and/or service involved. Include a brief description of the country proposed for trade, the rationale for selecting the country, identification of existing trade barriers, and identification of sources of information.

ANALYSIS OF THE INTERNATIONAL BUSINESS Research the economic, political and legal climate of the trading country. Describe the trading country's economic information that is important to your product or service, and the level of foreign investment. Describe its governmental structure and stability, and how the government controls trade and private business. Explain laws and governmental agencies that affect your product or service.

Prepare an analysis of the trade area and cultural analysis, including geographic and demographic information, important customs and traditions, other pertinent cultural information, and competitive advantages and disadvantages of the proposed business.

Conduct a market segment analysis of the target market. Describe the age, income level, population estimate, other specific demographic and economic information, and customer buying behavior related to the proposed business.

PLANNED OPERATION OF THE PROPOSED BUSINESS Prepare an analysis of the potential location. Prepare an analysis of the planned operation of the proposed business. Explain the type of ownership, the start-up steps, planned personnel needs, proposed organization chart, and brief job descriptions.

Describe the details of the product or services to be offered. Include potential suppliers, manufac-turing plans, and inventory policies. If the business provides a service, supply appropriate information about plans to provide the service. Explain how the product or service will be transported, the costs, benefits, and risks of transportation, and documents needed.

Summarize proposed strategies, including proposed pricing policies, what currency will be used, costs, markups, markdowns, relation to competition, and other factors that could affect the price of the product.

Detail the proposed promotional program, promotional activities, media availability, costs, one-year promotional plan outline, and local customs relating to business readiness.

PLANNED FINANCING This section will require several days for research and writing. Contact a banker, financial planner, and/or a retired executive from SCORE to gather additional information. Detail projected income and expenses. You should include projected income statements for first year's operation (sales, expenses, profit/loss); a projected balance sheet for the end of the first year; and a brief narrative description of the planned growth of the proposed business, including financial resources, needs, and a brief three-year plan projection.

CHAPTER 10

DEVELOP A NEW PRODUCT

LESSON 10.1 *WHAT IS A PRODUCT?*

LESSON 10.2 *COMPONENTS OF A NEW PRODUCT*

LESSON 10.3 *PRODUCT MARKET CLASSIFICATIONS*

LESSON 10.4 *DEVELOPING SUCCESSFUL NEW PRODUCTS*

NEWSLINE

REGULATING PRODUCT LABELING

ight. High fiber. No cholesterol. What do these terms mean? There is growing evidence that some companies have been more concerned about sales than about giving customers accurate information. For example, some products are labeled light to refer to their color rather than the amount of calories.

Many business people, consumer groups, and government officials are concerned about misleading or false nutrition labeling. The federal government has issued food-labeling rules that apply to every packaged food product sold to consumers. The rules require all food producers to use a standard label containing specific information that allows consumers to compare products and determine the impact of the product on their diets.

The information on each label must be based on a standard serving size and a daily consumption of 2,000 calories. The label must report the number of calories in each serving and the amount of fat, cholesterol, sodium, carbohydrates, and protein in both grams and percentage of the total daily diet requirements.

The use of terms is regulated as well. Specific meanings have been established for nutritional words like low-fat, high-fiber, and light. Companies cannot label their products as light unless fat and calories are substantially lower than the original product.

The labeling requirements are not viewed positively by everyone. Some believe it is too costly. Others think the rules are not totally effective since they apply only to the information on product packages and not to advertising. The information is not required on fresh foods or on restaurant menus.

THINK CRITICALLY

1. Examine three "light" products and compare the number of calories and grams of fat they contain to corresponding regular products.

2. Why are the packages of many "no cholesterol" products misleading?

CORPORATE VIEW

CAREER OPPORTUNITY
WEB SITE DEVELOPMENT MANAGER

POINT YOUR BROWSER

www.corpview.com

TeleView is looking for someone who possesses the following attributes.

- Excellent interpersonal and customer relations skills
- Problem solving and project organization abilities, time management proficiency, and technical communication skills
- Drive, flexibility, and a desire to work in an invigorating team-oriented environment
- Leadership skills to keep the Intranet and IT systems up and running efficiently with little or no downtime
- Willingness to relocate to Boulder, Colorado

TeleView's offices have state-of-the-art technologies at your disposal. All IT professionals receive a high-end portable computer with a docking station and remote access to the Intranet.

The main responsibilities of the job include the following.

- Share responsibility for drafting and implementing web site development and product marketing plans
- Work with the Product Marketing Manager and Brand Name teams to use the web site as an effective marketing and branding tool
- Manage changes and upgrades to the web site
- Work with artists, JavaScript and Java programmers, webmasters, and other IT professionals to maintain the web site
- Develop the content of the web site in conjunction with Corporate Communications and Marketing
- Work with Finance and Accounting to facilitate secure e-commerce transactions over the Web

- Work with Legal Services to enforce and comply with copyright and trademark rights
- Negotiate and manage contracts related to the web site, its servers, routers, bandwidth, connections, and maintenance
- Establish a system that enables changes to be implemented in a timely manner and with adequate prior notice to affected departments and mission-critical functions

The job requires the following education, skills, and experience.

- Minimum of three years Web/Intranet/Extranet experience, including at least a year in a managerial capacity
- Associate or Bachelors degree in marketing or corporate communications is preferred, but other degrees or the equivalent experience will also be considered
- Experience with JavaScript or Java is required, and a working understanding of ActiveX and other web technologies, both audio and video, are big pluses
- Excellent technical communication skills are a must

Please bring an electronic portfolio demonstrating your work with you at the time of the interview

THINK CRITICALLY

1. Prepare a cover letter written by a person who is qualified for this job and is seeking an interview.

2. What kind of future opportunities do you think a job like this would prepare you for?

3. Search want ads or the Internet for a job similar to this position. What type of compensation package is being offered for the job?

10.1 WHAT IS A PRODUCT?

- Explain that, for consumers, products are more than just the tangible objects that are offered for sale.
- Describe the role of marketers in keeping the focus on consumers during product development.

Businesses tend to view products as merely the tangible items that customers buy, while consumers see products as ways to satisfy their wants and needs. The role of marketers is to bridge that gap to make sure businesses stay focused on consumers' needs as products are being developed. Marketers' role in product development is to serve as the customers' representative by gathering information, designing strategies, and testing marketing mixes. By doing so, they assist others in the business to develop products that satisfy needs better than existing or competing products.

Find a product in your home that is no longer being sold because it failed to satisfy consumers' needs. Was it supplanted by a similar but superior competitive product? Or was it replaced by a new product that satisfied consumer needs in a different manner?

MORE THAN JUST A TANGIBLE OBJECT

A **product** is anything tangible offered to a market by the business to satisfy needs. It is important for marketers to realize that consumers view a product differently than business people. Business people often see their products as the first part of the definition—anything offered to a market. Businesses focus on what they offer—the tangible objects. Consumers have a different view of products. They are concerned about their needs and view products as ways to satisfy those needs. Those two views can result in problems when businesses develop and market products.

What are your motives when you go to a store to purchase a product? While you may plan to purchase a pair of shoes, a hamburger, or a book, you have reasons for each purchase that go beyond simply owning the product. People need shoes for protection of their feet. Beyond that, reasons for the purchase may be for style and image, to be able to play a sport, or to get durable footwear at a reasonable price. The purchase of a hamburger is typically a response to hunger. Additionally, taste, cost, and a social experience may be a part of your decision to buy the hamburger. When you purchase a book you are probably most interested in entertainment or education.

More Than an Item A product is more than a tangible item for consumers. It is a tangible item plus associated services that meet one or more important needs. The physical characteristics of the product are important. It must be durable, attractive, and safe. But beyond those qualities, the product must be useful to the consumer and meet the consumer's needs. If not, the consumer will be uninterested in buying the product no matter what its physical characteristics.

Business people make a mistake when they ignore consumer needs or believe the needs are so obvious that they are not particularly important to consumers when making purchase decisions. Some restaurant owners believe "food is food" and people will buy food when they are hungry. They fail to realize that hunger is a very basic need and few people who eat in restaurants are so hungry that it is the only factor they consider. Instead consumers decide on a restaurant on the basis of a large number of factors including menu, taste, speed and quality of service, atmosphere, location, and price. If restaurant owners are not aware of how consumers make choices on the basis of those needs, the business will probably not be successful. Few needs are really so obvious that business people can afford to ignore them.

Consumers Know Best

A second mistake is to believe that business people are better able to define needs than consumers. U.S. automobile manufacturers made that mistake years ago when they were convinced that consumers were much more interested in style and design than in safety and economy. They recognized their

Burgers with International Flavor

McDonald's hamburgers and french fries have been among the most successful products ever marketed. They are still the foundation of the company's U.S. menu, but the company has recognized that outside of its home market tastes can be quite different. Rather than merely trying to sell what it knows, the fast-food giant has been giving foreign customers what they want.

In India, where many people consider cows sacred, McDonald's sells beefless burgers. In Europe, many McDonald's outlets sell alcoholic beverages. In Mexico, the company began offering a hamburger with guacamole in 1999.

At about the same time, McDonald's began diversifying in other ways also. It acquired a minority ownership interest in a Denver-based chain of Mexican restaurants that specialize in burritos and tacos. Soon after, it bought a pizza chain. Meanwhile it boosted its promotions aimed at the African-American and Hispanic markets by initiating year-round programs to specifically address those market segments. Each segment accounts for about 15% of the company's U.S. sales.

THINK CRITICALLY

1. How do McDonald's actions demonstrate its understanding and application of the marketing concept?

2. Besides boosting sales in targeted market segments by developing products that reflect their traditional eating habits, how might McDonald's benefit on a wider scale from such practices?

mistake only after automobiles from other countries were designed to respond to the most important consumer needs and took away a large part of the U.S. automobile market. The teenage market is one that is often misunderstood by businesses. You can probably identify many businesses that try to sell products to you but make mistakes in trying to match their products with your needs and interests.

How does a consumer's view of a product tend to differ from that of a business?

PRODUCT DEVELOPMENT
AS A MARKETING FUNCTION

Who should be responsible for product development in a business? When thinking of new products, people often have an image of inventors, engineers, or scientists working in laboratories to create something new. Certainly those people are actively involved in most manufacturing businesses in developing new product ideas, but they can no longer afford to work alone.

The failure rate for new products is very high and very expensive. While the figures vary by the type of product, on average five of every 10 new product ideas will not be successful. The cost to a company for the development and introduction of a new product is typically at least several hundred thousand dollars and could be as high as several million dollars. Those figures mean that the time and money spent on developing new products that fail are lost and

can only be recovered from the successful products. Those successful products have to be very profitable in order to recover the large losses. The cost of a high rate of new product failure has to be passed on to the consumer in the form of higher prices on the successful products.

Why do products fail? Economic studies and consumer behavior indicate that products will be successful if they meet consumer needs better than other choices. Therefore, failed products are those that do not meet consumer needs or are not superior to competing products. Companies should be able to reduce the rate of product failure by improving their understanding of consumer needs and competition.

THE ROLE OF MARKETING

In the past, marketers were asked to sell the products that a business developed.

GET THE MESSAGE

Try It, You Just Might Like It

A problem with innovative new products is that it's hard for people to want something they have never tried or don't really have a feel for. Distributing free samples is a marketing tactic commonly used to familiarize people with new products and jump start consumer demand. It's particularly effective with consumable products targeted to young people. They are generally receptive to trying new things, especially if they're free.

General Mills included lots of free sampling in its marketing strategy for Yoplait Go-Gurt, a yogurt in a tube that was rolled out nationally in 1999. "They needed to sample it, see how it works, squeeze it, push it. We had to take it to them where they play and hang out to really make an impact," a company executive said.

More than a million samples were given out from late 1998 to early 2000 beginning with

cities such as San Francisco, Seattle, Houston, and Detroit. Kids on skateboards and scooters passed out the product at parks, festivals, and soccer and softball fields.

THINK CRITICALLY

1. A key to marketing new consumer package goods is getting retailers to devote shelf space to something that doesn't have a track record of sales. How can sampling help to persuade retailers to carry a product?

2. Mass sampling promotions such as Go-Gurt's work well because the product cost is low and the product is quickly consumed. So if people like it, they buy more. How could sampling work with more-expensive products or with a product that isn't quickly used up?

That was an easy task if consumers needed the product. But it was very difficult if the product did not meet consumer needs well. Put yourself in the position of a salesperson of a product for which the consumer does not see a need or a product that does not appear to be better than competing products. Yet your success depends on selling the product.

You can see why salespeople sometimes have a poor image. In this situation, the salesperson must try to convince the customer the product is needed or that it is better than the competitor's product even if it is not. That certainly is not easy and is probably not the right thing to do. The salesperson who successfully sells the product may still have problems. The customer may discover the product did not meet the needs described by the salesperson and return it for a refund. Even if the product is not returned, the consumer may be upset with the salesperson and the company and will not buy from them again.

To avoid that problem, the role of marketing has changed. A company that believes in the marketing concept uses the needs of customers as the primary focus during the planning, production, distribution, and promotion of a product or service. With that philosophy, marketers should not be in the position of having to sell products that do not meet customer needs. Marketers should be actively involved with others in the business in the design and development of new products.

MARKETING ACTIVITIES IN PRODUCT DEVELOPMENT

Marketing is the eyes, ears, and mouth of the customer in a business. Marketing is the direct link between a business and its customers. Marketers work with customers every day, whether in selling, promotion, product distribution, marketing research, or the many other marketing activities that occur in a business. Because of that close contact, marketers are in a good position to understand customers, what they like and do not like, how they view competing products, and whether they are satisfied with current products. Marketers must represent the consumer in the business as products are designed and developed.

There are three important roles for marketers in the product development process. Those roles are identified in Figure 10-1.

FIGURE 10-1
Marketers support product development in three important ways.

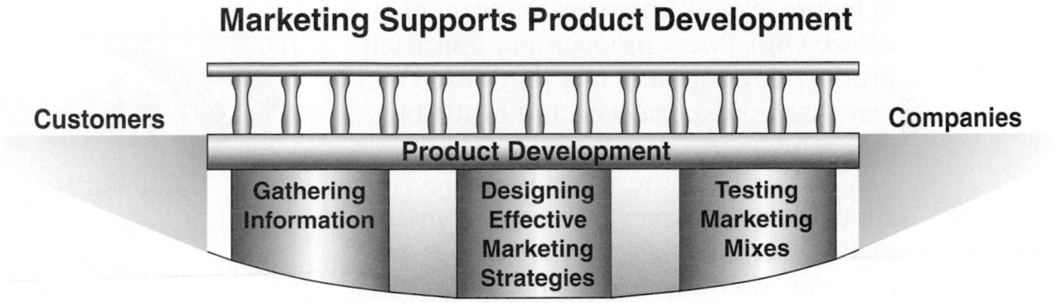

Marketing Supports Product Development

Customers — Product Development — Companies

Gathering Information | Designing Effective Marketing Strategies | Testing Marketing Mixes

Gathering Information The obvious role for marketers in product development is market research. Gathering market information, studying it, and using the results to assist in product planning keeps the focus on consumer needs and competition rather than the perceptions of the people involved in planning. Through research, marketers can study the competition, identify target markets, review alternative product designs and features, and analyze several marketing mix choices.

Information can be collected in many ways and from different sources. Feedback from salespeople is very important in understanding both customers and competitors. Analysis of sales data will determine items that have sold well in the past and those that have not. It will identify the areas of customer complaints and product returns. The marketing department might maintain one or more consumer panels that meet regularly to discuss new product ideas and their experiences as customers. The results of those discussions can provide important information for product changes and improvements.

Marketers that are actively involved in product planning usually develop and use a marketing information system. It allows the information from many sources to be collected, stored, and analyzed when needed to improve new product decisions.

Designing Strategies A new product is developed to meet company objectives. It becomes a part of a marketing strategy. If the company's goal is to increase its share of a specific market, it might develop a different product than if the goal is to enter a market it has never competed in before. A new company that cannot risk failure with a new product may approach product development in a very different way than an experienced and profitable company.

A marketing strategy combines decisions about a target market and an appropriate marketing mix. The actual product is only one part of the strategy. Marketers participate in developing an effective strategy by identifying target markets, determining company strengths and weaknesses, evaluating market positions, and suggesting alternative marketing mixes.

Testing Marketing Mixes After a product and the remaining parts of the marketing mix have been designed, most companies conduct tests to determine if the new product will be successful. Testing is a way to reduce the number of product failures and to avoid spending money on products that will not be successful.

There are several ways to test a new marketing mix. In the past, many companies used test markets. Test marketing has become very expensive so other ways of testing are being tried. Companies use focus groups and other consumer panels to review product ideas and marketing mix choices. There are very sophisticated computer programs that allow companies to simulate the marketing of products and

determine expected levels of sales and profits. Personnel from marketing are usually responsible for market testing activities.

THE PRODUCT PLANNING FUNCTION

Businesses using a marketing orientation involve marketing personnel in product planning. Therefore an important marketing function is *product/service planning*—assisting in the design and development of products and services that will meet the needs of prospective customers. The key parts of the definition are *assisting,* meaning that marketers work cooperatively with others in product development, and *meet the needs,* meaning that the products of a company are designed to satisfy customers.

What are the three important roles for marketers in the product development process?

1. What is a fundamental distinction between a product and a service?

2. Who is best able to define consumers' needs and what it takes to satisfy them, businesses or consumers themselves?

3. How has marketing's role in product development changed over the past few decades?

4. Why are marketers generally the best people in business to represent customers' wants and needs?

5. What is the product planning function of marketers?

6. What benefit does a marketing information system provide in regard to product development?

Every product is a complex blending of many parts, some tangible, some not. When a new product is developed, many decisions have to be made about its final form and the total product mix. Marketers start with a basic product, whether it's a toothbrush, an automobile, or a software program. Then they choose enhancements to make it more satisfying to a target market. Lastly, they decide which product extensions will make it even more satisfying.

Eventually, the product mix element may include related items in a product line, packaging that makes it easier to use or promotes safety, and a brand identification.

Find an item in your kitchen that comes in an innovative package. Describe the packaging and all the purposes it serves. Estimate how much of the product's total cost is for the packaging. How much does the packaging enhance the value you obtain from the product?

GOALS

● **Show how even a very simple product can be a complex mix of a basic item with assorted features.**

● **Describe the three steps of the product design process.**

● **Explain the importance of product lines, packaging, and brand development.**

PARTS OF THE PRODUCT
MIX ELEMENT

Even a product that seems very simple is made up of many parts. Think of the toothbrush you used this morning. Is it like every other toothbrush you could have purchased? What makes it unique? Why did you purchase it rather than one of the many other brands of toothbrushes available?

The basic product is easy to describe—a handle and head, typically plastic, with bristles. Even in that basic product, there are choices (see Figure 10-2). The handle may be long or short, contoured for an easier grip, bent to fit comfortably inside your mouth, and manufactured in several colors. It may have a hole drilled through it so you can hang the toothbrush when not using it, or it may have a rubber pick to massage your gums. The head also comes in various shapes and sizes. The bristles can be firm, medium, or soft. They can be short, long, or

varied with shorter bristles in the middle. One manufacturer includes a strip of

FIGURE 10-2
Even common consumer products offer many choices of features to make them different from competitors' products and more appealing to consumers.

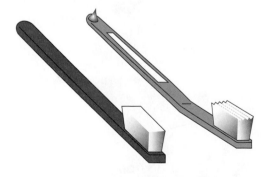

Analyzing a Common Product

colored bristles that indicate when the toothbrush needs to be replaced. Bristles can be manufactured from several different materials.

Even with the variations described above, many people believe that all tooth-brushes are quite similar. Yet there are still more features to choose from. There are compact toothbrushes that collapse into a small case that you can carry with you. There are disposable toothbrushes that come with toothpaste already applied. And there are electric toothbrushes in many varieties.

One electric toothbrush is part of a complete dental care system. The rechargeable handle can be used with the toothbrush, a tooth polisher, a water pick, and a flossing tool.

Most toothbrushes are sold with a brand name. Some are well-known brands under which many products are sold, such as Colgate. Others are brands specifically associated with tooth care, such as Oral-B.

Offering a guarantee is another way to give the product differences. Several tooth-brush manufacturers offer replacements to dissatisfied customers. Others will refund the purchase price to consumers who are not satisfied. A testimonial is similar to a guarantee. This is a recommendation from a professional group, such as the American Dental Association, about the quality of the product.

The toothbrush example demonstrates that every product can be quite complex and unique. Businesses have many choices in the development of new products. Those choices are reviewed in Figure 10-3.

Why does developing even a simple product like a toothbrush involve so many decisions?

FIGURE 10-3
Product planning involves the careful analysis of many factors in order to create the best possible product.

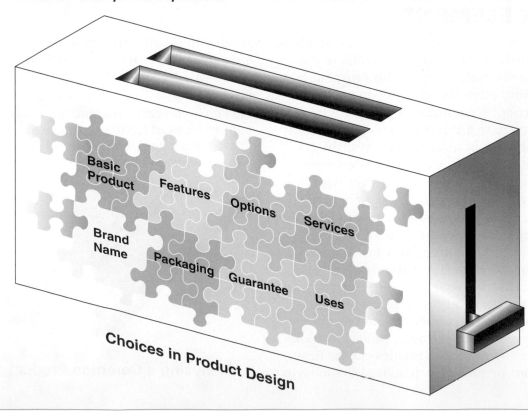

Choices in Product Design

DESIGNING A PRODUCT

Product design moves through three steps. It begins with the basic product. Then the basic product is modified and improved. Finally services and complementary products are developed to make it as useful as possible to consumers.

Basic Product   The most important part of the product is the basic physical product. It is a readily identifiable product in its simplest form. Consumers should be able to easily see the important need to which the product responds. The basic product is very much like that of competitors. Examples of basic products include a house, computer, shampoo, bicycle, microwave oven, or stereo.

Enhanced Product   The basic product responds to an important need of consumers. However, we know that consumers are usually trying to satisfy several needs with one purchase and evaluate products

to see which one provides the best and most specific satisfaction. Companies add enhancements to their basic products to meet those needs. Enhancements include features and options. For example, a bicycle can be manufactured in several frame sizes, in models ranging from mountain bikes to racing bikes, and with a single gear ratio or up to 24 speeds. Choices of materials used in manufacturing, seat design, and tire construction are available. Some bicycles have shock absorbers built into the frame. If you go to a large bicycle shop to consider all of the possible choices of features and options you may be able to select from several hundred different bicycles. Other types of enhancements to a basic product are levels of quality, styling differences, colors, brand names, and packaging.

Each type of enhancement changes the basic product. The change is likely to be viewed as an improvement by some customers, increasing the satisfaction they receive from the product. Other customers may view the change as unneeded or even dissatisfying. Enhanced products make it possible for companies to satisfy several target markets with one basic product. Different combinations of features, options, and even brand names are developed. Each alternative combination is designed with the specific needs of one target market in mind.

Extended Product Businesses can improve the satisfaction provided by a product in other ways in addition to product enhancements. That improvement can occur as the business offers services, guarantees, information on effective use of the product, and even additional products that improve the use of the product.

Services are an effective way to meet additional customer needs beyond those directly related to the use of the product. Examples of important services for some customers that could influence product choice are credit, delivery, installation, repair services, and technical support.

Suggesting additional products that should be purchased so the primary product can be used more effectively is often an important method of improving customer satisfaction. Would you like to purchase a new camera only to find out when you wanted to use it that a tripod and flash attachment are needed for certain types of pictures? A skilled photography equipment salesperson will talk with you about the types of pictures you plan to take and the conditions in which most will be taken. Based on that information, a recommendation of additional products will be made so you can get the greatest enjoyment and value from your purchase.

What are the three steps of the product design process?

PRODUCT MIX COMPONENTS

When consumers evaluate products to determine the most satisfying, they are interested in more than just the physical product. Three important considerations in planning the product mix are the product line, packaging, and brand development.

PRODUCT LINE

New or small companies often offer only one product to a target market. With more experience and as a company grows, it is possible to expand into other markets and consider the development of a product line. A **product line** is a group of similar products with slight variations in the marketing mix to satisfy different needs in a market.

Variation in Quantity Product lines can be developed in several ways. One of the easiest ways to expand from one product into several is to vary the product size. The identical food item may be packaged in three sizes—single serving, four servings, and 10 servings. Facial tissue may be sold in a pocket-sized cellophane wrapper, a box of 250 tissues, or a multiple-box pack. Another type of quantity variation is to have different sizes for the same basic product. For example, bed sheets are sold in twin, full, queen, or king size. In this case, the product itself is manufactured in varied sizes rather than just changing the quantity in a package.

Variation in Quality Differences in quality can also be used to develop a product line. Items such as paintbrushes, carpenter or mechanic tools, lawn mowers, and even clothing often are sold in two or three quality levels. Consumers who use the products infrequently may not need the best possible quality and would prefer to save money in exchange for accepting a slightly lower quality. Adding features to the basic product may produce several levels of product choices for consumers. Automobile and appliance manufacturers often have a

very basic model at a low price and several other models with selected features and options at higher prices.

As companies add items to their product line, they usually increase the satisfaction of individual consumers. However, the company is also adding to the costs of manufacturing, distribution, inventory control, and other related marketing activities. An expanded product line also requires additional display space for retailers. The retailer must make a decision whether to stock items from the complete product line or use the space for competing brands or entirely different products. In a supermarket display of soft drinks, you can see an example of very extensive product lines and the competition brands have for display space.

Assortments In addition to product line decisions, companies plan product assortments. A **product assortment** is the complete set of all products a business offers to its market. Retail stores provide the best example of product assortments. Some specialty retailers, lawn and garden centers for example, have a very complete assortment of products homeowners need in one category. Other general merchandise retailers, such as discount and department stores, stock products in many different categories. They will probably not have as complete an assortment in one line as the specialty store, but they respond to a broader set of the customers' product needs.

Some manufacturers specialize in one product category and have a full assortment of products in that line. Other manufacturers may have a product assortment in many different product categories.

PACKAGING

Most products are sold in a package. The package serves the dual purpose of protection and promotion. In addition, some packaging improves the use of the product. Containers with pour spouts built into the package, resealable liners, and handles for carrying are developed to solve customer problems with the use of the product.

Ease of Use   Manufacturers must carefully consider the ways customers use a product when designing the package. For example, if a cereal box is taller than the shelves in the customer's home, it will not be purchased. A manufacturer of a liquid cleaner found that people would not buy a large economy size because the container could not be lifted and poured with one hand in the way people were used to handling the product. Products that consumers use in a microwave oven must not have metal in the package.

Safety   Safety and protection are important concerns when planning the packaging of products. Products used by children certainly need to have safe packaging. A manufacturer of individual servings of puddings and fruits learned that children would lick the lid of the container when it was removed. The lid was changed from metal to plastic to prevent cuts. Glass and other fragile products need well-designed packages to insure they are not broken during shipment and display.

Attraction   The promotional value of packaging is also important for many products. Impulse items are often purchased because of an attractive package that clearly shows the use of the product. Perfumes and colognes usually have very expensive and uniquely designed containers to convey an appropriate image.

Handling   Packaging can also be helpful in the display and security of products. In stores where products are displayed for customer self-service, the package may need to be designed to hang from a hook or to lie flat on a shelf. Small or expensive items are often packaged in large containers to reduce the chance of theft.

Environment   There is growing concern about the type and quantity of materials used for packaging. Manufacturers are increasingly using recycled materials for packaging and developing materials that are biodegradable. Many retailers are reducing the amount of packaging used or are helping consumers reuse or recycle packages.

BRAND DEVELOPMENT

Do you know the brand names of the shoes and clothing you are wearing? Do you have a favorite brand of pizza or automobile? In what stores do you prefer to shop? Each of these questions demonstrates that the brand of products can be very important to consumers as they make purchase decisions. A **brand** is a name, symbol, word, or design that identifies a product, service, or company. A brand is very important to a company because it provides a unique identification for it and its offerings. To insure that others cannot use a brand, a company obtains a trademark. A **trademark** is legal protection of the words or symbols for use by one company.

Consider how difficult it would be to shop if there were no brand names. While some products are purchased without considering the brand (think of the paper you use for writing in school), in most cases consumers consider the brand as part of the purchase decision. Positive or negative experience with a brand will influence your future purchases. Business people know that brand recognition resulting from advertising often increases a product's sales.

The goal of a business in using branding is to gain customer recognition of the brand in order to increase the likelihood of a sale. There are several levels of consumer brand awareness as shown in Figure 10-4.

Brands can be developed by manufacturers or by retailers. Individual products can have their own brands or groups of products can carry a similar, or family brand. Some companies offer licensed brands to add prestige or a unique image to products. A **licensed brand** is a well-known name or symbol established by one company and sold for use by another company to promote its products. Disney and Sesame Street are examples of companies that license the use of character names and images for products ranging from toys to clothing. Professional and college sports teams license their names and mascot images for use on many products. Some

FIGURE 10-4

Businesses use brands to help consumers make choices. Branding is effective when consumers prefer or insist on a specific brand.

LEVELS OF BRAND RECOGNITION	
Non-recognition	Consumers are unable to identify the brand.
Rejection	Consumers will not purchase the product because of the brand.
Recognition	Consumers can recall the brand name but it has little influence on purchases.
Preference	Consumers view the brand as valuable and will choose it if it is available.
Insistence	Consumers value the brand to the extent that they reject other brands.

people prefer to purchase products with those brands rather than similar products that do not carry the licensed brand.

Registering a trademark protects which product mix component—a product line, packaging, or a brand?

LESSON REVIEW

1. What are the primary means that marketers use to enhance a basic product?

2. Why would a business add a product feature that lessens its usefulness or value to many consumers?

3. How have heightened environmental concerns affected the way consumer goods are packaged?

4. What are the five levels of consumer brand recognition?

5. Which type of retailer typically offers the widest assortment of products in a particular category such as bicycles, computers, sporting goods, or CDs?

10.3 PRODUCT MARKET CLASSIFICATIONS

GOALS

- Define consumer markets and describe what is meant by direct demand.
- Define business markets and explain the business product classification system.
- Understand the importance of product classifications for product planning.

MARKETING MATTERS

To be most effective, product planning should be based on an understanding of the market to which the product will be sold. Knowing who will use the product, the purpose for which it will be used, and the needs customers are attempting to satisfy with the product will result in the development of a product that's better designed for that consumer. Two broad market categories exist that are composed of prospective customers who have very different reasons for buying products. Those categories are consumer markets and business markets.

Name 10 businesses in your area and, for each, describe who its primary customers are, businesses or consumers. How would each business have to change if it was targeting the opposite category?

CONSUMER MARKETS

Individuals or socially related groups who purchase products for personal consumption are known as **consumer markets**. When you, your family, or your friends buy products for your own use or for others to use, you are a part of the consumer market. You make purchase decisions on the basis of the satisfaction you receive from the use of the product. If you are buying the product for use by a friend or family member, you are interested in buying something that person will find to be satisfying. The demand for consumer products is known as direct demand. **Direct demand** is the quantity of a product or service needed to meet the needs of the consumer.

Final consumers purchase products that they or people with whom they have social relationships will use. Therefore they have a clear idea of the reasons to purchase products. They locate and purchase the products that best meet their important needs.

FIGURE 10-5
Marketers develop more-effective products when they understand how consumers shop for them.

CONVENIENCE GOODS

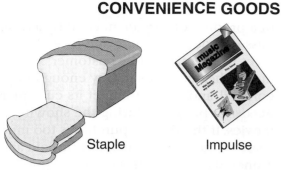

Staple   Impulse   Emergency

UNSOUGHT GOODS

SHOPPING GOODS

Attribute-based   Price-based

SPECIALTY GOODS

Classifying Products for the Consumer Market

To develop appropriate products for the consumer market, business people must be aware of consumers' needs and how consumers choose products to satisfy those needs. The product/service classification system, which assists businesses in consumer product planning, is reviewed in Figure 10-5. The system is based on two important factors:

1. The importance of the purchase to the consumer
2. The willingness of the consumer to shop and compare products before making the purchase

What is the connection between direct demand and consumer markets?

PRODUCT MARKET CLASSIFICATIONS   **10.3**

Restructuring Costs for Flexibility

Maximizing the chances of success for new products is crucial to a manufacturing company's profitability because so much of the cost of making tangible goods is in the form of fixed costs for things such as capital equipment. If sales fall short of expectations, fixed costs are incurred regardless. In industries where the ratio of fixed to variable costs is lower, launching new products is less risky. With variable costs, lower sales also mean lower expenses.

Unisys addressed that problem directly in the late 1990s when it outsourced the operation of its parts distribution warehouses. With the market for information systems changing so quickly, it wanted to build more flexibility into its cost structure. It also reasoned that a third-party operator would have

the ability to utilize space in the warehouses more efficiently by marketing excess space to other companies.

THINK CRITICALLY

1. If a new product sells for $100, and its maker incurs fixed costs of $300,000 to begin production and variable costs of $25 per unit, how many units does it need to sell in order to break even? How much gross profit would it generate if it doubled that volume?

2. If the company restructures its costs so that fixed costs are only $100,000 and variable costs are $60, how many units would it need to sell to break even? How much gross profit would it generate if it sold 8,000 units?

to be produced. Logs are purchased by lumber producers, oil by plastics manufacturers, and grain by cereal processors.

It is important that purchasers of raw materials have an adequate supply and a standard quality of the raw materials they use to produce their products. The price of the raw materials is also

important, since the cost has a big influence on what the company charges for its finished products. The purchasing company will want to sign a long-term contract with the supplier of the raw materials to insure they have a continuing supply and know what the cost of the materials will be.

COMPONENT PARTS

Component parts are also incorporated into the products that a business makes. However, component parts have been either partially or totally processed by another company. For example, a computer manufacturer will buy computer chips from a chip manufacturer. These chips are already carefully developed and simply are installed as a part of the computer assembly. The same manufacturer buys parts for a disk drive from another company. Those parts must be assembled before the disk drive can be installed into the computer.

Component parts can be specifically designed for the needs of one company or they can be a standard product that is used by many companies. As with raw materials, the purchasing company is concerned that a dependable source of supply is available when needed, that the component parts meet the quality standards of the company, and that costs are reasonable.

What are the five categories of the business product classification system?

PLANNING PRODUCTS FOR CONSUMER AND BUSINESS MARKETS

The classification systems for consumer and business markets are very useful to marketers as they complete product planning. Knowing whether the customer is a final consumer or a business consumer determines whether the product is being developed to meet a direct demand or a derived demand. For consumer markets, products treated as convenience goods require different planning than those treated as specialty goods. The product is less important than the location for convenience goods, so the company needs to develop a basic product at a reasonable cost. A specialty good is very important to the consumer, so care and attention must go into the product. It will probably require an enhanced and extended product to meet the consumer's needs.

For business customers, the type of product and its use are important factors to consider when planning products. Capital equipment is a major investment so the purchase is an important decision for the customer. The customer wants to work closely with the supplier in planning a product that will meet the company's needs, will have a long life, and that is affordable. Supplies, on the other hand, may be very routine purchases where the customer gives little thought other than price as long as the supply is the type needed by the company.

Some products are sold to both consumer markets and business markets. Consumers buy automobile tires for replacements when the original tires on their car become worn. Automobile manufacturers purchase thousands of tires to mount on automobiles they produce. Consumers purchase bottles of shampoo for personal care. Hotels buy large quantities of shampoo packaged in small bottles or packets to place in rooms as a service to their guests. You can see with both examples that while the basic product is the same, the extended and enhanced products may be quite different. Also, the reasons and methods of purchasing will not be the same. Marketers need to understand the differences in purchases between the two types of markets in order to develop effective products and marketing mixes for each.

Why is it important to understand the product classification of a product during its development?

LESSON REVIEW

1. On what two important factors are consumer product classifications based?

2. Which class of business products do you think tend to be the subject of the most intense negotiations before a purchase contract is concluded?

3. What is a key distinction between supplies, raw materials, and components? For instance, if a company buys paint thinner to mix paint that's sprayed on its basic product, is the thinner a supply, a component, or raw material?

4. Which type of business—manufacturers or service providers—typically have the highest capital equipment costs?

5. When the same basic product is sold both to consumers and to businesses, why would the product mix be different?

10.4 DEVELOPING SUCCESSFUL NEW PRODUCTS

GOALS

● **Understand what businesses mean by "new" products.**

● **Describe the six steps in new product development.**

Without new products, companies have a hard time keeping customers satisfied and maintaining a profit. Yet it is not easy to develop successful new products. The risk of failure is high and development and testing costs are great.

Describe a new product that you have tried in the past year. What did you like about it? What did you not like about it? Was the product successful in the marketplace? Describe what you imagine were the steps needed to bring the product to market.

WHAT IS A NEW PRODUCT?

Few products are really brand new in the sense that no other product like it has been available before. Many "new" products are changes and improvements to existing products. Others are new to a particular market but have been sold previously in other markets.

When the personal computer was first designed in the 1970s, it was completely new. Computers were not available to individuals before the development of the personal computer. People had to use large mainframe computers. Today, there are many new personal computers as features are added and technology allows machines to be developed that are smaller, faster, and easier to use.

You are probably very familiar with companies that introduce products as new and improved. Brands of laundry detergent, toothpaste, diapers, and potato chips often use new and improved in their promotions. In many cases it is difficult to see what really is new or better about the

product. Because some companies have misused the term "new" in order to attract customer attention, the Federal Trade Commission regulates how and when it can be used. A company can only call something "new" for six months after the introduction or change of a product. It must be entirely new or changed in an important and noticeable way.

Fashions, music, ethnic foods, and other specialized products may be new in some markets but well known in others. Much of the international trade in consumer products started by introducing into foreign markets products that had already proven successful in one country.

Who determines if a product is new or merely improved?

THE STEPS IN NEW PRODUCT DEVELOPMENT

Most companies have designed a very careful process to identify and develop new products. The process is used to screen out products that are not likely to be successful before the company spends too much money for production and marketing. The process is used also to make sure that the products meet an important market need, can be produced well and at a reasonable price, and will be competitive with other products in the market. The steps illustrated in Figure 10-7 are part of most companies' procedures for new product development.

IDEA DEVELOPMENT

The most difficult step in new product development is usually finding ideas for new products. You may see a new product on the market and say, "I could have thought of that." But few people have successful new product ideas. Since products are developed to meet consumer needs, gathering information from consumers may generate ideas for new products. Many companies have consumer panels whose members meet regularly to discuss ideas for new products.

One source of new product ideas is to identify problems customers are having, what they don't like about current products, or the complaints they make to the company. Often salespeople who work with customers every day have ideas for new products or product improvements.

Developing new product ideas can be a very creative process. Some people seem to be more creative that others, and those people are often involved in the new product planning process. Tools such as brainstorming, creative thinking exercises, and problem-solving are used to identify product ideas for testing.

IDEA SCREENING

To encourage a large number of new product ideas, companies do not evaluate ideas in the initial development stage. The second step is to carefully screen the ideas to select those that have the greatest chance of being successful. Businesses develop a checklist of criteria to be considered in deciding whether to proceed with product planning. Some of those criteria are listed below.

- Is there an identified market for the product?
- Is the competition in the market reasonable?
- Do we have or can we obtain the resources to produce the product?
- Is the product legal and safe?
- Can we produce a quality product at a reasonable cost?

FIGURE 10-7
A carefully developed process for new product planning will increase the chances that the new product will be successful.

Idea Development · Idea Screening · Strategy Development · Financial Analysis · Product Development & Testing · Product Marketing

New Product Development

Other criteria are not as straightforward and may be tailored to company circumstances. For example, some companies will not want to develop products that compete with their current products. Others will select products that can be developed with current equipment and personnel. Some companies are seeking opportunities to move into new markets, so they want product ideas that meet the new market needs. The initial investment required to produce the new product may be an important factor for some companies but unimportant to others.

STRATEGY DEVELOPMENT

After determining that the product idea seems reasonable, the business will create and test a sample marketing strategy. In this step, research is done to clearly identify an appropriate target market and insure that customers exist with the need and money for the product. Next, alternative marketing mixes are planned and analyzed to determine the possible combinations of product, distribution, price, and promotion. Again, each choice is carefully studied to determine if it is appropriate for the target market and if the company can effectively implement that mix. Often the study will involve presenting the product idea and mix alternative to a panel of appropriate consumers for their reactions. Based on that study, the best possible mix is selected. It is possible that the research in this step will determine that an effective mix cannot be developed, in which case the product idea would be dropped.

FINANCIAL ANALYSIS

If it is determined that a new product idea meets a market need and can be developed, the company will complete a financial analysis. Costs of production and marketing, sales projections for the target market, and resulting profits will be carefully calculated. Usually companies have computer models that help with the financial analysis. Several levels of analysis are completed to determine the best-case and worst-case possibilities. An understanding of the type of competition

Debugging New Products

For manufacturers, prototypes represent the Catch-22 of new product development. Building them is very expensive, takes lots of time, and requires the collaboration of many people who are rarely in the same place at the same time. That last factor inevitably causes misinterpretation and miscommunication errors. Not building prototypes or building fewer of them, on the other hand, often means that errors aren't caught until later in the development process, magnifying those same factors when late-stage design changes have to be made.

Innovations in computer-aided modeling systems are helping manufacturers address the dilemma. New systems allow various people at far-flung sites to view and examine a three-dimensional computer model simultaneously. Proposed changes can be experimented with and tested if necessary, and everyone can examine the results to make sure that errors haven't been introduced inadvertently.

As a result, less-error-prone prototypes can be built early in the product development cycle. They can be built at less cost and more quickly. Since more errors are eliminated with the modeling software, fewer expensive prototypes are needed before a product reaches the production stage.

THINK CRITICALLY

1. Why are prototypes so critical in developing new products, particularly machinery?

2. Why is it more expensive to incorporate design changes to a new product late in the development process?

(ranging from pure competition to monopoly) and the level of demand is important in determining what prices can be charged and the amount of sales to expect. The results of the analysis are matched against company goals and profit objectives to determine if the product should be developed and marketed.

PRODUCT DEVELOPMENT AND TESTING

After careful research and planning, the decision may be made to develop the product. For a manufacturer, that means designing the production process, obtaining the needed equipment and materials, and training the production personnel. For other companies such as a retailer, it involves identifying a producer or manufacturer that will supply the products and negotiating a contract for that production.

For very expensive or very risky products, the company may decide to develop a prototype, or sample, of the product. The prototype can be used to test quality and costs before beginning full-scale production. Another testing strategy in this step is a test market. A limited quantity of the new product is developed and the marketing mix is implemented in a small part of the market to determine if it will be successful. If the market test is not successful, the company can end production or change the product before a large amount of money is spent.

PRODUCT MARKETING

The last step in product development is full-scale introduction into the target market. A great deal of preparation is needed for this step. All of the marketing mix elements must be planned. Cooperating companies such as wholesalers, retailers, transportation companies, and advertising agencies need to be involved. Production levels must be high enough to have an adequate supply of the product available to meet the target market needs. Marketing personnel need to be prepared for their responsibilities. All of the activities must be coordinated and controlled by managers.

If the all of the steps in the new product planning process have been carefully completed, the opportunity for success is very high. However, marketers still need to be cautious and continue to study the market carefully. It is possible that conditions have changed, competitors may have anticipated the new product, or consumers will not respond in exactly the way predicted. Adjustments in the marketing strategy may be needed as the market develops.

Name the six steps in new product development.

1. Under Federal Trade Commission regulations, how long can a company promote a product as "new"?

2. Why do companies wait until the second stage—idea screening—to evaluate new product ideas that have been suggested?

3. Why do companies need new products if they already have enough successful products?

4. If a company adheres to a six-step new-product development process, doesn't it risk missing out on opportunities to competitors who bring products to market more quickly by skipping time-consuming screening, analyses, and testing?

5. What does a company do if a test market proves unsuccessful?

6. If financial analysis indicates that the best-case scenario for a proposed new product is marginal profitability, is the business likely to proceed on that basis?

SUMMARY

Lesson 10.1
A. Businesses and consumers have conflicting ideas about what a product is. Businesses think of the tangible object. Consumers see something that satisfies their needs. A business needs to remember that consumers know best what they want and need.

B. Marketers keep the focus on consumers during product development by gathering information, designing strategies, and testing marketing mixes with their needs in mind.

Lesson 10.2
A. Even a very simple product such as a toothbrush is a complex mix of a basic item with many features and options.

B. The three steps of the product design process are the basic product, product enhancements, and the extended product that includes associated services and complementary products.

C. Product lines, packaging, and brand development are three important components of the total product.

Lesson 10.3
A. Consumer markets are the individuals and groups who buy products for personal consumption. Direct demand is the quantity of a product demanded by consumer markets.

B. Business markets are the organizations that buy products to use in their operations or business activities. Categories of the business product classification system are capital equipment, operating equipment, supplies, raw materials, and component parts.

C. Product classifications are important because they indicate how products are used and what kinds of factors are involved in making purchasing decisions.

Lesson 10.4
A. Business use the term "new" to describe things that haven't been on the market before and existing products that have been altered or introduced to new markets.

B. New product development steps are idea development, idea screening, strategy development, financial analysis, product development and testing, and product marketing.

REVIEW MARKETING CONCEPTS

Match the products listed in the product column below with the correct product category.

Product	Product Category
a. $10,000 diamond ring	1. Convenience good
b. Boeing 767 airplane	2. Shopping good
c. One car battery	3. Specialty good
d. 500 gallons of window cleaner	4. Capital equipment
e. Loaf of bread	5. Operating equipment
f. 50 automobile tires	6. Supplies
g. Railroad car full of wheat	7. Raw materials
h. Cash register	8. Component parts

9. True or False: A preference level of brand recognition exists when a consumer values a brand and chooses it if it is available.

10. True or False: When a consumer refuses to buy a brand, it is an example of the insistence level of brand recognition.

11. True or False: A trademark protects a brand by prohibiting its use by unauthorized companies.

12. True or False: If a product is purchased both by consumers and businesses, it makes sense to use the same marketing mix for each market.

13. True or False: Marketers who represent consumers during product planning will usually jeopardize their positions within the company.

14. True or False: The Federal Trade Commission requires that new products be clearly labeled as such for at least six months after they are introduced.

15. True or False: As part of the financial analysis of a proposed new product, businesses look at best-case and worst-case scenarios.

16. True or False: The product planning process ends once a product goes into full-scale production.

REVIEW MARKETING TERMS

Match the terms listed with the definitions. Some terms may not be used.

17. A name, symbol, word, or design that identifies a product, service, or company.

18. The quantity of a product needed by a business to operate at a level that will meet the demand of its customers.

19. Anything offered to a market by a business to satisfy needs.

20. Individuals or groups who purchase a product for personal consumption.

21. A well-known name or symbol established by one company and sold for use by another company to promote its products.

22. The complete set of all products a business offers to its market.

23. Companies and organizations that purchase products for the operation of a business or the completion of business activity.

a. brand
b. business market
c. consumer market
d. derived demand
e. direct demand
f. licensed brand
g. product
h. product assortment
i. product line
j. trademark

APPLY MARKETING FUNCTIONS

MARKETING RESEARCH

24. Study advertisements, product catalogs, and merchandise available for sale in stores in your community. Identify at least three products that fit into each of the following categories:

   a. Products that are completely new

   b. Products that have significant changes or improvements

   c. Products that have been sold elsewhere but are new to this market

Using those products, create a poster or a display that illustrates the concept of new products.

25. The Games & U Company is planning to update the marketing strategy for its line of children's swing sets. The products are sold to families through toy stores and discount stores and to daycare centers and community centers through the company's sales-people. To assist with planning, the company conducted a telephone survey of 360 previous purchasers of the swing sets. One-third of those surveyed were business customers and the remainder were final consumers. The survey asked the respondents to identify what they liked most and what they liked least about the product. The results are shown in the table below:

   a. Calculate the percentage of responses by business customers, final consumers, and total purchasers for each of the items listed. Prepare a bar graph that compares the responses in all three categories (business, final, and total).

   b. Develop three specific recommendations for new product development based on the data. Make sure you apply the marketing concept when developing your recommendations.

MARKETING PLANNING

26. Business people often describe their products in terms of the physical characteristics and features. Consumers evaluate products on the basis of the needs that can be satisfied. For each of the following product descriptions, identify a consumer need that can be satisfied or a benefit the consumer will receive as a result of using the product.

Product Description

   a. cellular telephone

   b. automated bank teller machine

   c. credit card

   d. compressed digital audio player

   e. computerized tax preparation software

   f. rechargeable batteries

NUMBER OF RESPONSES

	Business Customers	Final Consumers
Liked Most		
A. Rapid delivery	15	0
B. Durability	50	28
C. Salesperson's product knowledge	30	12
D. Optional equipment	0	50
E. Safety features	20	110
F. Price	5	40
Liked Least		
G. Difficulty of assembly	10	95
H. Lack of credit terms	45	0
I. Limited product information when buying	0	40
J. Cost of replacement parts	60	35
K. Customer service	5	70

g. no-calorie sugar substitute
h. shampoo with conditioner
i. CDs that can be rewritten
j. stationary bicycle

Products are planned to respond to consumer needs. Those that best meet consumer needs are likely to be successful. For each of the common consumer needs listed below, identify a product that has been successful for several years because it meets the need very well.

Consumer Needs

a. health
b. economy
c. beauty
d. excitement
e. education
f. hunger
g. friendship
h. convenience
i. safety
j. status

27. Identify any consumer product that has been on the market for at least five years. On a large sheet of paper or poster board, draw three concentric circles to look like a practice target. Label the innermost circle BASIC PRODUCT. Label the middle circle ENHANCED PRODUCT. Label the outer circle EXTENDED PRODUCT. Study several brands of the product you selected to identify the components that are basic, enhanced, and extended parts of the product. Based on that analysis, use words or drawings to illustrate each part of the product in the appropriate circle.

or

Identify a manufacturing, retail, or service business that you can study. Identify the major products purchased by the business. Divide a large sheet of paper or poster board into five sections. Label each section with one of the categories of business products. In each section, use words or drawings to illustrate examples of the products used by the company that fit that category of business products.

MARKETING MANAGEMENT

28. Companies use product lines to be able to serve several target markets with the same basic product. Variations in the product's size, quality, features, etc. are used to meet specific needs of a market. Identify a consumer product that has a product line of at least four specific and different products. Prepare a chart that describes each of the specific products in the product line. For each one, identify the factors that make the specific product unique from the others in the product line. Then describe the characteristics of the target market to which you believe each product is designed to appeal.

29. A new company has started to take advantage of people's interest in nature and the environment. The company sells individual flowers that are no more than four inches tall and are planted in two-inch square plastic pots. The flowers are blooming and with proper care should live for several months or longer. They will be sold through supermarkets, gift shops, and even vending machines. You have been asked to help in the design of the package for the flowers. Create a package that will protect the flower, provide an appropriate display, and provide information on the care of the flower. Also develop a brand name for the product that will appear on the package.

MARKETING TECHNOLOGY

30. Search the Internet for web sites of marketing firms that specialize in new product development services. Describe in detail the kinds of services offered by one such firm. What kinds of experience does the firm offer to prospective clients? Describe the firm's target market.

31. Using a spreadsheet program or scheduling software, create a preliminary schedule for the development of a new product of your choice. Include all of the steps of new product development, and estimate the time it will take to complete each step. How long does it take from inception until the product is ready for the market?

COCA COLA—THE EXPANDING BRAND

Every day, 6 billion people decide what to drink. Every 10 seconds, 126,000 people reach for a Coke product at work, home, school, or at the street corner as they eat, study, dance, get dressed, or fill their vehicles with petroleum.

Coca Cola Company is the leading manufacturer, marketer, and distributor of non-alcoholic beverage concentrates and syrups. Nearly 34,000 people around the world are employed by Coca Cola and its subsidiaries. The company sells concentrates and beverage bases for its flagship brand and over 230 other soft-drink brands in nearly 200 countries.

Coca Cola faces new opportunities around the world. It is the favorite soft drink in China, where a tea-flavored beverage was added to the successful fruit-flavored lineup. The launch of Fanta Limette was extremely successful in Germany, while Apple Life is the #2 brand in Mexico. Sales of Minute Maid grew when calcium and vitamin C were added to the Minute Maid drink in boxes. Tian lu Di teas, waters, and fruit juices are big hits in China, while Mori No Mizudayori mineral water is in demand in Japan. Adding Schweppes to the Coca Cola empire brought 39 new brands in more than 160 countries.

Coca Cola believes that it is one of life's simple affordable pleasures, a sensory experience enjoyed by many people. Coca Cola was introduced to the marketplace in 1886. The 1960s saw the addition of Fanta, Sprite, Tab, and Fresca. Mr. Pibb, Sugar-free Sprite, Mello Yello, and Ramblin' Rootbeer joined Coca Cola in the 1970s. The 1980s brought Diet Coke, Caffeine-free Coca Cola, Caffeine-free Diet Coke, Caffeine-free Tab, and Sugar-free Sprite, renamed Diet Sprite. Other flavors that were added to Coca Cola's choices included Diet Fanta, Cherry Coke, Coca Cola with a new taste, Coca Cola Classic, Diet Cherry Coke, and Diet Mellow Yellow.

"New Coke" tasted sweeter like Pepsi and received a cool reception from soft drink enthusiasts. Pepsi proclaimed that "Coke was trying to be more like Pepsi." Coca Cola immediately added Coca Cola Classic as the original choice for consumers and turned what rightfully should have been a marketing disaster into a bonanza. The 1990s saw the addition of Caffeine-free Coca Cola Classic, Powerade, Nestea, Fruitopia, BarQs, Surge, Citra, and "New" Coke renamed Coke II.

Minute Maid, Coca Cola's juice business, has been the world's leading marketer of juices and juice drinks. Minute Maid products include Minute Maid Premium Orange Juice with Calcium, Minute Maid Premium Lemonade Iced Tea, Minute Maid Coolers, Hi-C Blast, and Five Alive. In 2001, Minute Maid was merged into a 50/50 joint venture with Procter & Gamble Co. P&G contributed its Sunny Delight juice drinks and its line of Pringles potato chips. The new company was expected to generate annual sales of $4 billion.

Coca Cola and Pepsi compete to be the only beverage offered at high schools, universities, airlines, and major hotels. A major school district can reap thousands of dollars in benefits by offering only Coca Cola products in vending machines and at school events. Kentucky Fried Chicken, Pizza Hut, and Taco Bell all offered Pepsi since they are part of the same conglomerate. Major hotels such as the Marriott may have vending machines that only carry Pepsi products while Continental Airlines offers only Coke products. Consumers tend to be loyal to

one brand over the other. Loyal Coca Cola customers are not pleased when they order Coke at a restaurant and the cola they get turns out to be a Pepsi.

During the 1970s Pepsi had the tasters' test to prove that consumers preferred Pepsi over Coke. Coke advertised its cola as the "Real Thing" while the Pepsi Generation gave people the freedom to be individuals. Pepsi added diet beverages and changed the look of its package to keep up-to-date. Pepsi even had a clear cola for a short period of time. Pepsi designed a line of clothes, while Coca Cola offered collectible items ranging from wooden cases for the bottles to Christmas ornaments.

Coca Cola Co. has a strong commitment to social responsibility and good citizenship. The company spent millions of dollars on drug education to totally separate its image from any association with the narcotic cocaine. The Coca Cola Foundation contributed $100 million to education in the 1990s, supporting programs at more than 400 schools, colleges, and associations around the world. Foundation grants are available for mentoring programs and for partnerships between public schools and universities.

Signature Coca Cola First Generation Scholarships help students become the first in their family to attend college. Each year, Coca Cola presents $1.4 million in scholarships.

Competition between Coca Cola and Pepsi goes well beyond the soft drinks each company offers. Each company determines a strategy to gain customer loyalty. Diversified product lines and good public image are major factors that contribute to the success of major soft drink manufacturers.

THINK CRITICALLY

1. Coca Cola currently sells more product than Pepsi. What strategy should Pepsi use to gain a larger share of the market? Why?

2. Why does a powerful corporation like Coca Cola have to spend so much money on public image?

3. Describe a new soft drink flavor for Coca Cola. Why will this flavor be successful?

4. Design a new container for Coca Cola. Describe the features that make this container desirable.

http://www.deca.org/publications/HS_Guide/guidetoc.html

LEARN TO EARN PROJECT

Your group has successfully earned a large sum of money baking cookies every Tuesday to sell in the cafeteria. Your principal has given you permission to expand your business operation in school and throughout the community. You must present a business plan for your extended operation. You may consider opening a school store, selling cookies outside of school, or diversifying your product line.

DESCRIPTION Give a thorough description of the type of project proposed, a brief description of the major product/service involved, sources of information (resource materials, presentations, etc.), and a brief description of advisors and their involvement.

BUSINESS SITUATION Prepare an analysis of the business situation. Include trading area analysis, which encompasses general data on geography, demographics, economics, and competition, as well as market segment analysis that looks at customer buying behavior related to the proposed project.

OPERATING PLAN Develop a plan of how the proposed project will operate. Explain the start-up steps, and the personnel needed to handle the managerial, financial, marketing, and production (if applicable) functions.

MARKETING STRATEGIES Propose marketing strategies, including a promotional program, promotional activities, media availability, and costs.

BUDGET Develop a projected budget for all costs that details operating costs and your rationale for the projected budget.

CHAPTER 11

SERVICES NEED MARKETING

LESSON 11.1 *WHAT ARE SERVICES?*

LESSON 11.2 *CLASSIFYING TYPES AND EVALUATING QUALITY*

LESSON 11.3 *DEVELOPING A SERVICE MARKETING MIX*

NEWSLINE

PROMOTING LAWYERS

The legal profession has long demonstrated the effectiveness of the marketing concept. Law firms target specific markets, such as criminal law or business law, and then provide the services their customers in those markets need.

They frequently solicit feedback regarding the needs and wants of their clients. Lawyers use various pricing methods depending on the market. Some require large retainers (money in advance), some charge by the hour, some agree to accept a percentage of any damage awards they are able to get for their clients, and some use a combination of methods. Lawyers commonly adjust their hours to be available to clients when they are needed, working around the clock if that is what a situation demands. Many law firms have multiple office locations, often including offices in Washington, D.C., and international offices.

The legal profession traditionally hasn't done as much with the mix element of promotion. Various laws as well as professional guidelines restricted advertising in the past. Most of those restrictions have since been changed. For many lawyers, especially those that serve businesses, an aversion to advertising still holds today. Lawyers who primarily serve individuals, however, promote their practices almost anywhere advertising appears.

While some states allow virtually unlimited advertising by lawyers, others still restrict the use of that marketing tool. Some places have laws that restrict the content of advertisements or require certain disclaimers.

THINK CRITICALLY

1. Why should lawyers be subject to restrictions on advertising that don't apply to any other profession or business?

2. Even after courts overthrew many restrictions on legal advertising as contrary to lawyers' rights to free speech, most lawyers still do not use mass media advertising to promote their practices. Why?

CORPORATE VIEW

CAREER OPPORTUNITY
GENERAL ADMINISTRATIVE
ASSISTANT

POINT YOUR BROWSER

www.corpview.com

TeleView is looking for someone who possesses the following attributes.

- Desire to work in a high-pressure, fast-paced position in a public environment
- Excellent interpersonal and customer relations skills
- Good problem solving, time management, and project organization skills
- Drive, flexibility, and technical communication skills
- Desire to work in an invigorating team-oriented environment
- Willingness to relocate to Boulder, Colorado

The main responsibilities of the job include the following.

- Process invoices, complete expense reports for team members, and check proper payments
- Help coordinate department events
- Maintain the supply room
- Post necessary forms on the Intranet for worldwide distribution to sales representatives
- Manage the general administration of the workgroups in the Sales and Support department, including overnight shipments
- Orchestrate equipment repair with Information Technology (IT) department
- Coordinate new-hire interviews and training schedules between the Sales and Support department and Human Resources (HR) department
- Facilitate paperwork with the HR benefits specialist and equity compensation specialist

- Work with Corporate Communications to insure Sales and Support content is appropriately posted and displayed on the Intranet
- Help fitness consultant organize and administer the Marketing Sales and Support fitness program for Boulder employees

The job requires the following education, skills, and experience.

- Associate degree in Corporate Communications, Business, English, Journalism or a related field
- One to three years of direct business experience in administrative support roles or in customer support services
- Experience supporting teams and workgroups
- Mastery of Microsoft Word, Excel, and PowerPoint is a must
- Excellent personal and workgroup management and organization skills required
- No sports fitness training required
- Must demonstrate an attention to detail

THINK CRITICALLY

1. Prepare a cover letter written by a person who is qualified for this job and is seeking an interview.

2. Prepare a list of questions to ask the interviewer to ascertain if this position can be used as a stepping stone to a better job at TeleView.

3. Search want ads or the Internet for a job similar to this position. What type of compensation package is being offered for the job?

UNIQUE QUALITIES OF SERVICES

There are four important characteristics that distinguish services from products. Services are intangible, inseparable, perishable, and heterogeneous (see Figure 11-2).

INTANGIBLE

The most important difference between goods and services is that services are intangible. **Intangible** means that the service cannot be touched, seen, tasted, heard, or felt. Examples of intangible services include haircuts, medical treatments, and legal services. Unlike products, they do not have a physical form.

The intangibility of services presents special challenges for marketers. Because people cannot see or handle a service, it is important for the marketer to focus on the benefits customers will receive. Promotional activities need to be carefully conceived to develop mental pictures of benefits provided by services. Tourism, for example, relies heavily on photos, posters, videos, and travelogues to entice customers to select vacation destinations. The objective and challenge of tourism marketing is to get customers to imagine what it is like to be at a particular tourist location.

INSEPARABLE

A second characteristic of services is that the production and consumption of the service are inseparable. **Inseparable** means that the service is produced and consumed at the same time.

Services such as a college class, a manicure, and a bicycle repair are produced and consumed simultaneously. In many cases, the customer is actually involved in the production of the service. When you drop money in a video game or pay an admission fee to watch your favorite football team, you are demonstrating the inseparability of production and consumption in a service business.

FIGURE 11-2
Services pose special challenges to marketers because they are intangible, perishable, heterogeneous, and inseparable.

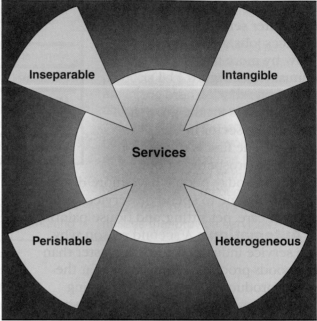

Unique Qualities of Services

This simultaneous production and consumption of services causes marketers to pay special attention to the distribution component of the marketing mix. As you learned previously, distribution involves having the service available where and when it is needed or wanted by the consumer. An example of ineffective distribution would be to locate a lawn mower repair service in a downtown area. Because of its location, it probably would not attract many customers. On the other hand, a hotel limousine service located at the airport would be a good distribution strategy.

PERISHABLE

Another characteristic of services is their perishability. **Perishable** means that services unused in one time period cannot be stored for use in the future. An example of this is a lawn care service. You cannot buy more than one grass cutting at a time. Though the person who cuts your grass might want to cut it 10 times in the spring when the weather is cool, the service cannot be purchased that way.

Because of perishability, marketers are concerned about lost opportunity. An empty seat in a theater or an airplane cannot be sold later. After the movie has been shown or the plane has taken off, the revenue that could have been generated by a paying customer is lost.

Airlines work very hard to fill seats on every flight. They recognize that money is lost on each empty seat and can never be retrieved. That is why the airlines offer discounted fares and special promotions to people willing to fly when they know there will be empty seats. This is the airlines' attempt to overcome the perishability of their service.

The pricing component of the marketing mix is crucial in the sale of perishable services. Prices must be set to assure the business the greatest number of sales while covering expenses and allowing for a profit.

Unified Currency Moves Europe Closer to Single Market

One reason the United States is the world's pre-eminent economic power is that it has long been the largest unified market. Europe is bigger, but Europe isn't—or at least hasn't been—a single market. That situation is changing.

When members of the European Union adopted the euro and got rid of their individual currencies at the beginning of this century, they simplified the marketing of products and services among themselves and also to other countries. Each member's central bank essentially turned over its role as supplier of money to the European Central Bank, which operates with much the same authority as the U.S. Federal Reserve.

Now if a German goes on a shopping trip to Paris, he doesn't have to exchange marks for francs and then change what's left over back again when he returns. So it's more convenient and also less expensive because there are no currency exchange fees to be paid.

Even more important, if a French dressmaker buys materials from Italy, buttons from Belgium, and contracts with a Spanish assembly shop, she doesn't have to worry about all those different currencies changing in value and eating up her projected profits before she ships the finished goods to U.S. buyers.

THINK CRITICALLY

1. For service businesses, what has been and continues to be an even bigger impediment to European economic integration than different currencies?

2. Why might some consumers and businesses have preferred to keep their separate currencies rather than adopt the euro?

amount of contact they have with customers, and the level of skill they require (see Figure 11-3).

TYPE OF MARKET

Just as with products, there are two types of markets for services—business consumers and individual consumers. A business consumer might employ a cleaning service, a grounds service, a maintenance service, and an equipment repair service. Businesses that provide these services to other businesses must offer services tailored to business needs that are available where and when the business wants them.

An individual consumer, like you or your parents, might also employ a cleaning service, a lawn service, a maintenance service, and an equipment repair service. For those consumer-oriented services, the target market and marketing mix will be quite different.

A marketing mix that is designed to reach business customers might stress personal selling and quantity price discounts. A marketing mix that is designed to reach individual customers might stress individualized attention, advertising through print and broadcast media, and more standardized prices. As a marketer, you need to know your market and the specific wants and needs of that market in order to satisfy it.

FIGURE 11-3
Service organizations satisfy the needs of individuals and businesses alike. The organizational goal, labor intensiveness, amount of customer contact, and level of skill of the service provider vary depending on the industry and organization.

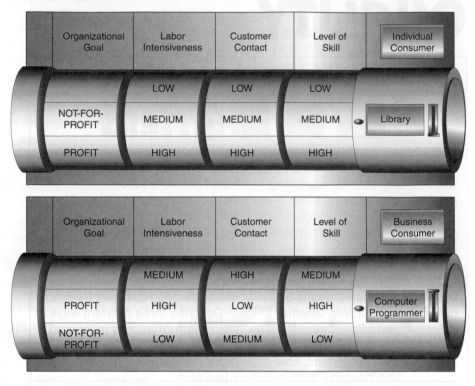

Service Organizations Satisfy Needs

GOALS OF THE ORGANIZATION

Some organizations have profit-making as a goal, while others operate as not-for-profit organizations. Most businesses that compete with each other in providing food, transportation, repairs, and other services for which people pay are profit-making organizations.

There are many not-for-profit organizations that also deliver services. Examples of these types of organizations are universities, libraries, museums, government programs, churches, and social agencies. These organizations have goals and motives that are different from profit-making organizations. Their goals might be public service, public awareness of a message or idea, or knowledge. Money is not normally a significant motivating factor for not-for-profit service organizations. Still, they are equally interested in delivering high-quality services that consumers need and want.

LABOR INTENSENESS

Labor intensiveness refers to the amount of human effort required to deliver a service. Services range from those that are extremely labor intensive to those that are totally reliant on equipment. Most combine labor and equipment and fall somewhere in between.

Equipment-based services are provided with the use of machinery. These services require few people to provide the services. Examples include automated car washes, dry cleaning, and automated teller machines. People-based services are provided through the work of people. Shoe shines, manicures, haircuts, and guided tours are examples of people-based services. These services are more labor intensive.

As a marketer, you will emphasize different parts of the mix depending on whether your service is labor or equipment intensive. When marketing equipment-based services, you will pay special attention to the distribution or location of your services. Locating an automatic car wash on a busy street is more appropriate than on a residential street. Placing an automatic bank teller machine in a safe, well-lighted place for a drive-through location gives customers a greater sense of security. You will also want to make sure the equipment is properly maintained.

With people-based services you will want to pay careful attention to the training of your personnel. You will train them in how to provide the service to satisfy your customers' wants and needs. A courteous and efficient waiter is a good example of well-trained personnel.

JUDGMENT CALL

Wireless Devices Raise Client Billing Issues

With the proliferation of wireless communications, providers of professional services such as lawyers and business consultants have the opportunity to drastically reduce down time. Now they can work—and bill clients for the time they spend doing it—virtually wherever and whenever they want. The troubling issue for clients is making sure they are getting their money's worth, because their business or affairs might not get a professional's undivided attention.

With Internet-enabled phones and personal digital assistants, a consultant can be driving down the highway at 75 mph and researching a client matter on the Internet or talking with clients on the phone. Safety issues notwithstanding, is it fair to a client to bill him for that time when the consultant simultaneously has to keep at least a few other things on her mind—such as the bridge abutments whizzing past and the semi in front of her that just hit its brakes?

The law and professional ethical standards aren't much help. As long as a professional is providing something of value to a client, it's permissible to bill that time. And as one lawyer noted, he can be just as distracted sitting at his desk as he can be behind the wheel of his car.

THINK CRITICALLY

1. If a lawyer is driving to a court appearance for client A and, while en route, also talking on the phone with client B about an unrelated matter, do you think it would be OK to bill both clients for that time?

2. Do you think it would be feasible to bill clients at a reduced rate for time during which the professional's attention is divided?

CUSTOMER CONTACT

The amount of customer contact a service provider has is another way to classify services. Some services have high customer contact. Examples of high-customer-contact services are barbers, doctors, schools, hotels, and restaurants. Other services, such as equipment repair, lawn maintenance, and movie theaters, have low customer contact.

Recognizing and responding to the level of customer contact is important if you are

Automated Teller Machines

Americans are increasingly placing a premium on their time and seeking greater control over how they use it. In many service organizations, convenience has emerged as a major marketing tool along with quality and customer service. This trend opens market opportunities for businesses that sell convenience, such as self-service dry cleaners that stay open 24 hours a day, dentists who work evenings and weekends, and banks that offer credit approval over the telephone.

One of the most competitive responses to the convenience factor has been the development of automated teller machines (ATMs). ATMs are now used by an estimated 150 million Americans who complete more than 300 million transactions each month. Originally ATMs only dispensed cash and accepted checks for deposit. Today they can issue monthly bus and rail passes, discount movie tickets, gift certificates, and store coupons. Besides being convenient for customers, they are profitable for businesses because they transform labor intensive services into highly automated services.

The merits of ATMs as a convenience tool are being realized by many businesses other than banks. Increasing numbers of ATMs are being installed in restaurants, department stores, and convenience marts. At a county fair in San Diego, $1.25 million was dispensed through ATMs in just 20 days. The ATMs were in trailers that could be placed in convenient locations.

THINK CRITICALLY

1. Do you think that the convenience of being able to withdraw money at an ATM increased the amount of money spent by fair-goers in San Diego?

2. Do you think it is fair that banks charge people fees when they use ATMs to withdraw their own money?

a service marketer. In general, the higher the contact, the more you must rely on personal selling as a promotional activity. With low-customer-contact businesses, it is important to stress planning to provide maximum customer satisfaction since there is not much opportunity to interact with customers.

LEVEL OF SKILL

Another way to categorize services is by the level of skill the provider possesses. The most common way to categorize based on skill levels is to divide the providers into professional and nonprofessional groups. Professionals include providers whose services tend to be more complex and more highly regulated than nonprofessional services. The professional category would contain accountants, lawyers, teachers, physicians, therapists, and others who are required to have a combination of high-level skill, education, and a license to practice. The nonprofessional service group would include providers such as pet sitters, personal shoppers, hotel clerks, and image consultants, whose jobs require limited preparation.

Identify the various ways marketers categorize service businesses and organizations in order to develop effective marketing mixes.

EVALUATING
SERVICE QUALITY

The United States is becoming a service-oriented country. People are continually finding new services to offer prospective customers, and consumers have more discretionary income to purchase these services.

With the large number of service businesses in the market today, a deciding factor for whether a company prospers or not is the quality of the service provided. **Service quality** is defined as the degree to which the service meets customers' needs and expectations.

Quality can be measured in a number of ways. Quality is controlled by the provider of the service. It might be in the qualifications of the provider or in the speed of service. It might also be measured in cleanliness, efficiency, safety, comfort, or any number of variables.

To improve quality, an organization must first understand how customers decide which service they want and how they will judge the quality of the service. Three types of service standards can be used to evaluate service quality—competition, performance standards, and customer satisfaction.

Competition   Marketers of services need to be aware of the nature and level of services their competitors are offering to customers. Organizations must provide services that are at least equal in quality to what their competitors offer for the same price. In addition, services must be positioned in a way that is unique and sets the business apart from its competition.

Performance Standards   A service organization should set its own service standards and communicate those standards to potential customers. Promotions used by airlines, car rental companies, delivery services, and telephone companies reinforce the commitment to quality service.

Just saying that the company is committed isn't enough. Each organization should have an actual list of standards that stands behind its advertising slogan. The standard should be measurable, such as the following: "Eighty-five percent of our arrivals will be on time," or "We will have no more than three customer complaints per month." The service should be evaluated to see if it meets that standard. It is important to find out if the service offered meets the standards, and to take corrective action if it doesn't.

Customer Satisfaction   The real test of service quality is customers' assessment of it. Firms use market research to find out exactly what customers think. One of the most important and useful indicators of customer satisfaction is repeat business. Do customers continue to come back to buy the service? If they do, it is a strong indication that they are satisfied with the service offered and that the organization is achieving its service standards.

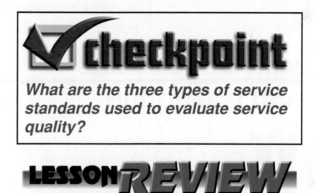

checkpoint

What are the three types of service standards used to evaluate service quality?

LESSON REVIEW

1. How does the level of customer contact affect the promotion element of a marketing mix?

2. With equipment-intensive services such as a dry cleaner or an automatic car wash, what is a crucial part of the distribution element of the marketing mix?

3. What is the most common way to categorize levels of skill?

4. Why is it important for businesses to evaluate the quality of the services they provide?

5. Name two ways that businesses use to determine what their customers think of the service they receive.

11.3 DEVELOPING A SERVICE MARKETING MIX

- Explain how businesses plan and promote services.
- Describe the importance of pricing and distribution of services.

The unique characteristics of services make developing a marketing mix very challenging. A customer's ability to make a buying decision about a product is enhanced by the tangible nature of products. The purchase decision is easier because customers can see the products, smell them, touch them, or taste them. Marketers of services, which are harder to grasp, must help their customers visualize their services. They do so by applying the principles of product/service planning, pricing, promotion, and distribution in ways that are suited to the nature of the services they provide. As with products, the objective is to satisfy their customers.

Make a list of five services that you have used in the past 24 hours, and describe how you arrived at your decision to use each of those services rather than competitive services or other alternatives.

SERVICE PLANNING AND PROMOTION

When dealing with services, business need to plan products carefully, keeping in mind the differences between services and products. Businesses also need to identify effective strategies for promoting their services.

SERVICE PLANNING

When developing the service to be provided, service marketers must recognize that their services cannot be defined in terms of physical attributes. Instead companies need to shape the attributes of the service to meet the needs and wants of consumers in the most satisfactory way possible.

FedEx sells a service and communicates the attributes of its service: fast delivery. Banks also sell their services such as checking accounts, savings accounts, and loans. The attributes of bank services are dependability, convenience, low interest rates on loans, and high yields on savings.

Both FedEx and a bank must develop favorable mental images of their services by communicating their benefits.

Services are intangible, but businesses also recognize that customers pay attention to certain tangible elements associated with the service. The delivery trucks for Federal Express are brightly painted, clean, and in good repair. The bank is in a building that reinforces the idea that it is a safe place for customers to deposit or borrow money. Imagine the image you would have of a bank if it was located in a building needing paint and repairs.

Recognizing that tangible products are important, many service organizations try to provide a physical item for customers to take along with them. Many times these items become a piece of specialty advertising as well. Dentists give patients toothbrushes, restaurants hand out mugs, and airlines may give away duffel bags. Banks provide checkbook covers, hospitals give out T-shirts, and professional baseball teams distribute team hats. In each case, the service organization is attempting to provide a tangible symbol and reminder of the service it provides.

PROMOTION

Services are sometimes thought to be difficult to promote. Something that cannot be touched is not as easily described in promotional strategies like print advertising or broadcast media. Services are also difficult to promote through personal selling since they are difficult to demonstrate. It is important to remember that, whether you are promoting a product or a service, you need to appeal to the buying motives of the target market and stress the benefits derived by use of the service.

One effective promotional strategy for services is to stress the tangible elements of the service. The well-dressed waiter, late-model rental cars, and high-quality furnishings in a law office are all tangible elements associated with intangible services.

Endorsements   Many services use endorsements as a promotional strategy. Satisfied service users describe their satisfaction in an advertisement. Sometimes endorsers are well-known role models for a target market. Celebrities often endorse telephone services, airlines, and credit cards.

Word of Mouth   Service organizations rely heavily on publicity and word-of-mouth promotion. People often consider information from friends to be very credible. Service sellers encourage word-of-mouth promotion in several ways. They ask satisfied customers to "tell a friend about us." They offer incentives to consumers who bring someone when returning for additional service. They also develop publicity activities that encourage people to talk about their business.

Personal Selling   Many marketers believe that personal selling is the most powerful promotional tool available. A well-trained sales staff can interact with customers to reduce their uncertainty, give

One-Stop Convenience

Personal computers liberated individuals and businesses from mainframes and computer operators by allowing them to process information from their desks. The Internet allowed people and businesses to buy and sell products via a web site. Now application service providers, or ASPs, give service businesses the ability to provide highly personalized services over the Internet.

Financial consultants can now subscribe to Internet-based planning services that allow them to merge clients' financial records in real time from multiple sources. Up-to-the-minute account data from banks, insurance companies, stockbrokers, mortgage lenders, and retirement plans are downloaded into a consolidated financial planning program with a few keystrokes.

With ASPs, clients and consultants no longer have to worry about working with outdated or incomplete information. Moreover, they can each view and analyze current data simultaneously from their own offices. So if someone wants to jump at a hot investment opportunity, the investor can run it by an adviser to see what overall affect it could have without either of them leaving their desks.

THINK CRITICALLY

1. How are Internet-based ASPs superior to software programs that are installed on stand-alone personal computers?

2. What kinds of concerns might arise from having highly personal and confidential data floating around cyberspace?

reassurance, reduce doubts, and promote the reputation of the service provider. Careful training and management of customer-contact personnel is crucial to the success of a service organization.

The last part of the promotion strategy is the nature and the timing of the message. The nature of the message should be such that it creates a mental image of the performance of the service. It must also foster the idea of satisfied needs in the customer. The timing of the promotional message must also be right. It must be close enough to the potential need and/or use for the service to be memorable and influence a decision.

What are the various strategies that marketers have found to be effective in promoting services?

PRICE AND
DISTRIBUTION

Price and distribution of services each have their own special considerations. Each needs to be carefully considered when developing marketing plans.

Speech-Recognition Software

Advances in speech-recognition software are opening up all kinds of new possibilities for marketers. Marketing research, customer service, telephone questionnaires, and desktop publishing of promotional materials can all be accomplished more quickly, more effectively, and much less expensively using software to translate spoken words into printed information or digital data.

Speech-recognition software now incorporates a feature that trains the program to better recognize what users are saying. The more a person uses the program, the fewer errors the program makes because it remembers various words and sounds that it has heard before. Programs also can be trained to recognize industry-specific terminology in order to translate frequently-used words and phrases accurately into print.

Coupled with automated dialers, speech recognition software can transform many marketing tasks that tend to be labor intensive and expensive. Now the challenge for marketers is to incorporate this technology into their work without offending customers who may not appreciate the idea of being questioned by a machine.

THINK CRITICALLY

1. How might marketers overcome customer objections to using speech-recognition software for handling orders or other customer communications?

2. Name three ways marketers might use speech-recognition software to accomplish common marketing functions.

PRICE

In the past, pricing was not viewed as particularly important among service providers. Services were perceived to be unique, much like a monopoly. With increased competition and government deregulation of many industries, businesses began to see pricing strategies as a way to improve their market positions and to differentiate themselves from their competition.

Service businesses are in a good position to alter their pricing strategies because they can change prices fairly easily. A hair salon in your neighborhood can change its pricing schedule to meet competition or to create a new image just by printing a new price schedule. If needed, the services can be altered to reflect the new prices. The amount or complexity of a service can be increased or decreased with the pricing strategy. For example, the neighborhood hair salon can add styling specialists or additional hair services to justify price increases.

One interesting pricing strategy that many service providers use is called bundling. **Bundling** is the practice of combining the price of several related services. Imagine that you are planning to spend a week in

Orlando, Florida. In this case, the airline would attempt to bundle the price of a ticket, a rental car, a hotel, and a four-day pass to the Magic Kingdom into one tour package for which you would pay one price. Another example of bundling is a college charging one price for a student's room, board, tuition, and fees covering library use, medical services, and insurance.

Bundling is a type of quantity discount. More services can be purchased for a lower price than if they were purchased individually. This has advantages for both the customers and the sellers of services. The customer pays a reduced price and has the advantage of one-stop shopping. The service marketer forms mutually beneficial relationships with other service marketers. The marketers are usually able to increase sales of their services using the bundling technique.

DISTRIBUTION

The distribution of services is primarily concerned with having the service in a location that is convenient for the consumer. Many services that people used to travel to are now provided in their homes. Pet grooming, tire changing, car maintenance, and television repair are examples of services that will come directly to your home.

An important point to remember in marketing services is that for many services, production and consumption happen simultaneously. That is, the service is performed and you receive it at the same time. Therefore, the channels of distribution for a service are very short. In many cases, the channel is the producer and provider all rolled into one. A restaurant is a good example of this. The food is cooked and served at one site.

Some types of services, however, make use of intermediaries. For example, you might drop off your film for developing at a supermarket or drugstore. The store then sends the film to a lab for actual developing.

In planning a distribution strategy for a service, the most important element of the strategy should be convenience for the consumers. Travel agents can usually bring the service of selling airline tickets closer to you than the airlines. Automated teller machines bring the services of banks to more convenient locations and more convenient hours. Video stores rent movies so people can watch them at more convenient times in the comfort of their own homes.

What is the key to the effective distribution of services?

LESSON REVIEW

1. Name five tangible elements that are associated with services provided by the federal government, such as making laws, printing money, and maintaining law and order.

2. What is bundling?

3. Why are services well-suited to altering pricing strategies to meet changing market conditions?

4. What does it mean when marketers say services have short channels of distribution?

5. Why do many service businesses give out some token product as part of their service, such as auto repair shops that give out calendars and restaurants that provide customers with matches?

CHAPTER 11

SUMMARY

Lesson 11.1

A. The service industry is growing rapidly in the United States. As people become increasingly prosperous and technology becomes more complex, America is quickly becoming a nation of service providers and service users.

B. Services differ from products because they are intangible, produced and consumed simultaneously, perishable, and heterogeneous. Marketers must emphasize specific elements of the marketing mix when preparing a marketing plan.

Lesson 11.2

A. Services can be classified by the type of market they serve, the service organization's goals, the amount of labor that is necessary to perform the service, the amount of customer contact, and the level of skill required to provide the service. It is important to understand these classifications because they help marketers determine the most appropriate marketing mixes for their businesses.

B. Because there are so many services available for customers to choose from, it is important that marketers understand how to evaluate

the quality of the service provided. Organizations evaluate quality based on their competition, their performance standards, and the satisfaction of their customers.

Lesson 11.3

A. Since a service lacks physical attributes, when developing the service to be provided, marketers need to shape the attributes of the service to meet the needs and wants of consumers in the most satisfactory way possible. Marketers promote services with various strategies that stress the benefits derived from using a service. Common strategies include emphasizing tangible elements of the service, using celebrity endorsements, relying heavily on word-of-mouth, and employing personal selling.

B. Pricing is gaining in importance as an element of services marketing because of increased competition and deregulation. Bundling several different services and selling them as a package has been an effective strategy. The distribution of services is primarily concerned with having the service in a location that is convenient for the consumer.

REVIEW MARKETING CONCEPTS

1. Services can be classified based on certain criteria: type of market, labor intensiveness, customer contact, level of skill, and organizational goals. Classify each of the following services by these criteria and create a chart to illustrate their appropriate classification.
   a. An insurance policy protecting a professional volleyball team from loss of the team's star player
   b. A new paint job for an old car
   c. Three empty horses on a circus carousel
   d. A manicure while the customer's hair is styled
   e. A heart bypass operation performed at the Mayo Clinic
   f. An opera performed by a local community group
   g. Clean uniforms provided by the employer
   h. A long-distance telephone call
   i. Renting a motel room
   j. A golf course
   k. A high school education
   l. Cable television installed in a new neighborhood

Read the following statements and supply the missing word or phrase.

2. __?__ are tangible objects that can be purchased and resold.

3. __?__ are intangible, perishable, and heterogeneous.

4. By 1999, __?__ percent of the workers in the United States were employed in service-producing industries.

5. When a service is produced and consumed at the same time, it is said to be __?__ .

6. Services are performed by people, and since people differ in their abilities and skill levels, services are said to be __?__ .

7. There are two types of markets for services: __?__ and __?__ .

8. Automated car washes, teller machines, and telephone calling cards are examples of services that are __?__ .

9. Whether you are promoting a product or service, you must remember to appeal to the __?__ of your target market.

10. With increased competition and government deregulation, businesses now use __?__ as a way to improve their market positions and to differentiate themselves from their competitors.

11. __?__ is the practice of combining the price of several related services.

12. Services characteristically have __?__ distribution channels.

13. The degree to which the service conforms to customers' specifications and expectations is called __?__ .

14. A service that is highly automated and involves little human effort is __?__ intensive.

REVIEW MARKETING TERMS

Match the terms listed with the definitions. Some terms may not be used.

15. Incapable of being touched, seen, tasted, heard, or felt.

16. Requires a substantial amount of human effort.

17. Produced and consumed at the same time.

18. An activity that is intangible, exchanged directly from producer to consumer, and consumed at the time of production.

19. The practice of combining the prices of several related services.

20. The degree to which a service meets customers' needs and expectations.

21. Incapable of being stored for use at a future time.

22. Dissimilar, characterized by differences.

a. bundling
b. heterogeneous
c. inseparable
d. intangible
e. labor intensive
f. perishable
g. service
h. service quality

SELLING LEGAL SERVICES IN CYBERSPACE

What happens when the legal profession turns to a new medium as the means to market its services? When the medium is cyberspace, old and new worlds collide. On the one hand, there's the Internet, the exciting information superhighway, offering an unbelievable amount of information with no limit on its content. On the other hand, there's the legal profession, steeped in tradition, self-regulating, slow to change, and skeptical of commercialism.

As a result, the legal profession has a tool limited only by the imaginations of those surfing cyberspace, yet ultimately constrained by the rules governing the conduct of lawyers and their marketing activities.

Originally, the American Bar Association (ABA) did not allow lawyers to advertise their services on television and the Internet. These types of advertising were viewed as being detrimental to the legal profession. Now lawyers frequently advertise on television, billboards, and the Internet. Legal advertisements on television range from poorly constructed soap operas to professional presentations. It is not uncommon to drive down an interstate highway and see a legal advertisement for handling a personal bankruptcy or a divorce for "as low as $500." Consumers now travel the information superhighway to obtain legal information they cannot find in the yellow pages.

While the U.S. Supreme Court lifted the ban on lawyer advertising in 1977, the Internet has only become a viable marketing tool for legal services in more recent years with the development of the World Wide Web. Law firms are making the leap from the yellow pages to home pages as they embrace the Internet at a phenomenal pace. Only five law firms had web pages in November 1994. Within a year, the figure had grown to almost 500 law firms.

DO THE RULES REALLY APPLY TO LAW FIRMS MARKETING ON THE INTERNET?

Some law firms have concluded that a web page is not advertising and that there is no need to comply with the profession's advertising rules. This is a dangerous assumption, since avoiding the rules also means avoiding the necessity of including disclaimers and labeling copy as advertising material. Some states prohibit client testimonials, illustrations, animations, and anything that sparks an emotional response. Avoiding the rules gives a law firm more room to present its message, and the marketing process becomes much easier and more likely to succeed.

Law firms sometimes try to avoid the ethical issue by labeling web sites as *commercial speech* but not *advertising.* The Supreme Court views a commercial speech as having the purpose of proposing a commercial transaction.

Legal firms use the Web to increase business. Whether something is commercial speech and subject to regulations is determined by its content. Most lawyers who use the Internet will be proposing the same types of commercial transactions that are also covered in law firm brochures—by defining the capabilities of the firm, the history of its success, and the expertise of its partners. It is likely that web pages of law firms and participation on the Internet by individual lawyers are subject to the rules of professional conduct governing the communication of legal services, especially those that prohibit misleading statements and control advertisements or solicitations.

Some lawyers have suggested that their presence on the Internet is different from other types of legal service marketing because the prospective client must seek it out. That differentiates it from invasive marketing media such as television commercials or targeted direct mail. The most feasible compliance alternative may be to include a statement on the home page like the statements found in advertisements for sweepstakes—in which sponsors comply with state laws by saying the game is "void where prohibited by law."

In any case, lawyers who choose the Internet as a marketing tool must understand that technology is ahead of the governing standards for that technology.

NOT ALL PROFESSIONALS ARE SOLD ON THE LATEST TECHNOLOGY

Jim and Judy Cada are a successful law team in Lincoln, Nebraska, that specializes in personal injury and medical cases. This married couple has built a strong law firm through hard work, customer service, and leads generated from satisfied customers and other lawyers. Jim believes that advertising in television commercials or poorly designed web sites tends to downgrade the profession. Their law firm wants to select cases they feel that they can win since they are paid a retainer. Advertising over the Internet would only magnify the number of prospective customers that the law firm would have to screen. Jim and Judy are successful because they specialize in areas of law where they have the most experience. Judy worked in the medical profession, while Jim worked at jobs during college that put him in contact with successful lawyers. Their business plate is full without generating more clients from the Internet.

THINK CRITICALLY

1. Make a two-column chart showing the pros and cons of using the Internet for legal services.

2. Why is the American Bar Association concerned with the types of marketing used by lawyers and the legal profession?

3. Do you think that marketing for the legal profession needs to be regulated? Why or why not?

---

http://www.deca.org/publications/HS_Guide/guidetoc.html

CREATIVE MARKETING RESEARCH PROJECT

You have landed an internship position in a prestigious law firm. Your first assignment is to prepare a customer survey to find out what clients expect from attorneys, what types of advertising bring the best results, and the level of knowledge clients have about legal fees charged by attorneys. The information you gather from this survey will be used to improve customer relations in the law firm and to improve advertisement of services. This survey should effectively gather the concerns prospective clients have when using legal services.

DESCRIPTION AND INTRODUCTION   Prepare a description of the project. Introduce the project by providing background information, including a description of the law firm. State the intention of the survey.

RESEARCH METHODS
Describe the procedures and research methods used. Describe any secondary research methods, such as looking up books, articles, and other resources at the library. Explain how the survey was prepared and who was involved.

SUMMARIZE FINDINGS   Present your findings, including data to support the findings. Present conclusions and the rationale to support those conclusions.

RECOMMENDATIONS   Explain recommendations resulting from the study. Outline a plan for implementing the recommendations, and outcomes you expect from implementing them.

CHAPTER 12

PRODUCTS FOR RESALE

LESSON 12.1 *BUSINESS-TO-BUSINESS EXCHANGE PROCESS*

LESSON 12.2 *MAKING PURCHASING DECISIONS IN BUSINESS*

LESSON 12.3 *BUSINESS PURCHASING PROCEDURES*

LESSON 12.4 *RETAIL PURCHASING*

NEWSLINE

CODING SYSTEM UNLOCKS BUSINESS MARKETS

The U.S. business market represents 20 million customers, many of whom spend millions of dollars each day on purchases. A few will budget several billion dollars each year to buy products and services. The market consists of producers, manufacturers, retailers, wholesalers, and service providers. They operate in such diverse areas as fishing, tourism, mineral extraction, and dentistry.

Sorting through all of the differences among businesses to find a target market can be difficult. But help is available in the form of a tool known as the North American Industry Classification System (NAICS). It was created to identify organizations in similar industries and to identify their primary activities, size, location, and other important descriptive information.

NAICS uses a six-digit code. It replaced the previous Standard Industrial Code (SIC) classification system in the late 1990s. The SIC system used four-digit codes and had become outdated with the creation of many new industries that didn't even exist when the system was designed by the U.S. government in the 1930s.

The NAICS system is also used in Canada and Mexico, facilitating trade between those countries and U.S. businesses.

To target business customers, most companies start with NAICS information. In that way they can identify businesses with similar purchasing needs. They can track increases and decreases in the numbers of businesses, the volume of sales in the industry, and even changes in levels of employment. It is an important tool for marketing planning. Reports on industry information using NAICS codes are prepared by government agencies as well as business, trade, and professional organizations.

THINK CRITICALLY

1. Using the Internet or library research, find an NAICS code for a business that makes engines for farm equipment. What do the component numbers of the code mean?

2. How do businesses use the NAICS to find markets for their products or services?

CORPORATE VIEW

POINT YOUR
BROWSER
www.corpview.com

CAREER OPPORTUNITY
CUSTOMER SERVICE
SPECIALIST

TeleView is looking for someone who possesses the following attributes.

- Well-developed interpersonal skills and an ability to work in an invigorating, team-oriented environment
- Excellent customer relations skills necessary to maintain customer loyalty
- Problem solving proficiency
- Up-to-date technical communications skills
- Ability to learn technical products quickly
- Proven project organization, time management, and interpersonal skills
- Drive and flexibility
- Desire to be in a high-pressure position working directly with some of the most important and influential corporate customers

This position has a base salary, benefits and a bonus structure. A portable computer with remote Intranet connection will be provided. A digital wireless phone and company account are also provided.

The main responsibilities of this job include the following.

- Supporting the sales team by working directly with their customers, particularly large account customers, prior to and for several months after a major sale
- Working as a member of a team to provide on-call, 24-hour support to specific major clients and large accounts
- Frequent travel may be necessary to solve some large account problems

- Handling any and all customer problems in a timely manner
- Effectively maintaining relationships with customers that will largely determine their long-term relationship with TeleView

The job requires the following education, skills, and experience.

- Bachelor's degree strongly preferred
- Two or more years in a previous customer support or direct sales role
- Ability to use the Intranet remotely to help solve problems
- PC experience required, Macintosh experience a plus
- Technical communications skill needed to instruct others via e-mail, through video conferencing, on the phone, and in person on how to use and troubleshoot TeleView products

THINK CRITICALLY

1. Prepare a brief cover letter of a person who is qualified for this job and is seeking to interview for it during an upcoming visit to Colorado.

2. Considering your own skills and career preferences, does this sound like a job you would be good at? Why or why not?

3. Search want ads or the Internet for a job similar to Corporate View's customer service specialist for large accounts. What is the job description and title? What type of compensation package is available for this job?

12.1 BUSINESS-TO-BUSINESS EXCHANGE PROCESS

GOALS

- Explain the various reasons businesses buy things from other businesses.
- Define the five major classifications of business consumers.
- Describe the common characteristics typical of business markets.

Any exchange of products and services involves a buyer and seller. People most often think about businesses as sellers and individual consumers as buyers. Actually, the majority of exchanges do not involve the final consumer. Instead, most exchanges take place between businesses. One business buys products and services from another business. Business-to-business marketing is a very important part of our economy.

Marketers should be aware that businesses buy products and services from other businesses for several distinct reasons. Also, there are five major types of business consumers. Business markets tend to share a number of characteristics that are significant for business-to-business marketing.

Every time a consumer buys a car, that one final exchange is the culmination of hundreds of business-to-business exchanges that had to take place in order for that car to be available at that time and place. List 10 business-to-business exchanges that routinely occur in the marketing of a car.

REASONS FOR BUSINESS PURCHASES

The business product classification system identifies various types of products and services that are bought and sold in business-to-business marketing. The categories of business products and services are shown in Figure 12-1.

There are many reasons why businesses purchase products. A producer or manufacturer usually does

FIGURE 12-1
The business products classification system describes the types of products and services that are bought and sold in business-to-business marketing.

CATEGORIES OF BUSINESS PRODUCTS

Capital Goods	The building and major equipment of business
Operating Equipment	Equipment used in the daily operation of the business
Supplies	Consumable materials used in the operation of the business
Raw Materials	Unprocessed materials that are incorporated into the products by the business
Component Parts	Partially or completely processed items that become a part of the products produced by the business
Services	Tasks performed in the operation of the business or to support the production, sale, or maintenance of the products and services

not own everything it needs to develop the products it sells. Some companies do not have the raw materials used in production. Many of the component parts that are used in manufacturing products are produced by other companies. Purchasing products to be incorporated into a production or manufacturing process is an important part of business-to-business marketing.

Some businesses purchase products for direct resale to other customers. It is not efficient to sell every product or service directly from the producer to the final consumer. Therefore, other businesses facilitate the marketing and sale of products. Typically, those businesses do not change the physical form of the product. They may repackage it. They may also provide a number of other marketing functions.

A third reason for business purchasing is to obtain products and services needed to operate the business. Buildings and equipment are produced by one company for sale to others. Companies need a variety of supplies for their day-to-day operations. Many businesses purchase professional services from attorneys and accountants, business services from advertising agencies and cleaning services, and services that support the products they sell such as repair services.

PURCHASING AS A MARKETING ACTIVITY

Purchasing is an important activity of marketing. Purchasing includes determining the purchasing needs of an organization, identifying the best sources to obtain the needed products and services, and completing the activities necessary to obtain and use them. Businesses must do an effective job

Minority Supplier Programs

Minority-owned businesses often have trouble gaining entry to corporate purchasing departments without contacts inside. As purchasing strategies increasingly emphasize greater reliance on fewer suppliers, getting a foot in the door is becoming harder even as it becomes potentially more lucrative. One way qualified minority suppliers can help to overcome barriers is to take advantage of diversity programs designed to increase purchasing from minority-owned firms.

Boeing's commercial airplane group has an active diversity program designed to encourage purchasing managers to buy from minority-owned and women-owned suppliers. Boeing's commercial airplane group buys more than $15 billion worth of goods and services annually from more than 3,000 suppliers. Procurement managers have to fill out a scorecard that rates their performance on 26 line items, such as the percentage of dollar volume purchased from minorities, women, and small businesses.

The program was initiated in 1999. Boeing's purchasing managers seem to like it because they rate themselves. The system also helps to identify top-performing minority suppliers so managers can direct more business to them.

THINK CRITICALLY

1. How do corporations such as Boeing benefit from diversity programs?

2. If you were the manager of a minority-owned manufacturer, how would you use diversity programs such as Boeing's to your advantage?

of purchasing the products and services they use if they are to be successful. If a business purchases the wrong products or products that are of poor quality, if it pays too much for the products it purchases, or if a supplier is not able to deliver products as promised, the business will be unable to operate effectively and serve its customers well.

Name three reasons that businesses buy products or services from other businesses.

TYPES OF BUSINESS PURCHASERS

Do you think marketing to businesses and organizations should be done in a different way than marketing to final consumers? If you just picture the two types of customers in your mind you might believe the answer is yes. Consider selling radios to an automobile manufacturer as compared to selling a radio to a consumer to be installed in that person's car. You see a very large business purchasing hundreds and thousands of radios versus one person buying a single radio. You can expect that the business has very different reasons for purchasing the radios than does the individual. It is reasonable to believe that quite different procedures would be used to gather information and make a decision about the radio that will be purchased.

Even though those differences are great, the basic marketing process is not different. It is necessary to identify the target markets, determine their characteristics and needs, and develop a marketing mix that meets their needs better than other companies. Just as all final consumers are not the same, businesses also have important differences that require different marketing strategies.

Internet Supplants EDI

Electronic data exchange (EDI) was supposed to revolutionize purchasing by freeing purchasing professionals from having to handle routine orders for parts and materials. Now it looks as if EDI may be supplanted by Internet-based procurement systems. With either process, a key to success is overcoming supplier resistance.

EDI is a two-way system by which a purchaser and a supplier can link their information systems to automate ordering, scheduling, tracking, and payment for parts and supplies. It is supposed to cut costs, reduce lead times, and eliminate shortages. Unfortunately, many small suppliers have found EDI systems too expensive, so in practice it has often been just a fancy way of sending and receiving orders via computers. Then suppliers print out the orders and fill them as they always have.

In part because of suppliers' noncompliance, many companies are shifting to Internet-based systems that are cheaper and require less expertise on the part of suppliers. A few years ago, Cessna attacked its suppliers' noncompliance head-on. It told them they had to use either EDI or the Internet, and that it would no longer do business by phone, mail, or fax.

THINK CRITICALLY

1. Why are EDI and Internet-based procurement systems usually more popular with large companies than small ones?

2. How can large companies convince small suppliers to adopt e-procurement systems, short of threatening to cut them off if they don't comply?

BUSINESS CONSUMER CLASSIFICATIONS

One way of classifying business consumers is by the type of organization. The major categories of businesses are producers, resellers, service businesses, government, and nonprofit organizations. All businesses and other organizations purchase the products and services that they need to operate, including capital equipment, operating equipment, and supplies.

They make purchases that are appropriate to the types of activities they perform.

Producers   Over six million businesses in the U.S. produce products. Those businesses range from farms and ranches, mining companies, and oil refiners, to manufacturers of business and consumer products. They can be very small businesses that employ only a few people and spend less than $10,000 a year on purchases or companies as large as General Motors Corp. or The Procter & Gamble Co. that each employ several hundred thousand people worldwide and may easily spend $10 million in one day on purchases. Producers are customers for raw materials and component parts as well as the other products and services needed for business operations.

Resellers   Wholesale and retail businesses are a part of the product distribution system connecting producers with consumers. They purchase products for resale. They maintain distribution and storage services, promote products through advertising and personal selling, extend credit to consumers, and complete a variety of other marketing activities to meet customer needs. More than 3 million businesses operate as resellers in the U.S. economy.

Service Businesses   There are more companies in the U.S. that produce services than produce products for resale. More than seven million service businesses were operating in 2000, and that number is growing faster than any other category of business. Most of the purchases made by a service provider are used in the operation of the business and the development of the services it sells. Some service businesses, such as rental firms, actually purchase products that are used by final consumers. Rather than selling the products to those consumers, they retain title and allow the consumer to use the product.

Some types of rental businesses are well known, like video stores, apartments, and stores that rent formal wear for proms and weddings. Other types of rental businesses are less well known. Businesses leased automobiles for many years, and it only later

became a popular option for individuals. When you go to an amusement park you can rent a video camera for the day. Investors build huge office buildings and then lease the space to companies.

Government   Federal, state, and local government offices and agencies provide services to citizens, and develop and enforce laws and regulations. If you total all of the purchases made by the U.S. government, it is the largest single customer in the world. From a supplier's viewpoint, the government is made up of thousands of separate customers with very different needs and purchasing procedures. Government agencies and institutions purchase the full range of products from raw materials to supplies and services. Some government organizations such as city utility companies purchase raw materials and operate very much like privately-owned producers. Part of the military operates like wholesalers and retailers when they purchase products for distribution and sale to military personnel and their families through commissaries and stores on military bases.

Nonprofit Organizations Many organizations in our communities do not operate in the same way as private businesses. They have specific goals or clients that they are organized to serve, and that service is the primary reason for their operations. While they need an adequate budget to operate, profit is not the primary motive for their existence. Most have a nonprofit designation from the U.S. Department of Treasury so that they are tax exempt. Common examples of these organizations are schools, museums, churches, social service organizations such as shelters and community centers, colleges and universities, professional organizations, and some social clubs.

As with government agencies, nonprofit organizations operate to provide services to specific client groups. Therefore, they need to purchase those things necessary to offer the services. Those purchases could be only a limited number of operating supplies and products or they could be the full range of products and services in the business products classification system.

What are the five major classifications of business consumers and their characteristics?

CHARACTERISTICS OF BUSINESS MARKETS

Businesses that sell to other businesses need to understand how those markets are different from final consumer markets. There are some common demographic characteristics and purchasing behavior that are typical of business markets.

Derived Demand Businesses do not buy products for final consumption. Instead they make purchases to be used directly or indirectly in meeting the needs of final consumers. Therefore the types and quantities of products and services demanded by the business are based on the level of demand of their customers. In other words, the business' demand is derived from their customers' demand.

Purchase Volume Business consumers tend to buy in much greater quantities than final consumers. While final consumers may buy the same product again, their needs change much more frequently than business purchasers. Because businesses are making purchases to be incorporated into other products or for operations, they usually purchase large quantities of those products. They are less likely to make major changes in the items purchased unless their customers' needs change dramatically.

Similar Purchases Businesses that produce or resell similar products and services usually have common purchasing needs. Consider two furniture stores serving the same target markets. They will likely purchase the same types of furniture and home accessories for resale and will buy similar capital and operating equipment for their stores. In most communities there will be several companies that mix concrete for use in construction projects.

They need to purchase the same raw materials, such as cement, sand, and stone, as well as similar equipment such as mixing facilities and trucks to operate the business.

Number of Businesses The number of business customers for specific products is usually smaller than the number of final consumers who will purchase a product. That is typically an advantage for those who sell to the business market. Fewer customers mean it should be easier to maintain contact with the customers and understand their needs. Because purchase volume for each customer is high, it should not restrict the amount of total sales a company can make in the business market.

Buyer/Seller Relationship

Businesses that produce products for sale to final consumers often have little contact with the customer. Because customers are located throughout the country and sometimes throughout the world, it would be difficult to distribute products directly from the buyer to the seller. Retailers and wholesalers are usually a part of the distribution system for consumer products. The retailer is responsible for selling the product and often for responding to customer problems with the product.

In business-to-business selling, direct distribution is used more frequently. The selling business is responsible for contacting prospective customers, selling the product, and providing follow-up support and service as well as solving customer problems. Those activities are possible because of the lower number of customers. Also, in some business markets, the businesses that purchase similar products are in the same industry and may be located in the same geographic area of a country.

checkpoint

What are common characteristics typical of business markets?

LESSON REVIEW

1. Describe three activities that are part of the purchasing function of marketing.

2. What distinguishes a producer from a reseller?

3. What type of business consumer is the most numerous in the United States?

4. What do government agencies and nonprofit organizations have in common?

5. What ultimately determines the type and quantity of products and services that businesses buy?

6. Why do businesses tend to have closer relationships with business customers than with final consumers?

company takes a great deal of time planning for the purchase. The company may develop purchase specifications that the selling companies must meet. **Purchase specifications** are detailed requirements for construction or performance of the product. The buyer will also have expectations in terms of the supply needed, delivery methods and schedules, and technical support required for use of the product.

Modified Purchase A company may find that the products purchased in the past do not totally meet current needs and so require changes. The company will identify the changes or improvements needed. The modifications will likely be communicated to the company that has been selling the original product and the opportunity provided for that company to meet the new requirements. Other companies may also be given the chance to supply the modified

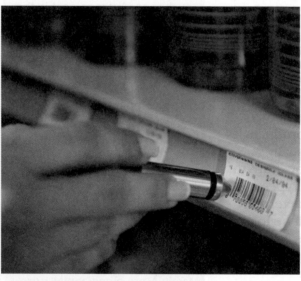

product, particularly if major changes are planned or if the buyer is not satisfied with products obtained in the past.

Retailers use modified purchasing when they have had success with a basic product and want to offer additional features and options to customers. Companies that have purchased computer systems may want to purchase additional computers, but want them upgraded with current technology. A company may have contracted with an accounting firm for bookkeeping services and now wants to extend the contract to include tax preparation.

Repeat Purchase Most business purchases are very routine. The same products and services are purchased over and over. The buyer is very aware of the needs that are being met with the purchase and has identified the product that meets those

needs. In many cases, the buyer has developed a good relationship with a seller and does not even consider buying from another company. When a new supply of the product is needed, the company just reorders from the same seller.

The purchasing process may become so routine that it is handled by a computer. The computer maintains the inventory level of the product. As the product is used or sold, the inventory level decreases until it reaches the reorder point. The **reorder point** is the level of inventory needed to meet the usage needs of the business until the product can be resupplied. When the reorder point is reached, the computer issues a purchase order to the supplier and the product is shipped.

When the product being purchased is not unique, with many companies offering the same product for sale, repeat purchasing becomes very competitive. Since the buyer realizes that the same product can be purchased from several sellers, price may become an important factor. The purchasing company may pressure the suppliers to reduce the price. This situation happens regularly with companies that sell to large retailers and companies selling common operating equipment and supplies to businesses.

PURCHASING REQUIRES SPECIALISTS

Purchasing in businesses occurs continuously and involves thousands and even millions of dollars each day in many businesses. Many of the products purchased are unique and very complex and technical. The purchasing process involves arranging delivery and payment schedules. Often lengthy and complex contracts are prepared between the buyer and seller. Because the process is so important and complicated, many businesses have departments and personnel that specialize in purchasing. Job titles for people involved in purchasing include buyers, product managers, merchandise managers, and purchasing agents.

Usually several people are involved in the buying decision the first time a product or service is purchased. The types of people most often involved in business purchases are shown in Figure 12-2. The department using the product plays an important role in the purchase decision. An experienced employee or the manager from that department will help to identify the need and prepare specifications for the purchase. For a very technical product or a new product, engineers or other people with technical

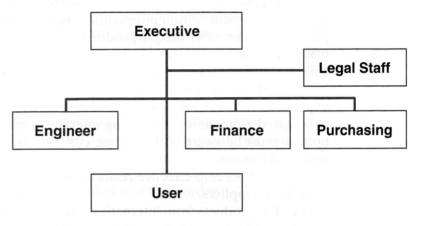

FIGURE 12-2
Important purchase decisions are typically made by various people representing different parts of the business.

Typical Members of a Business Purchasing Team

expertise may be involved to evaluate and test the product.

Financial personnel participate in purchases when the purchase is very expensive or the prices of competing products are quite different. Lawyers may help develop contracts and review all of the documents involved in the purchase.

The person or persons responsible for managing the purchasing procedure will be members of the purchasing department. They identify possible suppliers, communicate needs and specifications, gather needed information, and manage the paperwork. They are usually responsible for negotiating the price and terms of the sale. Finally, for very expensive or important purchases, one or more members of top management will participate in the purchasing process.

What are some of the jobs held by purchasing specialists?

12.3 BUSINESS PURCHASING PROCEDURES

The procedures that businesses use to make purchase decisions are similar to the procedures used by final consumers, except that business processes tend to be more detailed and systematic. Also, they usually involve a number of people rather than just a single individual. Like the process used by final consumers, the steps begin with identifying needs and include a post-purchase evaluation to gauge how well those needs have been met. When making purchasing decisions, businesses need to consider all of the costs that might be affected and what impact they will have on profits. Important records to maintain include inventory and purchasing records.

List all of your personal expenses that would be affected by a decision to buy or not buy a car. What costs would be affected by which model of car you choose?

STEPS IN THE PURCHASING PROCESS

The general process that business customers use in making a purchasing decision looks very much like that used by final consumers. The steps in the process are shown on the right side of Figure 12-3. The business purchasing process will be more detailed and involve more people. You can see that the steps businesses use generally match the final consumer process, but are more specific.

Identify Needs

Even the first step, need identification, is complex. Remember that the demand for business products is derived from the needs of the business'

customers. In addition, the needs of many parts of the business must be considered.

FIGURE 12-3
The decision-making process used by businesses is similar to that of final consumers. It is usually more detailed and involves a number of people in the business.

PURCHASING BY FINAL CONSUMERS AND BUSINESS CONSUMERS

Final Consumers	Business Consumers
1. Identify needs	1. Identify purchasing needs
2. Gather information	2. Determine alternatives
3. Evaluate alternatives	3. Search for suppliers
4. Make purchase decision	4. Select appropriate suppliers
5. Evaluate decision	5. Negotiate a purchase
	6. Make purchase decision
	7. Evaluate purchase

Those needs may not always be the same and might even conflict with each other. For example, a conflict in a company with declining sales affects the purchase of training services. The sales department believes that additional training will help salespeople more effectively serve customers and increase sales. The human resource department needs to reduce expenses because of lower sales, and wants to cut back on the amount spent for training. This conflict must be resolved before a purchase decision can be made.

Determine Alternatives In the second step, the business attempts to determine the types of products or services that will meet its needs. Here the business decides whether an existing product meets the needs best or whether a new product will be better. Money can probably be saved if suppliers do not have to develop a unique product, but that product may not be the ideal product. The business will develop product specifications in order to clearly describe the product needed. The business also determines the procedures to be followed in purchasing and the people to be involved in the process.

Search for Suppliers Next the business begins the search for suppliers. In some businesses, the purchasing department is responsible for maintaining lists of suppliers for various types of products and services. They may have catalogs or product lists that can be reviewed. Suppliers are selected for consideration based on criteria established by the purchasing business. Those factors include availability of products, quality, reliability, delivery, service, and price.

Select Appropriate Suppliers After possible suppliers have been identified, they are carefully evaluated. Often, several businesses offer acceptable products, but may vary on other factors important to the business. A decision will have to be made to determine

what combination of supplier characteristics best meets the buyer's needs. A procedure called vendor analysis may be used to help with the decision. **Vendor analysis** is an objective rating system used by buyers to compare potential suppliers on important purchasing criteria. An example of a vendor analysis for the purchase of automobiles is shown in Figure 12-4.

Negotiate a Purchase The purchasing team will review the information available and determine which of the products and suppliers best meet the business' needs. One or two vendors will be selected and the purchasing agent will begin negotiations with them. Here is another difference from the process used by final consumers. Usually, retail businesses specify the conditions of the sale and the consumer decides whether to accept those conditions or not. In business-to-business marketing, the buyer often specifies the requirements the seller needs to meet. The buyer and seller may discuss those criteria and there may be changes before the final decision is made.

Negotiations are completed in several ways. If the company is buying a standard product or one that has been purchased in the past, the negotiations are very simple. The buyer and seller will discuss price, quantity, and delivery, and agree on the terms of the sale. If the buyer has not developed a

FIGURE 12-4

If a company is planning to buy several new automobiles, it will usually analyze potential suppliers on important criteria in order to select the best vendor.

VENDOR	PURCHASE CRITERIA				
	Specifications	Warranty	Service	Price	Availability
Dodge	10	8	5	6	4
Ford	9	9	6	4	5
GMC	7	7	9	8	7
Toyota	8	4	7	5	6

VENDOR ANALYSIS

Scoring   10 = high   1 = low

TOTAL QUALITY MANAGEMENT

Another management tool that improves purchasing is total quality management. **Total quality management (TQM)** establishes specific quality standards for all operations and develops employee teams who are responsible for planning and decision-making to improve business activities. When TQM is used in purchasing, employees are involved in determining what needs to be purchased and how purchasing procedures can be improved to increase company performance.

Why do purchasing decisions need to take into consideration more than just the direct cost of products and services?

PROCESSING PURCHASES

From the time decisions are made to order products until they are ready for use or resale in a business, a number of procedures must be completed. A variety of records must be maintained to make sure the purchasing procedures are completed correctly. Some of the most important records related to purchasing involve inventory and purchasing records.

INVENTORY RECORDS

Inventory is the assortment of products maintained by a business. Inventory includes the products and materials needed to produce other products and services, to operate the business, or to be sold to customers. Inventory management is needed so managers are aware of the supply of products on hand at any time. That information helps to control costs and to insure that operations can continue without interruption.

Inventory records are maintained to provide information about the products on hand in the business. That information can include the type of products, their source, age, condition, and value. It should also indicate how rapidly the inventory is used, when it is reordered, and the sources of supply.

Two types of inventory systems are typically used by businesses: physical inventory and perpetual inventory. A **physical inventory** system determines the amount of product on hand by visually inspecting and counting the items. A physical inventory count is conducted on a regular basis, often every few months or each half-year.

A **perpetual inventory** system determines the amount of a product on hand by maintaining records on purchases and sales. Daily inventory levels determined through the perpetual system are often maintained on computers. Many businesses combine the use of physical and perpetual systems. There may be differences between the inventory levels of each system. The discrepancies can result from products that have been stolen or lost or from poorly maintained records.

PURCHASING RECORDS

A **purchase order**, a form describing all of the products ordered, is completed by the buyer and sent to the seller to begin the purchasing process. The seller fills the order and sends it to the buyer with a **packing list**, an itemized listing of all of the products included in the order. At the same time the seller sends an invoice to the buyer. The **invoice** is the bill for the merchandise. It lists all of the items purchased that are included in the order.

If the products are shipped by a transportation company, a **bill of lading** is sent with the merchandise identifying the products that are being shipped. When the merchandise is received by the purchasing company, it will be inspected and unpacked. A receiving record is completed, listing all of the merchandise in the shipment. The **receiving record** is sent to the accounting department where it is compared to the purchase order and invoice before payment is made.

Finally, the products that have been received are entered into the **inventory records** of the company, and the products are distributed to the departments where they will be used or sold. Some common purchasing records are identified in Figure 12-5.

FIGURE 12-5
The seller and buyer complete a number of forms in order to maintain accurate records of purchases.

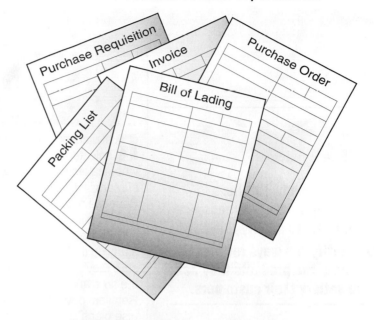

Common Purchasing Records

Why are accurate inventory and purchasing records so important to a business?

1. How does negotiating a business transaction differ from the process that typically takes place when a final consumer buys something?

2. If a business can get a substantial discount in price by buying a large quantity of an item that it purchases regularly, why might that not be a good purchase decision?

3. At what point in the purchasing process does a business prepare a purchase order for a product or service it wants to buy?

4. How do businesses inspect purchased goods or parts for quality assurance when there are too many of a purchased product to examine all of them?

5. Why do businesses keep both physical inventory records and perpetual inventory records? Why not just one or the other?

GOALS

- **Describe how retailers identify customer needs and how to satisfy them.**
- **Identify the ways retailers locate the products they need to satisfy their customers.**

Retailers buy products from selected manufacturers and wholesalers for resale to final consumers in their target markets. Because retailers make a relatively small profit on each item sold, they spend a lot of time and effort studying their customers to make sure they stock what they need at the time and place they need it. Retailers develop detailed merchandise plans to organize the hundreds or thousands of items they carry.

Retailers locate desirable products through manufacturers' and wholesalers' sales representatives, trade shows, catalogs, and increasingly through web sites maintained by the sellers. Once they decide what to buy, they have carefully developed procedures to get the products on their shelves in a timely fashion.

Make a list of eight things that you have purchased in the past month. For each item, name as many retailers as you can think of who carry that item or a very similar alternative.

PLANNING TO SATISFY CUSTOMER NEEDS

Retail businesses purchase products for resale. Market conditions for products sold by retailers change very rapidly. A buyer for a large supermarket chain may review more than 200 new products each week for possible purchase. Also, many of the products sold in retail stores are seasonal. That means the products sell well during a particular time of the year, but few customers want to buy them at other times. There is very little profit available to retailers on the sale of any one item in the store. Therefore if a product remains unsold, the business quickly loses money.

Customers and their needs are very important to retailers. Customers are studied carefully and their likes and dislikes considered when making purchase decisions. Retailing is also very competitive. If Company A offers a product that customers want and its competitors do not have that product, Company A has a real advantage. If a company is able to sell a similar product at a much lower price than its competitors, it will usually sell a larger quantity. Retailers evaluate their competitors to determine what products are being sold and the prices charged in order to remain competitive.

DETERMINING CUSTOMER NEEDS

Retailers use a great deal of marketing research to anticipate customer needs. Many have consumer panels and focus groups that meet regularly to evaluate new products. The business often contacts regular customers to determine what they like and dislike and to determine if the customers have needs that the business is not currently meeting.

Retail buyers and merchandise managers study market information including the economy, competition, and new product developments. They attend meetings and

High-Touch Communications

Communication between buyers and suppliers is critical for effective purchasing. A recent study by the National Association of Purchasing Management concluded that electronic media such as the Internet can be important communication tools. However traditional "high-touch" media are still necessary for many purchasing activities. High-touch media include face-to-face meetings and phone calls.

Face-to-face contact was judged to be the richest medium for purchasing communications. It allows nonverbal cues such as facial expressions and body language. It also facilitates two-way feedback and immediate responses or decisions. Internet procurement and electronic data exchange (EDI) systems were judged to be the least-rich media, more impersonal than even faxes, mail, and e-mail.

While impersonal electronic media may be best for routine communications such as purchase orders, richer media is preferred for nonroutine communications such as negotiation of large and critical needs contracts. In general, the study concluded that the right media for various tasks depend on the nature and purpose of what is being communicated.

THINK CRITICALLY

1. Based on this study, how important do you think interpersonal communications skills will be in the future as electronic communications via the Internet become more sophisticated?

2. What advice would you give to a small business regarding the development of its communications skills if it was trying to build better buyer-supplier relations with large international corporations?

---

trade shows and talk with salespeople and other representatives of manufacturers and wholesalers.

Comparison shopping is used to study competitors. In **comparison shopping**, people are sent to competitors' stores to determine products that are sold, prices charged, and services offered. In some cases, products are purchased from competitors and then analyzed to determine their quality.

Tracking Product Sales Retailers carefully track the sales of current products to determine which products sell rapidly and which do not. Computer technology aids in that process. Scanners at check-out counters are connected to computers that store inventory information. When a purchase is made by a customer, the scanner reads the bar code on each product purchased. The bar code is a distinct identifier for each product that provides information such as product name, product type, price, manufacturer, and the date the product was purchased by the business. That information is immediately analyzed by the computer. It is possible to identify sales levels by time of day and day of the week. Managers can determine if special displays, sales, or advertising programs affect sales volume of specific products.

Most retail store computer systems are connected to other computers in regional or national offices. Managers and buyers in those offices can monitor the performance of each store and each product in the store on a daily basis. With that information, purchasing decisions as well as marketing plans can be adjusted quickly to be sure that products are sold rapidly, products that do not sell are not reordered, and new purchases respond to customers' needs as demonstrated by past sales.

DEVELOPING A PURCHASING PLAN

Retail stores must offer an adequate assortment of products to meet the needs of their customers. Some stores, such as department stores, supermarkets, and discount stores, offer hundreds of different products in many merchandise categories. Specialty stores, such as apparel, office products, or sporting goods stores, offer less variety but a complete assortment in the specialty category.

A merchandise plan is developed by the business. The **merchandise plan** identifies the type, price, and features of products that will be stocked by the business for a specific period of time. The merchandise plan is like a budget in that it provides the basis for ordering merchandise and maintaining the store's inventory. The merchandise plan may be developed for a very short time period such as one or two months. It may also be developed for a specific season in which unique merchandise will be sold. While a general plan may be developed for a longer time period, few stores plan much longer than six months. Conditions can change dramatically in that time, causing the merchandise plan to be out of date quickly.

The merchandise plan is developed from a basic stock list or a model stock list. A **basic stock list** identifies the minimum amount of important products a store needs to have available to meet the needs of its target market. The basic stock list will not change a great deal over time. A **model stock list** describes the complete assortment of products a store would like to offer to customers. The model stock list is more complete and is subject to change more frequently based on economic conditions, the financial resources of the business, and the changing needs of customers.

How do retailers identify their customers' needs?

PUTTING PRODUCTS ON THE SHELVES

Retail buyers make purchases from many sources. Those purchases are made from both manufacturers and wholesalers. Many of the manufacturers and wholesalers have salespeople who contact managers at local stores. Or they may meet with regional or national buyers who make purchase decisions for several stores. Large retailers may have buying offices in major cities where many manufacturers are located. Some cities have trading centers for specific industries. For example, many furniture manufacturers open showrooms in High Point, NC, twice a year. Furniture retailers from all over the United States and the world come to see the offerings of many manufacturers at one time and to order merchandise for the coming season.

Trade shows also offer an opportunity for many manufacturers to show their merchandise to large numbers of wholesalers and retailers at one time. There is a large electronics trade show each year in Las Vegas. Companies spend hundreds of thousands of dollars on exhibits, demonstrations, and advertising for the show, because they know retailers will be looking for new products.

A final method of purchasing is the use of catalogs and web sites published by wholesalers or manufacturers. Catalogs are used frequently by very small retailers who cannot afford to travel to trade centers or trade shows and who do not purchase in enough quantity to warrant frequent visits from salespeople. Catalogs are also used to sell standardized and frequently purchased items that are purchased primarily on the basis of price and availability. Many small companies are now using web sites to replace or supplement catalogs. Most large companies are moving many of their sales and purchasing functions onto web sites.

COMPLETING THE PURCHASE PROCESS

The retail buyer studies several sources of supply before selecting the one from which to order merchandise. Specific criteria are used based on the retailer's needs. Those criteria may vary for different products in the store's merchandise assortment. Some products may be unique and can only be obtained from one source. Others may be products that have been purchased for some time and customers are very loyal to that brand. Again, one supplier is used.

Other products may be fast-selling, requiring the supplier to replace items in inventory rapidly. The retailer may want to purchase from a supplier who can guarantee

What If Buyers Become Too Close to Suppliers?

The trend toward more cooperative relationships between purchasing professionals and suppliers has increased opportunities for ethical problems. Most people recognize that bribes and kickbacks are wrong. The line between proper and improper behavior is clear. The real danger lies in gray areas where friendships mix with business.

Businesses that emphasize the development of strategic relationships with suppliers often have less objective procedures in place for awarding contracts. In such cases, it is easier for buyers to allow subjective personal feelings to interfere in the decision-making processes. Also, strategic relationships often involve sharing confidential internal information.

Only two-thirds of businesses have written ethics policies for purchasing personnel. Some corporate executives think such policies are not needed. They assume ethical people don't need rules and unethical people are going to ignore rules anyway. Some purchasing professionals believe policies are flawed because they are too lenient, not too strict.

THINK CRITICALLY

1. How do clearly defined policies help purchasing professionals and suppliers avoid problems?

2. What kinds of policies might a company adopt to prevent purchasing employees from feeling like they owe suppliers a favor for gifts?

---

rapid and reliable delivery. Some items may be very competitive products that can be purchased in many stores. The retailer's customers will shop for the lowest price, so a supplier must be located that will sell at competitive prices.

After the source of supply is determined, the order is placed. Most businesses have a standard procedure for ordering merchandise. The order must be placed far enough in advance to be sure it is delivered before the current stock is completely sold or in time for the selling season for the product. The timing of orders is often a difficult problem for retailers. If the order is placed too soon, the merchandise arrives before it is needed, taking up space and adding to storage and handling costs. If the order is late, the merchandise is not in stock when customers want it and sales are lost.

The seller ships the merchandise to the retailer's distribution center or store, where it is unpacked and prepared for sale. Again, each business has specific and careful procedures to be followed in receiving, unpacking, inspecting, and preparing products for sale. This is a very important part of the purchasing process. Large financial losses can occur in businesses that do not have effective procedures. Merchandise can be lost, stolen, or damaged during the receiving

process. Because most retail businesses have very low margins of profit, any significant loss at this time can mean that the business will be unable to make a profit.

checkpoint

Where do retailers find the products they want to offer customers once they have identified them?

LESSON REVIEW

1. What is a bar code and how does it help retailers know what their customers want?

2. What is a seasonal product?

3. What is the difference between a basic stock list and a model stock list?

4. For how long a time period are merchandise plans typically developed?

5. Why do retailers need careful procedures for receiving, inspecting, and preparing products for resale?

SUMMARY

Lesson 12.1

A. Most of the sales of products and services take place between businesses. Businesses buy products or services from other businesses to incorporate into their own products, to resell directly to their own customers, and for use in operating their businesses.

B. Marketers need to learn as much as possible about the reasons businesses buy products and services. The five major classifications of business consumers are producers, resellers, service providers, government, and nonprofit organizations.

C. Business-to-business markets rely on demand derived from their customers' demand. They tend to purchase in larger quantities than final consumers. Similar types of businesses buy similar things. Businesses that sell to other businesses sell to a relatively small number of purchasers and develop closer buyer/seller relationships.

Lesson 12.2

A. Businesses make new purchases when they haven't bought something before and require the most care. Modified purchases occur when needs change, new features are being added or a business isn't completely satisfied with a prior purchase. Repeat purchases are reorders of the same product or service.

B. Purchasing activities frequently require the hiring of purchasing specialists and the involvement of senior management. Jobs held by purchasing specialists include buyers, product managers, merchandise managers, and purchasing agents.

C. Some aspects of international purchasing that differ from domestic buying are checking supplier qualifications, examining the product, arranging financing, and transportation.

Lesson 12.3

A. Procedures businesses use to make purchase decisions are similar to procedures used by final consumers. Business processes tend to be more detailed and systematic and involve a number of people rather than just one. The steps in the business purchasing process are identify needs, determine alternatives, search for suppliers, select appropriate suppliers, negotiate terms, make a decision, and evaluate the purchase.

B. Purchasing decisions need to take into consideration more than just the direct cost of products and services. Purchasing decisions affect many other costs incurred by the business. Businesses must look at the big picture and the impact decisions will have on profits after all the affected areas are factored in.

C. Inventory and purchasing records are important because a business must know what it has on hand to meet production needs, to keep the business operating smoothly, or to fill customer orders in a timely manner.

Lesson 12.4

A. Retailers buy from manufacturers and wholesalers for resale to final consumers in their target markets. Retailers make a relatively small profit on each item so they study their customers carefully to make sure they stock what customers need at the time and place they need it. Retailers identify customers' needs by researching markets, tracking product sales, studying market conditions, and comparison shopping. Merchandise plans are used to organize the hundreds or thousands of items retailers carry.

B. Retailers locate desirable products through manufacturers' and wholesalers' sales representatives, trade shows, catalogs, and web sites. Once they decide what to buy, they have carefully developed procedures to get the products on their shelves quickly.

REVIEW MARKETING CONCEPTS

1. True or False: The majority of exchanges involving products or services are between businesses and final consumers.

2. True or False: Businesses that purchase products for resale to final consumers typically do not change the form of those products.

3. True or False: An example of a poor purchasing decision is selecting a supplier that is not able to deliver the product when promised.

4. True or False: The marketing process used for business-to-business marketing is very different from the one used to sell to final consumers.

5. True or False: The only types of companies classified as business consumers are producers.

6. True or False: The largest single customer for products and services in the world is the U.S. government.

7. True or False: The majority of products purchased by businesses are for final consumption.

8. True or False: Direct distribution from the producer to the customer is common in business-to-business marketing.

REVIEW MARKETING TERMS

Match the terms listed with the definitions. Some terms may not be used.

9. An objective rating system used by buyers to compare potential suppliers on important purchasing criteria.

10. The bill for the merchandise that lists all of the items purchased that are included in the order.

11. The level of inventory needed to meet the usage needs of the business until the product can be resupplied.

12. Determines the amount of product on hand by visually inspecting and counting items.

13. Contains a general description of the type of product or service needed and the criteria that are important to the buyer.

14. Detailed requirements for the construction or performance of a product.

15. A listing all of the merchandise in a shipment, recorded by the purchasing company when it is inspected and unpacked.

16. A form of bartering in which products or services of one company are used as payment for the products of another company.

17. The assortment of products maintained by a business.

18. The development of a relationship with suppliers to keep inventory levels low and to resupply inventory just as it is needed.

a. basic stock list
b. bidding
c. bill of lading
d. comparison shopping
e. inventory
f. inventory records
g. invoice
h. just-in-time
i. merchandise plan
j. model stock list
k. packing list
l. perpetual inventory
m. physical inventory
n. purchase order
o. purchase specifications
p. receiving record
q. reciprocal trading
r. reorder point
s. request for proposal
t. total quality management
u. vendor analysis

APPLY MARKETING FUNCTIONS

MARKETING RESEARCH

19. A vendor wanted to determine what factors were most important to its customers when they made purchase decisions. The company conducted a survey of purchasing agents and others involved in purchasing and asked them to assign a value from 0 to 5 for six factors they consider when purchasing products from the vendor. The meaning of the values ranged from *0 = not considered when making a purchase decision* to *5 = most important factor in the purchase decision.* The following results were obtained from 140 customers.

Factors	Value					
	5	4	3	2	1	0
Price	0	40	55	32	13	0
Delivery Schedule	45	38	36	20	1	0
Vendor Reputation	0	24	38	52	18	8
Past Experience with Vendor	7	10	68	55	0	0
Vendor Service after Sale	0	5	12	22	36	65
Product Quality	110	24	6	0	0	0

a. The vendor wanted to use the data to develop an average value for each of the factors. Calculate the mean value for each factor. The mean is determined by multiplying the value by the number of respondents selecting that value, totaling the result for all six value scores for the factor, and dividing the result by 140 (the total number of respondents). For example, the mean value of price is determined as follows: $(0 \times 5) + (40 \times 4) + (55 \times 3) + (32 \times 2) + (13 \times 1) + (0 \times 0) = 402$, and $402 \div 140 = 2.87$

b. The vendor asked a focus group to compare one of the vendor's products to similar products sold by two other competitors using the six factors from the research study. The focus group assigned each product a score ranging from 1 to 10 for each of the six factors, with 1 being the lowest rating and 10 being the

highest rating. The results of the focus group ratings are shown in the table.

Factors	Product		
	Vendor	Competitor A	Competitor B
Price	6	8	10
Delivery Schedule	8	5	7
Vendor Reputation	7	7	5
Past Experience with Vendor	3	9	6
Vendor Service after Sale	8	4	6
Product Quality	10	7	8

The vendor then used the information from the original marketing research study to develop a product score for each company. The mean score for each factor (calculated from the research study results in Part a) was multiplied by the rating assigned to that factor by the focus group (from the table above). Then the results for each of the six factors were totaled, giving each company a final score. That procedure would predict that the company whose product received the highest score would be the one that best met the purchaser's needs.

Calculate the total product score for each company using the procedure described. Then be prepared to discuss the meaning of the results in terms of customer perceptions of the three companies' products.

MARKETING PLANNING

20. Select one of the following topics related to purchasing procedures that is of specific interest to you. Research the topic by reading marketing books, current business magazines, and other business resources. You might be able to identify a business person or other resource person in your community who is an expert on the topic to interview. Prepare a 3-to-5-page written report on the topic.

a. Census data related to businesses and organizations
b. Gathering information on international businesses
c. Using benchmarking to develop product specifications
d. Sources of information that aid in identifying vendors
e. Just In Time (JIT) inventory management
f. Total Quality Management (TQM)
g. Technology related to inventory management
h. Ethics of comparison shopping
i. Developing a model stock list for a retail business
j. Manufacturers' markets and trade shows
k. Exporting and importing procedures

MARKETING MANAGEMENT

21. Identify a major purchase decision you might make within the next five years (college, new automobile, apartment, etc.). Then, using the information from the chapter, specifically outline the steps you could follow to make the purchase in the objective way followed by businesses. After you have outlined the steps, prepare a vendor analysis form. List the factors that you will consider when making the purchase. Develop numerical values for each factor that reflect the relative importance of each factor to you. Create the form so it can be completed as you evaluate several companies or organizations that provide the product or service you plan to purchase.

22. May Randall is the purchasing manager for Protective Insurance Company. The company has made a commitment to provide all employees who are involved with any type of information management or customer service and all company managers with a personal computer at their workstation. The company currently has a large mainframe computer where all major company records are maintained. It is important that the computers purchased for employees are compatible with the mainframe.

Working with managers from each of the major divisions of the company, May has developed purchase specifications for the personal computers and has identified four manufacturers who can provide personal computers that meet the specifications. One of the manufacturers is the supplier of Protective's mainframe computer, but each of the other manufacturers has assured May that their personal computers are compatible.

May is now faced with two important decisions. First, should Protective Insurance buy all of the personal computers from one manufacturer or order from more than one? May is concerned that if only one is used, there may be difficulties with the prices charged for service. Also, real problems could develop if the manufacturer changes products or goes out of business in the future. On the other hand, using more than one supplier can create other types of service and support problems. The second problem is whether to purchase from the company who sold the mainframe, since that product has worked well and the company has been very good about service and maintenance. However, that company has produced personal computers for only a short time, while the other manufacturers are well known for manufacturing high-quality personal computers. What recommendations would you make to May to help her with the two decisions?

MARKETING TECHNOLOGY

23. Use the Internet to find web sites for companies that are engaged in the types of businesses listed below. For each, list its name, its URL address, the specific products or services it sells, and how it markets those products or services to other businesses through its web site.

a. manufacturer of motor vehicles
b. insurance company
c. office supply chain
d. industrial supplies
e. chemicals
f. financial services
g. uniforms
h. machinery components
i. freight transportation
j. temporary personnel

MARKETING IN ACTION

CASE STUDY

FROM SMALL TOWN RETAILER TO THE NYSE

David Hirschfield founded Mills Clothing Store, Inc. in Kearney, Nebraska, in 1948. David's son Dan took over the company in 1965. A second store purchased in 1967 operated under the trade name "Brass Buckle." After trying several different names, the company changed its name to "The Buckle" in 1991.

The Buckle's image evolved from selling men's casual clothing in the late 1960s to a "jeans store" in the early 1970s. In 1977, The Buckle began offering both men's and women's casual apparel.

In May 1992, The Buckle Inc. began trading publicly under the symbol *BKLE* on the NASDAQ. Five years later it moved to the New York Stock Exchange, where it trades under the symbol *BKE*. By 2001 there were almost 300 stores located in 36 states, plus a corporate headquarters and distribution center in Kearney.

How has The Buckle succeeded while other

specialty retail clothing chains have fallen on hard times? The Buckle believes it is important to work hard to create lasting impressions with people who visit the store. Shoppers at The Buckle are treated like guests instead of customers. The goal of The Buckle is to make all guests feel welcome from the moment they walk through the door.

Building relationships, not merely making a sale, is the central theme for The Buckle. Creating an enjoyable shopping experience for the guest has resulted in great success. The store has a unique atmosphere created by innovative merchandise presentations, combined with upbeat music and creative visuals. This marketing mix generates excitement for guests and for employees, who are referred to as "teammates." The shopping experience is enhanced with promotions such as sweepstakes and special gift offers. The Buckle offers value-added

services such as free gift-wrapping, free alterations, layaways, and special orders.

In addition, The Buckle does not go into debt to open new stores. Much of The Buckle's success can be attributed to having no initial debt. The Buckle is a great example of how a small business can grow to national prominence by establishing good customer relationships and following wise financial strategies.

THINK CRITICALLY

1. What factors contributed to the success of The Buckle?

2. How can a small retailer like The Buckle compete with larger national chains like Banana Republic?

3. What does it mean when a business or company is publicly traded?

http://www.deca.org/publications/HS_Guide/guidetoc.html

APPAREL AND ACCESSORIES ROLE-PLAY

DECA PREP

After graduating from college, you have been hired as the new assistant manager for The Buckle in the upscale Galleria Mall. Duties of the assistant manager include scheduling and evaluating employees, incorporating goals of the company, teaching employees new sales strategies, and setting new goals for clothing sales.

Cameron has been employed by The Buckle for six years. For three years he had the highest sales among all associates. Cameron applied for the assistant manager position that you filled. He is not very pleased to have you as his boss since he has been with The Buckle much longer. Cameron's sales have dropped and he has been a negative influence on other employees.

Your manager has instructed you to talk to Cameron about his role with The Buckle. You must give Cameron his first warning that will be placed in his employment file. If Cameron receives a second warning, The Buckle will fire him. You must also devise a strategy to motivate Cameron to reach or exceed his previously high sales.

DESCRIPTION OF THE STRATEGY Outline your strategy for dealing with Cameron. Be sure to list objections that Cameron may bring up during your meeting with him, and prepare responses to those objections.

DESCRIPTION OF MOTIVATIONAL STRATEGY Outline your plan for motivating Cameron to reach or exceed his previously high sales.

ROLE PLAY Translate what you have learned into effective, efficient, and spontaneous action, demonstrated in a role-play.

CHAPTER 13

GET THE PRODUCT TO CUSTOMERS

LESSON 13.1 *MARKETING THROUGH DISTRIBUTION*

LESSON 13.2 *ASSEMBLING CHANNELS OF DISTRIBUTION*

LESSON 13.3 *WHOLESALING*

LESSON 13.4 *RETAILING*

LESSON 13.5 *PHYSICAL DISTRIBUTION KEEPS THINGS MOVING*

NEWSLINE

THE SHIFT FROM IMAGE TO VALUE

People who did not want to be seen shopping at discount stores a few years ago are now bragging about the bargains they find there. After years of believing that "image means everything," many customers now think "value means everything."

Customers are becoming more aware of product choices. They now realize that if they shop and compare before making a purchase, they can save up to 50 percent on many purchases and still get the quality they want.

What does this change in shopping behavior mean to business? Many traditional department stores have been struggling, while sales at discount stores are increasing. New leaders in retailing include factory outlets, off-price stores, and warehouse clubs. Manufacturers who in the past have been able to

command large markups by restricting their distribution to exclusive stores now find that consumers will accept off-brand and store-brand merchandise.

Will the trend toward low-price, high-value shopping continue? There are people with the resources to buy whatever they want and who are willing to pay for status and image. Other consumers have found that changing their behavior has not reduced their product choices or satisfaction levels. They are not likely to go back to their old ways.

THINK CRITICALLY

1. What can businesses do to attract both image-conscious and value-conscious customers?

2. What factors have contributed to the growth of value retailing?

POINT YOUR BROWSER
www.corpview.com

CAREER OPPORTUNITY
SUPPORT SPECIALIST

TeleView is looking for someone who possesses the following attributes.

- Excellent interpersonal and customer relations skills
- Outgoing and enjoys working with the public
- Strong problem solving, project organization, and time management abilities
- Drive and flexibility
- Technical communications skills
- Ability to organize and multitask
- Ability to work in an invigorating, team-oriented environment

This is a fast-paced position working directly with the public. If you like helping people, this is a position for you. It is located in Boulder, Colorado and may require occasional overnight travel.

This position has a base salary and benefits. A PC with Intranet connection will be provided.

The main responsibilities of the job include the following.

- Answering promptly daily customer inquiries via telephone, the Internet, and fax
- Researching customer problems and documenting resolutions on the Intranet
- Recording customer complaints, comments, and incident reports on the Customer Service database on the Intranet
- Helping Marketing, Sales, R&D, Testing, and Customer Support find and fix problems with TeleView products
- Contributing to the Marketing, Sales, and Support team
- Working on special assignments as needed

The job requires the following education, skills, and experience.

- Associate's degree or higher preferred
- Experience with database software programs and navigating a corporate Intranet
- Technical communications skills a big plus
- Previous Customer Support experience also a plus
- Aptitude with technical and electronic products
- Excellent interpersonal, teamwork, and customer relations skills are a must
- Must be organized

THINK CRITICALLY

1. Prepare a cover letter written by a person who is qualified for this job and interested in applying for it.

2. Which parts of this job appeal to you? Which do not?

3. Search want ads or the Internet for a job similar to TeleView's support specialist. What type of compensation package is being offered for the job?

13.1 MARKETING THROUGH DISTRIBUTION

GOALS

● Explain why the distribution function is so important to effective marketing.

● Illustrate how a well-planned distribution system supports the marketing plan.

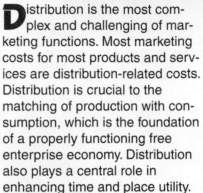

MARKETING MATTERS

Distribution is the most complex and challenging of marketing functions. Most marketing costs for most products and services are distribution-related costs. Distribution is crucial to the matching of production with consumption, which is the foundation of a properly functioning free enterprise economy. Distribution also plays a central role in enhancing time and place utility.

A distribution system can only work as planned if all the members of a distribution channel follow the plan. Because each member of a distribution channel has its own marketing strategy, it is especially important for a producer to choose its distribution partners wisely and manage its distribution system carefully.

Choose a product that you or your family bought recently for which the distribution channel involved a large number of businesses. How many separate steps in the distribution process can you identify?

THE IMPORTANCE OF DISTRIBUTION ACTIVITIES

Welcome to the world marketplace! U.S. consumers have access to hundreds of thousands of products. Products come from companies throughout the world. Any time of the day, and every day of the week, most people can locate a shopping center or store. Customers can find products they need or a business that performs a desired service. If a shopping area isn't convenient, other choices are available. Customers can purchase by telephone, through the mail or over the Internet.

The most complex and challenging part of marketing is distribution. With so many products and the convenience of shopping, this is difficult to imagine. Yet many people and companies are involved in the distribution of products and services from the producer to the consumer. Large percentages

of marketing budgets are spent on the activities involved in distribution. For most products and services, distribution activities account for over 50 percent of the cost of marketing.

Distribution is the oldest and most basic part of marketing. In fact, before the term marketing was even a part of business language, distribution was used to describe the activities that directed the flow of goods and services between producers and consumers. Today, because marketing activities have expanded, distribution is just one of the primary marketing functions. The **distribution function** involves determining the best methods and procedures to use so prospective customers can locate, obtain, and use a business's products and services.

When distribution works well, consumers are not really aware of its importance. Products and services are available where and when people want them and in a usable condition. However, when distribution does not work, it is very evident. Products are out of stock, backordered, available only in the wrong styles or sizes, out of date, or damaged. Prices are

incorrectly marked or missing. Salespeople do not have adequate product information, or products advertised in the newspaper are not the ones carried by the store. Much of the dissatisfaction consumers have with businesses results from poor distribution.

Paris Bread Maker Satisfies Customers Worldwide

Can it be that a Paris bread maker's secret to success is distribution? Yes, it must be when the bread is shipped all over the world every day, because bread this good has to be fresh. Since owner Lionel Poilane had no desire to keep opening more and more shops to meet rising demand, the Poilane bakery in Paris had little choice but to rely on distribution.

Instead of opening dozens of small shops, Poilane built a massive bread-making facility outside of Paris. It has 24 wood-fired, brick-and-clay ovens arranged in a circle. Company-owned trucks supply 2,500 local restaurants and food shops. Poilane relies on a FedEx hub at nearby DeGaulle Airport to deliver his oversized loaves of dark, chewy bread to eager customers worldwide. Loaves that emerge from his ovens this morning will be on someone's dinner table tomorrow evening, no worse for the thousands of miles of traveling in between.

The Poilane bakery sells 15,000 loaves of bread a day, each weighing about four pounds. One New York customer paid $100,000 so each of his children and grandchildren would receive a loaf each week for as long as they live.

THINK CRITICALLY

1. What attribute of bread makes Poilane's distribution system so important?

2. How does having an effective distribution system allow Poilane to maintain the high quality of his product?

DISTRIBUTION AS AN ECONOMIC CONCEPT

Distribution is an important activity for the effective operation of any economic system, and it is essential in a free enterprise economy. Free enterprise is based on the matching of production and consumption decisions. When a businessperson decides to produce a product, the product will not be successful unless consumers can obtain it. When consumers have a demand for a particular type of product or service, that demand will not be satisfied until they can locate the desired product. Distribution aids in the matching of supply and demand.

Another important concept is economic utility. Economic utility is the amount of satisfaction a consumer receives from the consumption of a particular product or service. Businesses can increase customer satisfaction by improving the form of a product or service, making it available at a more convenient time or place, or making it more affordable. As you consider the four types of economic utility, you can see that distribution directly affects time and place. Effective and efficient distribution can ensure a product is available in a usable form at a reasonable price. Distribution is important in increasing customer satisfaction.

DISTRIBUTION AS A MARKETING MIX ELEMENT

Another way of seeing the importance of distribution is to examine the marketing mix. The **marketing mix** includes all of the tools or activities available to organizations to be used in meeting the needs of a target market. Those activities are organized within the four mix elements—product, distribution, price, and promotion.

Distribution as a part of the marketing mix is the locations and methods used to make the product available to customers. When a marketer develops a marketing strategy and prepares a marketing plan, many ways to distribute a product or service to a specific target market need to be considered. The choices made can determine whether the customer is able to easily locate and purchase the products and services needed.

Why is distribution so important to effective marketing?

DEVELOPMENT OF A DISTRIBUTION SYSTEM

Edu-Games was a new company that produced high-quality board games for children. The company carefully researched the market and identified a target market of parents aged 25 to 45 with from one to three children under the age of 10. At least one parent had a college education, and total family income was over $45,000. The families in the target market were concerned about the quality of their children's education and spent an average of $2,000 a year on education-related purchases for their children, including educational toys and games.

Based on the target market information, Edu-Games prepared a marketing plan for its board games. The games were constructed of finished wooden pieces and packaged in sturdy boxes. Package designs illustrated the games in use and descriptions of the educational value were clearly printed on the outside of each box. Prices were set high ($56 per game) to match the quality image, and prices were printed on the package so customers could be certain that they would pay the same price no matter where they purchased the game.

Edu-Games used distributors of games and toys to sell the product to retailers, because Edu-Games was not large enough to have its own sales force. To help the distributors, the company identified the types of retail stores where the product should sell best. Those stores were primarily bookstores with special children's collections and stores specializing in children's apparel. The company did not want the games sold through large toy stores or discount stores, because those stores did not fit the image of the product as high-quality and high-priced. Besides, the target market did not do most of their purchasing of education products in those types of stores. To help the retailer successfully sell the games, Edu-Games produced an easy-to-assemble display that provided adequate space for 300 games and contained information and pictures clearly describing the games, how they are played, and their educational value.

Bar Codes with Brains

Bar codes are useful and cheap, but dumb. Smart labels are versatile and smart, but relatively expensive. In the market for scanner technology, both have a place. Because they are so inexpensive—all they require is the ink to print them—bar codes are employed everywhere to identify whatever it is that they are attached to. They can be used in applications ranging from grocery checkout lanes to inventory management.

Smart labels are the next generation of scanner labeling technology. They can carry much more information than bar codes, and unlike bar codes they can also receive and store new information after they've been put in place. Smart labels use thin computer chips that emit encoded information via radio signals. They can be imbedded into products or into transferable labels.

One innovative use of smart labels has been for routing luggage at airports. Scanners can read smart labels attached to luggage and direct the right pieces to each passenger's hotel. So instead of milling around waiting to pick up luggage and then having to carry it around all day until they can check into a hotel, business travelers can get off a plane in the morning, go about their business for the day, and meet up with their luggage later at their hotel. Smart stuff, indeed.

THINK CRITICALLY

1. Give an example of how smart labels might be used for a security application.

2. Why is it unlikely that smart labels will soon replace bar codes on consumer packaged goods like breakfast cereal or laundry soap?

decisions must be made in order for the exchange to occur. Those decisions include:

- Where and when will the product be produced, exchanged, and used?
- What are the characteristics of the product or service being exchanged that will affect distribution?
- What services or activities must be provided in order for the product to be exchanged?
- Is special physical handling needed?
- Who will be responsible for the needed distribution activities?
- When will each activity occur?
- Who is responsible for planning and managing distribution?

Disappointing Results Three months after beginning distribution, sales were much lower than expected. An evaluation of marketing activities discovered that the mix was not being implemented as planned. Most of the games had been distributed to large toy stores, because they were the traditional customers of the distributors, and the distributors believed higher sales would result from those stores. The toy stores used a mass marketing strategy and cut the suggested price by 10 percent or more. Even with the discounts, the price was much higher than the average board game sold by the stores. The unique displays were not used by many of the stores because of space limitations. Instead the games were stacked on shelves along with many other products that did not allow the customers to see the unique packaging that was designed to help them understand the new products.

The experience of Edu-Games shows that the success of a product or a business is usually influenced by many other businesses. Even businesses that apply the marketing concept and try to respond to the needs of a target market can have problems if the businesses they use to distribute products do not have the same philosophy and do not follow the marketing plan. An important part of marketing is the design and management of an effective distribution system.

Decision Time Any time a product or service is marketed to a customer, several

Why is merely designing an effective distribution system not enough to ensure that products will be where customers want them when they want them?

1. What portion of the marketing costs for most products is spent on distribution-related activities?

2. Why is effective distribution essential to a free enterprise economy?

3. Which types of economic utility does distribution affect most directly?

4. Which of the four marketing mix elements is most closely related to distribution issues?

5. Why does a distribution system become progressively more complex as additional members are added to the channels of distribution?

6. What does the distribution function of marketing entail?

ASSEMBLING CHANNELS OF DISTRIBUTION

MARKETING MATTERS

Channels of distribution are developed by businesses to perform the many marketing functions that have to be accomplished any time an exchange takes place with a final consumer. Direct distribution is used sometimes, as with catalog and Internet sales, but more often there are intermediate businesses such as wholesalers and retailers who move products from producers to final consumers. When there are businesses involved other than the producer, it is referred to as indirect distribution. Businesses often use both direct and indirect distribution methods to target various market segments. Channel members help adjust differences in quantity, assortment, location, and timing that would otherwise prevent a satisfying exchange.

Name a product that you have bought recently directly from its producer. Describe how you and the producer were brought together in order for the exchange to take place.

GOALS

- **Identify the differences between producers and consumers that are addressed by distribution channels.**
- **Describe the differences between direct and indirect channels of distribution.**

THE NEED FOR DISTRIBUTION CHANNELS

When products and services are exchanged, they move through a channel of distribution. A **channel of distribution** is made up of the organizations and individuals who participate in the movement and exchange of products and services from the producer to the final consumer. The channel can be very simple, involving only the producer and the final consumer, or it can be very complex, involving many businesses.

If you buy a local newspaper, it is often edited, printed, and distributed by one company. If you buy a copy of *USA Today*, it is written and edited by one company in Washington, D.C., printed by one of several other companies located in various parts of the country, then distributed and sold by other companies. There are several reasons that channels of distribution are needed in marketing.

ADJUSTING DIFFERENCES BETWEEN PRODUCERS AND CONSUMERS

There are many differences in what producers develop and what consumers need. Channels of distribution allow for adjustments to be made in those differences so the available products match the customers' needs. Consumers want to be able to buy products from many different companies (see Figure 13-1). Adjustments are usually needed in the quantity and assortment of products, the location of the products, and the timing of production and consumption.

FIGURE 13-1
Channels of distribution help to match supply and demand.

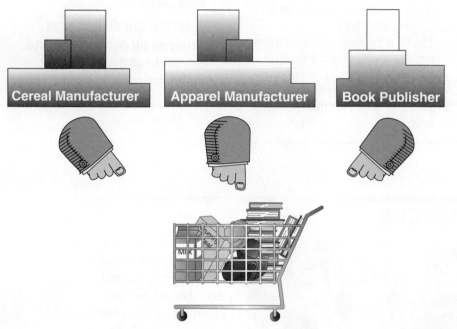

Adjusting Differences Between Producers and Consumers

Differences in Quantity   Businesses usually sell their products to large numbers of customers. They produce thousands and even millions of those products in order to meet the total market demand. Individual consumers usually buy only a very small quantity of a product at any time. Therefore, a channel of distribution must be able to adjust the large quantity produced by the business to the small quantity needed by a consumer.

Differences in Assortment   A producer or a manufacturer often specializes in production. A company typically produces only a limited variety of products in one or a few product classifications. Yet consumers have needs for a great variety of products. Another adjustment made through a channel of distribution is in the assortment of products. The channel will accumulate products from a number of manufacturers and make them available in one location to give consumers adequate choice and variety to meet their needs.

Differences in Location
Customers are usually not conveniently located next to the places where products are produced. They live throughout the country and throughout the world. It would be very difficult, if not impossible, for the manufacturer and final consumer to meet to complete an exchange. A channel of distribution is necessary to move the product from the place where it is produced to the place where it will be consumed.

Differences in Timing of Production and Consumption   In order to operate efficiently, most manufacturers operate year-round to produce an adequate supply of products. Consumers do not use many of those products year-round. Snow blowers, swimwear, gardening equipment, and children's toys are all examples of products that are purchased in much higher quantities during certain times of the year.

Producers of agricultural products often have products for sale only at specific times of the year. Consumers may want to consume products, such as fresh fruits and vegetables, throughout the year. This presents a challenge to distributors to match seasonal agriculture production with year-round consumer demand.

Making adjustments between the time of production and consumption is another responsibility of the channel of distribution. Walk through a supermarket and study the adjustments made for the products sold in the store. Food has been accumulated from throughout the world. Some is fresh and some is processed. The wheat used in the bread and cereal may have been produced many months ago, processed into the products you see on the shelf, and distributed to many stores. The fruit and vegetables may have been rushed by airplane and refrigerated truck from fields in the United States or South America and arrived at the store only a few days after being harvested. Eggs and meat are evaluated and sorted so you can purchase them in different quantities and grades. Soft drinks have been accumulated from several bottlers so you can have a variety of choices. If the channels of distribution have worked well, the supermarket will be well stocked with all of the products you want to buy.

PROVIDING MARKETING FUNCTIONS

In any exchange between producer and consumer, all of the marketing functions must be performed. If no other organizations or individuals are involved in the exchange, the functions will need to be performed by either the producer or consumer. Often neither of those participants is willing or able to provide some of the functions. Other organizations or individuals then have the opportunity to become part of the channel of distribution and provide the needed functions.

Downstream Activity Offers Clue to Future Sales

In order to gauge how well their products are doing in the marketplace, businesses that use intermediaries such as independent wholesalers and distributors need to distinguish between two measures of product movement. One is businesses' own sales and orders from their distributors. The other is the sales or deliveries that their distributors make to retailers. The latter measure of product movement is often referred to as "depletion," because it is a measure of the rate at which distributors are depleting their product inventories.

The relationship between sales and depletions can be a valuable indicator of future sales trends. If sales are lower than depletions, then inventories are decreasing. In that case, distributors will have to buy more products to maintain inventory levels. On the other hand, if sales are exceeding depletions, it means inventories are building. That might be a bad sign, indicating that sales will have to slow to keep inventories from becoming overstocked. Or it could be a favorable signal that distributors and retailers are building inventories because they anticipate a pickup in sales.

THINK CRITICALLY

1. If company sales for the just-completed quarter fell by 2,000 cases, and distributor depletions increased by 10,000 cases, what is the implied change in inventory levels at the company's distributors?

2. If a carmaker finds that its shipments to dealers for the past month increased by 25,000 cars while dealers' depletions increased by 15,000 cars, what is the implied change in dealers' inventory levels?

FIGURE 13-2
Unplanned channels require that many exchanges occur before consumer needs are satisfied. A planned channel makes the exchange process much easier and more efficient.

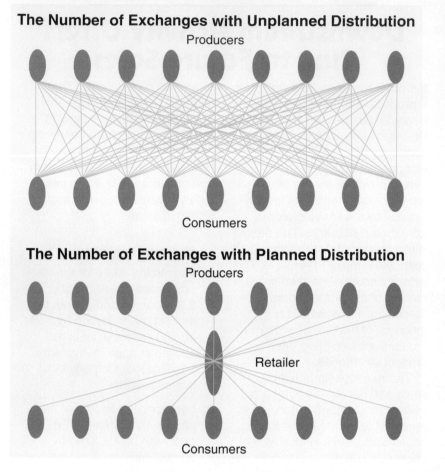

The Number of Exchanges with Unplanned Distribution

Producers

Consumers

The Number of Exchanges with Planned Distribution

Producers

Retailer

Consumers

INCREASING MARKETING EFFICIENCY

If all exchanges of products and services occurred directly between producers and consumers, a great deal of time would be required for marketing. Consider the number of products that you and your family purchase during one week. What if you had to locate and contact each producer and manufacturer, agree on a price, and find a way to get the product from the business to your home? You would spend most of your time on those marketing activities.

When other businesses enter the channel of distribution, they take over many of the responsibilities, saving you both time and money. The retailer determines your needs and the needs of many customers like you. It then contacts the manufacturers of the needed products and has all of the products shipped to their location. You can then make one shopping trip to the business and purchase the needed products. In addition to saving you and the manufacturers time, the other businesses are very effective at locating and purchasing the needed products and finding the most efficient ways to ship them to their locations. Therefore, the cost of the marketing functions should be reduced compared to the cost if you had to complete them yourself. Figure 13-2 shows a simple illustration of the efficiency of exchange that can result from a channel of distribution.

Consider marketing activities such as transportation, financing, or promotion. Some businesses do not have the special equipment or the personnel to complete those functions, but the functions must be performed if the product is going to be sold to the consumer. Trucking companies, railroads, and airlines can provide transportation. Banks and finance companies provide credit to businesses and consumers. Wholesalers and retailers purchase products from manufacturers, hoping to resell them at a profit. Advertising agencies, television and radio stations, magazines, and newspapers provide promotional assistance.

checkpoint

What are the four differences between producers and consumers that are adjusted by distribution channels?

PLANNING AND MANAGING
CHANNELS OF DISTRIBUTION

In order to have an effective distribution system, the channels of distribution must be carefully planned. Participants should be identified. Methods for developing and managing the channel should be considered. The channel of distribution will be most effective if all participants believe in the marketing concept and direct their efforts at satisfying customer needs.

CHANNEL PARTICIPANTS

The businesses and other organizations that participate in a channel of distribution are known as **channel members**. Businesses use either direct or indirect channels of distribution. In a **direct channel**, the product moves from the producer to the final consumer with no other organization involved. The producer and the consumer are responsible for providing or sharing all of the marketing functions. An **indirect channel** includes other businesses between the producer and consumer that provide one or more of the marketing functions. The typical types of businesses that serve as channel members are wholesalers and retailers. Wholesalers sell primarily to retailers and other businesses, while retailers sell to final consumers.

A business chooses between a direct and an indirect channel based on several factors. Indirect channels are used most often in the sale of consumer products, while direct channels are more typical in business-to-business marketing. There are many exceptions to that pattern. Some manufacturers use direct marketing methods such as catalogs, telephone sales, and factory outlets to reach final consumers. Also, manufacturers that sell to businesses across large geographic areas and in other countries often rely on other businesses to help them with selling, distribution, financing, and other marketing functions.

Direct channels of distribution are most often selected when

- there are a small number of consumers.
- consumers are located in a limited geographic area.
- the product is complex, developed to meet specific customer needs, or requires a great deal of service.
- the business wants to maintain control over the marketing mix.

If the opposite market characteristics exist, an indirect channel of distribution will usually be developed.

Many manufacturers use multiple channels of distribution for the same product. This decision is consistent with the marketing orientation because several target markets can exist for the same product. The needs and purchasing behavior of each target market can be quite different.

Think of all of the different customers and needs that must be met by a carpet manufacturer. The same basic product may be sold directly to a contractor who is building several large office buildings. To reach a variety of final consumers, the carpet might be sold through furniture stores, home improvement centers, and discount and department stores. Some of those businesses will be contacted by the company's salespeople, while some very small retail businesses might buy from a wholesaler or another business that sells carpets for several manufacturers. The possible channels of distribution for a carpet manufacturer are illustrated in Figure 13-3.

FIGURE 13-3
The same product may move through several channels of distribution before reaching the final consumer.

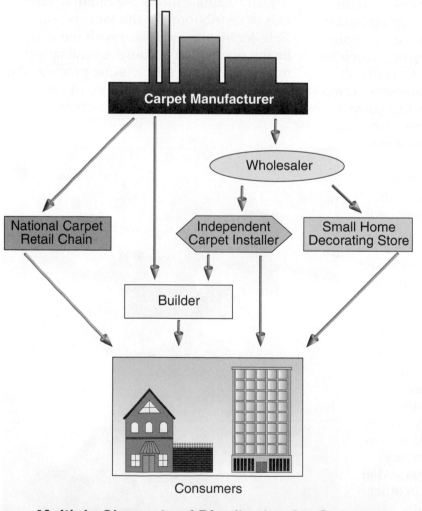

Multiple Channels of Distribution for Carpets

DEVELOPING AND MANAGING A CHANNEL SYSTEM

The Edu-Games example showed that developing an effective channel of distribution is important if a marketing strategy is going to be successful. Few products can be distributed using a direct channel. Therefore, channels must be developed carefully so that the product reaches the customers in the form they want, at the appropriate time and location, and at a price they can afford. Channel development and management is an important task for marketers.

Any business or individual can take responsibility for developing a channel of distribution. A manufacturer that develops a new product wants to find the best way to get the product to the target market. A retailer who discovers an important customer need will try to find a source of products that will satisfy that need. Even consumers can create channels of distribution by locating a supplier for a product they want that is not currently available in the market.

Channels of distribution are usually made up of independent businesses that treat each other as suppliers and customers as products move between them. They each have their own goals and customers and cooperate only when it is to their benefit. This often leads to problems and conflict. If a manufacturer has a very large inventory of one product and a limited supply of another, it is more likely to try to sell the first to

retailers without being too concerned about what the retailer will do with the product. However, if a retailer is competing with another business that is cutting prices, it will try to force manufacturers and wholesalers to cut the prices the retailer has to pay. The retailer will usually not worry whether those companies are able to make a profit.

When channel members do not cooperate, marketing problems may develop. Costs can increase, customer needs may not be met, and some marketing functions will not be performed well. Many businesses are concerned about the poor performance in channels of distribution and are developing ways to manage channels more effectively.

APPLYING THE MARKETING CONCEPT

Probably no situation provides a better example of the effectiveness of the marketing concept yet is more difficult to implement than a channel of distribution.

Businesses are used to competing with each other and working independently. Manufacturers make their profits from the sale of products and services to wholesalers and retailers rather than to final consumers. Wholesalers are concerned about selling to retailers and retailers to consumers. It is very difficult for all of the businesses in a channel of distribution to be concerned about satisfying the consumer and how they must work cooperatively to meet consumers' needs. It is not easy to change a business' philosophy toward a belief that all of the businesses in the channel must be successful if the channel is going to work well. If indirect distribution is going to be used, businesses that believe in the marketing concept must look for ways to operate the channel so the goals of the marketing concept can be met.

checkpoint

What is the difference between a direct and an indirect channel of distribution?

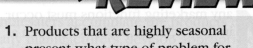

LESSON REVIEW

1. Products that are highly seasonal present what type of problem for businesses?

2. Which channel member is responsible for developing a channel of distribution?

3. When products are custom-made to order, what difference is eliminated?

4. Why is the marketing concept hard to apply effectively through an indirect distribution channel?

5. What factors tend to support the development of a direct channel of distribution?

6. How do channels of distribution increase marketing efficiency?

some wholesale businesses include financing the inventories of manufacturers until they can be sold and extending credit to retailers to enable them to make purchases.

Wholesalers can also be an effective source of information. They assist manufacturers in determining needs of retailers and final consumers and provide market and product information to retailers. Some support the promotional efforts of the manufacturers and retailers by promoting the products they sell.

Wholesale Clubs There has been a recent increase in the popularity of a unique type of wholesaler. **Wholesale clubs** are businesses that offer a variety of common consumer products for sale to selected members through a warehouse outlet. Well-known wholesale clubs include Sam's Club and Costco Wholesale. Large quantities of products are available, but often the variety of products and the choice of brands are very limited. Products are displayed in large warehouses with cartons

E-MARKETING

Invisible Packaging

Freight carriers now use the Internet to let their customers and clients know precisely where shipments are, when they're due to arrive at their destinations, and even what is inside of various packages.

Providing detailed shipping information is part of a larger trend toward integrating information among senders, freight carriers, and recipients. Properly executed, it can significantly reduce the amount of time that expensive components lie around in someone's warehouse waiting to be moved or put to use. In many cases companies are subcontracting the entire operation of parts warehouses to shipping companies and accessing what they need to know over the Internet.

For companies that send and receive sensitive cargoes, a big concern with so-called "invisible packaging" services has been security. It is convenient for them to be able to track the contents of en-route packages over the Internet, but that also opens up the possibility that someone who is not authorized might be able to get that same information. The services are particularly valuable for international shipping, where a package might change hands numerous times before reaching its destination.

THINK CRITICALLY

1. How can better information reduce the amount of time a component spends in inventory before it is put to a production use?

2. Search the Internet for a web site of an overnight package delivery company. What kinds of information can customers obtain from the web site?

stacked on the floor or on warehouse shelves. Customers search among the many products, select their purchases, pay cash, and are responsible for transportation.

The wholesale clubs initially targeted small businesses, and most also offer memberships to employees of large businesses and organizations and also to individuals. Individual customers must pay an annual membership fee to the wholesale club. Some clubs also charge a slightly higher price for products purchased for individual use rather than for use by a business.

Because individuals as well as businesses buy products from wholesale clubs, these companies cross the line between retailing and wholesaling.

What are the main benefits that wholesalers bring to members of a distribution channel and to final consumers?

THE CHANGING ROLE OF WHOLESALERS

As many manufacturers and retailers get bigger and as distribution and communication methods improve, it would seem that the need for wholesalers would decrease. In fact, some large retailers refuse to deal with wholesalers, believing they can get better service and prices if they work directly with manufacturers. As the nature of marketing has changed, wholesalers have adjusted some of their business practices in order to continue to participate in channels of distribution.

There are still many more small- and medium-sized retailers and manufacturers than there are large businesses. Those smaller businesses need effective purchasing and distribution methods if they are going to compete with the large businesses. Wholesalers provide those functions because they specialize in evaluating the products of many manufacturers, buying and shipping in large quantities, assisting with financing, and many other important marketing activities. For small businesses, wholesalers are more important today than ever before.

Access to Markets Wholesalers also provide access to new markets with less risk than if the retailer or manufacturer developed that market alone. Wholesalers help retailers become aware of new

Specialized Services Many wholesalers are adding marketing research and marketing information services. They help their customers gather information and provide them with data that will help the businesses improve their operations and decisions. Computer technology can process orders more rapidly and keep track of the quantity and location of products. New methods of storing and handling products reduce product damage, the cost of distribution, and the time needed to get products from the manufacturer to the customer. Wholesalers are providing additional services to their customers such as marketing and promotional planning, 24-hour ordering and emergency deliveries, specialized storage facilities, and individualized branding and packaging services.

products and new manufacturers. They make products available from businesses that are located long distances away. For manufacturers who want to expand into new markets or sell to different types of businesses, wholesalers may already have experience in those markets. They can develop the new business opportunities much more quickly and effectively than if the manufacturer attempts it alone.

Export and import organizations are very important in building international business. They are informed of the conditions and customer needs, as well as business procedures and legal requirements, for operating in the international market. Without the help of wholesalers, many companies would not be successful in international business.

Of the recent changes in wholesaling, among the most important are better communications, information, improved technology, and broader customer service. Effective wholesalers believe in the marketing concept just as other businesses do. They work to identify their customers and understand their needs. They learn of the problems the customers are having with products and with marketing activities and help them to solve those problems.

How are wholesalers adapting to consolidation in the marketplace, particularly the emergence of giant retail chains that prefer to bypass wholesalers altogether?

1. If a producer prefers to sell directly to retailers, but a wholesaler can do it more effectively, more quickly, and at a lower cost, what is likely to be the outcome?

2. What activities have traditionally accounted for the bulk of the things that wholesalers do?

3. What kinds of differences between producers and retailers do wholesalers bridge in order to get products to consumers when and where they want them?

4. Are wholesale clubs wholesalers or retailers?

RETAILING

MARKETING MATTERS

Consumers purchase most of their products and services from retailers. While retailers do not develop the product, they are responsible for the marketing mix that consumers see. Retailers select the location where consumers obtain products, determine prices, and control much of the promotion. They often provide customer service during the sale as well as service after the sale. Because retailers provide the consumer contact for all members in a channel of distribution, their role is critical.

Retailers are commonly distinguished by the types of products they carry and also by their locations. As consumer preferences and the business environment change, retailing also changes quickly in response. The growth of franchising and the adoption of new technologies are among the changes taking place in retailing.

Make a list of the 10 retailers that you have visited most recently. What products or product categories does each carry? In each case, is the store owned by a chain operator, franchised, or independent?

GOALS

● **Define retailing and describe ways to distinguish various types of retailers.**

● **Describe ways that retailing is changing in response to changes in consumer preferences and the business environment.**

WHAT IS RETAILING?

The final business organization in an indirect channel of distribution for consumer products is a **retailer**. While some large discount retailers sell products to other businesses, their primary customers are individual consumers purchasing to meet their own needs. Retailers accumulate the products their customers need by buying from manufacturers or wholesalers. They display the products and provide product information so customers can evaluate them. Many retail businesses help customers purchase products by accepting credit cards or providing other credit or financing choices. Additional services such as alterations, repairs, layaway, gift-wrapping, and delivery are available in some stores.

Managing the Mix or Restraint of Trade?

In September 1997, in a decision later upheld by a federal court, the U.S. Federal Trade Commission ruled that Toys "R" Us had acted improperly when it entered into agreements with toy makers that restricted the sale of popular toys to discount retail chains. The FTC said such agreements between toy makers and Toys "R" Us constituted illegal restraint of trade.

Toys "R" Us acknowledged that it sometimes declined to carry certain toys that were also being carried by other chains, but contended there was nothing wrong with forging exclusive marketing agreements in order to distinguish its merchandise mix from those of its competitors. It said it had not threatened to stop dealing with any suppliers. A big concern of Toys "R" Us is that discounters and wholesale clubs carry hot-selling toys only during the peak sales season, undercutting Toys "R" Us prices and getting a free ride from its advertising.

Discounters maintained that Toys "R" Us just wants to prevent consumers from being able to compare prices of identical merchandise at various retailers. In their view, by using its market strength to pressure toy manufacturers into restricting their distribution of certain toys, Toys "R" Us effectively deprives discounters of their ability to compete for consumers' business.

THINK CRITICALLY

1. It is common practice for manufacturers to manage which retailers handle their products in order to maintain an image of exclusivity. What is different about this case?

2. Why would toy makers agree to exclusive deals with Toys "R" Us if it meant losing business from discount retailers?

Retailers also help wholesalers and manufacturers. In addition to purchasing products for resale, retailers provide many other marketing functions. They store much of the inventory of products until the customer buys them. Because of that, the retailers are assuming a great deal of the risk and are providing financing for the products. Promotion is an important marketing activity of retailers. Increasingly, retailers are involved in marketing research and marketing information management. Some retailers even take responsibility for transporting products from the manufacturer to their stores.

TYPES OF RETAILERS

It is very difficult to describe retailing with precision because of the variety of businesses that sell to final consumers. Because there are so many consumers, and because their needs and purchasing behaviors are so different, retail businesses develop to respond to those differences.

Some consumers carefully plan their purchases, gather information in advance of shopping for products, and want to complete their shopping as quickly as possible. Other consumers use very little planning, gather information about products while they are in the store, and enjoy spending a great deal

of time shopping. You probably know people who make frequent trips to stores and make a large number of small purchases. There are other consumers who shop very infrequently but spend large amounts of money and make many purchases when they shop. Some people prefer to do their purchasing through catalogs or over the Internet rather than travel to the stores. Retail businesses are available that match each of these types of shopping behaviors. There are several ways to consider the types of retailing.

Product Mix of Retailers   One way of categorizing stores is by the types of products offered in the businesses. Some retailers specialize in one or a few product categories, while others offer customers a wide range of products.

Single- or **limited-line stores** offer products from one category of merchandise or closely related items. Examples include food, hardware, apparel, lawn and garden, or music. Some stores in this category offer a wide variety of types of products, while others may be very specialized. For example, within the category of food, it is possible to find businesses that sell only coffee, cookies, or fresh fruits while other businesses offer many varieties of food in hundreds of product categories.

Mixed merchandise stores offer products from several different categories. Common examples of mixed merchandise retailers are supermarkets in which you can buy many products other than food, department stores that may offer 50 or more distinct departments of products, and large drug stores that sell pet food, automotive products, electronic equipment, and health-related products in addition to drugs.

A relatively new concept in retailing is the superstore. **Superstores** are very large stores that offer consumers wide choices of products. Most superstores are mixed merchandise businesses offering a variety of product categories so consumers can use the business for one-stop shopping. Other superstores sell products in a limited category but offer consumers many choices of brands, product choices, and features within that category.

Two of the most popular types of limited-line superstores today are computer stores and consumer electronics stores.

Location of the Retail Business
An important characteristic of retailing is the location of the store. The location can be studied in relation to the customer or to other businesses. **Convenience stores** are stores located very close to their customers, offering a limited line of products that consumers use regularly. Most convenience stores sell gasoline, food, and household products. Other convenience stores are becoming popular, including businesses that provide packing and mailing, photocopy and printing services, and video rental.

Shopping centers are a set of stores located together and planned as a unit to meet a range of customer needs. There are several types of shopping centers, based on size and types of businesses. *Shopping strips* contain about 5 to 15 stores grouped together along a street. They offer a limited number of emergency and convenience products such as fast food, gasoline, laundry services, and so forth. *Neighborhood centers* have between 20 and 30 stores that offer a broader range of products meeting the regular and frequent shopping needs of consumers located within a few miles of the stores. *Regional shopping centers* contain 100 or more businesses. These large shopping centers attempt to meet most or all of consumers' shopping needs. The centers are developed around several large department or discount stores. They often attract customers from 10 or more miles away. The Mall of America in Minneapolis, Minnesota, offers customers the opportunity to shop in over 300 businesses at one location. It regularly attracts people from hundreds of miles away and is designed as an international shopping location. It promotes its location to travel agents that arrange tours for groups from around the world.

Stand-alone stores are large businesses located in an area where there are no other retail businesses close by and offering either a large variety of products or unique products. Stand-alone businesses must have products that customers cannot easily find in more convenient locations, or products so important or unique that consumers will make a special trip to the business. Examples of stand-alone businesses are some auto dealerships, superstores, and lawn and garden centers.

A unique category of retail businesses is non-store retailing. **Non-store retailing** sells directly to the consumer's home rather than requiring the consumer to travel to a store. Two of the oldest and most common forms of non-store retailing are door-to-door selling and catalog sales. Many years ago, traveling salespeople sold many consumer products. The salespeople traveled to the customer's home because consumers took infrequent shopping trips. This method is used less frequently today because of cost and changing shopping behavior, but organizations such as Avon Products and the Girl Scouts still use door-to-door selling. Catalog sales have regained much of their past popularity in many product categories as a result of express delivery services and strong guarantees and warranty programs by businesses.

Other types of non-store retailing include vending machines, telephone sales, televised shopping clubs, and direct mail selling. The newest and potentially the most lucrative form is Internet retailing such as Amazon.com. Numerous supermarkets now offer services that allow customers to place grocery orders from a home computer, pay by credit card, and have the groceries delivered.

What is retailing and what are two common ways to distinguish or classify various types of retailers?

HOW IS RETAILING CHANGING?

Retailing has always been known for variety as well as rapid change. There is nothing to suggest that change will not continue. Retailing is likely to be very different in the next 10 years than it is now. Also, because of the large number of retailers and the choices available to consumers, it will be increasingly difficult to compete in many types of retail businesses. Consumers expect variety, quality, service, and low price. Retailers will have to be very effective at purchasing, selling, and business operations. In addition, they will have to find the most efficient ways to operate in order to keep costs low if they are to be profitable.

Changing Types of Retailers It is likely that there will continue to be a need for both specialty and mixed merchandise stores. Some people predicted that specialty stores would disappear as people did more one-stop shopping. Yet there are a large number of consumers who are willing to invest more time in shopping and are looking for a wider choice as well as unique or unusual items that are not widely available. The number of small specialty retail businesses has begun to increase again after a time when the numbers were declining. The very large specialty businesses also continue to grow.

The Growth of Franchising

Franchising is becoming a very popular type of retail ownership (see Figure 13-5). In franchising, a company (the franchiser) develops a basic business plan and operating procedures. Other people (franchisees) purchase the rights to open and operate the businesses according to the standard plans and operating procedures. A franchise fee is paid to the franchiser for the business idea and assistance.

Franchises allow people with limited experience to enter a business. They are guided by the franchise plan, which can reduce the risk of failure. Popular franchise programs also increase customer awareness of a business, because many businesses operate in different locations using the same franchise name and promotions. Examples of successful retail franchises include restaurants, financial services, hotels, oil change services, auto repair shops, and printing and copying businesses.

Increased Use of Technology

Technology is having a big impact on retailers. Not only are most business operations managed with computers, but also new types of equipment are being used in businesses to store, distribute, and display products. For example, customers can shop for products using a computer screen on a kiosk rather than walking around a store. When a product is selected from the description and picture on the screen, the consumer inserts a credit card into the computer. The product is selected, packaged, and available for pickup at the front of the store when the customer is finished shopping.

The Global Marketplace

Global retailing holds a great deal of promise for the future. While many manufacturers and wholesalers have been involved in international marketing for a number of years, retailers are often reluctant to expand into other countries. Several types of retail businesses have successfully moved into Eastern and Western Europe and Asia. As countries of the former Soviet Union and Africa develop

FIGURE 13-5
Many successful businesses are operated as franchises, including Deck the Walls, Buffalo Wild Wings, and Maaco.

their economies, retail opportunities will expand there as well. Many of the U.S. fast-food businesses have been quite successful in international marketing, as have businesses in the travel industry, including hotels and automobile rental agencies. U.S. fashions have wide acceptance, so specialty stores are looking at other countries as likely places to expand their businesses.

checkpoint

In what ways is retailing changing in response to shifting consumer preferences and changes in the business environment?

LESSON REVIEW

1. How do retailers help other members of the distribution channel manage risk?

2. Name four types of locations that distinguish various retailers.

3. Which type or types of retailing have been experiencing the fastest growth lately?

4. What are some of the advantages that franchising offers to aspiring retailers, especially to businesses that have limited experience and start-up cash?

13.5 PHYSICAL DISTRIBUTION KEEPS THINGS MOVING

MARKETING MATTERS

It is important to have the right combination of businesses in a channel of distribution. Merely selecting the businesses does not insure that products will move effectively from the producer to the consumer. An important part of channel planning is physical distribution. Consider the number of activities that must be completed as a product moves through a channel.

All parts of the physical distribution process must be carefully planned and controlled if a marketing strategy is going to be successful and products successfully exchanged. The primary physical distribution activities are transportation—including by land, water, air, and pipeline—storage and product handling, and information processing.

List as many ways as you can think of that you have used to physically transport some product from one location to another during your lifetime.

THE IMPORTANCE OF TRANSPORTATION

When most people think of physical distribution, they probably think of transportation. It is more than just that. **Physical distribution** includes transportation, storage, and handling of products within a channel of distribution.

The process of moving a product through the distribution channel involves many activities, including a great deal of paperwork. The product is usually handled many times as it moves from manufacturing through several forms of

transportation and many locations to the business where it will be consumed or sold. It is likely that the product will be grouped into large units for transportation and then divided into smaller units for display and sale, all requiring further handling and packaging.

Usually products do not move continuously through the channel of distribution. They are stored as each business processes paperwork, sells to the next channel member, and determines the location of distribution.

Storage facilities must be arranged to hold and protect the product. Inventory control procedures must be developed so the product does not become lost.

Moving the Product The first step is deciding how products will be moved from producer to consumer. It seems like the decision is not difficult. There are common transportation methods used to move most consumer products—railroad, truck, airplane, ship or boat, and pipeline. As you consider those alternatives, some are automatically eliminated because they are not available in certain locations or are not equipped to handle the type of product to be shipped. You clearly would not send small packages by rail or by ship, and you wouldn't ship iron ore and coal by airplane. Other factors such as the speed of delivery that is needed, whether the products need special handling, and cost enter into the choice of transportation methods.

RAILROADS

Railroads are particularly useful for carrying large quantities of heavy and bulky items. Raw materials, industrial equipment, and large shipments of consumer products from the factory to retailers often are moved by rail. The cost of this transportation method is relatively low if a large quantity of a product is moved, but the total cost to ship one or more carloads of a product is high. Products move quite slowly on trains compared to other methods of transportation.

Problems exist in using railroads for shipping products. Equipment is not always available where it is needed, and it takes some time to move empty cars to new locations. Many areas of the country are not served by rail, meaning that other forms of transportation will be needed to and from the closest rail site. The time needed to load and unload freight from rail cars is long, particularly when a carload contains shipments from several companies or is intended for a large number of customers.

Railroads are responding to the need for improved service to customers. Railroad tracks and equipment are being upgraded and routes are being rescheduled to provide the services customers need. Newer methods of product handling have been developed, including packing products into large containers or truck trailers which are then hauled on flatbed cars. To speed rail shipments to customers, it is now possible for a business to send several carloads of products from the production point and redirect them to customers while en route as sales are made.

TRUCKS

Trucks are the most flexible of the major transportation methods. They can handle small or large shipments, goods that are very durable or require special handling, and products that are going across town or across the country. Trucks can reach almost any location and can provide relatively rapid service. Trucking costs are relatively low for short distances and easy-to-handle products but increase for longer or more difficult shipments.

Many companies own their own trucks. Small companies can often afford to own and maintain a delivery vehicle. Large manufacturers, wholesalers, and retailers often own fleets of trucks to be able to move products where and when needed. Trucking firms are important channel members. The firms provide the specialized service of transporting products to other channel members. They often have special product handling equipment, storage facilities, and well-trained drivers to insure that products are moved rapidly and safely.

SHIPS AND BOATS

A large number of products sold internationally are transported by water. While airlines move small shipments rapidly, ships can handle large quantities and large products very well at a much lower cost than air shipments. The major problem with this form of transportation is speed. Ships are relatively slow, and it may take several weeks after a product is loaded on the ship before it is delivered to the customer. Also, as accidents involving ships carrying oil has demonstrated, there is a risk of large losses if a ship is damaged by weather or other conditions. Ships usually must be used in combination with trucks or railroads, as they are limited to travel between shipping centers.

Boats on inland waterways such as lakes and large rivers are another type of water transportation used for shipping. Barges and boats that haul cargo handle a number of products such as coal, grain, cement, and other bulky and nonperishable items. Like ships, they are rather slow but can handle large quantities at relatively low prices.

AIRPLANES

If you want products delivered rapidly and can afford a higher cost, air transportation will often be the choice. Small parcels can be carried on commercial flights, while larger products or quantities of a product can be moved using cargo planes.

Because of the high transportation costs, many companies do not consider air as a transportation choice. When other factors are considered, air transportation may not be as expensive as it seems. For example, the speed of air delivery reduces the need for product storage. Products may need to be handled less and the speed of distribution reduces spoilage, damage, and theft. Companies that do not regularly use air transportation may choose that method for special or emergency deliveries.

PIPELINES

While not used for many products, pipelines are an important transportation method. Gas, oil, and water are moved in large quantities over long distances through pipelines. Even some products you would not think of move by pipe. Small coal and wood particles can be mixed with water into a slurry and sent through a pipeline between locations. Pipelines are expensive to construct and can be difficult to maintain. Once built, though, they can be a very inexpensive method to use when you consider the large volume of product that can move through the pipeline. It also may be the only choice to deliver products from some locations, such as crude oil from oil fields.

COMBINING METHODS

Products usually move through long channels among several businesses. It is likely that many will be transported using combinations of transportation methods. A shipment of appliances may be moved from a factory to a rail site by truck, moved across the country by rail, and then loaded on other trucks to be delivered to retailers. Shipments of grain from the Midwest may move by train or truck to a grain terminal at a river. The grain is loaded onto barges for shipment to an ocean port. It is then loaded onto ships for transportation to another country.

Companies like Federal Express, United Parcel Service, and the U.S. Postal Service employ their own fleets of cargo planes and delivery trucks to move small shipments between cities throughout the world overnight. Gasoline and other petroleum products are originally moved from a refinery to many locations across the country by pipeline. Then trucks are used to transport the products to wholesalers, retailers, and business consumers.

What are the common means by which products are transported within a channel of distribution?

STORAGE AND PRODUCT HANDLING

Since production and consumption seldom occur at the same time, products must be held until they can be used. This means that methods and facilities for storage must be developed as a part of marketing. Effective storage allows channel members to balance supply and demand, but it adds to the costs of products and adds the risk that products may be damaged or stolen while being stored.

Warehouses   Storage of most products is usually done in warehouses. Warehouses can be privately owned by any of the companies in the channel of distribution. Private ownership allows the company to develop the specific type of facility needed for the products being handled at the locations where they are most needed. For companies who need limited storage space or need it less frequently, public warehouses are available. Public warehouses are often used for overflow storage or for products that are seasonal.

If you live in a medium- to large-sized city, you may have an area of town that was a warehouse district. Large, old, multistory buildings were used in the past by many wholesalers and manufacturers. They were often located near the center of town to be close to the retail businesses. Today, you will find storage facilities located at the edge of town near transportation facilities such as interstate highways or airports. The buildings are quite different from the old warehouses. They are still large but are usually only one story tall. If you enter the building you will likely see long conveyor belts or chains that move products through the building. There may even be computer-controlled trucks and carts that move products from area to area without drivers. Special storage shelves and equipment can move products in and out without the need for handling by people. Bar codes on the shelves, containers, and packages allow computers to keep track of the location of products and the length of time they are in storage.

Distribution Centers   The newest kind of storage facility is known as a distribution center. A **distribution center** is a facility used to accumulate products from several sources and then regroup, repackage, and send them as quickly as possible to the locations where they will be used. A large retailer may have a number of distribution centers located throughout the country. Thousands of products are ordered from many manufacturers and shipped in huge quantities from the manufacturer to the distribution centers. The products are needed in various assortments and quantities in the hundreds of stores owned by the retailer. The costs of storage and transportation are quite high, so the distribution centers must be very good at receiving the products from the manufacturers, combining the many different products into shipments for each store, and routing those

shipments as quickly as possible so the merchandise can be sold. The goal of the distribution center is to reduce the costs of physical distribution while increasing the availability of products to customers. That can be done by careful and efficient product-handling methods and by reducing the amount of time products remain in the distribution center.

Packaging Another important part of product handling is packaging. Packaging is a part of product development in that it aids in the effective use of the product, and it also serves as a tool for promotion. The primary purpose of packaging, though, is to protect the product from the time it is produced until it can be consumed. A great deal of money is invested in products by manufacturers and other channel members that will be lost if the product is damaged or destroyed as it moves between companies.

Packaging materials need to be selected and packaging methods developed that protect the product and allow it to be shipped in appropriate quantities. The people planning the packaging need to consider the methods that will be used to handle the product and the method of transportation. A product that is handled with a forklift and shipped in large containers using trucks and rail cars needs to be packaged differently than a product that is shipped in small quantities directly to the consumer using a parcel service. Products being sent across town require different packaging and packing than those that are being shipped around the world.

checkpoint

What are the common options for storing and handling products while they are moving through the distribution channel?

INFORMATION PROCESSING

Physical distribution systems match the supply of products with the demand for those products. First, that requires that products are available. Then the inventory of products can be matched with the needs of consumers and channel members. An effective information system must be able to predict consumer demand to be sure that an adequate supply is available. The system must assure that the supply matches demand so there is not too much or too little of a product. Products must be routed to where they are needed as quickly as possible. The two important parts of the physical distribution information system are order processing and inventory control.

ORDER PROCESSING

Order processing begins when a customer places an order. Typically the order is placed with a salesperson, but the order may be called in by telephone, sent to the company by fax, or sent via computer using a direct connection or the Internet.

When the supplier receives the order, a system must be in place so the order can

be sent to the location in the business where it can be filled. At the same time, the order is being processed by the accounting department to determine the terms of the sale, method of payment, and cost of the products. Other people are determining the method, cost, and timing of transportation.

When the order is filled, it must be packaged and prepared for shipment. The order is checked to make sure it is complete and information is forwarded to accounting so an invoice can be prepared. The shipper is notified so transportation is available. The customer is informed that the order has been processed and shipped. This procedure is repeated at each stage of the channel of distribution until the product is delivered to the final consumer.

INVENTORY CONTROL

The level of inventory affects the cost of marketing and the level of customer satisfaction. If too much inventory is maintained, the cost of storage will be much higher than necessary. There is also a risk that customer needs will change or the product will spoil or become out of date and will not be sold. If not enough inventory is available, customers will not be able to buy what they need, and sales and goodwill will be lost.

An inventory control system must maintain several types of information. It is important to know what products are in inventory, what quantity of each product is available, and how long each has been in inventory. Effective inventory control methods maintain information in a computer so it is not necessary to look at the inventory each time there is a question about it. Perpetual and physical inventory systems help businesspeople keep track of the products on hand.

A second important feature of an inventory system is a method to determine what products to order and what quantities to order. An inventory control system should identify how much of each product is being sold and how rapidly. The people responsible for maintaining adequate inventory levels should know how long it takes to

process an order for each product so an adequate supply can be maintained. They should also be aware of products that are selling more rapidly or more slowly than planned. When sales are higher than expected, the company may want to order more to be able to meet customer needs. When sales are slow, reasons for the reduced level of sales should be determined and a decision made whether to reorder or not. The slow sales may indicate that the marketing mix for that product is not meeting consumer needs.

checkpoint

What are two important parts of the physical distribution information system?

LESSON REVIEW

1. What is the least expensive method of transportation commonly used to transport goods in a distribution channel?

2. What is the goal of a distribution center?

3. What is the primary purpose of packaging?

4. What advantages do trucks offer for transporting goods?

5. What kinds of information must an inventory control system maintain?

CHAPTER 13

SUMMARY

Lesson 13.1
A. Distribution is crucial to effective marketing. Customers will not be satisfied unless they can obtain a product or service when they want it in a convenient location.

B. A distribution system can only work if all channel members follow the plan. Each member has its own marketing strategy, so members should choose distribution partners wisely. If any member slips up, the system may not produce the desired results.

Lesson 13.2
A. Businesses develop channels of distribution to perform marketing functions needed any time an exchange takes place with a final consumer. Channels adjust for differences in quantity, assortment, location, and the timing between producers and consumers.

B. In a direct channel of distribution, the producer sells directly to the final consumer, and the producer or the consumer performs all marketing functions. In an indirect channel, wholesalers, retailers, and others perform some marketing functions.

Lesson 13.3
A. Wholesalers move products and services through channels of distribution on their way to final consumers. They often provide marketing services more effectively at lower cost because they specialize and achieve economies of scale by working with many producers and channel members.

B. As industries consolidate and producers and retailers deal directly with one another, effective wholesalers refocus on small- to medium-sized customers who need their services to remain competitive. Wholesalers provide access to new markets with less risk and serve as conduits for new technologies.

Lesson 13.4
A. Consumers buy mostly from retailers, who control the marketing mix consumers see. Retailers provide the consumer contact for all channel members. The products they carry and their locations distinguish retailers.

B. As consumer preferences and the business environment change, retailing also changes. The growth of franchising, the adoption of new technologies, and global retailing are among the changes taking place in retailing.

Lesson 13.5
A. The common means by which products are transported within a channel of distribution are rail, truck, ship or barge, airplane, pipe, or a combination of methods.

B. Common options for storing and handling products while they move through distribution channels are warehouses, distribution centers, and all sorts of packaging.

C. Two important parts of the physical distribution information system are order processing and inventory control.

REVIEW MARKETING CONCEPTS

1. Most producers make only a small number of goods, yet consumers need a wide variety of products and want to buy many of them at the same time and place. This disparity represents which kind of difference?
   a. quantity
   b. assortment
   c. location
   d. timing

2. True or False: The business that produces a product always has the primary responsibility for developing the channel of distribution that will get it to final consumers.

3. True or False: For a channel of distribution to work effectively, all of the channel members must adopt the same marketing strategy.

4. Which of the following factors supports the maintenance of a direct channel of distribution?
   a. a large number of consumers.
   b. consumers who are spread out over a wide geographical area.
   c. a complex product developed to meet specific consumer needs.
   d. the producer is not concerned with having control of the marketing mix.

5. An Internet service that sells custom-made CDs to individual consumers is an example of which kind of the following?
   a. non-store retailer
   b. indirect distribution channel
   c. limited-line store
   d. wholesale club

6. True or False: Retailers are responsible for the marketing mix that consumers see because they are the last business in an indirect channel of distribution.

7. Which type of shopping center typically has between 20 and 30 stores?
   a. shopping strip
   b. neighborhood center
   c. regional shopping center
   d. none of the above

8. True or False: Pipelines are only used to transport liquid products.

9. True or False: Transportation on inland waterways such as rivers and lakes has almost come to a halt in the United States because ground transportation of bulk materials such as coal, grain and gravel is faster, quicker, and less expensive by rail or truck.

10. The most flexible of the major transportation methods is
    a. railroad   c. ship
    b. truck   d. airplane

REVIEW MARKETING TERMS

Match the terms listed with the definitions. Some terms may not be used.

11. Includes other businesses between the producer and consumer that provide one or more of the marketing functions.

12. The final business organization in an indirect channel of distribution for consumer products.

13. Located very close to its customers and offers a limited line of products that consumers use regularly.

14. Offers products from one category of merchandise or closely related items.

15. Process by which products move from the producer to the final consumer with no other organization involved.

16. Involves determining the best methods and procedures to be used so that prospective customers are able to locate, obtain, and use the products and services of an organization.

17. A company that assists with distribution activities between businesses.

18. Located in an area where there are no other retail businesses close by and offers either a large variety of products or unique products.

19. A set of stores located together and planned as a unit to meet a range of customer's needs.

20. Offers consumers a very wide choice of customer's needs.

a. channel members
b. channel of distribution
c. convenience store
d. direct channel
e. distribution
f. distribution center
g. distribution function
h. indirect channel
i. limited-line store
j. marketing mix
k. mixed merchandise store
l. non-store retailer
m. physical distribution
n. retailer
o. shopping center
p. stand-alone store
q. superstore
r. wholesale club
s. wholesaler

APPLY MARKETING FUNCTIONS

MARKETING RESEARCH

21. Consumers often have different views about the types of businesses in which they can shop for products. Use the following steps to conduct a brief consumer survey that studies consumer preferences of stores and reasons for shopping:

    a. Using four note cards, write one of the following business categories on each card: factory outlet, specialty store, discount store, and Internet retailer.

    b. Using four more note cards, write one of the following reasons for shopping at a specific type of store on each card: convenience, service, price, variety.

    c. Use the following three products for your survey: jewelry, videocassette recorder, and digital music player.

    d. Ask at least 10 people to participate in the survey. For each of the products in Part C above, ask the respondent to choose from the first set of cards the store where they would most likely shop for that product. Then ask them to choose from the second set of cards the most important reason for their choice of a business.

    e. Record each respondent's decisions for all three products. To help you with the recording, develop a chart for each product containing a list of the types of businesses and a list of the shopping reasons. Record the frequency with which each type of business was chosen and the frequency with which each reason was chosen.

    f. Summarize the results by developing a table for each product that shows the respondent's preferences of businesses and reasons for shopping at those businesses. Prepare a one-half-page written discussion of each table.

22. There are many different types of wholesalers that provide a specific set of marketing functions or meet a particular marketing need. Several types of wholesalers that offer specific services are listed below. You will find that each one is very different from the others and provides marketing services in unique ways. Using resources in your library, locate information about each one and prepare a brief description (two or three sentences) of its activities.

    a. Industrial distributor
    b. Broker
    c. Drop shipper
    d. Truck wholesaler
    e. Commission merchant
    f. Manufacturer's agent
    g. Rack jobber
    h. Cash and carry wholesaler
    i. Producer cooperative

MARKETING PLANNING

23. When products are exchanged between producers and consumers, all of the marketing functions must be performed. In a direct channel of distribution, either the producer or the final consumer is responsible for marketing functions. In an indirect channel, other channel members will perform some of the functions. Two examples of common exchanges are listed below. For each of the examples, think about the activities that will occur as the product moves through the channel of distribution. Then identify which of the channel members will be responsible for each of the seven marketing functions. Prepare a brief written justification for each of your decisions. (It is likely that more than one channel member can perform some of the functions.)

    a. A consumer travels to a strawberry farm to pick and buy fresh fruit.

    b. A homebuilder orders a truckload of plywood from a building supply wholesaler to be delivered to the job site by the supplier. The supplier fills the order from a shipment of plywood delivered last month by rail car from the plywood manufacturer.

24. The number of franchises is growing rapidly. There are franchise opportunities available in manufacturing and service development, wholesaling, and retailing. There are probably many franchises operating in your community. Identify a franchise you would like to study. Gather information about the franchise through library research, by writing to the company that sells the franchise, or by interviewing the owner of a local franchise. Gather the following information:

  a. Is the franchise a manufacturing, wholesale, retail, or service business?

  b. What are the primary products and services offered?

  c. Who are the customers?

  d. What other businesses does the franchise work with?

  e. Where is the franchise located in the channel of distribution?

  f. What marketing functions does the franchise perform?

  g. What types of physical distribution activities are completed in the business?

  Gather additional information you believe will help you understand the franchise business. Prepare a written or oral report from the information you collect.

MARKETING MANAGEMENT

25. The location of a retail business is very important to its success. Unless the product is extremely important to customers and they do not have choices of where to buy, they will not want to spend a long time and a great deal of effort looking for a place to purchase it. For each of the products listed, consider who the typical consumer would be and then determine whether the store that sells this product or service should be located in a neighborhood shopping strip, a regional shopping center, or a stand-alone store. Develop a written justification for each decision.

  a. Homeowners' and renters' insurance

  b. Personal computers for home and business use

  c. New automobiles

26. Edu-Games was trying to develop an effective channel of distribution for its unique product. The company was having difficulty because the distributors and retailers were not implementing the marketing mix the way it was planned. If a manufacturer is unable to get the necessary cooperation from other channel members, it is difficult to successfully market the products. To solve the problem, Edu-Games is considering three alternatives:

  a. Selling the games directly to customers by mail.

  b. Developing its own sales force to replace the distributors.

  c. Finding ways to work more closely with its current distributors to implement the marketing plan that was already developed.

  Prepare a written analysis of each of the three alternatives, identifying advantages and disadvantages of each. Then select the alternative you believe is best and develop a rationale for your choice based on principles of marketing and distribution.

MARKETING TECHNOLOGY

27. Using a computer spreadsheet program, compile a list of 15 to 20 household products that you and your family purchase regularly. Find the per-unit prices that these or comparable products sell for at a wholesale club, a mixed merchandise store such as a supermarket or discount department store, limited-line specialty stores, and at a superstore. Compute the average difference in prices between each of these types of retailer. Note any special requirements such as a need to buy in large quantities at wholesale clubs or any special services each retailer offers.

28. Use the Internet. Research the various types of transportation services that serve businesses in your area. Write a two-page report on them, including which types of services are available (rail, trucks, barges, etc.), how many of each there are, and which are the primary means of freight and package transportation used in your area.

DETERMINING THE BEST PRICE

LESSON 14.1 *THE ECONOMICS OF PRICE DECISIONS*

LESSON 14.2 *DEVELOPING PRICING PROCEDURES*

LESSON 14.3 *PRICING BASED ON MARKET CONDITIONS*

NEWSLINE

ESTABLISHING VALUE AT HMOs

The rising cost of health care is one of the most serious problems facing the United States, where costs now top $1 trillion a year. Stressing preventive health care can help control costs. If people see doctors regularly, problems can be identified and treated before they become more expensive.

Preventive health care is a key characteristic of health maintenance organizations (HMOs). HMOs offer medical services to subscribers for a flat fee rather than requiring patients to pay based on the services they receive. In the past, people visited physicians infrequently, seeking attention only when they were sick or injured. Now people go to HMOs to prevent illness.

A problem is that some subscribers go to HMOs without good cause, raising costs unnecessarily. Costs that had been brought under control by HMOs are now increasing again. Studies of subscribers' attitudes identify two reasons for the increasing costs. First, they view the services as "free." Second, they strongly believe in preventive care and they visit HMOs regularly to ensure that they remain healthy.

HMO managers needed a way to increase the perceived value of their services without diminishing the importance of prevention. So they introduced small service fees for each visit. Ideally, the fee is low enough that it does not discourage people who need to see a doctor, yet high enough to discourage unneeded visits. Subscribers will not visit unless their problem is worth at least the amount of the service fee.

Attitudes and perceptions are an important part of marketing. Marketing personnel for HMOs need to be concerned about their customers' views of price and value if they are going to continue to reduce the cost of health care.

THINK CRITICALLY

1. What do you think is a good amount for an HMO service fee? Why?

2. How do HMO subscribers benefit from service fees?

CORPORATE VIEW

CAREER OPPORTUNITY
CREDIT MANAGER AND ANALYST

POINT YOUR BROWSER

www.corpview.com

TeleView currently has a career opportunity. They are looking for someone who possesses the following attributes.

- Strong problem solving skills
- Proven financial organization and financial management skills
- Up-to-date technical communication skills
- Excellent interpersonal skills to coordinate financial issues with each department and workgroup in the corporation
- Drive, flexibility, and a desire to work in an invigorating, team-oriented environment

The main responsibilities of the job include the following.

- Prepare collection forecasts and risk reports for multiple accounts, and maintain information for certain international accounts
- Research and seek resolution for debt issues, and approve release of sales orders that have been placed on hold
- Perform credit risk analysis on new and assigned accounts, issue credit lines to customers, and establish acceptable limits to those credit lines
- Help manage the bad debt reserve
- Support and implement Corporate View's credit and collection policy, and help establish a similar TeleView policy based on the needs and realities of the telecommunications, electronics, and computer industries
- Track outstanding receivables and doubtful accounts
- Prepare cash-flow forecasts, and help with month-end and quarter-end close activities

Note: This job may eventually be split into two positions, but for headcount reasons the responsibilities are broad at this time.

The job requires the following education, skills, and experience.

- B.S. degree or equivalent experience
- 10 years of experience needed, including management and teamwork experience
- Experience in credit issues in Asia, Europe, or Latin America a big plus, including the ability to analyze foreign financial statements
- Ability to work with accounts where English is not the primary language
- Ability to evaluate international as well as domestic credit risks
- Experience in collections and reconciliation for large accounts would also be a plus
- Minimum of three years Web/Intranet/Extranet experience, including at least a year in a managerial capacity

TeleView's headquarters in scenic Boulder, Colorado, are modern with state-of-the-art technologies at your disposal. All Finance and Accounting department professionals receive a high-end portable computer with a docking station and remote access to the Intranet. Getting to and from the TeleView office complex is facilitated by two freeway exits that provide easy access from picturesque communities to the north and south.

THINK CRITICALLY

1. Prepare a cover letter written by a person who is qualified for this job and is seeking to interview for it while in Boulder on other business next week.

2. The job responsibilities seem very broad, as even the company itself points out. How do you think that affects the desirability of this position?

3. Search want ads or the Internet for a job similar to this position. What type of compensation package is being offered for a similar job?

GOALS

- Explain the reasons why price is an important marketing tool.
- Demonstrate how the economic concept of elasticity of demand relates to pricing decisions.
- Describe the three primary ways in which government influences prices.

Price is an important part of marketing because the prices people pay largely determine how they value an exchange and how satisfied they are with purchase decisions. Expectations of value are closely tied to the price of a product or service. Sellers and buyers devote a lot of attention to prices because prices are easy to change, unlike other elements of the marketing mix.

Price also is central to the economic concepts of supply and demand. Marketers who understand how elastic or inelastic demand is for a product are better able to set the optimum price for it.

Government in a free enterprise economy plays a limited role in setting prices. The main ways it influences prices are by regulating competition, taxing, and regulating pricing practices.

Make a list of all the things you bought in the last week. For which ones did the price significantly affect your purchase decision?

PRICE AS A MARKETING TOOL

"That was a great value!"
"You didn't get your money's worth."
"Is that the lowest price available?"
"It can't be very good at that price."

People make many decisions about what to buy based on the prices they pay. Their satisfaction with purchases is often based on the prices they pay. The lowest price is not always the best price for every customer. The Yugo was a very inexpensive automobile, but did not offer most people the size, quality, or features they expected in a car. K-Mart was very successful in establishing an image of offering low-cost merchandise, but that image made it difficult to attract customers that considered factors other than price when they made purchases. You can probably think of many products you buy that could be purchased at a lower price. Why do you decide to pay a higher price?

The prices charged for products and services are important to the businesses selling them as well as to consumers. The price determines how much money a business will take in to cover the costs of designing, producing, and marketing. If the price is not high enough to pay those costs and provide a profit, the business will be unable to continue to offer that product.

THE IMPORTANCE OF PRICE

We know that effective marketing results in satisfaction for both the consumer and the business. A satisfactory price means that the consumer views the purchase as a value. It also means that the business makes a profit on the sale.

What Is Price? *Price* is the money a customer must pay for a product or service. But price is much more complicated than that. Think of the various words used to identify the price of something. They include admission, membership, service charge, donation, fee, retainer, tuition, and monthly payment. You can probably identify other words used to communicate the price of a product, service, or activity. In some cases, money is not used at all. In bartering, people must agree on the value of the items being exchanged rather than setting a monetary price.

Price is such an important part of marketing that it is one of the four elements of the marketing mix. **Price** is the actual cost and the methods of increasing the value of the product to the customers. As one of the seven functions of marketing, *pricing* is defined as establishing and communicating the value of products and services to prospective customers. When planning any marketing activity, business people must consider the impact of the cost to the business, the price customers must pay, and the value that is added to the product or service as a result of the activity.

Adjustability Price is an important tool because it can be changed much more quickly than other marketing decisions. Once a product is designed and produced, it is very difficult to change its form or features. A channel of distribution takes a great deal of time to develop. After the wholesalers and retailers are selected and the product is distributed, it is not easy to change the locations where customers can purchase the product. Even promotion is not easy to adjust. Advertisements must be written and produced, time or space in media is purchased well in advance, and salespeople have to be hired and trained. It is difficult to quickly change the types of promotions for a product or service.

By contrast, changing a price is often as simple as adding a new price sticker or

Technology Transforms Buying and Selling of Stocks

Information technology continues to shake up the way American investors buy and sell stocks and other financial securities. Before computers, virtually all shares were traded on stock exchanges where exchange members gathered and arranged trades for their clients through an auction process. For the most part, individual investors were far removed from the process and had little information about pricing.

Today, most trading takes place away from auction-based stock exchanges, the New York Stock Exchange being a notable exception to their demise. Instead, securities dealers are linked electronically through computer networks such as the NASDAQ (National Association of Securities Dealers Automated Quotation) system. On NASDAQ, dealers known as market makers post the prices at which they are offering to buy or

sell various securities. When investors place their orders, they are filled at the best price available in the system.

Even computerized trading still left individual investors mostly in the dark about the prevailing prices. They might place an order at $10 and by the time it was completed only minutes later, the price could conceivably have doubled. The growth of the Internet and regulatory reform in the 1990s began giving individual investors access to the kinds of information that dealers and large institutions have.

THINK CRITICALLY

1. Use the Internet to access a stock quoting service, and get a quote for a stock that's listed on the NASDAQ system. What kind of information does it provide?

2. Why is price such a critical element of securities markets?

marking out an old price. Even manufacturers can change the price charged by a retailer by offering a coupon or a rebate. Because prices can be changed more rapidly and easily than other marketing tools, marketers must be careful not to make mistakes with price changes.

Cite three reasons why price is an important marketing tool.

PRICE AS AN
ECONOMIC CONCEPT

Price is also an important economic concept. People have unlimited wants and needs that they try to satisfy with the limited resources that are available to society. Price allocates available resources among people. If there is a small quantity of a product or service but a very large demand, the price will usually be quite high. On the other hand, if there is a very large supply of a product or if demand is low, the price will be low. Figure 14-1 illustrates how supply and demand affect price.

FIGURE 14-1
At a price of $3, demand (90) is greater than supply (30). At a price of $7, supply (90) is greater than demand (30). At a price of $5, supply equals demand (60) and the market is in equilibrium.

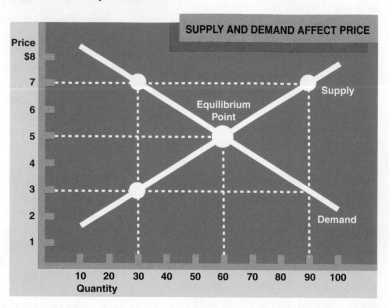

ECONOMIC UTILITY

The value customers receive from a purchase results from more than just the product or service itself. The concept of economic utility demonstrates that value is added through changes in form, time, place, or possession. Therefore, customers believe a product is a greater value and will often pay a higher price if the product is available at a better time or place than other choices, or if it is more accessible or affordable. Figure 14-2 demonstrates how marketers can add to the value of a product by increasing the economic utility.

FIGURE 14-2
A business can increase its economic utility for customers through improvements in form, time, place, and possession.

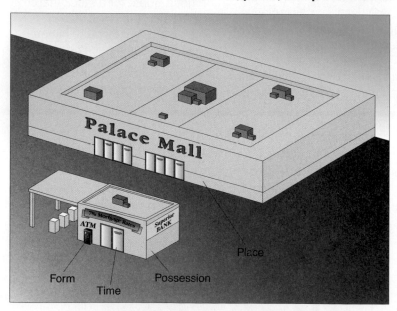

Economic Utility Adds to the Value of a Product

ELASTICITY OF DEMAND

It may seem that an easy way to get consumers to buy your product is to decrease the price. It seems logical that if the price decreases, more products will be sold. Many people believe that if sales increase, profits will increase as well. That is not always the result.

The table in Figure 14-3 shows several prices charged by a supermarket for one dozen eggs. The table also shows the quantity sold and the total revenue the store received from the sales. As you can see, the decrease in price does not result in enough additional sales to increase the total amount of money received.

A different result is shown in Figure 14-4. When the supermarket decreases the price of ice cream, the additional quantity sold increases total revenue.

The difference between these examples illustrates a key economic concept. **Elasticity of demand** describes the relationship between changes in a product's price and the demand for that product. Elasticity is based on the number of good substitutes for a product and the willingness of consumers to go without a product if the price gets too high. In Figure 14-3, the result occurs because there are few substitutes for consumers who purchase eggs. When consumers need to purchase eggs, they will do so even if the price is increased. If the price decreases, they will not buy many more eggs than they would at the higher price. This is an example of inelastic demand. In **inelastic demand**, a price decrease will decrease total revenue.

Figure 14-4 illustrates elastic demand. In **elastic demand**, a price decrease will increase total revenue. Demand is elastic when customers have several good substitutes for a product. Consumers view ice cream as one choice among many desserts. If the price of ice cream increases, some customers will not buy ice cream or will buy other products like cake or candy that are now a better value. If the price of ice cream decreases, people who were buying other products may switch now that ice cream seems more affordable.

If price changes are too great, the type of demand elasticity may change. If eggs become extremely expensive, people will stop buying them. There is a limit to the amount of ice cream people will buy no matter how inexpensive it is. Therefore, marketers can use price elasticity only for price changes that consumers believe are reasonable.

FIGURE 14-3
When the price is decreased for one dozen eggs, a larger quantity will be sold. The increase in quantity is not enough to increase the total revenue from the sales.

INELASTIC DEMAND

Price of a Dozen Eggs	Quantity Sold	Total Revenue
$0.65	305	$198.25
$0.68	300	$204.00
$0.71	292	$207.32
$0.74	285	$210.90
$0.77	277	$213.29
$0.80	264	$211.20

FIGURE 14-4
When the price of one gallon of ice cream decreases, the quantity sold increases a great deal. The increase in quantity results in higher total revenue.

ELASTIC DEMAND

Price of a Gallon of Ice Cream	Quantity Sold	Total Revenue
$3.65	180	$657.00
$3.70	165	$610.50
$3.75	158	$592.50
$3.80	147	$558.60
$3.85	136	$523.60
$3.90	122	$475.80

How are prices related to elasticity of demand for a product or service?

GOVERNMENT'S EFFECT ON PRICES

In private enterprise economies, businesses and consumers interact to determine prices and what is bought and sold. Governments play a role only when laws or regulations are needed to prevent unfair competition or to encourage activities that benefit society. When governments are involved in the economy, they often affect prices. The most important methods governments use to influence prices are by regulating competition, prices, and taxation.

REGULATING COMPETITION

A foundation of private enterprise is that competition benefits both businesses and consumers. Whenever one business is large enough to control a market or when a few businesses cooperate to take advantage of smaller businesses or consumers, the government will regulate that business. Several years ago, the federal government believed that AT&T had too much control of the telephone service industry. A court ruling required AT&T to divide itself into several smaller independent companies. This allowed other businesses such as MCI and Sprint a better chance to offer competing telephone services.

The government also wants to encourage the development of new products and services so consumers have additional choices to satisfy their needs. One way to help businesses is to protect new products from competition until they can become profitable. Patents are granted to inventors of unique products for a period of 20 years. During that time, no other business can market exactly the same thing unless the inventor grants permission or the patent is sold. In the same way, people who develop artistic works such as books, films, recordings, or art work can be protected by copyrights. If a company has a patent or copyright, it has greater control over the price it charges since there will be no product just like it for a period of time.

JUDGMENT CALL

Prosecutor Proffers Amnesty for Anxious Price Fixers

In the United States it is illegal for two companies to get together and agree on how much they will charge for their products or services. It's called price-fixing or bid-rigging. The offending companies are subject to penalties. They could also be forced to sell off parts of their businesses under federal antitrust laws. Also, company executives who participate in price-fixing schemes are subject to criminal prosecution and can be sentenced to as much as a year in jail.

In the mid-1990s, the Justice Department's chief antitrust prosecutor began offering to let price-fixers off the hook if they confessed. The only catch was that only the first company to admit to a particular price-fixing arrangement went free. If another conspirator got there first and confessed, then any other participants would be penalized. Early cooperation might earn a conspirator a reduced penalty.

The amnesty offer was designed to encourage a race to the courthouse by conspirators afraid that other conspirators would beat them to it. It helped also that when a company was given amnesty, so were its employees. The plan worked. Numerous conspiracies were uncovered and hundreds of millions of dollars in fines levied. About half of the companies that confessed revealed schemes that the government didn't know about.

THINK CRITICALLY

1. If a company that owns a chain of stores is not required to compete against itself, why should two independent stores be subject to penalties if they agree to charge the same prices, just as the chain stores do?

2. Do you see any potential problems with this amnesty offer as a permanent policy? Explain.

TAXATION

Taxes are another way that governments affect the products and services marketed, the prices paid, and the level of competition. An increase in the tax on a product makes it less attractive to consumers and reduces the level of sales. Taxes on products such as tobacco and liquor not only collect revenues for the government, they also reduce the consumption of products that are believed to be harmful. In the same way, import taxes increase the price of foreign products, making domestic products a better value for consumers. For products that are considered luxuries such as furs and jewelry, a tax may not reduce the quantity of the products purchased, but it increases the amount of taxes collected from people who are most able to pay.

Occasionally, the government wants to encourage a particular type of business or the development of certain products or services. Legislators use a tax reduction for that purpose. When businesses disappear from the central part of cities, city and state governments may reduce or eliminate taxes for several years to encourage businesses to relocate in those areas. To promote the use of alternative fuels, some states reduced the tax on ethanol-based gasoline. When the price of ethanol-based gasoline dropped several cents per gallon lower than other gasoline, the consumption of it increased.

REGULATING PRICES

The federal government has specific legislation to regulate the pricing practices of business. Some of the most important areas regulated by laws include the following:

- Price fixing: Competing companies at the same level in a channel of distribution (manufacturers, wholesalers, retailers) cannot cooperate in establishing prices.
- Price discrimination: Businesses cannot discriminate in the prices they charge to other businesses in their channel of distribution. A manufacturer must offer equivalent prices, discounts, and quantities to all wholesalers or retailers rather than giving an unfair advantage to one or a few companies.

- Price advertising: Businesses cannot mislead consumers through the advertising of prices. Examples of misleading advertising include using phony list prices (price at which the product is never sold), incorrect comparisons with competitors' prices, or continuous promotion of a sale price. Companies must also clearly communicate the terms of credit offered to customers.
- Bait-and-switch: Companies cannot lure customers into a store with offers of extremely low prices and then tell the customer the low-priced product is unavailable or inferior.
- Unit pricing: Many products that are sold in varying quantities or package sizes must carry a label listing the price for a basic unit of measurement, such as a liter, ounce, or pound, so consumers can make price comparisons.

What are the three main ways that government influences prices in a free enterprise economy?

1. Which condition do producers prefer, elastic or inelastic demand? Why?

2. Which condition benefits consumers, an elastic supply curve or an inelastic supply curve? Why?

3. Why should marketers be so concerned about pricing mistakes if prices are so easy to change and simple to correct?

4. What ways do governments use to encourage new product development?

5. Retailers often try to attract shoppers by advertising a "sales event" rather than a "sale." Why?

14.2 DEVELOPING PRICING PROCEDURES

GOALS

- Describe three objectives businesses commonly choose from when setting a price.
- Explain how businesses establish a price range for a product.
- Identify the three components that must be covered by the selling price.

In order to achieve optimal results, businesses need to carefully plan the prices they charge for their products and services. Price planning begins with establishing price objectives. Three common objectives are maximizing profits, increasing sales, and supporting an image.

To narrow down their choices, businesses analyze demand to determine the maximum price that customers will pay. Breakeven analysis helps to determine the minimum price at which a business can cover its fixed and variable costs. In the end, the selling price must cover product costs, operating expenses, and leave room for a profit. Some businesses, especially retailers, set prices by applying markups such as a fixed percentage of product cost to a range of merchandise.

Make a list of three things you've owned that you subsequently sold, how you determined the prices you asked for, and the prices you eventually received from buyers.

SETTING PRICE OBJECTIVES

It is not easy to determine the best prices to charge for products. Companies want prices that cover their costs and contribute a reasonable profit. Consumers are not particularly concerned about the company's costs or whether the company makes a profit on the sale. Consumers want to get the best value and expect the product to be comparably priced to other similar products. Because it is not easy to determine the actual costs for marketing a product or what customers are willing to pay, many companies do not take enough care in setting prices. They may set their prices based on what competitors are charging. Or they may set their prices high, believing that they can reduce them if customers are unwilling to pay the original prices. Such practices are risky and may result in unsold products or loss of profits. Prices should be planned as carefully as the other mix elements.

To begin price planning, marketers need to determine what objectives they want to accomplish with the product's price. Examples of possible objectives are to maximize profits, increase sales, or maintain a company image.

Maximize Profits Companies that seek to maximize profits carefully study consumer demand and determine what customers in the target market are willing to pay for their products. The prices are set as high as possible while still satisfying customers. In this way, there is more money to cover the costs of production and marketing and return a profit. Companies that want to maximize profits usually select smaller target markets where unique products can be developed. Their products are quite different from competitors' and meet important customer needs in those markets.

Increase Sales Sales-based pricing objectives result in prices that achieve the highest possible sales volume. Companies that want a greater share of the market or have high levels of inventory may choose this objective. Prices will usually be quite low to encourage customers to buy. Companies using a sales-based objective need to set the price high enough to cover costs. Also, they must have an adequate supply of the products to meet customer demand. They will usually sell their products in markets with a large number of available customers.

Maintain an Image

Companies can use the prices of products to create an image for the product or the company. Many consumers believe that price and quality are related, that higher prices mean better quality while lower prices suggest poorer quality. Therefore, companies that are building a quality image use higher prices than those on competing products. Companies trying to appeal to cost-conscious customers need to keep their prices as low as or lower than competitors' prices. Some companies advertise that they will "meet or beat" their competitors' prices. The intention of that strategy is to convince customers that the company will always have the lowest prices.

Have you shopped at a business where no prices were posted by the products? Have you eaten at a restaurant where the menu did not contain prices? These businesses are creating an image that price is unimportant in the purchase decision. They are using non-price competition to sell their products and services.

Calculating the Cost of Coupons and Rebates

Rebates and coupons can be very effective forms of promotion, and they don't necessarily cost businesses nearly as much as consumers might imagine. Although a coupon that gives a shopper $1 off the purchase price reduces or eliminates the profit margin on that particular transaction, overall profits can increase with a well-planned campaign.

Key issues for businesses issuing coupons or offering rebates include determining the face value of the coupon or rebate, the percentage of buyers likely to redeem coupons or claim rebates, the number of coupon or rebate users who would not have made a purchase except for the promotion compared to the number who would have made the purchase anyway, and the cost of distributing and handling coupons.

Companies attempt to maximize publicity generated by a campaign while limiting the number of customers who actually redeem coupons or claim rebates. For example, mail-in rebate offers attached to product packages have proven very effective. They provide a strong point-of-purchase incentive for shoppers to buy a product, but only a small percentage of them take the time to fill out and mail in the necessary form. After all, is a $1 or $2 rebate really worth 10 minutes of someone's time, plus a 34-cent stamp and a trip to the mailbox?

THINK CRITICALLY

1. A maker of breakfast cereal prints a $1 rebate offer on each box, and sales increase by 100,000 boxes, or 25% compared to the previous period. If 3% of all purchasers bother to claim the rebate, how much will the company have to pay out in rebates?

2. If the company makes a profit of 50 cents per box sold before the rebates are paid out, how much will it gain or lose as a result of the rebate promotion?

checkpoint

What are the three objectives that businesses commonly choose from in setting prices?

DETERMINING
A PRICE RANGE

fter a company determines the basic objective that will guide pricing, the next step is to determine the possible prices for products and services. It is likely that there is more than one price that can be charged for a product. Study almost any product and you will see that it is sold at various prices depending on the brand, store, time of year, and other factors. To set an effective price, maximum and minimum prices for the product must be determined. Those prices determine the price range.

Maximum Price   The highest possible price that can be charged is determined by the target market. It is based on demand analysis. Marketing research is used to identify the customers in the target market and determine their needs. Then alternative products and services that the target market will consider in satisfying their needs are identified. Finally, the customers in the target market are asked to identify what they would be willing to pay for each of the alternatives. The highest price that results from this analysis of demand is the maximum price. Customers will not be willing to pay more than that amount as long as needs and alternatives do not change.

Minimum Price   The lowest price in the price range is determined by the costs of the seller. A company can sell a product at a loss only for a short time and then only for a very few products. Most prices must be set so that when all products are sold the company has covered its costs. The minimum price should also contribute profit to the company.

To determine the minimum price, calculate all production, marketing, and administrative costs for the product. That is difficult because some costs cannot be directly related to specific products. Also, costs are often highest for new products and then go down as more products are sold.

Breakeven Analysis   One way that companies determine the minimum price is through breakeven analysis. The **breakeven point** is the quantity of a product that must be sold for total revenues to match total costs at a specific price. The breakeven point is calculated using the following information.

- Fixed costs: The costs to the business that do not change no matter what quantity of the product is produced or sold
  - Variable costs: Those costs that are directly related to the quantity of the product produced or sold
  - Total costs: Fixed costs plus variable costs for a specific quantity of the product
  - Product price: Price at which the business plans to sell the product
  - Total revenue: The anticipated quantity that will be sold multiplied by the product price

The formula for finding the breakeven point is

$$\text{Breakeven point} = \frac{\text{Total fixed costs}}{\text{Price} - \text{Variable costs per unit}}$$

Figure 14-5 illustrates a breakeven analysis table for an Ascroe Garden Weeder. Using the information in

FIGURE 14-5
The breakeven point is the quantity where total costs equal total revenue. Based on the figures in this table, that quantity would be about 7,589 units.

BREAKEVEN ANALYSIS FOR ASCROE GARDEN WEEDER

Units Sold	Variable Costs per Unit	Fixed Costs	+	Total Variable Costs	=	Total Costs	Price	Total Revenue
5,522	$2.80	$85,000	+	$15,462	=	$100,462	$14	$77,308
6,054	$2.80	$85,000	+	$16,951	=	$101,951	$14	$84,756
6,998	$2.80	$85,000	+	$19,594	=	$104,594	$14	$97,972
7,589	$2.80	$85,000	+	$21,249	=	$106,249	$14	$106,246
8,225	$2.80	$85,000	+	$23,030	=	$108,030	$14	$115,150
9,110	$2.80	$85,000	+	$25,508	=	$110,508	$14	$127,540

Figure 14-5, you can calculate the break-even point if the weeder sells for $14. The total fixed costs for the product are $85,000. The variable costs for each tool are $2.80. Ascroe wants to determine how many weeders must be sold to break even if the price is set at $14. Using the formula:

$$\text{Breakeven point} = \frac{85,000}{14.00 - 2.80} = \frac{85,000}{11.20} = 7,589 \text{ units}$$

Ascroe must determine if they will be able to sell this number of units. If so, they can set the price at $14. Additional calculations can be made at other possible prices to determine the relationships between prices, costs, and demand.

Price Range Figure 14-6 shows a price range that was calculated for a pair of shoes. Using demand analysis, it was determined that customers in the target market would pay as much as $87 for the shoes when they are compared to all of the other choices. The company must charge at least

$53 to cover fixed and variable costs. The shoes can be sold at any price between the maximum and minimum. The company will select a price that meets its pricing objective and gives it the flexibility to increase or decrease the price as market conditions change.

If the goal is to sell the greatest quantity of shoes possible, the company will set the price near $53. If the goal is to establish a high-quality image and provide a higher level of customer service, the price will be closer to $87. A goal of being competitive with the price may result in a price that is close to the prices of other companies' brands.

FIGURE 14-6
A company can price its product anywhere between its total cost per unit (minimum price) and the amount customers are willing to pay (maximum price). All of the possible prices are known as the price range.

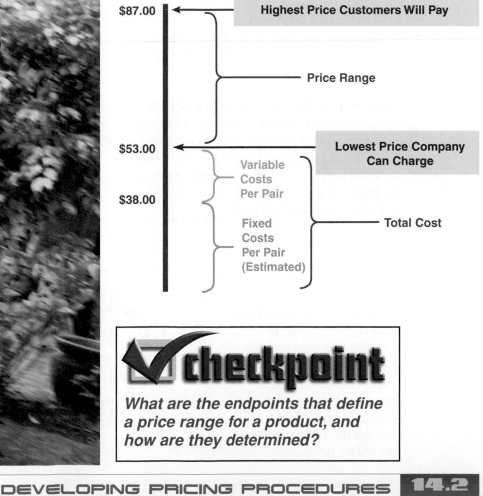

Price Range for a Pair of Tennis Shoes

$87.00 — Highest Price Customers Will Pay

Price Range

$53.00 — Lowest Price Company Can Charge

Variable Costs Per Pair

$38.00

Fixed Costs Per Pair (Estimated)

Total Cost

✓checkpoint

What are the endpoints that define a price range for a product, and how are they determined?

CALCULATING
A SELLING PRICE

The price charged for a product or service is known as the selling price. For a successful product, the selling price has three components. The largest part of the selling price for most products is the cost of producing (or buying) the product. That cost should include the cost of parts and raw materials (or the price paid to a supplier for finished products), labor, transportation, insurance, and an amount for damaged, lost, or stolen products. The difference between the cost of the product and the selling price is known as the **gross margin**. The gross margin is the amount that is available to cover the business' expenses and provide a profit on the sale of the product.

The next component of the selling price is operating expenses. **Operating expenses** are all costs associated with actual business operations. The costs of buildings, equipment, utilities, salaries, taxes, and other business expenses need to be calculated and added to the product cost. Marketing costs are incorporated into the operating expenses or included as a separate amount.

The final component of the selling price is profit. **Net profit** is the difference between the selling price and all costs and operating expenses associated with the product sold. Profit is not guaranteed to businesses when they sell products. Often costs and expenses are higher than anticipated, or the selling price has had to be reduced to make the sale. In those cases, the business may not be able to make a profit or might even lose money on the sale. Businesses try to set selling prices high enough that reasonable profits are possible even when some costs are higher than expected or prices are reduced. Figure 14-7 summarizes the components of the selling price.

Figuring Markups To simplify the process of determining the selling prices for products, some businesses, especially retailers, use markups. A **markup** is an amount added to the cost of a product to determine the selling price. Markups are usually stated as a percentage rather than a dollar amount. Businesses determine the percentage needed to cover operating expenses and provide a profit and use that percentage to determine the selling price.

Markup can be calculated as a percentage of the product cost, or sometimes it is determined as a percentage of the selling price. A box of 500 envelopes is sold at an office supply store for $3.50. The cost to the store is $2.80. The markup as a percentage of cost is 25 percent ($0.70 ÷ $2.80). The markup as a percentage of the selling price is 20 percent ($0.70 ÷ $3.50).

A few businesses use a standard markup for most products. All products are originally marked up the same percentage, such as 45 percent, to determine the selling price. Other businesses determine the differences in operating and marketing costs or differences in the type of competition for various product categories. Then they develop a separate markup percentage for each product category.

Effect on Profit High markups do not always mean that the business will make a larger profit on the product. Usually a high markup reduces the quantity sold or results in slower sales and higher costs to the business. On the other hand, business people must be careful in using very low markups. While the lower price may result in higher sales, the markup may not cover all expenses. In some cases, expenses increase because of the costs of handling a larger quantity

FIGURE 14-7
The selling price is made up of the cost of the product, operating expenses, and net profit.

Selling Price

Product Cost

Net Profit

Operating Expenses

Components of the Selling Price

of products. Marketers must carefully study the effects of different markup percentages before determining the one to be used.

For retailers, usually all products will not be sold at the original selling price. When products are not selling as rapidly as a business expects, a markdown will be used. A **markdown** is a reduction from the original selling price. Markdowns can be expressed as specific dollar amounts or as a percentage of the original selling price. Markdowns are usually viewed as business mistakes since the product did not sell at the planned price. The mistakes may be a result of poor product quality or from misunderstanding customer demand. They can also result from poor marketing mix decisions such as the location and promotion of the products or from changes made by competitors.

Internet Advertising Services

The advent of Internet shopping has rattled many businesses, because it is now so much easier for buyers to comparison shop. They no longer have to leave their desks or talk to salespeople to get an accurate idea of the range of prices and products that are on the market. They can quickly get the information they need to satisfy almost any need by searching the Internet. Web sites can also inform about availability, including how long it takes to ship a product or locations where they can pick up something in person.

With so much pricing information in consumers' hands, many businesses are forced to focus on other elements of the marketing mix to attract customers. Fortunately, the Internet has also made that easier for them. Advertising services are available that can send ads directly to potential buyers while they are shopping on a competitor's web site. The ads are sent via the shopper's web browser when they sign up for the service. They enable businesses to, in effect, steal customers away from their competitors with better offers, while those very customers are most likely to be making buying decisions. It takes the idea of targeting promotions to a whole new level.

THINK CRITICALLY

1. How do you think businesses like the idea that a competitor can reach their prospects while they are viewing their web sites?

2. The Internet businesses that offer these services have very strict privacy policies. Why do you think those policies are necessary?

What are the three components that have to be covered by the selling price if a product is to be successful?

1. Why would a business establish an objective to increase sales at the expense of maximizing profits?

2. How do businesses determine the maximum price that customers will pay for a product?

3. What are the three variables that businesses commonly analyze using break-even analyses?

4. Why do companies usually select a price somewhere in the middle of the price range and not at either extreme?

5. If operating expenses exceed the gross margin, what happens to profits?

6. If a bookstore applies a uniform markup of 60 percent of the product cost to all the books it sells, what is its gross margin?

14.3 PRICING BASED ON MARKET CONDITIONS

GOALS

- Identify two marketing tools that illuminate competitive conditions and help marketers set prices.
- Describe the various criteria businesses use in establishing the final price a customer pays.
- Explain why extending and managing credit is important to marketing.

Determining the best price is as much a function of the target market as it is a matter of marketing objectives. Much depends on conditions in the market, and product life cycles and consumer purchase classifications help marketers tailor prices to the competitive environment. Depending on the type of market being targeted and the expectations of customers, various criteria can be used to adjust the final price for each transaction.

Credit is a component of the price element that businesses use to facilitate transactions and to enable customers to make purchases that they otherwise might not be in a position to complete. Businesses need to manage credit effectively, or it can be costly.

Make a list of 10 items purchased by you, a friend, or a family member. For how many of those 10 items was the final price the same as other people paid who purchased the same item at about the same time? How did prices paid differ?

COMPETITIVE ENVIRONMENT

When planning the prices of products and services, marketers need to be aware of the type of competition in the market. If customers see many good alternatives for the product being marketed, the prices of those products will remain very similar. If customers view a product as having few substitutes, the price of that product can be set at a different level than competing products.

There are certain types of market conditions where customers view products as very similar. Consider the difference between pure competition and monopoly. In pure competition, customers see all product choices as identical. Therefore it is almost impossible for a business operating in pure competition to charge more for its products than other companies are

charging. On the other hand, a business operating in a monopoly has the advantage that customers have no good substitutes. Therefore the company has much control over the price. That is why government often regulates monopoly markets.

Product life cycle analysis and consumer purchase classifications are two marketing tools that are helpful in making pricing decisions.

PRODUCT LIFE CYCLE

Throughout the stages of a product life cycle, the type of competition changes. Those changes affect the prices that companies can charge. In the introductory stage, only one brand of a new product is available, allowing the business to control the price charged. Some companies enter the market with a skimming price. A **skimming price** is a very high price designed to emphasize the quality or uniqueness of the product, even though it attracts fewer customers. Other companies use a penetration price in the introductory stage of the product life cycle. A **penetration price** is a very low price designed to increase the quantity sold of a product by emphasizing the value. A skimming strategy usually results in higher profits for the company and encourages other companies to enter the market. A penetration price may result in higher total revenues, but the initial level of profit is much lower. Companies use a penetration price to attract a large share of the market early and discourage other companies from entering the market.

In later stages of the life cycle, competition increases and there is an emphasis on price competition. In the maturity stage, customers see many choices that look very similar. Therefore a small price change might encourage them to switch from one brand to another.

CONSUMER PURCHASE CLASSIFICATIONS

Consumer purchase classifications also provide an example of different levels of price competition. Staple convenience goods and price-based shopping goods illustrate intensive price competition. In each case, customers see few product differences. They often choose the lowest-priced product if they see a reasonable price difference. For products such as emergency or specialty goods, price is not as important to customers. Other factors cause them to purchase products at much higher prices than competing products.

Companies selling products with many similar competitors (common household products, basic clothing items, business supplies) have to be very careful of the prices they charge. They must pay close attention to the prices of competitors. On the other hand, companies with unique products (special jewelry or fashion designs, expensive automobiles, personal services) can be less concerned about the prices of competing products or services.

GM Drives Home the Value of Co-Branded Credit Cards

When General Motors Corp. teamed with MasterCard in the early 1990s to issue credit cards, co-branding suddenly gained a lot of marketers' attention. General Motors Corp. wanted to establish its brand name in consumers' minds so they would be more likely to buy a GM car than another manufacturer's brand. GM management believed a credit card carrying the company's name would help.

People use credit cards regularly for purchases. If they use the GM MasterCard, the name GM will become a part of their buying process. When the customer receives a credit card bill each month, the name GM appears. The bill provides a regular opportunity for GM to put promotional information in front of a highly targeted audience of prospective customers.

A major incentive related to auto purchasing is also built into the use of the credit card. Each time the card is used, 5 percent of the purchase amount charged is credited toward a rebate on the purchase or lease of a GM automobile. Card users have a strong incentive to purchase a GM product and take advantage of the rebate. GM believes this will keep customers focused on GM products for several years rather than just when they visit a showroom to purchase an automobile.

THINK CRITICALLY

1. How much do you think credit card sponsors such as GM need to award on credit card purchases in order to be effective as a promotional tool?

2. What other types of businesses might benefit from co-branded credit card programs?

NON-PRICE COMPETITION

When businesses emphasize price as a reason for customers to buy a product or service, two problems can result. First, the emphasis on price may encourage customers to view price as the most important reason for buying. That view causes them to see the other parts of the marketing mix as less important. Second, the emphasis on price means that businesses must keep prices as low as possible. With low prices, there is less profit available on each product sold. With lower profits, the company has less money to spend on marketing research, other marketing activities, or new product development.

To avoid those problems, some companies use non-price competition. **Non-price competition** de-emphasizes price by developing a unique offering that meets an important customer need. Few people ask the price to be charged when they go to a physician with an illness. Price is not an important factor when purchasing a one-of-a-kind painting, applying for admission to an exclusive college, or planning a weekend getaway to celebrate a wedding anniversary.

Companies using non-price competition need to carefully study the needs of a target market. The products and services that people in the target market view as possible alternatives must be examined. Market research can identify the things customers find dissatisfying about the competition. The company uses that information to develop a better marketing mix that is more satisfying to those customers. If the company is successful in developing a unique marketing mix that meets important customer needs, price will not be an important factor in the decision to purchase.

What are two tools that help marketers to identify the competitive environment and make better pricing decisions?

PRICING
POLICIES

Few people expect to pay the price that is listed on the window sticker of a new automobile. Yet, when you go bowling or play miniature golf, you pay the price set by the business. Companies develop policies based on various criteria to establish how the final prices are derived.

Price Flexibility   Customers may not have a choice of the price they pay for a product. They either pay the price set by the business or they do not buy. A **one-price policy** means that all customers pay the same price. In other cases, such as the purchase of a new car, the price paid by customers is based on how effectively they negotiate with the salesperson. A **flexible pricing policy** allows customers to negotiate the price within a price range.

It may seem unfair to offer different prices for the same product. In some cases it is actually illegal to use flexible pricing. But consider a farmer selling fresh vegetables at a market. On days when there are a number of other farmers with the same products at the market, the farmer may need to lower the price in order to sell all of the products on hand. If the weather is bad and fewer customers come to the market, the price will likely be reduced. On the other hand, a high demand will result in higher prices.

Automobile dealers traditionally have used flexible pricing to extract the highest price possible from each customer. They often reduce the price in order to sell a car to a customer who refuses to pay the sticker price. Some customers enjoy negotiating for a lower price, while others do not. Recently many auto dealers have begun using a one-price policy, in part because so many customers have been obtaining dealer cost information on the Internet. With this policy, a lower initial price is set and all customers are expected to pay the price listed for the automobile. The dealers believe they can reduce the costs of selling and that customers will believe they are being treated more fairly with the new policy. It will be interesting to see if the one-price policy becomes standard in auto sales.

Price Lines Many companies offer several choices of the same product to appeal to different customer groups. Appliance stores sell refrigerators, stoves, and dishwashers with several choices of features ranging from basic to full-featured. To make it easier to analyze the choices, the products are grouped into two or three price lines. **Price lines** are distinct categories within which products are organized based on differences in price, quality, and features. Companies must decide whether or not to offer price lines, the number of different lines to offer, and the difference in prices among those lines.

Geographic Pricing

Increasingly, companies sell products in different parts of the country and throughout the world. Costs of distribution and selling are quite different at various locations. Customer expectations of price, as well as the level of competition, are often different. Companies must determine how prices will be set in each area.

Some companies keep the product price the same but charge a different amount to cover transportation costs. A method for setting transportation costs based on geographic location is known as FOB (free on board) pricing. **FOB pricing** identifies the location from which the buyer pays the transportation costs and takes title to the products purchased. For example, "FOB factory" means the customer pays all transportation costs from the point where the product is manufactured. A seller can

Clip a Coupon, Save a Billion

How does Mexico help U.S. consumers save almost $5 billion each year on their grocery bills? Not by providing low-cost food products. Rather, Mexico is the location of most of the companies known as *clearinghouses* that process more than 8 billion manufacturer's coupons annually. The United States still leads all other countries in coupon usage, but coupons are a global shopping experience. Yet no matter where they are distributed, most of the coupons end up in Mexico.

Each year over 300 billion coupons are distributed. It is estimated that nearly three-fourths of all U.S. households regularly use coupons. Those coupons are given to retailers, who send them to the manufacturers in order to receive payment. Handling coupons after they have been redeemed is as important as handling cash. If they

are lost or misplaced, the retailer will not receive credit. If they are miscounted, the manufacturer may end up paying too much to the retailer.

Most coupons are sorted and counted by hand in large warehouses in Mexico. Often the coupons are recounted for accuracy and security. The records are sent to the manufacturers, or to companies called *paying agents,* where checks are issued to the retailers. All of the work must be done rapidly so retailers get their payments as quickly as possible.

THINK CRITICALLY

1. Why do coupon issuers have to be careful about counterfeiting and fraud?

2. Why do you think most of the coupon warehouses ended up in Mexico?

negotiate with the customer by agreeing to pay some or all of the transportation costs by identifying a selected city between the buyer's and seller's locations for the FOB designation. Another type of geographic pricing is zone pricing. With **zone pricing**, different product or transportation costs are set for specific areas of the seller's market.

Discounts and Allowances Sellers may choose to offer discounts and allowances to buyers. **Discounts and allowances** are reductions in a price given to the customer in exchange for performing certain marketing activities or accepting something other than what would normally be expected in the exchange. Some common discounts and allowances include the following:

● Quantity discount: Offered to customers who buy large quantities of a product

- Seasonal discount: Offered to customers who buy during times of the year when sales are normally low
- Cash discount: Offered to customers who pay cash rather than using credit or who pay their credit accounts quickly
- Trade discount: Specific percentage reduction in price offered to businesses at various levels in a channel of distribution (wholesalers and retailers)
- Trade-in allowance: Reduction in price in exchange for the customer's old product when a new one is purchased
- Advertising allowance: Price reduction or specific amount of money given to channel members who participate in advertising the product
- Coupon: Specific price reduction offered by a channel member through a printed promotional certificate
- Rebate: Specific amount of money returned to the customer after a purchase is made

Added Values The customer's perception of value can be changed by making additions to the purchase. This is typically done through services provided during and after the sale. Another way of adding value is to provide complementary products or a larger quantity for a reduced unit price, such as "buy two and get a third item free." Some businesses offer prizes and premiums for purchases or use incentives for regular purchasing. An example of such incentives are the frequent flyer programs used by airlines. Customers are given free tickets after they have traveled a certain number of miles on one airline. Contests like the one sponsored by Publisher's Clearinghouse are used to encourage people to buy. In that particular contest, the company gives away money and prizes to a few people selected from the many who send in an entry form or order magazines during the year.

Name three techniques or criteria businesses use to determine the final price a customer pays.

OFFERING
CREDIT

Companies marketing very expensive products or services may have a difficult time selling them even if customers believe the price is fair. Few companies have the cash to pay for a $30 million building. Few individuals are able to pay the full amount for a new car, whether it costs $7,000 or $70,000. Credit makes it possible for expensive purchases to be made. A company must determine if credit is necessary as a part of the price mix element.

TYPES OF CREDIT

Retail or **consumer credit** is credit extended by a retail business to the final consumer. The credit may be provided by the seller or may be offered by another business that is participating in the marketing process, such as a bank, finance company, or a credit card company like VISA.

Most sales between businesses are made on credit. **Trade credit** is offered by one business to another business. This happens because of the time lag between when a sale is negotiated and when the products are actually delivered to the business. Also, credit sales are a traditional business practice in many channels of distribution. Businesses rely on waiting 30 or 60 days or longer before making payment.

DEVELOPING CREDIT PROCEDURES

Credit provides a method for obtaining additional customers and sales that otherwise might not be possible with cash sales only. If credit is poorly managed, though, costs may be very high and the money from the sale of products may never be collected from some customers. Business people responsible for credit sales must plan procedures carefully to be sure that credit is a successful part of a marketing strategy. The procedures include developing credit policies, approving credit customers, and developing effective collection procedures.

Credit Policies   The first decisions for a business are whether to offer credit and whether credit will be offered on all products and for every customer. Next, the credit plan is developed. The business decides whether it will offer its own credit plan or rely on other companies to offer credit. Finally, the credit terms are developed. The terms include the amount of credit that will be extended, the rate of interest to be charged, and the length of time given to customers before payment is required.

Credit Approval   Not all customers are good credit customers. If a customer is unable to pay for purchases, the seller loses all of the money invested in producing and marketing the product as well as the cost of extending credit. Even if the product is recovered from the customer, it is not likely that it can be resold for an amount that will cover the costs.

A business that plans to offer credit must determine the characteristics and qualifications of the customers that will be able to make credit purchases. Those factors typically include customers' credit history, the

resources they have that demonstrate their financial health, and the availability of the money with which they can make payments. Most businesses have a procedure through which customers apply for credit and provide financial references. These references include banks and other businesses from which they have obtained credit in the past. Commercial credit services such as Dun & Bradstreet can be used to provide information on the credit history of businesses and consumers.

Collections   Effective collection procedures are an important part of a credit plan. The procedures are needed so that customers are billed at the appropriate time and pay their accounts when they are due. Because some customers are unable or unwilling to pay their accounts, procedures for collecting overdue accounts are an important part of a credit system. Most businesses that offer credit have a small percentage of their accounts that are never collected. Even a small percentage of uncollected funds can make a credit plan unsuccessful. This results in losses and the need to increase prices to other customers.

Why should businesses bother with extending credit, since it exposes them to a risk of not being paid?

LESSON REVIEW

1. When high-tech companies bring out new products and initially charge very high prices that they know only a relatively few technology enthusiasts will pay, what kind of price are they setting?

2. Why is non-price competition more prevalent among luxury products and services targeted to very affluent consumers?

3. Name a set of established price line-based brands in the automobile industry.

4. Why do you think frequent-flyer programs and similar buyer-loyalty incentives are so popular in industries that target mainly business people?

5. Why do businesses traditionally allow 30 to 60 days before payment is due for a business transaction?

6. Why does it make sense to offer consumers seasonal discounts, such as off-season rates at resort hotels or airlines?

CHAPTER 14

SUMMARY

Lesson 14.1

A. Prices largely determine how customers value an exchange and how satisfied they are with purchase decisions. Prices get a great deal of attention because they are easily changed, unlike other elements of the marketing mix.

B. Price is central to the economic concepts of supply and demand. Elasticity of demand describes the relationship between changes in price and corresponding changes in the quantity consumers demand. Elastic or inelastic demand for a product determines the optimum price for it.

C. The main ways government influences prices are by regulating competition, taxation, and discouraging detrimental activities or encouraging beneficial activities.

Lesson 14.2

A. Price planning begins with establishing price objectives. Three common objectives are maximizing profits, increasing sales, and supporting a carefully planned brand image.

B. Demand determines the maximum price. Breakeven analysis finds the minimum price. The maximum and minimum prices form the endpoints of the price range. The selling price is set somewhere within the price range.

C. Some businesses set prices by applying markups to entire ranges of merchandise. The amount of the markup (the difference between the cost and the selling price) is the gross margin. Use of markups is most common among retailers and wholesalers.

Lesson 14.3

A. Determining the best price is a response to competitive conditions in the target market. Where a product is in its life cycle and how customers regard it help marketers tailor prices to the competitive environment.

B. Depending on the type of market being targeted and the expectations of customers, various criteria can be used to adjust the final price for each transaction.

C. Credit is a price component that can facilitate transactions and enable customers to make purchases they otherwise might not be able to. Some credit accounts will always be uncollectable, but if they become too much, the business can wipe out its profit.

REVIEW MARKETING CONCEPTS

1. A(n) __?__ is offered to customers who buy large numbers or a large amount of a product.

2. A(n) __?__ is a specific price reduction offered by a channel member through a printed promotional certificate.

3. A(n) __?__ is a specific percentage reduction in price offered to businesses at various levels in a channel of distribution.

4. A(n) __?__ is a specific amount of money returned to the customer after a purchase is made.

5. A(n) __?__ is offered to customers who pay without using credit or who pay their credit accounts quickly.

6. A(n) __?__ is offered to customers who buy during times of the year when sales are normally low.

7. A(n) __?__ is a price reduction or cash payment given to channel members who participate in advertising a product.

8. A(n) __?__ is a reduction in price in exchange for the customer's old product when a new one is purchased.

REVIEW MARKETING TERMS

Match the terms listed with the definitions. Some terms may not be used.

9. A reduction from the original selling price.

10. Describes the relationship between changes in a product's price and the demand for that product.

11. The difference between the selling price and all costs and operating expenses associated with the product sold.

12. Increases total revenue when prices decrease.

13. All customers pay the same price.

14. A very high price designed to emphasize the quality or uniqueness of the product, even though it attracts fewer customers.

15. A very low price designed to increase the quantity sold of a product by emphasizing the value.

16. De-emphasizes price by developing a unique offering that meets an important customer need.

17. The quantity of a product that must be sold for total revenues to match total costs at a specific price.

18. Costs associated with business operations.

19. Allows customers to negotiate price within a price range.

20. Distinct categories within which products are organized based on differences in price, quality, and features.

21. The actual cost and the methods of increasing the value of the product to the customers.

22. Different product or transportation costs are set for specific areas of the seller's market.

23. The difference between the cost of the product and the selling price.

24. An amount added to the cost of a product to determine the selling price.

25. Extended by a retail business to the final consumer.

a. breakeven point

b. consumer credit

c. discounts and allowances

d. elastic demand

e. elasticity of demand

f. flexible pricing policy

g. FOB pricing

h. gross margin

i. inelastic demand

j. markdown

k. markup

l. net profit

m. non-price competition

n. one-price policy

o. operating expenses

p. penetration price

q. price

r. price lines

s. skimming price

t. trade credit

u. zone pricing

APPLY MARKETING FUNCTIONS

MARKETING RESEARCH

26. There are many terms used to present the price of products and services. Also, the price or value of a product or service can be represented in a variety of ways with numbers, graphics, and pictures. Look through newspapers, magazines, direct mail advertisements, and other print materials from businesses and organizations and find examples of the many ways prices are communicated to consumers. Cut out examples and create a collage of price and value on a sheet of poster board.

27. Identify at least 10 consumers who will participate in a study of the importance of price. Ask each person to respond to the following three items and record their answers:

   a. Identify five products or services that you purchase regularly for which price is one of the most important factors in the decision.

   b. Identify five products or services that you purchase regularly for which price is not one of the most important factors in your decision.

   c. Compare the products from the two lists and identify up to three reasons why price is more important for the first list than for the second.

   After you have collected the information, analyze the responses and develop several conclusions about the importance of price in consumer purchase decisions.

MARKETING PLANNING

28. The goal of businesses when pricing products is to set a price that provides a reasonable profit after all products are sold. Calculating the breakeven point identifies the minimum quantity that must be sold in order to cover the costs of the product. Using the following price and cost information for four products, determine the breakeven quantity. Then construct a graph for each product that illustrates total fixed costs, total variable costs, total revenue, and total costs. Identify the breakeven point on each graph.

Product	Price	Total Fixed Costs	Variable Costs Per Unit
A	$42.00	$20,000.00	$18.00
B	550.00	980,500.00	86.00
C	1.20	1,500.00	0.90
D	150.50	75,250.00	102.00

29. Identify one form of consumer credit to study. It can be a credit plan from a retail store, a credit card from a retailer or a manufacturer, a bank credit card such as MasterCard or VISA, installment credit, a loan plan from a bank or finance company, or other types of credit plans. Collect information by interviewing a credit manager or other person from the company who understands the credit system. Collect a copy of the credit application and other print information that explains the terms of credit. If possible, interview one or more people who use that particular form of credit. When you have finished your study, prepare a written report on the credit policies and procedures. Include the following information: who is offered credit, the application and approval procedure, the type of credit plan, the major credit terms, how billing is done, and the collection procedures for past due accounts.

MARKETING MANAGEMENT

30. Jerry Englebrecht has operated a successful dog grooming service for 10 years. Each year his number of customers has grown as satisfied customers have told others of his service. His expenses have always been quite low since he is the only employee, and he operates the business from one-half of his garage that he remodeled into a small office and grooming area. For many years, the number of dog owners has increased in his town, but that growth has now almost stopped.

   In the past two years, three other competing grooming services have started. One is being offered by a veterinarian, Dr. Humble, to serve primarily her customers. Another is part of a chain of pet grooming stores that is about three times as big as Jerry's business and is located in a larger city 15 miles away. The newest competitor is a small partnership consisting of two people who are doing grooming on a part-time basis. They are only open two evenings a week and on Saturdays.

   Until recently, Jerry has not been too concerned about the competition. He believed he had loyal customers and was regularly getting inquiries from new pet owners. Recently he has noticed few new people calling to ask about grooming, and some of his regular customers have not returned for their regular grooming appointments. In talking to some of his current customers, he learns that the chain store and the partnership are both offering grooming services at a much lower price than Jerry.

Jerry does not want to lower his price because that will decrease his profits. His goal has always been to use the profits to buy a building and expand his business. Also he believes his service is better than that offered by competitors.

a. How can Jerry decide whether he should lower his price?

b. If Jerry wants to emphasize non-price competition, what are some recommendations you would make to him in the areas of product, place, and promotion that could help him increase customer satisfaction?

31. A small company has just created a new type of greeting card. It looks the same as the typical greeting card you can buy in most retail stores. The unique feature is a microchip in the card on which the sender can record a 30-second personalized message. Initially, the cards are being produced in two categories—Valentine cards and New Year's cards—for times when people may want to send more unique and personalized messages. If these cards are successful, the company may choose to expand into other holidays, seasons, and categories of cards.

Because of the computer technology and special envelopes needed to protect the card, the company's cost before distribution is higher than other cards—$3.40 each. It has been decided that the cards will be sold to a select set of specialty retailers throughout the world. A few wholesalers may be used for distribution if they follow a carefully developed marketing plan. The

cards will also be sold to individual consumers who purchase in quantities of at least 50 cards. Those cards will be distributed by a parcel delivery service.

Your task is to develop a proposed set of pricing policies for the company. Develop a specific policy for each of the following items that is consistent with the product, its image, the type of competition that will exist, and the marketing strategies described: price objective, price range, price flexibility, price lines, geographic pricing, discounts and allowances, and added value.

MARKETING TECHNOLOGY

32. Make a list of five new CDs released by recording artists you like to listen to. Go to two different stores and find out the prices of the CDs. Use the Internet to shop three additional retailers and get prices from them. Note shipping and handling charges also.

Input the data you have collected into a spreadsheet program and have it calculate the total cost for the five CDs from each retailer, including shipping and handling charges. Also have it calculate the high, low, and average prices for each CD. Make a printout of the calculations.

33. Using the information in the following chart, calculate the missing amounts.

Product Cost	Gross Margin	Operating Expenses	Selling Price	Net Profit	Markup (Selling Price)	Markup (Cost)
$120.00	$	$40.00	$	$15.00	%	%
	36.00	16.00	58.00			
0.75	0.30	0.12				
865.00			995.00	27.50		
		12.75	38.50	5.25		
10.00				2.00		50
	25.00	25.00	80.00			
		27.00		64.00	70	

MARKETING IN ACTION

BRAND RECOGNITION: THE PERSONALITY OF A PRODUCT

Nike Inc. markets its products in more than 100 countries and is a leading sports and fitness company. The company donated $28 million in cash and products to community-based organizations globally in 2000. Adidas, the top brand in the sporting goods industry, is entering a new frontier in sporting apparel with its "customization experience" project. What sets Nike and Adidas apart from numerous competing brands? Each of these popular brands has an image that is enhanced with the latest styles, unique advertising, and good publicity.

Many consumers associate Nike with Michael Jordan, widely considered to be the best professional basketball player in history. Commercials featuring this basketball icon kept consumers aware of the latest trends at Nike and linked the product line with a winner. Consumers consciously or subconsciously purchased Nike products because they wanted to be like Michael Jordan. Parents and youth were willing to spend over $100 on a pair of athletic shoes associated with Jordan.

Every company takes a risk when they use a celebrity as a spokesperson for their product. They are assuming that the celebrity will maintain a positive public image. Hertz Rent-a-Car had O. J. Simpson as its spokesperson for many years. The company compared its service in airports to the speed of O. J. on the football field. Controversy caused Hertz to disassociate itself altogether with Simpson. Once Jordan retired, both the NBA and Nike lost some of their luster.

At about the same time, reports of Nike products being manufactured in sweatshops in South America gave the company negative publicity that was difficult to overcome. Nike focused attention on several positive campaigns to restore the public's confidence in its integrity. When India suffered a magnitude 7.9 earthquake in January 2001, Nike shipped nearly 20,000 articles of Nike clothing. One month earlier, Nike had partnered with Federal Express to ship products to earthquake victims in El Salvador. Nike officials realize that they cannot respond to every disaster worldwide, so the company limits its efforts to disasters affecting the Nike family. Nike has an office in Bangalore, India, and two factories in Ahmebadad.

Growing popularity of the WNBA and women's soccer have triggered growing opportunities for Nike and other sporting goods marketers. Prominent Olympians such as Marion Jones have generated more interest in women's sports and fitness. Nike has set a top priority to capture a larger share of women's business, a major growth area in the United States and internationally. Nike plans to increase investment in all facets of the women's product market, from television advertising to retail development.

In the sporting goods industry, Nike is not the only game in town. Adidas recently initiated a successful campaign to take over the #1 spot in U.S. athletic retail sales. Adidas realized that it would not be easy to keep the #1 ranking, so it launched its own aggressive international marketing strategy. The company paid attention to what youth were demanding and provided popular merchandise.

In February 2001, Adidas opened a "Megastore" in Paris, France. Appearances by sports celebrities such as Zinedine Zidane, Jackson Richardson, and other gold medal Olympians made the grand opening a big success. Ever since the French national soccer team won the World Cup in France in 1998, image and awareness of the Adidas brand has been enhanced. The Megastore gives Adidas a great opportunity to showcase over 400 different models of shoes. Each of the three floors in the store highlights a specific category of merchandise.

After a successful pilot project in six European countries in 2000, Adidas has launched a "customized experience" in footwear in Herzogenaurach, Germany. It gives consumers the opportunity to create footwear to their exact personal specifications in terms of function, fit, and appearance. The project started with soccer and is being expanded into other major sports.

Big-name companies such as Nike and Adidas realize the importance of international markets, product creativity, and association with winners. Large sums of money are spent to put the Nike or Adidas emblem on the jersey or cap of a champion. Positive public image is also an important element for corporate success.

How can smaller brands compete with the big corporations? Success depends on offering a product having similar features to the popular big brands, while charging lower prices. The winning sporting brands will step up to the plate to manage product design, international markets, and publicity.

THINK CRITICALLY

1. What three major issues covered in this case study help to determine the success of a sporting goods company?

2. What male and female athletes would you choose to endorse a sporting goods company's products? Why did you choose these athletes?

3. Explain the importance of a corporation participating in charities.

http://www.deca.org/publications/HS_Guide/guidetoc.html

RETAIL MARKETING RESEARCH EVENT

DECA PREP

Nike has been extremely concerned with the public's perception of the company due to recent media reports on sweatshops in South America. Design a survey with the goal of collecting information about the public's perception of Nike. This survey should determine if the public is aware of the relief efforts conducted by Nike in earthquake disaster areas. You want to find out whether Nike has a positive or negative public image. Nike also wants recommendations to strengthen its image.

PROPOSAL DESCRIPTION   Prepare a one-page description of the proposed survey. Include a description of the business or organization, as well as a description of the community (geographic, demographic, and psychographic factors).

RESEARCH METHODS   Describe the research methods used. This might include sample questionnaires, letters sent and received, general background data, etc. What steps did you take to design the survey and the instrument? How did you conduct the survey?

FINDINGS AND CONCLUSIONS   Prepare a geographic, demographic, and psychographic description of customers. Explain the buying behavior of customers. Summarize customer familiarity with the business. What conclusions can you make based on the findings of the survey?

PREPARE BUSINESS OUTLINE   The outline should include goals/objectives and rationale, proposed activities and timelines, the proposed budget, and a plan to evaluate the effectiveness of marketing the services offered by the company.

CHAPTER 15

PROMOTION MEANS EFFECTIVE COMMUNICATION

LESSON 15.1 *PROMOTION AS A FORM OF COMMUNICATION*

LESSON 15.2 *TYPES OF PROMOTION*

LESSON 15.3 *MIXING THE PROMOTIONAL PLAN*

NEWSLINE

INFLUENCING WHAT YOU EAT

"**B**uy me!"
"Try me!"
"Take me home for dinner."

Do you ever get the feeling that the supermarket shelves are talking to you? Companies go to great lengths to convince you to buy their brands. Promotion is the tool they use and the payoff can be big. Some estimates suggest that as much as 80 percent of the purchases made by the average supermarket shopper are unplanned.

Businesses use a variety of promotional tools to make sure their products are the ones consumers select. Large-screen television monitors at checkout aisles broadcast a news channel with plenty of ads thrown in. The goal is to get consumers to watch the advertisements while waiting in line. Electronic bulletin boards display advertised specials and other information with moving messages. Flashing buttons located on the shelves under featured products can be pushed to play a 10-second commercial and dispense a coupon.

One company has developed a video shopping cart. The monitor on the cart can display a map of the store, identify locations of specific products, print receipts, compare prices, and provide product information. The cart needs to be effective. It costs $100,000 per store to install the system.

Why the interest and investment in unique methods of promotion? Competition among products and brands in supermarkets is intense. Customers make many spur-of-the-moment decisions. The new types of point-of-purchase promotions are much more effective than an advertisement in the morning paper or a radio commercial.

THINK CRITICALLY

1. Why do you think point-of-purchase promotions are more effective than newspaper or radio ads?

2. In what ways do retailers benefit from all the new promotional tools that are on the market?

CAREER OPPORTUNITY
PUBLIC RELATIONS SPECIALIST

POINT YOUR BROWSER
www.corpview.com

TeleView is looking for someone who possesses the following attributes.

- Proven problem solving, project organization, and time management skills
- Well-developed interpersonal skills
- Public-speaking skills
- Drive and flexibility
- Up-to-date technical communication skills
- Excellent customer relation skills to help us maintain product loyalty
- A sincere desire to work in an invigorating team-oriented environment

The main responsibilities of the job include the following.

- Creating, implementing, and managing public relations campaigns for TeleView products
- Furnishing regular, positive, and consistent information for media coverage of TeleView and its products
- Working closely with Marketing, Sales, and Support teams
- Maintaining a consistent and positive interaction with industry analysts, press, and media publications
- Conducting press tours of the Corporate View research park and TeleView corporate offices
- Sending TeleView products to industry analysts for their review
- Preparing press releases and developing press kits
- Demonstrating press kits to Marketing, Sales, and Support team members
- Tracking competitive products and preparing competitive analysis reports
- Preparing new feature highlight sheets

- Attending trade shows, industry meetings, and conferences to support and popularize TeleView brands and products
- Monitoring press coverage and working with the Intranet team to post timely press reports to TeleView's management and employees over the Intranet
- Planning strategies that will promote TeleView's industry leadership and brand-name recognition

The job requires the following education, skills, and experience.

- An Associate's, B.S., or B.A. degree in either public relations, corporate communications, journalism, marketing, or in a liberal arts or equivalent field of study
- Two to four years of public relations experience, preferably in high-tech industries
- Must be able to demonstrate strong verbal skills
- Must be able to demonstrate up-to-date technical communications
- Contacts within the press and with industry analysts are a plus

Applicants will be expected to bring a portfolio of writing samples to the job interview.

THINK CRITICALLY

1. Prepare a cover letter written by a person who is qualified for this job and interested in applying for it.

2. Write an essay of 300 to 400 words explaining why good public relations are essential for a company in the communications industry.

3. Search want ads or the Internet for a job similar to TeleView's public relations specialist. What type of compensation package is being offered for the job?

15.1 PROMOTION AS A FORM OF COMMUNICATION

GOALS

● Explain the three roles of promotion in marketing.

● Describe how the communication process works in marketing.

● Define the two types of communication that are important to marketers.

MARKETING MATTERS

Because of its power and pervasiveness, promotion is the marketing mix element that often comes to mind when people think of marketing. Consumers are bombarded with promotional messages from marketers about products and services. They are carried over many media and delivered in various forms. Promotion has three roles in marketing—to inform, to persuade, and to remind.

For marketers to communicate effectively, they need to understand the communication process. The communication process is the transfer of a message from a sender to a receiver. The process comprises seven basic elements—a sender who originates the message, encoding by the sender, a message channel, decoding, a receiver, noise along the way, and feedback or response.

Identify an important message that you have received in the past 24 hours. Describe the process by which it was sent from the sender to you. What action or result occurred or will occur because of that communication process?

THE ROLE OF PROMOTION IN MARKETING

It is estimated that the average person is exposed to over 3,000 promotional messages every week. These messages occur through such media as television, radio, direct mail, personal selling, coupons, and rebate offers. Their purpose is to tell the consumer about products and services that are available and to encourage exchanges in the marketplace. Though not all of the messages are received by consumers, they remember those that have meaning for them.

Promotion is any form of communication used to inform, persuade, or remind consumers about an organization's goods or services. Because of its high visibility, promotion is the mix element that often comes

to mind when a person thinks of marketing. It is a powerful element that can be strategically combined with product/service development, pricing, and distribution to satisfy the overall marketing objectives of the organization (see Figure 15-1).

As a vital component in the marketing mix, promotion has three different roles in marketing: to inform, to persuade, and to remind.

INFORM

The first task of promotion is to inform potential and current customers of a new product or service or of an improvement to an existing product. The information task of promotion is often used when a product is in the introduction stage of the product life cycle. During this stage, a great deal of emphasis is placed on providing information to the customer. Usually people will not purchase a good or service until they know its characteristics and benefits. The expectation is that the information provided through promotion will help consumers make more intelligent purchasing decisions.

Some products and services require complex and detailed promotion. For instance, the promotions for automobiles, electronic equipment, hospital services, and bundled vacation packages are more lengthy and complex than promotions for simpler items, such as books or candy.

Promotions that inform are not used just for new products and services. Established brands that are in the later stages of the product life cycle can be improved or reformulated. Promotional messages are used to inform consumers about changes to these products. Also, new uses for old products are common. For example, Johnson & Johnson created a promotional campaign to reach a new segment of users—adults—for its baby shampoo. Arm & Hammer created an informational campaign to get consumers to put baking soda in refrigerators and on carpets. These are examples of promotion in its role of informing consumers.

PERSUADE

Persuasion attempts to encourage a customer to take a specific action, such as purchasing a product. It is designed to stimulate action. This term has a negative meaning for some people, but it should not be seen as negative. An example of persuasion is encouragement to buy healthier bread products.

Persuasion is often an important task of promotion during the growth stage of the product life cycle. At this point, customers should have a general awareness and some knowledge of how a product can fulfill their needs. The promotional task moves from informing the customer about a product to persuading the customer to buy. The marketer emphasizes the product's advantages over competitors' products. Persuasive promotions often use coupons, rebates, or free samples to provide additional incentives to buy.

Persuasion is used throughout the life cycle for products that are very competitive and similar to other brands. For example, marketers of soft drinks and toothpastes flood their markets with promotional activities that are designed to persuade people to switch brands. For these products, the need for new product information is not particularly strong.

Noise Though the communication process seems to be a direct path between the sender and the receiver, not all messages are clearly communicated. One of the major problems is called noise. **Noise** is interference that can cause the message to be interpreted by the receiver incorrectly. Noise occurs in all stages of the communication process. Examples of noise are competing messages, misinterpretation, radio static, poor quality printing, or the use of ambiguous or unfamiliar words. Marketers are continually working at identifying sources of noise and attempting to reduce and eliminate them.

Feedback The last concept associated with the communication process is feedback. **Feedback** is the receiver's reaction or response to the source's message. The concept of feedback is extremely important to the implementation of the marketing concept. Feedback, or the response to the promotional message, is how marketers measure the effectiveness of their promotional strategies.

Feedback may not take place immediately. For example, Pepsi-Cola may choose to send a message through the newspaper that includes a coupon to be redeemed for 50 cents off the purchase of a six-pack of a new Pepsi product. The feedback going from the receiver back to the sender does

GET THE MESSAGE

Magazines Put Readers Under the Microscope

Magazine advertising has long been one of the most effective message channels for businesses to deliver promotional messages to market segments. Now magazine publishers are helping their advertiser clients to really zero in on their targets by meticulously researching who their readers are.

Gourmet magazine went so far as to invade the homes of 30 of its readers—with their permission, of course—to grill them about their lifestyles, search through their cupboards for clues to their purchasing habits, and photograph their prized possessions. *Esquire* decided to do away with giveaways to media planners, such as umbrellas with the magazine's logo, and instead pour all available funds into reader research.

Time magazine, a general-interest weekly news magazine with very broad readership, is concentrating its research efforts on identifying three core groups of readers: families, businesspersons, and older readers. It even publishes special editions of the magazine with extra pages aimed at those market niches. The extra pages are not included in newsstand copies.

These research and development efforts are intended to differentiate magazines' readers from those of their competitors, so that advertisers can target their promotions ever more precisely. In that way, the chances of their messages reaching receptive receivers, who respond by buying their products, is greatly enhanced.

THINK CRITICALLY

1. Why would a magazine publisher want to narrowly define its readership base, since that would seemingly limit the advertisers who would be interested placing ads in the magazine?

2. How would you like it if a magazine that you subscribe to wanted to come into your house and go through your desk and cupboards?

not take place until the receiver uses the coupon to purchase the product. Feedback or lack of feedback is used to modify or change promotional messages.

What are the seven elements of the marketing communication process?

TYPES OF COMMUNICATION

Marketers study the communication process to determine the types of communication necessary for their products or services. The type of communication used depends on the product or service and the intended target market characteristics. There are two kinds of important communications for marketers, interpersonal and mass communication.

INTERPERSONAL COMMUNICATION

The first type of communication is interpersonal. **Interpersonal communication** involves two or more people in some kind of person-to-person exchange. This type of communication is usually two-way, with the communicators having the ability to respond to each other. An example of this type of communication is personal selling. When you walk into a department store and a salesperson assists you in selecting your purchase, interpersonal communication is occurring. The salesperson is asking questions and is receiving immediate answers from you.

Interpersonal communication is frequently used in business-to-business marketing. Many businesses have a professional sales staff to provide customers with information about available products and services. The salesperson's job is to meet the wants and needs of the customers by working one-on-one with each customer. This type of communication keeps the sales personnel in close contact with their customers and in a position to receive immediate feedback, both positive and negative, about their products or services.

MASS COMMUNICATION

Mass communication involves communicating to huge audiences, usually through mass media such as magazines, radio, television, or newspapers. Mass communication is one way. It does not provide the audience with a method of directly communicating with the sender.

An advertisement in a newspaper is an example of mass communication. A department store might place an advertisement in the local newspaper to inform customers of an upcoming sale. In this case, the senders do not know exactly who will and who will not read the advertisement. There is little opportunity for readers to ask direct questions about the sale or express pleasure or displeasure with it.

In an effort to overcome this lack of direct feedback, many businesses use other techniques to gauge the effectiveness of their promotions. They use coupons or directives to the consumer, such as "tell them Joe sent you," to gauge the effectiveness of their mass communications. Marketing research is also used to track consumer reactions to advertising and other mass communication techniques.

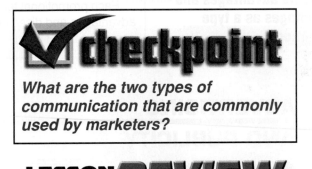

checkpoint

What are the two types of communication that are commonly used by marketers?

LESSON REVIEW

1. What are persuasive promotions designed to do, and at what stage of a product life cycle are they most likely to be used by marketers?

2. How does the promotional role of reminding differ from that of informing?

3. Why is proper encoding so important to the process of communicating a promotional message?

4. What does the phrase "the medium is the message" mean in the context of a promotional message?

5. In terms of mass vs. interpersonal communications, what is the advantage of using electronic communication through an Internet web site?

Big Advertisers Find Better Role for Internet

The world's largest advertisers are among the biggest users of Internet promotions, but they aren't doing it with banner ads. Instead, companies such as Unilever, Procter & Gamble, Coca-Cola, and General Motors Corp. are finding innovative ways to use sites of their own to serve their customers. They're using traditional media such as TV and magazine ads to draw people to their sites, where they can provide more detailed information in a highly targeted fashion, and also collect information about their customers for other marketing activities.

After a few years of experimenting with various Internet strategies, the companies found that traditional passive media are good for planting an idea in someone's mind. An active medium such as the Internet works better with people who already know they have an interest in a product and want more information.

At Unilever's SlimFast.com site, customers can find diet tips, keep track of their weight, and exchange messages about diet topics with other site users. Unilever and P&G use various product sites to gather customer information that is then used for both e-mail and direct mail promotions. Users of GM's site can get detailed information about its cars and trucks, including which dealers have the models they want in stock.

Rather than using the Internet merely as another advertising medium, these big advertisers are using e-marketing in conjunction with offline media to take advantage of the specific strengths each has to offer.

THINK CRITICALLY

1. What are the implications of this trend for general interest Internet sites that rely on banner advertising revenue?

2. Search the Internet for a music recording label's site and describe how it uses the communication abilities of the Web to promote its products.

disadvantage is cost. Though the cost per viewer might be low, there is no escaping the fact that McDonald's pays millions of dollars to send its messages through advertising.

The second disadvantage is that the target audience might not be in the right place to receive the message. Consumers might decide to watch a videotape instead of television, turn off the radio, or switch to a different station. What if the intended audience doesn't read a specific issue of the magazine or the newspaper on the day the advertisement appears? The advertiser cannot control consumers' viewing or reading habits. They can only predict consumers' tendencies. If they are wrong, the money is wasted.

The final disadvantage is advertising's impersonal nature. It communicates to you, but you cannot respond immediately. You cannot tell McDonald's that you like or dislike the advertisements or the product or service mentioned. Feedback returns to the advertiser very slowly, in terms of increased or decreased sales or other consumer actions.

PUBLICITY

Another type of promotion, publicity, is often overlooked. **Publicity** is a nonpaid form of communication about a business or organization (or its products and services) that is transmitted through a mass medium. Publicity is often a news story about an organization or its products or services.

Though the company receiving the publicity does not pay directly for the cost of the media used, there are still costs associated with publicity. A company often has a publicity or a public relations department with staff that work on developing the news stories and identifying opportunities for publicity. Those people will work closely with the media to try to get free coverage of their important information.

Advantages of Publicity The major advantage of publicity is the goodwill it can create for an organization, product, or service. **Goodwill** is the customer's positive feelings about an organization, product, or service. One example is the Disney Co. Disney works very hard to maintain a positive image as a good, wholesome source for family entertainment. As a result, Disney enjoys the goodwill of the public.

When the public hears or reads about the latest safety innovations developed by an auto manufacturer, that is also an example of positive publicity. All organizations are eager to receive good publicity. It keeps their products, services, or ideas in front of the public in a positive way.

Disadvantages of Publicity   The major disadvantage of publicity is that the organization has little control over it. Since it is generated by the media, the organization cannot cancel or change the reports. The same automobile manufacturer that enjoys publicity when the media reports new safety features does not welcome a report about the high incidence of accidents with its cars.

Name some advantages and disadvantages of advertising as a type of promotion.

PERSONAL
SELLING

The third major type of promotion is personal selling. **Personal selling** is person-to-person communication with potential customers in an effort to inform, persuade, or remind them to purchase an organization's products or services. Personal selling is commonly used in industry, where vendors meet with clients to inform them of potential products or services. This type of selling, *professional selling,* usually requires a large amount of information about the product or service and the customer's needs. It also requires a lot of follow-up even after a sale is made to insure that the client is satisfied with the product or service and will place a reorder.

Telephone companies have salespeople whose job is to call on large businesses to sell complete telephone systems. To sell a telephone system is a complex, time-consuming process that works best on a person-to-person basis. Another type of personal selling that you might be more familiar with is retail sales. As you walk into a sporting goods store, you are approached by a salesperson to assist you with your purchase. It is this person's job to question you about your needs and suggest a product that will satisfy them. As with professional selling, this salesperson can provide immediate feedback to your questions and concerns.

JUDGMENT CALL

Cause-Related Marketing Requires PR Savvy

Cause-related marketing has become so popular that marketing disciplines have been fighting over whose turf it is. It used to be that cause-related promotions typically were one-time affairs—maybe an event sponsorship by a corporation that benefited a national charity. The corporation put up some cash to underwrite expenses, tying in its products or brand name and garnering some favorable exposure, and the charity got the event proceeds. Then both went their separate ways, at least until the next promotion.

Then the emphasis shifted to building deeper relationships with long-term campaigns. Charities and causes now go to great lengths to market themselves to corporations as worthy partners, even going so far as retaining marketing firms themselves. Companies carefully analyze the implications and potential benefits of identifying themselves with various worthy causes before selecting one suitable for a long-term relationship.

Increasingly, businesses rely on publicity and public relations specialists rather than sales promotion agencies to manage cause-related marketing. The thinking is that PR experts are experienced in complex corporate citizenship issues and better able to deal with the full implications of cause-related marketing. They recognize, for example, that if a company develops an initiative to aid an environmental cause while itself engaged in environmentally questionable practices, the campaign might draw hostile media coverage and quickly backfire. Since longer relationships with causes seem to deliver more benefits on both sides, it is crucial that such campaigns be thoroughly planned.

THINK CRITICALLY

1. If a company has engaged in unpopular practices in the past and now wants to clean up its image and repair the damage, would a cause-related marketing initiative be a good idea?

2. Is the growth of cause-related marketing good for society, or just an expression of corporate opportunism masquerading as corporate citizenship?

ADVANTAGES OF PERSONAL SELLING

The first advantage of personal selling is personal contact. It can be much more informative and persuasive than advertising because of the person-to-person interaction. The salesperson in the sporting goods store can attempt to satisfy your needs immediately.

The second advantage is that with person-to-person contact, feedback from the customer is immediate. Positive responses can be acted on immediately, and hopefully a sale can be made. Negative reactions can be responded to with additional questions, or alternative suggestions.

DISADVANTAGES OF PERSONAL SELLING

There are also disadvantages to personal selling. The major disadvantage is the per-person cost. Though the cost of advertising is high, advertising reaches millions of people. Personal selling reaches one customer at a time, one sale at a time. The cost per customer can be extremely high. In professional sales it might take several months of planning and sales calls involving many people before a company decides on a telephone system. Every sales encounter doesn't result in a sale. There are many meetings, calls, and interactions with customers that do not result in a sale.

Name an advantage and a disadvantage of personal selling as a type of promotion.

SALES PROMOTION

The last type of promotion available to marketers is called sales promotion. **Sales promotions** are activities or materials that offer consumers a direct incentive to buy a good or service. Examples of sales promotions are coupons, sweepstakes, contests, free samples, and rebates. Sometimes products are given away with services, such as a toothbrush from your dentist or a refrigerator magnet with a dry cleaning service. These are examples of sales promotions.

It is important not to confuse the term *sales promotion* with *promotion*. Sales promotion is only one aspect of the larger area of promotion, which includes advertising, publicity, and personal selling.

ADVANTAGES OF SALES PROMOTION

There are more advantages than disadvantages to the use of sales promotion. The first advantage is that it generates immediate, short-term sales. The offer of a free product or a cents-off coupon is often enough incentive to the customer to purchase a product. Fast food restaurants such as Hardee's and McDonald's have had continued success with their toy promotions.

The second advantage of sales promotion is its use to support other parts of the promotional campaign. For example, a television advertisement introduces a new fat-free ice cream. Later that week, the consumer receives a coupon in the mail for the new ice cream. On Saturday, when the potential customer is doing the weekly shopping, a representative of the ice cream company is offering

free samples at the supermarket. The potential customer tastes it, puts a gallon in the shopping cart, and uses the coupon at the register. A product is sold with the help of sales promotion.

DISADVANTAGES OF SALES PROMOTION

The main disadvantage of sales promotion is the cost. It is estimated that over $90 billion is spent every year on sales promotion activities. If the promotion does not result in a significant sales increase, the business will lose money on the product or service.

Name an advantage and a disadvantage of sales promotion as a type of promotion.

1. In what sense is the impersonal nature of advertising an advantage?

2. How do marketers attempt to overcome the disadvantage created by the expense of mass-media advertising?

3. While personal contact is generally an advantage of personal selling, how might it work to a business' disadvantage in some circumstances?

4. Why is good publicity often more effective than advertising?

5. Why is reliance on publicity an inherently risky promotional strategy for a business?

6. What response from potential customers do most sales promotions try to generate?

GOALS

- Explain the four major factors that affect the promotional mix.
- Describe the seven steps in the promotional planning process.

Marketers usually do not rely on one type of promotion to market a product or service. They combine types of promotion in a promotional mix to take advantage of the benefits of each. The specific ingredients of the promotional mix depend on a number of factors, including the target market, the marketing mix, the business' promotional policies and objectives, and costs and available financial resources.

Develop a promotional mix for a part-time business that you could operate out of your home. Include elements of all four of the principal types of promotion. Explain how the target market, the marketing mix, and the financial resources of the business drive the promotional mix.

THE PROMOTIONAL MIX

Marketers combine promotional tools to develop a promotional mix (see Figure 15-4). The **promotional mix** is a blend of the promotional elements of advertising, personal selling, publicity, and sales promotion into a strategy for delivering a message to the target market.

It would be very unusual for an organization to rely on only one type of promotion. For example, it is not likely that an airline would rely only on advertising, a university only on personal selling, a lawn mower manufacturer only on publicity, or a restaurant only on sales promotion. Yet it does happen. In a highly unusual one-medium campaign, Motel 6 reached millions of consumers. With one announcer, radio spots that promised to "leave the light on" were very successful.

FIGURE 15-4
Advertising, personal selling, publicity, and sales promotion work together to create a promotional mix.

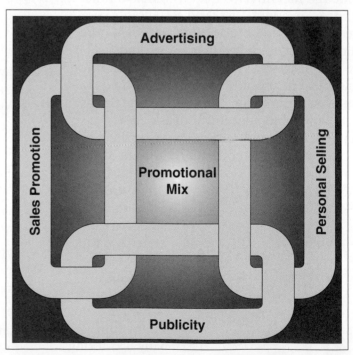

Elements of a Promotional Mix

FIGURE 15-5
Developing a promotional mix is a major responsibility of marketers. Many factors affect the choices they make about the blend of advertising, sales promotion, personal selling, and publicity.

Factors that Affect the Promotional Mix

| Marketing Mix | Target Market | Promotional Policy and Objectives | Financial Resources |

Promotional Mix

Target Market The second factor in determining an appropriate promotional mix is the target market. It is critical to remember the target market's characteristics so that the promotional campaign can be focused on their needs. It would be inappropriate to advertise furniture on MTV, because MTV viewers are not the primary target market for furniture. The marketer needs to develop a specific promotional mix that reaches each target market.

Policy and Objectives The third factor in determining a promotional mix is the company's policy and objectives for promotional activities. Some companies have specific promotional guidelines. Hershey Foods Corp. did not advertise its product at all until after 1950.

In most cases, businesses rely on a mix of all four elements to bring their products or services to the attention of the target market. How firms blend these activities and which elements they use depend on several factors (see Figure 15-5).

Marketing Mix First, the promotional mix depends on the characteristics of the marketing mix that was developed for the product or service. The stage of the product life cycle might dictate the best promotional strategy. The price of a product also determines the type of promotional mix. A very expensive product might need more personal selling and less television advertising. If the product is seasonal, it changes the characteristics of the promotional mix. Consumers do not hear very much about snow blowers until winter. Then there is often a media blitz to inform consumers about them and to encourage them to buy. Advertising may be accompanied by a coupon or rebate. There will usually be a salesperson in the store to help the customer. The company will try to get publicity to support the other types of promotion.

Chuck E. Cheese's Goes Bilingual to Target Hispanics

Chuck E. Cheese's, the fun-and-games pizza chain targeted to kids, has begun zeroing in on a growing market segment it felt it was missing with mainstream promotions. Now with bilingual commercials in English and Spanish, the Texas-based company hopes to reach the Hispanic children who make up at least 16 percent of the U.S. youth market. The ads began running on the Nickelodeon cable channel during shows that are based on Latino characters and culture.

In one of the commercials, some Hispanic kids are showing their parents how to play the games at a Chuck E. Cheese's restaurant. Their generous assessment of the old folks' skills: "No esta mal novatos."—"Not bad for beginners."

Chuck E. Cheese's operates nearly 400 restaurants across the country. They are known for their kid-friendly games and entertainment and have become a birthday party tradition in many families. The chain has been working more Spanish-language elements into its promotions and operations for several years. The next step is more Spanish on its web site. Hispanics are the largest and fastest-growing minority group in the United States. Much of the U.S. Hispanic population is located in the Southwest.

THINK CRITICALLY

1. Do you think non-Spanish-speaking kids will be confused or turned off by the bilingual ads?

2. Why is it important for Chuck E. Cheese's to promote its restaurants to Hispanic children and families?

---

might be scaled down or eliminated because of the expense. Promotional financing should not be done with "whatever money is left over." It requires careful planning and managerial commitment to be effective. Promotional budgets are often based on the expenditures for the previous year or a certain percentage of expected sales.

Select the Promotional Mix   After the budget is set, the marketing manager must determine the most appropriate promotional strategies to reach the target market, achieve organizational

objectives, and remain within the budgetary guidelines. In this stage the mix of advertising, personal selling, publicity, and sales promotion will be decided.

Implement the Promotional Plan   After the promotional mix is determined, the implementation schedule must be set. This includes naming people or departments responsible for implementation of various parts of the plan and determining the timetable for each promotional strategy. Specific dollars from the total promotional budget will be allocated to each activity.

Evaluate the Results The final step in promotional planning is to evaluate the plan against the objectives that were set.

Marketing managers must carefully evaluate their strategies to determine if they should be continued, altered, or changed completely. Each promotional activity will be measured against the promotional plan. Research will be used to gather information about consumer perceptions and actions before and after the promotion has occurred.

Gauging Effectiveness

The success of most promotions ultimately depends on the effect they have on business profits. The tricky part is figuring out which parts of a complex promotional mix are responsible for what portion of subsequent changes in revenue and profits. In most cases, there is no way to tie changes in revenue directly to a specific promotion, so marketers have to use indirect means to estimate a promotion's effectiveness.

Magazines and newspapers track paid circulation, total circulation, and readership estimates, the latter factoring in how many people typically read each copy.

Electronic media have developed new ways of measuring success. Web site hits are the number of people who log on to a site. Clickthrough rates are the portion of viewers who click on an ad to see the sponsor's site, where the amount of time each spends at the site is also tracked. Conversion rates are the portion of viewers who follow through by buying something or registering for whatever is being promoted.

THINK CRITICALLY

1. If the weekly Rabbit Hash Business Journal has a paid circulation of 5,000, gives out 800 free copies, and estimates that 5.5 people read each, how many people read the paper each week?

2. If a popular web site averages 10 million hits a day, and an advertising agency figures a banner ad for a contest promotion on the site will yield a clickthrough rate of 3% and a conversion rate of 22%, how many people per day can it expect to register for the promotion?

checkpoint

What are the seven steps in the promotional planning process?

LESSON REVIEW

1. How does the marketing mix affect the choice of the best promotional mix?

2. If a business has numerous target markets, should it develop one promotional mix suitable for them all?

3. What characteristics should promotional objectives possess?

4. Why should budgeting be done only after promotional objectives have been established?

5. What is involved in evaluating a promotional plan?

CHAPTER 15

SUMMARY

Lesson 15.1
A. Promotion is only one element of the marketing mix. To be used effectively, it must be blended with decisions made about product, price, and distribution. Promotion is designed to inform, persuade, and remind consumers.

B. The communication process is the transfer of a message from a sender to a receiver. The process comprises seven basic elements—a sender who originates the message, encoding by the sender, a message channel, decoding, a receiver, noise along the way, and feedback or response.

C. The two types of communication commonly employed in marketing are interpersonal and mass communication. Interpersonal communication is characterized by a person-to-person exchange. Mass communication is a one-way exchange from a sender to a large number of receivers.

Lesson 15.2
A. Types of promotion include advertising, publicity, personal selling, and sales promotion. Advertising is any paid form of non-personal communication sent through a mass medium by an organization about its products or services. Publicity is a non-paid form of communication about a business or its products that is transmitted through mass media.

B. Personal selling is person-to-person communication with potential customers to inform, persuade, or remind them to purchase an organization's products or services.

C. Sales promotions are activities or materials that offer consumers a direct incentive to buy a good or service. Examples include coupons, sweepstakes, and free samples.

Lesson 15.3
A. Marketers usually combine types of promotion in a promotional mix to take advantage of each. The specific ingredients of the mix depend on factors like the target market, the marketing mix, the business' promotional policies and objectives, and costs.

B. The seven-step promotional planning process helps develop and implement successful focused, consumer-driven promotions based on achievable goals.

REVIEW MARKETING CONCEPTS

There are four types of promotional activities within marketing: advertising, personal selling, publicity, and sales promotion. Read the following activities and identify which type of promotional activity is involved.

1. A press conference announcing a new automobile safety feature.
2. A coupon for 50 cents off the purchase price of toothpaste.
3. A shoe salesperson suggesting the purchase of shoelaces to a customer.
4. Skywriting over a football stadium.
5. A full-page ad in a newspaper devoted to the sale of seafood products.
6. A hospital inviting people to visit its new pediatric wing.
7. An end-of-aisle display offering a free cooler with the purchase of a case of bottled water.
8. A telemarketing call encouraging you to buy a magazine subscription.
9. A lobbyist encouraging a legislator to vote for a particular bill.
10. The offer of a chance to win a free trip to purchasers of a new automobile.
11. A school sending its drama troupe to entertain in a retirement home.
12. A billboard depicting a new golf course.

REVIEW MARKETING TERMS

Match the terms listed with the definitions. Some terms may not be used.

13. Interference that can cause the message to be interpreted by the receiver incorrectly.

14. The blend of the promotional elements of advertising, personal selling, publicity, and sales promotion into a strategy for delivering a message to the target market.

15. The medium the sender chooses to transmit the message.

16. Involves communicating to huge audiences, usually through mass media such as magazines, radio, television, or newspapers.

17. Interpreting the message or symbols and converting them into concepts and ideas.

18. The receiver's reaction or response to the source's message.

19. The person or persons to whom the message is directed.

20. Involves two or more people in some kind of person-to-person exchange.

21. The carefully arranged sequence of promotions designed around a common theme responsive to specific objectives.

22. Paid form of nonpersonal communication sent through a mass medium by an organization about its products or services.

23. Any form of communication used to inform, persuade, or remind consumers about an organization's goods or services.

24. Person-to-person communication with potential customers in an effort to inform, persuade, or remind them to purchase an organization's products or services.

25. The source or originator of the message in the communication process.

26. Nonpaid form of communication about a business or organization (or its products and services) that is transmitted through a mass medium.

27. The customer's positive feelings about an organization, product, or service.

28. An activity or material that offers consumers a direct incentive to buy a good or service.

29. Putting the message into language or symbols that are familiar to the intended receiver.

30. In marketing, the transfer of a message from a sender to a receiver to facilitate an exchange.

a. advertising
b. communication process
c. decoding
d. encoding
e. feedback
f. goodwill
g. interpersonal communication
h. mass communication
i. message channel
j. noise
k. personal selling
l. promotion
m. promotional mix
n. promotional plan
o. publicity
p. receiver
q. sales promotions
r. sender

APPLY MARKETING FUNCTIONS

MARKETING RESEARCH

31. Marketers use a variety of media when creating a campaign for a product. Pick one product that you are familiar with and track its campaign for one week. Write down all television and radio commercials that relate to the product. Check the newspapers for coupons, print advertisements, or publicity pieces about your product. After one week, determine the target market and the theme of the campaign. Be prepared to report your findings to the class.

32. Four magazines that direct their messages at a similar target audience are *Vogue, Harper's Bazaar, Elle,* and *Mirabella.* The following chart shows the number of ad pages sold between January and June for each of these publications over a three-year period.

THE IMPACT OF ADVERTISING

Magazine	Year 1 Ad Pages	Year 2 Ad Pages	Year 3 Ad Pages
Vogue	885.12	906.26	832.43
Harper's Bazaar	376.90	301.14	499.19
Elle	553.58	490.06	367.96
Mirabella	323.12	264.83	268.27

a. Calculate the total number of pages sold every year.
b. Calculate the percentage share each magazine has for each time period.
c. Create a bar graph comparing Year 1, Year 2, and Year 3 for the four publications, based on total pages sold.

MARKETING PLANNING

33. Every community has residential real estate marketing activity occurring in it. Real estate marketers all use some form of promotion. Those forms of promotion cover the whole range of promotional methods. For this activity, you are a residential real estate marketer. You must decide what percentage of your promotional effort should be expended on each of the methods for your community. You have 100 percent of your money and effort available for promotion. It is your task to divide that 100 percent among advertising, publicity, personal selling, and sales promotion efforts. Tell how you would divide your budget and effort and give reasons for your decisions.

34. Promotional techniques are not just for businesses that are selling products and services and hoping to make a profit. Many organizations, such as the American Lung Association, the Red Cross, and political parties, use promotional techniques to communicate their messages and ideas.

Choose a not-for-profit organization with which you are familiar. Demonstrate how you believe they use each of the promotional techniques by preparing a written or oral report.

MARKETING MANAGEMENT

35. Marketing managers and planners understand that a good management plan that includes promotional activities requires well-written objectives. Objectives help focus the campaign and allow the results to be measured and analyzed.

The following list contains several products and services. It is your task in this activity to develop two promotional objectives that are appropriate for these products or services. Make certain the objectives are achievable through promotion. You may want to focus on a specific role of promotion: to inform, persuade, or remind.
a. General Motors four-wheel drive vehicles
b. Gourmet jelly beans
c. Wooden stepladders
d. Guided tours of South American Mayan ruins
e. Artificial tanning lotion

36. A good marketing or promotional manager can demonstrate talent, skill, and intuition by developing promotional strategies to achieve promotional objectives. For each one of the objectives you developed in the previous activity, suggest one promotional strategy that you think would be most effective in helping to achieve the objective. Explain why you think it would be most effective.

MARKETING TECHNOLOGY

37. Search the Internet for product sites that provide information or promotional tools related to the products listed below. Write a half-page summary for each product site, indicating address (URL) of the web site, the operator of the site, and the kinds of information or tools that can be accessed.
a. automobile
b. diet food
c. hair care products
d. lawn and garden supplies
e. medicine
f. interior design products

38. Search the Internet for recent industry data on business spending for promotional activities. Write a one-page report summarizing the information you find.

MARKETING IN ACTION

CASE STUDY

"WE LOVE TO SEE YOU SMILE"

Richard and Maurice McDonald of San Bernardino, California, converted a barbecue drive-in with carhops into the world's first McDonald's in 1948. In 1954, the brothers granted Ray Kroc exclusive franchising rights to their limited-menu, self-service concept. Kroc opened his first McDonald's restaurant in Des Plains, Illinois, in April 1955 and founded the company that evolved into McDonald's Corp. McDonald's commitment to high standards and strictly enforced cooking procedures helps to ensure uniform quality of McDonald's food wherever customers visit.

McDonald's has successfully expanded its operations around the world. The corporation now has over 28,000 restaurants in 120 countries. Sales for 1999 totaled $38 billion, with 60% of operating income coming from restaurants outside the United States. When McDonald's opened in Moscow, excited people lined up in the cold for hours before the grand opening. Thousands of applications were received for approximately 700 jobs.

CAREFULLY CRAFTED MARKETING CAMPAIGNS

McDonald's carefully chooses its marketing strategies. Television programs are analyzed to determine the best environment for the airing of McDonald's commercials. McDonald's wants to associate its advertising with entertaining, responsible programs. Before a commercial is placed nationally, prime-time programs are previewed by a screening service. Then McDonald's advertising agency reviews the screening reports to make decisions regarding the placement of commercials within a show.

McDonald's is very aware of the influence that young children have on their parents. Happy Meals with toys from popular kids' movies attract the attention of many youngsters. McDonald's introduced its Playland to further entertain youngsters while they visit their favorite restaurant. Ronald McDonald is a well-recognized character for children and adults.

A large part of McDonald's success is due to the corporation's positive public image. Ronald McDonald Houses provide a "home-away-from-home" for families of seriously ill children receiving treatment in nearby hospitals. The first Ronald McDonald House opened in Philadelphia in 1974. Kim Hill was undergoing treatment for leukemia, and her parents grew tired of sleeping in the hospital waiting room and eating meals out of vending machines. Fred Hill, who was a player for the Philadelphia Eagles at the time, rallied support from his teammates, Children's Hospital's general manager, and local McDonald's franchisees to create the Ronald McDonald House. There are now 206 Ronald McDonald Houses in 19 countries. Each house relies on the people and businesses in its own community to provide the additional funds, goods, and services necessary for its operation.

Ronald McDonald Mobile Care Program works with local hospitals and health systems to bring education, preventive medicine, and dental services into neighborhoods with unmet healthcare needs. This special program is literally a positive promotion campaign on wheels.

Ronald McDonald's national and global network has awarded more than $225 million in grants to children's programs worldwide. Ronald McDonald House Charities has partnered with *Prevent Child Abuse* to play an important role in ensuring the health, safety, and successful development of American children through Healthy Families America (HFA). This unique program gives support to new parents nationwide with intensive home-visiting services for those at greatest risk. With Ronald McDonald House Charities' help, HFA grew from 20 sites in 1992 to 345 sites in 41 U.S. states and Canada.

SATISFYING CUSTOMERS WITH MORE CHOICES

McDonald's launched a "new tastes menu" in January 2001 to counter declining sales in the United States. The menu offers more than 40 new tastes, a number that will grow as new products are developed and added. Local markets will select up to four of these menu items to be featured in their individual markets and rotate them with other selections throughout the year. Some of the new items include Big N' Tasty, Crispy Chicken McClub, Arctic Orange Shake, and Bacon Ranch Crispy Chicken. McDonald's has also diversified its operations, with hotels in Switzerland and McCafes in Portugal and Austria. McDonald's ketchup is sold in German grocery stores.

McDonald's new U.S. advertising campaign focuses on delivering customer smiles. One of the initial broadcast spots is called "A Day in the Life" and tells the story of a crew person and customer experiencing the benefits of the new "Made for You" kitchen system. Another commercial entitled "Are We There Yet?" shows a father alone in his car at a McDonald's drive-through, having children speak through his cell phone to directly place their orders from home. McDonald's customer-order display screens allow the father to view and confirm the children's orders. The advertising campaign is intended to show the best of both worlds—specific improvements and changes McDonald's has made, as well as a reminder to customers of their love affair with McDonald's.

McDonald's also is aware of a maturing population. More senior citizens now appear in McDonald's commercials as both workers and customers. These commercials serve two purposes—to show that McDonald's is an equal opportunity employer and that it's a good place for senior citizens to eat.

THINK CRITICALLY

1. What major challenges does McDonald's face in the United States?

2. Why do you think McDonald's takes part in so many community service projects?

3. Why do you think McDonald's has to adjust its menu for a global marketplace?

---

http://www.deca.org/publications/HS_Guide/guidetoc.html

DECA PREP

CIVIC CONSCIOUSNESS PROJECT

McDonald's realizes the importance of community service or commitment to the community. In that spirit, you and a partner must propose a community service project.

PROJECT DESCRIPTION Write a one-page description of the project.

INTRODUCTION Explain the background of your project.

PURPOSE Describe the purpose of the project. Give rationale for selecting the community service project. Describe the benefits of the project.

ORGANIZATION
Prepare an organizational chart that shows who will be involved in the effort, and their job descriptions. Describe the project and show necessary documentation. What is the impact goal for the beneficiary (community, young people, citizens)?

EVALUATION Evaluate the project. What was the impact of the community service project? Give recommendations to improve the project in the future.

BE CREATIVE WITH ADVERTISING

LESSON 16.1 *WHAT IS ADVERTISING?*

LESSON 16.2 *DEVELOPING AN ADVERTISING PLAN*

LESSON 16.3 *PUTTING THE AD PLAN INTO ACTION*

NEWSLINE

WHERE'S THE CONSUMER?

The New York Department of Consumer Affairs analyzed over 2,000 advertisements in 10 magazines to determine minority representation. The results of the analysis show that more minority group members are being included in magazine advertisements. The percentage of minority group models used in advertisements rose from 3.4 percent in one year to 5.2 percent the following year. That's the good news.

The bad news is that advertisers presented minority models in stereotypical roles. They were often shown as musicians, athletes, or objects of pity in corporate philanthropy advertisements. Minority models were seldom portrayed as consumers. One car company showed minority group members in 24 of its 134 ads. However, only one of those ads showed a minority group member as a car buyer. That buyer was a professional basketball player.

A separate study of 14 of the most frequent advertisers in the magazines showed that half included no minority group members in their advertisements at all. Finally, two of the magazines that have over 25 percent minority readership had less than 6 percent of their advertisements containing minority group members.

THINK CRITICALLY

1. Why is it important for advertisers to include members of minority groups in their advertisements if they want minorities to buy and consume their products?

2. Why do you think some advertisers continue to exclude minorities or portray them only in stereotypical roles?

CAREER OPPORTUNITY
SENIOR GRAPHIC ARTIST

POINT YOUR BROWSER

www.corpview.com

TeleView is looking for someone who possesses the following attributes.

- Problem solving, project organization, and time management skills
- Excellent interpersonal skills
- Drive and flexibility
- Up-to-date technical communication skills
- Excellent customer relation skills, which help us maintain product loyalty
- Desire to work in an invigorating, team-oriented environment

TeleView's offices are modern, with state-of-the-art technologies at your disposal. Commuter access to the TeleView office complex is facilitated by two freeway exits that provide easy access from picturesque communities to the north and south of the TeleView offices.

Location: Boulder, Colorado

The main responsibilities of the job include the following.

- Working with Corporate Communications writers, editors, designers, and other artists to generate conceptual art using a variety of platforms and graphics software
- Maintaining project workflow documents and coordinating with workgroup teams
- Meeting deadlines
- Producing accurate work of high quality, including conceptual illustrations and page layouts, both online and in hard copy
- Creating, or assisting in the creation of, a variety of Web and Intranet online art
- Creating art to be used as online graphics, for online movies, and for hard copy publications
- Proofing illustrations and text in documents

- Checking film proof, bluelines, crops, and color
- Supervising work conducted by outside photo and film labs and suppliers

The job requires the following education, skills, and experience.

- Associate's degree in Graphic Arts, B.A. or M.A. preferred
- Minimum of three years professional experience
- Computer experience with the latest Macintosh and Windows platforms required
- Graphic file conversion skills are a must

Portfolio required at the time of the interview.

THINK CRITICALLY

1. Prepare a cover letter written by a person who is qualified for this job and interested in applying for it.

2. This position is part of the Corporate Communications department rather than the Marketing department. How do you think that affects the desirability of the job?

3. Search want ads or the Internet for a job similar to TeleView's senior graphic artist. What type of compensation package is being offered for the job?

16.1 WHAT IS ADVERTISING?

GOALS

- Explain the advantages and disadvantages of advertising as a type of promotion.
- Define organizational advertising and product advertising and distinguish between the two types.
- Describe the ways in which advertising is regulated by the government.

Advertising is any form of non-personal promotional communication by an identified sponsor. The distinguishing characteristics of advertising are that the organization pays for the message, and that it is sent to an audience through a mass medium. The name of the sponsor of the advertising is clearly stated, and that sponsor controls the message that is sent.

Advertising as a promotional device has several distinct advantages over other types of promotion, including that it can reach large numbers of people in diverse locations at a relatively low cost per person. Among its disadvantages is that advertisers have little control over who actually sees their ads. Ads come in two basic types, those that promote an organization and those that feature a product or service. Advertising is regulated by government and is also subject to self-regulation by advertisers.

Cut out an advertisement from a newspaper or magazine and write a 300-word explanation of why you think it is effective.

THE PROS AND CONS OF ADVERTISING

Ask someone how wave theory applies to acoustical engineering and you will probably get a blank stare. Ask someone how the writings of Montaigne apply to modern-day problems and you will probably get another blank stare. But ask someone what makes effective advertising and it's a good bet that you will get a lengthy response. People may tell you what they believe and do not believe in the ads they have seen. They will often have an opinion about the amount of advertising they are exposed to and the quality of the ads. Even though advertising is technical and complex, most people believe they know a great deal about it.

Advertising is very big business. The expenditures for advertising in the United States are more than $200 billion per year.

Over the last few decades, the leading advertising media have been newspapers and television, although television advertising has been increasing at a faster rate. The Internet and direct mail are growing in importance, while outdoor advertising has declined as a percentage of total advertising spending. Radio has remained relatively constant.

Billions of dollars are spent on advertising every year, with some industries advertising more than others. For example, businesses that sell games and toys spend a large percentage of their sales dollars on advertising. Businesses that sell beverages also spend a lot of money on advertising. Pepsi, Coca-Cola, Folgers, and Maxwell House, for example, all have extensive advertising plans and budgets.

Businesses are not the only organizations that use advertising. Churches, educational institutions, political organizations, and government agencies advertise.

ADVANTAGES OF ADVERTISING

There are many advantages to advertising as a method of promotion. Advertising can be used to communicate to a large audience in various geographic locations. A single television ad might reach 30 million viewers or more. Several large city newspapers reach over one million readers every day. In the case of magazine ads, the audience reached is increased when more than one reader reads the magazine. For example, several dozen people may read a single copy of *Time* in a dentist's office. Each of those people is exposed to advertisements contained in the magazine.

A second advantage is that the cost per viewer for advertising is relatively low.

★★★★★★★★★ JUDGMENT CALL

Vying for Control of TV Screens

The advent of digital personal video recorders that can manipulate TV programming has brought a long-simmering conflict to a head. Who should control what viewers watch when they turn on their TV sets? The individual viewer? The network or station operator? Or the advertisers?

Viewers have been able to watch free television programming for decades, but only because advertisers assumed that, when people sat down to watch The Ed Sullivan Show or the latest episode of The Sopranos, most of them would also watch the commercials interspersed with the programming. As ad clutter grew, viewers became less tolerant of interruptions, so inevitably technology was developed that allowed them to skip over the ads.

First VCRs enabled them to do it, but it was a very cumbersome process. Among other things, it required them to prerecord an entire show on a videocassette and then manually fast-forward through commercials while watching at a later time. PVRs (personal video recorders), which unlike VCRs use digital technology, now make ad avoidance much easier. There are no cassettes to fumble with, no manual fast-forwarding is required, and the necessary time delay is minimal so you can watch programming almost as it is being broadcast.

PVRs make ad avoidance so easy that counter-technology was developed. Essentially, it encodes programming in a way that makes it impossible for PVRs to skip the commercials. Advertisers maintain they should have the right to do that because they're paying for the programming. Viewers contend that they wouldn't be watching the shows at all without PVRs, so advertisers aren't any worse off if they use them to skip the commercials.

THINK CRITICALLY

1. Why might advertisers be better off just giving in to viewers and dealing with ad avoidance by other means?

2. What is the likely outcome if advertisers come to the conclusion that TV ads are not reaching the desired audiences?

A television ad that costs $300,000 to produce and broadcast may reach as many as 30 million viewers. That results in a cost per 1,000 viewers of only $10.

A third advantage is that the advertiser can target the ad to a specific audience. The organization can customize the words, medium, graphics, timing, size, or length of the advertisement based on the target market. For example, if an advertiser wants to reach Spanish-speaking women in Tucson, Arizona, the ad can be placed on a Spanish radio station, a Spanish-language television channel, or in a Spanish-language newspaper.

DISADVANTAGES OF ADVERTISING

Advertising also has some drawbacks. First, the communication is one-way—advertiser to consumer. If a customer asks a salesperson a question, there is an opportunity for a discussion. A customer seeing an advertisement on television is unable to ask questions about the product or service being advertised.

A second drawback is that advertisers have no control over who might be watching, reading, or listening to their advertisements. Though they work very hard to make sure the ad is directed at the appropriate target market, whether consumers see or hear the ad is another question. Television commercials are often a good time to get something to eat, have a conversation, or start the laundry. Another barrier to reaching the target audience is the use of VCRs and personal video recorders (PVRs) to delete commercials from prerecorded shows. This is bad news for advertisers who have spent millions of dollars trying to attract the viewers' attention.

A third disadvantage is the total cost of placing advertisements. Although the cost per viewer is quite low for a $200,000 ad on national television, the advertiser must have the $200,000 to spend. This sometimes eliminates small and local businesses from many types of mass media advertising.

What are two advantages and two disadvantages of advertising as a promotional device?

TYPES OF ADVERTISING

The three purposes of advertising are to inform, persuade, and remind customers. The message can communicate information about products and services or about the businesses that sell the products and services. These objectives are accomplished by using two types of advertising—organizational advertising or product advertising.

ORGANIZATIONAL ADVERTISING

The first type of advertising is called organizational advertising. **Organizational advertising** is designed to promote ideas, images, and issues associated with a company or organization. The most prominent characteristic of organizational advertising is that specific products, services, or prices are not featured in the advertisement. Instead, the benefits of the business or organization to customers or society are the main themes of the advertisement.

For years, the DuPont Chemical Co. used the slogan, "Better things for better living through chemistry." This advertising slogan was used to promote and strengthen the image of DuPont. BASF promoted its business with advertisements that said, "We don't make the product, we make the product better." During the halftime of televised college football games, the colleges whose teams are playing in the game often show promotional messages about the schools. These video promotions, a form of organizational advertising, are designed to promote the image of those universities.

PRODUCT ADVERTISING

The second type of advertising is product advertising. **Product advertising** is used by organizations to sell specific products. A product advertisement can be identified by the presence of a specific product, service, or price in the advertisement. The

U.S. Postal Service sells stamps. Soft drink companies sell colas. The Schwinn bicycle company sells bicycles. The Sierra Club invites you to go on one of its tours. In each case, the organization is promoting a product or service in its advertisements and not just its organizational image.

What is the major distinguishing characteristic between organizational advertising and product advertising?

REGULATING
ADVERTISING

Advertisers must be honest and ethical in their professional activities. Almost all advertisers follow regulations established by federal, state, and local government agencies, as well as their own professional code of ethics. The rules are designed to protect consumers and competitors from unfair and inappropriate promotional practices.

The Federal Trade Commission and the Federal Communications Commission use several approaches to guard against inappropriate advertising practices. These approaches include the requirements of full disclosure, substantiation, cease and desist orders, corrective advertising, and fines.

Full Disclosure   The requirement of full disclosure demands that all information necessary for a customer to make a safe and informed decision be provided in a promotional message. For example, if a product is promoted as being a diet product, the label must tell the number of calories and the amount of fat contained in the product.

Substantiation   Substantiation requires that an organization be required to

prove all of the claims it makes in its promotional messages. If an audiotape is promoted as suitable for recording music, then the advertiser must be able to prove that it has tested the tape for that purpose.

Cease and Desist   Cease-and-desist orders require firms to discontinue a promotional activity that is considered deceptive. The organization may not be forced to admit guilt or pay fines, as long as it obeys the cease-and-desist order.

Corrective Ads   Corrective advertising demands that an organization run a new advertisement to correct any false impressions left by previous ones. For example, Listerine was told to spend $10.2 million in advertising to correct prior messages claiming that the product was a cold remedy. Listerine ran ads with the following phrase: "Listerine will not help prevent colds or sore throats or lessen their severity."

Fines   The final remedy to inappropriate promotion is a fine. Fines are monetary penalties imposed on an organization for deceptive promotion. A company may be required to pay a large sum of money to

DIGITAL DIGEST

Ad Avoidance Technology

The digital technology used in personal video recorders (PVRs) is about to revolutionize television advertising, transforming it from a mass media to one that permits precise targeting of ads. Since people are no longer required to watch commercial advertisements on television—and research indicates that many of the viewers who are most desirable demographically are active ad avoiders—advertisers will have to get people's permission beforehand. That might not be all bad, from either side of the exchange.

Technology now allows people with PVRs to skip over commercials, essentially by prerecording programming and playing it back without the clutter. The next step is for viewers to opt to watch commercials for certain products or services in which they are interested. The same technology that now allows viewers to avoid watching commercials can also be used to feed them only those that they want to watch.

It works in a manner somewhat similar to e-mail message services that recipients register to receive. For example, if a person is in the market for a new convertible, he or she would punch a few buttons to program the TV set, and all the fast food and laundry detergent ads would be replaced with car ads that are downloaded to that set. Advertisers will pay for the service, but in return they'll be connected to a highly targeted market segment. Most importantly, it will be a viewer who has willingly chosen to see its ads, and who is eager to buy the product.

THINK CRITICALLY

1. What kinds of privacy concerns might viewers have using these opt-in advertising services?

2. What is this practice likely to do to television advertising production costs?

the government if it is found guilty of engaging in deceptive promotions.

Self-Regulation In addition to government restrictions, media have developed voluntary standards for advertising practices. For example, the National Association of Broadcasters monitors the ads placed on television and radio for truth in advertising. Other groups such as the Better Business Bureau and the American Association of Advertising Agencies also participate in the self-regulation of advertising.

What are the five ways the federal government guards against inappropriate advertising?

1. What is advertising?

2. How much money do companies and organizations spend on advertising annually in the United States?

3. How can it be that cost is both an advantage and a disadvantage of advertising as a promotional method?

4. What type of advertising is it when GE runs TV ads with the slogan "GE. We bring good things to life"?

5. Why would a company spend money on organizational advertising rather than promoting specific products or services that it wants businesses and people to buy?

6. If a company runs advertising that purposely creates a false impression of a product's benefits, what kind of regulatory response is likely?

DEVELOPING AN ADVERTISING PLAN

MARKETING MATTERS

When a company decides to include advertising as part of its promotional mix, the first step is to develop an advertising plan. An advertising plan describes the activities and resources needed to prepare and present a series of related advertisements focusing on a common objective. It is usually part of a larger overall promotional plan that includes several promotional mix elements.

The first steps in developing an advertising plan are setting objectives, working out a budget, and developing a theme. The next step is analyzing which type or types of media (radio, TV, newspapers, billboards, etc.) will be most effective, and then selecting the specific media outlets (*The Wall Street Journal* or MTV, for example) in which to run advertising.

Select an ad that you think would be much more effective if it ran in a different medium and/or at different times. Explain why.

GOALS

● **Describe the process of setting objectives, determining a budget, and developing an advertising theme.**

● **Explain the four major characteristics of various types of media that are analyzed in determining which media are best for a particular advertising plan.**

LAYING OUT THE PARAMETERS

An **advertising plan** describes the activities and resources needed to prepare and present a series of related advertisements focusing on a common objective. It centers on a specific product, service, or group of products and services. Since advertising involves huge sums of money, plans are carefully developed. Developing an advertising plan requires seven steps.

● Set objectives
● Determine the budget
● Develop the theme
● Select media
● Create the advertisements
● Develop an advertising schedule
● Evaluate the plan's effectiveness

SET OBJECTIVES

The first step in the development of an advertising plan is to determine the advertising objectives. **Objectives** are the desired results to be accomplished within a certain time period. The advertising objectives should support the marketing mix. The advertising objectives state what specific message the plan should communicate, to what target audience, and in what specific period of time. Objectives should be very specific and they should be measurable.

Objectives for a specific advertising plan will vary from organization to organization and from product to service. For example, an advertising plan for a municipal library might have as its objective to attract 1,000 new library cardholders between the ages of five and 10 during the next month. An advertising plan for the Mazda Miata might have as its objective the sale of 3,000 new Miatas to Spanish-speaking residents of Texas and Arizona in the months of June, July, and August.

SETTING OBJECTIVES

Elements of Objectives	Plan for Seaside Resorts
Desire or needed results	Increase reserved summer rentals by 10 percent by February 15
Advertising message to be communicated	Make reservations early to assure availability and save $100 off the weekly rate
Target market	Families who spend one week or more at the beach every year

It has been said that without objectives you will never know when you have arrived. This cliché is certainly true in advertising. Figure 16-1 presents objectives for the advertising plan of Seaside Resorts.

DETERMINE THE BUDGET

Once the advertising objectives are defined, the budget can be developed. Managers identify a total advertising budget early in the planning process. A more detailed budget is prepared as planning is completed. There are four common methods of determining budgets for advertising as shown in Figure 16-2.

What You Can Afford   One method of determining the ad budget is called the *what you can afford* approach. In this system, organizations account for all of their other expenses and whatever is left over is budgeted for advertising. This method does not properly support the advertising objectives.

FIGURE 16-2
Without a budget, it is hard to develop a theme, select the media, or create the advertisement.

Four Methods of Budgeting for Advertising

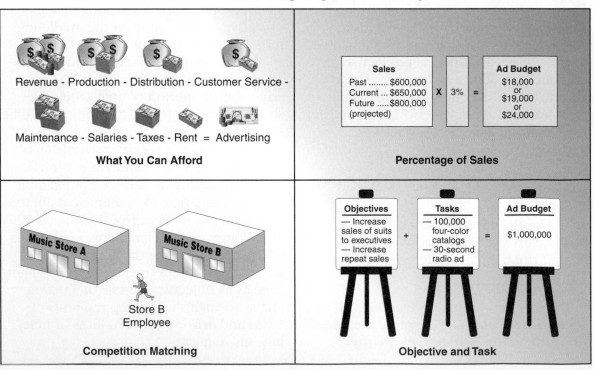

Percentage of Sales A second method used to determine an advertising budget is called the *percentage of sales* approach. The percentage of sales approach budgets a percentage of past, current, or projected future sales for advertising. For example, a firm that sold $50 million of tractors last year and allocated five percent of sales to advertising would budget $2.5 million for advertising.

One drawback of this method is that advertising varies directly with sales. If sales are low, advertising expenditures will be limited. However, when sales are low, advertising expenditures might need to be increased, not decreased, in order to help improve sales volume.

Firms need to be very cautious about using *past* sales to determine the *current* or *future* budget. What has happened in the past will not necessarily be repeated in the future. For example, an independent video store might be facing a more difficult year because a large chain has just opened nearby. The advertising budget should be determined based on the current and future situation, taking into consideration any new competitive challenges.

Competition Matching A third method of determining an advertising budget is called the *competition matching* approach. This approach suggests that an organization should spend a similar amount of money on advertising as its competitors. Though it is reasonable to be aware of what your competitors are doing in terms of advertising, this method of budgeting has serious drawbacks. One drawback is that competitors may have different advertising objectives and different resources. Also, it is difficult to determine competitor's budgets until after the fact. Therefore, using this approach can result in serious mistakes.

Objective and Task The *objective and task* approach involves determining the objectives to be achieved, identifying the tasks required to accomplish the objectives, and then computing the costs of each task. This is usually the best method to use in determining an advertising budget, if accurate information is available. The advertising manager determines the specific objectives and strategies needed to meet those objectives. Then the cost of advertising to meet the objectives is determined.

DEVELOPING THE THEME

To provide a focus for its advertising, an organization will develop a theme next. A **theme** is one idea, appeal, or benefit around which all advertising messages in a plan revolve. All pieces of advertising in the plan should feature the theme so that a consistent message is sent to the target audience. Advertising is expensive and critical to the success of a product or service. The message being sent to the receiver must be carefully planned and coordinated.

Pepsi focused advertisements on people who think young, whom it dubbed "the Pepsi Generation." Pork, "the other white meat," is positioned as an alternative to chicken or fish. Kellogg's appeals to adults when it advertises its cereals with the theme "taste them again for the first time."

What are the four common methods of determining an advertising budget, and which one is usually the most effective?

their sales to coincide with the beginning of winter and summer.

Pulsing allows advertisers to be more focused with their advertising messages. Advertisers direct their messages at their target audience when the audience is in a mood to buy. Pulsing can save advertisers money if they limit their advertising expenditures to specific times.

checkpoint

What type of format is exemplified by a McDonald's ad featuring Ronald McDonald?

GAUGING ADVERTISING EFFECTIVENESS

The final step in advertising planning is to measure effectiveness. **Evaluation** is measuring how well the advertising plan achieves its original objectives. Advertising activity is difficult to evaluate, but this step should not be avoided just because it is difficult. The evaluation procedures employed depend on the objectives. When advertising objectives are described in terms of changing attitudes or increasing awareness, for example, then the evaluation should attempt to measure whether these changes have occurred.

CHOOSING EVALUATION TECHNIQUES

If the advertising has a built-in evaluator, like a redeemable coupon, a rebate offer, or a two-for-one offer, then the advertisement's effectiveness can be determined from the usage rate for these promotional items. Many advertisements, though, do not have built-in measures. They need to be evaluated using other techniques.

Advertisements should be evaluated throughout the development and use of the ad. Pretesting occurs before an advertisement is run. Advertisers might evaluate advertising using pretesting to determine the best choice among several preliminary designs. Posttesting occurs after an advertisement is run. Advertisers are interested in finding out the strengths and weaknesses of advertisements in various media.

Focus Groups   There are several different methods used to posttest ads. Focus groups are structured discussions with groups of potential customers lead by a facilitator. Advertisers use focus groups to obtain information about advertisements that have just been run. Some of the things that advertisers can learn from focus groups are whether the advertisement appeals to the target audience, whether the message is clear, and ways to make the ads more effective.

Recall Testing   Recall testing can be conducted on a sample of consumers from the target market. They are asked to recall certain parts of an advertisement. Often recall tests are done at different time intervals to determine how long recall lasts.

Recognition Testing   Recognition testing is another evaluation method. Individuals are shown the actual ad and asked if they recognize it. If they can recognize the ad, they are asked additional questions about it.

However advertising is measured, it is important to evaluate all parts of an advertising plan. Evaluation shows advertisers what they did well and what they did not do well. It provides information that can aid in future decision making.

USING ADVERTISING AGENCIES

Advertising plans are often the responsibility of advertising agencies hired by the business. These agencies can handle all or part of the advertising function. Almost all advertising agencies coordinate their work with the company's marketers when preparing an advertising plan.

Advertising as a Game of Chance

To see how difficult it can be to accurately predict the effectiveness of an advertising plan, look at the number of variables and calculations involved. Most plans rely on getting a message out to a huge number of people with the hope that a minute percentage of them will buy the product. All it takes to throw it out of whack is a few small changes in the factors that determine the size of the audience or the response rate.

Consider a company that buys a TV spot during the World Series, expecting to reach 30 million baseball fans with a pitch for a credit card co-branded by their favorite club. Based on prior experience, the plan estimates that one in every 200 people (0.5%) will call the toll-free number and apply for a card. That yields 150,000 card applications, of which 120,000 (80%) can be expected to qualify, which satisfies the objective of 100,000 new cards.

But what happens if the game is a blow-out by the end of the 2nd inning, and the ad runs in the 5th when only 60% of the viewers are still watching? And what if 25% of them drift out of the room during the break? The audience has shrunk to 13.5 million. Now suppose that because of overexposure to prior promotions the response rate is weak, and only 1 in 500 (0.2%) apply. Moreover, since those still watching tend to be people with nothing better to do, they also tend to have below-average credit. So, only 67% qualify. All of these factors leave the company with only 18,000 new cards, nowhere near its objective.

How could it have been so far off? It is the result of cumulative changes in a long series of variables.

THINK CRITICALLY

1. A banner ad is seen by 20 million Internet users, and 0.4% of them click through to the sponsor's site, at which point 2% buy the product being promoted. How many product sales result?

2. By what percentage do product sales decrease if the clickthrough rate is reduced by 0.3 percentage points?

Each advertising agency has account executives. These are individuals who work directly with the business' marketing department. Advertising agencies typically provide creative services and purchase space or time for the company's advertising in the various media. Advertising agencies also do research to help determine the effectiveness of the advertising plan. Agencies are often compensated by a percentage of the cost of media purchases.

However, agencies may also bill the client for the cost of their time and other expenses.

When should the effectiveness of an advertising plan be evaluated?

LESSON REVIEW

1. Do advertisement formats have to conform to one and only one of the recognized format types?

2. Which is more expensive, continuity scheduling or pulse scheduling?

3. What efficiencies can be derived by companies that market seasonal products if they develop an array of seasonal products whose peak demand times are spread out over the entire year?

4. What is a built-in advertising evaluator?

5. What are focus groups?

6. What responsibilities does an advertising agency have?

SUMMARY

Lesson 16.1

A. Advertising is any form of nonpersonal promotional communication by an identified sponsor. Advertising has several distinct advantages over other types of promotion, including that it can reach large numbers of people in diverse locations at a relatively low cost per person. Among its disadvantages is that advertisers have little control over who actually sees their ads.

B. Ads come in two basic types, organizational advertising and product advertising. The major distinguishing characteristic between organizational advertising and product advertising is that the former focuses on a company or other organization rather than on a product or service, while the latter highlights a specific product or service that a business wants consumers to use.

C. Advertisements must be truthful and ethical. Advertisers are regulated by many government agencies, as well as their own professional organizations. Sanctions used by government to regulate advertising include requiring the full disclosure of relevant product information and substantiation of advertised claims, issuing cease-and-desist orders, ordering offending advertisers to run corrective advertising, and levying fines for untruthful or unethical practices.

Lesson 16.2

A. When a company decides to include advertising as part of its promotional mix, the first step is to develop an advertising plan. An advertising plan describes the activities and resources needed to prepare and present a series of related advertisements focusing on a common objective. It is usually part of a larger overall promotional plan that includes several promotional mix elements. The first steps in developing an advertising plan are setting objectives, working out a budget, and developing a theme.

B. The next step is analyzing which types of media will be most effective, and then selecting the specific media outlets in which to run advertising. The four primary considerations in selecting the types of media in which to run an advertisement are cost, reach, frequency, and lead time. Each advertising medium offers particular strengths and weaknesses in terms of those four considerations as well as other factors that determine how effective an ad can be.

Lesson 16.3

A. After setting objectives, budgeting, and developing a theme, the next step in an advertising plan is creating the ad. There are various formats that are commonly used, each of which focuses on an element or technique to catch consumers' attention and make the message stick in their minds. Popular formats include slice-of-life, fantasy, musical, technical expertise, testimonial, lifestyle, mood or image, character, and scientific evidence. Once ads are created, they are then scheduled to run in the various media outlets that have been preselected. Two common strategies for scheduling are continuous scheduling, which generates consistent, year-round exposure for a product or service; and pulse scheduling, which concentrates resources on peak demand times of the year for seasonal products.

B. The final step is evaluating how effective an ad plan has been. Evaluation should take place before, during, and after ads run so that adjustments can be made to keep the plan on target based on the objectives. Methods of evaluating effectiveness include focus groups, recall testing, and recognition testing. The advertising function, in whole or in part, can be handled by an outside advertising agency that works with marketing personnel in the business. Agencies are often involved in evaluating the effectiveness of an ad campaign in meeting plan objectives.

REVIEW MARKETING TERMS

Match the terms listed with the definitions. Some terms may not be used.

1. Idea, appeal, or benefit around which all advertising messages in a plan revolve.

2. Desired result to be accomplished within a certain time period.

3. Used by organizations to sell specific products.

4. Measuring how well the advertising plan achieves its original objectives.

5. Describes the activities and resources needed to prepare and present a series of related advertisements focusing on a common objective.

6. Means that advertisers increase their advertising efforts during a specific period of time and decrease or even withdraw their advertising during another period of time.

7. Designed to promote ideas, images, and issues associated with a company or organization.

8. Means that advertising will be scheduled regularly throughout the year.

a. advertising plan

b. continuity

c. evaluation

d. objective

e. organizational advertising

f. product advertising

g. pulsing

h. theme

REVIEW MARKETING CONCEPTS

9. Advertising is any form of __?__ promotional communication by an identified sponsor.

10. With the what-you-can-afford approach to budgeting, organizations account for all of their other expenses, then whatever is __?__ is budgeted for advertising.

11. The __?__ approach budgets a percentage of past, current, or projected future sales for advertising.

12. The competition-matching approach to budgeting suggests that an organization should spend a similar amount of money on advertising as its __?__ .

13. The objective and task approach to budgeting involves determining the objectives to be achieved, identifying the tasks required to accomplish the objectives, and then computing the __?__ of each task.

14. Reach refers to the number of readers or viewers in a medium's __?__ .

15. __?__ refers to the number of times a member of the target audience is exposed to the advertising message.

16. Lead time is the amount of time required to __?__ an advertisement prior to the time it runs.

17. A(n) __?__ is usually a half-hour television program that looks like a talk show, although in reality it is a 30-minute commercial.

18. The __?__ format shows people using the product or service in an everyday setting.

19. __?__ use either celebrities or everyday people to endorse a product.

20. A scientific evidence format uses __?__ and scientific information to demonstrate to the consumer why a product is superior.

21. Pretesting occurs __?__ an advertisement is run. Posttesting occurs __?__ an advertisement is run.

22. Substantiation requires that an organization be required to __?__ all of the claims it makes in its promotional messages.

23. The requirement of __?__ demands that all information necessary for a customer to

make a safe and informed decision be provided in a promotional message.

24. __?__ advertising demands that an organization run a new advertisement to correct any false impressions left by previous ones.

APPLY MARKETING FUNCTIONS

MARKETING RESEARCH

25. Annual advertising costs in the United States exceed $200 billion. Clearly, marketers spend a great deal of money on advertising. Your task in this activity is to become acquainted with advertising costs in a local market. Select an advertising medium used by marketers in your community, such as a radio station, a newspaper, a shopper's guide, an outdoor advertising agency, or a television station.

Contact the organization or use reference materials to obtain information regarding its advertising rates. Be prepared to report to your class regarding the cost of advertising per minute, per inch, per week, per day, or whatever measurement is used.

26. One of the major concerns of organizations that advertise is the effective use of their advertising dollars. A recent survey of 259 successful companies asked what type of evaluation techniques they use. The responses are summarized in the following table. (Respondents could select more than one type of approach.)

Type of Approach	Number of Respondents
Coupon redemption	179
Toll-free customer line	114
Focus groups	114
Customer survey	44
Rebate redemption	41
Recognition tests	26

a. Calculate the percentage of each of the response types and create a bar graph to illustrate the results.

b. Based on these results, how have the companies decided to allocate evaluation dollars? Do you think this is the best approach for all companies? Explain your answer.

MARKETING PLANNING

27. You are the owner of a taxi company in a city of 100,000 people. Until recently you were the only cab company in town. You have been able to reduce your promotional efforts because of the lack of competition.

Recently, a new cab company with five taxis has acquired a license to operate in your city. Describe your marketing response in terms of price, product, distribution, and promotion. Emphasize the type of advertising planning you would do.

28. Many businesses experience seasonal fluctuations in sales. Listed below are three products or services that often experience high and low sales periods. Suggest two advertising strategies for each product/service that could help reduce these sales fluctuations.

   a. Lawn maintenance

   b. Pet grooming

   c. Toy manufacturer

MARKETING MANAGEMENT

29. You are the chief executive officer of a company that manufactures golf equipment. Your marketing research determines that there is a large market for an oversized driver golf club. Your company invests heavily in designing and manufacturing this new driver.

    The advertising agency you have hired is developing an advertising plan for the new golf club. As CEO, develop one good question you will ask the account executive for each step of the advertising plan. An example for the "set objectives" step might be "What audience are you targeting with the advertisements?"

30. Research one of the laws or agencies that deal with illegal advertising and prepare a 200-word report. Be prepared to present your findings to the class.

MARKETING TECHNOLOGY

31. Log on to the web site of one of the organizations listed below and prepare a one-page report of the services it offers to its members and the kinds of information available on its site. Be prepared to give a presentation to the class.

   a. Advertising Mail Marketing Association

   b. Advertising Research Foundation

   c. American Advertising Federation

   d. Association of National Advertisers

   e. Audit Bureau of Circulations

   f. Direct Marketing Association

   g. Internet Advertising Bureau

   h. Outdoor Advertising Association of America

   i. Radio Advertising Bureau

   j. Television Bureau of Advertising

32. Search the Internet for a web site that carries a lot of online advertising. Browse the site for 15 minutes and count the number of different ads that you see. Write a one-page report on the ad content of the site, including the types of advertisers you see and the formats of the ads they display on the site.

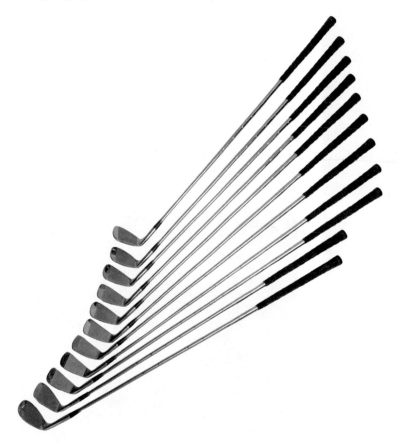

USING PERSONAL SELLING

There are advantages and disadvantages to personal selling. Those advantages and disadvantages are summarized in Figure 17-2. Business people need to understand when personal selling is needed and when it may not be the most effective promotional tool.

FIGURE 17-2
Personal selling is not appropriate for all exchanges. Organizations need to consider the advantages and disadvantages of personal selling when deciding whether to use it.

WHEN TO USE PERSONAL SELLING	
Advantages of Personal Selling	**Disadvantages of Personal Selling**
More information	Cost per customer
Flexible	Time required
Uses feedback	Less control
Persuasive	Skilled personnel
Follow-up	

ADVANTAGES

When a business provides information through an advertisement, there is a limited amount of information that can be included. An outdoor billboard or electronic display is usually restricted to fewer than 10 words, because viewers pass by very quickly. Television and radio commercials last no more than a minute, with most fitting into even shorter time slots. While newspaper and magazine advertisements can be longer, few people will spend more than a minute or two reading a print advertisement.

Information Salespeople spend considerably more time with customers. Even in the very shortest sales presentation to a customer, the conversation may last for several minutes. Effective salespeople often meet with customers several times. Each meeting may last from 10 minutes to one hour. With that amount of time, a great deal of information can be provided.

Flexibility Personal selling is very flexible. The sales presentation is typically scheduled at a time and place that is convenient for the customer. During the meeting, if it is clear that a customer understands certain information or if that information is not important to the customer, the salesperson moves on to another topic.

Feedback Because personal selling is two-way communication, the customer provides feedback. An effective salesperson asks questions, listens to customers' concerns, and determines if additional information is needed. That feedback is used to make the information even more specific to the individual needs of the customer. In addition to obtaining feedback from the customer, the salesperson provides feedback to the company. If the customer is dissatisfied with any part of the marketing mix or if competing products appear to meet customer needs better, the salesperson can inform the company.

Persuasion Selling is typically used near the end of the consumer decision-making process. At that time the customer is deciding whether or not to make the purchase. The customer may be comparing one or two very similar products before making a final decision. A salesperson is able to be persuasive at that time. By knowing the important needs of the customer, those needs can be matched with the qualities of the company's product and compared to those of competitors. The salesperson needs to be sure the product will satisfy the customer. If it does, the salesperson is in a position to help the customer make the decision to purchase.

Follow-Up A sale is not completed at the time the customer makes a purchase. The customer must use the product and decide if it meets the needs for which it was intended. If the customer is dissatisfied with the product, it will probably be returned. The customer may not want to buy other products from the company. An important responsibility of a salesperson is to follow up with the customer after the sale. The follow-up provides an opportunity to insure that the customer is able to use the product correctly, has everything needed, and is satisfied.

DISADVANTAGES

While there are many advantages of personal selling, there are also some disadvantages. One of the most important disadvantages is cost. You often hear of the high cost of advertising. A magazine ad can cost tens of thousands of dollars and a nationwide television advertisement on a popular show can cost hundreds of thousands. It doesn't seem possible that personal sales

Selling Yourself with Internet Job Services

The development of the World Wide Web and the proliferation of Internet-based employment and personnel services has been a boon for freelancers. Instead of wasting nonbillable hours and dollars searching classified listings and networking for contacts of questionable value, they can now post their qualifications and requirements on the Internet and clients will come to them.

Even better, their search is no longer as limited by geography as it used to be. With a few keystrokes, they can send their personal information to millions of potential clients around the world. Meanwhile, they can also conduct highly targeted searches of Internet databases for assignments to pursue. The same technology that allows freelancers to find work easily will also permit them to perform many tasks in the comfort of their hometown rather than at a client's office hundreds of miles away.

Almost all Internet services geared to freelancers are available without charge to job seekers. A key to success is writing a profile or resume that includes the right buzzwords. Companies conduct their own searches to find qualified freelancers, and you will draw their attention only if your information matches their search criteria. Another key is to include realistic expectations so that you aren't wasting time with offers that don't meet your requirements. When you're selling yourself, qualifying customers is most important.

THINK CRITICALLY

1. What keywords might you include in a personal profile if you wanted to find freelance marketing work?

2. Does the advent of Internet job services mean that face-to-face networking is no longer necessary?

could be more expensive, but businesses are concerned about the cost per customer as well as the total cost.

Pay-for-Performance Incentives

Salespeople are paid to sell, and many have compensation packages that provide incentives based on sales. The more they sell, the more money they make. Some receive base salaries plus incentives. Others are entitled to compensation only based on what they sell.

Common forms of incentives include sales quotas, commissions, bonuses, long-term incentives, and contests. Various methods are often combined to provide an array of incentives to keep salespeople hungry for more sales. For example, car salespeople are commonly paid a flat fee for each car they sell, plus a commission based on a percentage of the gross profit from each sale. If they reach a certain level—say, 20 cars in a month—their percentage of the profit is increased. So they have a strong incentive to sell as many cars as possible, and also to negotiate the highest possible price.

Given that kind of pay structure, it is no wonder that car salespeople are notorious for high-pressure tactics. Many businesses have found that such compensation systems tend to hurt customer relationships. They try to balance compensation packages with long-term incentives and management systems that keep a rein on overly aggressive salespeople.

THINK CRITICALLY

1. A salesperson is paid $100 for every car she sells, plus 10% of the gross profit from each sale, plus a bonus of $100 for each car in excess of 20 in a given month, plus an additional 1% of her total gross profits for each car she sells in excess of 25 cars in a month. How much will she be paid if she sells 28 cars for a total gross profit of $65,000?

2. A salesperson is paid $2,000 per month plus a 5% commission on sales in excess of $40,000 in a month. If he already has booked sales of $31,000 by the last day of the month, how much is it worth to him if he can close on a $10,000 order by the end of the day? If he is confident of getting a $50,000 order from another customer the following month, what might he be tempted to do with the $10,000 order?

Cost Per Customer If an advertisement reaches thousands of potential customers, the cost per person might be as low as one dollar or less. A salesperson's expenses can include the cost of salary, travel, time spent with a customer, equipment and materials needed for sales presentations, and so forth. A salesperson may only talk to a few customers each day. Therefore, the cost per customer can be very expensive. For sales of products to businesses, the cost is often more than a hundred dollars. Occasionally costs are as high as a few thousand dollars per customer before a sale is made.

Time Because a salesperson meets with customers one or a very few at a time, it takes a great deal of time for a large number of customers to be contacted. Compare that to an advertisement that reaches millions of people at the same time. The length of time needed to reach a large number of customers is a disadvantage of personal selling. A company can solve that problem by employing a large number of salespeople, but that adds to the costs of selling.

Control The salesperson is responsible for deciding what information to provide as well as how and when activities are completed. Therefore, the company's managers have limited control over the sales process. Salespeople often work alone or in small selling teams. During the time they are with a customer, they provide the information they believe is needed to help the customers decide to buy. When salespeople are not meeting with customers, they can plan additional sales calls, follow up on previous sales, and complete a variety of record-keeping tasks.

Skill The last disadvantage involves the knowledge and skill required to be an effective salesperson and the difficulty of the selling job. Salespeople need to understand selling procedures, communications, psychology, accounting, and management. In addition, they need a great deal of knowledge about their products and services and those of their competitors. The selling process requires people who are outgoing, creative, able to adjust to different people and situations, and good at solving problems. The job often requires long work hours and travel. Because of the complex and difficult job, it is not easy for companies to find and hire skilled salespeople.

CHOOSING PERSONAL SELLING

Personal selling should be used when it improves the marketing efforts. It can be the only method of promotion used by a company. Usually it is combined with other methods as a part of a promotional plan.

Characteristics of products and markets that indicate the need for personal selling include the following.

- Complex or expensive products
- Markets made up of a few large customers
- New or very unique products with which customers are unfamiliar
- Customers located in a limited area
- Complicated or long decision-making process
- Customers who expect personal attention and help with decision-making

How can time be both an advantage and a disadvantage of personal selling?

PERSONAL MANAGEMENT FOR SALESPEOPLE

Personal selling is a very demanding career. Most salespeople are responsible for their own time and activities, with limited direction from their managers. Often they are paid on commission. This means they are not paid unless they sell something.

A sales career can also be very rewarding. Professional salespeople who do their jobs well are paid more than many other business people. Because salespeople are responsible for the sales presentation, there is a great deal of satisfaction when a sale is made and the customer is satisfied. Successful professional salespeople are good managers. The important areas of management are self-management, customer management, and information management.

Self-Management   Selling requires motivation and an effective use of time. It is difficult to call on another customer at the end of a long day. It is demanding to complete the necessary research needed to plan a sales presentation. Much of a salesperson's time is spent on non-selling activities—paperwork, research, solving customer problems. A salesperson must be able to determine what needs to be done, set a work schedule, and devote the necessary time to complete all of the work.

Salespeople need to be emotionally and physically healthy. A great deal of stress is involved in the job. Salespeople may feel stress because success depends on customers deciding what to purchase and when they will purchase. Long hours of work leave little time for exercise and relaxation.

Finally, an important part of self-management is personal development. Salespeople must be well educated and informed. They need to continue to learn about new selling procedures, the use of technology such as computers, and information about products, customers, and competitors.

Customer Management   Selecting and scheduling customers is a difficult challenge for salespeople. Some customers offer a greater potential for sales because they purchase more frequently or in larger quantities. Certain customers require a greater amount of time from salespeople because they are at an earlier stage in decision-making. Some customers require more time because their needs are not well identified or they ask for a great deal of information. Salespeople must be able to decide how much time to spend with each customer to maximize their sales.

When salespeople travel to meet customers, they have to carefully schedule their time. They need to limit the amount of time they are traveling in order to spend more time selling. Also they need to keep their travel costs as low as possible to increase profits.

Information Management   The Newsline at the beginning of the chapter describes how today's salespeople manage information using a laptop computer.

It illustrates the importance of information to salespeople. Consider the salesperson who does not have access to information about specific customers and attempts to develop a sales presentation. That presentation will be very general and based on the salesperson's assumptions. In the same way, if the salesperson does not have immediate access to updated product information, price changes, distribution schedules, service records, and the like, it will be difficult to respond to customer needs and answer customer questions.

Salespeople must be able to identify needed information, develop effective record-keeping systems, and use the company's information system. In addition, salespeople must complete orders and other sales records carefully and completely.

What three things do salespeople need to manage well in order to be effective at selling?

1. What is accomplished, for customers and for businesses, when successful sales occur?

2. Why is personal selling more appropriate, or potentially more profitable, when it involves expensive products or services or when markets are made up of a few large customers?

3. Name three advantages of using personal selling.

4. Name three disadvantages of using personal selling.

5. Why is effective customer management necessary for successful personal selling?

6. What crucial tasks do salespeople perform when they are not selling?

PREPARING FOR EFFECTIVE SELLING

The success of a salesperson is typically measured by the sales that are made and the satisfaction of the customers. That success is often determined well before the salesperson ever meets with the customer. Many salespeople spend more time preparing for sales than they do in actual contact with customers. In addition to developing effective selling skills, three areas are important—understanding the customer, understanding the product, and understanding the competition.

Imagine that you are preparing to interview for a well-paying job that you want very badly. You need to sell yourself to the employer, who in this situation is the *customer* to whom you want to sell your services. You are the *product*, and other job applicants are the *competition*. Make a list of two points each about the customer, the product, and the competition that will determine your chances of success.

GOALS

- Describe the way effective salespeople qualify prospective customers and use their decision-making processes to plan their sales presentations.
- Explain why salespeople need to know their product thoroughly and how product features will benefit their customers.
- Demonstrate why it is important to understand the competition's products and marketing plans.

UNDERSTANDING THE CUSTOMER

Marketing is responsible for creating satisfying exchanges. Because salespeople negotiate the sale of products and services with the customer, they need to ensure that the customer is satisfied with the purchase. Understanding the customer helps organize the sales presentation to meet the customer's needs. Figure 17-3 illustrates that effective selling requires a great deal of preparation.

IDENTIFYING CUSTOMERS

Salespeople need to identify appropriate customers. Information is needed about who the customers are and where they are located. A great deal of time is wasted if the salesperson is talking to people who are not interested in the company's products or are not able to buy them.

FIGURE 17-3
A salesperson needs to understand effective selling as well as customers, competitors, and the products and services being sold.

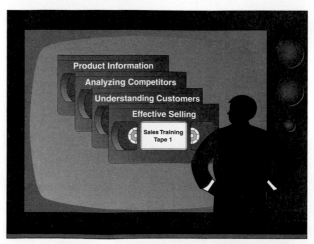

Requirement for Effective Selling

Some salespeople use a process called cold calling. With **cold calling**, a salesperson contacts a large number of people who are conveniently located, without knowing a great deal about each person contacted. A business products salesperson may call on every business listed in a city business directory with annual sales over $1 million. A telemarketer may use a computer dialing system programmed to randomly call all residential numbers in a telephone directory. A door-to-door salesperson stops at every home on a block to try to locate customers for a carpet-cleaning business.

You can imagine that using cold calling is difficult and discouraging. A large number of customers may

Web Sites for Distributor Communication

For many industrial supply distributors, the World Wide Web is evolving into the key medium for getting their message out to prospective customers. Since they are dealing with standard parts and supplies that can usually be obtained through a number of distribution channels, successful selling frequently hinges on price, availability, and reliability. Getting up-to-date information out to customers is vital to staying competitive in what many believe has become an "information transfer" business.

Even for small distributors, the Web opens the door to a potential worldwide market for products, particularly those for which shipping is not a big expense. Its big advantages are cost-effectiveness and timeliness. Distributors can publish a web-based catalog that is available to anyone with a web browser, 24 hours a day, seven days a week. Unlike print catalogs, it can be updated continuously, so product listings can always be current, and pricing and other terms can be adjusted instantaneously to respond to market conditions.

From a buyer's perspective, online catalogs allow a business to query dozens of suppliers by e-mail at the touch of a few keystrokes. Distributors have learned to reply promptly or risk losing an order to a competitor.

THINK CRITICALLY

1. What role does personal selling have in an "information transfer" business that relies heavily on a web site to generate sales?

2. What are the advantages and disadvantages of web-based catalogs vs. printed catalogs?

have to be contacted before finding someone who is interested in the salesperson's products. Also, the salesperson has a difficult time beginning the selling process when little is known about the prospective customer, whom the salesperson has just met. Most importantly, people contacted by the salesperson may be quite upset if they are not interested in the products being sold. They may not want to be bothered by a salesperson at that time. The salesperson is wasting the time of people who have no current needs related to those products. Also wasted are the resources of the company that could be better spent on interested consumers.

A marketing oriented business does not use cold calling. Salespeople gather information on possible customers and determine if they fit the characteristics of the company's target market. Often, through the company's marketing information system or marketing research, information is already available to assist the salesperson. Also, other promotional or marketing efforts such as coupons and product registration cards are used to identify customers and gather other information. If the salesperson knows who prospective customers are, where they are located, some of their important needs, and when and how to contact each customer, the selling process is much more productive.

QUALIFYING PROSPECTIVE CUSTOMERS

Not all people in a target market are prepared or able to purchase a product at a particular time. A salesperson will complete a procedure known as qualifying a customer. **Qualifying** involves gathering information to determine which people are most likely to buy.

Three characteristics qualify a person as a prospective customer. Without all three characteristics, the person will not purchase the product. The characteristics include:

1. A *need* for the product.
2. The *resources* to purchase the product.
3. The *authority* to make a decision to purchase.

While everyone in a target market has a general need for the product being marketed, that need may not be as important as other needs. The customer may have already purchased another product to meet the need. Salespeople identify customers who have the strongest need and who are ready to make a purchasing decision.

Most people have many more needs than they can satisfy at a given time. A common limitation on purchasing is a lack of resources to buy the product. It is possible that a customer does not have the money or adequate financing through the use of credit. No matter how hard the salesperson works or how effective the sales presentation is, a sale is not possible if the customer is unable to afford the product. Part of the information-gathering process of salespeople is determining if the customer has adequate resources.

Many times people want to buy a product but do not have the authority to make the decision. A child may have to ask a parent, a manager may need to get approval from the purchasing department, or a partner in a business may need to have the agreement of the other partners. Salespeople often need to work with several people before a purchase decision is made. It is important to determine which person or people will make the final decision and to make sure they are included in the selling process.

UNDERSTANDING CUSTOMER DECISIONS

Consumers go through a series of steps when they make a decision. Those steps include identifying a problem or need, gathering information, evaluating alternatives, making a decision, and evaluating the decision. Consumers need specific types of information as they move through each step. If the consumer is gathering information on possible products to satisfy a need, information on financing alternatives will not be helpful. On the other hand, if the customer has already narrowed the choice to two products and is comparing them, it will not help to provide general information on the needs a product satisfies.

Salespeople often translate the consumer decision-making steps into a series of mental stages that lead to a sale. Those mental stages are summarized with the letters AIDCA. The meaning of each letter is shown in Figure 17-4.

A salesperson knows that the customer must first focus attention on the salesperson and the sales presentation. It is important to get the customer's interest in the product early in the presentation. A customer moves from interest to desire when it is clear that the product meets important needs. The desire turns to conviction when the customer determines the product is a good value and the best choice. That leads to action, or the purchase of the product.

A salesperson who understands consumer decision-making and is able to determine which of the AIDCA stages each customer is in will be able to provide the specific information that each customer needs. An important advantage of personal selling is the capability of providing specific information to each customer.

FIGURE 17-4
Consumers complete a series of mental decisions as they decide whether to make purchases. Salespeople who understand the mental stages can use the information to plan their sales presentations.

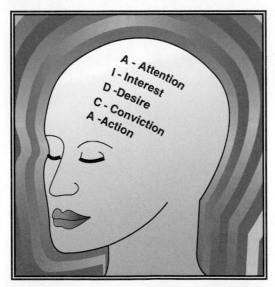

A - Attention
I - Interest
D - Desire
C - Conviction
A - Action

Mental Stages of Consumer Decision-Making

Why is it important to qualify prospective customers before engaging them in a sales presentation?

UNDERSTANDING
THE PRODUCT

As the representative of the company to the customer, the salesperson is responsible for providing the information needed for the customer to make a good decision. There are two parts to that responsibility. The salesperson must have adequate product knowledge. Also, the salesperson must be able to communicate the information effectively to the customer.

not interested in all of the information, the salesperson must be able to tailor the presentation to the needs of each customer. One customer may want to know about the construction and durability of a product. Another may be concerned about the warranty and repair services. Still another needs to know about financing. A salesperson who does not know that information or who is unable to

PRODUCT KNOWLEDGE

Choosing the best product to satisfy a customer's needs is often not an easy task. Customers may not be able to determine by examining a product, or even by reviewing the information that accompanies a product, whether it is the one they should buy. Salespeople need to know a great deal about the products they represent. They need access to additional information so they can answer customers' questions and demonstrate the product effectively.

Salespeople must be familiar with all parts of the marketing mix. Customers are concerned not only about the product but also about price, availability, and promotion. While an individual customer is

Sales Force Technology Encounters Latin Resistance

Using technology to increase the effectiveness of salespeople is a growing trend in the United States and Europe. In Latin America, it faces several cultural hurdles that are putting Latin companies several years behind the curve. One hurdle is the attitude of salespeople themselves. While the United States' business culture is all about advancing the interests of the organization by sharing and integrating information, Latin attitudes—particularly among salespeople—are more individualistic. Salespeople in Latin American countries tend to resist sharing customer information for fear that they will lose their edge or that someone else might reap benefits that rightfully belong to them (not the company).

Cost also is more of a factor in Latin America, where companies are smaller, less well-financed, and where sales forces tend to be larger because personal

selling is more prevalent than other forms of promotion. Moreover, the high cost of updating technology means that the latest sales technology won't work with outdated systems.

Another barrier to technology is language. Most software is written and operates in English, which many field-level personnel do not speak or understand well. Rather than struggle with devices they do not understand—or worse, with devices that make them look stupid in front of their customers—salespeople find excuses not to use them.

THINK CRITICALLY

1. What effect does resistance to technology have on the competitiveness of Latin companies?

2. How might companies in Latin America overcome barriers to sales force technology to increase sales efficiency?

FIGURE 17-5

Features have little meaning to customers until they understand how each feature provides a benefit. To communicate the benefits of the product, salespeople need to understand customer needs.

Feature-Benefit Comparison

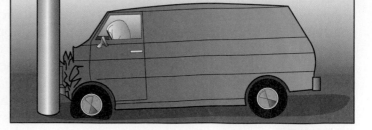

obtain it quickly will not be able to satisfy potential customers. The salesperson will lose sales to salespeople who can provide the information the customer needs.

Information Sources A variety of sources of product information are available. Companies prepare information sheets and product manuals. Advertisements and other types of promotion often contain valuable information including price changes, special promotions, and so on. The product's marketing plan and marketing research reports are sources of useful information, as are other salespeople and company personnel.

Many companies offer training for salespeople that emphasizes important product information. They also prepare sales aids and other materials for salespeople to use. Effective salespeople regularly read business publications, attend conferences and trade shows, and study other information sources to keep up-to-date on the products and services they sell.

COMMUNICATING PRODUCT INFORMATION

Which of the following statements is more effective as a part of a sales presentation?

"The standard engine in this vehicle is a 4.3 liter V6."

"Our standard engine offers the best combination of efficiency and power. You will average 26 miles per gallon. You will

have enough acceleration so you won't have trouble merging into faster traffic when entering the freeway."

The statements provide examples of features and benefits. Figure 17-5 illustrates this difference. A **feature** is a description of a product characteristic. The first statement describes a feature—the standard engine. A **benefit** is the advantage provided to a customer as a result of the feature. The second statement describes how the customer will benefit from the engine—efficiency and acceleration. Salespeople communicate most effectively when they can describe the benefits of a product for a customer.

Many of a product's features are similar to those of competitors. Other features are different, and a few may be unique. Customers want to know how various products and brands are similar and how they are different. They also want to know how the features will meet their needs. The salesperson needs to understand the features, translate them into customer benefits, and communicate the important benefits in an understandable way to each customer.

Why is merely reciting a product's features not enough for an effective sales presentation?

UNDERSTANDING
THE COMPETITION

Seldom will a customer make a purchase without considering several choices. The consumer wants to buy the most satisfying product and the best value. It is not always easy to make the best choice. With products that are very similar, quite complex, or for which little information is available, consumers may have a difficult time determining which is best. It is not unusual for a customer to buy one product only to realize later that another choice would have been better.

Salespeople want to sell the products and services they represent, but they will be more successful in the long run if the customer is satisfied with the purchase. The salesperson who is familiar with competitors' products can help the customer understand differences among the choices. Customers will view that kind of salesperson as quite different from the salespeople who can only describe the products of one company. It is not unusual for customers to study several brands or similar products before making a decision. A knowledgeable salesperson can explain important differences to customers to assist them with the comparison. The customer will often look at those differences when examining a competitor's product and will be able to see the advantages of the original brand. Just as with their company's products, it is important that salespeople study all parts of the marketing mix for competitors' products.

Why is it necessary for a salesperson to understand competitors' products?

LESSON REVIEW

1. Why is cold calling often a wasteful activity?

2. What three characteristics must a prospective customer possess before he or she will make a purchase?

3. What do the letters in the acronym AIDCA stand for?

4. What is the critical distinction between a feature and a benefit?

5. Why do salespeople need to have more information about a product than any customer will ever want to know?

6. Why would a salesperson want to point out a superior feature of a competitor's product, possibly losing a sale that he or she would otherwise make?

17.3 THE SELLING PROCESS AND SALES SUPPORT

GOALS

- Detail the six steps of the selling process.
- Explain why salespeople need support from other areas of the business.

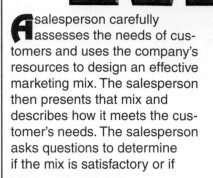
STEPS OF THE SELLING PROCESS

The selling process that is based on the marketing concept may not fit your perception of selling. Remember that not all companies and salespeople understand or believe in the marketing concept. It is not unusual to find salespeople who believe their responsibility is to convince the customer to buy their company's products. They look at the selling process as a type of contest between the customer and the salesperson. Each tries to negotiate the best deal possible. The salesperson uses information and the resources of the business to persuade the customer to buy.

Effective selling is a very demanding profession. People who are skilled at selling are in high demand in business. They are well compensated for their abilities. The skills needed by salespeople can be summarized in the six steps of the selling process. Those steps are listed in Figure 17-6.

FIGURE 17-6
Effective salespeople follow a specific procedure to match customer needs with the company's products and services.

STEPS IN THE SELLING PROCESS

Step	Purpose
Preapproach	Studying the customer and his or her needs
Approach	Contacting the customer to determine information needs and establish a helping relationship
Demonstration	Presenting the marketing mix in an interesting way that emphasizes customer benefits
Answering Questions	Helping the customer resolve concerns and ensure the marketing mix meets the customer's needs
Closing the Sale	Obtaining a decision to purchase from the customer and suggesting other products and services the customer may see as valuable products
Follow-up	Continuing contact with the customer to determine if the mix was provided as promised, if needs were satisfied, and if the customer has additional needs

PREAPPROACH

We are often told that time spent in preparation leads to successful performance. Whether it involves studying for a test, practicing for a musical performance, or training for an athletic event, people who spend time learning and perfecting their skills are usually more successful. Salespeople are no different. Preparation during the preapproach improves the chances for a successful sale.

The **preapproach** includes gathering needed information and preparing for the sales presentation before contacting the customer. Salespeople study target market information and any other information available on the specific customer they are meeting. They also review and organize all of the information about the company, its products and services, and the other parts of the marketing mix. Based on customer information, the salesperson prepares for the first meeting with the customer.

Most good salespeople outline and practice their sales presentation before meeting with the customer. The intention is not to memorize the information. Instead, the salesperson organizes the presentation to lead the customer effectively to a decision. Practice makes the salesperson more comfortable. It allows the salesperson to concentrate on the customer during the sales presentation.

APPROACH

The **approach** is the first contact with the customer when the salesperson gets the customer's attention and creates a favorable impression. The approach might be initiated by the customer or by the salesperson. In either case, the salesperson is responsible for the result. The approach provides the opportunity for the salesperson to attract the customer's attention and create an interest in the product or service.

Consider the situation in which a customer enters a retail store. The salesperson must decide whether to approach and greet the customer or to allow the customer to look around the store. Some customers have a particular product in mind. Others are simply spending time in the store without any real interest in making a purchase. A salesperson who approaches the customer in a pleasant and courteous way can quickly determine if the customer wants assistance. The salesperson can also determine where the person is in the mental stages of decision-making.

For the customer who is just beginning to search for a product, the salesperson provides information on the basic characteristics of products that might meet the customer's needs. The salesperson allows the customer to examine several choices. If the customer is nearing a decision, the salesperson might review payment methods, advantages of certain product features, or any final important factors that will help the customer decide to buy.

Salespeople who call on business customers have different factors to consider when planning an approach. Since several people may be involved in making a purchasing decision, the salesperson must decide whom to contact. A method of contacting the person must be developed that will result in the opportunity to meet with the customer for the sales presentation. Business people have frequent contacts from many salespeople. They do not have time to meet with all of them, so they select only those that they believe can be of help. Telephone calls, letters of introduction, or special promotional materials sent to the prospective customer can be used to make the customer aware of the salesperson, the company, and its products.

DEMONSTRATION

The major part of the sales presentation is the demonstration. The **demonstration** is a personalized presentation of the features of the marketing mix in a way that emphasizes the benefits and value to the customer. The real value of personal selling is shown in the demonstration. The salesperson tailors the product information directly to the customer and emphasizes the parts of the mix that best meet the customer's needs. The demonstration is designed to turn the customer's interest into desire.

Effective Technology Boosts Sales

Increasing the productivity of a sales force takes more than just handing out hand-held digital organizers to manage their appointments and contacts. If information technology merely streamlines administrative tasks to give salespeople more time to make unproductive sales calls, it's not worth the investment in money or time. Technology consultants stress that truly productive systems provide salespeople with the very latest information on products, customers, competitors, orders, and market conditions. And they include training salespeople to get the most out of the technology. Otherwise, salespeople are likely to suspect that new technology is just another way for management to keep tabs on them.

The best-regarded information systems not only give salespeople the latest information available, but also integrate any new information that they come across. This two-way movement of information ensures that everyone in an organization, including independent dealers, can access the latest information when and where they need it. It also ensures that everyone is working with the same information at all times.

As a result, salespeople can target their sales presentations more precisely and, if appropriate, make adjustments to the marketing mix to fit the situation. That results in a reduction in unproductive activities and an increase in effective selling.

THINK CRITICALLY

1. What kinds of information about a customer would you want to have before making an important sales call?

2. Why is sales force information technology most beneficial for large organizations?

As soon as the customer makes the decision to buy, the salesperson should take the opportunity to reinforce that decision. Customers want to believe they made the right choice but often have concerns about the decision after it is made. The salesperson can emphasize the value and summarize the benefits the customer will receive from using the product or service.

One of the responsibilities of the salesperson at the completion of a sale is to be certain the customer's needs are satisfied. It is possible that the product can be used more effectively if the customer purchases related merchandise. A bicycle rider needs a bicycle helmet. Sheets and blankets may be useful for someone who just purchased a bedroom suite. When a pet is purchased, the family may need food, grooming supplies, and so on. If customers go home without all of the things needed to use the product, they will probably be dissatisfied. Offering addition products and services after an initial sale in order to increase customer satisfaction is known as **suggestion selling**.

FOLLOW-UP

Customers who purchase products and services from a company and are satisfied with their purchases are likely to buy from that company again. Making contact with the customer after the sale to ensure satisfaction is known as **follow-up**. It is the responsibility of the salesperson to follow up with each customer to ensure that the customer is satisfied. Follow-up also provides another opportunity to reinforce the customer's decision as well as to determine if the customer has additional needs that the business can meet.

Part of the follow-up responsibility may include checking on delivery schedules, making sure warranty or product registration information is accurate, scheduling product installation and maintenance, or completing paperwork for financing. If the customer has any problems, the salesperson can arrange to resolve them quickly. When the customer sees the salesperson completing the follow-up activities, it will be clear that the customer is important to the business.

What are the six steps in the selling process?

PROVIDING
SALES SUPPORT

For selling to be effective, the salesperson must receive support from many parts of the business, including other marketing personnel. To meet customer needs, the salesperson must have products and services that are well designed, readily available, and priced competitively. People in production, finance, and management need to coordinate their work with the salespeople to match the supply of products with sales. Order processing, customer service, and many other business activities are needed in order for the selling process to be successful.

Each of the other marketing functions demonstrates how salespeople depend on marketing activities for support.

1. Marketing-Information Management: Salespeople need access to a wide variety of information throughout the selling process. In the preapproach, the salesperson needs information on customers and their needs. During the sales presentation, the salesperson may need to gather additional information about products and their availability, pricing, or other matters to answer customer questions.

2. Financing: Many customers need to finance their purchases. Salespeople must have access to credit services that they can offer to their customers. Salespeople may also need assistance in explaining financing and completing the necessary paperwork.

3. Pricing: Many prices are not set but can be negotiated by the customer working with the salesperson. Offering discounts, accepting trade-ins, and other methods can be used to adjust the price. A salesperson must have the authority to negotiate the price or must be able to get pricing information quickly.

4. Promotion: Usually customers obtain information from sources other than the salesperson to aid in making a buying decision. Other types of promotion,

including advertising and publicity, can create interest, inform potential customers of product choices, or reinforce a purchase decision after the sale is completed.

5. Product/Service Management: Salespeople can provide information on customer needs and customer reactions to the current products and services offered by the business. That information can be used to improve existing products and develop new products so the salesperson can meet customer needs.

6. Distribution: Products and services often need to be delivered to customers. Salespeople rely on transportation services to get the products delivered at the time the customers want them. Salespeople need to have information on transportation schedules and costs when they work with their customers.

Why do salespeople need support from other areas of the business?

LESSON REVIEW

1. Why should salespeople practice their sales presentations before they meet with customers?

2. How does approaching a business customer differ from approaching a consumer in a retail setting?

3. Name three ways to make a demonstration more effective.

4. Why is the follow-up step so important for effective personal selling?

5. In what sense do salespeople rely on distribution activities to perform their jobs effectively?

CHAPTER 17

SUMMARY

Lesson 17.1

A. Professional, personalized communications, which are at the core of selling, are an effective promotional tool for many businesses. Personal selling allows a company to respond to the unique needs of customers with specific messages designed to help customers make purchasing decisions.

B. Selling is not the best promotional method for every situation. There are distinct advantages and disadvantages that need to be weighed to determine where and when personal selling fits a business's needs, either alone or in conjunction with other promotional methods. Advantages include the ability to provide more information, flexibility, a feedback mechanism, the opportunity to persuade, and the ability to follow up with customers. Disadvantages include a high cost per customer, high time requirements, less control, and the need for skilled personnel.

C. Management skills are important to salespeople because of the difficult job they must perform. Salespeople need to develop skills in self-management, customer management, and information management.

Lesson 17.2

A. Effective selling requires a great deal of preparation. Many salespeople spend more time preparing for sales than they do in actual contact with customers. In addition to developing effective selling skills, three areas are important, the first of which is understanding the customer. Salespeople must qualify prospective customers to ensure that they have a need for the product, have the resources to buy it, and have the authority to make a purchase decision. Customer buying decisions follow a series of mental stages represented by the acronym AIDCA—attention, interest, desire, conviction, and action.

B. A salesperson's second area of concern is understanding the product. Salespeople need thorough knowledge of all parts of the marketing mix, and must have access to a variety of information sources to answer customer questions. Communicating product information is best accomplished by emphasizing the particular benefits that each customer will derive from various product features.

C. The third area of concern for salespeople is understanding the competition. They need to know competitors' products as well as their own, including the entire marketing mix. That way they can explain the significant differences to customers, who might see the products as essentially the same and not realize that one is better suited to their needs.

Lesson 17.3

A. Personal selling involves a series of steps. Those steps match the consumer decision-making process. The selling process includes preapproach, approach, demonstration, answering questions, closing the sale, and follow-up. Nothing demonstrates the marketing concept better than the selling process when it is completed effectively. A salesperson assesses the needs of a customer and presents the marketing mix to the customer, asking questions to determine if it satisfies the customer or if adjustments must be made. The salesperson helps the customer make the best decision.

B. To be effective, salespeople also need support from other parts of the company to meet customer needs with well-designed products that are readily available for a competitive price. Selling will not be effective unless it is supported by other business and marketing functions to design and deliver an effective marketing mix for each customer. Salespeople can assist the company in designing products and services to meet customer needs.

REVIEW

REVIEW MARKETING CONCEPTS

1. True or False: Cold calling is usually a cost- and time-effective method of finding sales leads.

2. Personal selling is __?__ in that a salesperson can provide additional information or move on to another topic depending on a customer's reaction to her sales presentation.

3. True or False: Personal selling generally has a higher cost per customer than other methods of promoting a product or service.

4. The mental stages of consumer decision-making are represented by the letters of the acronym __?__.

5. In the past, the step of the selling process now referred to as *answering questions* was known as __?__.

6. When a customer indicates that he or she has decided to place an order, the salesperson should take the first opportunity to __?__ the decision to assure the customer that he or she has made the right move.

7. True or False: Successful salespeople are often lacking in self-discipline and self-management skills but succeed because they are good conversationalists.

8. Successful sales occur when customers are able to buy what they need and the business is able to __?__.

The following concepts are examples of personal selling. Match each example with the correct selling concept.

   a. assess and satisfy needs
   b. benefit
   c. customer decision-making process
   d. feature
   e. feedback
   f. flexibility
   g. follow-up
   h. product knowledge
   i. qualifying customers
   j. time

9. During a sales presentation, the salesperson has the advantage of responding to the customer's questions or determining if specific information is needed.

10. In personal selling, salespeople can adjust their sales presentations to include information that is most useful to the customer.

11. Effective salespeople often meet frequently with their customers to provide information and support for products and services they have sold.

12. Lin Chung estimates that she spends about one-third of her time with customers who have previously purchased her products.

13. "The excellent print capability of this machine will make your correspondence look professional at half the cost of a printing service."

14. Rosa Garcia likes to make sure her customers get the best products possible to solve their problems.

15. Using marketing research information to determine the appropriate customers who are interested in and able to buy the company's products or services.

16. Fred March works closely with his customers so he can understand when they are ready to make decisions to purchase.

17. Sales publications, manuals, promotional pieces, conferences, trade shows, and trade publications are studied and used by effective salespeople.

18. "This telephone system has a 200-call capacity."

REVIEW MARKETING TERMS

Match the terms listed with the definitions. Some terms may not be used.

19. Gather information to determine which people are most likely to buy.

20. Lead the customer to a decision to purchase.

21. An advantage provided to a customer by a product characteristic.

22. Make contact with the customer after the sale to ensure satisfaction.

23. Gather needed information and prepare for the sales presentation before contacting the customer.

24. Direct, personal communications with prospective customers in order to assess needs and satisfy those needs with appropriate products and services.

25. The first contact with the customer when the salesperson gets the customer's attention and creates a favorable impression.

26. Provide the customer with the opportunity to buy during the sales presentation.

27. A description of a product characteristic.

28. A personalized presentation of the features of the marketing mix in a way that emphasizes the benefits and value to the customer.

29. Offer addition products and services after an initial sale in order to increase customer satisfaction.

30. Resolve concerns and provide additional information needed by a customer.

31. Contact a large number of prospective customers who are conveniently located, without knowing a great deal about each person contacted.

a. answer questions
b. approach
c. benefit
d. close
e. cold call
f. demonstration
g. feature
h. follow-up
i. preapproach
j. qualify
k. selling
l. suggestion selling
m. trial close

APPLY MARKETING FUNCTIONS

MARKETING RESEARCH

32. Salespeople are often paid bonuses or commissions on their total sales. Each of the following salespeople earns $60,000 per year and earns 2 percent commission on all sales over $250,000 per year.

  a. What is each salesperson's total salary for the year?

  b. What is the average amount of each salesperson's sale?

  c. What percentage of calls resulted in a sale for each salesperson?

Salesperson	Total Sales	Number of Sales Calls Per Year	Number of Sales Per Year
Chin Mueller	$2,345,200	250	107
Jane Brown	3,395,200	350	120
Marcus Gonzalez	2,930,400	400	99

33. Before making a sales call, the salesperson should be armed with information about the customer, the product, and the competition. Assume you are a salesperson for an industrial firm. List three pieces of information that would be helpful to know about your customer, your product, and the competition. List three ways that you can find the necessary information.

MARKETING PLANNING

34. It is important to remember that effective salespeople solve customer problems by explaining how a product or service will benefit the consumer. In preparing for a sales call, it is best to prepare a feature-benefit chart for the product. Assume you are a salesperson selling a video camera. For each of the following features, describe a customer benefit.
  a. automatic focus
  b. date and event imprinter
  c. soft-sided case with strap and handle
  d. lightweight
  e. three-hour battery
  f. fade-in and fade-out
  g. detachable microphone
  h. lens cover
  i. tripod attachment
  j. zoom-in capabilities

35. AIDCA is a series of mental stages that customers go through in the decision-making process. Draw a diagram of the steps of a sale and add the AIDGA model to the steps to show how the selling process can aid customer decision-making.

MARKETING MANAGEMENT

36. Identify a product or service of your choice and prepare a sales presentation. Use a classmate as a customer. Be prepared to role-play your presentation to the class.

37. As the CEO of a computer technical support company, you understand how important it is to provide sales support to your sales staff. For each of the marketing functions listed below, specify one activity that each area can do to provide the necessary support for your sales staff.
  a. Distribution
  b. Financing
  c. Marketing Information Management
  d. Pricing
  e. Product/Service Management
  f. Promotion

MARKETING TECHNOLOGY

38. Search the Internet for six entry-level job openings in sales positions. Describe the kinds of compensation packages they are offering and the level of pay they advertise. Note in particular if the pay advertised is a base salary, estimated commissions and bonuses, or a combination of compensation methods.

39. Pick one of the following types of products listed below, and go comparison shopping for a particular brand and model of that product at five different retailers or dealers. Obtain data on the list or sticker price, the price a salesperson says you can buy it for, and any other available incentives. Input the data into a computer spreadsheet program and have the spreadsheet calculate the average list price, the average offered price, and the difference between each list and offered price. Using a word processing program, write a one-page report of the actions taken by salespeople you encountered.
  a. new car
  b. bicycle
  c. portable or hand-held computer
  d. digital music recorder
  e. used car
  f. video camcorder
  g. personal computer
  h. digital camera

through the purchase of products than it is receiving from the sale of products abroad. It also demonstrates that businesses from other countries are satisfying the needs of consumers better than the country's own businesses.

What is the difference between indirect and direct exporting?

FOREIGN PRODUCTION, INVESTMENT, JOINT VENTURES

FOREIGN PRODUCTION

Another example of international trade is foreign production. With **foreign production**, a company owns and operates production facilities in another country. Rather than manufacturing a product in one country and then shipping the product to another country, the entire process is completed in the country where the product is to be sold. Nearly $4 trillion of products and services are developed by companies using foreign production each year. Foreign production has advantages over exporting in that the major business activities are performed within the country in which the products will be sold. This reduces the amount of distribution activities and the time needed to move products from one country to another.

People in some countries are becoming concerned about the amount of products being purchased from other countries. For example, some people in the United States believe too many automobiles produced in Japan and Germany are being sold in this country. So manufacturers such as Honda, Toyota, and BMW now have dozens of automobile assembly plants in the United States. The use of foreign production allows those companies to continue to sell their products while responding to the consumer concern about where the products are manufactured.

Currency Rates

One of the trickiest aspects of international trade is dealing with changing values of various national currencies. Any time a company buys or sells something in a foreign country it also has to sell or buy foreign currency used in the exchange. Currency exchange rates can be highly unpredictable. They can change much more quickly than companies' marketing plans.

When a U.S. company sells American-made products in Europe, the success of its marketing plan depends on the value of the euro remaining stable compared to the dollar. If the value of the euro falls sharply, then it has to either raise its prices and risk losing sales, or keep prices the same and accept lower profits.

Whatever its decision, any profits will be worth less after the euros have been converted to dollars. That would also be the case if a company owned factories in Europe. Multinational companies that operate and market products in dozens of countries face multiple variations of that situation all around the globe.

To control the effect of currency fluctuations, companies often enter into contracts that offset the risk. A contract might give a company the right to sell euros at a given price, regardless of their value on foreign exchange markets. Then if the euro falls in value, the company is protected.

THINK CRITICALLY

1. If one Canadian dollar is worth 75 U.S. cents, how many Canadian dollars is a U.S. dollar worth?

2. If a company pays $50,000 for the right to sell 10 million euros for $9 million, how much does it gain if one euro is worth 85 cents at the end of the contract period?

FOREIGN INVESTMENT

Some companies have identified businesses in other countries that have already developed production or marketing capabilities. Rather than entering the country and starting a new business, the company purchases the existing business. Owning all or part of an existing business in another country is known as **foreign investment**. Through foreign investment, businesses can move more quickly into another country. They can also use the business' past records to determine whether it is a good investment. The new owners may decide to change the business or continue to operate it in the same way as the previous owners. That decision will be based on the past success of the business and the needs of the company making the foreign investment. Figure 18-2 lists some recent examples of companies that have been purchased by organizations from other countries.

American companies have been active in foreign investments in the past, but in recent years other countries have also increased their foreign investments. In 1960, the United States had half of the world's total foreign investment. While the actual dollars invested in the businesses in other countries has increased from that time, today the United States has only about a third of the world total. In addition, the United States is an attractive country in which foreign businesses like to invest. Currently it is the leading host country for foreign investments. Just as the types of exports are changing, so are the types of businesses in which foreign companies invest. At this time about half of all foreign investments are in manufacturing businesses, with 20 percent in mining and oil companies and 30 percent in marketing, finance, and service businesses. The percentage of manufacturing investments is declining while marketing investments are increasing.

JOINT VENTURES

When two or more companies in different countries determine that they have common interests, they may form a venture. In a **joint venture**, independent companies develop a relationship to participate in common business activities. The agreement may be in the form of a contract where the companies agree to a specific set of activities for a predetermined period of time. Another form of joint venture is where each company actually agrees to purchase a portion of the other company to create joint ownership. They then have a continuing relationship based on that ownership. A few years ago, three large airlines, Delta Air Lines, SwissAir, and Singapore Airlines, agreed to purchase 5 percent of the stock in each of the other airlines in order to

FIGURE 18-2
Many well-known businesses have been acquired by companies from other countries.

EXAMPLES OF RECENT FOREIGN INVESTMENTS

Purchaser	Investment	Type of Business
Phillip Morris Co., Inc (United States)	Jacobs Suchard Ltd. (Switzerland)	Chocolate/Coffee
Ford Motor Company (United States)	Jaguar (United Kingdom)	Automobiles
PepsiCo, Inc. (United States)	Empresas Gamesa SA de CV (Mexico)	Snack Foods
Bass PLC (United Kingdom)	Holiday Inns (United States)	Motels
Investcorp International (Bahrain)	Saks Fifth Ave. (United States)	Retailing
Accor SA (France)	Motel 6 (United States)	Motels

develop an international venture. Consider the advantages that type of relationship could offer when the three companies compete with other airlines for international travel. It also creates some problems in managing the three companies since they are still independently operated companies with different markets and customers.

checkpoint

If an American company wants to expand manufacturing overseas, what options does it have?

MULTINATIONAL COMPANIES

Some companies have been involved in international business for a long time. They may use several of the strategies described above and sell services and products in a large number of countries throughout the world. They probably are purchasing products and services from companies in many countries to use in production and operations. Businesses that are heavily involved in international business usually develop factories and offices in several countries in order to keep operations closer to the customers. Businesses that have operations throughout the world and that conduct planning for worldwide markets are **multinational companies**. Multinational businesses no longer think of themselves as located in one country selling to customers in other countries. They think globally.

WORLDVIEW

Hypermarkets Vying for Asian Retailing

Western discount retailing giants such as America's Wal-Mart, Britain's Tesco, and France's Carrefour are trying to transform Asian retailing. Not long ago, Asian retailing was dominated by traditional outdoor markets comprised of hundreds of independent stalls. Lately, warehouse-style hypermarkets have been taking over leadership. According to the *Economist* magazine, what had until recently been a local business run by locals is quickly becoming an international industry run by foreigners. By matching the locals' prices with the help of centralized purchasing and other economies of scale, the hypermarkets are drawing away customers in droves with the lure of air conditioning and convenient one-stop shopping.

The multinational retailers have moved in so quickly and so aggressively that local competition no longer appears to be much of a threat in most markets. In some cases, aided by a regional financial crisis in the late 1990s that softened up the locals, the western companies bought them out. Now the real competition is among the multinationals themselves. In many cases they are building stores virtually right next to each other.

Such developments demonstrate the need for companies engaged in international marketing to keep close tabs on the markets they are moving into. Conditions change very rapidly, especially when they are the catalysts for most of the changes.

THINK CRITICALLY

1. How has the nature of the competition changed for Wal-Mart and Carrefour since they first entered Asian markets in the 1990s?

2. If western retailers succeed in taking over the industry in Asia, can they then be less concerned about satisfying customers' needs and devote more attention to building profits?

FIGURE 18-3
Multinational companies offer many employment opportunities throughout the world.

THE LARGEST WORLDWIDE EMPLOYERS

Company	Country	Employees (Estimated)
General Motors (vehicles)	United States	750,000
Coal India (mining)	India	670,000
IRI (metals)	Italy	410,000
Siemens (electronics)	Germany	400,000
Daimler-Benz (vehicles)	Germany	380,000
IBM (computers)	United States	350,000
PepsiCo (food, beverages)	United States	340,000
Ford Motor Co. (vehicles)	United States	330,000
Hitachi (electronics)	Japan	310,000
Unilever (food)	United Kingdom	300,000

they work for the multinational company. Figure 18-3 shows that there are many employment opportunities in multinational businesses.

Competitors for multinational businesses also come from many different locations. A business may compete with one set of companies in Australia and another in Africa or South America. There may be a few large multinationals that compete for customers in all parts of the world. Thinking globally opens up many opportunities for businesses but also makes business and marketing decisions even more complex.

There are many businesses that you may think of as U.S. companies that are really multinational. They operate throughout the world and derive a large part of their sales and profits from countries other than the United States. General Motors Corp. is an example of a multinational company. At one point in the 1990s, it was earning more than 70 percent of its profits from outside the United States. Other examples of well-known multinational companies that started in the U.S. are Coca-Cola, Hilton Hotels, John Deere, 3M Corp., Nike, and IBM. There are also many multinational firms that started in other countries. Some familiar examples are Nestle S.A., DaimlerChrysler, Panasonic, Seiko, Hyundai, L'Oreal, and CibaGeigy. These are just a few of the growing number of multinational businesses.

Multinational companies hire employees, including managers, from many countries. They expect their employees to be able and willing to work with people from all over the world.

Employees often travel and some even relocate and live in other countries while

checkpoint

Why do multinational companies operate in so many different markets and hire employees and managers from so many countries?

LESSON REVIEW

1. What are some of the advantages and disadvantages of indirect exporting?

2. Why is the United States such an attractive host country for foreign investment?

3. Why do companies form joint ventures rather than merge into a single company?

4. What does it mean if a country has a positive balance of trade?

5. What are the advantages of foreign investment over foreign production?

6. Where do multinational companies maintain their headquarters?

18.3 UNDERSTANDING INTERNATIONAL MARKETS

GOALS

- Explain how economic development and conditions affect the ability to successfully market within a country.
- Describe the factors that determine the best marketing mix for particular countries.
- Examine how conditions and customs in international markets can affect the successful completion of marketing functions.

The marketing concept applies in other countries' markets like it does in the United States. While the same marketing functions are completed in international business, there are differences in the specific marketing activities that are effective from one country to another. Business people often work with marketing experts from the foreign country to be sure they use the most effective procedures.

Name three consumer products that are popular in foreign markets but which are not in demand in the United States. Why are these products popular overseas, but not in the United States?

ECONOMIC ENVIRONMENT

The concept of a market in other countries is the same as a market in this country. A market refers to the description of the prospective customers a business wants to serve and the location of those customers. It is important to remember that just as markets are not all alike in your own country, there are differences in markets within other countries as well. Business people should not assume that all countries have the same kinds of markets or that all people in a country have the same characteristics, needs, and interests (see Figure 18-4).

FIGURE 18-4
Businesses must gather a great deal of information in order to determine if they can successfully market their products and services in another country.

Information Needed for International Markets

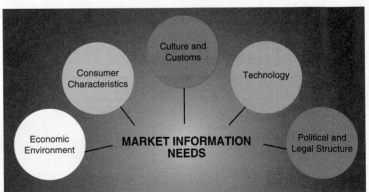

FIGURE 18-5
There are three types of economies in the world. Each economic stage requires a different type of marketing.

The Three Stages of Economic Development

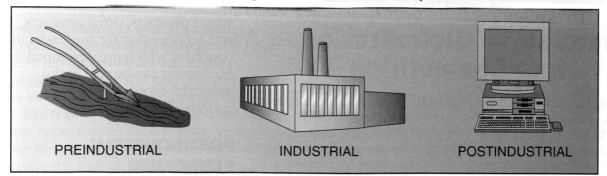

PREINDUSTRIAL INDUSTRIAL POSTINDUSTRIAL

There is a great deal of similarity but also some difference between marketing internationally and marketing within one country. The idea of identifying markets and developing a marketing mix remains the same. So does the need to complete each of the marketing functions. The characteristics of markets, the information needed and how it is obtained, and the procedures used in developing each of the marketing mix elements will change as companies concentrate on markets in other countries.

The level of economic development of a country and the current condition of the economy must be understood for effective marketing. A country that has a high standard of living will usually manufacture and sell a variety of consumer products and services. That country will offer very different marketing opportunities than a country that is struggling to meet basic consumer needs. Economies of the world's countries can be grouped into three broad categories: preindustrial, industrial, and postindustrial (see Figure 18-5).

PREINDUSTRIAL ECONOMIES

The **preindustrial economy** is based on agriculture and raw material development through activities such as mining, oil production, and cutting timber. Many of the country's citizens provide for all of their own needs and have a very low standard of living. Manufacturing, distribution, and retail systems are just beginning to develop. This makes it difficult to produce, distribute, or sell products.

Leaders in a country at the preindustrial economy stage recognize the importance of moving to the next stage. They see their natural resources being consumed and few choices of jobs for their citizens. Those countries are unable to participate in the international economy except through the sale of raw materials. The leaders of the countries are looking for help in developing their economies.

Countries with preindustrial economies were once viewed as offering few opportunities for foreign businesses. Some companies purchased raw materials in the countries. Others actually developed mining, lumbering, or oil drilling activities. Often those companies were accused of exploiting the countries. Some companies took natural resources and returned very little to the economies. Today, many preindustrial countries provide opportunities for companies that want to sell manufacturing equipment or cooperate in the development of manufacturing businesses.

Many of the countries also seek assistance in developing distribution systems. There must be effective methods of getting products to customers and places for the products to be sold. Without distribution systems, businesses will not be successful. Roads, railroads, and airports are needed to distribute products as manufacturing develops. Developing distribution systems

JUDGMENT CALL

Bribery Common but Not Legal

Offering bribes or demanding kickbacks to facilitate international business transactions is widespread, even though it is outlawed in virtually every country. Because it is so common and so difficult to fight, it is one of the toughest barriers to international trade faced by American businesses.

Unlike in other countries, United States law makes it illegal for a U.S. company to bribe a foreign official. So Americans generally have no good choices when they encounter foreign officials who demand payment before they will award them a contract or issue necessary permits. They can either break the law to get the contract, or they can decline to pay and lose the business.

Some U.S. businesses opt to transact foreign business through foreign partners or subsidiaries. Then foreign employees handle the distasteful transactions while the parent company looks the other way and avoids violating U.S. laws.

THINK CRITICALLY

1. If a businessperson encounters a foreign citizen who expects an illicit payment to facilitate a business deal, what options does he or she have?

2. Why are attempts to combat bribery in international trade so difficult?

of money they have to spend, and other characteristics such as age, income, employment, and education. Businesses must determine where prospective customers are located in the country, where they typically buy products, methods of transportation, and communications media available. This information that helps identify and locate people is known as demographics.

CULTURE AND CUSTOMS

The culture and customs of a country may determine whether certain products or marketing methods will be appropriate or acceptable. **Culture** is the common beliefs and behaviors of a group of people who have a similar heritage and experience. Family structures, religion, beliefs and values, language, personal habits, and daily activities may be quite different from what the marketers are used to in their own culture. Failure to recognize differences that are important to people from other cultures may result in misunderstanding and mistrust.

For example, certain words can have very different meanings when translated into

another language. In some countries it is important to be exactly on time for an appointment, while in other countries people are not concerned if they are late.

The types of communications that are acceptable in business and the meaning of communications are important in international business. Some cultures require a great deal of personal or social conversation preceding the discussion of business, while others are offended by conversations that are too personal. Other cultural factors include understanding of ethics, male/female relationships, and the importance of age, education, and income.

TECHNOLOGY

The technology of business and marketing is changing rapidly. Businesses are adopting new methods of manufacturing, transportation, product handling, and communication. Consumers have access to computers, new types of appliances, and changing technology for work and leisure time.

Once these new technical products are developed in one country, they are usually distributed and accepted in many other countries. Businesses cannot assume, though, that the same technology used in their home country is available or used in other countries. Even if the technology is used, there might be important differences in those countries. Even basic technologies that have existed for many years may be different. An excellent example is the metric system. Several years ago, there was an attempt to convert most of the measurement systems in the United States to the metric system, which is widely used throughout the rest of the world. That attempt was not successful, although metric measures are used more widely than before. If it is the standard in another country, customers there will expect it to be used on all products. It will affect everything from tools, to container sizes, to measurements for replacement parts.

POLITICAL AND LEGAL STRUCTURE

One of the most important factors that can affect the success of international marketing is the type of political and legal systems in a country. The types of political systems range from democratic, in which the citizens of the country control the decisions of the government, to autocratic, where power is in the hands of a very small group of people. In the recent past, one of the major political structures, communism, was rejected in many Central European countries and in the former Soviet Union. Those countries reorganized their political systems to adopt more democratic principles.

The stability of the political system is important for businesses. If a country is unstable, it is very possible that business ownership and operating procedures may be threatened. There have been many examples of countries in which the government was overthrown and the businesses owned by people from other countries were destroyed or taken over by the new government.

Countries develop laws to regulate business. Many of those laws affect international business operations. Some countries have laws that provide strong support for their businesses in the sale of products and services in other countries or protect the country's businesses from foreign competition. Because the leaders of industrial economies want the businesses in their country to be successful, they may try to restrict the amount of imports through the use of quotas or tariffs. **Quotas** are limits on the numbers of specific types of products foreign companies can sell in the country. **Tariffs** are taxes placed on imported products to increase the price for which they are sold. As an example, the United States has laws that regulate the number of trucks and motorcycles that can be imported into the country. Some categories of vehicles are charged an import tax to increase their price. This makes the American vehicle a better value for many consumers, effectively limiting the number of foreign products sold.

Countries may also support their businesses through subsidies. A **subsidy** is money provided to a business to assist in the development and sale of its products. European countries provide financial support to airplane manufacturer Airbus so it can compete with U.S. manufacturers. The company has signed contracts to produce nearly a third of all commercial airplane orders in a recent year.

Name four factors that can affect the success of a marketing plan in a foreign country.

INTERNATIONAL MARKETING ACTIVITIES

Before a business can begin to develop a marketing mix for an international market, it needs to secure reliable information about that market. The procedures for gathering and analyzing market information are quite similar for international markets to those used in a business' home country. The business needs to develop a marketing information system to collect and analyze information. It also needs to complete marketing research or work with research companies to answer specific questions about customers and competitors.

GATHERING MARKET INFORMATION

The characteristics of specific countries require special attention to both marketing information management and marketing research. The sources of information, the types of technology and research capabilities, how people respond to research

FIGURE 18-6
*The same marketing functions must be completed by businesses whether marketing
nationally or internationally. There will often be important differences in how those
functions are completed in foreign markets.*

Marketing Functions in International Business

Product/Service Management
Distribution
Selling
Marketing-Information Management
Financing
Pricing
Promotion

procedures, and the laws relating to information collection will likely be quite different. For example, in the United States much of the consumer research today is completed using telephone calls. In some countries, technology is not as well developed and fewer people have telephones. In other countries, asking personal questions using the telephone is considered very rude.

Businesses often work with marketers and marketing businesses from the country in which they hope to market products to gather information. This helps to insure that those doing the research have a better understanding of the unique characteristics of the country and that the research will be completed in a way that does not harm the image of the business. People in international business need to listen carefully to people from the countries they want to serve in order to avoid biases and stereotypes.

DEVELOPING THE MARKETING MIX

After business people have gathered the necessary information to understand the new market, they can develop the marketing mix. With this information, the mix can be specifically designed to meet the needs of the international market. Again, the types of marketing activities often will be the same or similar to those previously used by the company, but there are some important differences in international marketing. Reviewing

the functions of marketing reveals some of those differences. (See Figure 18-6.)

Product/Service Management
Products and services must be developed to meet the needs of customers. Important activities for international markets include packaging for protection and for easy use by customers. In addition, brand names must be carefully selected to fit the language of the country. Finally, any product information or instructions must be written to meet the laws of the country and to clearly communicate with the customers.

Distribution   Effective distribution of products to and within other countries may be the most challenging marketing function. Decisions need to be made on the appropriate shipping method from country to country and within the country of the new markets. Selection of the types of businesses in which the product will be sold is part of distribution. It is important to know the amount of time it will take from processing an order until the product is available to customers. Also, laws regulating distribution, including taxes, tariffs, and quotas, must be observed. Most countries require inspection of imported products, which must be arranged either before the product is shipped or when it reaches the country.

Selling   Personal contact between a business and its customers is very important in many countries. Once again, customs play an important role in successful selling.

Salespeople must be aware of the need to be formal or informal, who initiates conversations, how a business card is presented, and whether it is appropriate to conduct business during a meal. In some cultures, it is expected that salespeople present a gift to a prospective customer, while in other countries the gift would be seen as a bribe and would be illegal or offensive.

Marketing-Information Management Businesses need to identify information needs, create methods of collecting and analyzing that information, and set procedures for ensuring the information is up-to-date. In the United States, the government is an important source of information about many other countries. The U.S. Foreign Commerce Service is an agency of the Department of Commerce. It collects business information from a large number of international sources that is updated very frequently. The information is available on an electronic database and is easily accessible by businesses.

Financing In most cases, the business needs to extend credit to wholesalers or retailers who distribute the products in the country. The accepted credit practices for consumers will also have to be considered. The procedures used to assist customers in purchasing will need to conform to the country's laws and customs. The types of contracts and forms used, as well as the monetary system, may be different. While some credit cards are used internationally, they may not be the typical form of payment used by consumers in each country. The business will usually need to develop relationships with banks and other financial organizations in the new country.

Pricing It is not likely that customers from another country will have the same perception of value as those in the business' home country. Even if that perception is similar, a different money system is used and the costs of marketing are often higher. Therefore, prices will have to be changed. The business may have been used to offering discounts or other types of price reductions. The customs of the new country may require a new approach to determining the way prices are set, changed, and communicated to the customer.

Promotion Promotion is the marketing function where a country's customs and culture are very important. Promotion relies on effective communication. Language and pictures communicate a business' message to customers. There are many examples of promotional mistakes where words were not translated correctly or had very different meanings after translation.

Promotional planning for international markets includes careful selection of the media to be used. Mass media may not be as available in some countries or may not be used for promotion. In many countries, television is not used as extensively for advertising as it is in the United States.

✓ checkpoint

What must be done before developing a marketing mix for a targeted international market?

LESSON REVIEW

1. Why do preindustrial economies present very challenging conditions for the marketing of products and services by foreign businesses?

2. Besides the stage of economic development of a country, what other economic factor is important to effective international marketing?

3. Why is political stability an important consideration in international marketing?

4. What happens when you plug an American hair dryer into a German electrical outlet without using a transformer to reduce the voltage? What is this an example of?

5. Why do prices typically have to be adjusted for foreign markets?

CHAPTER 18

SUMMARY

Lesson 18.1

A. International trade is the sale of products and services to other countries. Products or services purchased from another country are imports. Products and services sold to another country are exports.

B. Businesses try to sell products or services in international markets when they run out of new customers in their home markets. They also seek to equalize competition from foreign firms in their home markets. They want to satisfy increased demand from foreign consumers for a greater variety of products.

Lesson 18.2

A. Indirect exporting is done through an agent representing the exporting company. Direct exporting happens when a company controls the marketing of its own product overseas. The difference between a country's imports and exports is known as its balance of trade.

B. If an American company wants to expand its manufacturing base overseas, it can build a new plant, buy a company already in production, or form a joint venture.

C. Businesses with operations throughout the world are known as multinational companies. Multinationals operate in many markets and hire employees from many countries to stay in touch with local markets, respond quickly to changing conditions, and promote long-term, stable growth by diversifying various economic and financial risks.

Lesson 18.3

A. Preindustrial economies are based on agriculture and raw materials, industrial economies on manufacturing, and postindustrial economies on high-tech products and services and the global marketplace. Economic development and current economic conditions are important to marketers.

B. Companies successfully using the marketing concept have an advantage in international markets. A quota is a limit on how much of an import foreign companies can sell. Tariffs are taxes on imported products.

C. Business people often work with marketing experts from the foreign country to ensure effective procedures are used. Factors that can affect marketing in a foreign country include traditions, language, standards, and customary business procedures.

REVIEW MARKETING CONCEPTS

1. True or False: Preindustrial economies can offer good opportunities for foreign businesses, although the economies' needs and resources limit the opportunities.

2. True or False: Most of the countries in the world have industrial economies.

3. True or False: Because of cultural and language barriers, international trade in services is not significant.

4. True or False: The marketing concept does not apply in some foreign markets that do not encourage consumer choice.

5. True or False: Many multinational corporations have exploited information technology to develop worldwide monopolistic power over their respective industries.

6. True or False: The United States produces a much larger share of the world's goods and services than is represented by its share of world population.

7. True or False: Regional trade pacts can both increase and decrease international trade barriers at the same time.

REVIEW

REVIEW MARKETING TERMS

Match the terms listed with the definitions. Some terms may not be used.

8. Occurs when prices increase faster than the value of the goods and services.

9. Products and services that are sold to another country.

10. Occurs when a business takes complete responsibility for marketing its products in other countries.

11. The difference between the amount of a country's imports and exports.

12. Products or services purchased from another country.

13. Occurs when a company owns and operates production facilities in another country.

14. Tax placed on imported products that has the effect of increasing the price for which they are sold.

15. The per capita value of resources produced by a country.

16. The exchange of products and services among people in different countries.

17. Money provided to a business to assist in the development and sale of its products.

18. The amount of goods and services that can be obtained with a specific amount of money.

19. Carried out through agents that arrange for the sale of products in other countries.

20. Limit on the number or amount of a product that foreign companies can sell in the country.

21. The total value of the goods and services produced in a country during the year.

a. balance of trade
b. culture
c. direct exporting
d. exports
e. foreign investment
f. foreign production
g. GDP
h. imports
i. indirect exporting
j. industrial economy
k. inflation
l. international trade
m. joint venture
n. multinational company
o. postindustrial economy
p. preindustrial economy
q. purchasing power
r. quota
s. recession
t. standard of living
u. subsidy
v. tariff

APPLY MARKETING FUNCTIONS

MARKETING RESEARCH

22. It is important to learn as much about a country as possible before making a decision about marketing products and services there. Your task is to develop a market research report about a country.

Select any country you believe might provide potentially attractive markets for U.S. businesses. Gather facts and information about the country using the library, Internet, or other sources. Collect information about the following factors—population characteristics, geography, culture, economy, government and politics, and business statistics. If possible, interview someone from your school or community who is familiar with the country.

When you have completed the data collection, prepare a written report describing the country and its potential for international business. Include several tables or figures in your report. Also make sure to use footnotes and attach a bibliography.

19.1 ASSESSING BUSINESS RISKS

GOALS

- Explain why businesses take risks and how they are classified.
- Describe the four ways available for businesses to deal with risks.

MARKETING MATTERS

Risks can be classified in three ways—based on whether taking the risk presents an opportunity for gain, whether the risk is controllable, and whether the risk is insurable.

Business people deal with risks in one of four ways or in a combination of ways. They can avoid a risk by choosing an alternative that does not entail that risk. They can transfer a risk to someone else, usually at a cost. They can insure the potential loss from a risk. Or they can assume the risk and accept the consequences.

Describe a risky course of action that you chose to undertake in the recent past and the potential losses and gains that it entailed. What was the outcome?

THE NATURE OF BUSINESS RISK

Every year thousands of people decide to open their own businesses. Most entrepreneurs will use all of the money they have saved. They will borrow thousands of additional dollars. They may quit their current jobs to devote all their time to the new business. Each believes he or she has an idea that will attract customers, earn a living, and maybe even make a lot of money.

At the same time that thousands of entrepreneurs are opening new businesses, many others are closing their doors. Their dreams did not come true. They are disappointed and discouraged. Most lost the money they invested in the business. Many will never attempt a new business again.

When a person decides to open a business or a company decides to develop a new product, there is a chance for success and a chance for failure (see Figure 19-1). The

possibility that a loss can occur as the result of a decision or activity is known as **risk**. Why do people invest a great deal of time and money in new businesses or products when there is a risk of loss? The typical answer is that while there is a chance of loss, there is also an opportunity. An **opportunity** is the possibility for success.

FIGURE 19-1
A business is willing to take risks because of opportunities. It may lose money, but it has a chance to make a profit.

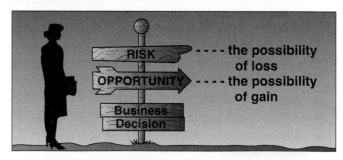

The Outcomes of a Business Decision

Success takes many forms. For both individuals and businesses, it can mean recognition, being viewed as a leader, or providing personal satisfaction and satisfaction for others. An important measure of success in business is profit. The private enterprise economy is organized to encourage risk-taking. People invest money and take risks in business in order to make a profit.

Each of us takes risks every day. You might decide whether to speak to a new person you meet. The risk is that the person might not respond in a positive way. The opportunity is that you will establish a new friendship. You may have spent a great deal of time and effort in the past few years selecting difficult courses, completing homework, and preparing yourself for college. There is a risk that all of the effort will not pay off. Your grades might not be high enough, or you may not have the money needed to attend the college you have chosen. You are willing to take the risk for the opportunities provided by a college education.

CLASSIFICATION OF RISK

Marketers need to understand the risks involved in order to deal with them. There are three classifications of risk. The classifications are based on the result of the risk, control of the risk, and insurability of the risk.

Result of the Risk Some risks, known as **pure risks**, present the chance of loss but no opportunity for gain. When you are driving, you are at risk of being in an accident. If you have an accident you will likely suffer a loss. You could be injured, you could injure others, or there could be damage to the vehicles. If you avoid an accident you do not have an opportunity for gain.

GET THE MESSAGE

Serious Business That's Only a Game

Some people take risks when there is little chance for success. Others seldom take risks even when everything seems to be in their favor. Analyzing risks and opportunities is an important skill for business people and consumers alike. Brian Wiersema believes everyone should know how to take financial risks. As a former teacher, he knows that games can be an important teaching tool. He developed *The Reward Game*.

The game helps players understand the influence the economy has on investments. Wiersema found that using *The Reward Game,* even elementary school students could understand it. After playing the game, younger students could do as well as many adults, including some stockbrokers.

The Reward Game is played on a board much like *Monopoly.* Every player starts with cash, stocks, and bonds. During the game, inflation can increase the value of those assets, or downturns in the economy can reduce their value. As each player moves

around the board, there are opportunities to make purchases and investments, or increase savings. Some decisions will be profitable while others will not. Money can be borrowed when needed, but players might be surprised by a sudden jump in interest rates.

People who have played *The Reward Game* come away with a new appreciation for how the economy works. They see that the best decisions can be ruined or poor decisions improved by changes in the economy. They also learn that it is possible to understand the factors that can influence the success or failure of investment decisions. Learning through a game is not as risky as spending your own money for the lesson.

THINK CRITICALLY

1. Why is a game a particularly good way for young people to learn about the risks of investing?

2. What sorts of risks do changes in the economy pose for businesses?

Insure the Risk If a financial loss is possible from the risk and that loss can be predicted, the risk can be insured. The company facing the risk pays a small amount of the potential loss to an insurer. If the loss occurs, the insurer guarantees payment to the company. The company is willing to accept a small, certain loss (the cost of insurance) for protection from a larger, uncertain loss. Remember that many risks are not insurable because they are speculative.

Assume the Risk A company that assumes a risk faces the risk and deals with the result. Some risks are quite unlikely to occur. Other risks have relatively small losses compared to the opportunities.

There are risks that are a normal part of business. In each case, it may be best to assume the risk because it will not have a serious negative effect on the business.

There are other risks that a business has to assume because they cannot be avoided, transferred, or insured. Once a product is in the market, many things can happen that may result in much lower sales than expected. The business accepts that possibility and attempts to make the product as successful as possible. Occasionally, conditions change rapidly and the business faces a risk that was not anticipated. There is not enough time to make changes, so the business must assume the risk.

What are the four ways people deal with the risks that are inherent in operating a business?

LESSON REVIEW

1. When a gambler goes to a racetrack or a casino, what kind of risk is he or she assuming?

2. Why is the private enterprise economy organized to encourage risk-taking?

3. What conditions are necessary in order for a risk to be insurable?

4. Why must a risk be faced by a large number of people in order for it to be insurable?

5. Why would a business assume a risk that it could avoid?

6. How might the formation of a joint venture be a form of dealing with risk? What method of dealing with risk does it represent?

IDENTIFYING MARKETING RISKS

MARKETING MATTERS

Marketing poses many different kinds of risks. Many factors combine to determine whether a business is successful or not. Those factors include the type of competition, the economy, laws and regulations, technology, and customer demand. As factors change in unpredictable ways and market conditions shift, each poses risks and also offers opportunities. Marketers try to take advantage of the opportunities before conditions change at the risk of making a decision that ends up being ill-suited by the time it is implemented.

When a company has choices of marketing mixes, the company often selects the one that emphasizes its strengths and can be completed successfully. Yet each of the marketing mix elements—product, distribution, price, and promotion—is subject to certain risks. Marketers consider those risks when planning and implementing marketing decisions.

Make a list of five factors in the current economy and legal environment that pose serious risks to area businesses. Explain each.

GOALS

- **Explain how changes in the economic and competitive environment create marketing risks.**
- **Describe the marketing risks associated with each of the marketing mix elements.**

THE RISK OF CHANGE

Business people, including marketers, face a variety of risks. An important part of the product/service management function is risk management. **Risk management** in marketing includes providing security and safety for products, personnel, and customers, as well as reducing the risk associated with marketing decisions and activities. It is possible to analyze the marketing environment and marketing mix to identify the areas where risks are likely to occur.

Many factors combine to determine whether a business is successful or not. Those factors include the type of competition, the economy, laws and regulations, technology, and customer demand. Each factor poses risks and also offers opportunities. Marketers are always looking for profitable new opportunities. They are willing to take a risk if there is a real possibility of success. They evaluate opportunities to determine which provide the greatest opportunities with the least risk.

Economy Businesses regularly face the risk of a change in the economy. Sales may be high and customers may value the product until faced with a recession. Suddenly, the business is unable to maintain sales, and profits fall. The same result can occur after a government action. Increases in taxes, implementation of new laws, or a court ruling can require a major change in operations.

New Products New technology and products can enter the market at any time. Those changes can have an immediate effect on a business. Consider how quickly a new video game or a new version of computer software makes existing products out of date. When a few supermarkets and other retail stores converted to scanner technology to speed customer checkouts, other stores had to install the equipment quickly or risk losing customers.

Customer Needs Customer needs can change with little notice. Marketing responds to customers' needs, so such a change will cause a loss of business. Product life cycles illustrate how demand changes for products. Some life-cycle stages last only a very short time and require the business to make changes to maintain sales and profits.

✓ **checkpoint**

How do changes in the economic environment affect marketing risks?

RISKS TO ELEMENTS
OF THE MARKETING MIX

When selecting from among several target markets, a company reduces its risk if it works with markets that can be clearly identified and located. The company should choose a market for which adequate information is available. A group of customers that has purchased a company's products before and has been very satisfied presents a better opportunity for introducing a new product than a group that has no previous experience with the company. When a company has choices of marketing mixes, the company will often select the one that emphasizes its strengths and that can be completed successfully.

Each of the marketing mix elements is subject to some risks. Marketers should consider those risks when planning and implementing marketing decisions.

PRODUCT

The product itself faces several risks. Probably the most obvious is the risk of damage before the product is sold or used. The product needs to be designed so it is sturdy and durable. Packaging needs to protect the product while it is transported and stored. You have probably purchased products that were damaged or broken when you opened them. Perhaps they did not perform the way you expected when you used them. It is likely that you returned the product for a refund. You may have lost confidence in that product and others with the same brand name. A company risks a great deal with a poorly designed product.

Businesses must study how the consumer will use the product. They must be sure it is designed to meet consumer expectations for use. Also if the product will not be consumed immediately, it must not spoil or deteriorate before it is used. Many food products are dated to tell consumers when they were processed or when they should be used. Restaurants that prepare foods in advance have to discard food if it sits too long before being ordered.

The product design must be up to date. If competing products have improvements or incorporate new technology, customers will quickly see the differences and switch to those brands. There are many examples of businesses that failed because their products did not change with the times. Even the most loyal customers will not continue to buy the same product when they see that a superior design is available.

The product risk that concerns businesses most is liability. **Liability** is a legal responsibility for loss or damage. You frequently hear or read of a company that has to pay millions of dollars to a person who was injured while using the company's products. Companies are responsible for the design and use of their products. When injury, death, or financial loss occurs that involves a company's product in any way, the company may be held legally liable. Even services are subject to that risk. One of the highest expenses for physicians is the cost of malpractice insurance. The insurance is needed for protection from the cost of lawsuits brought by patients who believe they were mistreated or injured while under the doctor's care.

DISTRIBUTION

When planning for the distribution of products, businesses need to be concerned about safety, security, and performance of distribution activities. Safety risks include the safety of products, buildings, and equipment. They also include the safety of people involved in distribution activities and customer safety. Whenever products are moved from one location to another, there are opportunities for damage or injury. Procedures for product handling, storage, and transportation are planned carefully to reduce that possibility. People are trained in proper handling procedures. Safety standards are used in the design of facilities and equipment.

WORLDVIEW

Coke Returns to Angola

A country embroiled in a long-running civil war, where even major roads are too risky for transporting goods because of guerilla attacks, would not seem to be much of a market for a soft drink company. Still, Coca-Cola already makes money in Africa, and there's much more room for growth there than in highly developed markets such as Europe and North America. So in 2000, it opened a $33 million bottling plant in Angola, 25 years after pulling out of the then newly independent former Portuguese colony.

Coke has operations throughout Africa. Some are limited to distribution of product made elsewhere. Others involve both production and distribution. The potential rewards for Coke are clear, and so are the risks. To offset some of those risks, it formed a joint venture with the Angolan government and South African Breweries.

Since the Angolan government has a 45% stake in the Coca-Cola venture, it has a strong incentive to see it succeed. That's one reason government soldiers protect the new plant in Bom Jesus, 30 miles from the nation's capital. It also puts a damper on black-market suppliers of canned Coke who can undercut prices by evading import duties.

THINK CRITICALLY

1. How does the formation of a joint venture with South African Breweries and the Angolan government help to reduce Coke's risks?

2. What political risk has Coke taken by investing in a country where a civil war is being fought?

As products move through a channel of distribution, there are many opportunities for theft. Products can be stolen by burglars, by customers who shoplift, and by employees. Security equipment and procedures and security personnel are used to protect against theft. You can see the importance that is placed on security when you visit most retail stores. Well-designed merchandise displays, security tags, video monitors, security personnel, and electronic sensors at all exits are used to reduce shoplifting and employee theft. Even with the thousands of dollars invested in security, shoplifting in many businesses is as much as 10 percent of sales. That loss adds tremendously to the price of products. It also requires special product handling procedures that are an inconvenience to customers and an extra expense to the business.

The final area of business risk related to distribution is the performance of the distribution system. Products need to be available to the customer at the place and time they are needed. If the product is not there, a sale is missed. Products must move through the distribution system efficiently.

Mobile Technology 'Next Big Thing'

Even as most businesses are still coming to grips with e-commerce as a means of conducting marketing activities, m-commerce is being touted as the next big thing. The "m" stands for "mobile," which means "wireless."

Once people get used to buying things and performing other activities online, allowing them to do it from wherever they are seems to be the inevitable next step. Instead of sitting at a desk using a personal computer to access the Internet, they will use a cell phone, personal digital assistant, or some other mobile device yet to be created.

In the minds of most industry forecasters, the question is not *whether* m-commerce will eventually supplant PC-based e-commerce, but only the *form* it will take. Will m-commerce be carried out by dozens of different devices, each designed to perform certain specialized tasks, or will the PC be replaced by some other multifunctional mobile device similar to a handheld organizer? Because the United

States has led the world in wired Internet commerce, it may lag behind other parts of the world in adopting m-commerce.

Gartner Group, an information technology research firm, has projected that more than a quarter of all online transactions would be made over mobile devices by 2005. In its opinion, it is only a question of when accessing the Web over wireless devices becomes more convenient than other options.

THINK CRITICALLY

1. Why is wireless Internet access expected to replace wired access?

2. What is the biggest hurdle for wireless technology to overcome?

3. Why is the United States' lead in wired technology a hindrance to the development of m-commerce, at least compared to other areas that are less wired?

Ordering and order processing, inventory control, materials handling, and transportation must all work effectively. If an order is misplaced, a shipment is sent to the wrong location, or inventory levels are not maintained correctly, customers cannot obtain the products they want. Product damage is another concern in the distribution system. Procedures and equipment are used that protect the products while they move through the channel of distribution.

It is even possible for factors outside the control of a business to interfere with distribution. Poor weather conditions can slow transportation or damage or destroy buildings, equipment, and inventory.

PRICE

Customers must see the product price as a value. They also must be able to afford the product. Companies face two risks when pricing products and services. The price can be set too high, reducing demand and causing products to remain unsold. On the other extreme, if products are priced too low, the company is unable to make a profit.

Setting a product price is very difficult. A number of factors enter into the price, including the costs of production, marketing, and operations. Any services offered, discounts, markdowns, and the cost of credit must be figured into the price in order for a profit to be earned. Every business in a channel of distribution must be able to make a profit after paying its costs. Finally, customers will usually compare the cost of a product with those of competitors.

PROMOTION

The goal of promotion is to communicate with consumers to influence them to purchase the company's products. Anything that interferes with that goal is a business risk. The media need to perform as planned. If a radio or television commercial is not aired as planned, or if a newspaper or magazine is not distributed on schedule, the promotional plan is less effective. If a salesperson cannot meet with a customer or does not communicate effectively, sales are lost.

Just as companies are subject to product liability, there are legal responsibilities related to promotion. Information must be honest and accurate, or the company may be liable for the harm caused by inappropriate or illegal promotion.

Another area of risk is the damage that can result from the promotion of other businesses or information communicated by people or other organizations. Sometimes other companies' promotions contain misleading or incorrect information about a competitor's products. While it may be possible to get the company to stop using those promotions, damage may already be done. It is difficult to correct misinformation. Customers who have had a negative experience with a product will often tell many other people about their experiences. That word-of-mouth publicity can be very damaging.

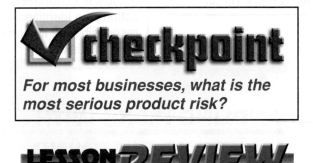

checkpoint

For most businesses, what is the most serious product risk?

LESSON REVIEW

1. What kinds of activities does risk management in marketing encompass?

2. What risks do the courts pose for marketers?

3. In what way is a product life cycle associated with or a reflection of marketing risks that businesses encounter?

4. What are some of the risks associated with the distribution element of the marketing mix?

5. Why is it just as risky to set prices too low as it is to set them too high?

6. Is the risk of having damaging information disseminated by a competitor higher or lower today than it was 25 years ago?

Risks, Rewards, Expected Value

With almost any business or investment activity, the results are uncertain but not wholly unpredictable. In most cases, there is a known range of possible outcomes. For example, investing in a company's stock will result in a complete loss if the company goes bankrupt. On the other hand, if it does very well, the value of the stock might double or triple over a period of time.

Through detailed analysis, reasonably accurate estimates can be made of the likelihood of the various possible outcomes. Those estimates, expressed as probabilities, can be used to derive what is known as the "expected value" of a course of action. Expected value is calculated by multiplying each possible outcome by the probability of its occurrence and then adding up all of the subtotals. That final sum is the expected value, although "expected value" is something of a misnomer, since for any single action the outcome is not likely to be the expected value. Still, the expected value can then be used to determine whether a course of action is a worthwhile risk. For a large number of actions, the average outcome should approximate the average expected value.

Business people need to keep in mind that an expected value is only as good as the probability estimates from which it is derived. If a highly favorable outcome is given an unreasonably optimistic (high) probability, a risk might seem well worth taking when it actually is not.

THINK CRITICALLY

1. In a game of chance played by flipping a coin, when a coin comes up heads the player wins $5 and if it comes up tails the player pays $5. If there is a 50% chance of getting heads or tails, what is the expected value of each flip?

2. What would the expected value be if the player had to pay $6 when the coin came up tails?

Action The final section of the marketing plan is the action plan. In this section the activities and responsibilities for the marketing strategy are identified. Some of the activities and responsibilities will relate to risk reduction. For example, people are given responsibility for quality control, scheduling and coordinating distribution activities, checking promotional plans to make sure they meet all legal requirements, and the many other activities that deal with the risks in marketing. A responsibility of the marketing manager is to carefully review each part of the action plan to determine if risks are adequately addressed.

What are the three sections of the marketing plan that can be used to identify and develop plans to manage marketing risks?

OTHER WAYS OF DEALING WITH MARKETING RISK

In addition to planning, most businesses implement specific security and safety plans, purchase insurance to protect against financial loss, and regularly review marketing activities and operations to identify and reduce risks.

SECURITY AND SAFETY

Because of its importance, security and safety planning is often a responsibility of people specifically trained in that area. In many businesses, security and safety management is part of the operations area. It must be coordinated throughout the business, including marketing activities. Marketers will work with security and safety experts to identify areas needing attention

Pace of Change Heightens Risks

For marketers of digital information products such as computers and computer microprocessors, perhaps the biggest risk they face is getting stuck with outdated products. The second biggest risk they face is not having enough of the latest products to meet demand. Balancing those complementary risks is a key to their survival.

Faster and more powerful products are developed so quickly that any miscalculation can result in either excess or inadequate inventories. Excess inventories that can't be sold soon become virtually worthless inventories. When a slowdown hit the industry in 2000-2001 following years of steady growth, company after company was forced to write off inventories of components. Compaq Computer Corp. announced in April 2001 that $550 million worth of its inventory was essentially worthless. The inventories had been built up to meet ever-growing demand that suddenly came to a screeching halt. Only a few months earlier, many of the same businesses had been furiously trying to increase inventories to keep up with soaring demand.

The problem was exacerbated by a fierce battle for market share between Intel and Advanced Micro Devices, makers of the microprocessors that are the guts of personal computers. The two were locked in a price-and-development war. Often, faster and more powerful microprocessors were introduced at prices substantially less than the prices of less powerful chips that had been introduced only months before. The competition forced companies to sell inventories of existing, inferior chips at steep discounts and, in turn, slashed the value of those chips in computer manufacturers' storerooms.

THINK CRITICALLY

1. When the computer industry was hit by an abrupt slowdown in demand, why did it pose a much greater risk for the most aggressive marketers of personal computers?

2. If building inventories too aggressively is risky, why don't businesses play it safe and keep inventories lean?

and procedures to use that will reduce those problems.

All marketing personnel should receive special training in safety and security procedures (see Figure 19-4). They should know how to recognize problems and prevent accidents and injuries. They should be aware of company policies regarding security, shoplifting, and theft prevention. Salespeople and customer service personnel need to discuss risks and safety concerns related to product use with customers. Products and packaging should be analyzed to insure that they meet all safety and health requirements. Information should be supplied with all products informing customers about safe handling and use of the products.

PURCHASING INSURANCE

One method of transferring risk is to purchase insurance. The payment of insurance premiums transfers some or all of the financial loss for the insured risk to the insurance company. There are some common areas of marketing in which businesses

FIGURE 19-4
It is important that all employees of a business receive training in safety and security. Well-trained employees can be very effective in reducing the losses suffered by a business.

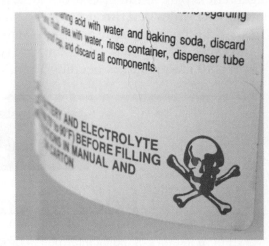
1. Know how to recognize problems
2. Know how to prevent accidents and injuries
3. Be aware of company policies

Employee Training in Security and Safety

purchase insurance. Those areas are shown in Figure 19-5.

Insurance on marketing personnel includes health and life insurance as well as surety bonds. A **surety bond** provides insurance for the failure of a person to perform his or her duties or for losses resulting from employee theft or dishonesty.

Property insurance protects the buildings, equipment, and in some cases, the inventory of the business. Liability insurance pays for damage caused to other people or their property. Theft insurance also provides property protection. There are several types of insurance available to protect against damaged and lost merchandise while it is being transported. Another important type of

FIGURE 19-5
Purchasing insurance is an important way of reducing risk in marketing. There are a variety of specialized policies that insure against common marketing risks.

Common Types of Insurance for Marketing Risks

insurance is **product liability insurance**, which provides protection from claims arising from the use of the company's products. Similar insurance is available for service businesses. An example is the malpractice insurance for physicians discussed earlier.

REDUCING RISKS

Marketers are constantly searching for opportunities. Those opportunities include

new target markets and improved marketing mixes. With every opportunity comes a certain amount of risk. Risks can never be eliminated entirely in marketing. However, careful planning and effective marketing management can avoid some risks and reduce the negative effects of others.

The most important way to reduce risks is with careful planning. The marketing plan provides a useful structure to identify risks and develop ways to deal with them. Another important method of reducing risk is with the careful selection and training of marketing personnel. Employees should be selected who are concerned about customers and their needs. Employees should want to perform their jobs effectively. Then they should be trained to follow safety and security procedures. Finally, all marketing employees should be constantly alert to possible risks that can cause problems for the business or harm to customers or other people. When problems are identified, changes should be made to reduce the risk and avoid damage or loss.

checkpoint

Which marketing personnel should receive special training in dealing with safety and security risks?

LESSON REVIEW

1. Name several types of insurance that cover marketing-related risks.

2. How can marketing risks be minimized in conjunction with developing a marketing strategy?

3. What kinds of marketing risks are dealt with during marketing analysis?

4. Malpractice insurance is an example of what type of marketing-related insurance?

5. What type of insurance might a company purchase if it handles large amounts of cash and wants to cover potential losses that might arise from employee theft?

CHAPTER 19

SUMMARY

Lesson 19.1

A. Risk is inherent in any business. Being able to identify risks and develop strategies for dealing with those risks is a critical marketing skill. People accept the risk of failure and financial loss because the other side of the coin is that they gain the opportunity to achieve success and profits. If there were no risks involved in a business, then there would be no opportunity. Everyone would want to be in a business with no risk, and it would quickly become an overcrowded market. Risks can be classified in three ways—based on whether taking the risk presents an opportunity for gain, based on whether the risk is controllable, and based on whether the risk is insurable.

B. Business people deal with risks in one of four ways or in a combination of ways. They can avoid a risk by choosing an alternative that does not entail that risk. They can transfer a risk to someone else, usually at a cost. They can insure the potential loss from a risk, accepting a certain small loss (the cost of the insurance premiums) in order to avoid a potential loss that might be much greater. Or they can assume the risk and deal with whatever consequences transpire. In many instances, the latter alternative is the most practical one because so many risks cannot be avoided, transferred, or insured.

Lesson 19.2

A. Marketing poses many different kinds of risks because various factors combine to determine whether a business is successful or not. Those factors include the type of competition, the economy, laws and regulations, technology, and customer demand. Those factors change in unpredictable ways and market conditions are constantly shifting. Each poses risks and also offers opportunities. Marketers try to take advantage of the opportunities before conditions change, at the risk of making a decision that proves to be wrong because conditions change too quickly or in a way that was not adequately anticipated.

B. When a company has choices of marketing mixes, the company tries to fashion a mix that emphasizes its strengths and that can be completed successfully as planned. Yet each of the marketing mix elements—product, distribution, price, and promotion—is subject to a number of risks. Marketers consider those risks when planning and implementing marketing decisions.

Lesson 19.3

A. Marketers work with other people in the business and in the channel of distribution to develop effective plans for managing risks. Risk management should be incorporated into a company's marketing planning process, as each step of that process presents opportunities for identifying risks and developing ways to manage risks. An important part of risk management is gathering and studying information. Information is needed about the marketing environment and the marketing strategy in order to identify the types of risks that are likely to occur. When action plans are developed for implementing a marketing strategy, each action should be examined for potential risks.

B. In addition to managing risks through the marketing planning process, businesses can effectively manage risks by training marketing personnel in safety and security policies and making sure they know how to recognize problems and how to prevent accidents and injuries. Businesses also manage risk by purchasing a number of different types of insurance to cover potential damages that arise from risks that cannot otherwise be avoided.

REVIEW MARKETING CONCEPTS

1. If a business chooses an alternative strategy because the strategy does not pose a particular risk, what kind of risk management strategy is it practicing?
   a. Avoiding risk
   b. Transferring risk
   c. Insuring risk
   d. Assuming risk

2. When a business hires another company to perform a risky activity that it does not want to undertake itself, it is practicing which type of risk management strategy?
   a. Avoiding risk
   b. Transferring risk
   c. Insuring risk
   d. Assuming risk

3. True or False: A surety bond is a financial security that pays a guaranteed rate of return and cannot decrease in value over the stated term.

4. True or False: Marketing plans are usually not effective in managing marketing risk because market conditions change too quickly and the premises on which plans are based become outdated before they can be implemented.

5. Weather is a big risk factor in farming, but since farmers can't do anything to change it, it is a(n) __?__ risk.

6. Business people assume the risk of failure in order to gain the __?__ for success.

7. A business that takes full responsibility for its actions and is prepared to accept possible adverse consequences is practicing which type of risk management strategy?
   a. Avoiding risk
   b. Transferring risk
   c. Insuring risk
   d. Assuming risk

8. When a business forms a joint venture with other companies that are better prepared to handle certain risks, it is practicing which type or types of risk management strategy?
   a. Avoiding risk
   b. Transferring risk
   c. Assuming risk
   d. All of the above

9. if a business figures it has a two-out-of-three chance of doubling the value of a $10 million investment in a year's time and a one-out-of-three chance of losing everything it puts into it, what is the expected value of the investment gain after a year?

10. The three sections of a marketing plan are marketing __?__, marketing __?__, and __?__.

11. When businesses buy insurance to cover their risk of financial loss, they exchange the certain cost of the __?__ for the uncertain cost of the covered damages.

12. Employees should be trained to
    a. be aware of company safety policies.
    b. know how to recognize problems.
    c. know how to prevent injuries.
    d. all of the above.

NAPSTER, THEFT OR INGENUITY?

More than 50 million people downloaded free music from the Internet using a program called Napster. For a time, virtually unlimited musical choices were just a mouse click away. Napster expanded the musical horizons of users while also changing their buying habits. It was one of the most important things to happen on the Internet, although most of the music initially shared on the Napster site was unauthorized. Recording companies claimed that CD sales declined because of the use of Napster.

The ethical issue of not paying musicians for their music was clouded over by the convenience that Napster provided. It allowed individuals to search for any song on any other Napster user's hard drive, and then copy it for free.

Recording companies wanted to see Napster's top managers thrown in prison for racketeering and copyright infringement. Others regarded them as Silicon Valley heroes after they accumulated $15 million in venture-capital funds. The fight over Napster involved the future of music publishing, copyright law, ethics, and the relationship of artists to their audience.

Napster was created by Shawn Fanning, a 19-year-old college dropout and entrepreneur. "Napster" was his nickname in his hairier days. He had survived a difficult childhood, with his

family on welfare during his early years. Periodically, he and his siblings lived in foster homes. Shawn's uncle, John Fanning, took a special interest in his nephew, letting him work in his computer game company and purchasing a personal computer for him. Shawn quit college out of boredom and dedicated all of his time to creating software. The project turned into a business in 1999.

Napster reignited the controversy over unauthorized copying of artistic works by consumers, an issue that had flared up years before when videocassette recorders became popular. A key distinction with Napster was that the Internet makes it easy to produce multiple copies of CDs, something most VCRs can't do with videotapes. Fanning claimed that Napster was ethical and legal because it simply allowed users to share their personal files. Record companies understandably had a different viewpoint—they claimed they were being ripped off—although some observers argued that Napster might actually boost CD purchases by people who had first "sampled" music online for free.

The first notable lawsuit against Napster was filed by the Recording Industry of America. Then the heavy-metal group Metallica sued. Major universities, including Yale and the University of Southern California, whose students used Napster, were also sued. All of the lawsuits did not thwart the growing popularity of Napster. Some colleges eventually banned Napster because music files were using up more than half of the computer resources at some schools.

Finally, the survival of Napster was threatened by a lawsuit for copyright infringement brought by the recording industry. On Feb. 21, 2001, the Ninth Circuit Court of Appeals in San Francisco ruled that Napster had to stop helping its users exchange unauthorized copyrighted material. The court put the burden on Napster to prevent unauthorized copying that used its file-sharing capabilities. The court wanted Napster to act as a traffic cop, sorting through music files and identifying the ones protected by copyright.

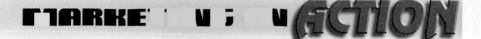

Napster countered by offering to pay $1 billion over five years to the recording industry. Through this agreement, Napster would pay $150 million per year in licensing fees to independent labels and artists. Napster's offer received a cool reception from the recording industry, which contended that $1 billion over five years did not even come close to the money it lost because of Napster. The recording industry was willing to talk only if Napster came up with a business model that paid for copyrighted materials and allowed the recording industry to be an active player.

Napster needed to develop screening technology fast if it hoped to survive. A digital-rights management architecture allowed Napster to keep track of and impose restrictions on music shared over its system. Napster II was developed to operate as a pay-subscription service. Subscription fees would then be passed on to performers and record labels.

This technology dramatically changed the Napster experience. When a user sends a music file, it is "wrapped" in a protective layer that acts as a digital lock similar to the encryption that keeps credit card numbers secure on the Internet. In order to open the file and access the music, another user needs a digital key provided by Napster. Napster can charge different fees for different keys.

In the meantime, big music companies also developed their own plans. For example, Vivendi Universal and Sony Music developed a subscription-based online music service. Charging customers a fee is a major obstacle to overcome, however. When companies try to convert web sites from free to fee, consumers usually choose to flee.

THINK CRITICALLY

1. How did Napster gain so much success?

2. What ethical issues are involved in this case?

3. Would you be willing to pay a fee for music from a web site, when previously you could get it for free?

4. What do you propose as the ultimate solution for this problem that will make both Napster and recording companies happy?

---

http://www.deca.org/publications/HS_Guide/guidetoc.html

BUSINESS SERVICES ROLE PLAY

You are a sales representative for a major insurance company. Much of the success of your business can be attributed to personal customer service. Many of your clients choose to have their insurance premiums automatically deducted from their checking accounts. One of your best customers during the past ten years has just called, very upset about having her automobile insurance deducted twice from her checking account. The $158 charge was deducted twice when it only should have been deducted once. The customer is so upset that she is considering a different insurance company to meet her needs.

OUTLINE A STRATEGY You have 15 minutes to outline a strategy to take care of the customer in order to keep her business.

ROLE PLAY Be prepared to role play the situation with another student or businessperson.

You will have 10 minutes to explain your strategy.

CHAPTER 20
MARKETING REQUIRES MONEY

LESSON 20.1 *MARKETING AFFECTS BUSINESS FINANCES*

LESSON 20.2 *TOOLS FOR FINANCIAL PLANNING*

LESSON 20.3 *BUDGETING FOR MARKETING ACTIVITIES*

NEWSLINE

FRITO-LAY FOCUSES ON FINANCE

If your company was a top financial performer, would you be worried? Many companies would be satisfied, but not PepsiCo.

PepsiCo's Frito-Lay division has long been a top company in the U.S. salty-snack market. In the late 1980s, several competitors of Frito-Lay became very aggressive. At the time, Frito-Lay was increasing its prices and continuing with traditional marketing strategies. PepsiCo's managers noticed the efforts of competitors, and they decided to act.

Market research showed that competing chips were beating Frito-Lay products in taste tests. Cost analysis indicated that money being spent on administration and management cut into the funds available for marketing. PepsiCo's top management knew that marketing, not administration, had the greatest impact on sales.

New strategies were put in place. Product research led to improved texture and taste for existing products. New types and flavors of chips were created. Manufacturing and distribution operations were streamlined. The number of factory managers was reduced by 40 percent, with many shifted into selling jobs. Salespeople worked more closely with retail outlets. Advertising was designed to create an exciting, fast-paced image. Prices were set at more competitive levels.

It was projected that the streamlined company would increase its profits by 15 percent each year. Attention to competition, marketing strategy, and financial performance should keep the company ahead of the competition.

THINK CRITICALLY

1. What incentive does a market leader have for improving its performance?

2. How can the top company in a product category improve its market position?

CORPORATE VIEW

CAREER OPPORTUNITY
FINANCIAL ANALYST

POINT YOUR BROWSER

www.corpview.com

TeleView is looking for someone who possesses the following attributes.

- Strong problem solving abilities
- A natural aptitude for number crunching and financial analysis
- Proven financial organization and financial management skills
- Drive and flexibility
- Excellent interpersonal skills to coordinate financial issues with other departments and workgroups within the corporation
- A desire to work in an invigorating team-oriented environment

At TeleView, we pride ourselves on a Finance & Accounting team that really counts!

TeleView's offices in Boulder, Colorado, are modern with state-of-the-art technologies at your disposal. Access to the office complex is facilitated by two freeway exits that provide easy access from picturesque communities to the north and south.

The main responsibilities of the job include but are not limited to the following.

- Preparing monthly financial statements as well as formal quarterly and year-end reports
- Organizing a workgroup team and supervising the completion of team tasks
- Solving assorted financial problems as they come from the workgroup you supervise
- Coordinating and supervising the preparation of mid- and long-range forecasts for the corporation as well as for individual departments
- Drawing up budget and performance evaluation methods and standards for various departments

- Overseeing departmental budget analyses to make sure they conform to corporate standards
- Completing an annual corporate review of financial accounting practices to ensure that they meet company needs, are consistent among various departments, and meet regulatory and industry standards
- Working directly with IT to improve reporting tools
- Helping to determine system report requirements throughout the company

The job requires the following education, skills, and experience.

- Bachelor's degree minimum in business, management, accounting, or a related field
- CPA designation preferred but not required
- Three years of experience in accounting or corporate finance
- Experience with spreadsheets and forecasting systems a must
- Up-to-date technical communication skills
- Performance analysis background also a plus

THINK CRITICALLY

1. Prepare a cover letter written by a person who is qualified for this job and is seeking an interview.

2. Write a 250-word essay describing how you would use this position to improve the financial management and monitoring of an innovative company such as TeleView.

3. Search want ads or the Internet for a job similar to this financial analyst position. What type of compensation package is being offered for the job?

20.1 MARKETING AFFECTS BUSINESS FINANCES

GOALS

- Explain how marketing affects a business' financial planning.
- Define short- and long-term marketing expenses and the various types of financing for marketing activities.

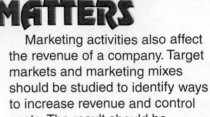

Marketing can be very expensive. There are several important categories of marketing costs including capital expenses, inventory costs, and operating costs. Sources of financing need to be developed for each category of costs. Those sources include financial institutions, credit offered by sellers, cash available in the business, and money obtained from the sale of products and services.

Marketing activities also affect the revenue of a company. Target markets and marketing mixes should be studied to identify ways to increase revenue and control costs. The result should be increased profits for the company.

Choose a local business or non-profit organization in your area. Talk to the top manager and outline the organization's primary sources of revenue and its primary expenses. What are its main sources of funding?

MARKETING COSTS AFFECT
BUSINESS SUCCESS

Marketing costs money. On average, 50 percent or more of the retail price of products and services is needed to pay the cost of marketing activities. Therefore managing marketing costs is important to the profitability of a business. If marketing costs are carefully controlled, there is more money available to use for important activities such as marketing research, product improvement, and customer services. The result should be greater customer satisfaction. On the other hand, if marketing costs are not well managed, the company does not have the money to improve the marketing mix. Production costs may need to be reduced, marketing activities cut back, or prices increased to customers. The result is a product or service that is less satisfying to customers and not as competitive with other brands. In the end, there will be reduced profits for the company. This makes financial management an important marketing skill.

THE IMPORTANCE OF FINANCES

One of the results of effective marketing is **revenue**—the money received from the sale of products and services. In order to sell products, money must be spent to pay for the products and services to be sold. The cost of operating and managing the business must be covered. The expenses of the marketing activities needed to facilitate the exchanges between the business and its customers must be paid. When all of those costs are subtracted from the revenue, the result

FIGURE 20-1

Successful businesses must be able to offset the costs of operating with the revenue received. If revenue is higher than expenses, the business makes a profit. If costs are greater than income, the business loses money.

The Basic Financial Equation

is a profit or loss for the business. This basic financial equation is illustrated in Figure 20-1.

Even in non-profit businesses or other organizations, finances are important. If the expenses of those organizations are higher than the available funds, they cannot operate at the level they would prefer. If expenses exceed revenue, they cannot offer the products and services their clients need or expect.

For example, a day-care center might operate as a non-profit organization, but it is still involved in marketing. The center must offer the appropriate services in a safe and comfortable facility. It must be open when clients need day-care services, and it must offer affordable prices. The organization needs to communicate with current and prospective clients about the center's services. If the revenue collected from the clients is not adequate to support the marketing mix, the center will not be able to continue to operate. Therefore, it is important that the manager of the day-care center carefully plans and controls the finances in order to keep the center open and available to families in the community.

THE ROLE OF MARKETING IN FINANCIAL PLANNING

We know that most large organizations have a part of their organization that deals specifically with financial planning and management. Experts in finance and accounting are responsible for maintaining the best possible financial position for their company. These experts assist other managers with planning. They maintain the financial resources and records, and they provide information on revenue and expenses.

Even small businesses and other organizations usually have assistance to help managers with financial planning and record keeping. A business may employ an accountant full- or part-time, use an accounting service, or consult a financial planner. There are easy-to-use computer software programs that can help even the newest and smallest organizations with financial decisions.

While marketers may have people and other resources to help them with financial planning, they are still responsible for the revenue and expenses related to marketing activities. Marketers need to identify ways to increase revenues while controlling the costs of marketing. They must decide which markets present the most profitable opportunities and which choices in a marketing mix are the most cost effective.

Target Markets   A variety of decisions that marketers make affect the financial performance of a company. One example is the choice of target markets. A company may have a choice between two markets. One market has a smaller number of potential customers, but they spend a higher percentage of their incomes on the product, and there are fewer competitors. In another situation, a new international market seems very risky. It may be difficult and expensive for the business to enter a market that is far from their location and with which they have no experience. If the business is not successful in the market, a great deal of money will be lost. On the other hand, successful entry could mean a very profitable market for many years to come and opportunities to enter adjoining markets in other countries. In each of these examples, the decisions about the target markets determine the amount of sales and revenue that can be obtained.

Marketing Mix   In the same way, decisions about the marketing mix have an important impact on the company's financial resources. As the product element of the marketing mix is developed, marketers may decide that additional customer services or improved packaging to prevent product damage are needed. Each of those choices increases the cost of the product. The changes may also result in increased sales or customers who are willing to pay more because of the improvements.

Distribution decisions can also increase expenses. Examples include using several channels for distribution or operating regional warehouses to reduce the time needed to get products to customers. Expenses involved with the pricing element include offering credit, coupons, or rebates.

Expenses associated with the promotion mix element are more frequent advertising, direct marketing efforts such as telemarketing, or additional training for salespeople. Each time marketers consider changes in the marketing mix, they need to study the costs of those changes and predict the effect of the change on sales.

Why are marketing and its effectiveness so important to an organization's financial planning process?

MANAGING
MARKETING COSTS

To determine the amount of money needed for marketing, marketing expenses need to be classified as either long term or short term. Long-term expenses are for items that the company can use for several years. Short-term expenses are for current activities or items used within a short time, typically less than a year. Long-term expenses are usually paid for over an extended period of time. They are often financed by borrowing money from a bank or other financial institution. Normally, short-term expenses must be paid for when they are purchased. Sometimes they are financed with credit from the seller that will be paid within one or a few months. Figure 20-2 illustrates examples of long-term and short-term marketing expenses.

Long-Term Expenses
Most of the long-term costs to a business are used for production or for operations rather than for marketing. The costs of land, buildings, and equipment are the typical expenses in this category. Some marketing plans identify land and building needs. A company that distributes products may need buildings, vehicles, and equipment for product storage and handling. Manufacturers using direct sales to customers

FIGURE 20-2
Marketing expenses are both long term and short term. Long-term expenses are paid for over a number of years, while short-term expenses are usually paid for in less than one year.

Long-Term Marketing Expenses

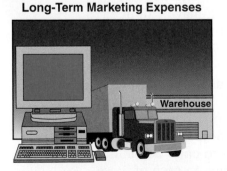

Short-Term Marketing Expenses

Classifying Marketing Expenses

through factory outlet stores need to build or rent facilities and equipment for retail operations. The increased use of technology in other parts of marketing will require investments in special equipment. For example, computers are essential for effective marketing research and marketing information management. Companies that use telemarketing or provide customer information and service often invest in telephone systems, computers, and other office equipment. Advertising and other types of promotion require sophisticated audio, video, and print production equipment and facilities. While most companies hire advertising agencies and production companies to develop their advertising and promotional materials, some larger companies maintain their own facilities, equipment, and personnel for those tasks.

Short-Term Expenses   Most marketing expenses result from performing specific marketing activities that are completed in a short period of time. Those types of expenses depend on the marketing mix, but there are common short-term expenses that most businesses have. They include the cost of salaries and wages, administrative costs, operating expenses, order processing, customer services, advertising and promotion, and transportation costs.

FINANCING MARKETING ACTIVITIES

An important part of financial planning is identifying the sources of money needed to pay for marketing activities and expenses. Marketers work with the executives and financial managers of a business to identify financial needs. They must also identify the methods that will be used to obtain the needed money. The three main types of financial needs, shown in Figure 20-3, are capital expenses, inventory expenses, and operating expenses.

FIGURE 20-3
Money is needed to finance marketing activities. Marketing managers must work with finance personnel and other managers to determine the amount and sources of funds necessary for effective marketing operations.

Financing Marketing Activities

| Capital Expenses | Inventory Expenses | Operating Expenses |

Goodbye Sears Catalog

Ask anyone who lived in the United States between 1885 and 1993 and they will remember the Sears catalog. It was the store at home offering access to thousands of products through the convenience of the telephone and mailbox. For future generations, the Big Book will only be a memory. Sears decided to get out of the catalog business, and 1993 was the last year the catalog was published.

How can a company abandon a product that was successful for 97 years and was the market leader for most of that time? Even in its last full year of operations, it garnered $3.3 billion in sales. Yet the catalog continued to lose more and more money.

Industry experts suggest that the catalog concept had not died, but that Sears could not adjust to changing market conditions. Customers no longer have to rely on catalog sales as in the first half of the century. Customers in rural areas and small towns used the Sears catalog to see what was new and to have a full range of products to purchase. Today, most people are less than 15 minutes from a major department or discount store, or they can shop on the Internet 24 hours a day.

Sears has always appealed to the broad shopping needs of the middle class, and the Sears catalog followed the same strategy. It sold some of everything but was neither top-of-the-line nor lowest cost. Even into the 1990s, Sears' huge catalog offered everything from tires to appliances to lawn care products to family fashions. At the same time, other catalog businesses were moving to limited lines of specialty items with very high-quality visual presentations. In catalog sales the new emphasis is on niche marketing, low-cost operations, quick customer response, and high levels of service.

THINK CRITICALLY

1. How could Sears financially justify shutting down an operation that generated more than $3 billion in annual revenues?

2. How do the target markets of today's specialty catalogs differ from the market that Sears has traditionally targeted with both its retail stores and its catalog?

Capital Expenses Capital expenses are long-term investments in land, buildings, and equipment. They are usually financed by money borrowed from a financial institution such as a bank or insurance company. Some manufacturers participate in long-term loans to their customers to help finance a major equipment purchase. It is also possible to lease equipment and buildings instead of buying them. The financial personnel of an organization are usually responsible for arranging for financing of capital purchases.

Inventory Expenses Inventory is the assortment and quantities of products the company maintains for sale to customers. Inventories for manufacturers are produced with the anticipation that they will be sold to customers. For other channel members, inventories are purchased and then resold to their customers. The cost of the inventory is not recovered until the products are sold and the customer pays for the purchase.

Financing of inventory is usually done in one of two ways. Short-term loans may be obtained from financial institutions. Most banks will not loan the full value of the inventory, since it may not sell as expected. The other common method of financing inventory is through credit extended by the seller. Since most sellers will only finance the sale for a short period, often 30–60 days, the purchasing company must be able to sell the inventory quickly in order to pay for the order on time. In both cases, the purchaser pays interest on the money borrowed and factors the cost of financing into the price of the products.

Operating Expenses The final category of marketing expenses are operating expenses. **Operating expenses** are the costs of the day-to-day activities of marketing. They include salaries and wages, materials and supplies, advertising and special promotions, and customer services. Marketing expenses include the variety of other marketing activities completed regularly to sell products and services and to meet customer needs. The operating costs are normally paid as they are incurred or shortly thereafter. The money for payment of operating expenses comes from the cash on hand in the business and the income from sales. Monthly and weekly budgets and financial reports monitor operating expenses and income to ensure that money is available to pay the expenses. Marketing managers pay careful attention to operating budgets and make changes rapidly if it appears that operating expenses are too high or revenues are too low.

What is the difference between capital expenses and operating expenses in terms of how they typically are financed?

LESSON REVIEW

1. What happens to a business in which costs consistently exceed revenues?

2. How does a business' choice of target markets affect its finances?

3. How do a business' marketing mix decisions affect its finances?

4. How are inventory expenses usually financed?

5. What kinds of capital expenses might a marketing department require?

6. How are capital expenses typically financed?

FIGURE 20-4

An income statement is an important financial tool for marketers. It shows the relationship between sales and expenses in order to determine if operations are profitable.

Dendum Products, Inc.
Income Statement
For the Six-Month Period Ending June 30, 20—

Revenues:
  Gross Sales:
    NE region..................................$123,528
    NW region.................................195,426
    SE region...................................232,965
    SW region..................................148,258
      Total Gross Sales.................................$700,177
  Less Sales Returns:
    NE region ....$ 6,123
    NW region....................................5,896
    SE region.....................................8,344
    SW region....................................7,421
      Total Sales Returns 27,784
  Net Sales $672,393
  Cost of Products Sold:
    Inventory, Jan. 1, 20—...........................$ 86,593
    Purchases $583,226
    Less: Purchase Returns...............-6,048
        Purchase Discounts ....-3,582
    Net Purchases.......................................573,596
  Total Cost of Products For Sale.........................$660,189
    Inventory, June 30, 20— ....-78,190
    Net Cost of Products Sold 581,999
Gross Margin ....$ 90,394
Operating Expenses:
  Rent Expense ....$ 8,225
  Bad Debts Expense 695
  Credit Card Fee Expense 1,200
  Transportation Expense 10,150
  Equipment Purchases...............................860
  Equipment Depreciation.............................620
  Insurance Expense 1,050
  Salaries and Wages.................................12,845
  Payroll Taxes 1,926
  Supplies Expense 734
  Advertising Expense 18,040
    Total Operating Expenses.......................$ 56,345
Net Income Before Taxes ....$ 34,049

Those tools are known as financial statements. **Financial statements** are detailed summaries of the specific financial performance for a business or a part of the business. The important financial statements for marketers are income statements and balance sheets.

Income Statement

An **income statement** reports on the amount and source of revenue and the amount and type of expenses for a specific period of time. The purpose of an income statement is to determine if the business earned a profit or loss on its operations. A sample income statement is shown in Figure 20-4.

An income statement can be developed to analyze the profitability of the entire company or just one operating unit of the company. For example, Toys "R" Us operates stores in many different countries. It can develop an income statement for the entire corporation, which includes the income and expenses of all stores in every country. It can also analyze the performance of all of the stores operating in a specific country or region of a country. Additionally, each store will have its own income statement. Managers may also want to determine the profitability of specific parts of the business operations. An income statement can be developed for a specific market, a category of customers, or a product or product category. The income statement in Figure 20-4 analyzes the financial performance of a company for a six-month period, with sales figures broken out for four different regions of the country.

generated by them. Two common examples of budgets used in marketing are sales and advertising budgets. Separate budgets are usually developed for each product, market, and major marketing activity.

OPERATING TOOLS

Managers use several financial tools to determine the effectiveness of operations.

FIGURE 20-5
A balance sheet shows the relationship between the assets and liabilities of a business.

Froerich Fundamentals
Balance Sheet
December 31, 20—

ASSETS

Current Assets:

Cash	$ 95,436	
Accounts Receivable	42,827	
Product Inventory	135,673	
Supplies	21,128	
Prepaid Insurance	2,442	
Total Current Assets		$ 297,506

Capital Assets:

Buildings	$647,545	
Vehicles	97,221	
Equipment	228,322	
Capital Assets	$973,088	
Less: Depreciation of Capital Assets	13,286	
Total Capital Assets		959,802
Total Assets		$1,257,308

LIABILITIES

Current Liabilities:

Accounts Payable	$ 92,286	
Mortgage Payable	296,243	
Notes Payable	63,552	
Payroll Taxes Payable	71,074	
Insurance Payable	6,995	
Total Liabilities		$ 530,150

CAPITAL

Retained Earnings	$286,680	
Owners' Equity	440,478	
Total Capital		727,158
Total Liabilities and Capital		$1,257,308

Balance Sheet A balance sheet describes the type and amount of assets, liabilities, and capital in a business on a specific date. Assets include the things the business owns. Liabilities are the amounts the business owes. The difference between the amount of assets and the amount of liabilities is the actual value of the business, or capital. Managers must be able to identify changes in those amounts to determine if the financial condition of the business is improving or declining. Figure 20-5 shows an example of a balance sheet.

Marketers use income statements to determine if marketing activities are resulting in an adequate volume of sales. Income statements are also used to identify the costs of the activities needed to achieve that sales volume. Important information that marketers obtain from balance sheets includes the value of assets used for marketing activities, the levels of inventory of products for sale, and the amount owed by customers who have been offered credit. A balance sheet also identifies whether the company has money available to spend on such things as new product development, buildings, equipment, and other resources needed to improve marketing activities.

What kinds of financial information do income statements and balance sheets contain?

USING FINANCIAL TOOLS

Marketers work with finance and accounting experts to develop and use financial tools. Some of the information used to prepare forecasts, budgets, and financial statements comes from the marketing department and its operations. Marketers help to collect and report the necessary information. When the reports are prepared in accounting and finance, they are distributed to marketing personnel for use in decision-making. Marketers must be able to understand and interpret financial statements. Marketers use the information to develop marketing plans and to improve marketing operations.

DEVELOPING FORECASTS AND BUDGETS

Financial plans are not helpful unless they are reasonably accurate. Planners use several methods to develop good forecasts and budgets. The most common planning method to use is past performance. By com-paring the forecasts and budgets from previous years with the actual results, planners can see which ones were accurate and which were not. Using that past experience makes planning more accurate.

A second method is to use information from comparable businesses and markets to develop plans. Often trade associations or information services collect and report on the financial performance of businesses in a particular industry. Some government agencies, including the U.S. Department of Commerce, also gather and report financial information on businesses.

Additionally, planners can look for related figures that help to predict performance. For example, the number of tires that an auto service business might sell can be based on the number of cars in a market and the age of those cars. The original tires on a car will normally need to be replaced between two and three years after the car is sold. Identifying the number of those cars in the shopping area of the business will help in developing a forecast for tire sales.

Marketing Plan   The most effective way to develop a budget for marketing expenses is to calculate the costs of performing the necessary marketing tasks. Here again, the marketing plan is an effective tool. A marketing plan describes the marketing activities necessary to implement the marketing mix. The marketing manager analyzes each of the planned activities to determine what personnel and resources will be needed. Then the wages, costs of resources, and the amounts of all other expenses are matched with each activity. When all of those items are totaled, the marketing manager has a specific estimate of the amount that needs to be budgeted for that activity. An example of that type of budget development is shown in Figure 20-6.

FIGURE 20-6
This budget helps the manager analyze the costs and benefits of operating a customer service department.

DEVELOPING A BUDGET FOR A MARKETING ACTIVITY

Planned Monthly Customer Service Department Expenses

Management Salary	$ 4,028
Personnel Wages	18,840
Facility Expense (space and utilities)	3,526
Office Equipment	305
Telephone Expense	498
Computer Expense	295
Postage	86
Supplies	175
Travel Expense	830
Product Returns and Replacements	644
Total Budgeted Expenses	$29,227

GATHERING INFORMATION FOR FINANCIAL STATEMENTS

The information needed to prepare income statements and balance sheets is the actual financial performance of the business. Therefore, the marketing department is responsible for maintaining accurate records on sales, expenses, inventory levels, customer accounts, and equipment. This information is then available to prepare the statements.

Traditionally, employees were asked to record information while completing a marketing activity or after the activity was completed. For example, when a sale was made, information about the customer, product, and terms of the sale would be recorded on a purchase order, invoice, or sales receipt. In retail businesses, the information may have been recorded by punching keys on a cash register or a point-of-purchase computer.

Today much of the information is captured through electronic scanners and bar codes on products and then automatically entered into computer databases. As products move through a manufacturing and distribution process, the bar codes are scanned automatically or by employees using scanning equipment. Additional information can be entered along with the bar code data using a keyboard, a touchscreen, or an electronic pen.

Federal Express, United Parcel Service, and other delivery companies track each item they handle using this kind of technology. From the time packages are received to the time they are delivered, information on each item at each step along the way is maintained in computers. Reports on numbers of items delivered, speed of delivery, costs, and location can be obtained at any time.

Where does the information come from that businesses use to develop financial statements, forecasts, and budgets?

ANALYZING FINANCIAL INFORMATION

Information available from financial tools can be very valuable in improving marketing decisions. Forecasts and budgets are evaluated to determine their accuracy. The projections are compared with actual performance. When differences are found, they are studied to determine why the differences occurred and what can be done to reduce the amount of difference in the future. It is possible that the projections proved to be inaccurate, indicating that methods used to develop the forecasts and budgets need to be modified. Or it could be a sign that marketing activities were less effective than anticipated and need to be improved.

USING FINANCIAL INFORMATION

Financial statements are evaluated to determine the changes that occur from one period of operations to the next. A marketing manager studies various markets to determine if sales are increasing or decreasing. Inventory levels can be compared from year to year, as can the amounts owed by customers. If the information shows that the financial performance is improving, the marketing manager will want to continue with the same activities. If sales are decreasing or inventories and customer accounts are increasing too quickly, marketing activities may need to be changed to correct the problems.

Another method of analysis is to compare one type of financial performance to another. For example, sales volume can be compared to advertising expenses. If expenses are going up at a faster rate than sales, a problem may be developing. Other important comparisons in marketing are the level of inventory to sales, costs of transportation compared to costs of product handling and storage, and product cost compared to marketing expenses.

FIGURE 20-7

When the goal of a business is increased profits, marketers have two basic ways of getting there. (1) They can increase sales while holding costs steady. (2) If sales are not increasing, they can reduce the cost of achieving those sales.

Marketing Strategies to Increase Profits

Information is essential for effective marketing. Marketing research provides information to aid in understanding customers. Financial information is needed to determine what marketing activities the organization can afford to complete and the impact of those activities on profits.

Marketers need to understand accounting and finance, because financial planning is a critical marketing skill.

Marketers use financial information to identify how to increase revenue and reduce costs. As shown in Figure 20-7, if a greater volume of sales can be achieved while controlling expenses, profits will increase. In the same way, if sales can be maintained while reducing the costs of marketing, the company will also be able to increase profits.

INCREASING REVENUES

Increased revenue results from selling more products and services. Financial information is analyzed to determine the products that sell the best and the customer groups who buy the most products. Efforts are directed at the best products and markets. Poorly performing products and markets are either improved or dropped. Each time a new marketing plan is developed, the marketing manager will identify the most important products and markets for that planning period.

JUDGMENT CALL

Stock Options

Financial statements can be valuable tools for analyzing marketing plans and performance, but accountants and financial analysts sometimes have a tough time keeping up with innovative financing techniques. A debate has been raging in the financial community for more than a decade over how to treat employee stock options. Stock options have emerged as one of the primary ways of attracting and keeping valued management employees, particularly for young, fast-growing companies that are not yet able to pay huge cash salaries.

The problem, as some people see it, is that the value of stock options never shows up on a company's income statement as an expense, as do other types of compensation. Yet they obviously have value—cashing in stock options worth millions of dollars is a common practice among top corporate managers. That value ultimately comes out of other shareholders' pockets. When options are converted the value of existing shares is diluted proportionately.

So when marketing managers analyze income statements to see how efficient their marketing plans have been, millions of dollars in would-be expenses may never show up in their calculations. Some people are concerned that such accounting sleight-of-hand can distort decision-making processes. The Federal Accounting Standards Board has recommended that companies factor the value of stock options in their public financial statements, but under heavy pressure from businesses that don't want to see their profits evaporate it has declined to make it a requirement.

THINK CRITICALLY

1. How might including the value of employee stock options in a marketing budget affect a marketing plan?

2. Why do businesses that issue lots of employee stock options prefer to not include them in their financial statements?

Marketers are also concerned that an effective price for a product is maintained. It is possible that more products can be sold to customers if discounts are offered or the price is reduced. Some salespeople who have control over price are quick to reduce the price, believing that is the only way the customer will buy. Yet the lower price may reduce revenue to the point where a profit cannot be made. Salespeople who understand customer needs make an effective presentation of the entire marketing mix in response to those needs. They know that customers look for the best value, not the lowest price.

CONTROLLING COSTS

Marketing managers are very concerned about reducing and controlling the costs of marketing activities. When businesses are in very competitive markets, it is often the company that operates most efficiently that makes a profit. Businesses that are concerned about satisfying customer needs must be very careful in cutting costs. Marketing activities that are important to customers cannot be eliminated without considering the impact on customer satisfaction. It is often possible to find ways to perform marketing activities in a less costly way while keeping the same level of customer service. For example, an insurance company provided its salespeople with personal computers to reduce the number of forms to be completed. The company also wanted to cut the time it took for information to be exchanged between the salesperson and the company. The company found that the use of computers not only reduced expenses by over 15 percent but also cut the number of errors on insurance applications by nearly 5 percent.

Another example of reducing marketing expenses comes from a large supermarket in the Southeast. They operate a very large fleet of trucks to deliver products from their warehouses to their stores. The trucks would deliver the products and return to the warehouse empty. The transportation manager started to identify suppliers of products that were located in the towns where the supermarket had stores. When a truck was delivering a load from the warehouse to a store,

the manager would determine if a nearby supplier had an order to be sent to the warehouse. If so, the supermarket's truck would pick up the order and bring it back rather than driving back empty. This procedure saved the company several thousands of dollars each month in transportation costs.

Marketing employees as well as managers need to be aware of the costs of marketing activities and identify ways to reduce expenses. It is often possible to identify ways that marketing activities can be performed more efficiently, the amount of supplies or materials can be reduced, or waste can be eliminated. Many companies provide incentives for employees who can identify important cost savings.

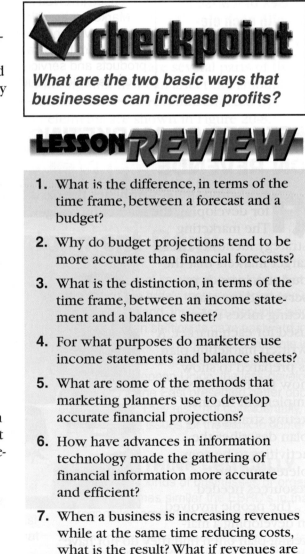

✓ checkpoint

What are the two basic ways that businesses can increase profits?

LESSON REVIEW

1. What is the difference, in terms of the time frame, between a forecast and a budget?

2. Why do budget projections tend to be more accurate than financial forecasts?

3. What is the distinction, in terms of the time frame, between an income statement and a balance sheet?

4. For what purposes do marketers use income statements and balance sheets?

5. What are some of the methods that marketing planners use to develop accurate financial projections?

6. How have advances in information technology made the gathering of financial information more accurate and efficient?

7. When a business is increasing revenues while at the same time reducing costs, what is the result? What if revenues are shrinking while costs are going up?

businesses, products must be purchased from other companies, so their costs are determined by the prices paid for the merchandise.

There are other expenses related to the product mix element. The expenses associated with offering a guarantee or warranty, as well as the costs of repairing items that are damaged or fail, must be included. In addition, many businesses offer customer services, some of which can be very expensive.

Some services are offered as part of the actual sale, such as delivery and set up or training. Other services are provided for a long time after the sale while the customer is using the product. For example, many computer software companies have technicians who will work with a customer if they are having problems with a product. General Electric has a toll-free telephone number that customers can call to get information about the use of any product the company manufactures, ranging from small appliances to large industrial equipment.

Several automobile manufacturers offer 24-hour-a-day roadside repair service for their customers.

Distribution Expenses   Distribution costs are a major area of marketing expenses. Companies have the costs of transportation, storage, and display for their products. These costs include long-term expenses, such as buildings and equipment, and short-term expenses, such as wages and supplies. Even service businesses have expenses associated with delivering the services to customers or operating the location where customers come to purchase the services. In addition to the obvious costs of distribution, other expenses for most businesses include the costs of developing and managing the channels of distribution, inventory control costs, materials handling expenses, and the costs of order processing.

Price Expenses   The major expense related to the price mix element is the cost of offering credit. Another price expense item is the cost of communicating prices to customers. This may seem like an unimportant item, but consider the thousands of items that a business stocks and sells during one year. If each item has to have the price identified on it, the cost of printing the stickers or tags and the expense of placing the price on the item can be high. Then if a price change has to be made, the cost increases. Many retail businesses, such as supermarkets, found the time and expense of pricing products so great that they have introduced other methods. The products no longer carry price stickers. Instead the price is posted on the display shelf. The price is stored in the company's computer and is identified through the bar code on the product package. A price change is made by changing the amount in the computer and updating the price on the product display.

Promotion Expenses   There are many costs associated with promotion. Few inexpensive ways are available for companies to communicate with customers. Each type of promotion has its own set of expenses.

Advertising is the most common type of promotion. The major cost of advertising is the expense of purchasing space in newspapers or magazines or buying time on television or radio. It is also expensive to create and produce the advertisements. Those expenses include the salaries of a variety of creative people as well as the equipment and materials they need for their work.

Selling is also an expensive promotional method. An important cost of selling is the salaries of salespeople. Additional costs include training and management as well as the equipment, materials, and product samples salespeople use. Salespeople for manufacturers often travel regularly to meet with customers. Their sales territories can cover several states or countries. The costs of operating an automobile, airplane tickets, hotel rooms, meals, and other related expenses can be hundreds of dollars each day. Salespeople need to be very effective in order to make enough sales just to cover their expenses.

It is said that the most inexpensive form of promotion is word of mouth. But companies that want customers to help sell their products often spend money to insure that it is done well. When a customer buys a product, the company may make a follow-up telephone call to make sure the customer is satisfied. Letters and gifts may be sent to show that the company appreciates the customer's business. Some companies offer satisfied customers money or other incentives if they identify a prospective customer who ends up buying a product.

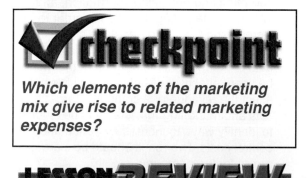

checkpoint

Which elements of the marketing mix give rise to related marketing expenses?

LESSON REVIEW

1. Name an industry that generates a substantial amount of its profits from products and services that would not normally be considered its primary products and services.

2. When Starbucks sells "Starbucks" T-shirts in its coffee shops or when the Chicago Cubs peddle Cubs-branded merchandise at Wrigley Field, why are their marketers so happy?

3. What are some of the expenses associated with the price element of the marketing mix?

4. If making a change to the marketing mix would increase revenues, why would a company not make the change?

5. Although most businesses do not make substantial profits from offering credit to their customers, and many in fact lose money by doing so, what industry is a notable exception?

6. Why is word-of-mouth promotion not really free?

CHAPTER 20

SUMMARY

Lesson 20.1

A. The basic financial equation is REVENUE – COSTS = RESULTS. When all of the costs are subtracted from revenue the result is either a profit or loss for the business. The financing function of marketing involves planning for the effective use of resources, collecting and analyzing information, and improving marketing activities in order to increase revenue and decrease costs. Because marketing activities cost a great deal of money, it is important that the money be spent effectively. Marketing activities also affect the revenue of a company. Target markets and marketing mixes should be studied to identify ways to increase revenue and control costs. The result should be increased profits for the company.

B. Marketing can be very expensive both in short-term and long-term expenditures. There are several important categories of marketing costs, including capital expenses, inventory costs, and operating costs. Sources of financing need to be developed for each category of costs. Those sources include financial institutions, credit offered by sellers, cash available in the business, and money obtained from the sale of products and services.

Lesson 20.2

A. Three factors contribute to the financial performance of a business—revenue, costs, and results (profit or loss). Managers are responsible for operating the business so that customers are satisfied and the business makes a profit. Several financial tools help managers meet that responsibility. Those tools can be classified as planning tools and operating tools. The primary planning tools are forecasts and budgets. Forecasts predict long-term financial performance, generally for periods of a year or longer. Budgets are shorter-term tools used to develop detailed plans for specific activities.

B. The primary operating tools are income statements and balance sheets. Managers use these detailed summaries of financial performance to determine the effectiveness of business operations. An income statement reports the amount and source of revenue and the amount and type of expenses for a specified period of time, usually a year or less. The purpose of an income statement is to determine if the business earned a profit or loss. A balance sheet describes the type and amount of assets, liabilities, and capital in a business on a specified date.

C. Marketers must be able to interpret financial statements in order to develop marketing plans and improve decision-making. Marketers use financial information to identify how to increase revenue and reduce costs. The two basic ways to improve results are to increase revenue while holding costs steady, or hold revenue steady while cutting costs.

Lesson 20.3

A. Marketing activities generate revenue. Most of the revenue comes from the sale of primary products and services. The marketing plan identifies the markets to serve, and activities are developed to persuade customers to purchase the products or services. Secondary and after-sale products and services can also contribute to revenues and profits. Offering credit can generate interest revenues.

B. Completing marketing activities also incurs costs, and there are expenses associated with each of the four marketing mix elements—product, distribution, price, and promotion.

REVIEW MARKETING CONCEPTS

From information provided in the chapter, list two examples for each of the following:

1. Parts of the basic financial equation that determine whether a company makes a profit or not
2. Types of financial plans
3. Types of financial statements
4. Methods used to develop good forecasts and budgets
5. Ways that marketing personnel can gather financial information
6. Sources of revenue resulting from marketing activities
7. Categories of marketing expenses based on length of time
8. Types of financial analysis that will be helpful in marketing decision-making
9. Ways that an understanding of financial information can be used by marketing managers in order to increase profits
10. Main types of financial needs in marketing
11. Categories of financial data included on a balance sheet

REVIEW MARKETING TERMS

Match the terms listed with the definitions. Some terms may not be used.

12. The money received from the sale of products and services.
13. A long-term investment in land, buildings, or equipment.
14. A cost of day-to-day marketing activities.
15. A numerical prediction of future performance related to revenue and expenses.
16. A detailed summary of the financial performance for a business or a part of a business.
17. A description of the type and amount of assets, liabilities, and capital in a business on a specified date.

a. balance sheet
b. budget
c. capital expense
d. financial forecast
e. financial statement
f. income statement
g. inventory
h. operating expense
i. revenue

APPLY MARKETING FUNCTIONS

MARKETING RESEARCH

18. Two important methods of planning and analyzing financial information are (1) comparable information from similar businesses and (2) the costs of performing specific marketing tasks and activities.

There are a number of reference books published by the federal government, trade and professional associations, and private businesses that contain this information.

Using the library in your school, a business information encyclopedia, other business reference books, the Internet, or the resources of a businessperson you know, identify at least two sources of specific financial information available to marketers. After you have identified the sources, review one and prepare a written summary of the information that is contained in the reference. Provide examples of the specific information.

19. Business people are sometimes reluctant to use marketing research because of its cost. Marketing research is a marketing expense item and does not directly contribute to

revenue. Therefore, some people believe that the use of marketing research reduces profits. Marketing managers must be able to develop a budget for marketing research and be able to justify the expenses.

Assume you are the marketing manager for the franchiser of a chain of family hair-cutting centers that are located in major shopping malls in 10 states. You want to complete a marketing research project to determine if the company's pricing strategy should change. Currently the price of hair-cuts is $18, but coupons are frequently distributed through newspaper ads and direct mail offering $5 discounts. You believe customers may be more satisfied with a one-price policy in which haircuts are always $15 with no coupons. You plan to survey customers in the 10 states using mall intercepts done by employees from the franchises. People would be stopped in malls and asked to complete a five-item questionnaire. The questionnaires would be returned to your office for analysis.

a. Using Figure 20-6 as a model, make a list of the items you believe should be included in a budget for the marketing research project. Think of all of the types of expenses that would be involved from the time the project is started until you have a report on the results of the research.

b. You do not have to develop estimates of the amount of money you would budget for each item in the budget. Instead, for each item, identify the method you would use to determine the amount to budget for each item. Write a one- or two-sentence explanation of the method you would use beside the item.

c. Now prepare a brief oral presentation to give to the president of the franchise. Explain the purpose of the research, how you will develop the budget, and why the expense for the marketing research is justified even though it does not contribute directly to revenue. Be prepared to make your oral presentation to your instructor and other class members. You may want to develop some visual aids to support your presentation.

MARKETING PLANNING

20. You are the marketing manager for EnviroSaf, a company that has developed a new type of lawn care product that controls weeds and insects without chemicals. The product is currently sold through garden centers in eight states in the northwestern United States. You are responsible for all distribution and promotion activities, and for completing marketing research. You work with other managers to set product prices, to develop and provide customer services, and to complete new product planning. You believe that you can make the most effective decisions if you have financial information available related to the marketing activities you control.

Write a one-page memo to Frances Payton, chief financial officer of EnviroSaf. In the memo, identify the types of financial information you need, the financial tools that will help you with planning and operations, and why it is important for the marketing manager to be involved in financial planning for the business. Use information from the chapter to help you prepare the memo.

21. One of the methods of forecasting sales for products and services is to identify relationships between two products or services. In the chapter, it was suggested that the volume of automobile sales can be used to predict the sale of automobile tires. If business people can identify similar relationships among products and services, they can increase the effectiveness of their forecasts. List at least 10 other product/service relationships where you believe the sale of one affects the sale of the other. Two more examples are given to help you.

The sale of	Is related to the sale of
Computers	computer software
Winter coats	gloves and hats

MARKETING MANAGEMENT

22. One of the school clubs to which you belong needs to raise funds to pay for a trip to a state conference. The members are tired of the old ways of fund raising and want to do something that will be fun, provide a community service, and result in a reasonable profit for the club. The idea

being considered is an Ethnic Food Celebration. Your club would be responsible for contacting community groups who would agree to staff a booth in which a specific type of ethnic food would be prepared and sold. The group would also develop a display representing the ethnic culture or provide a short presentation (dance, historical story, and so on) about the culture. The ethnic celebration would be held on a Saturday afternoon for three hours in the school's gymnasium. People would come to sample the food and to enjoy the presentations going on throughout the afternoon.

For financial planning, some of the anticipated costs are:

Gymnasium rental $300
Table rental for booths ....$3 per table
     (minimum of 50 tables)
Security ....$45 per hour
Insurance...................................$80
Cost of possible promotional materials:
Flyers..$.08 each
Posters......................................$.45 each
Envelopes and postage ....$.32 each
30-second radio ad...................$58 each
    (10 for $500) + $80 production
    costs (fixed)
Salesperson commission ....$8/booth sold
Labor costs
  (Set up, tear down, cleaning)..$6 per hour

The plan is to sell booths for the celebration. There is space for up to 40 booths in the gymnasium if three tables are used per booth. The groups would be able to sell their foods and keep all revenues from the sale after paying the booth fee. Also, an admission could be charged to the celebration. Other products could be sold as a part of the celebration as well (T-shirts, souvenir cups, and so on).

Develop a plan of activities to be followed by your class in planning and managing the celebration. Include all aspects of a marketing mix (product development, distribution, pricing, promotion). Based on the plan of activities, prepare a budget for the celebration using the income statement format illustrated in the chapter. Include projections of all types of revenues and reasonable expenses. Estimate those expenses for which no costs are given. Develop at least three projections of revenues using alternative prices charged for the booths, varying admission prices, or different attendance levels. Calculate the impact of the change on the profit or loss from the celebration.

23. A hardware store decides to add free delivery as a service for customers who purchase over $250 of merchandise in one order. Delivery will also be available to other customers, but a delivery fee will be charged. The store can purchase a delivery van for $18,000. Three methods of financing the van are being considered.
    a. The store's bank will provide a one-year capital improvement loan at 9 percent interest. To qualify for the loan, the company must maintain 120 percent of the value of the vehicle in checking or savings accounts with the bank.
    b. A finance company will purchase all of the company's accounts receivable for 86 percent of their value. The store's accounts receivable currently are valued at $26,500.
    c. The store can use cash on hand to make the purchase. The current balance sheet for the store shows the cash balance is $31,800. The cash budget for the coming 12 months shows that the highest projected cash total during that time is $38,000 and the lowest projected cash total is $12,200.

    Analyze the three sources of financing to determine the direct cost of each to the business and the possible advantages and disadvantages of each method. Prepare a written recommendation of the method you believe the store should use to finance the delivery van.

MARKETING TECHNOLOGY

24. Search the Internet for a public corporation's annual report, and find the section that discloses its revenues, costs, and results for five or 10 years. Using a spreadsheet program, calculate the percentage increase in sales revenue for each year. Also, calculate the ratio of sales revenue to earnings or net income. Print the results of your calculations.

FINANCING A START-UP COMPANY

Why does it seem like many businesses can attract start-up capital effortlessly, while some entrepreneurs with great ideas struggle to find money to get them off the ground? It is true that some of the best ideas never get financed. There is still hope if family, friends, and the bank can't fill the financial needs of an entrepreneur's start-up business. There are other services available to help entrepreneurs achieve their goals, even when a business incubator is not available.

What are investors looking for in a business venture? Lenders and investors have always been interested in the five Cs of credit—character, capacity, conditions, collateral, and capital. Character is the financial responsibility possessed by an entrepreneur. Financial character is determined by how an entrepreneur has handled past debts, bank accounts, and employment. Investors and lenders want to be assured that the prospective entrepreneur is trustworthy, consistent, and dedicated to making the business successful. Lenders want assurance that the loan will be repaid, and investors or venture

capitalists expect a positive financial return on their investment.

Capacity is the financial ability of the business owner to meet financial commitments. Amount of savings, business potential, and the entrepreneur's level of education are factors that influence capacity. Level of education may be an indicator of earning potential.

Conditions reflect the economic situation that a new business will face. Prosperity will draw the attention of potential investors, while recession tightens the purse strings. A slowdown in the economy will probably result in a slowdown in investment by venture capitalists who are uncertain about the future of new business.

There are two forms of collateral—loan and investor. Loan collateral consists of identifiable business and personal assets such as land, buildings, vehicles, and machinery. If an entrepreneur can't pay, the bank can take away those assets and sell them. With investor capital, if an entrepreneur doesn't achieve growth predictions, investors can take over the company. Venture investors usually choose between two ownership control concepts. They may choose to take a minority interest that can increase if profitability targets are not met, or they can start with controlling interest that declines when financial targets are met.

Capital involves risk sharing. Equity capital shows how much owners have risked in the company. Prospective investors are interested in the capital commitment of the business owner. Venture capitalists want to know that they have potential to get out of an investment. Equity is like a cushion to absorb possible losses. Debt capital must be repaid in good and bad times.

So how do entrepreneurs find start-up funds if family members, friends, and banks are inadequate? A number

of possibilities exist. Worthington-Cabott maintains a database of private equity funds, one-stop shops, venture capital funds, endowments, and foundations to which entrepreneurs can submit business plans. The funding sources are broken down by various preferences—industry, geography, type of investment, and stage of investment. The service comes at a price of $200 to submit the plan to the first five prospects.

Another financial service, Vcapital.com, determines appropriate venture capitalists for a business opportunity through its matching process and guides the project, from drafting a basic proposal to setting up a meeting with potential investors. Its web site allows the entrepreneur to prepare an iDeal Summary (synopsis of the business plan), while staffers provide feedback on the complete business plan. Vcapital.com charges a one-time fee of $200.

BusinessFinance.com is designed to assist entrepreneurs in locating funding sources. The site directs entrepreneurs to venture capital, investment funds, and equipment leasing or financing. BusinessFinance.com even helps the entrepreneur secure a loan or government funds. The site has a capital search engine to find funding sources that specialize in the entrepreneur's industry, size, stage, and

amount of funds being requested. A free workbook is provided to teach the entrepreneur how to prepare and present a funding request. The workbook also discusses government programs and suggests other resources and experts that the entrepreneur should consider. There is no charge because the entrepreneur is expected to do most of the work.

Do you want to obtain funds for a start-up business and don't know where to begin? Entrepreneurs beat the bushes and pound the pavement to locate venture capital. After searching high and low, many entrepreneurs are ready to throw in the towel. Help may be as close as the Internet, however.

THINK CRITICALLY

1. What are the traditional sources of venture capital for a business start-up?

2. What has made the task of searching for start-up capital much easier?

3. Which Internet company mentioned in the article do you think is the most helpful for a start-up business? Why?

4. What are the five Cs considered by investors? Describe how you stack up for each of the Cs.

http://www.deca.org/publications/HS_Guide/guidetoc.html

FINANCIAL SERVICES TEAM DECISION-MAKING EVENT

You and a partner are executives for BusinessFinance.com. Your Internet service has become very popular since the service is free to entrepreneurs searching for start-up capital. The financial success of BusinessFinance.com can be attributed to advertisements on the web site. The company wants to boost earnings by increasing the cost of advertising on the site, increasing the number of advertisers, and charging a minimal fee to entrepreneurs who choose to use the service. You will probably need to convince entrepreneurs that you have increased the financial services available on your web site.

STUDY THE SITUATION   Take 30 minutes to study the situation and outline your marketing strategy for accomplishing the three goals to boost earnings. Organize an analysis of your strategy, using a management decision-making format. During the preparation period, teams may only consult with one another about the management situation.

PRESENT YOUR ANALYSIS   Prepare a 10-minute presentation that describes your analysis of the situation. You may use printed reference materials, audio or visual aids, and notes made during the preparation time to enhance the presentation. You may use a laptop computer for the presentation.

CHAPTER 21

WHAT IS ENTREPRENEURSHIP?

LESSON 21.1 *WHAT IS ENTREPRENEURSHIP?*

LESSON 21.2 *ENTREPRENEURS' CHARACTERISTICS*

LESSON 21.3 *BUSINESS OWNERSHIP OPPORTUNITIES*

LESSON 21.4 *LEGAL NEEDS FOR ENTREPRENEURS*

LESSON 21.5 *DEVELOPING A BUSINESS PLAN*

NEWSLINE

AVOIDING THE GLASS CEILING

A problem faced by many people in business is known as the "glass ceiling." In many companies in the past it was very difficult for women and racial or ethnic minorities to move beyond a certain point in their career. Older white males held the top management and executive spots. When they retired or moved to other positions, other white males usually replaced them. While businesses have attempted to make changes, there is still a belief that the glass ceiling remains.

Entrepreneurship has been a way for women and other minority businesspeople to get to the top of a company. When you start your own business, no one can place a glass ceiling over your head. Statistics bear out the diversity of small business ownership.

According to the Small Business Administration (SBA), the number of women-owned businesses increased by 89 percent from 1987 to 1997. Eight and a half million businesses had women owners in 1997. Those businesses sold $3.1 billion of products and services and employed 24 million employees.

In that same 10-year period, the number of minority-owned businesses increased 168 percent for a total of 3.25 million companies. Those companies sold $495 billion dollars of products and services. Of all small businesses, 5.8 percent are Hispanic-owned, 5.8 percent have an African-American owner, and 4.5 percent have Asian ownership.

THINK CRITICALLY

1. Why do you believe successful women and minority employees have experienced the glass ceiling in the past?

2. Do you believe the glass ceiling is a major reason for the growth in new business ownership by the groups identified? Why or why not?

3. If the glass ceiling disappears in large businesses, do you believe the growth in minority-owned small business will slow? Why or why not?

4. While the number of woman-owned and minority-owned businesses is increasing, the percentage is much smaller than the percentage of the total U.S. population that each group accounts for. Why do you believe that percentage remains low?

CAREER OPPORTUNITY
INVENTORY ANALYST/
INVENTORY MANAGER

POINT YOUR BROWSER

www.corpview.com

TeleView is looking for an employee who possesses the following skills.

- Time management, problem-solving, project organization and interpersonal skills
- Customer relations skills that help to maintain a high level of customer loyalty
- Internet, technical communications, and computer skills are essential
- Ability to work in an invigorating, team-oriented environment

The main responsibilities of the job include the following.

- Analyze inventory value, turns, and efficiency
- Identify ineffective procedures and spot slow-moving inventories to reduce excess inventory
- Develop cycle count methods and procedures
- Work directly with the Product Marketing and Manufacturing Managers responsible for the specific products in inventory via the Intranet
- Train subordinates in inventory control and management to create an efficient inventory team

The job requires the following education, skills, and experience.

- Bachelor of Science degree in business management or administration or the equivalent training in inventory management from a professional organization
- 3-5 years of experience in manufacturing or warehouse inventory control
- Spreadsheet, email, and database entry skills a must

THINK CRITICALLY

1. Prepare a sample resume of a person who is qualified for this job and interested in applying for it.

2. Considering your skills and preferences, does this sound like a job you would like to have one day? Why or why not?

3. How could you use the skills and experience developed in this job to become an entrepreneur? What types of businesses do you think someone with these qualifications and interests could start?

21.1 WHAT IS ENTREPRENEURSHIP?

GOALS

- Define the characteristics of entrepreneurship.
- Describe the importance of entrepreneurship to the U.S. economy.

MARKETING MATTERS

Entrepreneurs are unique people. They are willing to take risks to start businesses. Successful entrepreneurs often start several companies during their business careers. They are usually not content to start the business and then continue to operate it for years and years as the manager. In fact, many entrepreneurs are not successful if they have to manage a growing business for many years.

Consider the following questions. Why is it important in a free-enterprise economy to have people who are willing to take risks to start new businesses? How do the skills needed to start a business differ from those needed to manage a business? Do you believe you would rather be an entrepreneur responsible for a new company or a manager responsible for an existing company? Why?

STARTING A BUSINESS

You may have heard the story of Henry Ford, who created Ford Motor Co. Today, Ford is a giant international corporation. But it had its beginnings in 1896, when Henry Ford produced his first automobile in a Michigan garage.

Bill Gates provides another example of a man who started with an idea and developed a successful large business, in his case Microsoft. The idea for the company began when, as college students, Bill and his friend Paul Allen developed a computer program to operate the first personal computers.

Many other people have put their personal stamps on the U.S. economy with business ideas and the initiative to bring the ideas to life in new companies. Examples include Madame C. J. Walker, who started a business in the early 1900s to produce and distribute hair-care products and cosmetics for African-Americans who were not being served by other businesses. Levi Strauss

Making Convincing Presentations

A new business will not be successful if the entrepreneur cannot obtain funding from investors, loans from banks, or financing from other companies to be able to purchase or lease buildings, equipment, and materials needed to operate the business.

The entrepreneur prepares a business plan to provide the information needed by others in deciding whether to invest or provide financing. Most people will not read the full plan, though, until they are interested in the business idea.

So an entrepreneur must be able to make a short oral presentation when meeting with potential investors and business people that will cause them to be interested in the new company. If the presentation does not get their attention in the first minute and present two or three meaningful points and supporting information in the first few minutes, it will probably not be successful.

THINK CRITICALLY

1. Why do prospective investors and other business people want to hear a short presentation from the entrepreneur?

2. If you were an entrepreneur, what would be your first statement to generate interest in your new company?

3. Create a presentation outlining the major topics you would cover in 3-5 minutes to interest investors in a new business.

Ice Cream is known worldwide for its high-quality products and its unique company environment. Margaret Rudkin developed the Pepperidge Farms company that she later sold for several million dollars. The business idea grew as she baked and sold bread and cookies from her home in the 1930s.

THE AMERICAN DREAM

Starting your own business has been called the American Dream. People go into business to make a profit, but they also start their own businesses to have the freedom to do work that they enjoy and to take responsibility for the success or failure of the business. There is little that is more rewarding than seeing your ideas and efforts grow into a profitable business, offering jobs to others, and providing products and services that satisfy customers. On the other hand, there is a continuing challenge in business ownership to meet a payroll, pay the bills, and find ways to compete successfully.

An **entrepreneur** is someone who takes the risk to start a new business. That risk involves investing his or her money in the business. **Entrepreneurship** is the process of planning, creating, and managing a new business.

An entrepreneur is different from a business manager. A manager is responsible for a business created and owned by others. The manager is an employee and so takes direction from the owners of the business.

invented a process in 1873 to use rivets in the manufacturing of denim work pants to add strength to the seams, creating a clothing company that still manufactures blue jeans today. Ben Cohen and Jerry Greenfield began mixing unique flavors of ice cream in a renovated Vermont garage in 1978. Ben and Jerry's

The owners must approve any major change in the business. Conversely, the manager does not take on risks like the owners. If the business fails, the manager will lose a job but will not have lost any money invested in the business.

While entrepreneurship is an important part of U.S. business, there are entrepreneurs starting businesses around the world. In developing economies, entrepreneurs are often the first to start businesses to produce and sell products and services. Some of the most renowned global businesses, such as Sony, Mercedes-Benz, and IMAX theatres, were originally the ideas of international entrepreneurs.

ENTREPRENEURSHIP OPPORTUNITIES IN MARKETING

Entrepreneurs start all types of businesses. Manufacturing businesses tend to be the most recognized, but marketing opportunities also exist for entrepreneurs. Some of the best-known entrepreneurs had marketing ideas.

Sam Walton developed an efficient method to distribute products from manufacturers to his discount retail stores. He grew his small Arkansas business into today's Wal-Marts and Sam's Clubs. Fredrick Smith wrote a paper as an undergraduate student at Yale on how packages and other deliveries could be moved rapidly by airfreight through a system of hub cities. From that idea, he created FedEx, which today is the world's largest express transportation company. Mrs. P.F.E. Albee took the products of the California Perfume Co. and pioneered the now famous door-to-door selling and distribution methods of the Avon Products Co.

Those are just a few examples of people who had ideas for how to distribute, sell, promote, and service the thousands of products consumers demand. Retail and wholesale businesses, finance and credit companies, transportation businesses, advertising agencies, and many other organizations are involved in the distribution and exchange of products and services between producers and consumers. All provide opportunities for entrepreneurs.

What is the difference between an entrepreneur and a manager?

THE IMPORTANCE OF ENTREPRENEURSHIP

It is sometimes easy to confuse small business with entrepreneurship. Not all small businesses are owned and operated by entrepreneurs. Many people buy an existing small business or operate a franchise and may not be considered entrepreneurs. Nevertheless, almost all businesses developed by entrepreneurs start out as small businesses.

ECONOMIC ROLE

Entrepreneurs develop small businesses, and small businesses are important to the U.S. economy. Some important small business statistics are shown in Figure 21-1.

FIGURE 21-1
The role of small businesses in the United States.

Small businesses . . .
- make up over 90% of all businesses
- employ 52% of all non-government workers and 38% of workers in high-tech occupations
- provide about 75% of the all-new jobs
- are responsible for over half of all goods and services produced
- make up over 95% of all companies involved in exporting

Another benefit provided by small businesses is that they are the source of most of the initial job training people receive. Most of us started working for a small business where we learned important lessons such as time management, human relations, good work habits, and the skills to perform the job for which we were hired.

Small businesses are more likely to hire younger and older workers and workers who need part-time jobs. Most entrepreneurs start their first business while they are still working for another company. They often start the business at home on a part-time basis and expand it to a full-time business if it is successful.

Small businesses provide ownership opportunities for people from minority groups. By 2000, almost 10 million women owned their own businesses. Hispanic-owned businesses total over 1.5 million; African-American ownership is nearing 1 million businesses; and Asian business ownership is also about 1 million.

PERSONAL BENEFITS

Entrepreneurs work long hours to make their businesses successful. They sacrifice to invest their savings and often have very little if any income for the first few years of operations. They are responsible for the success of the business, so they have to handle complaints and solve problems. With all of those difficulties, why would anyone want to be an entrepreneur?

Owning a small business offers many personal benefits. Many people are able to add to their income by operating a part-time business in addition to their full-time job. Entrepreneurs receive a great deal of personal satisfaction from developing an idea into a business and completing work that is interesting and uses their skills.

Watching a business grow, opening new businesses, providing jobs for people in the community, and being able to control the profits from the company are all identified by entrepreneurs as reasons they prefer business ownership.

Why are small businesses an important part of the U.S. economy?

LESSON REVIEW

1. Why do people start their own businesses?

2. What is the key risk that entrepreneurs take when starting a business?

3. Why is a manager not an entrepreneur?

4. What types of marketing opportunities are available to entrepreneurs?

5. Provide examples of businesses from other countries started by entrepreneurs.

6. What types of small-business owners are not necessarily entrepreneurs?

7. What percentage of all businesses are small businesses?

8. How do small businesses contribute to the U.S. economy?

21.2 ENTREPRENEURS' CHARACTERISTICS

- Identify personal characteristics of entrepreneurs.
- Describe the education needed to prepare for entrepreneurship.

Some characteristics that make a successful marketer also make a successful entrepreneur. Creativity, determination, risk-taking, and willingness to take responsibility and make decisions are all important both in marketing and in starting a new business.

You are often involved in activities in school, in clubs and other organizations, and in part-time jobs that demonstrate the qualities needed for success as an entrepreneur and as a marketer.

List the characteristics identified above. Now make a list of the school activities, clubs, organizations, and jobs in which you have participated.

Compare the lists and identify specific assignments, activities, and leadership roles that gave you an opportunity to develop and demonstrate each of the characteristics. After you have finished, consider which of the characteristics are personal strengths and which are not.

WHAT DOES IT TAKE?

Why is it that some people have started several successful businesses and other people have never considered starting one? What makes one person suited to be a business owner and other people managers or employees? Researchers have studied successful entrepreneurs and identified qualities that make them different from other people.

CHARACTERISTICS OF ENTREPRENEURS

It is important to recognize that anyone can be an entrepreneur. Women and men of all races, older and younger people, and those who have never completed high school as well as college graduates are successful entrepreneurs. People are not born with entrepreneurship skills. They can be developed if you want to start your own business.

Successful entrepreneurs usually have the following characteristics.

- **Entrepreneurs are focused and goal oriented.** Many successful entrepreneurs thought about and planned their business for many years. Often they dreamed of starting their own business when they were very young. They may have faced a number of obstacles before they were able to succeed, but they did not give up on their plan.

- **Entrepreneurs are risk takers.** They are willing to take a chance that the business will fail in order to be successful. They invest time and money in an idea that others may not have tried. Yet entrepreneurs are not gamblers. In other words, they carefully consider the risk to see if it is possible. They work hard to reduce the risk and increase the chances of success.

- **Entrepreneurs want to achieve.** They set high personal goals and then do everything they can to meet those goals. They will be unhappy if they don't achieve what they want and may stubbornly keep working at the goal even when it doesn't seem likely they will succeed.

FIGURE 21-2
Checking my entrepreneurship characteristics.

___ I usually set realistic and achievable goals for myself.
___ I like to take responsibility for my own actions.
___ I like to solve problems and identify new ways to do things.
___ I'm willing to take risks when I know there is a chance to be successful.
___ I am able to manage my time well and usually complete the tasks I start.
___ When I am doing something I enjoy I will commit long hours to the work.
___ I like challenges and don't mind the pressure.
___ Things do not have to be simple; I can manage several things at the same time.
___ I usually have confidence in the things I choose to do.
___ I often put personal activities ahead of socializing.
___ When I don't have the answer to something, I will go out and find it.
___ I understand my strengths and weaknesses.

- **Entrepreneurs are independent.** They are often not involved in team activities and may not do well when asked to cooperate with others. They are more comfortable when they are in charge and responsible for results and so may seek activities where their individual skills are important.

- **Entrepreneurs have a high level of self-confidence.** They believe in themselves and their abilities and expect to be successful. If they do not succeed at an activity, they will either decide it wasn't important, put the responsibility for failure on others, or work hard to improve so they will succeed the next time.

- **Entrepreneurs are creative.** They are interested in challenges and finding ways to solve problems. They often approach problem-solving differently than others and are likely to come up with unique ideas and solutions. That creativity is often the reason that entrepreneurs come up with business ideas others have not considered.

You can see by looking at the list of characteristics that not everyone is suited to be an entrepreneur. Also it is apparent why an entrepreneur may not make a good business manager or team player and may prefer to work independently rather than for someone else.

Often the business started by an entrepreneur fails when it begins to grow and the owner has to spend time managing the growing business. The entrepreneur may not have the patience or the interpersonal skills needed to successfully manage the business. It is not unusual for an entrepreneur to sell the business after several years and then begin the process of starting a new business all over again.

DO YOU WANT TO BE AN ENTREPRENEUR?

Most people know if they want to be an entrepreneur or not. Remember you can be a small business owner without being an entrepreneur. You can buy a business that was successfully started by another person and operate it. You can become a franchisee where you operate a business using the standards and procedures developed by the people who started the franchise.

If you have thought about starting your own business, you should assess your potential. Determining whether you have what it takes to be a successful entrepreneur is an important step. If you want to start a business, you can develop the characteristics and skills that are necessary.

Use the checklist in Figure 21-2 to determine if you have the qualities needed to successfully start your own business. For the items for which you cannot place a checkmark, plan ways to develop the quality so you can improve your chances for success as an entrepreneur.

Why do some businesses started by entrepreneurs fail when they begin to grow?

PREPARING FOR ENTREPRENEURSHIP

You can begin planning now if you want to become an entrepreneur. In fact you have probably already done several things that improve your chances for successfully starting a new business. Education and business experience are both important parts of your preparation.

In the early part of the 20th century and before, many entrepreneurs did not have a great deal of education. It was not unusual for an entrepreneur to drop out of school, work in business for many years, and then start a business. However, that was a time when business was not as complex and fewer people were educated. It was possible to run a business based on what the person learned through experience.

Today, consumers and other business people are more educated, and business procedures and technology are more complex. While we still hear examples of young entrepreneurs, most of the people who start successful businesses today have completed high school and often have one or more college degrees.

Education is an important part of preparing to become an entrepreneur. The classes you select should develop academic abilities, technology skills, and an understanding of business principles and procedures.

ACADEMIC PREPARATION

To plan and start a business you will need to work with many people, develop and communicate your business plans, seek financing, prepare and review financial documents, make decisions, and solve problems. A strong academic preparation will provide the knowledge and skills needed for these tasks.

Communications Skills Writing and speaking are essential entrepreneurial skills. You will write business letters, memos, and reports. You will prepare written materials such as employment advertisements, job descriptions, and product information. Use classes in English and composition to develop your ability to write clearly and efficiently using the form and style expected by the reader.

Oral communications are especially important to entrepreneurs. You will make

An Inventor and an Entrepreneur

Combine the curiosity of an inventor and business skills of an entrepreneur and you have multimillion-dollar international business success.

Enro Rubik was a Hungarian designer who was intrigued by mathematical problems. He developed a cube made up of 26 smaller six-colored cubes that were connected but could be rotated independently. Mr. Rubik wanted to determine how to solve the problem of aligning all of the same-colored sides of the small cubes on the same side of the larger cube. He invented and applied for a patent for the cube.

When Hungarian businessman Tibor Laczi saw the cube, he believed there was potential for both a children's toy and an adult puzzle. Working with Enro Rubik, Mr. Laczi signed agreements with companies in several countries to produce and market the Rubik's Cube.

It has become the most popular puzzle in history and made both men multi-millionaires. Over 1/8 of the entire world's population has played with a Rubik's Cube.

THINK CRITICALLY

1. What personal characteristics do you believe are similar and different between an inventor and an entrepreneur?

2. Why do you believe the Rubik's Cube was such a successful international product?

presentations to investors, bankers, lawyers, business people who are needed to provide products and services for your business, and prospective customers. You must communicate effectively with employees to conduct meetings, give directions, explain procedures, and build enthusiasm and commitment to the company. Public speaking, speech, and other oral communications courses are important to you if you are planning to be an entrepreneur. In addition, find leadership roles in class projects, become an officer in clubs and other organizations, and participate in activities in which you are responsible for formal and informal presentations.

Math Skills   As an entrepreneur, you are responsible for the profitability of your new business. If the business is not profitable in a short time, it will fail. If there is no profit, you will not be able to pay yourself and so will need to work at another job to receive a paycheck.

Basic math skills are used to develop financial plans for the business as well as in day-to-day business operations. You will need to make calculations quickly and accurately involving the mathematical functions of addition, subtraction, multiplication, and division. You will frequently calculate percentages and use fractions and decimals. The ability to estimate the accuracy of a calculation will allow you to quickly check a budget, an invoice, or a sales estimate for a customer.

Advanced math skills including statistics and accounting will be useful in conducting research and in preparing and analyzing financial reports. You will be able to select the best investment opportunities, negotiate favorable loan terms, and compare the performance of your business with other similar businesses. To develop the needed skills you should take a number of mathematics classes, including algebra, and business classes that include mathematics, such as accounting, finance, business statistics, or marketing research.

Scientific Skills   You may believe that science classes cannot contribute a great deal to helping you become an entrepreneur unless the business is a scientific business. Yet science classes are an important way to learn to complete problem-solving, conduct research, and make decisions based on careful and objective analytical procedure.

Scientific skills include problem identification, information review, considering alternative solutions, and basing decisions on objective information. Science classes also teach careful observation skills, note taking, and the preparation of written reports.

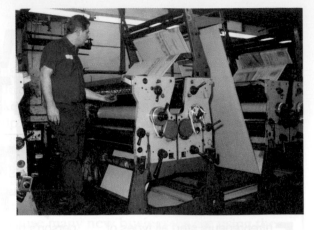

for entrepreneurs. Each of the marketing functions needs to be performed as products and services are exchanged between producers and consumers. Each of those functions offers possibilities for starting your own business.

Promotion   Several types of businesses offer promotional services. Advertising agencies, public relations firms, graphic design, copywriting, and printing companies are examples of businesses involved in promotion. Companies build displays for stores or malls or design billboards and electronic signs to be placed in high traffic areas to promote businesses and products.

Selling   Sales agencies are hired to sell the products and services of companies. This is often done when it is not profitable for a company to employ its own sales force. Another type of business opportunity related to selling is offering sales training or developing resources that are used by salespeople, such as computer programs, films and videotapes, or product models.

Distribution   One of the most important marketing functions is distribution. Many types of companies move and store products from producer to consumer. Trucking companies, express delivery businesses, and couriers handle thousands of products each day. Warehouses and storage centers are distribution businesses that ensure that products are held safely until they are needed.

Pricing   Pricing is a function for which it is difficult to identify related businesses. Yet a number of companies help determine the value of products and negotiate agreements between the buyer and seller. An example of that type of business is an auction house, where products are presented and sold to the highest bidder. eBay is an example of an Internet business that helps buyers and sellers negotiate a fair

Small Business Takes to the Net

Some of the luster went out of the Internet as a place for business with the failure of many of the new e-businesses in the late 1990s. But a look at those failures suggests many were caused by poor business planning and management rather than by the Internet being a poor place for business. Many businesses are successfully using the Internet.

ZdNet recently surveyed small businesses about their Internet use. Nearly 50 percent use the Web as a regular part of their business. There were four primary uses of the Internet: 35 percent use it for research; 19 percent had their own home page; 18 percent used it for e-mail; and 13 percent had an internal network (Intranet) to support the work of their employees.

Other research studies summarized by the Small Business Administration report that 1 in 3 small businesses use the Internet for business transactions, either to sell or buy products. A very small percentage of small companies use the Web for one of the popular large business tools, to recruit new employees. Popular reasons reported by small business owners in moving to the Web are to reach new customers and to expand globally.

THINK CRITICALLY

1. Why do you believe small businesses are choosing to use the Web for business even though there has been a high failure rate among new e-commerce companies?

2. Research has found that small businesses that use the Web are slightly more profitable than those companies not using the Web. What could be some reasons for the difference?

3. Use the Internet to find examples of a variety of uses of the Internet by small businesses.

price for products. Other companies provide pricing information to prospective buyers so they know how much they should pay for products such as new and used cars, real estate, or travel.

Finance Banks and credit card companies are marketing businesses that provide financial services to businesses and consumers. Financial advisors help in obtaining credit and making investments.

Marketing-Information Management Gathering and analyzing information and conducting marketing research are important marketing activities. Many types of businesses perform this marketing function. Some companies pay consumers to test products, conduct surveys in malls, or send shoppers into businesses to determine the effectiveness of customer

service. Businesses gather information, prepare reports for businesses, or provide data security services for other companies.

Product/Service Management You can find a company that will provide assistance to other businesses in new product research and design. Other companies will provide testing to make sure of the quality of a product or to compare the strengths and weaknesses of competing products.

Why are retailers and wholesalers considered to be marketing businesses?

IDENTIFYING BUSINESS OWNERSHIP OPPORTUNITIES

Understanding marketing gives you an important set of skills to be able to identify possible business opportunities if you want to be an entrepreneur. Many entrepreneurs select a business idea based solely on their interests, skills, and experience. It is important to choose a business that you like and for which you have the interests and skills to operate successfully. But that is not enough.

Successful marketing uses a two-step process. The first step is to identify customers and their needs. The second step is developing a marketing mix to meet the needs of the customers.

A successful business should follow the same procedure. Rather than starting with an idea for products and services, an entrepreneur should begin by studying the market. Are their prospective customers available that the business can serve? Do you understand their needs? Can you develop products and services that will meet those needs? Can you operate the business and serve your customers at a profit?

If that approach is used, there is a much greater chance that the business will be successful than if you develop a business and then try to find and attract customers to the business.

Identify a Target Market Before you decide to start a business, you should determine if a target market exists for the business. What are their specific needs?

Study the Competition A new business will have difficulty competing with an existing business unless that business has a weakness. Identify companies offering similar products. Determine the prices they charge and the services they offer. Find out whether customers are generally satisfied or dissatisfied with the business.

Develop a Unique Offering Based on a study of the customers and competitors, determine if you can provide a competitive product. What can you offer that customers will view as satisfying their important needs better than what is being offered by your competitors? Unless you can identify something your business will offer that is better than the competition in some important way, it is not likely that your new business will be successful. Using your understanding of marketing planning will help you identify successful business opportunities.

Return on Investment

To finance a new business, an entrepreneur was able to invest $75,000 of her own money. She obtained $490,000 of additional funds from a group of people who owned a venture capital company. The venture capital company looked for attractive new business ideas where they could get a good return on the money they invested. The table shows the amount of money invested and the profit received at the end of three years of operation.

	Entrepreneur	Investors
Amount of Investment	$75,000	$490,000
3-Year Profit	$9,500	$112,000

THINK CRITICALLY

1. What was the 3-year return on investment of the entrepreneur and of the Investors? (profit ÷ investment × 100).

2. What was the total amount of money invested in the business and the total amount of profit?

3. Why would an entrepreneur be willing to accept a smaller return on investment than the venture capital group is willing to accept?

What is the two-step marketing process that can be used to identify business opportunities?

LESSON REVIEW

1. Identify several examples of non-marketing businesses that can be started by entrepreneurs.

2. What marketing function would an advertising agency perform?

3. How does an auction house improve the exchange process between buyers and sellers?

4. What problems result when an entrepreneur decides on a business idea based on skills, interest, and experience only?

5. Why is it important to identify a target market as the first step in developing a new business idea?

6. What makes it possible for a new business to successfully compete with existing businesses?

LEGAL NEEDS FOR ENTREPRENEURS

MARKETING MATTERS

Entrepreneurs are quite independent and want to be totally responsible for business decisions. This makes it difficult to share ownership of a new business with other people. However, having multiple owners in a business often increases the chances that the business will be successful.

Form small groups with other students and discuss the advantages and disadvantages of each of these three scenarios:

1. An entrepreneur starts a new business with his or her own money and is the sole owner and decision maker.

2. An entrepreneur identifies another person to be a partner in a new business. The partners contribute an equal amount of money and share in the ownership and decision-making.

3. An entrepreneur sells stock to four other people to finance a new business. The entrepreneur owns half of the stock and the other four own equal amounts of the remaining stock. The entrepreneur manages the business and the other owners serve as the board of directors to approve major plans for the business.

GOALS

● **Describe the legal forms of ownership for a business.**

● **Discuss legal steps to be followed in starting a new business.**

THE OWNERSHIP DECISION

One of the very first decisions made by an entrepreneur is the legal form of ownership for the new business. While it would seem that an entrepreneur would be the sole owner, there are three common ownership choices. Each offers advantages and disadvantages.

PROPRIETORSHIP

A business owned and managed by one person is a **proprietorship**. A proprietor is a person who has sole ownership of a business. Proprietorship is the most common form of business ownership, with over three-quarters of all businesses organized in this way.

Under the proprietorship form of organization, the owner is responsible for the money needed to start and operate the business as well as all business planning and management. As a result of being the sole

Internationalize Your Web Site

It may seem easy to go global with your business through the Internet. Just develop a web site, add it to international search engines, and you are in business. But that won't do it.

While English is used as a language of business in many countries around the world, many potential customers do not read English. Even for those who do, word meanings and symbols may be misinterpreted. If you are planning to market your product internationally through the Web, you must start by thinking about the web site design.

Many companies start with a very basic home page that allows the viewer to select the language they prefer. Then a link from the home page takes them to the "localized" web pages in that language. When developing the web site, make sure to avoid images that can be misinterpreted and technical information that may not translate well. It is best to get people who are skilled in each language to help translate the web site and review the content to make sure it is meaningful.

Other important considerations in developing a truly global web site are:

- Date and time formats
- Currency
- Credit card submission systems
- Phone numbers and area code formats
- Address and postal codes

THINK CRITICALLY

1. Why should a company think about the global business before it begins developing its web site?

2. How will the perception of your company by international customers change if they can access your web site in their own language rather than just in English?

3. Use the Internet to find examples of companies that have developed web sites in multiple languages to improve global business.

can make all decisions. That feature suits many entrepreneurs, who are generally quite independent.

The proprietor receives all profits of the business. Because of the profit motive, entrepreneurs work very hard to make their businesses successful.

The owner can make decisions without consulting others and so can act quickly when needed. As a result, proprietorships are quite flexible and can adjust rapidly to changing conditions.

Forming a proprietorship is relatively easy. There are few legal requirements to start the business or to end it. People are encouraged to use this form of business ownership as a result.

Disadvantages of Proprietorships Running a business successfully requires many skills. A proprietor is solely responsible for the business and may not have all of the skills needed. There is a greater chance that the business will fail due to lack of planning and management skills.

While a few businesses can be started without a lot of money, most new businesses are quite expensive to form. One person may not have the needed money and may not be able to borrow adequate funds.

A proprietorship requires the owner to assume a great deal of risk. While the owner receives all the profits of the business, that person also suffers all the losses if the business is not profitable. Creditors have a claim against the owner's personal assets, not just the assets of the business if it fails.

The business will not be able to continue to operate for long if the owner becomes ill or dies. The business will either have to be sold or must close.

owner, that proprietor is entitled to all profits earned by the business.

If there are no debts, a proprietor has full claim to all of the business' assets. If there are debts, people to whom the business owes money have the first claim against the assets if the business is sold or if it fails.

Advantages of Proprietorships The owner of the business is the boss and

PARTNERSHIP

A **partnership** is owned and operated by two or more people who share in the decision-making and profitability of the company. A partnership is formed using a **partnership agreement**, a legal document that specifies the responsibilities and financial relationships of the partners.

Advantages of Partnerships
Partnerships pool the knowledge and skills of all the owners. There are more people available to manage the business.

Because more than one person owns the business there is usually more money available. Also, banks are more likely to loan money to companies when more than one person is responsible for repaying the loan.

If one person decides to leave the business or dies, the business does not have to close. Partnership agreements specify how a partner can be replaced. The remaining partners can continue to operate the business until a new partner is located.

Disadvantages of Partnerships
Disagreements can occur among partners on important decisions. It may take time for partners to discuss issues and agree on the best solution.

In a partnership, all partners are responsible for any actions and decisions made by another partner. If money is owed, each partner is liable for the debt.

CORPORATION

A **corporation** is a business owned by people who purchase stock in the company. Corporations are granted a charter by the state in which they are formed. A **charter** is a legal document allowing the corporation to operate as if it were a person. The business can borrow money, enter into contracts, and is liable for its decisions and actions.

Advantages of Corporations
A corporation is most often formed by an entrepreneur to raise money and to limit the liability faced by the owners. Because an owner invests in stock, the losses suffered by the business in case of failure are limited to the amount of the investment.

The life of a corporation does not depend on any one owner. If an owner decides to sell his or her stock, another person can buy it and the business continues to operate.

Disadvantages of Corporations
Because corporations operate based on a charter, they face more rules and regulations than other forms of businesses. They are watched more carefully by the states in which they operate and must file regular reports.

The people who own the company's stock usually do not have as much interest in the business as the entrepreneur. They may be more concerned about the profits earned by the company than day-to-day operations. No one individual has to take responsibility for business operations and decisions.

Corporations usually are taxed at a higher rate than the other forms of business. In addition to corporate taxes, individual investors must pay taxes on any profits distributed to the owner.

What are the three forms of ownership to consider when starting a new business?

STARTING YOUR BUSINESS

Once you have decided to start a business, several legal steps need to be completed before you can open for business.

● Select the form of ownership. Decide if your business will be a proprietorship, partnership, or corporation. If it is a partnership, prepare and sign the partnership agreement. If it is a corporation, prepare and file a charter and complete the other forms required by the state.

● Decide on a business name and register it with the state and local government.

● Determine the licenses and permits that are needed to operate your business. Complete the procedures to obtain each one.

● If you are creating a new product, determine if a patent, copyright, or trademark can be obtained. If so, file an application.

● Purchase or lease buildings and equipment. Obtain necessary financing for the purchases and for business operations. Complete mortgage, lease, and loan applications and final documents.

● Develop necessary business records.

● Identify insurance needs and purchase the necessary policies.

● Prepare personnel policies and procedures if employees will be hired. Identify and comply with all employment and tax laws.

● Prepare forms and procedures you will use to sell products to customers, and make sure they meet all legal requirements. Be prepared to collect and report all local, state, and federal taxes.

You can see that starting a business involves many steps and requires a great deal of legal information. An entrepreneur should work with a lawyer skilled in business startups and seek assistance from experienced business people, business associations, and government offices to make sure all procedures are followed and all legal requirements are met.

Why is it important to get assistance from a lawyer and others when starting a new business?

1. Why do entrepreneurs often prefer a proprietorship as a form of business ownership?

2. How does a partnership increase the chances of success for a new business?

3. What amount of financial liability does a partner in a business have?

4. Who are the owners of a corporation?

5. What is a charter?

6. Why is it important to carefully follow legal steps when starting a new business?

7. Who should an entrepreneur work with to understand the procedures to follow in starting a business?

DEVELOPING A BUSINESS PLAN

MARKETING MATTERS

The characteristics of entrepreneurs make them more interested in operating the business than developing plans for a business. Yet studies have identified that one of the most important tools to the success of a new business is a carefully developed, written business plan.

Consider all of the information needed and all of the decisions that must be made before a business can open. Consider the business activities that must be completed to successfully operate a business.

Before you study this lesson, make a list of all of the things you believe should be a part of a business plan. For each item listed, write one or two sentences describing why you believe it would help an entrepreneur to complete that planning before starting the business. As you complete this lesson, compare your list to the information in the lesson.

GOALS

● Discuss the importance of a business plan for a new business.

● Identify and describe the parts of a business plan.

THE IMPORTANCE OF PLANNING

An entrepreneur will make many decisions before the business ever opens. Many more decisions must be made after the business begins operations. If the correct decisions are made, the business will be successful, but if enough of the owner's decisions are incorrect, the business will join the thousands that fail each year.

An experienced business owner may know enough about the business to make many of the important decisions rapidly with the information available at the time. A new entrepreneur does not have that experience or the information to easily make decisions. It will be valuable if the entrepreneur has help readily available when problems are encountered and decisions must be made.

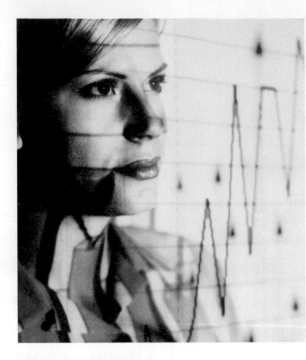

THE BUSINESS PLAN

A **business plan** is a written document prepared to guide the development and operation of a new business. It contains the information used and the initial decisions made to manage each of the major areas of the business.

Each new business will have a slightly different plan. It is prepared by the business owner and reflects the owner's knowledge, ideas, and experience. But all business plans must communicate several things:

- The purpose of the business and the types of products and services it plans to offer
- Descriptions of the business' customers and their important needs
- Major business activities that will be completed
- Resources needed including materials, equipment, and people
- Sources of financing and the amount of money needed to start and operate the business
- The type of competition to be faced and major competitors
- Financial requirements and profit projections

USING THE BUSINESS PLAN

A business plan would be important even if only the entrepreneur used it. By gathering and studying information and using that information to make decisions about the business, the owner will usually be more careful and more objective in determining how the business will operate. Moreover, other people who are involved in starting the business also use the business plan.

Prospective Partners and Stockholders If the entrepreneur wants to organize the business as a partnership or a corporation, potential owners will want information about the business to determine if they want to participate.

Bankers and Investors Most new businesses will need to borrow money to finance buildings, equipment, product purchases, and several months of operations. Bankers and other people who might consider making loans will need detailed information to make sure the business is a solid investment.

Employees of the Business The owner of a new business works many hours each week and is very busy making sure the business is successful. Employees are an important part of the operations. The business plan provides information to employees so the owner will not have to orally communicate all of the information.

Other Business People Other businesses will be a part of the success of the new business. If the new business manufactures products, it will need cooperation from retailers to sell products. It will need to purchase raw materials, supplies, and equipment and usually will want credit from suppliers. The new business may need the help of lawyers, accountants, advertising agencies, and others. A business plan assures the cooperating businesses that the owner is well prepared to work with them.

Why is it important for a new entrepreneur to have a written business plan?

DEVELOPING A BUSINESS PLAN

A business plan is used to make important decisions about business operations, to communicate those decisions to others to build understanding and support, and to serve as a guide for business operations. The parts of a business plan are shown in Figure 21-3.

FIGURE 21-3
Outline of a business plan for a new business.

I. **Introduction to the Business**
   A. Description of products and services
   B. Owners and form of ownership
   C. Business organization
   D. Long- and short-term objectives
   E. Strengths and weaknesses

II. **Description of the Industry**
   A. Economic conditions
   B. Type of competition
   C. Strengths and weaknesses of competitors
   D. Anticipated changes in the industry

III. **Market Analysis**
   A. Description of target markets
   B. Analysis of needs and purchase behavior
   C. Sales forecasts for major markets

IV. **Operations**
   A. Organization of operations and departments
   B. Descriptions of major activities
   C. Identification of equipment, materials, and other operating resources needed
   D. Staffing requirements and management plans

V. **Marketing**
   A. Description of marketing mix
   B. Procedures for implementing marketing activities
   C. Resources needed for marketing

VI. **Financial Plans**
   A. Startup costs
   B. Semiannual income and expense projections
   C. Monthly cash flow budgets
   D. Annual balance sheet projections
   E. Analysis of financial plan
   F. Sources of financing and funding requests

The sections of the business plan identify the decisions made and describe how the business will be organized and managed. It shows the resources that will be needed to operate the business successfully.

Financial plans describe the money that will be needed to operate the business and what the money will be used for. Detailed financial projections are made to show income, expenses, profit, and the return investors can expect on financing they provide.

After the business plan is completed, the owner should prepare a one- or two-page summary of the plan. The summary provides an overview of the business and the major decisions. The written summary is useful when the owner needs to present the plan to others in order to build understanding and support for the new business.

What are the major parts of a business plan?

1. What happens when an entrepreneur makes a number of incorrect decisions about the new business?

2. What is a business plan?

3. What are several things that need to be communicated with a business plan?

4. Identify several groups of people that need to know the information contained in a business plan.

5. What information is included in the financial section of a business plan?

6. In what section of the business plan are staffing needs described?

7. Why should a written summary of the business plan be prepared?

SUMMARY

Lesson 21.1

A. People go into business to make a profit. They also start businesses to have the freedom to do work they enjoy and to take responsibility for the success or failure of their efforts.

B. Entrepreneurs start all types of businesses. Manufacturing businesses are the most often recognized, but marketing opportunities exist for entrepreneurs as well. Some of the best-known entrepreneurs had marketing ideas.

Lesson 21.2

A. Researchers have identified the qualities that make successful entrepreneurs different from other people. Anyone can become an entrepreneur if they develop those characteristics.

B. Begin planning now if you want to become an entrepreneur. Education and experience are both important parts of your preparation. You will need academic, technology, and business skills for a new business.

Lesson 21.3

A. There are many marketing opportunities available for entrepreneurs. Each of the marketing functions needs to be performed as products and services are exchanged between producers and consumers. Each of those functions offers possibilities for starting your own business.

B. Understanding marketing gives you an important set of skills to be able to identify possible business opportunities if you want to be an entrepreneur. Successful marketing first identifies customers and their needs, then develops a marketing mix to meet them.

Lesson 21.4

A. One of the very first decisions made by an entrepreneur is the legal form of ownership for the new business. There are three common ownership choices—proprietorship, partnership, and corporation.

B. An entrepreneur should work with a lawyer skilled in business startups and seek assistance from experienced business people, business associations, and government offices to make sure all procedures are followed and all legal requirements are met before starting a business.

Lesson 21.5

A. A business plan is a document prepared to guide the development and operation of a new business. It contains the information used and the initial decisions made to manage each of the major areas of the business.

B. A business plan is used to make important decisions about the business operations, to communicate those decisions to others to build understanding and support, and to serve as a guide for business operations.

REVIEW MARKETING CONCEPTS

1. True or False: It is not possible to be an entrepreneur today due to the competition from large international businesses.

2. True or False: One of the reasons people start businesses is to have the freedom to do work they enjoy.

3. True or False: All small businesses are owned by entrepreneurs.

4. True or False: Small businesses represent about half of all of the businesses operating in the United States.

5. True or False: Often a business started by an entrepreneur fails when it begins to grow.

6. True or False: A disadvantage of small business ownership is that successful small businesses are seldom owned by people from minority groups.

7. Which of the following is NOT a characteristic of entrepreneurs:
   a. Entrepreneurs want to achieve.
   b. Entrepreneurs are independent.
   c. Entrepreneurs are wealthy.
   d. Entrepreneurs are risk takers.

8. When selecting an idea for a business to start, an entrepreneur should choose one that:
   a. has never been tried before.
   b. meets his/her interests and skills.
   c. requires only a small investment.
   d. friends and family recommend.

9. True or False: Unless an owner can identify something a business will offer that is better than the competition in some important way, it is not likely that the business will be successful.

10. The form of business ownership in which the owners assume the least amount of risk is:
    a. entrepreneurship
    b. partnership
    c. proprietorship
    d. corporation

11. True or False: A disadvantage of a partnership is that if money is owed, each partner is responsible for the debt.

12. True or False: When a new business is started, the business name needs to be registered with state and local governments.

13. True or False: The business plan should be shared with prospective customers so they are more confident in the business's success.

14. The financial section of a business plan includes:
    a. an analysis of customer needs.
    b. a description of the marketing mix.
    c. identification of startup costs.
    d. staffing requirements.

15. True or False: The complete written business plan should be no more than two to three pages long.

REVIEW MARKETING TERMS

Match the terms listed with the definitions. Some terms may not be used.

16. Someone who takes the risk to start a new business.

17. The process of planning, creating, and managing a new business.

18. A business owned and managed by one person.

19. A business owned and operated by two or more people who share in the decision-making and profitability of the company.

20. A legal document that specifies the responsibilities and financial relationships of business partners.

21. A business owned by people who purchase stock in the company.

22. A legal document allowing the corporation to operate as if it were a person.

23. A written document prepared to guide the development and operation of a new business.

a. business plan
b. charter
c. corporation
d. entrepreneur
e. entrepreneurship
f. partnership
g. partnership agreement
h. proprietorship

APPLY MARKETING FUNCTIONS

MARKETING RESEARCH

24. The number of businesses formed as proprietorships, partnerships, and corporations is identified and reported by state and federal governments each year. Use the Internet to obtain the most recent information on the number and type of businesses for the entire United States and for your state.

Develop a spreadsheet to report the information you obtained. Use the spreadsheet to calculate the total number of businesses in the country and in your state. Calculate the percentage of U.S. businesses in each category represented by your state. Prepare national and state pie charts to illustrate the number and percentage of businesses in each category. Make sure to label the charts and all data presented.

25. Use a word-processing program to develop a questionnaire using the items in Figure 21-2. Add three additional items asking respondents to identify their age, gender, and number of years of education.

Give a copy of the questionnaire to five people and ask them to complete it. When you have all of the completed questionnaires, enter the items into a spreadsheet. Calculate the totals for each item. Prepare a report of your findings.

Working with other students in your class, enter the information from all questionnaires into one spreadsheet and calculate the class totals for each item. Discuss the results. Identify any differences in responses that seem to relate to age, gender, and education.

MARKETING PLANNING

26. Identify a small business you would be interested in starting as an entrepreneur. Use the Internet to locate the following information about that type of business:

- Two existing businesses that offer the same type of product or service.

- Two businesses that could supply products or services needed by the business for its operations.
- Two sources of small business assistance available to a new entrepreneur.
- Two financial institutions in your area that may provide startup financial support for the new business.

27. Working in small groups and with the help of your teacher, identify a small business owner from your community. Contact the person and arrange an interview. If possible, obtain a video camera and videotape the interview. If it is not possible to meet the business owner in person, it may be appropriate with the permission of your teacher to complete the interview using the telephone or e-mail. Make sure to take careful notes during the interview.

Ask the business owner the following questions:

1. How did you start your business?
2. What is your target market?
3. Who are your main competitors?
4. What are the characteristics of your marketing mix: product, price, distribution, and promotion?
5. What do you believe are the most important factors in being a successful small business owner?

When your interview is completed, summarize the information your team obtained and prepare an oral report of your findings to present to your class.

MARKETING MANAGEMENT

28. Becoming a successful entrepreneur requires a person who has the necessary personal characteristics, education, and experience, as well as the financial resources to be able to provide some of the initial financing of a new business.

Prepare a personal analysis of your current status as a possible entrepreneur and a plan to improve your preparation. Use a word-processing program and prepare a two-column table titled "My Entrepreneurship Preparation." The heading of the left column is "What I Have." The heading of the right column is "What I Need."

Using information from the chapter, complete the table to describe what you have already done to prepare to be an entrepreneur and what you need to do to continue your preparation. Use the following headings as rows in your tables:

Entrepreneurship Characteristics

Academic Preparation
    Communication skills
    Math skills
    Scientific skills

Using Technology
Business Skills
    Education
    Work experience

29. Using your school or city library or the Internet, identify an historic or current entrepreneur of interest to you. Find books, magazine articles, or other sources of information on the entrepreneur. Study the information to learn as much as you can about the entrepreneur. Prepare a 200-word report on the entrepreneur and the business or businesses the person started.

Obtain pictures of the entrepreneur, the business, and products by photocopying from books and magazines or downloading images from the Internet. Working with your classmates, prepare a class bulletin board on the entrepreneurs studied.

MARKETING TECHNOLOGY

30. Using an Internet browser or search engine, locate an example business plan or outline for a business plan. Compare the sections of the plan or outline you locate with those listed in Figure 21-3. Identify the information that is similar and that is different.

Assume that you are a venture capitalist who invests in small businesses. Using the information you have collected, prepare an outline of a business plan that you would want an entrepreneur to present to you so you would have the information needed to make a decision about investing in the business. For each major section, describe why the information is important to you as a venture capitalist.

31. Entrepreneurship opportunities often result from the design of new products or the development of improvements in existing products. Select one of the following products or identify another product category approved by your teacher:

    Portable CD player
    Computer keyboard
    Personal digital assistant
    Cellular telephone

Use a computer graphics program or craft materials to create a new design for the product that you believe improves on current design (added features, easier to use, more portable or efficient, etc.). When you and your classmates have finished your designs, display the new products around the classroom. Have a "gallery walk" where small groups walk from product to product and the designer describes the product, its features, and benefits.

MARKETING IN ACTION

CASE STUDY

THE RISE OF SUCCESSFUL ENTREPRENEURS

What do Dave Thomas, Mary Kay Wagner, and Debbi Fields have in common? They are all successful entrepreneurs who had meager beginnings.

Dave Thomas was adopted in 1932 by Rex and Auleva Thomas of Kalamazoo, Michigan. Auleva died unexpectedly when Dave was five, and the family moved several times as Rex looked for work. Dave got a job as a busboy at the Hobby House Restaurant in Fort Wayne when he was 15 years old. When the family announced that they planned to move one more time, Dave dropped out of high school and rented a room at the YMCA to work full time at the Hobby House.

Thomas enlisted in the U.S. Army at age 18, and after attending cooking school, he managed an enlisted men's club. When Dave was discharged from the military, he returned to the Hobby House, where he met and married one of the waitresses, Lorraine Buskirk, in 1954. The couple raised five children.

In the early 1960s, Thomas was given a chance to turn around four failing Kentucky Fried Chicken (KFC) restaurants in Columbus, Ohio. Dave cut the menu down to chicken with side dishes. By 1967, Dave was part owner of KFC in Columbus, and in 1968 he made his first $1 million when the restaurants were sold back to KFC.

Most experts said that America did not need another hamburger restaurant, but Dave Thomas forged ahead by opening the first Wendy's Old Fashioned Hamburger restaurant in Columbus in 1969. The restaurant is named for his daughter. The success of the first restaurant led to franchising in 1973. During the first 100 months, more than 1,000 Wendy's were opened. By 2001 there were more than 5,000 Wendy's worldwide, employing over 130,000 people.

Mary Kay Wagner grew up in Hot Wells, Texas. Mary Kay's father was an invalid, and her mother worked as a restaurant manager in Houston to support the family. Mary took care of her father, cooked, cleaned, and shopped. Each note left by Mary's mother ended with "Honey, you can do it."

Mary Kay did not have enough money to attend college. She married at age 17, and by the time her husband was called to serve in WW II, she had three children to support. Mary and her husband divorced shortly after that war. To support herself and her children, Wagner became a direct sales representative for Stanley Home Products. Three parties each day reaped a total of $30 to $36. Mary received the "Miss Dallas" ribbon for successful recruitment of new dealers. This award convinced her that recognition for achievement is just as important as financial achievements.

While selling Stanley products in the 1950s, Mary Kay met a woman who made her own skin care lotion. The woman's father worked as a hide tanner and he had amazing skin tone that he attributed to constant exposure to hide tanning lotion. After experimenting with the formula, the daughter developed creams and lotions for women's skin. Mary Kay and her 20-year-old son, Richard, launched Mary Kay Cosmetics in a Dallas storefront in 1963. She used her life savings of $5,000 to purchase used furniture, supplies, and the rights to skin care products owned by the tanner's heirs.

Mary Kay used a unique sales method to sell her products. Well-educated consultants provided instruction to small groups of customers. First-year sales of $200,000 quadrupled the following year. The importance of personal recognition at Mary Kay Cosmetics continues today, and beauty consultants are presented with jewelry, dream vacations, and cars for their successes and achievements. Sales reached $1 million in 1966, and by 2001, there were more than 475,000 independent Mary Kay beauty consultants in 25 countries, generating sales of more than $2 billion.

Debbi Fields was a young mother with no business experience who made delicious chocolate chip cookies. When she opened her first store in Palo Alto, California, in 1977, business experts

told her she was crazy. Debbi Field's success can be attributed to determination, a dynamic personality, and a sincere concern for people. From humble beginnings, Mrs. Fields has become a premier cookie and baked-goods company. Mrs. Field's mission has always been to create the highest quality product every time. Cookies must pass a thumb-press test for freshness. The end results of this commitment are satisfying products that consumers keep demanding.

Mrs. Fields began franchising in 1990, giving others dynamic opportunities backed by name recognition and approval from worldwide customers. Debbi Fields believes in the following philosophy, "The important thing is not being afraid to take a chance. Remember, the greatest failure is to not try. Once you find something you love to do, be the best at doing it."

THINK CRITICALLY

1. Do you have to be rich to succeed as an entrepreneur? Explain your answer.

2. Give examples of two additional entrepreneurs who worked hard and achieved great success.

3. What entrepreneurial idea do you think would be profitable to pursue? Why?

---

http://www.deca.org/publications/HS_Guide/guidetoc.html

ENTREPRENEURSHIP WRITTEN EVENT

DECA PREP
An Association of Marketing Students

These entrepreneurs' successes came from hard work, determination, sound ideas, and a good business plan. Guides for writing a business plan can be found on the Internet, in books, and at SCORE. Now it is your turn to write a business plan for your entrepreneurial idea.

DESCRIPTION OF BUSINESS   Prepare a summary of your business plan. Give a one-page description of the business. Briefly describe your product/service, your sources of information (interviews and research sources), and a brief description of advisors and their involvement.

ANALYZE BUSINESS SITUATION   Prepare an analysis of the business. This should include a self-analysis that explains your personal business experience and training/education in the proposed field, personal business strengths and weakness, demonstrated willingness to take risks, and a brief plan for personal development in the proposed field. It should also include a trading area analysis describing the general geographic, demographic, economic, and competitive data for the area where you will locate the business; as well as a market segment analysis that explains the characteristics of your target market, customer buying behavior related to your proposed business, and analysis of potential location (availability, cost, traffic patterns, proximity to competition).

OUTLINE OF OPERATIONS   Prepare the planned operation of the business. This section should include the proposed company organization, proposed product/service, and proposed marketing strategies.

FINANCIAL STATEMENTS   You are now ready to prepare the toughest part of your business plan. This section must include planned financing and a proposed plan to meet capital needs. You will want to consult a banker or retired businessperson from SCORE to complete this portion of your paper. Charts and tables should be used to show your financial statements.

CONCLUSION   Finish the business plan with a conclusion (specific request for financing) using a summary of key points to support your financial request.

CHAPTER 22

TAKE CONTROL WITH MANAGEMENT

LESSON 22.1 *MANAGING WITH A PURPOSE*
LESSON 22.2 *MANAGING EFFECTIVELY WITH A PLAN*
LESSON 22.3 *MANAGING MARKETING ACTIVITIES*

NEWSLINE

QUALITY IS TOP MANAGEMENT RESPONSIBILITY

One of the most important responsibilities of a retail manager is maintaining quality. Even the lowest prices will not attract customers to a store if they are not satisfied with the shopping experience. What are the factors that indicate quality?

A survey asked almost 1,000 shoppers to rate 21 specific factors that influenced their attitudes about a store. The most important quality feature to consumers is time. Time was rated twice as important as any other category. Time includes how long it takes to check out, total time to complete shopping, and how quickly the store processes credit cards and checks. Second in importance was customer treatment. Consumers want to feel that the store is concerned about their needs and that each employee is helpful, friendly, and courteous.

Efficiency, including the number of checkout lanes or registers and the ease of locating merchandise, was rated third. Price and the physical environment were tied for fourth place. Customers are concerned that prices are clearly marked and specials are easy to locate. They want to shop in a pleasant, roomy atmosphere. Finally, consumers are concerned about technology. They want stores to use modern technology. They also want employees to know how to use the cash registers quickly and accurately.

Managers can rate their own stores against these quality factors. Areas where ratings are high should be maintained while managers work to improve the lower-rated factors. Improving quality is one of the best ways to ensure customer satisfaction.

THINK CRITICALLY

1. How can managers find out what their customers think of their stores?

2. Why do you think time was so important to the survey respondents?

CORPORATE VIEW

CAREER OPPORTUNITY
ACCOUNTS PAYABLE MANAGER

POINT YOUR BROWSER

www.corpview.com

TeleView is looking for someone who possesses the following attributes.

- Attention to detail
- Problem solving and project organization abilities
- time management proficiency
- Up-to-date technical communication skills
- Excellent interpersonal and customer relations skills
- Drive, flexibility, and a desire to work in an invigorating team-oriented environment

TeleView's offices in Boulder, Colorado, are modern with state-of-the-art technologies at your disposal. Access to the TeleView office complex is facilitated by two freeway exits that provide easy access from picturesque communities to the north and south.

The main responsibilities of the job include the following.

- Managing invoice processing and other issues involved in the Accounts Payable (AP) function of our department
- Dispersing payments for employees, suppliers, vendors, and outsource consultants in a timely and efficient manner
- Supervising a team of six to ten full-time, part-time, and temporary team members and directing all reporting activities for the workgroup
- Analyzing and delegating the workgroup's workload in an equitable manner
- Supervising and assisting with the annual 1099 filing process
- Processing paperwork for the bi-weekly check run

- Assisting internal and outside auditors by supplying the information they need to do their jobs
- Managing petty cash payments and accounting procedures for the HR, Corporate Communications, IT, and R&D departments
- Helping to upgrade and train on the software used by Corporate View for financial reporting
- Supplying monthly information on the efficiency of your AP workgroup
- Making improvements according to world-class benchmarks

The job requires the following education, skills, and experience.

- An Associate degree or higher
- Fve years of recent experience in accounts payable
- Some management background and training
- Must be able to interpret accounting policies for your workgroup
- Experience with online, Intranet-based integrated accounting systems
- Ability to research and solve problems with the accounting system

THINK CRITICALLY

1. Prepare a cover letter written by a person who is qualified for this job and is seeking an interview.

2. What kind of future opportunities do you think a job like this would prepare you for?

3. Search want ads or the Internet for a job similar to this position. What type of compensation package is being offered for the job?

22.1 MANAGING WITH A PURPOSE

GOALS

- Explain the importance of management in business and the role of managers in effective marketing.
- Define the five functions of management.

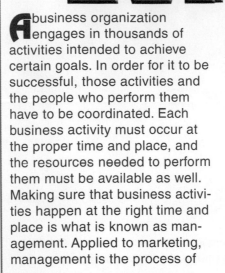

MARKETING MATTERS

A business organization engages in thousands of activities intended to achieve certain goals. In order for it to be successful, those activities and the people who perform them have to be coordinated. Each business activity must occur at the proper time and place, and the resources needed to perform them must be available as well. Making sure that business activities happen at the right time and place is what is known as management. Applied to marketing, management is the process of coordinating resources to plan and implement an efficient marketing strategy.

Business management entails five basic functions—planning, organizing, staffing, leading, and controlling. They apply to all organizations, large and small, and to every manager from the chief executive officer down to the lowest-level supervisor.

Make a list of 10 activities that must be coordinated in order for this marketing class to be effective and successful. Compare lists among your classmates.

COORDINATING PEOPLE AND RESOURCES

The work of an organization consists of thousands and thousands of activities. Those activities often seem unrelated to each other. Many employees in a business and most customers are unaware of the variety of activities that go on every day in many different locations. However, all of that work is necessary for products and services to be produced and distributed and for customer orders to be received and processed. Each activity needs to be completed on time and accurately. Each activity must be coordinated with other related activities.

KEY TO SUCCESS

What makes a company successful? A quality product? Satisfied customers? Well-trained and motivated employees? Efficient operations? Profit? Each of these is an

E-MARKETING

Will New Ad Formats Stimulate Traffic?

Facing a dramatic falloff in Internet advertising sales at the beginning of 2001, the Internet Advertising Bureau (IAB), an online advertising trade group, announced standards for seven new Internet ad formats—two vertical "skyscrapers" and five large rectangles. The new formats were in addition to existing standard formats for banner and button ads.

The new formats were designed to enable marketers to utilize greater interactivity as well as expand the creativity in their online messaging, according to the IAB. The IAB said a task force would meet every six months to examine the effectiveness of existing ad units, review proposed new ad units, and issue updated guidelines as appropriate.

"The goal is to help publishers, advertisers, and their agencies make the Internet a more effective marketing medium. The innovations we are recommending offer the industry greater flexibility and expanded capabilities and choice for the creative community. We believe that their wide adoption will create a more effective medium, for cohesive branding and direct marketing campaigns," said the task force's chairman.

The new standards came in the wake of widespread disappointment with the effectiveness of Internet ads among advertisers and ad agencies. Response rates, known as "click-through rates," in most cases were only one or two per thousand. As a result, ad rates had fallen substantially and many sites that depended on ad revenue experienced financial difficulty.

THINK CRITICALLY

1. What are the likely effects of lower ad rates for Internet advertising in terms of the supply of ad space and advertiser demand?

2. What purposes are served by establishing standard ad formats for Internet advertisements?

important ingredient in success. Successful organizations have another important factor—management.

Effective managers are able to organize the resources and work of a company in ways that result in success. Companies with effective managers usually have good products, employees, and operations resulting in satisfied customers.

Management is one of the most important functions of a business. Very simply, **managing** is getting the work of an organization done through other people and resources. How can businesses make sure the resources and people work as well as possible so that they are successful? If the resources available are not the ones needed for a task, that task cannot be performed. If employees are dissatisfied with their jobs or are not well trained, they will not work effectively. If customer service is not performed well, salespeople may receive complaints. If someone in order processing is not careful in calculating prices on an invoice, someone in accounting will face

The Work of Management

Without Management

With Management

MARKETING MANAGEMENT

Consider the many resources and people involved in marketing. Products need to be planned, priced, distributed, and promoted. Each of the mix elements must be coordinated with the others. If a product is not distributed in the time or the way that is expected by

the problem of explaining an overcharge or the need for an additional payment to a customer. These are the types of challenges facing managers (see Figure 22-1).

salespeople or advertisers, customers may be promised a product that cannot be delivered. If product development costs much more than budgeted, pricing decisions will need to be changed. **Marketing management** is the process of coordinating resources to plan and implement an efficient marketing strategy.

The work of more than one company usually needs to be coordinated as products move through a channel of distribution. The channel may include a manufacturer, transportation company, finance company, wholesaler, retailer, advertising agency, and others. The work of marketing managers can be very complex.

Now that you understand what a marketing strategy is, you are able to describe the work of marketing managers. Marketing managers are responsible for identifying markets and planning marketing mixes. You also know how to determine if marketing managers are doing a good job. According to the marketing concept, effective marketing results in satisfying exchanges. Marketing managers are successful when customers in the target markets are satisfied and the company is profitable.

What is the role of marketing managers in achieving effective marketing?

MANAGEMENT FUCTIONS AND ACTIVITIES

The definition of managing provided earlier is quite general. It is hard to determine specifically what managers do from that definition. A better understanding of management comes from examining the five functions of management. Those functions are illustrated in Figure 22-2.

PLANNING

Planning involves analyzing information, setting goals, and determining how to achieve them. The president of a company is responsible for determining the direction of the business and making sure that plans are in place to move forward. Supervisors determine what their work groups need to accomplish each day and assign duties to each person. Even though the two managers work at different levels in the organization, both have planning responsibilities as a part of their jobs. There are two types of planning that managers complete—long-range planning and short-term planning.

Long-Range In long-range planning information is analyzed that can affect the business over a long period of time (typically one year or more). Long-range planning includes setting broad goals and direction. Examples of long-range planning in a business are the strategic plan and business plan. In marketing, the marketing plan is a long-range plan because it sets direction and goals for all marketing functions and personnel.

Long-range planning is difficult because it relies on information from a variety of sources that may not be totally accurate. Managers need to anticipate what might

FIGURE 22-2

Five functions are common to all managers. This is true whether managers work in small or large businesses; whether they are company presidents or beginning supervisors.

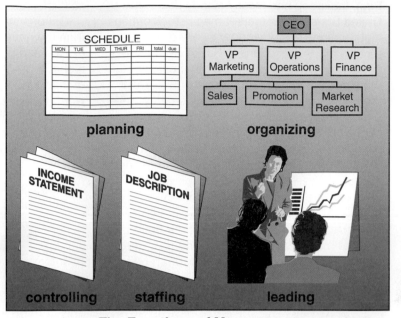

The Functions of Management

occur over the time that the plan will be in place. They must use their experience, marketing data, and the help of planning experts to make decisions. Using management skills, they will make decisions that will guide the business in the future.

Short-Term Short-term planning (often known as operational planning) identifies specific objectives and activities for each part of the business. Short-term planning is based on the long-range plan, so that all of the areas of the business are coordinated with each other. The marketing plan identifies the target markets that the business plans to serve. It identifies the marketing mix that must be developed to meet the needs of each market. It also sets goals that the company will use to evaluate whether the plan is successful.

The managers of each specific area of marketing (research, distribution, sales,

MANAGING WITH A PURPOSE **22.1**

593

Managers Counting on Stock Options

Stock options have become an increasingly popular component of management compensation in the past two decades or so. There are two main reasons for that development. First, the steep and mostly steady rise of the United States stock market made stock options highly valuable, so managers were glad to receive grants of options in lieu of cash compensation. Options entailed a bit of risk, but most people figured the added risk was worth the heftier payoff, and in most cases they were proven correct. Second, businesses liked awarding stock options in lieu of cash compensation because the options were, in a sense, free. Options grants did not require the expenditure of any cash, and they did not have to be charged as expenses against profits.

The value of an option basically depends on two factors—the exercise price of the option and the market price of the underlying shares. The exercise price, or strike price, of an option is the amount that has to be paid when an option is converted into a share of stock. The underlying value of an option is the difference between the exercise price and the market price, because that is the amount which the owner of an option will gain if he or she converts an option into a share of stock and then sells the stock for cash.

Options that have an exercise price lower than the corresponding market price are said to be "in the money." Those with an exercise price higher than the market price are said to be "out of the money." Out-of-the-money options are not worth exercising because it costs more to convert them to stock than the stock itself is worth.

THINK CRITICALLY

1. If you have been granted options to purchase 1,000 shares of your company's stock, and the options have an exercise price of $12 a share, how much are the options worth if the stock has a market value of $24 a share?

2. If that same stock increases in value by $6 a share, how much of a percentage gain is that for the value of the stock? For the value of your options?

---

customer service) use the information from the marketing plan to determine the objectives and activities for their areas. They meet regularly to coordinate their plans and activities. In this way, each of the short-term plans will coordinate to meet the long-range goals.

Research managers determine the information needed to make good decisions in each part of marketing. They plan the studies or collect the data at the appropriate time so it is available for the managers who are making the decisions. The distribution managers determine what products need to be moved to specific locations in what quantities.

Sales managers provide training and product information to salespeople. They help identify target markets and prepare the salespeople to work with those customers. They provide appropriate information about the marketing mix to meet the customers' needs. Customer service managers insure that personnel and resources are available to respond to customer needs after a product purchase. They make sure problems are solved and the customers are satisfied with their purchases.

ORGANIZING

Organizing resources is important so work can be accomplished effectively and efficiently. Organization charts in a business divide work into divisions or departments and show the relationships among those work units. There are many ways to divide up the work in a business. Managers organize by assigning responsibility and authority to others to get work done. Managers must develop effective working relationships within the work group and with other work groups.

STAFFING

The activities needed to match individuals with the work to be done are known as **staffing**. Managers prepare job descriptions, recruit and select employees, determine how personnel will be compensated, and provide the necessary training so employees can complete their work well.

Staffing is often considered the most difficult of the management functions. There are a number of activities involved in staffing, and the manager must be able to work well with a variety of people. It may be difficult to find people with the skills that match the jobs in a company. Effective training requires time and money. Some companies are not willing to invest in good training programs, making the manager's job more difficult. Managers are also responsible for evaluating the performance of each employee. They can reward those who are doing well but may need to terminate employees who cannot meet the requirements of their jobs.

LEADING

Is there a difference in being a manager and being a leader? Who do you identify as leaders—in your class, school, community, or country? What are the characteristics of an effective leader? Today in business, leadership is identified as one of the most important qualities of effective management. **Leading** is the ability to communicate the direction of the business and to influence others to successfully carry out the needed work. Effective leadership includes commitment and motivation, effective communications, establishing good working relationships, and recognizing and rewarding effective performance.

CONTROLLING

When **controlling**, managers measure performance, compare it with goals and objectives, and make corrections when necessary. A company establishes a goal that 95 percent of all customer orders are delivered within 24 hours. The manager tracks the orders to be certain that the goal is met. When the manager sees that fewer than 95 percent of the orders are being delivered on time, quick action must be taken. The manager must determine why orders are late and take steps to improve performance.

Specific controlling activities include setting standards, collecting and analyzing information, considering methods of improving performance, changing plans when necessary, solving problems, and resolving conflicts. Several common tools are used by managers to control operations, including plans, budgets, financial reports, and management information systems.

What are the five functions of management?

1. What happens if someone makes a mistake on a price when filling out an order for a product or service?

2. What types of businesses or companies are involved when managing the marketing activities required to complete a typical business transaction?

3. How do marketing managers who follow the marketing concept measure success?

4. Describe the two types of planning that business managers complete.

5. Name three specific controlling activities performed by managers and three common tools used by managers to effectively control business operations.

22.2 MANAGING EFFECTIVELY WITH A PLAN

GOALS

- Describe how a marketing plan serves as a guide for effective marketing management.
- Explain how marketing managers determine effectiveness by gauging satisfaction.

MARKETING MATTERS

Marketing plans, which are by definition written and detailed documents, help marketing managers to perform each of the management functions effectively. The act of developing and writing a marketing plan in many ways entails the performance of management functions such as planning and supports functions such as staffing, leading, and controlling. So the act of developing a marketing plan in itself furthers many management functions. A marketing plan also provides a means for evaluating the effectiveness of management activities and spotting changes in the business environment that warrant change in management functions.

Marketing effectiveness needs to be determined in relation to how well customers and the organization itself are satisfied. Customers include both individual consumers and business consumers, including members of a distribution channel. Organizational satisfaction is gauged by how well goals are being met.

Work with a group and draw up a list of five goals, activities designed to accomplish those goals, and ways to determine how well those goals are met.

IMPROVING MANAGEMENT WITH A MARKETING PLAN

Studies have been done that compare successful companies with unsuccessful companies. While there are many things that affect success, one of the most important differences typically seen is that successful companies develop written plans, while unsuccessful ones do not. Figure 22-3 shows the outline of a typical marketing plan.

INFORMATION FOR PLANNING

It is easy to see how the marketing plan is related to the planning function. It is a long-range plan that sets goals and direction for the company for the length of time that the plan is in effect. The first part of the

FIGURE 22-3

Each section of a marketing plan is important to a marketing manager in completing the five functions of management.

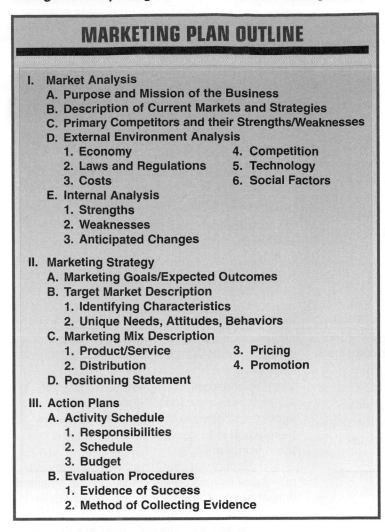

MARKETING PLAN OUTLINE

I. **Market Analysis**
  A. Purpose and Mission of the Business
  B. Description of Current Markets and Strategies
  C. Primary Competitors and their Strengths/Weaknesses
  D. External Environment Analysis
    1. Economy   4. Competition
    2. Laws and Regulations   5. Technology
    3. Costs   6. Social Factors
  E. Internal Analysis
    1. Strengths
    2. Weaknesses
    3. Anticipated Changes

II. **Marketing Strategy**
  A. Marketing Goals/Expected Outcomes
  B. Target Market Description
    1. Identifying Characteristics
    2. Unique Needs, Attitudes, Behaviors
  C. Marketing Mix Description
    1. Product/Service   3. Pricing
    2. Distribution   4. Promotion
  D. Positioning Statement

III. **Action Plans**
  A. Activity Schedule
    1. Responsibilities
    2. Schedule
    3. Budget
  B. Evaluation Procedures
    1. Evidence of Success
    2. Method of Collecting Evidence

at implementing that strategy and achieving those goals and objectives. The managers responsible for each marketing function must determine how their function supports the marketing strategy. The goals and objectives they develop for their part of the business must also support the goals identified in the marketing plan.

In the final section, the Action Plan, specific activities and responsibilities are identified to guide short-term operations. All of the managers of marketing activities contribute to the development of this section. It identifies the work needed in their part of the business and guides them in planning day-to-day activities, including schedules and budgets. Most companies require each manager to prepare written operational plans and to show how their plans support the marketing plan.

DIRECTION FOR ORGANIZING

plan, Market Analysis, reviews internal and external information that affects marketing. By studying that part of the plan, managers learn about the competition, the economy, and other important factors that can affect the success of their plans. They are made aware of strengths and weaknesses so weaknesses can be improved and strengths can be emphasized.

The second section of the marketing plan is the Marketing Strategy. In this section target markets are identified and the marketing mix is described. Most importantly, the goals and outcomes that will be used to measure the success of the marketing plan are described. Every manager who has marketing responsibilities needs to be very familiar with this section of the plan. Every planning activity in the company is directed

Much of the organizing work in a company is done before a marketing plan is developed. A company decides which marketing functions and activities it will perform and which will be left to other companies. It develops a structure that organizes marketing personnel and activities into departments. It identifies the responsibilities of managers for the various departments and activities. Those decisions usually will not change a great deal even though many marketing plans will be written. If a company is successful with its target markets and makes only minor adjustments in the marketing mixes, it will not want to change its basic organizational structure unless it sees ways to improve performance or save money with the change.

SUPPORT FOR STAFFING DECISIONS

Effective marketing requires people with the skills necessary to perform the required marketing activities. Again, the marketing plan provides a useful tool for managers to determine staffing needs. The Action Plan is particularly important since specific activities and responsibilities are described in that section.

Managers match those activities with the current marketing employees. If the employees do not have the necessary skills to perform the activities, managers develop training programs. If there are not adequate numbers of employees to perform the necessary work, new employees must be hired, or other businesses can be brought into the marketing channel to perform those activities. In some instances current employees may not be needed for new marketing activities. If they cannot be retrained to perform other necessary work, they may have to be terminated.

Using the marketing plan to evaluate staffing needs is an important way for managers to determine where problems are likely to occur. You are probably familiar with businesses that had problems because they did not have adequate numbers of employees or the employees did not have the needed skills or were not motivated to serve customers well. Managers who pay careful attention to staffing needs, training, and employee motivation often have a decided advantage over their competitors.

MANAGERS AS LEADERS

Many marketing efforts fail because the people responsible for the activities do not perform them well. Poor performance does not always occur because people do not have the skills to do the work. It may be due to a lack of leadership. Even though a manager has developed an effective plan and has the people and resources needed to carry out the plan, another ingredient is necessary—leadership.

Employees need to be a part of the business. They want to be involved and understand why the work they do is important. A marketing manager who is a leader involves employees in developing the plan, and discusses the plan with employees

Japan's Quandary: Ethics vs. Loyalty

Saddled with a decade-long economic downturn in the 1990s, numerous Japanese companies were also stung with ethics scandals that highlighted some of the weaknesses in the Japanese management style. According to the *Economist* magazine, Japanese companies in the early 2000s were still grappling with basic ethical issues, including drawing up codes of conduct, which Western companies had long since resolved. It said many companies were trying to shake off the Japanese tradition of "administrative guidance" under which managers didn't have to think for themselves but merely had to observe a strict set of rules laid down from above.

The *Economist* also noted two complementary Japanese corporate traditions that inhibited ethical conduct and exposure of misdeeds—employment for life, and promotion by seniority. The two practices combined tend to stifle any questioning of decisions made by an employee's superiors. Pressure for change is starting to come from foreign and individual shareholders, who do not have the same conflicts of interest that cross-shareholding Japanese banks have. Japan still lacks a broad community of ethical investors such as exists in the United States and Britain, the magazine said.

THINK CRITICALLY

1. How do practices such as employment for life and strict seniority promotion stifle exposure of wrongdoing?

2. Why are foreign and individual shareholders more likely to press for reforms than Japanese banks that share ownership with many of the Japanese companies they lend to?

when it is completed. In that way, the employees see why the plan is important. They understand how it can lead to success for the business and the people who work for the business.

The marketing manager also determines the working relationships that are necessary to implement the plan. Those relationships may be among people in the same department, in different departments in the company, and even among people in other businesses. A good leader develops effective working relationships and finds ways to recognize and reward the people who do their work well. When activities are completed that are an important part of the marketing plan, the people who are responsible need to know that they are doing the right things and that their manager and co-workers appreciate the good work.

GAINING CONTROL OF MARKETING

An old proverb says, "if you don't know where you're going, you will never know when you get there." A marketing plan states clearly whom the business wants to serve, what marketing activities are required, and the goals the business expects to achieve. Each of those decisions is used to measure the effectiveness of marketing.

Evaluating Effectiveness   Marketing managers study how well they are reaching and serving each target market. They determine the market potential, the company's market share, and the share held by each competitor. Most businesses evaluate customer satisfaction with products and services as well as with other parts of the marketing mix. They want to see high satisfaction levels. A business becomes concerned if satisfaction begins to decline or if customers rate competitors higher.

The marketing mix is identified in the marketing plan. The activities needed to implement each mix element are specifically described. Schedules, budgets, and other planning tools are prepared. Most businesses develop standards of performance for marketing activities and evaluate

each to see if the performance standards are being met. Whenever managers receive information that shows activities are not being performed as expected, they must take immediate action to correct problems.

Environmental Change   There is another valuable way that the marketing plan helps managers with the controlling process. The first part of the marketing plan carefully describes the internal and external environment on which the plan is based. A change in any part of that environment could affect the success of the marketing plan. Managers read research reports, magazines, and newspapers. They attend conferences, talk to colleagues, and review other information so they will be up-to-date and prepared to respond to changes.

The types of environmental factors that often change are the economy, technology, competition, and laws and regulations. For example, during 2000 and early 2001, many economic signs indicated that businesses were changing their spending patterns, particularly for technology and related products and services. Manufacturers immediately began to adjust their own inventory levels and production capacities so that they would not be caught carrying too much or have to write down the value of outdated products.

Why is a marketing plan a key to effective marketing management?

DETERMINING MARKETING EFFECTIVENESS

Remember that managers are responsible for getting the work of the business done through other people and resources. If the work is not done well, the manager has not been successful. An important management responsibility is determining the effectiveness of marketing.

How can managers decide if marketing is effective? Is it based on the highest sales, largest market share, or most profit? Is the company with the best products or the products that have been on the market longest the most effective?

Managers may not always agree on what is effective marketing. Figure 22-4 shows some of the variables marketers need to consider. The definition of marketing presented at the beginning of the book states that effective marketing results in satisfying exchanges. That means that both the customer and the business must be satisfied. If you agree with that definition, then you need to be able to determine when the customer and business are satisfied.

MEASURING CUSTOMER SATISFACTION

Customers are satisfied when they select a company's product or service to meet a need, use it, and choose it again when they have the same need. Because of this process, an increasing level of sales is usually a good indication of customer satisfaction. Companies should be careful to gather information on repeat purchases and use. They should be able to identify the level of sales for specific target markets.

Many companies spend a great deal of time and money studying customer satisfaction. They telephone customers or ask them to complete surveys. Some companies develop customer service centers to make sure they identify and solve customer problems. It is important to keep records of customer questions, problems, and complaints. Positive responses from customers should also be recorded. You are probably familiar with businesses that have customer

FIGURE 22-4

If you were the marketing manager of a company, what would you use to determine the effectiveness of marketing?

Measures of Marketing Effectiveness

Sales, Profits, Costs, Employee Performance, Channel Effectiveness, Customer Satisfaction

suggestion cards and other methods of regularly gathering consumer information.

Companies should not ignore the satisfaction of other businesses in the channel of distribution. Retailers and wholesalers are customers of manufacturers. If they are not satisfied with the products and services provided by the manufacturer, they may decide to work with a competitor. Retailers and wholesalers need to inform manufacturers of any problems customers have with their products so the problems can be resolved. Many businesses now involve other channel members in planning. They regularly check with those businesses to make sure they are receiving the support needed to be effective.

MEASURING BUSINESS SATISFACTION

Every business operates for a purpose. For many businesses, the purpose is to make a profit for the owners. For some businesses, however, profit is not the most important purpose. Some people start and operate a business because they enjoy the work. Some organizations are developed because of the contribution they make to the community. The success of schools, churches, city missions, public health centers, and other similar organizations is usually not measured by the level of profit. They certainly need enough money to operate. These organizations have to operate very efficiently, but profit is not their primary reason for existing. They determine their success by looking for improvements in the community or society that result from their work.

Analyzing Goals   The success of a business is determined by its goals. If the goal of a business is to increase sales or market share, it will not be successful if sales and market share decline. If a business sets a goal to achieve a profit of 4 percent of all sales or an 11 percent return on the money the owners have invested, it will be successful when it achieves that goal. Even if the goal of an organization is to change the attitudes or behavior of a group of people (stop smoking, stay in school), it will be successful only if the people it works with have changed.

Most goals of businesses and organizations are quite specific and can be measured. Businesses gather information on sales, costs, market share, and profits to determine their success. Non-profit organizations gather information on increases in attendance, use of services, changes in behavior, or differences in attitudes and beliefs.

Financial Analysis   When people think of marketing, they often fail to recognize the importance of budgets and financial performance. Marketing managers must pay careful attention to those factors. They need to understand financial information and use it to determine the success of marketing activities. Sales of products in various markets can be compared from one year to the next. Costs associated with specific activities can be analyzed. Profits from one target market can be compared with those from another. The profitability of a specific marketing strategy can be analyzed.

Employee Satisfaction   Managers also need to be concerned about the satisfaction of the people who work for the business. There is a great deal of evidence that employees who enjoy their work are more productive. They want to contribute to the success of their employer. When employees are not happy, they will often find reasons not to do as well as they could.

Marketing managers need to determine the level of employee satisfaction. Some companies ask their employees to complete surveys. Others hold regular meetings where employees can discuss problems and make suggestions. Today, many companies form work teams. The teams have a great deal of responsibility for setting goals. They may determine the ways that work should be completed or how to solve customer problems. They may even be responsible for hiring other members of the work team and determining how bonus money should be distributed. Involving employees in important decisions usually increases their satisfaction.

checkpoint

When marketing managers use the marketing concept, what gauge do they use in determining marketing effectiveness?

LESSON REVIEW

1. Which management function is least affected by the marketing plan as long as the marketing plan is successful?

2. Which part of the marketing plan is most helpful in carrying out the staffing function of management?

3. How does a marketing plan help a marketing manager effectively control a business in the face of a changing business environment?

4. What is the result of effective marketing?

5. If a business' goal involves something other than maximizing profits, how does that affect its marketing management?

6. Why is employee satisfaction so important to marketing management, and how can marketing managers determine if their employees are satisfied?

GOALS

- Describe the kinds of activities managers perform in carrying out planning and organizing functions.
- Detail the way in which business managers staff, lead, and control their organizations effectively.

MARKETING MATTERS

The activities managers perform while carrying out business management functions vary. They depend largely on the specific position and the type of organization. Senior executives tend to do long-range planning and developing strategy. Lower-level managers often spend time effectively implementing the decisions made by senior executives. Most managers perform many common or similar activities at all levels of an organization and in all kinds of organizations.

Choose an organization with which you are familiar or interview managers at an area organization. Cite three activities common to that organization that senior managers perform but that lower-level supervisors do not. Name three activities that all managers perform regardless of their managerial level.

PLANNING AND ORGANIZING

Oyang Chen is the executive vice president of marketing for an international automobile manufacturer. James Swathmore is a field sales manager for a food products wholesaler. He supervises five salespeople in a large northeastern state. The partial organization charts in Figure 22-5 illustrate the differences between Chen's and Swathmore's positions.

Planning Ms. Chen spends most of her time planning with four other top executives and the CEO to set

FIGURE 22-5
Oyang Chen and James Swathmore hold very different positions within their companies. Both must be effective at planning, organizing, staffing, leading, and controlling.

The Work of Two Marketing Managers

International Automobile Manufacturer
- Chief Executive Officer
- Executive Vice-President of Marketing—**Oyang Chen**
- Seven Regional Managers

Food Products Wholesaler
- Chief Executive Officer
- Vice-President of Marketing
- National Sales Manager
- Manager of Institutional Sales
- Field Sales Manager—**James Swathmore**

FIGURE 22-6

Marketing activities can be organized by function, product, market, sales, or geography. Managers' responsibilities will vary depending on the organization of their businesses.

Organizing Marketing Operations

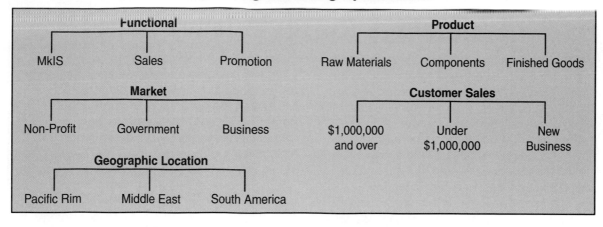

Functional				Product		
MkIS	Sales	Promotion		Raw Materials	Components	Finished Goods

Market				Customer Sales		
Non-Profit	Government	Business		$1,000,000 and over	Under $1,000,000	New Business

Geographic Location		
Pacific Rim	Middle East	South America

direction for the company. She is involved in strategic planning, which identifies how the company must change over the next five to ten years. Ms. Chen studies consumer purchasing trends throughout the world and how the economies of various countries are developing. She is very concerned about international trade agreements, increases and decreases of quotas, and changes in tariffs among several countries that have a major impact on the international automobile industry. Energy sources and prices, inflation, and the values of world currencies are also concerns for Ms. Chen.

The major responsibility of Ms. Chen's office is to prepare the company's marketing plan. The plan is developed for a five-year period, with specific plans for each of the five years. The marketing plan is used by seven regional managers to prepare more specific plans for their regions of the global market.

Mr. Swathmore is also involved in planning, but he concentrates on short-term plans. He develops quarterly plans, but implements monthly and weekly plans. While Mr. Swathmore must be familiar with the entire company's marketing plan, he is most concerned with the promotional mix element and the selling responsibilities.

Mr. Swathmore spends most of his planning time identifying customers, assigning

them to salespeople, developing schedules and budgets for each person, and helping salespeople to develop specific sales strategies for major customers.

Organizing   Mr. Swathmore and Ms. Chen have very different organizing responsibilities. The overall marketing structure of each company is already set. The automobile manufacturer is organized into seven worldwide regions. The food wholesaler is organized by customer type and geographically by state. Several common ways that companies organize their marketing operations are shown in Figure 22-6.

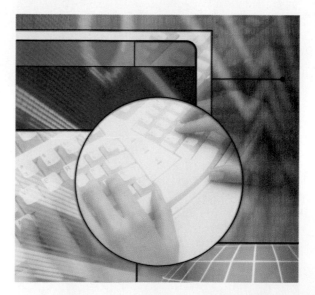

Technology Raises Privacy Issues

The development and spread of digital information technologies in the workplace has greatly increased the ability of employers to monitor employees' work habits. While the technology has raced ahead, the ethical issues raised by those advances have multiplied. In many cases, the issues have arisen much faster than businesses and managers have been able to confront and resolve them.

Typically, the legality of employers' actions is not in question because the actions they are monitoring (or capable of monitoring if they choose to do so) are conducted on company time and using company equipment or property. Telephone records, e-mail and Internet traffic records, and computer files are all kept and stored as standard business practices by many if not most businesses. The information has many possible business uses aside from the monitoring of employee activities.

The ethics of using those resources to evaluate employees, however, is far from clear. On one hand, employers have openly used timekeeping and surveillance systems for decades to monitor workplace activities. Moreover, the availability of phone and computer records should be no secret to employees in today's working environment. Still, there are lines that most employers would not think of crossing, such as recording phone conversations or placing hidden cameras in offices. The question is, where should those lines be drawn as technology advances?

THINK CRITICALLY

1. What guidelines would you set for businesses in establishing privacy policies for management and employees?

2. What responsibilities do managers and employees have in preserving ethical behavior and respect for privacy in the workplace?

Ms. Chen's organizing activities focus on developing company policies and procedures. Those policies and procedures will determine the organizational structure for marketing, the functions that are performed, and the types of companies that will participate in marketing the automobiles.

Mr. Swathmore must work within the policies and procedures established by his manager. He is responsible for determining what activities need to be performed and assigning those duties to the salespeople. He delegates authority and responsibility to each salesperson to complete the necessary selling tasks.

✓checkpoint

What are the key distinctions between the types of planning and organizing activities engaged in by Ms. Chen and Mr. Swathmore?

MANAGING MARKETERS

Both of the managers are responsible for getting the work of the organization done through other people. Therefore they need to identify the need for personnel and fill those positions with the most qualified people.

Staffing   Ms. Chen will hire a few people to be her assistants. Her main responsibilities for staffing are to develop policies and procedures. She makes decisions about the percentage of the marketing budget that will be allocated to employee salaries, benefits, and expenses.

Mr. Swathmore is directly responsible for the salespeople who work in the territory

GET THE MESSAGE
These Bank Managers Deliver . . . in Person

What is your image of bank executives—gray suits, large offices, conservative attitudes? A work schedule that includes meeting in plush conference rooms or on the golf course with top business leaders? You may be surprised to meet the managers of Fifth Third Bank in Cincinnati. You may even have difficulty meeting them. It certainly won't be on the golf course. It will more likely be in their cars as they travel to meet with current or potential customers.

Fifth Third Bank has discovered the value of involving managers as salespeople for the bank. Each manager is assigned a number of area businesses. The managers don't wait for the businesses to call and inquire about banking services. They don't even rely on telephone calls to the business. Instead, each manager has a daily "call book." Armed with information about Fifth Third's products and services, the managers visit each customer. They discuss the customer's business and financial needs and determine the level of satisfaction with the customer's current bank.

Often prospective customers will meet with them simply because they are surprised and

impressed with personal contact from the manager of a bank. If they switch to Fifth Third, they continue to receive the same personal attention and a variety of financial services particularly tailored to small- and medium-sized businesses.

The results of this personalized marketing approach to banking have been effective. While Fifth Third Bank is small compared to many other banks, it has a higher performance rating than banks that are over 100 times its size and significantly higher than the industry average. In addition to adding customers, it has grown by purchasing other regional banks. One of the first strategies in each of the new banks is to teach marketing and selling skills to the managers.

THINK CRITICALLY

1. What are the advantages of putting bank managers out on the streets to sell bank services to business customers?

2. Which function or functions of management are most affected by Fifth Third's practice of having all bank managers sell its services?

he manages. He may not have total responsibility for hiring each person, but he identifies when an opening exists and describes the requirements for any open position. He helps with recruiting, interviewing, and selecting the person to fill the position. Most sales managers are very active in training new salespeople and helping to improve the selling skills of experienced employees.

Leading   Leading is an important responsibility for each of the managers. Some people would expect that Ms. Chen has more leadership responsibilities because she is the top marketing executive in the company. Yet Mr. Swathmore must be an effective leader if the selling team is to be successful in its territory. Each manager must be able to involve people in planning, communicate expectations, and build effective teams to accomplish the work. They need to be able to recognize performance that contributes to the goals of their company and provide rewards that encourage people to continue to perform well.

Managing Innovation Through Teamwork

The lone scientist or maverick engineer has a grip on the popular imagination, but many technological breakthroughs are created by teams of researchers. For high-tech companies, getting teams to reach seemingly impossible goals is much more challenging than nurturing someone with a high IQ.

A case in point is the IBM team that created an ingenious memory device, the "millipede," that stores digital information using microscopic levers that make minute marks on plastic. IBM's Zurich research lab began the millipede project in 1995 under the leadership of two scientists who approached their work in two very different ways. Gerd Binnig, a Nobel Prize-winning inventor, was an out-of-the-box thinker who would rush to the lab to test a new idea with a soldering iron. Peter Vettiger was an experienced team leader who appreciated the rigorous long-term planning needed to bring a new microchip design to fruition.

Outside criticism of the project helped knit the team together. In five years, it successfully demonstrated a chip with 1,000 levers that could store data on a plastic surface, read it back, and erase it. The team was expanded to develop a complete storage device. One possible market for the millipede is as low-power memory for mobile devices. As a testament to the team's success, IBM's competitors soon launched their own projects to build similar micromechanical devices.

THINK CRITICALLY

1. Why is managing a team more challenging than nurturing an individual?

2. What advantages did IBM's team derive from having two leaders with very diverse leadership styles?

Controlling Controlling is another area of marketing where both managers have similar responsibilities. Each prepares objectives and specific plans to guide their work. They have developed standards for performance of the various marketing activities for which they are responsible. The major controlling activity is to gather and review information to determine if the objectives, plans, and standards are being met.

An effective marketing information system is important to each manager. The marketing information system gathers and analyzes information. It identifies when problems arc occurring. Both Mr. Swathmore and Ms. Chen spend a great deal of time studying reports. They must identify the parts of their plans that are working well and the areas where problems may be developing. Ms. Chen concentrates on products or regions that have high and low performance. Mr. Swathmore is concerned about individual customers and salespeople.

When a specific problem is identified, each manager works quickly to correct it. They review budgets, schedules, and activities from their plans to see if some are not being performed in the way that was expected. They may have to revise the plans if it is clear that the original plans will not work.

For which management functions do Ms. Chen and Mr. Swathmore tend to have similar responsibilities?

LESSON REVIEW

1. Who has more responsibilities for hiring and evaluating the work of specific employees, Ms. Chen or Mr. Swathmore?

2. Which marketing mix element is Mr. Swathmore most concerned with in carrying out the planning function?

3. Why is Ms. Chen more concerned with consumer purchasing trends and economic conditions around the world than with problems a dealer in India might be experiencing in getting needed parts?

4. How are Ms. Chen's and Mr. Swathmore's responsibilities regarding the controlling function similar?

5. What would be the result if Mr. Swathmore did not exhibit effective leadership skills?

6. Which manager has more management responsibilities, Ms. Chen or Mr. Swathmore?

CHAPTER 22

SUMMARY

Lesson 22.1

A. A business organization engages in thousands of activities intended to achieve certain goals. In order for it to be successful, those activities—and the people and resources needed to accomplish them—have to be coordinated. That is the responsibility of managers. Marketing management is a complex combination of functions and activities. If the activities are well planned and coordinated, customers will be satisfied, and the company will make a profit.

B. Managers have the responsibility to accomplish the work of an organization through the use of people and other resources. While each manager in a business performs very different activities from other managers, all managers are responsible for the same five management functions—planning, organizing, staffing, leading, and controlling. They apply to all organizations, large and small, and to every manager from the chief executive officer down to the lowest-level supervisor.

Lesson 22.2

A. The marketing plan is a guide for marketing management. It is used to gather and analyze information, determine goals, develop a marketing strategy, and describe action steps for implementing the plan. Managers must be familiar with the marketing plan and use the information in it as a basis for their own planning. In this way, the many marketing activities and management decisions will be coordinated with each other. Developing a marketing plan in itself furthers many management functions. A marketing plan also provides a means for evaluating the effectiveness of management activities and spotting changes in the business environment that warrant changes in management functions.

B. Marketing managers are responsible for determining the effectiveness of marketing. Each business and organization will identify the factors used to measure effectiveness. Both customer satisfaction and business or organizational satisfaction are important to successful marketing. Customers include both individual consumers and business consumers, including members of a distribution channel. Organizational satisfaction is gauged by how well its goals are being met, whether those goals are related to making a profit or otherwise.

Lesson 22.3

A. The various activities that managers perform in carrying out the five management functions depend on the position held by a specific manager as well as the type of organization. Senior executives tend to do similar things such as long-range planning, developing strategy, and monitoring the business environment for changes that might warrant organizational restructuring. Lower-level managers often spend more time on shorter-term duties aimed at effectively implementing the decisions made by senior executives.

B. In performing the staffing function, high-level managers may be responsible for hiring and evaluating a few staff members that work in their office, but for the most part the function is concerned with policies and procedures. By contrast, a mid-level manager may find that staffing is the most important part of his or her job. They have direct responsibility for making sure that the right people are on staff to accomplish the detailed activities of the marketing plan. All managers have crucial roles to play in leading people to accomplish their tasks effectively.

REVIEW MARKETING CONCEPTS

Read each of the following statements and determine if it is a planning, organizing, leading, controlling, or staffing function.

1. The home office of a drugstore chain sends directions on how merchandise should be displayed on the shelves.

2. The owner of Norma's Hardware surveys her customers regarding the hours she should be open and decides to open her shop one hour earlier.

3. Aries Stavros holds a staff meeting every week to make sure that the staff understands their job assignments and to hear any complaints and questions they may have.

4. The owners of a dog grooming service decide to offer training classes to their employees in customer service.

5. Su Lee Han finds it necessary to review the budget allocations for her department once a week.

6. Jack Erbinsky attends a training session to learn about a new line of refrigeration products his company will carry.

7. Julio Chavez fires all of his employees except one assistant after deciding that he can move into a smaller office and do the work better and more efficiently without them.

8. A multinational corporation restructures its marketing operations by product lines rather than by countries or regions.

9. The sales manager at Bruno's Auto Sales holds a weekly meeting with his sales staff to keep them focused on their sales targets.

10. Marketing executive Carol Hoerst combs five newspapers every morning for news that might affect the competitive environment for her company's products.

11. Melvin B. Goode hires an executive assistant in order to free up more of his own time for strategic planning.

12. The 65-year-old CEO of an international conglomerate, anticipating retirement in two years, launches a search for his replacement.

13. The general manager of a restaurant reviews menu prices every three months to determine if changes are needed to keep prices in line with fluctuating food costs.

REVIEW MARKETING TERMS

Match the terms listed with the definitions. Some terms may not be used.

14. Involves analyzing information, setting goals, and determining how to achieve them.

15. The process of coordinating resources to plan and implement an efficient marketing strategy.

16. Assigning responsibility and authority to others (including individuals, divisions, and departments) so work can be accomplished effectively and efficiently.

17. Carrying out the activities needed to match individuals with the work to be done.

18. Includes measuring performance, comparing it with goals and objectives, and making corrections when necessary.

19. Getting the work of an organization done through other people and resources.

20. Communicating the direction of the business and influencing others to successfully carry out the needed work.

a. controlling
b. leading
c. managing
d. marketing management
e. organize
f. planning
g. staffing

THE PERFECT MARRIAGE TURNS SOUR

Firestone and Ford are major corporations that had solid reputations for quality and service to their consumers. "Quality is Job 1" was Ford's theme for many years. Yet the positive reputations of these two corporate giants evaporated almost overnight when it was revealed that failed tires produced by Firestone for Ford vehicles were causing numerous accidents resulting in destruction, serious injuries, and death.

The publicity nightmare was fueled by numerous heart-wrenching consumer experiences. Two examples of such horror stories involved Victor Rodriguez and Donna Bailey. Victor loaded his family into their Ford Explorer over Labor Day weekend to visit a sick aunt in Laredo, Texas. Cruising down Interstate 35, Victor was startled by a thump, and tread began shredding off a Firestone Wilderness AT tire on his Explorer. Victor was unable to control the vehicle, which flipped and ejected five of its passengers. Victor's 10-year-old son, Mark Anthony, died instantly as the Ford Explorer crushed his body. Mark had become the latest victim of a growing crisis that eventually took the lives of dozens of Americans and worried thousands of

motorists who used sports utility vehicles as family cars.

Donna Bailey still remembers the beautiful Saturday in March when she and a friend planned to climb Enchanted Rock north of Austin, Texas. Their Ford Explorer took a dramatic swerve, and the tire started separating. Donna's friend lost control of the vehicle and the Explorer skidded and rolled on dry pavement. Bailey's friend walked away from the accident while Bailey was left suspended by her seatbelt, paralyzed from the neck down. Today Donna struggles with a wheelchair she directs with a breathing tube. Bailey's lawyers planned to take on Ford and Firestone in court, contending that a defective tire and car took away her livelihood. The lead attorney said "you cannot divorce the two companies. It's a bad tire on a bad car." Donna Bailey sought millions of dollars in damages to meet her yearly medical costs of $600,000.

Ford and Firestone both led massive recalls to make the public aware that they wanted to resolve the deadly problem. Ford had hoped that an efficient, well-publicized recall and a contrite approach toward customers would enable the company to put the crisis behind it as it prepared to introduce the redesigned 2002 Explorer. The nation's second-largest automaker underwent intense public interrogation over the extent to which flaws in the Explorer's design caused or contributed to accidents. Remarkably, however, Ford's sales of Explorers were up 3.8% in 2000 compared to 1999.

The once amiable marriage between Ford and Firestone turned into a blame game. Some of the facts and accusations that surfaced:

● In 1990 Ford introduced the Explorer and recommended inflating tires to 26 psi. Critics believed that this recommendation did not solve an instability problem that might have contributed to rollovers. Firestone's ATX tires passed requirements that same year, but

critics suggested that the tests were not strict enough and were based on different tires.

- The first recorded accident in a Ford Explorer caused by a Firestone tire-tread separation occurred in 1992, and the first lawsuit related to such an incident was filed in 1993.

- Workers went on strike against the Bridgestone/Firestone Decatur plant from 1994 to1996. It was later discovered that tires made in the plant during that time period were more likely to have tread separation.

- During 1995-1997 Ford used Goodyear tires on some Explorers and reported that it had just one complaint about treads.

- Bridgestone/Firestone received many complaints about tire separation in 1997, but Ford was never notified.

- In 1998 State Farm Insurance alerted the government to a growing number of claims involving Firestone tires on Ford Explorers. The government performed rollover tests and informed Ford about instability problems. Also, Ford received first reports of tread separations in Saudi Arabia. Ford asked Firestone to investigate problems in Venezuela. Firestone reported no problems.

- Firestone's 1999 annual analysis found Decatur tires accounting for more than half of all separations. Ford recalled tires in the Middle East. Firestone ran more tests at Ford's request, but found no problems.

- In 2000, Ford offered free tire replacements in Malaysia. It later recalled tires in Venezuela, Ecuador, and Colombia. Firestone announced a recall in the United States and Congress conducted an investigation, requiring Firestone and Ford to testify.

Which company is accountable for the terrible accidents, injuries, and deaths? Could the arrangement between Firestone and Ford lead to the downfall of one or both companies? In the end, consumers will determine the fate of both corporations.

THINK CRITICALLY

1. After studying the chain of events with Firestone and Ford, which party do you think should take the greatest share of blame? Why?

2. How can these corporations overcome the negative publicity from this disaster?

3. What would you do as corporate president for Firestone and Ford to regain the trust of consumers?

4. Do you think that either corporation failed to respond appropriately to reports from 1990 to 2000? Explain.

http://www.deca.org/publications/HS_Guide/guidetoc.html

PUBLIC RELATIONS PROJECT

DECA PREP

You are a public relations specialist for Ford. Design a public relations plan (campaign) to overcome the negative publicity that resulted from the injuries, destruction, and deaths caused by rollovers of vehicles and defective tires.

DESCRIBE THE PROJECT Prepare a one-page description of the project. Write a campaign theme or focus that includes a statement and description of the issue to be addressed, rationale for selecting the issue, and description of the target population.

EXPLORE PROMOTIONAL POSSIBILITIES Describe the local media and other promotional possibilities. Summarize the campaign organization and implementation.

FINDINGS AND RECOMMENDATIONS Prepare an evaluation of the process and recommendations for future campaigns.

CHAPTER 23

CAREERS IN MARKETING

LESSON 23.1 *BENEFITS OF A MARKETING CAREER*
LESSON 23.2 *JOB LEVELS IN MARKETING*
LESSON 23.3 *MARKETING EDUCATION AND CAREER PATHS*
LESSON 23.4 *BEGINNING CAREER PLANNING*

NEWSLINE

WHAT DO EMPLOYEES WANT?

It's a startling statistic. In a recent survey, only three percent of employees said they were satisfied with their current job. Half of the respondents said they would consider changing their careers to entirely different types of work; almost one-fourth are planning to make changes in the next year. Fewer than one in five employees said they would never consider a career change.

What are people looking for? Nearly 30 percent want to be able to make more money and don't believe their current job offers that opportunity. Coming in second was to increase their personal happiness. Nearly 25% of the people wanting a career change believed they would be happier in another job. The third and fourth reasons for changing careers were greater job satisfaction (7%) and better working hours (4%).

Do people who change careers obtain the things they are looking for? Almost three quarters of job changers do make more money. In order to get those increases in pay, though, most had to complete additional education or training.

The results related to the other reasons for change are less encouraging. Respondents were nearly evenly divided about whether they were happier with their new jobs. Most reported the new job was more challenging and satisfying but believed they spent too many hours working and had only limited control over the hours they worked. One of the greatest values is that the individuals who changed jobs believed they were in a better position to withstand changes in the job market and to take advantage of other job opportunities that might become available.

THINK CRITICALLY

1. Does the number of people who report that they are dissatisfied with their jobs surprise you? Why or why not?

2. What does the information about job satisfaction say about the way that people choose their careers? Why do you believe people choose careers that they later find dissatisfying?

3. Why do you think "to make more money" is cited so frequently as the most important reason for wanting to change jobs?

4. If people report being dissatisfied with their jobs, why do only seven percent want to change jobs to increase job satisfaction?

5. If you were an employer reading this report, what would you do about it?

CORPORATE VIEW

CAREER OPPORTUNITY
RESEARCH AND
INFORMATION SPECIALIST

POINT YOUR BROWSER

www.corpview.com

TeleView is looking for an employee who possesses the following skills.

- Proven ability to analyze and synthesize data from multiple sources for meaningful reports
- Must be a self-starter and team player
- Ability to manage multiple projects simultaneously
- Ability to work in an invigorating, team-oriented environment

The main responsibilities of the job include the following.

- Identifying information needs of all mission-critical functions and gathering data related to those needs
- Using market research and online information services, standard reference tools, survey results, and government census sources to gather market and business trend data
- Preparing reports based on data collection activities in formats useful to internal customers
- Posting data on the corporate Intranet for use by employees around the world
- Cooperating with HR to train employees and teams in the use of research services and online research techniques

The job requires the following education, skills, and experience.

- A Masters in Library Science (MLS) or equivalent degree
- Technical communications skills

- Three years of experience in data collection, analysis, and reporting
- Experience with HTML development software tools is a plus

THINK CRITICALLY

1. Prepare a sample resume of a person who is qualified for this job and interested in applying for it.

2. Considering your skills and preferences, does this sound like a job you would like to have one day? Why or why not?

3. Search want ads or the Internet for a job similar to TeleView's Research and Information Specialist. What type of compensation package is available for this job?

GOALS

- Identify the impact of marketing careers on the economy.
- Describe the benefits of choosing a marketing career.

Marketing jobs exist in every community and almost every business. Many people get their first job while they are still in high school or even earlier. That first job is often a marketing job. It may be delivering newspapers, taking tickets at a movie theater, or serving customers in a fast-food restaurant.

While those jobs do not require a great deal of education and experience, they are important in developing an understanding of business operations as well as important career skills that are used even by people who hold the highest jobs in a company.

Make a list of any part-time or full-time jobs you have held. For each job, identify two or three things you learned that will be helpful in advancing into higher positions in a business. Compare your answers with other students to see what the jobs have in common in preparing people for careers in business.

THE IMPORTANCE OF MARKETING CAREERS

Marketing is one of the most important functions of business today. It provides employment for millions of people. Many of the fastest growing and highest paying jobs in our economy are marketing jobs. Whether you are still in high school, have a two- or four-year college degree, or even have a graduate degree such as an MBA or PhD, there are employment opportunities in marketing that match your interests and skills.

Between one-fourth and one-third of all jobs in the United States are marketing jobs. The people who are employed in marketing are responsible for research and product planning, advertising and selling, distributing products from manufacturers to consumers, providing customer service, assisting with financing and credit procedures, and

Career Competence

In the 1990s the U.S. Department of Labor appointed a commission to identify the most important competencies employees needed to perform their jobs well. The Commission's report was called SCANS and is viewed as an important guide to career preparation.

Communications skills stand out in the report. Important competencies for today's "knowledge" worker are:

- Acquires and evaluates information
- Organizes and maintains information
- Interprets and communicates information
- Uses computers to process information
- Ability to read, write, listen, and speak

THINK CRITICALLY

1. Why would the Department of Labor want to identify the most important competencies needed by employees?

2. If you were an employer, how would you determine if a prospective employee has the communications skills described in the SCANS report?

3. Why is the use of computers considered a part of effective communications?

activities. They are responsible for one or more of the marketing mix elements or marketing functions. Most of the jobs in those businesses are marketing jobs.

Other businesses have a non marketing activity as their primary purpose. Those businesses include manufacturers and service providers as well as government agencies, schools, public utilities and many other types of organizations. Even in those businesses, however, many people are employed to complete marketing activities that are an important part of the regular operations of those businesses.

Even people who are not directly employed in marketing jobs often need to understand marketing and use marketing skills as a part of their work. Physicians and dentists often operate practices by themselves or in partnership with other professionals. Owners of small businesses—from daycare centers to catering to landscaping businesses—need to be able to plan, promote, price, and distribute their products and services in order for the enterprises to be successful. Marketing is an important part of almost every business and many jobs. You will find an understanding of marketing useful to you as you choose and prepare for a career.

Marketing is a part of every industry. Therefore you can combine your interest in that industry with your marketing background for a choice of jobs. Important marketing jobs are found in the airline industry, entertainment, the military, healthcare, agriculture, and construction. Marketers are an essential part of the newest industries, including e-commerce and biotechnology. If you want to work in science, research, publishing, or education, you can find numerous opportunities to combine those interests with your marketing skills.

many other activities. Because of people who effectively perform their marketing jobs every day, customers are able to obtain the products and services they need at a fair price, and businesses are able to sell their products and services at a profit.

MARKETING AND BUSINESS OPPORTUNITIES

Marketing jobs are found in all types of businesses. The primary purpose of some businesses, such as advertising agencies and retail stores, is to complete marketing

MARKETING JOBS IMPROVE THE ECONOMY

Consider what our lives would be like without people employed in marketing jobs. Our views would not be heard in business as new products are planned without marketing researchers. Fresh fruit and vegetables would

not be available year-round in the local supermarket without people who work in distribution to ship those products from other states and countries. We could not use the newspaper, magazines, radio, or television to gather information about the products we want to buy if people didn't work in advertising and promotion.

Marketers who work with us when we make hotel or rental car reservations or reschedule a flight on an airline help to ensure that we enjoy business travel or vacations. Customer service personnel solve problems with a product that we've just purchased, realtors help us rent an apartment or purchase a home, buyers for retail stores get the latest fashions for us, and automobile salespeople locate and arrange financing for the car we have always wanted to own.

Marketing people are involved in many of our daily activities as we purchase products, enjoy restaurants and entertainment, and use the services of businesses and other organizations. We notice, and often are not very happy, when marketing activities are not performed well. Marketing activities performed effectively by business people who are concerned about customer satisfaction save us time and money and make our lives more enjoyable.

There are thousands of marketing jobs that most of us know little about because we don't come into contact with the people performing that work. Those jobs are in business-to-business marketing.

Many businesses provide products and services to other businesses rather than to consumers. Farmers sell the products they grow to food processors. Steel and plastic producers develop materials used by the auto industry, appliance manufacturers, large construction firms, and many other types of businesses. Transportation companies move the products of one company to other companies to be used in their businesses or to be resold to consumers.

Each of those companies is involved in marketing and employs many people to complete the marketing activities needed to satisfy their business customers. The same types of jobs described earlier that are performed to meet consumers' needs are also completed in business-to-business marketing.

While you may not be aware of those jobs, if they are not performed well you would not be able to purchase your morning cereal or lunchtime sandwich. Automobiles, microwaves, and shopping malls would not be built. And the computers and paper needed to print your favorite magazine would not get to the publisher.

We are more familiar with the marketing jobs in our town or city and even many of the marketing jobs in our country. But marketing occurs worldwide to meet the needs of the citizens of every country and to support international trade. Locate the names of the countries in which the products you use every day are produced and you will quickly realize the importance of marketing around the world. Those products would not be available to you and U.S. companies would not be able to sell their products in other countries without the daily work of thousands and millions of people in marketing careers. International marketing is providing more and more career opportunities.

Why are marketing jobs important to businesses that have non-marketing activities as their primary purpose?

WHY CHOOSE A MARKETING CAREER?

This may be your first experience studying marketing. You may not have understood marketing very well before beginning this class and may not have been aware of the variety of marketing career opportunities. It is not unusual for people to end up in marketing careers without careful planning or without being aware of the benefits of those careers. Understanding marketing will allow you to select a career that is exciting, challenging, and rewarding. You can also plan the education you will need and the types of work experiences that will help you prepare for the career of your choice.

BENEFITS OF WORKING IN MARKETING

You have a choice of many different jobs and careers. With careful planning and preparation, including continuing your education, additional choices are open to you. While you may choose to work in another type of career, you should nevertheless be aware of the many benefits of working in marketing.

Many Choices Marketing jobs exist in every industry and within most companies. Marketing jobs are found at the lowest and highest levels of a company and are available for people with varied amounts of education and experience. No matter what your interests, job opportunities in marketing are available that match those interests.

Interesting Work Marketing is usually not boring. Marketers work with customers and people from other businesses as well as with people in their own company. Most marketing jobs involve creativity and decision-making. Marketers are involved in planning, communicating, evaluating, and problem solving. As companies develop new products and services or identify new market opportunities, marketers will be involved from the beginning.

Financially Rewarding Some beginning marketing jobs will pay no more than minimum wage. Yet employees in those jobs who prove to their employer that they understand business operations and have a customer-service attitude are promoted quickly to higher-paying jobs with more responsibility. Marketing jobs are among the highest-paid positions in most companies. Because effective marketing results in higher profits for a company, effective marketers are often compensated with commissions, bonuses, or profit sharing to increase the salaries they earn.

Stable Employment As the economy changes, people may find that job opportunities change as well. People worry that they will lose their jobs when the economy is poor. Because marketing activities are so important to most businesses, marketing employees are often the last to be reduced and the first to be rehired. Marketing skills are useful in many types of businesses and industries. If one industry is not doing well economically, there are likely to be marketing jobs available in industries that are experiencing better economic conditions.

CAREER PATHS

Most people will change jobs many times during their lifetime. Marketing skills are useful in a number of jobs. Beginning jobs in marketing usually lead to advanced jobs with greater responsibility and higher salaries. A clerk in a store can become a department manager, store manager, and regional manager. Survey specialists working in marketing research can become product and brand managers. A sales associate can progress to salesperson, sales manager, and vice-president of sales and marketing. A recent study of the largest businesses in the United States found that people who started in marketing are frequently chosen to lead the entire company as the chief executive officer, or CEO.

CAREER PLANNING

No matter if you choose marketing or some other career, careful planning is important. You will need to identify the knowledge and skills you will need for the career you select, the educational preparation needed, and the jobs you will likely hold as you progress through your career. Lack of appropriate preparation is often cited as the reason why a person is not considered when a position is filled in an organization.

There are a number of important resources available to help you plan a career in marketing. Libraries and the Internet provide many career planning resources and references. Business organizations and many individual businesses provide materials that describe career opportunities and the preparation necessary for each career. People with experience in the careers that interest you are often willing to discuss their work, provide career advice, and even serve as mentors to people who are beginning their careers. Career centers and counselors are also valuable resources for planning.

You are now familiar with marketing and the many career opportunities available in marketing. You can decide if you want to consider a career in marketing and the career planning activities you will need to complete to prepare for the career of your choice.

What are the major benefits of working in marketing?

LESSON REVIEW

1. Why is marketing an important career area in business?

2. What percentage of all jobs are marketing jobs?

3. What are some examples of ways that consumers benefit from people performing marketing jobs?

4. Why are we unaware of many business-to-business marketing jobs?

5. How do individual consumers and businesses benefit from people working in international marketing?

6. Why does marketing provide an area of stable employment?

7. What are some resources that are useful if you want to complete planning for a marketing career?

JOB LEVELS IN MARKETING

GOALS

- Identify the five employment levels for marketing jobs.
- Describe the skills needed to progress through the marketing employment levels.

JOB PROGRESSION IN MARKETING

Many people have an idea of their ideal job. However, the job in which you will spend the most time in your career will not be your first or second job. Each of us will hold many jobs before we find the job we really want. Some people will never achieve the job of their dreams because the do not develop and follow a career plan.

COMPLETING CAREER PLANNING

Planning for a marketing career involves a number of choices. A way to increase your chances for a successful career is to complete career planning. Career planning in business is made up of several components. First you identify a career area. A **career area** is the area of business or the business function in which you plan to work. Examples include marketing, accounting, information management, production, and others.

The next step is to consider a career path in the career area. A **career path** is a series of related jobs with increasing knowledge and skill requirements and greater amounts of responsibility.

The third step is to compare your current academic preparation and experience with the jobs in the career path and prepare a career plan. A **career plan** identifies the progression of jobs in your career path, your plans for education, training, and experience to meet the requirements for those jobs, and a tentative time schedule for accomplishing the plan.

It may seem to be an almost impossible task to develop a realistic career plan when the business world is changing so much. There are likely going to be jobs available

10 years from now that don't exist today. The knowledge and skills needed to be successful in a job will likely be quite different in a few years.

A career plan cannot be totally accurate and will likely change several times in the future. However, without a plan you will not be aware of those changes and will seldom be prepared to pursue promotions, advancements, and job changes. People who complete career planning are more likely to have jobs they like and are better prepared to perform them than those who do not have a career plan.

EMPLOYMENT LEVELS IN MARKETING

Employment opportunities in marketing are available to people with a range of education levels, work experience, and interests. To help with career planning, those opportunities are organized within five levels. The levels of marketing employment are entry-level, career-level, specialist, supervisor/manager, and executive/entrepreneur. The five levels are illustrated in Figure 23-1.

FIGURE 23-1
The levels of employment in marketing.

Executive/Entrepreneur

Supervisor/ Manager

Specialist

Career

Entry

Entry-Level Marketing   People employed in entry-level marketing jobs perform routine activities with limited authority and responsibility. Entry-level jobs require limited education and experience. They are often held by individuals who are still enrolled in high school or who have only a high school diploma. You can often obtain an entry-level marketing job with no previous experience.

Entry-level jobs usually pay an hourly wage, often beginning at the minimum wage level. Some examples of entry-level jobs in marketing are clerk, cashier, stockperson, and delivery person.

Quite often, people who hold entry-level positions do not view the job as the first step in a career path. They just want part- or full-time employment to earn money. They may move from job to job with no specific plans for the future. Career planning helps people select entry-level jobs that will be interesting, use existing knowledge and skills, and help prepare them for career advancement.

Career-Level Marketing   Career-level jobs are more complex than entry-level positions. People in career positions have more control over their work, have a variety of tasks to complete that require specific knowledge and skill to perform well, usually are involved in problem-solving and decision-making, and may have some limited supervisory responsibilities over a few entry-level employees.

To qualify for career-level jobs, a person will need a year or two of experience in the company or a similar business. In lieu of or in addition to that experience, a person may need to complete education beyond high school such as a two-year or four-year degree.

People in career-level jobs usually view the work as more than a job to earn money. They work in an area of general interest and in a job they believe will lead to career advancement. Businesses hire people for career-level positions in marketing who demonstrate understanding of marketing principles and business operations and who have an enthusiasm for developing skills in the area of work that will contribute to the business' success.

Specialist-Level Marketing   Marketing specialists perform very specific work in a business that requires advanced knowledge of a particular area of business

operations. They will generally have special training and considerable experience in one particular area of marketing or a type of marketing activity required by the business in which they work. They will usually have a four-year college degree or even a graduate degree or advanced training in their area of work.

Marketing specialists are often considered the most skilled and expert people in their part of the business. Examples of marketing specialists include brand and product managers, advertising account executives, lead sales representatives, marketing research specialists, and buyers.

Marketing specialists will usually continue to work in the specific area of marketing and be promoted to advanced positions. They may be hired by other companies because of their specialized marketing expertise.

Supervisor/Manager-Level Marketing

People who work for some time in a business and have held career or specialist positions may want to move into management. They will usually begin as a supervisor or assistant manager with responsibility for a few people in a specific area of the business. If they like the responsibility of managing others and do it well they will likely be moved to higher levels of management and be responsible for a broader set of marketing activities.

Supervisors need to have an understanding of and usually some experience working in the area for which they have management responsibilities. They also must have effective communications, human relations, and leadership skills. People promoted to the position of supervisor or manager usually have several years of experience in the company. However some people are hired as supervisors or managers with less experience but specific education or training in management. Companies often have management training programs to help employees learn to be effective managers.

Supervisors and managers are needed in all areas of marketing. Examples include sales manager, inventory manager, customer service manager, marketing information systems manager, and many others.

Executive/Entrepreneur-Level Marketing

The people with the greatest amount of authority and responsibility for marketing are executives and entrepreneurs. They hold the top marketing positions in a company, such as vice-president of marketing or president of international marketing operations. People who start their own marketing businesses are entrepreneurs.

Marketing executives and entrepreneurs need to have a thorough understanding of business principles and procedures, management, and all areas of marketing. They are responsible for all of the major marketing plans and decisions made and the implementation of the plans. They spend most of their time gathering and reviewing information, planning, and evaluating marketing effectiveness to make sure it is contributing to the profitability of the business.

Executives will have spent many years in the business often working in many different marketing jobs. They often will have a graduate degree in business. Entrepreneurs do not always have as much experience or education. They do have a strong desire to start their own business. Today, many entrepreneurs without academic preparation in business and marketing and some business experience will find it difficult to develop a business that continues to grow and make a profit.

What are the five levels of employment in marketing?

SKILLS FOR
MARKETING SUCCESS

Marketing today is becoming very complex. It involves many specialized but related activities. The people asked to complete marketing activities in companies must be more knowledgeable than ever before. Although in the past people could learn how to perform marketing on the job, that is seldom possible today.

To prepare for a marketing career, you need to understand the skills that will be required for the job that you want. Marketing jobs demand two types of skills. First you will need foundational skills that are useful in all business careers. Then you can develop skills in the specialized area of marketing in which you want to work.

MARKETING FOUNDATIONS

Marketing is necessary for business success. At the same time, marketing cannot be effective without the support of many other business activities. In companies that apply the marketing concept, marketers work closely with people in other parts of the business such as accountants, production personnel, engineers, and information management specialists. Understanding business fundamentals will allow people from across

the company to communicate and work effectively together.

Business Principles Important business foundations on which marketing is based are economics, accounting, law, technology, and management. Marketers do not have to be expert in those areas, but they need to understand basic operations, use business information and reports, and make marketing decisions that support the business's strategy and plans.

Interpersonal Skills Marketers interact with other people. They work with people on their marketing team and with their managers, they often communicate with customers to provide information and solve problems, and they are involved regularly with other people inside and outside of the company. Interpersonal skills including communications, teamwork, human relations, decision-making, and problem solving are all important in developing and maintaining effective work relationships.

Academic Preparation People who choose careers in marketing know that they need strong academic preparation. Today most career positions in marketing require education beyond high school. Marketers need to have effective mathematics, writing, and speaking skills. Preparation in science, psychology, and technology are very helpful in many areas of marketing. Because of the diverse society in which marketers work and the growth of international business, the study of foreign languages is very important.

MARKETING FUNCTIONS

Building on the foundations, marketers add skills in one or more of the marketing functions to prepare for a career. Some marketing jobs are very specialized and are a part of one of the seven marketing functions. For example, a person involved in marketing research is responsible for one aspect of marketing-information management. A

person who designs and constructs window displays in a retail mall is performing a specialized promotion activity. In other jobs, the employee must be skilled in several marketing functions. Brand managers for a consumer products manufacturing company need to understand all of the marketing functions. A buyer for a wholesaler or retailer will use skills in finance, pricing, and product management.

Every marketer needs a general understanding of marketing and must be familiar with marketing terms and concepts. In addition, each person will need to develop specialized skills in one or more of the marketing functions.

Product/Service Management Product/service management is responsible for planning new products and services and making improvements to existing products. It requires an understanding of consumer needs and attitudes as well as competitors' products and services. Marketers involved with this function make sure that products are safe, easy-to-use, and are perceived as a value by the target market.

Pricing Marketers that specialize in the pricing function are ultimately responsible for the profitability of a product. They need to analyze supply and demand and set a price that will result in the sale of the company's products at a profit. They plan pricing policies and determine how the price will be communicated to the customer. If markdowns are needed they will determine the amount of the markdown and when it will be offered.

Distribution Distribution is a very complex marketing activity. Many marketing jobs are a part of distribution, and distribution specialists need a number of skills. People who plan distribution need to know where customers are located and where they prefer to purchase the products or services. Channels of distribution must be planned including building relationships with other companies involved in the channel. Procedures for order processing, inventory management, packaging, shipping, and customer service need to be developed.

Marketing in the Dot.Com Age

Traditional marketing jobs are not disappearing because of the growth of the Internet. On the contrary, many traditional jobs in distribution, credit, marketing research, and advertising have increased in numbers as e-commerce companies recognize the need for a variety of marketing services.

Most of the traditional marketing jobs have an equivalent job within e-commerce businesses. In fact, the jobs are so similar that monster.com created an online tool to compare traditional and e-commerce jobs. (dotcom.monster.com/articles/jobconverter/ie.asp). Examples of comparable jobs include:

TRADITIONAL JOB	E-COMMERCE JOB
outside sales rep	e-commerce sales account executive
marketing manager	interactive marketing manager
PR coordinator	online community manager
customer service representative	online customer care representative
business development manager	web business development manager

The major difference between the two types of jobs is the need to understand and use the technology of e-commerce. Marketing professionals who recognize that they must identify and meet customer needs and make sure all marketing functions are provided effectively can be effective in either a traditional business or an e-commerce business.

THINK CRITICALLY

1. Why are the numbers of traditional marketing jobs continuing to grow even as e-commerce expands rapidly?

2. In addition to understanding and using Internet technology, in what other ways do you believe marketing jobs in e-commerce are different from traditional marketing jobs?

3. Use the Internet to identify the job titles of several e-commerce marketing jobs.

Financing Financial planning is an important marketing responsibility. Budgets must be prepared and adequate financial resources identified to pay for the marketing activities of the company. If customers want or need to purchase on credit, credit plans and policies will need to be developed. Some products will be leased rather than sold, so financial specialists will work with customers to explain the lease terms and complete the necessary paperwork.

Promotion Communication and promotion needs to be carefully planned in order to make customers aware of the company's product, provide them with the necessary information so they will make a purchase, and follow up to make sure they are satisfied with the product. There are many skills used in planning promotion including writing, editing, design, graphics, media, and technology.

Selling When more personal and direct communications are needed to encourage customers to buy, selling is used. A salesperson often has the most direct contact with customers, so he or she is considered the representative of the company. Salespeople must be able to build and maintain successful relationships with their customers. They need skills in oral and written communications, time management, human relations, planning, and budgeting. Today, technology skills are very important because salespeople use computers, projectors, PDAs, cell phones, and the Internet in their work.

Marketing-Information Management Marketing is scientific and relies on data. Marketers need to be able to instantly obtain and review information. Telemarketers need product information to answer customer questions. Marketing researchers select a sample of consumers to survey. Product managers analyze the daily sales of a brand in an important market.

People involved in marketing information need skills in mathematics and statistics, computer skills, an understanding of research procedures, and the ability to manage and analyze large amounts of data. They also need communication skills in order to provide reports to other people responsible for decisions that use the information collected.

Why is an understanding of marketing foundations important to people planning a career in marketing?

LESSON REVIEW

1. What are the three steps in career planning?

2. Why is a career plan important even though jobs and job requirements are changing?

3. Why is it important to carefully select an entry-level job if you are planning a marketing career?

4. How is a career-level job different from a specialist-level job?

5. What are the two types of skills demanded by marketing jobs?

6. What are reasons that a person may need skills in more than one of the marketing functions?

MARKETING EDUCATION AND CAREER PATHS

MARKETING MATTERS

Some people have a career goal of becoming a manager in a business. Others would prefer not to manage other people but want to spend all of their time on marketing activities. Companies need effective managers but they also need people who are experienced and skilled in particular areas of business operations.

In the past many companies identified the people who were the best performers in each area of the business and made them the managers. Managers were often paid more than other employees.

List the advantages and disadvantages of selecting the best employees to become managers and paying managers more than other employees. What are reasons why a business might want to let superior employees continue to work in the areas where they are skilled, rather than making them managers? How do you believe each of those practices would affect career planning of employees? Share your ideas with other students.

GOALS

● Describe the importance of marketing education.

● Identify non-management and management career paths in marketing.

THE BENEFITS OF MARKETING EDUCATION

How do you prepare for a marketing career? When is the best time to begin career planning? Preparing for a career in marketing will require a combination of education and experience. It is never too early to start that preparation even if you are unsure if you want a career in marketing. Marketing skills are useful in many jobs. An understanding of marketing principles and the marketing skills you have will make you a valued employee in most businesses and organizations.

You have already begun your preparation for a marketing career with this course and others you have completed in high school. It is likely that you and many of your classmates have held entry-level marketing jobs giving you some experience and an opportunity to understand many of the ideas you are studying. You will need to decide if you want to continue your marketing education and what knowledge and skills you need to develop for the career of your choice.

WHAT IS MARKETING EDUCATION?

You can learn about marketing and develop marketing skills at almost any point in your education. Marketing education begins in middle schools with career exploration programs, job shadowing experiences, and introductory business courses.

High School Marketing Education At the high school level, many schools offer business and marketing classes as electives designed to develop general knowledge of marketing principles. Specialized marketing courses may be available to allow study of topics ranging from personal selling and advertising to sports marketing or fashion.

Career programs in Marketing Education provide the most comprehensive preparation opportunities for high school students considering full time employment in marketing after graduation or for those considering additional education after high school. A **Marketing Education program** incorporates three types of complementary learning experiences—introductory and advanced courses in marketing, structured work experiences through internships and cooperative education, and a student organization called DECA. The three components of Marketing Education provide a model for career development. The classes offer understanding of marketing principles in an applied academic environment. Work experience through cooperative education gives students the chance to practice and test their marketing skills in a business, interacting with experienced employees, managers, and customers. DECA complements the classes by providing student-led opportunities to build teamwork and leadership skills, participate in professional development experiences including conferences and seminars, and enhance and test marketing skills through individual and group competitions.

Community College Programs

Marketing education opportunities continue and expand at the college level. Community colleges offer business and marketing courses as a part of an academic curriculum through which students can earn an Associate of Arts degree. The courses and degree will qualify graduates for a number of career-level positions in marketing. In addition, most four-year colleges and universities will accept the Associate of Arts degree, so students can use it as a step toward a Bachelor's degree.

Community colleges also offer one-year diploma programs that provide very specialized study of a specific set of marketing skills (selling, inventory management, small

business management) for immediate employment. Two-year career programs that earn an Associate of Applied Science (AAS) degree are structured in a similar way to the high school Marketing Education programs. They include coursework in English, math, natural science, and social science. Then students can choose to complete a general marketing curriculum or a specialized program such as Hospitality Marketing, Food Marketing, E-Marketing, Professional Selling, and Fashion Marketing. Many two-year career programs offered by community colleges include structured part-time or full-time work experiences in marketing jobs and a student organization, Delta Epsilon Chi.

College Study   You can earn a baccalaureate degree in Marketing at most colleges and universities. Those programs incorporate study of advanced marketing skills that prepare graduates for career-level and specialist-level positions in business. Popular marketing courses in colleges today include international marketing, entrepreneurship, e-commerce, and sports marketing.

Lifelong Learning   Marketing education is a lifelong experience. Companies spend thousands of dollars each year to offer training to improve the skills of marketing personnel. Marketers participate in conferences and seminars and read business and marketing magazines to update their knowledge about the best marketing practices. Marketers who want to move into executive management positions will usually complete a graduate program in business such as a Master of Business Administration (MBA). Executive education programs are offered to the top marketing managers in companies to improve their understanding of the changing economy, to introduce the latest technology, and to improve decision-making abilities.

What are the three types of learning experiences in a Marketing Education program?

CHOOSING A CAREER PATH

The career opportunities in marketing are so vast that it may be difficult to choose the career path you will follow. However, because of the many opportunities, it is possible to develop a more general career path and make it more specific in the future as you gain experience and complete further education. One of the decisions that will guide career planning is whether you want to prepare for a management or non-management career.

MOVING INTO MANAGEMENT

In the past it was expected that most people planning a career would prefer to move into a management position if given the opportunity. Businesses were organized as hierarchies with promotions leading to more and more responsibilities and ultimately into supervisory and management positions. While those expectations have changed in many companies, a management career is still desired by many people.

In marketing, managers are needed for each of the major marketing functions. There will usually be several supervisor positions available in every marketing department. Most companies have one or more executive-level marketing management positions at the top of the company.

Preparing for International Jobs

Companies frequently offer employees international work assignments. To make sure the assignments are successful, employees and their families need to be prepared through education and training. It is estimated that more than a quarter of all overseas work assignments end early because the employee or family members cannot adjust to the assignment.

The education programs need to include basic information about the country to which the employee is assigned, immersion in the language to provide writing and speaking skills, and awareness of cultural differences to allow comfortable interactions with new coworkers and neighbors. The family needs to be prepared for basic living skills, including shopping, travel, entertainment, and education.

Less than a third of large U.S. companies report providing formal education and training for employees given international work assignments. Nearly half of comparable companies in Europe and Asia offer training prior to overseas assignments.

THINK CRITICALLY

1. What do you think are reasons overseas work assignments often end early?

2. What would you like to know about another country before you accepted an international work assignment there?

23.4 BEGINNING CAREER PLANNING

- Describe the steps in preparing a career plan.
- Discuss how to successfully apply for a job.

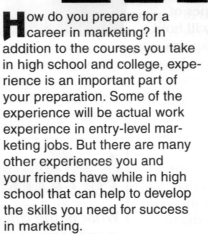

How do you prepare for a career in marketing? In addition to the courses you take in high school and college, experience is an important part of your preparation. Some of the experience will be actual work experience in entry-level marketing jobs. But there are many other experiences you and your friends have while in high school that can help to develop the skills you need for success in marketing.

Start by making a list of 5 to 8 skills you believe will be important for people who want a career in marketing. Examples could be human relations and communications skills.

For each of the skills you have listed, identify experiences you believe are available in your classes, in clubs and other extracurricular activities, and in outside-of-school activities that can contribute to the development of the skills. Be very specific in describing the experiences.

Discuss the experiences with other students and decide which of the experiences seem to be most useful in preparing for a career in marketing.

CHOICES AND DECISIONS

Right now you may believe that preparing for a career in business is like trying to assemble a jigsaw puzzle. Hundreds of pieces to the puzzle lay before you, but it is almost impossible to envision how they fit together. You know that marketing careers require a combination of education and experience. It is difficult to decide what types of education and experience you need as well as where and when to obtain them.

You may know right now that you want a career in marketing and even may have decided on the specific job that is of most interest to you. On the other hand you may have decided on a non-marketing career but see how an understanding of marketing will benefit you. Or you may be undecided on a

career and are just beginning to consider your choices.

Don't be too concerned if you haven't made specific career choices at this time. People change jobs many times during their lifetimes and often move into totally different areas of work than they originally planned. Still, it is important to focus on the impact that education and the employment choices you make will have on your career.

COMBINING EDUCATION AND EXPERIENCE

Today, it is less likely that a person will achieve their career goal without planning and preparation. A successful business career is more likely for you if you understand the requirements for the job you want and plan to develop the necessary skills. Career planning becomes a process of determining your interests and abilities, studying the requirements for the job you want, and planning the education and experience you will need to qualify for the job. Employers value both education and experience.

You will need strong academic skills (reading, writing, mathematics) as well as knowledge of business and marketing. The courses you have already completed as well as the remaining courses you will take in high school will prepare you for your career choice. College coursework can add to your academic and career preparation.

Experience in business is always an advantage. Employers value experience because it demonstrates your interest in business, your motivation, interpersonal skills, and the ability to apply what you have learned in your classes. It is relatively easy to find an entry-level job in marketing if you are not too concerned about the type of work. Even though those jobs do not always pay as much as you would like and it is difficult to manage a work schedule with school and extracurricular activities, a good work record provides a decided advantage when you apply for other jobs.

If you have successful entry-level experience in high school, you may be able to qualify for more advanced jobs when you seek full-time employment after high school or for jobs you hold while in college. You can add to your work experience by completing internships, working on projects and activities in school organizations, and by volunteering in community organizations.

DEVELOPING A CAREER PLAN

Planning is an important marketing skill as well as necessary to obtain the job you want. Many people do little planning even for things that are important to them. Without a plan, however, you are less likely to achieve your goals. By developing a career plan, you will not only increase the chances of obtaining the job you really want, but you will be practicing an impor-

Changing Job Market

Between 1990 and 2000, the types of jobs in the U.S. economy have changed. The following table shows the number of employees (in millions) in four industries.

	1990	2000
Manufacturing	19,000	18,400
Retail	19,600	23,100
Wholesale	6,200	7,000
Service	29,900	40,400

THINK CRITICALLY

1. What was the increase or decrease in employment during the 10 years for each industry?

2. What is the percentage increase or decrease in employment during the 10 years for each industry?

3. Calculate the total number of employees in all industries for 1990 and then for 2000. How much did employment increase during the 10-year period in all of the industries combined?

4. Why do you believe manufacturing employment decreased while employment in service businesses increased during the decade?

tant business skill. Employers will be impressed with the efforts you devote to career planning.

If you want to develop an effective career plan, follow these steps:

1. Complete an assessment of your current knowledge, skills, and interests. Work with teachers, counselors, and others to identify tests and other resources that will improve your self-understanding in order to make the best matches with possible careers.

2. Study marketing careers in depth to determine the industries and types of marketing jobs available and the work that is required in the jobs of interest to you.

3. Identify the education and experience requirements for the marketing careers that interest you. Interview employees and visit businesses to add to your knowledge. Compare the results with your current education and experience to determine what you will need to qualify for the jobs in the career area that interests you.

4. Make a list of the knowledge and skills you will need to develop. Meet with experienced people (teachers, counselors, business people) who are familiar with education and work opportunities to gather advice on the possible choices for additional education and work experience. Share your career plans with them and have them help you make the best matches to help you achieve your career goals.

5. Prepare a written career plan. The plan may be general at first, but you can make it more specific as you gather more information. The plan should identify the career area of interest to you and possible jobs that make up a career path. You should list the knowledge and skills you will need and the choices of education and experience that you have made to assist you with your career development. You may want to include a timeline that projects how long it will take to complete the experiences listed.

checkpoint

Why do employers value work experience when hiring a new employee?

OBTAINING THE JOB YOU WANT

The importance of career planning will become apparent when you apply for the job you want and are hired because the employer was impressed with your preparation and planning. The information in your career plan will be helpful in completing applications for jobs or for schools.

PREPARING A CAREER PORTFOLIO

Portfolios are a common tool used by artists, models, and advertising people to visually

demonstrate their abilities and their past work. You may have been asked to develop a portfolio for a class that included the major projects and activities you completed during the year.

A career portfolio is an excellent resource to help you with career planning and job applications. A **career portfolio** is an organized collection of information and materials developed to represent yourself, your preparation, and your accomplishments.

Select and organize items for your portfolio that you believe provide the best evidence of your marketing knowledge and skills. Those items can include tests, reports, and projects completed in classes, summaries of aptitude or interest tests you have taken, projects and activities you completed in a club or organization, and even work done for a hobby if it demonstrates important business or marketing skills. For example you may have developed a personal web site on your computer that demonstrates technology skills.

If you have worked for a business, you may have work reports or performance reviews that can be incorporated into your career portfolio. If you completed a special

Online Employment

While only four percent of web users report obtaining a job online, the use of the Internet by companies to locate new employees and by individuals to find jobs is becoming more and more important. Over 80 percent of Fortune 500 companies use their web sites to post available jobs. Nearly all of them allow prospective employees to submit an application and resume online.

For people looking for a job, the Internet provides more than the opportunity to go to a company's web site to obtain job listings and make a job application. Three types of Internet resources are available to job seekers:

- Job seeking preparation sites
- Career information sites
- Job and resume posting sites

Job seeking preparation sites provide support to the job seeker in completing a self-assessment to determine interests and skills. Help in resume development and writing a letter of application is also provided. Articles and books related to career selection, finding the right job, and interviewing are listed. The

site might have career counselors or a chat room to talk with other job seekers.

Career information sites provide information on the job market, salaries, education requirements, and the top employers. The sites often provide information on cities and links to community resources to help job seekers learn about the locations where they might want to live.

Job and resume posting sites provide an "employment service" online. Employers can provide job listings, and individuals can post resumes in order to make career matches.

THINK CRITICALLY

1. If only four percent of web users find their jobs online, why are there so many career web sites online?

2. What do you believe are the advantages for companies in posting available jobs online? Can you identify any problems that could result from the practice?

3. Would you feel comfortable in finding and accepting a new job totally online without visiting the company? Why or why not?

project on the job and your employer allows you to have a copy, it should be included. Photos of work you have completed provide interesting evidence of skills. Any awards or recognition you have received in school or on the job should be included as well.

Make sure your portfolio is well organized so you can easily locate items when needed and so others can quickly review your work. You will add to the portfolio as you continue your education and work, so design the portfolio so items can easily be added or removed.

APPLYING FOR THE JOB YOU WANT

Once you have prepared your career plan and portfolio, you are ready to begin your job search and then apply for the marketing job you want.

Identify Jobs The first step in a job search is to identify available positions. Newspapers are one of the best sources for listings of available jobs. They are usually organized by the type of job or job title.

The Internet has become a very important tool for job searches. Most companies maintain a listing of open positions on their web sites. There are specific web sites where companies can list their job openings. Examples are Monster.com and HotJobs.com. Many of the web sites allow you to search for jobs by job category, specific job title, company name, or geographic location. Many sites let individuals develop and post their resumes online. Some will even match the resumes to available jobs

and send matching resumes to the businesses with job openings.

Other sources of job openings are career centers in schools, employment agencies, and recommendations from family members and friends.

Make a Career Match Your career plan will help you identify the companies and select the jobs that most closely match your current interests and abilities and fit your long-term career goal. From the available jobs, select those for which you are qualified and interested.

After you have selected a few jobs, gather information about each of the companies on the list. You will want to know more about the business if you plan to work for it. In addition, by learning about the company you can show the employer how your skills will specifically benefit the company. Businesses want to hire people who will contribute to their operations. By preparing in advance with information about the company, you will be able to clearly communicate the benefits you can provide as an employee.

Prepare Application Companies will usually ask you to complete a written application on a form they provide. In addition they may request a resume outlining your preparation and experience. Make sure all materials are carefully and professionally prepared and that all of the information you provide is accurate.

The work you have done in preparing a career plan and portfolio will be very useful in completing the job application. You will have very specific information available and can select the information that most closely matches the job requirements for your resume and application.

Many resumes are quite general because they are not prepared for a specific job. Through the use of a computer and the materials you have assembled as a part of your career planning, you can prepare a specific resume for each employer. They will be impressed by the specific information you are able to provide and the evidence that you have studied the company and job.

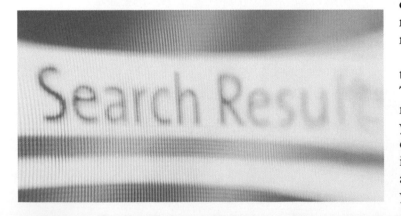

Complete a Successful Interview

If you have not had a lot of experience with job interviews, you may be nervous. Once again, the careful and thorough preparation you have completed will help give you confidence if you are selected for an interview. You know a great deal about yourself and the job for which you are applying.

It is important to make a professional appearance in an interview. You want to wear appropriate business apparel that is compatible with what employees in the business normally wear at work.

Make sure you are on time for the interview. If possible, identify the name of the person who will interview you in advance so you can ask for that person and use their name during the interview.

Unless you are told not to do so, you can bring selected items from your portfolio. You will probably be given the opportunity to show and describe them during the interview if you are carrying them. Don't hesitate to refer to examples of your work when answering questions.

Communicate your interest in a marketing career and how the job fits into your career goals. Make sure the employer knows you are interested in working for the company and want to do a good job because of your interests in marketing.

Demonstrate confidence and professionalism during the interview. Do not be afraid to ask questions about the company and the job. In fact, you should prepare several questions in advance and be prepared to ask them.

When the interview is finished, thank the interviewer for the opportunity. Clarify what will happen after the interview and when you can expect to hear from the company. Send a personal note of thanks to the interviewer as soon as possible. Use the note to highlight one or two unique qualities you can offer.

The Decision Don't expect that you will be offered every job for which you apply. Your preparation increases the likelihood that you will be hired if you select jobs that are good matches with your interests and qualifications.

You also will need to decide if you will accept the job if it is offered to you. You should use the interview to gather information to be able to make that decision. If the job isn't what you expected or does not fit your career plan, you may choose to decline an offer. The person making the offer will probably be impressed if you clearly communicate why you don't believe the job is the best choice for you. If you decide to accept the job, you will do so with the confidence that it is the job that best meets your career plans.

What are several useful sources to identify available marketing jobs?

1. Do people need to have specific career plans to be successful in marketing? Why or why not?

2. Why are entry-level jobs important even though they may not be the most interesting or the highest paying?

3. What are two advantages of preparing a career plan?

4. What types of people can be helpful to you as you develop a career plan?

5. What is a career portfolio?

6. What is the first step in a job search?

7. What is the advantage of preparing a specific resume for each employer?

SUMMARY

Lesson 23.1

A. There are many job opportunities in marketing. People can be employed directly in marketing jobs, or they may use marketing knowledge and skills in non-marketing positions.

B. Marketing careers provide many benefits. There are many interesting jobs available. Marketing careers are usually financially rewarding as well as stable sources of employment. Marketing opportunities range from entry-level positions to the top executive positions in a company.

Lesson 23.2

A. Careful career planning is important in achieving the job that you want. Career planning involves selecting a career area, identifying a career path, and preparing a written career plan.

B. There are five career levels in marketing. They are entry-level, career-level, specialist-level, supervisor/management-level, and executive/entrepreneur-level.

Lesson 23.3

A. You can learn about marketing and develop marketing skills at almost any point in your education. Marketing education opportunities can be found at all levels of education from middle school to graduate programs in colleges and universities.

B. A career path is a series of related jobs with increasing knowledge and skill requirements and greater amounts of responsibility. You can select a career path in one of two ways—either by industry or by marketing function.

Lesson 23.4

A. Success in marketing requires a combination of education and experience. You will need strong academic skills as well as an understanding of business and marketing concepts. Employers are more likely to hire you if you have work experience in addition to your education.

B. An effective tool for obtaining a job is a career portfolio. The portfolio helps you select jobs that match your abilities and interests. It also is a source of information and materials that will be useful in developing a resume, completing a job application, and preparing for an interview.

REVIEW MARKETING CONCEPTS

1. True or False: While there are a large number of marketing jobs available in our economy, they are generally low paying.

2. True or False: Companies that have non-marketing activities as their primary purpose will usually employ some marketing employees.

3. True or False: If you are interested in a professional career such as a physician or dentist, an understanding of marketing is useful in your work.

4. True or False: Two types of businesses that are not involved in marketing are manufacturers and farmers.

5. True or False: Marketing jobs are found at the lowest and highest levels of a company.

6. True or False: The first step in career planning is to select a broad career area that interests you.

7. True or False: Once you have prepared a career plan, it should not be changed.

8. True or False: Most entry-level marketing jobs require at least a high school diploma.

9. True or False: The people with the greatest amount of authority and responsibility for marketing are executives and entrepreneurs.

10. True or False: Marketing jobs demand two types of skills—foundational skills and specialized skills in a marketing function.

11. True or False: Today, someone who has a high school diploma but no college education can still obtain most marketing jobs.

12. True or False: Marketing education is actually a lifelong experience since you can study marketing from middle school through graduate school and beyond.

13. True or False: To be successful, a career path must end in a management job.

14. True or False: Once you have chosen an industry in which to work, it will be very difficult to switch to a marketing job in another industry.

15. True or False: Career planning is much more important to career success today than it was in the past.

16. True or False: Employers are more likely to hire someone with academic experience and work experience than someone with just academic experience.

17. True or False: A self-assessment of your knowledge, skills, and interests is a good starting point for career planning.

18. True or False: A career plan will not be useful unless it is very specific.

19. True or False: A career portfolio should include information and materials from any jobs you have held but not from your academic work.

20. True or False: Since little information on the Internet is accurate, it is not a good source to look for employment opportunities.

21. True or False: Whenever possible you should prepare a specific resume for each prospective employer.

22. True or False: Even if a job does not fit your expectations after the interview, you should accept it if it is offered to you.

REVIEW MARKETING TERMS

Match the terms listed with the definitions. Some terms may not be used.

23. The area of business or the business function in which you plan to work.

24. Incorporates three types of complementary learning experiences—introductory and advanced courses in marketing, structured work experiences through internships and cooperative education, and a student organization, DECA.

25. Identifies the progression of jobs in your career path, your plans for education, training, and experience to meet the requirements for those jobs, and a tentative time schedule for accomplishing the plan.

26. A series of related jobs with increasing knowledge and skill requirements and greater amounts of responsibility.

27. An organized collection of information and materials developed to represent yourself, your preparation, and your accomplishments.

a. career area
b. career path
c. career plan
d. career portfolio
e. Marketing Education program

APPLY MARKETING FUNCTIONS

MARKETING RESEARCH

28. Many marketing occupations are among the jobs employing the most people in the U.S. economy. Also marketing careers are normally among the fastest growing occupations.

Use the Internet to locate employment statistics for the United States and also for your state. Identify any jobs you believe are marketing occupations that are among those employing the most people and the fastest growing occupations. List the jobs and identify those you would be interested in for your own employment and those that would not interest you. Provide reasons for your decisions.

29. Using your library or the Internet, locate information on three 2-year or 4-year colleges that offer degrees in marketing. Study the courses you would have to complete to earn the degree.

Prepare a table that identifies the college, the title of the marketing degree, the total number of credits needed to earn the degree, and the total number of marketing credits needed to earn the degree. Now determine the combined total number of credits in the academic subjects of English, speech, writing, and mathematics.

Calculate the percentage of total credits that will be marketing courses, the percentage of credits in the academic subjects, and the percentage of total credits for all other course work. Prepare a pie chart to illustrate your findings. What conclusions can you draw from the table and chart?

MARKETING PLANNING

30. Select one of the seven marketing functions that interests you as a possible career area. Using career resources in your school's library, career center, or the Internet, identify three jobs that would make up a career path in the marketing function you selected. One of the jobs should be an entry-level job, one should be a career- or specialist-level job, and one should be a supervisor/manager or executive entrepreneur-level job. Prepare a detailed job description of each the jobs you identified. For each position, identify:

- a detailed job description
- the amount of education you believe is necessary to obtain the job
- the amount and type of work experience that you believe would be expected of a person hired for the job
- an approximate wage or salary you believe the job would pay

31. Form two teams of students and prepare to debate the following issue:

"Companies should select the most skilled employees to become managers."

vs.

"Companies should recognize and reward their most skilled employees but keep them working in the areas where they are the most skilled rather than promoting them to management."

Each team will be assigned one of the two positions. The team members will work together to develop arguments for their position and against the opposing position. Each team will be given 5 minutes to present the reasons for their positions. Then each team will have 5 minutes to present reasons against the opposite position or to directly rebut the arguments of the other team.

At the end of the debate, the entire class should discuss the issue based on the arguments presented.

MARKETING MANAGEMENT

32. You are the manager of a customer service team for the local telephone service provider in your city. Your customer service representatives respond to telephoned and e-mailed questions from customers who want to add or change their local services or are experiencing problems and are calling for help. The customer service representatives will have specific training so they know the information about the services provided, and can access a computer program that will provide suggested answers to customer problems. If the problem cannot be solved, the representative will schedule an appointment with a technician who can go to the customer's home to make a repair.

You will be hiring 15 new customer service representatives. Based on the information provided, write a classified advertisement for the position. Include an overview of the position and a description of the qualifications you would require of job applicants.

What procedures would you follow and what materials would you require of job applicants in order to make the best choices for your new employees?

33. The two marketing careers at the top of many career paths are executive and entrepreneur. An executive typically works in a large organization and is responsible for the effective performance of many of the marketing functions in the company. An entrepreneur owns his or her own business and is responsible for the success of the business. That includes all of the business functions including marketing.

Research the similarities and differences between the positions of executive and

entrepreneur. If possible, interview a person who is a marketing executive and a person who is an entrepreneur. Prepare a 2–3 page report comparing the two marketing jobs including their similarities and differences. Conclude the report by indicating whether you would prefer to be an executive or an entrepreneur and why.

MARKETING TECHNOLOGY

34. Begin the development of a career portfolio. Prepare a 3-ring binder or some other useful means of organizing and maintaining your portfolio materials. Identify the categories of materials that you want to include in your portfolio such as class projects, work products, and others you believe are important as evidence of your career preparation. Begin to add items to the portfolio. Prepare a list of the types of items you would like to develop and include in your portfolio. Use word processing and computer graphics programs to prepare the portfolio materials so they have a professional look.

35. Using an Internet browser or search engine, identify five marketing jobs that are directly related to e-commerce and Internet businesses. For each job, identify the marketing function or functions that are the focus of the jobholder's work.

Select at least two of the jobs that interest you. Again using the Internet, locate two companies that are currently attempting to hire a person for the identified positions. For each company located, print the job announcement that identifies the company, location, job description, requirements, and any other information provided.

MARKETING IN ACTION

CASE STUDY

YOUNG ENTREPRENEUR IN THE WEB DESIGN WORLD

Matt Douglas became interested in designing web sites when he was 13 years old. He liked the idea of making information available to the entire world, and the thought of designing his own web pages was exciting.

Learning how to design web sites was a fun challenge for Matt. He started with a small site about himself. Even though Matt did not have much experience with the Web, he was eager to learn something new. Through hours of trial and error, Matt taught himself the essentials of web site development.

Locating customers is the most difficult part of a web designer's job. Matt's experience taught him the most effective method of finding customers is networking. He was very fortunate because his dad was a very successful manufacturer's representative with hundreds of contacts, many of whom needed web sites. About half of the sites Matt has created have been related to manufacturing. Friends and family have been a huge asset to Matt's business, because their contacts have accounted for most of his work.

Another less-effective method Matt used was cold calling. Matt learned that people either want a web site or they don't. In most cases, he found that there was little he could say or do to change someone's mind in that regard.

Once a web developer manages to get his foot in the door, it is important to ask the right kinds of questions in order to design a site that meets the client's requirements. A web designer must determine what type of site customers are looking for. Is it a general information site for their business, or do they want to use the site to sell products?

When young Matt started designing web pages, he often faced the problem of gaining the trust of older clients. It was difficult for some of them to accept Matt as a serious businessperson because he was so young. Matt helped overcome this obstacle by being extremely polite and professional and responding to customer requests immediately.

Matt learned the hard way that the price should be established before beginning work on a site. When he began working as a web designer, Matt did not quote prices up front. Then when he wrote up his final invoices, he would under-price them to avoid any bad feelings from clients. Consequently, clients would get great sites for half what they should have paid. Now Matt establishes a price range at the outset.

Often a site will take a month or more to complete. Clients are usually busy, and Matt might be out of contact with them for weeks. When this happens, Matt sends an invoice for the work that he has completed, even though the site is not finished. This helps to remind a client that work is in progress, and it brings money into Matt's business in the meantime.

To keep up to date with the latest Internet market information, Matt pays close attention to the news. Many articles proclaim new products as the "future of the Internet." Matt analyzes these articles and researches products to find out if they could help his business grow. Also, Matt learns new techniques of web design by searching the Web and studying other business web sites.

Matt has served many clients since he launched his web design venture in the summer of 2000. Although prices vary for individual sites, Matt generally charges between $800 and $1,500 per site—a low cost considering the quality of his work.

Matt has learned to balance his business activities and the demanding workload of high school. At first it was difficult. Matt would spend either too much time on his business, or too much time on schoolwork. While one would receive all of Matt's attention, the other would suffer. Once Matt realized this, he trained himself to balance the two by designating certain times for each. By sticking to a time schedule, Matt has been successful with business and school.

THINK CRITICALLY

1. List three obstacles Matt had to overcome as an entrepreneur.

2. What factor has allowed young web designers to create work for people around the world?

3. How should billing be handled for a web design business? Why?

4. How does a young person balance school and a challenging career?

http://www.deca.org/publications/HS_Guide/guidetoc.html

DECA PREP

TECHNICAL MARKETING REPRESENTATIVE EVENT

One of your clients is a specialty grocery store called Ideal Grocery, located in Waverly, population 25,000. Waverly's population represents two primary marketing targets: families who still own working farms, and wealthy families who commute to the nearby city for work but choose to live in spacious homes on large lots. Customers demand the grocery basics, but they also have sophisticated tastes and often request international foods and unique items. Ideal Grocery has established good relations with vendors and has been able to satisfy its customers' requests reliably. Ideal also makes a nice profit margin on all special requests.

Because it is the sole supermarket in town, Ideal Grocery can be very busy, especially on weekends. There are six cashiers using scanners that were installed 10 years ago, but all produce still needs to be weighed on a separate scale. Despite experienced cashiers, the older technology causes lines to build.

The owners of Ideal Grocery want to improve the checkout system of their store to make the lines move faster. They are interested in learning more about new cash registers and other electronic equipment for maintaining inventory, pricing, scanning, weighing, and processing checkout transactions.

Feedback from cashiers shows a need for a more user-friendly transaction display so customers can easily check price accuracy; a desire by customers to use credit cards for purchases; and a desire to continue the popular Ideal Bonus Card that provides discounts, check approval, and buying points for customer loyalty. There is also a need for at least one wider aisle to accommodate wheelchairs, strollers, and bulky items. Aisles cannot be added due to the store's size; however, increasing the width of an existing aisle would not be a problem. Due to the high profit margin on special requests, Ideal has been able to budget $100,000 for the project.

DEFINE THE PLAN Describe the product(s) and define the target customer.

PREPARE THE SALES PRESENTATION Organize appropriate information, and present/defend a sales presentation.

GLOSSARY

A

accounting and finance function plans and manages financial resources for businesses and maintains records and information related to businesses' finances

advertising any paid form of nonpersonal communication sent through a mass medium by an organization about its products or services

advertising plan the activities and resources needed to prepare and present a series of related advertisements focusing on a common objective

analysis the process of summarizing, combining, or comparing information so that decisions can be made

approach the first contact with the customer when the salesperson gets the customer's attention and creates a favorable impression

B

balance of trade the difference between the amount of a country's imports and exports

balance sheet accounting statement that describes the type and amount of assets, liabilities, and capital in a business on a specific date

bartering exchanging products or services with others by agreeing on their values

basic stock list identifies the minimum amount of important products a store needs to have available to meet the needs of its target market

benefit the advantage provided to a customer as a result of a feature of the product

benefits derived segmentation technique that divides the population into groups depending on the value they receive from the product or service

bidding several suppliers develop specific prices at which they will meet detailed purchase specifications and other criteria prepared by the buyer

bill of lading form sent with the merchandise identifying the products that are being shipped

boycott an organized effort to influence a company by refusing to purchase its products

brand a name, symbol, word, or design that identifies a product, service, or company

breakeven point the quantity of a product that must be sold for total revenues to match total costs at a specific price

bricks and mortar business company that completes most of its business activities by means other than the Internet

budgets detailed projections of financial performance for a specific time period, usually a year or less

bundling the practice of combining the price of several related services

business consumer buyer of goods and services to produce and market other goods and services or for resale

business markets the companies and organizations that purchase products for the operation of a business or the completion of a business activity

business plan a written document prepared to guide the development and operation of a new business

buying behavior the decision processes and actions of consumers as they buy and use services and products

buying motives the reasons that consumers buy products

C

capital expenses long-term investments in land, buildings, and equipment

career area the area of business or the business function in which you plan to work

career path a series of related jobs with increasing knowledge and skill requirements and greater amounts of responsibility

career plan identifies the progression of jobs in your career path, your plans for education, training, and experience to meet the requirements for those jobs, and a tentative time schedule for accomplishing the plan

career portfolio an organized collection of information and materials developed to represent yourself, your preparation, and your accomplishments

central market a location where people bring products to be conveniently exchanged

channel members businesses and other organizations that participate in a channel of distribution

channel of distribution the organizations and individuals who participate in the movement and exchange of products and services from the producer to the final consumer

charter a legal document allowing the corporation to operate as if it were a person

close point point in the sales process when a customer makes a decision to purchase

closed-ended questions survey questions that offer two or more choices from which respondents can select answers

code of ethics a statement of responsibilities for honest and proper conduct

cold calling method of selling where a salesperson contacts a large number of people who are conveniently located, without knowing a great deal about each person contacted

communication process the transfer of a message from a sender to a receiver

comparison shopping people are sent to competitors' stores to determine products that are sold, prices charged, and services offered

consumer behavior the study of consumers and how they make decisions

consumer credit credit extended by a retail business to the final consumer

consumer markets markets made up of individuals or socially related groups who purchase products for personal consumption

consumerism the organized actions of groups of consumers seeking to increase their influence on business practices

continuity scheduling an advertisement regularly throughout the year; a common timing technique for products that do not have seasonal swings

controllable risks risks that can be reduced or even avoided by actions a person takes

controlled economy the government attempts to own and control important resources and to make the decisions about what will be produced and consumed

controlling management function that measures performance, compares it with goals and objectives, and makes corrections when necessary

convenience stores stores located very close to their customers, offering a limited line of products that consumers use regularly

cookies small files that a web server sends to your browser when you access a site

corporation a business owned by people who purchase stock in the company, granted a charter by the state in which they are formed

culture the common beliefs and behaviors of a group of people who have a similar heritage and experience

D

database a collection of data that is arranged in a logical manner and organized in a form that can be stored and processed by a computer

decoding interpreting the message or symbols and converting them into concepts and ideas

demand the quantity of a product consumers are willing and able to purchase at a specific price

demand curve graph showing the relationship between a product's price and the quantity demanded

demographics the descriptive characteristics of a market such as age, gender, race, income, and educational level

demonstration a personalized presentation of the features of the marketing mix in a way that emphasizes the benefits and value to the customer

derived demand the quantity of a product or service needed by a business in order to operate at a level that will meet the demand of its customers

direct channel movement of a product from the producer to the final consumer with no other organization involved

direct competition competition in a market segment with businesses that offer the same type of product or service

direct demand the quantity of a product or service needed to meet the needs of the consumer

direct exporting a company takes complete responsibility for marketing its products in other countries

discounts and allowances reductions in a price given to the customer in exchange for performing certain marketing activities or accepting something other than what would normally be expected in the exchange

discretionary spending the amount of total income left after paying taxes and basic living expenses

distribution a part of the marketing mix that is the locations and methods used to make the product available to customers

GLOSSARY

distribution center a facility used to accumulate products from several sources and then regroup, repackage, and send them as quickly as possible to the locations where they will be used

distribution function involves determining the best methods and procedures to use so prospective customers can locate, obtain, and use a business's products and services

dot.com business company that does almost all of its business activities through the Internet

E

e-commerce the exchange of goods, services, information, or other business through electronic means

economic market all of the consumers who will purchase a particular product or service

economic resources natural resources, capital, equipment, and labor

economic utility the amount of satisfaction a consumer receives from the consumption of a particular product or service

elastic demand market situation in which a price decrease will increase total revenue

elasticity of demand the relationship between changes in a product's price and the demand for that product, based on the number of good substitutes for a product and the willingness of consumers to go without a product if the price gets too high

emergency goods convenience goods that are purchased as a result of an urgent need

emotional motives reasons to purchase based on feelings, beliefs, or attitudes

encoding putting the message into language or symbols that are familiar to the intended receiver

entrepreneur someone who takes the risk to start a new business

entrepreneurship the process of planning, creating, and managing a new business

ethics decisions and behavior based on honest and fair standards

evaluation measuring how well the advertising plan achieves its original objectives

experiments tightly controlled situations in which all important factors are the same except the one being studied

exports products and services that are sold to another country

external information provides an understanding of factors outside of the organization

F

feature a description of a product characteristic

feedback the receiver's reaction or response to the source's message

final consumer buyer of a product or service for personal use

financial forecasts numerical predictions of future performance related to revenue and expenses, usually made for a period of at least a year or more into the future

financial statements detailed summaries of the specific financial performance for a business or a part of the business

financing budgeting for marketing activities, obtaining the necessary financing, and providing financial assistance to customers to assist them with purchasing the organization's products and services

flexible pricing policy that allows customers to negotiate the price of a product within a price range

FOB (free on board) pricing a method for setting transportation costs based on geographic location; it identifies the location from which the buyer pays the transportation costs and takes title to the products purchased

focus group a small number of people brought together to discuss identified elements of an issue or problem

follow-up making contact with the customer after the sale to ensure satisfaction

form utility increasing economic utility by changing the tangible parts of a product or service

foreign investment owning all or part of an existing business in another country

foreign production a company owns and operates production facilities in another country

form utility results from changes in the tangible parts of a product or service

free economy resources are owned by individuals rather than the government, and decisions are made independently with no attempt at regulation or control by the government

G

GDP (gross domestic product) the total value of the goods and services produced in a country during the year

geographic segmentation dividing consumers into markets based on where they live

gross margin the amount that is available to cover the business' expenses and provide a profit on the sale of the product

H

heterogeneous differences between services

I

image a unique, memorable quality of a brand

imports products or services purchased from another country

impulse goods convenience goods that are purchased without advance planning

income statement accounting form that reports on the amount and source of revenue and the amount and type of expenses for a specific period of time

indirect channel movement of a product that includes other businesses between the producer and consumer that provide one or more of the marketing functions

indirect competition occurs when a business has a product that competes outside its product classification group

indirect exporting the process in which marketing businesses with exporting experience serve as agents for a business with less international experience and arrange for the sale of products in other countries

industrial economy economy in which the primary business activity is the manufacturing of products

inelastic demand market situation in which a price decrease will decrease total revenue

inflation economic situation where prices increase faster than the value of the goods and services

input the information that goes into the system that is needed for decision-making

inseparable the service is produced and consumed at the same time

intangible the service cannot be touched, seen, tasted, heard, or felt

internal information information developed from activities that occur within the organization

international trade the sale of products and services to people in other countries

interpersonal communication two or more people in some kind of person-to-person exchange

inventory the assortment and quantities of products the company maintains for sale to customers

inventory records record of the products that have been received by a company

invoice the bill for the merchandise, which lists all of the items purchased that are included in the order

J

joint venture business relationship in which independent companies participate in common business activities

just-in-time purchasing method of purchasing in which a company develops a relationship with its suppliers to keep inventory levels low and to resupply inventory just as it is needed

L

labor intensiveness the amount of human effort required to deliver a service

law of demand when the price of a product is increased, less will be demanded, and when the price is decreased, more will be demanded

law of supply when the price of a product is increased, more will be produced, and when the price is decreased, less will be produced

leading the ability to communicate the direction of the business and to influence others to successfully carry out the needed work

liability a legal responsibility for loss or damage

licensed brand a well-known name or symbol established by one company and sold for use by another company to promote its products

M

macroeconomics study of the economic behavior and relationships of the entire society

management and administration function develops, implements, and evaluates the plans and activities of a business

managing getting the work of an organization done through other people and resources

markdown a reduction from the original selling price

market the description of the prospective customers a business wants to serve and the location of those customers

market opportunity analysis studying and prioritizing market segments to locate the best potential based on demand and competition

market position the unique image of a product or service in a consumer's mind relative to similar competitive offerings

market potential the total revenue that can be obtained from the market segment

market price the point where supply and demand for a product are equal

market segment a group of individuals or organizations within a larger market that share one or more important characteristics

market share the portion of the total market potential that each company expects to get in relation to its competitors

marketing the creation and maintenance of satisfying exchange relationships

marketing concept using the needs of customers as the primary focus during the planning, production, distribution, and promotion of a product or service

Marketing Education program incorporates three types of complementary learning experiences—introductory and advanced courses in marketing, structured work experiences through internships and cooperative education, and a student organization called DECA

marketing information system (MkIS, pronounced M-K-I-S) an organized method of collecting, storing, analyzing, and retrieving information to improve the effectiveness and efficiency of marketing decisions

marketing mix all of the tools or activities available to organizations to be used in meeting the needs of a target market; the blending of the four marketing elements (product, distribution, price, and promotion) by a business

marketing plan a clear written description of the marketing strategies of a business and the way the business will operate to accomplish each strategy

marketing research a procedure designed to identify solutions to a specific marketing problem through the use of scientific problem-solving

marketing strategy the way marketing activities are planned and coordinated to achieve an organization's goals

markup an amount added to the cost of a product to determine the selling price

mass communication communicating to huge audiences, usually through mass media such as magazines, radio, television, or newspapers

merchandise plan identifies the type, price, and features of products that will be stocked by the business for a specific period of time

merchandising offering products produced or manufactured by others for sale to customers

message channel the medium the sender chooses to transmit the message

microeconomics study of relationships between individual consumers and producers

mixed merchandise stores stores that offer products from several different categories

model stock list describes the complete assortment of products a store would like to offer to customers

money system the use of currency as a recognized medium of exchange

monopolistic competition market situation in which there are many firms competing with products that are somewhat different

monopoly a type of market in which there is one supplier offering a unique product

multinational companies businesses that have operations throughout the world and that conduct planning for worldwide markets

N

NAICS (North American Industry Classification System) a tool for identifying organizations in similar industries and classifying their primary activities, size, location, and other descriptive information

need anything required to live

neighborhood centers shopping centers having between 20 and 30 stores that offer a broad range of products to meet the regular and frequent shopping needs of consumers located within a few miles of the stores

net profit the difference between the selling price and all costs and operating expenses associated with the product sold

noise interference that can cause the message to be interpreted by the receiver incorrectly

noninsurable risks risks for which it is not possible to predict if a loss will occur or the amount of any loss that might occur

non-price competition occurs when businesses de-emphasize price by developing a unique offering that meets an important customer need

non-store retailing selling directly to the consumer's home rather than requiring the consumer to travel to a store

O

objectives the desired results to be accomplished within a certain time period

observation collecting information by recording actions without interacting or communicating with the participant

oligopoly a type of market in which a few businesses offer very similar products or services

one-price policy all customers pay the same price

open-ended question a type of survey question that allows respondents to develop their own answers without information about possible choices

operating expenses all costs associated with actual business operations

operations the ongoing activities that support the primary function of a business and keep a business operating efficiently

opportunity the possibility for success

organizational advertising ads designed to promote ideas, images, and issues associated with a company or organization

output the result of analysis given to decision-makers

P

packing list an itemized listing of all of the products included in the order

partnership a business owned and operated by two or more people who share in the decision making and profitability of the company

partnership agreement a legal document that specifies the responsibilities and financial relationships of the partners

patronage motives buying motives based on loyalty

penetration price a very low price designed to increase the quantity sold of a product by emphasizing the value

perishable services unused in one time period cannot be stored for use in the future

perpetual inventory inventory system that determines the amount of a product on hand by maintaining records on purchases and sales

personal selling person-to-person communication with potential customers in an effort to inform, persuade, or remind them to purchase an organization's products or services

personality a well-defined, enduring pattern of behavior

physical distribution includes transportation, storage, and handling of products within a channel of distribution

physical inventory inventory system in which the amount of product on hand is determined by visually inspecting and counting the items

place utility making products and services available where the consumer wants them

planning management function that involves analyzing information, setting goals, and determining how to achieve them

population all of the people in the group the company is interested in studying

possession utility results from the affordability of the product or service

postindustrial economy economy that is based on a mix of industrial and consumer products and services produced and marketed using high-tech equipment and methods that are purchased and sold in the global marketplace

preapproach gathering needed information and preparing for the sales presentation before contacting the customer

predatory pricing setting prices artificially low in order to drive out competitors

GLOSSARY

preindustrial economy economy that is based on agriculture and raw material development through activities such as mining, oil production, and cutting timber

price the actual amount that customers pay and the methods of increasing the value of the product to the customers

price competition competition among businesses on the basis of price and value

price lines distinct categories within which products are organized based on differences in price, quality, and features

pricing establishing and communicating the value of products and services to prospective customers

primary data information collected for the first time to solve the problem being studied

private enterprise a market situation in which independent decisions are made by businesses and consumers with only a limited government role regulating those relationships

product anything offered to a market by a business to satisfy needs, including physical products, services, and ideas

product advertising used by organizations to sell specific products

product assortment the complete set of all products a business offers to its market

product liability insurance provides protection from claims arising from the use of the company's products

product line a group of similar products with slight variations in the marketing mix to satisfy different needs in a market

product usage the frequency with which consumers use a product

product/service planning assisting in the design and development of products and services that will meet the needs of prospective customers

product/service purchase classification system a description of the way consumers shop for products based on their needs and perception of products

production function creates or obtains products or services for sale

profit motive a decision to use resources in a way that results in the greatest profit for the producer

promotion any form of communication used to inform, persuade, or remind consumers about an organization's goods or services

promotional mix a blend of the promotional elements of advertising, personal selling, publicity, and sales promotion into a strategy for delivering a message to the target market

promotional plan a carefully arranged sequence of promotions designed around a common theme responsive to specific objectives

proprietorship a business owned and managed by one person

psychographics a way of segmenting a market according to people's interests and values

publicity a nonpaid form of communication about a business or organization (or its products and services) that is transmitted through a mass medium

pulsing advertisers increase their advertising efforts during a specific period of time and decrease or even withdraw their advertising during another period of time

purchase order a form describing all of the products ordered; it is completed by the buyer and sent to the seller to begin the purchasing process

purchase specifications detailed requirements for construction or performance of the product

purchasing power the amount of goods and services that can be obtained with a specific amount of money

pure competition a type of market in which there are a large number of suppliers offering very similar products

pure risks risks that present the chance of loss but no opportunity for gain

Q

qualifying gathering information to determine which people are most likely to buy

quotas limits on the numbers of specific types of products foreign companies can sell in the country

R

random sampling a procedure in which everyone in the population has an equal chance of being selected in the sample

rational motives buying motives based on facts or logic

receiver the person or persons to whom the encoded message is directed

receiving record a list of all of the merchandise in the shipment

recession a period of time in which production, employment, and income are declining

reciprocal trading a form of bartering in which products or services of one company are used as payment for the products of another company

reference groups groups or organizations from which people take their values and attitudes

regional shopping centers large shopping centers that contain 100 or more businesses attempting to meet most or all of consumers' shopping needs

regulated economy a type of market in which the resources and decisions are shared between the government and other groups or individuals

reorder point the level of inventory needed to meet the usage needs of the business until the product can be resupplied

request for proposal a general description of the type of product or service needed and the criteria that are important to the buyer

retailer the final business organization in an indirect channel of distribution for consumer products

revenue the money received from the sale of products and services

risk the possibility that a loss can occur as the result of a decision or activity

risk management providing security and safety for products, personnel, and customers, as well as reducing the risk associated with marketing decisions and activities

Rule of 72 a tool for estimating how fast a market share can be doubled

S

sales promotions activities or materials that offer consumers a direct incentive to buy a good or service

scarcity unlimited wants and needs, combined with limited resources

secondary data information already collected for another purpose that can be used to solve the current problem

segments components of a market in which people have one or more similar characteristics

self-regulation taking personal responsibility for actions

self-sufficient not relying on others for the things needed in order to survive

selling direct, personal communications with prospective customers in order to assess needs and satisfy those needs with appropriate products and services

sender the source or originator of the message in the communication process

service quality the degree to which the service meets customers' needs and expectations

services activities that are intangible, exchanged directly from producer to consumer, and consumed at the time of production

shopping center a set of stores located together and planned as a unit to meet a range of customer needs

shopping goods purchases that satisfy important needs, are of a significant cost, and for which real differences exist between products

shopping strip small shopping center containing about 5 to 15 stores grouped together along a street, offering a limited number of emergency and convenience products such as fast food, gasoline, and laundry services

simulations experiments operated in laboratories where researchers create the situation to be studied

single- or limited-line stores stores that offer products from one category of merchandise or closely related items

skimming price a very high price designed to emphasize the quality or uniqueness of the product, even though it attracts fewer customers

social class the lifestyle, values, and beliefs that are common to a group of people

social responsibility concern about the consequences of actions on society

specialization of labor concentrating effort on one or a few related activities so that they can be done well

INDEX

Business ownership
  deciding on, **575–577**
  identifying opportunities,
    573–574
  starting new business, **562–564,
    578**
Business plan, **580–581**
Business planning, for
  entrepreneur, **579–580**
Business practices, improving,
  46–47
Business publications, **123–124**
Business purchasing. *See*
  Purchasing
Business risk, nature of, **508–511**
Business roles, differentiating,
  103–105
Business skills, for entrepreneurs,
  570
Business success, measuring,
  600–601
Business-to-business, reasons for
  purchases, **312–313**
Buyers, **317**. *See also*
  Consumer(s); Customer(s)
Buyer/seller relationship, in
  business-to-business, **317**
Buying behavior, **152–153**
Buying motives, **150–151**

C

Calvin Klein, **442**
Capital equipment, **275**
Capital expenses, **536**
Career area, **621**
Career path
  choosing, **629**
  defined, **621**
Career plan
  defined, **621**
  developing, **633–634**
Career planning, **620–621**
Career portfolio, preparing,
  634–636
Cause-related marketing, **414**
CBS, **450**

Cease-and-desist orders, **433**
Central markets, **12**
Century TV, *This Old House* and,
  478
Channel members, **104, 351**
Channel of distribution. *See*
  Distribution channels
Character format, **443**
Charter, **577**
Checkers restaurant, **112**
Children's Hospital, **426**
Chiquita, **84**
Chrysler, **47, 84**
Chuck E. Cheese's, **420**
Cingular, **450**
Clearinghouses, **393**
Closed-ended questions, **134**
Closing, **471**
Clutter, **443**
Co-branding, **391**
Coca-Cola Company, **286–287, 515**
Codes of ethics, **46**
Cohen, Ben, **563**
Cold calling, **462**
Collections, **395**
Collins, Key, **30–31**
Communication
  importance of skills, **568–569**
  media, high-tech and high-touch,
    331
  promotion as, **406–408**
  types of, **409**
Company
  changes outside, **242**
  multinational, **490–491**
  performance, marketing plan
    and, **242**
Compaq Computer Corp., **521**
Comparison shopping
  defined, **331**
  Internet, **389**
Competition, **115**
  in airline industry, **56**
  benefits of, **179**
  Coca Cola versus Pepsi,
    286–287

  direct versus indirect, **176–177**
  globalization and, **494**
  government regulation of, **382**
  handling, **64–65**
  intense, **100–101**. *See also*
    Oligopolies; Pure competition
  limited, **101–102**
  for new business, **574**
  non-price, **392**
  performance of, **428**
  positioning strategy and, **174**
  price versus non-price, **177–178**
  pricing and, **390–392**
  primary, **246**
  responding to, **100–102**
  salesperson's understanding of,
    467
  services and, **299**
  types of, **68–74**
  understanding, **74**
  See also Comparison shopping
Competition matching approach,
  437
Competitor positioning strategy, **173**
Component parts, **276**
Consumer(s), **61**
  behavior of, **146–147**
  final and business, **324**
  in foreign markets, **495–496**
  information about, **117**
  personality of, **154–155**
  producers and, adjusting differ-
    ences between, **348–349**
  stages in decision-making,
    98–100
Consumer Bill of Rights, **45**
Consumer information, online,
  208–209
Consumerism, growth of, **45–46**
Consumer markets, **272–273, 277**
Consumer perceptions, positioning
  strategy and, **174**
Consumer protection, **44–46**
Consumer purchase classifications,
  391
Continental Airlines, **286**
Continuity scheduling, **443**
Controllable risks, **510**

Controlled economy, **59**

Controlling
as management function, **595**
responsibilities, **607**

Convenience, ATMs, **298**

Convenience goods, **236–239**

Convenience stores, **361**

Cookies, **204**

Co-pays. *See* Health maintenance organizations (HMOs)

Corporation, **577**

Corrective advertising, **433**

Costco Wholesale, **356**

Cost per thousand (CPM), **439, 441**

Costs
advertising media, **439**
average and incremental, **319**
distribution, **552**
effects of marketing on, **36**
inventory, **536–537**
marketing mix and, **551–553**
operating, **388, 537**
of personal selling, **457–458**
reducing and controlling, **545**
See also Marketing costs

Coupons, **385**
online, **209**
processed in Mexico, **393**

Credit, **549–551**
developing procedures for, **394–395**
offering, **394–395**
types of, **394**

Credit approval, **395**

Credit cards, **549–550**

Credit policies, **395**

Croemers department store, **218**

Culture
defined, **155**
in foreign markets, **496**

Currency, euro, **293**

Currency rates, **488**

Customer(s)
cost per, for personal selling, **458**
identifying, **461–463**
information about current and prospective, **242–243**

knowledge of, **92–94, 461–464**
qualifying prospective, **463**
responsibility toward, **48**
satisfied versus hard-to-please, **539**
understanding decisions of, **464**
See also Consumer(s)

Customer contact, **297–298**

Customer feedback, Internet services for, **37**

Customer management, **460**

Customer needs
consequences of not meeting, **18**
determining, **330–331**
different levels of, **149**
focusing on, **90**
identifying, **92–94**
personal selling and, **455**
products and, **260–261**
recognition of, **99**
risk of change and, **514**
satisfying, **17–18, 94, 330–332**
See also Hierarchy of needs

Customer records, **120–121**

Customer retention, through e-mail promotions, **407**

Customer satisfaction, **35, 535**
measuring, **600**
service, **299**

Customer service, online, **204–205**

Customs, selling and, **499**

D

Daddy-O's restaurant, **112**

Data. *See* Information

Databases
direct mail, **157**
household purchasing, **172**
scanner-based information, **93**
uses in marketing, **22, 59**

Data-collection procedure, developing, **129–130**

Data services, **124**

Decision-making
consumer's process of, **152–153**
extensive, **157**

influences on consumer, **154–155**
limited, **156**
marketers' response to, **157**
MkIS and, **127**
routine, **156**
stages in, **98–100**
types of, **156–157**
understanding customers', **464**

Decoding, **407**

Dee's Designs, **90**

Demand
defined, **61, 312**
derived, **274**
direct, **272, 351**
elasticity of, **381**
factors affecting, **63**
microeconomics and, **62–64**
See also Customer needs; Supply and demand

Demand curve
analyzing, **63–64**
measuring, **73**

Demographics, **167**

Demonstration, **469**

Derived demand, **274**

Direct demand, **272, 351**

Direct exporting, **487**

Direct mail, databases, **157**

Discounts and allowances, **393**

Discovery Channel, *The Christopher Lowell Show* and, **478**

Discovery Home and Leisure, *This Old House* and, **478**

Discretionary spending, **222**

Disney Co., **84, 412**

Distribution, **6–7, 227**
business opportunities in, **572**
career in, **625**
competitors', **181**
decisions regarding, **95–96**
defined, **20, 344**
for e-commerce, **201–203**
as economic concept, **344**
expenses related to, **552**
in foreign markets, **498–499**
importance of, **342–344**

INDEX

as marketing mix element, **344**
online, **203–205**
physical, **364**
risks to, **515–517**
sales support and, **473**
of services, **302–303**
See also Transportation

Distribution centers, **367–368**

Distribution channels, **347–350**
developing and managing system, **352–353**
planning and managing, **351–353**

Distribution function, **343**

Distribution system, development of, **344–346**

Diversity programs, **313**

Dominique Designs, **116–117**

Dot.com businesses, **193**

Douglas, Matt, **642–643**

Dun & Bradstreet, **124**

DuPont Chemical Co., **432**

E

eBay, **374**

E-commerce, **192–194**
advantages and disadvantages of, **195–196**
defined, **192**
distribution for, **201–203**
marketing concept applied to, **196**
promotion for, **209–211**
stages of development, **194**
See also E-marketing

Economic concept, price as, **380–381**

Economic environment, of foreign markets, **492–495**

Economic forces, interplay of, **61**

Economic market, **64**

Economics, importance of understanding, **58–59**

Economic systems
types of, **59**
See also Private enterprise economy

Economic utility, **75**

Economy
foreign market's state of, **495**
importance of entrepreneurs to, **564–565**
marketing jobs and, **617–618**
risk of change and, **514**

Education
experience and, **632–633**
See also Marketing education

Edu-Games, **344–346**

Elastic demand, **381**

Elasticity of demand, **73, 380–381**

Electronic data exchange (EDI), **314**

E-mail lists, **209**

E-mail promotions, **407**

E-marketing, **5**
ad formats, **591**
application service providers, **301**
banner advertising, **441**
basic Internet business models, **5**
e-procurement systems, **326**
free Internet services, **548**
global opportunities, **149**
Internet advertising, **389**
Internet job services, **457**
Internet use by small businesses, **572**
m-commerce, **516**
online auctions, **60**
Procter & Gamble's Whitestrips, **88**
providing details on web sites, **412**
searching for information, **39**
value of "dot.coms," **177**
wireless technology in Asia and Europe, **484**
See also E-mail promotions; Internet promotion

Emergency goods, **233–234**

Emotional motives, **150–151**

Employee satisfaction, **561, 614**

Employment
applying for, **636–637**
getting right job, **634–637**

international, **629**

Employment opportunities, **36**
in marketing, **617**
online, **635**

Encoding, **406**

Endorsements, **301**

English, as language of international trade, **483**

Entrepreneur
characteristics of, **566–567**
defined, **563**
presentations by, **563**
women and minority, **560**

Entrepreneurship
defined, **563**
importance of, **564–565**
preparing for, **569–570**
See also Business ownership; Partnership; Proprietorship

Environment, packaging and, **270**

Equifax, **124**

Esquire magazine, reader research, **408**

Ethics, **47–49**
billable time, **297**
buyer-supplier relationships, **333**
defined, **47**
"dumpster diving," **123**
in Japanese companies, **598**
price fixing, **382**
respecting confidentiality, **236**
super squirt guns, **32**
technologically monitoring employees, **604**
See also Codes of ethics

Ethnic media, **440**

E-Trade, **450**

Euro, **293**

European Bank for Reconstruction and Development (EBRD), **547**

Evaluation, **444**

Evaluation procedures, for marketing plan, **251**

Expected value, **520**

Expenses. *See* Cost(s)

Experiments
marketing research, **136–137**
See also Testing

Exporting, importance of, **487–488**

Exports, **484**

External environment analysis, **247**

External information sources, **122–124**

Eye-tracking research, **246**

F

False advertising. *See* Advertising, regulating

Fanning, Shawn, **528**

Fantasy format, **442**

Feature, **466**

Federal Express, **300, 400, 564**

Feedback
  defined, **408**
  with personal selling, **456**

Feldman, Ed, **479**

Fields, Debbi, **586–587**

Fifth Third Bank, **605**

Final consumer, **146**

Finances, importance of, **532–533**

Financial analysis, **601**
  new product, **280–281**

Financial forecasts, **537**

Financial information, analyzing, **543–545**

Financial planning, marketing and, **533–534**

Financial statements
  defined, **540**
  gathering information for, **533**

Financial tools, using, **542–543**

Financing, **6**
  business opportunities in, **573**
  career in, **626**
  foreign markets and, **498**
  international purchasing, **323**
  sales support and, **473**

Firestone, **612–613**

Fisher-Price, **84**

Flexibility, with personal selling, **456**

Flexible pricing policy, **392**

Focus group
  defined, **134–135**
  to evaluate ad's effectiveness, **444**

Follow-up
  defined, **472**
  to personal selling, **457**

Ford, Henry, **562**

Ford Explorer, **612–613**

Forecasts, **538–539, 542**

Foreign investment, **489**

Foreign markets
  designing web site for, **576**
  economic environment of, **492–495**
  finding right mix for, **495–497**
  gathering information about, **497–498**
  See also International trade

Foreign production, **488**

Form utility, **75**

Franchising, growth of, **363**

Free on board (FOB) pricing, **393**

Free economy, **59**

Free samples, **262**

Frequency, advertising media and, **440**

Frito-Lay, **450, 530**

Full disclosure, **433**

G

Gates, Bill, **562**

General Electric, **47, 552**

General Mills, **112, 262**

General Motors Corp., **7–8, 391, 412, 491**
  Saturn division, **164**

Geographic pricing, **393**

Geographic segmentation, **165–166**

Glass ceiling, **560**

Global market, **115**
  advertising, **148**
  business purchasing, **322–323**
  international jobs, **629**
  retailing, **363**
  See also Foreign markets; International trade

Goals. *See* Objectives

Gourmet magazine, reader research, **408**

Government
  assistance with international marketing, **486**
  as business consumers, **315**
  effect on prices, **382–383**
  in foreign markets, **497**
  in private enterprise economy, **61**

Government regulation, **45–46**
  of competition, **382**
  of credit, **551**

Government reports, **122–123**

Gray marketing, **95**

Greenfield, Jerry, **563**

Gross Domestic Product (GDP), **495**

Gross margin, **388**

Gross profit margin, **104**

Guarantee/warranty, **226**

H

Harm and accountability, **48–49**

Health maintenance organizations (HMOs), establishing value at, **376**

Healthy Families America, **427**

Hershey Foods Corp., **417–418**

Hertz, **8, 400**

Heterogeneous, **294**

Hierarchy of needs, **147–148**

Hill, Kim and Fred, **426**

Hirschfield, David, **338**

Hispanic market
  Chuck E. Cheese's appeal to, **420**
  reaching, **153**

Home and Garden Television, *This Old House Classics* and, **478**

Home Depot, **478–479**

HotJobs, **450**

Hypermarkets, in Asia, **490**

I

IBM, teamwork at, **606**

Idea development and screening, **279–280**

INDEX

Ideal Summary, 559

Image
- brand name and, **226**
- price's effect on, **385**
- versus value, **340**

Imports, **483**

Impulse goods, **233**

Income statement, **540**

Incremental cost, **319**

Indirect channel, **351**

Indirect exporting, **487**

Industrial economies, **494**

Industry, marketing careers in, **630–631**

Inelastic demand, **381**

Inflation, **495**

Infomercials, **441**

Information
- analyzing, **131–132**
- categories of, **116–118**
- collecting, **130**
- about competitors, **180–183**
- consumer's search for, **152**
- for developing marketing plan, **242–243**
- gained through personal selling, **456**
- gathering, for product development, **263–264**
- internal sources of, **120–121**
- marketing research, **130–132**
- numerical, **131**
- online security, **203–204**
- as promotion task, **405**
- salesperson's sources of, **466**
- sources of, **119–124**
- using Internet to gather, **199–200**. See also Cookies
- See also Databases; Marketing research; Marketing information system (MkIS)

Information management, for salespeople, **460**

Information processing, physical distribution, **368–369**

Input, for MkIS, **125**

Inseparable, **292**

Insurability of risk, **510–511**

Insurance, as risk management, **522–523**

Intangible, **292**

Intel, **521**

Interest, credit and, **549–551**

Internal analysis, **247**

Internal information sources, **120–121**

International trade, **38**
- changing nature of, **484–485**
- defined, **483**
- economic environment for, **492–495**
- marketing activities, **497–499**
- supplier qualifications, **322**
- U.S. and, **482–485**
- why businesses enter into, **485–486**
- See also Trade agreements

Internet
- businesses, **193**
- business uses of, **198–200**
- countries' use of, **197, 202**
- feedback services, **37**
- growth of, **197–198**
- marketing and, **195–196**
- promotion, **206–209**
- users, communicating with, **206–209**
- See also E-commerce; E-marketing; Web site

Interpersonal communication, **409**

Interview, job, **637**

Inventory
- defined, **328, 536**
- expenses, **536–537**
- tracked by scanner, **93**

Inventory control, **369**

Inventory records, **328, 329**

Investment
- foreign, **489**
- return on, **574**

"Invisible packaging" services, **356**

Invoice, **329**

J

J'Borg Apparel, **116–117**

JC Penney, ethnic media campaign, **440**

Jennings, Lynette, **478–479**

Johnson & Johnson, **405**

Joint venture, **489–490**

Jones, Marion, **400**

Jordan, Michael, **400**

Just-in-time (JIT) purchasing, **327**

K

Kellogg's, ad theme, **437**

Kentucky Fried Chicken, **286, 586**

Kickbacks, **496**

Kmart, **378, 478**

Kodak, **84, 169–170**

L

Labeling
- bar codes and smart labels, **345**
- regulating, **258**

Labor intensiveness, **297**

Laczi, Tibor, **568**

Law of supply, **65**

Lawyers, promoting, **288**

L'Erario, Joe, **479**

Leadership skills, **606**

Leading, as management function, **595**

Lead time, of advertising media, **440**

Learning Channel, **478-479**
- *Furniture to Go*, **478–479**
- *Men in Toolbelts*, **478–479**

Levi's, **84**

Liability, **515**

Licensed brand, **271**

Lifestyle format, **443**

Lifetime, *Next Door with Katie Brown*, **478**

Limited-line stores, **361**

Listerine, corrective ads, **433**

Living.com, **374**

Location, producers and consumers and, **348**

Lowell, Christopher, **478–479**
Lowe's Home Improvement, **478–479**

M

Macroeconomics, **62**

Mad cow disease, **227**

Management
coordinating people and resources, **590–592**
functions and activities of, **593–595**
of marketers, **605–607**
moving into, **629**
for salespeople, **459–460**

Management and administration function, **14–15**

Managers, as leaders, **598–599**

Managing, **591**

Markdowns, **389**

Market(s)
analyzing, **244–247, 419**
business. *See* Business markets
central, **12**
changing, **115–116**
consumer. *See* Consumer markets
Hispanic, **153, 416**
identifying, **19**
international. *See* Foreign markets; Global market; International trade
targeting, **218**
test, **137**
type of service, **296**
wholesalers' access to, **357–358**
See also Target market

Marketing, **15**
benefits to people, **35–36**
benefits to society, **37–38**
business development and, **11–12**
business opportunities in, **571–573**
cause-related, **414**
changes in, **21–25, 86–88**
common complaints about, **39–42**
defining, **8–9**

determining effectiveness of, **600–601**
effects on businesses, **34–35**
effects on revenue, **546–551**
entrepreneurship opportunities in, **564**
gaining control of, **599**
importance of, **25**
improved standards of living and, **38**
increasing efficiency of, **350**
international, assistance with, **486**
Internet and, **195–196**. *See also* E-marketing
job levels in, **622–623**
misuse of, **17**
as money-waster, **41**
need for, **10–11**
in non-business organizations, **25, 105**
as problem-solver, **42–43**
product, **281**
product development and, **263–264**
reasons for studying, **4–6**
relationship, **30–31**
response to consumer decisions, **157**
role of, **262–263**
role of promotion in, **404–406**
to segments, **114–116**
U.S. expertise in, **2**
See also Advertising; E-marketing; Promotion

Marketing career
importance of, **616–618**
job progression, **621–623**
non-management, **630**
paths, **630–631**
reasons for choosing, **619–620**
skills for, **624–626**

Marketing concept, **16–18**
adjusting to, **88–90**
applied to distribution channel, **353**
applied to e-commerce, **196**
changing role of, **23–24**
effect on planning, **92**
implementing, **19–20**

Marketing costs
business success and, **532–534**
financing activities, **535–537**
long- and short-term, **534–535**
managing, **534–537**

Marketing department, changing role of, **22–23**

Marketing education, **624**
benefits of, **627–628**

Marketing education program, **628**

Marketing Ethics, Channel One News, **48**

Marketing function(s), **6–7**
career paths in, **631**
careers specializing in, **625–626**
channels of distribution and, **349–350**
companies' use of, **7–8**
product development as, **262–264**
purchasing as, **313**

Marketing-information management, **7**
business opportunities in, **573**
career in, **626**
for foreign markets, **499**
sales support and, **473**

Marketing information system (MkIS), **124–127**

Marketing management, **592**

Marketing mix, **19–20**
costs associated with, **551–553**
creating right, **95**
distribution as element, **344**
effects on finances, **534**
for foreign markets, **498**
information about, **117**
promotional mix and, **417**
risks to elements of, **514–517**
specifying, **249**
testing, **264**

Marketing plan, **239–240**
activity schedule, **250**
developing budget in, **542**
evaluation procedures, **251**
improving management with, **596–599**
outline, **245, 597**
planning for action, **250–251**

INDEX

Marketing planning
  benefits of, **238–240**
  handling risk with, **518–520**
  information for, **596–597**
  positions and responsibilities, **602–603**
  preparing for, **241–243**
Marketing research, **99–100, 128**
  gathering information, **130–132**
  magazine readers, **408**
  product development and, **263–264**
  proposing solution, **132–133**
  selecting participants, **130**
  surveys, **134–135**
  when to use, **133**
  See also Eye-tracking research; Testing
Marketing strategy
  defined, **220**
  marketing plan and, **239–240**
  review of current, **245**
  risk management and, **519**
Market opportunity analysis, **94**
Market position, competitors', **182**
Market potential, **169**
Market price, **67**
Market segments
  analyzing, **169–170**
  common characteristics, **221–222**
  defined, **94**
  differences between, **221**
  differentiating, **220–222**
  identifying, **165–167**
Market share, **169–170**
Markups, **104, 384**
Marriott, **286**
Mary Kay Cosmetics, **586**
Maslow, Abraham, **147–148**
Mass communication, **409**
Math skills, **569**
McDonald's, **47, 112**
  advertising, **411–412**
  direct and indirect competition, **177**
  international business, **504**
  Ronald McDonald House, **426–427**

understanding of marketing concept, **261**
Mean, **136**
Median, **136**
Megastore, **401**
Members Only, **47**
Merchandise plan, **331**
Merchandising, **13**
Message channel, **407**
Metallica, **528**
Microeconomics
  consumer demand and, **62–64**
  defined, **63**
Mills Clothing Store, Inc., **338**
Minorities
  depictions in advertisements, **428**
  entrepreneurship and, **560**
  See also African-Americans; Ethnic media; Hispanic market
Mission statement, **244**
Mixed merchandise stores, **361**
Model stock list, **332**
Modified purchase, **320**
Money systems, **12**
Monopolies, **69–70**
Monopolistic competition, **72–74, 102**
Monster.com, **450**
Mood format, **443**
Motel 6, **416**
Mrs. Fields, **587**
Multinational companies, **490–491**
Musical format, **442**

N

Naming rights, **35**
Napster, **528–529**
NBA, **400**
NASDAQ, **379**
NFL, **118**
Needs
  defined, **147**
  identifying, **324–325**
  See also Customer needs
Neighborhood centers, **361**

Netpliance.com, **450**
Net profit, **388**
New York Stock Exchange, **379**
NFC, **451**
Niches, restaurant, **112**
Nike, **47, 400–401**
Noise, in communication path, **408**
Non-business groups, marketing by, **25, 105**
Non-insurable risk, **510**
Non-numerical data, **131–132**
Non-price competition, **392**
Non-profit organizations, as business consumers, **316**
Non-store retailing, **362**
North American Industry Classification System (NAICS), **310**
Numerical data, **131**

O

Objectives
  advertising plan, **435–436**
  analyzing, **601**
  determining outcomes, **248**
  organization, **296**
  pricing, **384–385**
  promotional, **417, 419**
Objective and task approach, **437**
Observations, research information through, **135–136**
Oligopolies, **71–72**
Olive Garden, **112**
Omidyar, Pierre, **374**
One-price policy, **392**
Online advertising, **207–208**
Online catalogs, **462**
Online employment, **635**
Open-ended questions, **134**
Operating equipment, **275**
Operating expenses, **388, 537**
Operating tools, **540–541**
Operations
  defined, **14**
  using Internet to improve, **200**

Operations reports, **121**

Opportunity, **508**

Options, features added as, **225–226**

Order processing, **368–369**
online, **202**

Organizational advertising, **432**

Organizations
classifying services, **295–298**
goals of, **296**
non-business, **25, 105**

Organizing
direction for, **597**
as management function, **594–595**
responsibilities, **603–604**

Output, MkIS, **126**

P

Package size, **173**

Packaging, **226**
considerations in, **270**
as product protection, **368**
See also Labeling

Packing list, **329**

Partnership, **577**

Partnership agreement, **577**

Pass-along rate, **439**

Patronage motives, **151**

Pay-for-performance incentives, **459**

Paying agents, **393**

Penetration price, **391**

Pepperidge Farms, **563**

Pepsi-Cola, **286–287, 406–407**
ad spending, Super Bowl, **450**
ad theme, **437**
Pepsi Max, **129**

Percentage of sales approach, **437**

Performance
improved, **327**
measuring services', **294**
See also Pay-for-performance
incentives; Quality; Success

Performance information, **121**

Performance standards, service, **299**

Perishable, **292–293**

Perpetual inventory, **327**

Personal selling, **301–302, 413–414**
advantages and disadvantages of, **414**
by managers, **605**
understanding, **454–455**
using, **456–459**
when to use, **459**
See also Salespeople

Personal video recorders (PVRs)
ad avoidance and, **431**
ad selection and, **434**

Persuasion
personal selling and, **457**
promotion as, **405**

Pets.com, **190, 374**

PetSmart Inc., **118**

Physical distribution
defined, **364**
information system, **368–369**
pipelines, **366**

Philadelphia Eagles, **426**

Physical inventory, **328**

Pizza Hut, **286**

Place utility, **76**

Planning
career, **620–621**
defined, **593–594**
entrepreneurial, **579–580**
financial, **533–534**
marketing. See Marketing planning
product/service, **6, 94–97, 181, 264, 277**
promotional, **97, 418–421**
service, **300–301**
tools, **537–540**
up front, **91–92**
See also Advertising plan; Merchandise plan; Product/service planning; Promotional plan

Poilane bakery, **343**

Point-of-purchase promotions, **402**

Population, **130**

Positioning
bases for, **171–173**

competition for, **175–178**
statement, developing, **249**
strategy, selecting, **173–174**

Possession utility, **76**

Postindustrial economies, **494**

Postpurchase evaluation, **153**

Preapproach, **469**

Predatory pricing, **49**

Preindustrial economies, **493–494**

Presentations, by entrepreneurs, **563**

Price, **227–228**
adjustability of, **379**
defined, **20, 378–379**
determining range for, **386–387**
as economic concept, **380–381**
expenses related to, **552**
government's effect on, **382–383**
as marketing tool, **378–379**
as positioning strategy, **172**
regulating, **383**
risk management and, **517**
selling, **388–389**
setting objectives for, **384–385**

Price fixing, **382–383**

Price lines, **393**

Pricing, **7, 95–96**
business opportunities in, **572–573**
career specializing in, **625**
in competitive environment, **390–392**
competitors', **180–181**
cooperative, **72**
in foreign markets, **499**
geographic, **393**
policies, **392–394**
sales support and, **473**
services, **302–303**

Primary competitors, analyzing, **246**

Primary data, **130**

Private enterprise, **60**

Private enterprise economy, **60–61**

Problem
consumer's recognition of, **152**
defining and analyzing, **128–129**

Procter & Gamble, **412**
marketing expertise, **240**
Whitestrips, **88**

Producers, **61**
 as business consumers, **311**
 consumers and, adjusting differences between, **348–349**
 manufacturers and, role of, **103**
Product(s)
 basic, **225, 267**
 business. *See* Products,
  business
 decline of, **231**
 defined, **20, 260**
 effects of marketing on, **36**
 enhanced, **267–268**
 expanded uses of, **226**
 expenses related to, **551–552**
 extended, **270**
 features of, **225**
 finding and buying online,
  201–202
 fine-tuning, **224–226**
 growth stage, **230**
 life cycle of, **390–391**
 maturity stage, **230–231**
 new. *See* Products, new
 putting on shelves, **332–333**
 risks to, **514–515**
 salesperson's understanding of,
  465–466
 storing and handling, **367–368**
 supplying, **64–67**
 transporting, **365**
 See also Shopping goods;
  Specialty goods
Product advertising, **432–433**
Product assortment, **269–270**
Product classification, as positioning strategy, **173**
Product design, **267–268**
Product development, **95**
 marketing activities in, **263–264**
 as marketing function, **262–264**
 steps in, **279–281**
 testing and, **281**
 See also Prototypes
Production, **13**
 changing role of, **21–22**
 foreign, **488**
Production function, **13**
Production reports, **121**

Product liability insurance, **523**
Product liability lawsuits, **267**
Product life cycle analysis, **229–231**
Product line
 defined, **269**
 variations in, **269–270**
Product marketing, **281**
Product mix
 components, **269–271**
 parts of, **265–266**
Products, business
 categories of, **312**
 determining alternatives, **325**
 See also Purchasing
Products, new, **277–279**
 failure rate of, **506**
 improved and, **37**
 introducing, **229–230**
 risk of change and, **514**
 See also Product development
Product/service management
 business opportunities in, **573**
 career in, **625**
 for foreign markets, **498**
 sales support and, **473**
Product/service planning, **6, 94–97**
 competitors', **181**
 for consumer and business
  markets, **277**
 as marketing function, **264**
Product/service purchase classification system, **232**
Products and services
 developing unique, **574**
 pricing, **95–96**
 sales of, **548**
Product usage, **168**
Product user, as positioning
  strategy, **172**
Professional selling, **413**
Profit motive, **60**
Profits, maximizing, **384**
Promotion, **7, 228**
 business opportunities in, **572**
 career in, **626**
 as communication process,
  406–408
 defined, **20, 404**

 for e-commerce, **209–211**
 e-mail lists, **209**
 expenses related to, **552–553**
 in foreign markets, **499**
 on Internet, **206**. *See also*
  E-marketing
 of lawyers, **287**
 risks to, **517**
 role in marketing, **404–406**
 sales, **415**
 sales support and, **473**
 service, **301–302**
 in supermarkets, **402**
 See also Advertising; Coupons;
  E-mail promotions; Publicity;
  Rebates
Promotional mix, **416–418**
 selecting, **420**
Promotional plan
 defined, **418**
 implementing, **420**
Promotional planning, **97, 418–421**
Promotions
 company's policy and objectives,
  417–418
 competitors', **181**
 gauging effectiveness of, **421**
 long- and short-term impact of,
  172
 tissue pack handouts, **126**
Proposal, request for, **326**
Proprietorship, **575–576**
Prosperity, growth of service
  industry and, **291**
Prototypes, **280**
Psychographics, **167**
Public Broadcasting System,
  This Old House, **479**
Publications, business, **123–124**
Public awareness, increasing, **42**
Publicity
 advantages and disadvantages
  of, **412–413**
 defined, **412**
Publisher's Clearinghouse, **394**
Pulsing schedule, **441–444**
Purchase classifications, consumer,
  391

Purchase classification system, **232–235**

Purchase order, **329**

Purchases
decisions regarding, **153**
negotiating, **325–326**
processing, **328**
unneeded, **40–41**
See also Business purchasing

Purchase specifications, **320**

Purchasing
buying decision, **318–320**
completing process, **332–396**
improving procedures for, **327**
international, **322–323**
as marketing function, **313**
new products, **319–320**
specialists, **321**
steps in process, **324–327**

Purchasing plan, developing, **331–332**

Purchasing power, **495**

Purchasing records, **329**

Pure competition, **68–69**

Pure risk, **509**

Q

Qualifying, **503**

Quality
evaluating service, **299**
as positioning strategy, **172**

Quantity, differences in, between producers and consumers, **347**

Questions, answering, as part of selling process, **470–471**

Quotas, **497**

R

Radio, **77**

Railroads, for physical distribution, **365**

Rally's restaurant, **112**

Random sampling, **130**

Rational motives, **151**

Raw materials, **275–276**

Reach, advertising media, **439**

Rebates, **385**

Recall testing, **444**

Receiver, message, **407**

Receiving record, **329**

Recession, **495**

Reciprocal trading, **322–323**

Recognition testing, **444**

Recording Industry of America, **528**

Reference groups, **155**

Regional shopping centers, **361–362**

Regulated economy, **59**

Regulation. *See* Government regulation; Self-regulation

Relationship marketing, **30–31**

Reliable Auto Service, **89**

Reminder, promotion as, **406**

Reorder point, **320**

Repair to Remember, A, **478**

Repeat purchase, **320**

Reports, marketing research, **132–133**

Request for proposal, **326**

Resellers, as business consumers, **315**

Restaurant niches, **112**

Retail or consumer credit, **394**

Retailers
hypermarkets in Asia, **490**
kiosks use by, **115**
location of, **361–362**
product mix of, **361**
quality of shopping experience, **588**
satisfying customer needs, **330–332**
types of, **360–363**

Retailing
changes in, **362–363**
defined, **359–360**
non-store, **362**

Retail sales, tracking, **331**

Revenue
after-sale and related, **549**
defined, **532**

effects of marketing on, **546–551**
increasing, **544–545**

Reward Game, The, **509**

Richardson, Jackson, **401**

Risk
of change, **513–514**
classification of, **509–511**
dealing with, **511–512**
defined, **508**
entrepreneurs and, **566**
reducing, **523**
result of, **509–510**

Risk management
defined, **513**
insurance as, **522–523**
through marketing planning, **518–520**
through security and safety planning, **521–522**

Robbins, Tony, **479**

rocketcash.com, **374**

Ruffman, Mag, **478**

Rubik, Enro, **568**

Rubik's Cube, **568**

Rudkin, Margaret, **563**

Rule of 72, **170**

Ryan's Family Steakhouse, **418**

S

Safety, in packaging, **270**

Sales
career in, **626**
changing role of, **22**
closing, **471–472**
effects of marketing on, **548**
of products and services, **548**
retail, **331**. *See also* Retailing
unit, **550**

Sales-based pricing objective, **385**

Sales information, **120–121**

Salespeople
personal management for, **459–460**
product knowledge and, **465–430**
skills of, **459**
understanding of competition, **467**

Sales promotions, **415**

INDEX

Sales support, providing, **473**

Sam's Clubs, **356, 564**

Scarcity, **59**

Scientific evidence format, **443**

Scientific skills, **569**

Sears, **536**

Sears Auto Centers, **470**

Secondary data, **130**

Security, online, **203–204**

Segments, **221**

Self-management, for salespeople, **460**

Self-regulation, **46–47**
   of advertising practices, **434**

Selling, **7**
   business opportunities in, **572**
   defined, **455**
   in foreign markets, **499**
   process of, **467–473**
   See also Personal selling; Sales

Sender, communication, **406**

Service planning, **300–301**

Service promotion, **301–302**

Services
   associated, **226**
   as business consumers, **315**
   commercial data and information, **124**
   defined, **290**
   evaluating quality of, **299**
   growth and importance of, **290–291**
   measuring performance of, **294**
   organization classifications, **295–298**
   price and distribution, **302–303**
   role of, **104–105**
   specialized, **358**
   unique qualities of, **292–294**
   See also Products and services

Seven-Up, "Uncola" campaign, **173**

Shabby Chic, **478**

Ships and boats, for physical distribution, **366**

Shopping centers, **361–362**

Shopping goods, **238–240**

Shopping strips, **361**

Simmons, Richard, **479**

Simulations, **137**

Simpson, O.J., **400**

Single-line stores, **361**

Skills
   for marketing career, **624–626**
   communication, **617**
   entrepreneurial, **568–570**
   interpersonal, **624**
   leadership, **606**
   for sales, **459**
   for service organization, **298**

Skimming price, **391**

Slice-of-life format, **442**

Smart labels, **345**

Smith, Fredrick, **564**

Social action, **47**

Social class, **155**

Social responsibility, **44**

Software, speech-recognition, **302**

Sonic restaurant, **112**

Sony, **7, 144, 504**

Sony Music, **529**

Specialization of labor, **11–12**

Specialty goods, **234, 236–237**

Speculative risk, **510**

Speech-recognition software, **302**

Staffing
   management of, **604–606**
   as management function, **595**
   support for decisions about, **598**

Stand-alone stores, **362**

Standard Industrial Code (SIC), **310**

Standard of living, **495**

Stanley Home Products, **586**

Staple goods, **233**

Stewart, Martha, **478–479**

Stock options, **544, 594**

Stocks, electronic trading, **379**

Storage
   MkIS, **125–126**
   product handling and, **367–368**

Strategy
   deciding on, **248–249**
   defined, **91**
   new product, **264**

product development, **264**
   See also Marketing strategy; Planning; Positioning strategy

Strategy development, new product, **280**

Strauss, Levi, **562–563**

Subsidy, **497**

Substantiation, of advertisements, **433**

Success
   key to, **590–591**
   marketing costs and, **532–534**

Suggestion selling, **472**

Super Bowl, **450–451**

Supermarket promotions, **402**

Superstores, **361**

Suppliers, finding and choosing, **325**

Supplies, **275**

Supply, **61, 64–67**

Supply curve, **65–66**

Supply and demand
   intersecting, **66**
   matching, **43**

Surety bond, **518**

Surveys, conducting, **134–135**

Survivor: The Australian Outback, **450**

T

Taco Bell, **286**

Target market
   defining, **248**
   identifying, **419**
   for new business, **574**
   profitability of, **533**
   promotional mix and, **417**
   selecting, **223**

Tariffs, **497**

Taxation, prices, **383**

Teamwork, **606**

Technical expertise format, **442**

Technology
   to boost sales, **472**
   entrepreneurs' use of, **570**
   foreign trade and, **496**

growth of service industry and, **291**

increased use of, **363**

Latin American resistance toward, **465**

monitoring employees with, **604**

risks of, **521**

selling with, **452**

Testimonials, **443**

Testing
advertisement effectiveness, **444**
marketing mix, **264**

Test markets, **137**

Theme, advertising, **437**

Thomas, Dave, **586**

Time magazine, reader research, **408**

Time utility, **76**

Timing, differences in, between producers and consumers, **348–349**

Tools
financial, **542–543**
operating, **540–541**
planning, **358–540**
price as, **378–379**
utility as, **77**

Total quality management (TQM), **328**

Toysmart.com, **374**

Toys "R" Us, **360**

Trade agreements, **480**

Trade credit, **394**

Trade and professional associations, **123**

Transportation
importance of, **364–366**
international purchasing, **323**

Trial close, **471**

Trucks, for physical distribution, **365**

U

Uncontrollable risk, **510**

Unilever, **412**

Unisys, **276**

United States Bureau of the

Census, as information source, **122**

international trade and, **482–485**

Supreme Court, **308**

See also Government

Unit sales, **550**

Universal MGM, **450**

University of Southern California, **528**

Unpaid credit, **551**

Unsought goods, **235, 237**

UPS, **84**

Use or application strategy, **172**

Utility, **75–77**

V

Value
added, **394**
defined, **60**
image versus, **340**

Vcapital, **558–559**

Vendor analysis, **325**

Verizon, **450**

Vettiger, Peter, **606**

VISA, **450**

Vivendi Universal, **528**

Volkswagen, **450**

W

Wagner, Mary Kay, **586**

Walker, Madame C.J., **562**

Wal-Mart, **564**

Walton, Sam, **564**

Wants, **147**

Warehouses, **367**

Web site
distributors' use of, **462**
effective promotion methods, **211**
internationalizing, **576**
measuring effectiveness of promotions, **421**
priority placement, **212**
shopping experience, **214**
sponsorship, **212**
stages of e-commerce development, **194**

using offline media in conjunction with, **412**

Wendy's, **112, 586**

What you can afford approach, **436**

Wholesale
activities, **355–356**
benefits of, **354–355**

Wholesale clubs, **356–357**

Wholesalers
changing role of, **357–358**
defined, **354**

Wholesaling, who needs? **354–357**

Wiersema, Brian, **509**

Wireless ads, location-sensitive, **221**

WNBA, **400**

Word of mouth, **301**

World Cup, **401**

Worthington-Cabott, **558**

Y

Yahoo, **374**

Yale, **528**

Z

Zidane, Zinedine, **401**

Zone pricing, **403**

PHOTO CREDITS

Cover Photo. *VCG/FPG International, LLC.*

Chapter 1. 6: © 2000, *Marketing Education Resource Center (Mark ED)*, Columbus, Ohio. Used with permission. 3, 7, 8, 10 , 13, 15, 16, 18, 20, 24, 30, 31: © *PhotoDisc, Inc.*

Chapter 2. 33, 34, 37, 38, 40, 51, 53, 54: © *PhotoDisc, Inc.*

Chapter 3. 57, 63, 65, 66, 67, 69, 70, 74, 82, 83: © *PhotoDisc, Inc.*

Chapter 4. 84, 86, 91, 95, 98, 99, 102, 105, 107, 108, 109, 110, 111: © *PhotoDisc, Inc.*

Chapter 5. 115, 121, 124, 129, 133, 142, 143: © *PhotoDisc, Inc.*

Chapter 6. 162: © *CORBIS* 145, 146, 147, 148, 150, 151, 152, 154, 158, 159, 160, 161, 163: © *PhotoDisc, Inc.*

Chapter 7. 165, 169, 170, 172, 174, 175, 176, 177, 178, 179, 180, 181, 182, 183, 186, 187, 188, 189: © *PhotoDisc, Inc.*

Chapter 8. 191, 192, 194, 196, 200, 209, 210, 211, 214, 217: © PhotoDisc, Inc

Chapter 9. 221, 223, 224, 228, 230, 234, 235, 236, 237, 238, 239, 241, 242, 243, 244, 245, 246, 248, 249, 250, 251, 255, 256, 257: © *PhotoDisc, Inc.*

Chapter 10. 261, 267, 268, 269, 270, 272, 273, 276, 283, 286, 288: © *PhotoDisc, Inc.*

Chapter 11. 290, 291, 293, 295, 303, 307: © *PhotoDisc, Inc.*

Chapter 11. 308: © *PhotoDisc, Inc.*

Chapter 12. 315, 316, 317, 318, 319, 320, 321, 322, 323, 328, 338, 339: © *PhotoDisc, Inc.*

Chapter 13. 363: *Courtesy of Deck the Walls* 363: *Courtesy of Buffalo Wild Wings* 363: *Courtesy of Maaco* 340, 341, 342, 343, 345, 346, 347, 349, 351, 353, 356, 357, 358, 359, 360, 361, 364, 365, 366, 367, 368, 369, 374: © *PhotoDisc, Inc.*

Chapter 14. 376, 387, 400: © *PhotoDisc, Inc.*

Chapter 15. 404, 407, 410, 411, 413, 415, 417, 418, 419, 420, 421, 424, 425, 426: © *PhotoDisc, Inc.*

Chapter 16. 428, 429, 430, 433, 437, 439, 440, 441, 448, 449, 450, 451: © *PhotoDisc, Inc.*

Chapter 17. 452, 454, 456, 457, 459, 462, 463, 464, 467, 478: © *PhotoDisc, Inc.*

Chapter 18. 481, 483, 484, 485, 504: © *PhotoDisc, Inc.*

Chapter 19. 507, 509, 510, 511, 512, 513, 514, 516, 518, 519, 520, 521, 522, 523, 525, 528, 529: © *PhotoDisc, Inc.*

Chapter 20. 530, 535, 536, 537, 539, 546, 548, 549, 550, 551, 552, 553, 558: © *PhotoDisc, Inc.*

Chapter 21. 565: © CORBIS 562, 563, 571, 572, 573, 575, 577, 578, 579, 580, 584: © *PhotoDisc, Inc.*

Chapter 22. 590, 591, 592, 594, 596, 599, 603, 604, 605, 606, 607, 610, 611, 612: © *PhotoDisc, Inc.*

Chapter 23. 615, 616, 618, 619, 620, 623, 624, 626, 629, 630, 631, 634, 635, 636, 637, 640, 641, 642, 643: © *PhotoDisc, Inc.*